Public Administration in Canada:
Selected Readings

Public Administration in Canada: Selected Readings

edited by

A. M. Willms
W. D. K. Kernaghan

Methuen

Toronto   London   Sydney   Wellington

Public Administration in Canada: Selected Readings

Published in Toronto by Methuen Publications
(A Division of the Carswell Co. Ltd.)
and in London by Methuen & Co Ltd

Library of Congress Catalog Card Number 68-8673

SBN 416 99510 1/42

Printed and bound in Canada

Contents

Chapter Four
Canadian Government Organization

Chapter Five
Planning and Financing

Chapter Six
Control in Administration

Chapter Seven
Decision-Making and Communicating

Chapter Eight
Human Relations and Leadership

Chapter Nine
Personnel Administration

Chapter Ten
Administrative Responsibility

Preface

Almost two decades have passed since the founding of the Institute of Public Administration of Canada — the professional association of students and practitioners of public administration. Among the achievements of the Institute has been the publication since 1958 of the quarterly journal, *Canadian Public Administration*. The contributions to this journal, combined with the publication of a substantial volume of other writings on administration in Canada and the United States, are now sufficient to justify the preparation of this book of readings. Virtually all the selections date later than 1960 and several, especially those on the organization and machinery of the Canadian public services, are published here for the first time.

The primary purpose of this book is to examine the institutions and processes of public administration in Canada, to promote their understanding and stimulate further study. The readings, based on an extensive search of the literature and taken from a number of disparate sources, are designed to satisfy several objectives. They will serve the needs of a wide audience as a textbook on Canadian public administration. Students in universities and in the burgeoning colleges of applied arts and technology need to study public administration to understand the general concepts of administration and to appreciate the challenges and opportunities offered by a career in Canadian government. The readings are also intended to meet the demands of increasing numbers of public servants engaged in training and development courses conducted by the public service commissions or individual departments at all levels of government.

Within the limitations of concentrating on Canadian writings, the editors have provided a broadly representative selection of concepts, issues and developments in modern public administration. In the absence of Canadian material, particularly on theoretical questions, American literature has been included to ensure comprehensive coverage. In view of the wide range of subjects in the field, the editors have occasionally been obliged to choose summaries of administrative concepts and structures instead of more detailed analyses. Moreover, to achieve a representative sampling of the literature, substantial editing was necessary. An effort was made, however, to avoid editing which would distort the substance or the style of the author's contribution. Although strictures of space and available material have forced the editors to focus primarily on the federal public service, the theoretical material is applicable not only to the provincial and municipal levels of government but to private administration as well. Evidence of the relevance of the readings to private administration is manifested in the selection of articles from such professional business journals as the *Advanced Management Journal, The Business Quarterly* and the *Harvard Business Review.*

Traditional writings on administration have been supplemented by recent materials representing the behavioural approach to the study of administration. These approaches are not mutually exclusive but complementary and a sampling of both approaches is indispensable for an over-all survey of the field. The book includes contributions which reflect the various orientations to the study of administration. The readings have been arranged so that a separation may be made between the theoretical and the more descriptive or practically-oriented writings. Teachers and students may therefore follow their own inclination for one group of readings over another. The comments preceding each chapter are intended not as succinct summaries but as general introductions and background material to the selections. To encourage continued reading by the student, each of these introductory sections includes a brief annotated bibliography of the central works available in that subject area.

This volume emphasizes concepts of administration rather than detailed explications of managerial techniques applicable generally to government operations or particularly to the operations of the Canadian public services. An analysis of important support services, embracing descriptions of such areas as purchasing and stores, records management, engineering services and legal advice, has been omitted because of space limitations and the very technical nature of such services. Nevertheless, several of the departmental services have been examined either through the allocation of an entire chapter as in the case of personnel management, or through their relationship to other subjects as in the case of budgeting, information and operations research.

The essays in Chapter 1 introduce the student to public administration by examining definitions of administration and bureaucracy, comparisons between public and private administration, and unique features of the study, teaching and practice of public administration in the Canadian environment. The next two chapters are theoretical in content. Through a review of the major contributions to administrative thought, Chapter 2 traces the development of the longstanding debate on the limits and approaches to the study of administration. The fundamental question of whether administration is an art or a science is examined in the context of the behavioural sciences. Chapter 3, on organization theory, treats the crucial problems of hierarchy, span of control, decentralization, line-staff-service relationships and the use of committees.

This theoretical foundation prepares the student for an inquiry in the next several chapters into government organization and management functions. Chapter 4 examines the most important elements of organization in the federal government. Then, in the following two chapters, finance, planning and control are considered. Chapter 5 assesses new concepts of planning and finance in the federal public service and the exercise of control over financial management by Parliament and the public service. The theme of Chapter 6 is internal control. This section examines not only the enforcement of control but the means of measuring the performance of public or private administration in terms of economy and efficiency. Valuable new insights into the traditional administrative functions of decision making and communication are contained in Chapter 7. Attention is also drawn to the revolutionary managerial technique of operations research and the implications for management of computers and automation.

Chapter 8 centres on the enormous influence of human relations in administration and specifically on the critical questions of leadership approaches and styles, managerial behaviour and employee motivation. In Chapter 9, the significance of developing and maintaining skilful and zealous public employees is evaluated through an analysis of the elements of personnel management and its organization within the Canadian federal public service.

Finally, Chapter 10 explores the traditional responsibilities of the bureaucrat to the public. The readings investigate the issues of the delegation of quasi-legislative and quasi-judicial powers to public servants and the legal means available to guard against abuse of such discretionary powers. This concluding chapter also explains the political character of public administration and focusses on the perennial and increasingly crucial difficulty of holding government officials accountable to the public.

In conclusion, the editors would like to acknowledge their indebtedness to the authors and publishers who granted permission to reprint their material and to those authors who wrote articles especially for this volume.

Carleton University
Ottawa

A. M. Willms

Brock University
St. Catharines, Ontario

W. D. K. Kernaghan

June 1968

Chapter One
Introduction to Public Administration

Advances in the study of public administration have been so rapid during the postwar period that a one-sentence definition of the subject is now impracticable. The longstanding difficulty of delimiting the scope and content of public administration has been immensely compounded by an increasing number of cross-disciplinary research contributions which continue to expand its boundaries. In the first two essays of this chapter, the enduring problems of definition are examined and the evolution of various approaches to the study of public administration is discussed.

The explication in the third selection of the characteristics of contemporary public bureaucracy and the elimination of the invidious connotations of the term *bureaucracy* is critical to an understanding of the nature and purposes of public administration. The unique features of public bureaucracy are further described by a comparative analysis of government bureaucrats and their counterparts in private administration.

The significance of the growth of the public bureaucracy and of the theoretical and methodological progress in administrative studies in Canada is outlined in the final three essays. A description of the Canadian public service in retrospect is followed by an assessment of teaching and research in Canadian public administration today and the prospects for their future development.

The initial chapters of the major textbooks on public administration invariably provide an introduction to the study of the discipline. Among the most useful texts for this purpose are

M. E. Dimock and G. E. Dimock, *Public Administration*, Holt, Rinehart and Winston, New York, 1964.

E. N. Gladden, *The Essentials of Public Administration*, Staples Press, London, 1964.

F. Morstein Marx (ed.), *Elements of Public Administration*, Prentice-Hall, Englewood Cliffs, New Jersey, 1959.

Felix A. Nigro, *Modern Public Administration*, Harper & Row, New York, 1965.

J. M. Pfiffner and R. V. Presthus, *Public Administration*, Ronald Press, New York, 1967.

Aside from the articles included in Chapter 1 of this book, two important articles published recently on the problems and changing nature of public administration are

Lynton K. Caldwell. "Public Administration and the Universities: A Half-Century of Development", *Public Administration Review*, Vol. 25, No. 1, March 1965, pp. 52-60.

Helen C. Hilling, "Public Administration: Study, Practice, Profession", *Public Administration Review*, Vol. 26, No. 4, December 1966, pp. 320-328.

1   What is Public Administration ?*

Dwight Waldo

When announcement of the first atomic explosions was made there was a deep sense of awe at the power unleashed. Imagination and reason strained to comprehend what had happened and how it had been brought to pass. The sense of awe was extended to the physical science and engineering which had made this stupendous phenomenon possible.

Along with an account of the general principles of physics involved and how they had been conceived and brought to successful test by the various physicists, the government of the United States gave also an account of the human science and engineering that lay behind the achievement. In brief, a special administrative system named the Manhattan Engineer District had been set up as a subdivision of the government of the United States. The Manhattan Engineer District spent two billion dollars, under conditions of such great secrecy that comparatively few Americans knew it existed and many of its own employees did not know its purpose. It brought together thousands of variously and highly trained men, and many and rare materials and objects, from all over the earth. It built extensive facilities and created specialized subadministrative systems across the continent, tying them together in intricate ways with the administrative systems we know as business enterprises and universities. The success of the Manhattan Engineer District lies before all: its purpose was the achievement of militarily usable explosions based on nuclear fission.

---

* Reprinted with permission of author and publisher from D. Waldo, *The Study of Public Administration*, Random House, New York, 1955.

Now it is a reasonable conclusion, based upon evidence, that most people regarded the atomic bomb as an achievement of physical science alone, and that the account of the Manhattan Engineer District did not make much of an impression — and has been generally forgotten. *But might we not seriously entertain another point of view: that the atomic bomb was as much an achievement on the human side as on the side of physical science?*

Not that the atomic bomb was a triumph of human morality. Perhaps the reverse was true, though judgment upon the atomic bomb cannot be dissociated from judgment upon war itself and all its modern machinery. What should be noticed is that in the perspective of history the human technology in achieving the bomb was a remarkable thing — perhaps as far removed from the social experience and imagination of any primitive people as the bomb itself from their physical experience and imagination.

To be sure, the all-but-universal judgment of the day is that our physical science is progressive or mature, while our social science is backward, infantile, or adolescent. This may be true. Certainly it is true by definition if the criteria commonly used in making this judgment are accepted as the proper ones: these criteria (for example, mathematical sophistication) are the distinguishing marks of the physical sciences! But though it may be true, this judgment tends to obscure and to depreciate what we have achieved in the area of human "technology," to use a word not as hard and argumentative as science.

Because we have lived from birth in a society with an advanced technology of cooperation and have learned so much of this technology without awareness, we accept the miracles of human cooperation all about us as though they were natural or indeed inevitable. But they are not. Far from it. This technology was achieved through incalculable human industry, much systematic thought, and the flashes of inspiration of occasional geniuses. The technology of human cooperation must be learned afresh with each generation. Still fuller achievement of human purposes depends upon its extension by study and invention.

This essay is intended as an introduction to the study of one phase or aspect of human cooperation, namely, public administration. Public administration is much less than the whole process or concept of human cooperation. Those who study law, or anthropology, or economics, for example, are also studying human cooperation. There are specialized technologies within the technology of human cooperation; and there are also varying conceptual apparatuses by which study *in* or the study *of* these technologies may be approached. Public administration in our society is one of the technologies within the technology, and has its own special conceptual apparatuses in its practice and in its study.

The Problem of Definition

Logic and convention both require that we now deal more carefully with the problem of definition, What is public administration? But in truth there is no good definition of public administration. Or perhaps there are good short definitions, but no good short explanation. The immediate effect of all one-sentence or one-paragraph definitions of public administration is mental paralysis rather than enlightenment and stimulation. This is because a serious definition of the term — as against an epigrammatical definition, however witty — inevitably contains several abstract words or phrases. In short compass these abstract words and phrases can be explained only by other abstract words and phrases, and in the process the reality and importance of "it" become fogged and lost. With this warning let us consider two typical definitions:

(1) Public administration is the organization and management of men and materials to achieve the purpose of government.

(2) Public administration is the art and science of management as applied to affairs of state.

These are the ways public administration is usually defined. There is nothing wrong with such definitions — except that in themselves they do not help much in advancing understanding. Perhaps these definitions do evoke sharp concepts and vivid images in the reader's mind. But if they do not, it is better to proceed, rather than puzzle over each word, in the hope that the following explanations, descriptions, and comments will bring understanding in their train.

Administration: Art or Science?

Let us give a moment's attention to a traditional dispute in the definition of public administration, and a related source of frequent confusion in the use of the term. The conflict has concerned whether public administration is an art or science. Some students and administrators, impressed with the achievements of the natural and physical sciences, have been insistent that public administration can and should become a science in the same sense. Other students and administrators, impressed with a fluid, creative quality in actual administration, with such intangibles as judgment and leadership, have been equally insistent that public administration cannot become a science, that it is an art.

Much nonsense has resulted from the debates of the science-art controversy, but also considerable clarification of concepts and agreement on usage. It is fashionable nowadays to refer to the "art *and* science" of public administration, in the manner of the second definition above. This usage reflects a general conclusion that public administration has important aspects of *both* science and art. It reflects also, however, a desire to bypass the definitional problems, to compromise the issues by yielding to both sides, to get on with the study and practice of public administration, whatever it is. This disposition to get on is no doubt healthy, and diminishes a picayune and wasteful squabbling over words alone. But it must not be forgotten that definitions are important to fruitful study and effective

action. The problem of how people are to be educated or trained for participating in public administration, for example, is one that can be solved only
after a decision as to what, after all, is meant by public administration.[1]

Dual Usage of the Words Public Administration

A fertile source of confusion and error, closely related to the science-art
controversy, is the fact that the words "public administration" have two
usages. They are used to designate and delineate both (1) an area of intellectual inquiry, a discipline or study, and (2) a process or activity — that
of administering public affairs. While the two meanings are of course closely
related they are nevertheless different; it is a difference similar to that
between biology as the study of organisms and the organisms themselves.

Now if this distinction seems so obvious as not to warrant the making,
the excuse must be that it is nevertheless a distinction often missed. It is
obvious, in retrospect, that a great deal (but not all) of the controversy
over whether public administration is a science or an art stemmed from
failure to agree on which public administration was being discussed, the
discipline or the activity. It is quickly apparent that it is easier to make the
case for science on the *systematic study*, and the case for art on the *practice*,
of public administration.

A student of public administration must cultivate a sharp eye for the two
usages of the term. Sometimes the meaning will be clear from definition
or context, but often there is simply ambiguity and confusion. Sometimes
this is true because a writer begins with a definition of public administration as a process or activity, and then proceeds, abruptly or gradually, to
use the term also to refer to the systematic study of public administration.
Sometimes too the attempt is made to embrace both meanings within the
same definition, which opens great opportunity for confusion. (Turn back
now and scrutinize the two definitions given on an earlier page. In terms
of the distinction made, is their intent clear?)

Let us confess that in attempting to clarify a distinction which is important we have made it sharper than it is in fact. To explain, recall the
analogy drawn above between biology as the study of organisms and the
organisms themselves. In this case the distinction is sharp, because while
biology includes the study of man as an organism, this is but a small part
of the whole; and on the other hand, no organism except man makes much
of a study of other organisms. In the case of public administration, however, the central concern of the study is man himself, in certain aspects and
sets of relationships; and on the other hand, much studying of public
administration is carried on by men while engaged in the activities and pro-

---

1 Another distinction, related and similar to the distinction between science and art, is
that between pure and applied, or theoretical and practical, science. This distinction,
which has important uses, is discussed below in connection with logical positivism. For a
statement of it see Herbert A. Simon, *Administrative Behavior: A Study of Decision-
Making Processes in Administrative Organization*, Macmillan, New York, 1947, Appendix.

cess of public administration. The file clerk meditating on a better filing system for his needs, the supervisor deciding upon a new distribution of work among his staff, the group of publicly employed social scientists making an elaborate study of how employee morale can be maintained, are all studying public administration in some sense or aspect.

The Concept of Rational Action

The point will be made clearer by the introduction of the concept of *rational action*, defined here as action correctly[2] calculated to realize given desired goals with minimum loss to the realization of other desired goals. We will use the concept somewhat crudely, and not pause here to consider such interesting and important questions as whether man does wish or should wish that all his actions be rational. We will be content for the moment with the general observation or belief that man can and does maximize his goal achievement by taking thought, by correctly relating means to ends.

Now public administration in *both* senses is rational action as just defined. It is action designed to maximize the realization of goals that are public by definition. In public administration *as an activity* there is continuous calculation of the means to maximize public goals, although there is great variation in the goal awareness, knowledge, and level of abstraction of those engaged in the activity. A top leader may be highly trained and spend his time and energy in a conscious and careful calculation of means to realize given public goals. A machine-operator, on the other hand, may not know or care about the "public" goals of the agency for which he works. Still, the work of the machine-operator will be rational, in the sense that it is a joining of means to ends — say, the operation of a calculating machine for the solving of arithmetical problems. Rationality may be built into a mechanical operation or even a profession. The task of a leader or administrator is then to relate such built-in rationality to goals which *he* seeks in such a way that these goals are maximized.

In public administration *as a study* there is also continuous calculation of the means by which public goals may be maximized. In fact this is not only a central concern of the discipline but, many would say, its sole legitimate concern. In this case too, however, there is great variation — in types of approach, in level of abstraction, in size of problem, in the generality or particularity of goals to be maximized, and so forth. Time-and-motion studies of mechanical operations, leadership decision-making, community value-structures affecting administration, auditing procedures, trade-union

2 This is an important — and difficult — word. One source of difficulty lies in the fact that given actions may produce desired results for the wrong reasons. Thus actions enjoined by superstition are found sometimes to be correct (*i.e.* goal-maximizing) by science, but the explanations in the two systems of interpretation are quite different.

characteristics in public administration — these are random examples suggesting the range and variation of studies.

To visualize how study and action can blend together in the concept of rational action, let us imagine a case. Suppose that a firm of management consultants is hired on contract by a state department of public works, with the specific task of determining whether use of mechanical equipment might be made more rational. The persons assigned to the study would observe and gather data and enlist the interest and support of those employees in the department who are concerned with mechanical equipment. Eventually they would present recommendations, and these recommendations might be accepted and put into effect immediately, by the consultants working together with those in the department. In such a case, study and action are so blended that the distinction does not make much sense; and of course study is also a form of action, in the final analysis. Still, at the extreme instead of at the mean. the distinction is a very useful one. A helpful analogy is the familiar range of the spectrum: between the extreme bands are many variations and gradations.

The Meaning of Administration: Cooperative Rational Action

Up to this point we have invariably dealt with the expression *public administration* and at no time with the noun *administration* alone. An appropriate next step is to examine into the meaning of the noun alone, and then into that of the adjective.

We may proceed by analogy: Public administration is a species belonging to the genus administration, which genus in turn belongs to a family which we may call *cooperative human action*. The word *cooperative* is here defined in terms of results: human activity is cooperative if it has effects that would be absent if the cooperation did not take place. Thus — to take a frequently used illustration — when two men roll a stone which neither could roll alone, they have cooperated. The result, the rolled stone, is the test. But what if one of the two men has lent his effort unwillingly, perhaps under threat of bodily harm from the other: Is this cooperation? It is, in the meaning here assigned. Cooperation as ordinarily used suggests willingness, even perhaps enthusiasm; so we are straining the customary meaning. But the English language seems to have no word better adapted to the meaning here desired. The expression *antagonistic cooperation*, incidentally, is sometimes used in the social sciences to distinguish unwilling from willing cooperation.

We are now in a position to describe administration. Administration is a type of cooperative human effort that has a high degree of rationality. This description in turn needs some qualification.

First, administration is not necessarily the only type of human cooperation that is rational. For example, the American economic system utilizes competition between companies — antagonistic cooperation — as well as administration within them to achieve rational action in the production and distribution of economic goods.[3]

Second, there is an important question implicit in the phrase "high degree of rationality." It is well to note this question, though it cannot be discussed fully here. Whose goals or ends shall be used in assessing rationality? A little reflection will suggest that the *personal* goals of many if not all of the people in a particular administrative system are different from the formally stated goals of that system; sometimes, indeed, a product (for example, a military item) may be secret, its use unknown to many of those engaged in its manufacture. The idea of purpose or goal is essential to the definition of administration. But like quicksilver it is hard to grasp; it eludes and scatters. What shall we say is the purpose or goal of the Chevrolet Division of General Motors? In one sense certainly to make automobiles; and in another sense certainly to make profits for the stockholders. But the personal goals of all officers and employees are certainly in some senses neither of these, or at least not wholly these.[4]

Administration was described as a type of cooperative human endeavor with a high degree of rationality. What distinguishes it as a *type*? The answer depends in part upon the perspective. In one perspective the sociologist views the distinguishing characteristics as those he subsumes under the concept of *bureaucracy*. In the conventional perspective of the student of administration these characteristics are best subsumed under the two terms *organization* and *management*.

The Nature of Organization

The terms *organization* and *management* require explanation in turn. We may begin with another analogy: organization is the anatomy, management the physiology, of administration. Organization is structure; management is functioning. But each is dependent upon and inconceivable without the other in any existing administrative system, just as anatomy and physiology are intertwined and mutually dependent in any living organism.[5] We are close to the truth, in fact, when we assert that organization and manage-

---

[3] See Robert A. Dahl and Charles E. Lindblom, *Politics, Economics and Welfare*, Harper & Bros., New York, 1953 for a discussion of different forms of rational cooperation.

[4] Sometimes a distinction is made between *purposes* and *function* in an attempt to deal with this problem. Dahl and Lindblom (p. 38) apply the idea of *net* goal achievement to the problem of multiple goals. "What do we mean by 'rationality'? And how can one test whether one action is more rational than another? The first question is easier to answer than the second. An action is rational to the extent that it is 'correctly' designed to maximize goal achievement, given the goal in question and the real world as it exists. Given more than one goal (the usual human situation), an action is rational to the extent that it is correctly designed to maximize *net* goal achievement."

[5] This analogy is for introductory and explanatory purposes, and is to be viewed in this light. The definitions of organization and management that follow in the text admittedly comprehend less than the whole of societal anatomy and physiology respectively. And we are not here concerned with the familiar sociological distinction between patterns and consequences, or with distinguishing between static and dynamic models.

ment are merely convenient categories of analysis, two different ways of viewing the same phenomenon. One is static and seeks for pattern; the other is dynamic and follows movement.

More precisely, organization may be defined as *the structure of authoritative and habitual personal interrelations in an administrative system*. In any administrative system some persons give orders to others, for certain activities if not for all, and these orders or instructions are habitually followed by other persons; that is to say, some have more power than others, as evidenced by habitual command-obedience or instruction-response relationships. Usually there is an official theory or statement of what the authoritative interrelationships should be in a given administrative system. In an army unit, for example, authority is officially exercised according to the ranks (lieutenant, major, etc.) in the chain of command.

There may be considerable discrepancy, however, between the official theory or statement of authoritative interrelations and the actual, habitual exercise of authority, as evidenced by the actual giving and following of orders or directions. In truth, in any actual administrative system there is usually some discrepancy between the official theory or statement and the facts of authority as evidenced by customary action; and in some cases the official theory or statement may even be no more than a polite fiction, so far do the facts depart from it. Moreover, all or nearly all so-called subordinates, those we think of as docilely taking orders, have means or techniques for changing the behavior of their superiors — for example, the workers' slowdown, or the secretary's smile or frown. A pure one-way power relationship in human affairs is very rare, if indeed it exists. In short, the word *authoritative* in the above definition is ambiguous, since the test of authority may be either the official theory or habitual response. The definition was framed in the knowledge of this ambiguity, which is important but cannot be explored further here. In any case — this is our present point — there are more or less firm structures of personal interrelationships in an administrative system, and these we designate *organization*.

The Nature of Management

Turning to *management*, we may define it as *action intended to achieve rational cooperation in an administrative system*. An administrative system is what we are seeking to explain, and rational cooperation has already been defined. Our attention focuses, then, upon the phrase *action intended to achieve*.

Action is to be construed very broadly: *any change intended to achieve rational cooperation*. It includes self-change or activity, all effects of man upon man, and all effects of man upon nonhuman things. In the postal system, for example, action includes the deliberations of the Postmaster General on such a matter as the desirability of a system of regional postal centers, the instructions of a city postmaster in supervising his staff, and the activities of a deliverer in sorting his daily batch of mail. There is an authoritative quality involved in many of these actions: some men habitually give more instructions (which are followed) than others. Hence some writers define management in terms of direction or control. But this definition is likely to lead to an undesirable narrowing of attention.

The word *intended* in the definition has this significance: there may be a distinction between actions intended to achieve rational cooperation and actions which in fact do so. The reason for this is that in terms of given goals, actions intended to be rational may fail because not all the relevant facts and conditions are known or properly included in judgments and decisions — something which occurs in private life as well as in group activity. On the other hand, actions which are not part of any conscious rational calculation may nevertheless contribute to rational cooperation. Such actions may be sheerly accidental, or they may be actions we associate with emotions, personality, and so forth — areas beyond full scientific statement and calculation, for the present at least. *Management* is customarily used of actions *intended* to achieve rationality (and carries the presumption that the intention is usually realized), but of course an astute practitioner or student will be aware of the difference between intention and actuality and will never forget the large area still unmanageable. Incidentally, a great deal of political theory, especially in modern centuries, has concerned itself with the question of the general scope and the particular areas of human manageability. Students of administration can profit from the literature of this debate. And their findings and experience are in turn an important contribution to it.

The Meaning of Public

After this attempt at a formal definition of administration we return to the question. What is *public* administration? What qualities are signified by the adjective? How is public administration distinguished from administration in general, the species differentiated from the genus?

This is a difficult question. We might begin by defining *public* in terms of such words as *government* and *state*, as is often done. An attempt to understand these words in turn leads to an inquiry into such legal and philosophical concepts as sovereignty, legitimacy, and general welfare. These are important matters, and a student or practitioner of public administration ought to have made serious inquiry into general political theory. Such inquiry helps in understanding various phenomena, such as the coercions sometimes exercised in public administration.

Or we might take a quite different, empirical tack and attempt to define *public* simply by the test of opinion: In a particular society what functions or activities are believed to be public? This proposal has a certain crude truth or usefulness. In the United States, for example, there is certainly a general opinion that, say, the administration of military affairs is public, whereas the administration of automobile sales is private. But complications arise quickly in following this approach. People's opinions differ and are extremely hard to determine and assess (and to suggest another type of complication, the administration of automobile sales is subject to much public control, even in peacetime).

Or we might take the common-sense approach and ask simply, Does the government carry on the function or activity? For many common-sense purposes this approach is quite adequate. It will satisfy most of the purposes of the citizen, and many of those of the student and practitioner of administration. But for many purposes of study, analysis, and informed action it is quite inadequate. Even at the level of common sense it is not completely adequate. For example, there are unstable political situations in which it is difficult to identify "the government" and what is "legal." And there are borderline activities of which one is hard put to it to say whether the government carries them on or not, such are the subtleties of law and circumstances. For example, the development of atomic energy is public in the sense that the government of the United States is in charge. Indeed, there is much secrecy, and tight controls; the situation is sometimes referred to as a monopoly. Yet this program involves an intricate network of contractual relationships, not only with state and local authorities, but with private corporations and individuals. Shall we call development programs carried on under contract by Union Carbide and Carbon Corporation public administration?

The most fruitful approach to the meaning and significance of *public* for the student of administration is through use of certain concepts which have been developed most fully in such disciplines as sociology and anthropology. The ones suggested as being particularly useful are associated with the expressions *structural-functional analysis* and *culture*. The concepts involved in these terms are by no means completely clear and precise. About them highly technical and intense professional debates are carried on. Nevertheless they are very useful to the student of administration even if used crudely. They provide needed insight, if not firm scientific generalizations.

Clarification through Structural-Functional Analysis

Structural-functional analysis seeks the basic or enduring patterns of human needs, wants, dispositions, and expressions in *any* society. Recognizing the great diversity in human societies, it yet seeks for common denominators for the universal grammar and syntax of collective living.

Such studies provide the basis for a meaning of *public* which one could designate universal or inherent. What is indicated — if not precisely concluded — is that institutions and activities that are associated with the identity of a group, with group life as a whole, have special coercive, symbolic, and ceremonial aspects. There is inevitably a sacred aura surrounding some aspects of government. In some societies, of course, Church and State are one, or closely joined. But even where they are officially separated, and even indeed when religion, as such, is officially proscribed by the government, the government — if it is "legitimate" — has this sacred quality. (Nationalism is, of course, often described as a secular religion.)

This approach helps us to understand the special public quality of certain functions of government, for example, the apprehension and trial at law of persons accused of crimes, and the punishment or incarceration of the convicted; the manufacture and control of money; the conduct of foreign relations or the recruitment, training, and control of armed forces. There is about such activities a monopoly aspect, and they are heavily vested with special coercions, symbolisms, and ceremonies. It is especially in such areas of activity that when a private citizen becomes a public official we expect him to play a new role, one which gives him special powers and prestige, but also requires of him observance of certain proprieties and ceremonies.

Incidentally, though the concept of rational action seems the most useful one in defining administration, we could also use the ideas and findings of structural-functional analysis for this purpose. We could, that is to say, construct a model of what an administrative system is like as a general type, using the concepts and idiom of structural-functional analysis.

Clarification through the Concept of Culture

The concept of culture is used in the social sciences — especially anthropology and sociology — to denote the entire complex of beliefs and ways of doing things of a society. We may analyze it as follows for our purposes: By *beliefs* is meant the systems of ideas held with respect to such matters as religion, government, economics, philosophy, art, and personal interrelations. By *ways of doing things* is meant patterns of activity with respect to food, clothing, shelter, courtship and marriage, child-rearing, entertainment, aesthetic expression, and so forth. The concept implies or asserts that there is a close connection between beliefs and ways of doing things — for example between ideas concerning art, and modes of aesthetic expression. It further implies or asserts that the various beliefs and ways of doing things in a particular culture are a system in the sense that they are dependent one upon the other, in such a way that a change in one sets off a complicated (and given the present state of our knowledge, at least, often unanticipated and uncontrollable) train of results in others. For example, the introduction of firearms or of the horse into the culture of a primitive people is likely ultimately to affect such matters as artistic expression and marriage customs.

Now the concept of culture tends somewhat to turn attention in the opposite direction from structural-functional analysis. It emphasizes the variety of human experience in society rather than the recurrent patterns. Indeed, the concept has been used in arguing the almost complete plasticity of human beings and of society — and this is the source of one of the professional controversies referred to above. The professional controversies as to the *limits* of the truth or usefulness of concepts should not mislead us, however. The two concepts or sets of concepts we are dealing with here are not necessarily antithetical, but rather are customarily supplementary over a large area of social analysis.

As structural-functional analysis provides tools for dealing with recurrent phenomena, the concept of culture provides tools for dealing with *variety*. The feeling or intuition that administration is administration wherever it is comes very quickly to the student of administration; and this theme is heavily emphasized in the American literature dealing with administration. Yet the student will also become aware, as he advances, that there are important *differences* between administrative systems, depending upon the location, the tasks, the environment, and the inhabitants of the system. And he needs handles by which he can grasp and deal with the differences.

Our present concern is with the differences between private and public administration. The thesis here is that unless we take the broad view provided by intercultural comparison, we are likely to fall into error, designating a distinction as universal when it is a true or important distinction only in our own country or cultural tradition. There come to mind here the common generalizations of writers in the United States which are true of a significant part or aspect of public administration in liberal democratic societies, but are by no means true of public administration by definition, as is implied or suggested. Precisely, consider the generalization that public administration is distinguished by special care for equality of treatment, legal authorization of and responsibility for action, public justification or justifiability of decisions, financial probity and meticulousness, and so forth. It does not take much knowledge of comparative administration to appreciate the very limited applicability of these characteristics to some "public" administration.

The concept of culture — plus knowledge about the actual culture — enables us to see administration in any particular society in relation to all factors which surround and condition it: political theories, educational system, class and caste distinctions, economic technology, and so forth. And enabling us to see administration in terms of its environment, it enables us to understand differences in administration between different societies which would be inexplicable if we were limited to viewing administration analytically in terms of the universals of administration itself. *For as the constituent parts of culture vary within a society, or between societies, so does administration vary as a system of rational cooperative action in that society, or between societies.* Administration is a part of the cultural complex; and it not only is acted upon, it acts. Indeed, by definition a system of rational cooperative action, it inaugurates and controls much change. Administration may be thought of as the major invention and device by which civilized men in complex societies try to control their culture, by which they seek simultaneously to achieve — within the limitations of their wit and knowledge — the goals of stability and the goals of change.

What is Public Administration? A Summary Explanation

Let us return again to the question: What is *public* administration? The ideas associated with structural-functional analysis and culture will not enable us to *define* public with precision, but they help us in understanding the significance and implications of the term. They help us to understand why public administration has some general or generic aspects but also why the line between public and private is drawn in different places and with differing results — why "public" doesn't have precisely the same meaning in any two different cultural contexts. They help make some sense of the undoubted facts of similarity in diversity and diversity in similarity that characterize the Universe of Administration.

Whether public administration is an art or a science depends upon the meaning and emphasis one assigns these terms. The answer is affected too by the kind of public administration referred to — the study or discipline on the one hand, the activity or process on the other.

The central idea of public administration is rational action, defined as action correctly calculated to realize given desired goals. Public administration both as a *study* and as an *activity* is intended to maximize the realization of goals; and often the two blend into each other, since in the last analysis study is also a form of action.

Administration is cooperative human action with a high degree of rationality. Human action is *cooperative* if it has effects that would be absent if the cooperation did not take place. The significance of *high degree* of rationality lies in the fact that human cooperation varies in effectiveness of goal attainment, whether we think in terms of formal goals, the goals of leaders, or the goals of all who cooperate.

The distinguishing characteristics of an administrative system, seen in the customary perspective of administrative students, are best subsumed under two concepts, organization and management, thought of as analogous to anatomy and physiology in a biological system. *Organization* is the structure of authoritative *and* habitual personal interrelations in an administrative system. *Management* is action intended to achieve rational cooperation in an administrative system.

The significance of *public* can be sought in varying ways, each having some utility. For some purposes, for example, a simple determination of the legal status of an administrative system will suffice. For some important purposes, however, it is desirable to go beyond the boundaries of public administration as it has conventionally been studied and to adopt some of the concepts and tools of sociology and anthropology. *Structural-functional analysis* helps to identify the generic meaning or enduring significance of *public* in all societies. The concept of culture, on the other hand, helps in identifying and dealing with the varying aspects of *public* between societies, as well as with various relations of administration within a society.

The Importance of Nonrational Action

In this attempt to define and explain public administration in brief compass we have constructed a simple model. Of necessity many concepts of importance in the study of public administration have been omitted, and some of the concepts included have been dealt with rather summarily. This is the appropriate place, however, to deal with what is perhaps a bias or distortion in our model, since the basis or source of the distortion largely lies outside of the later discussions.

The point is this: perhaps the model, by stressing rational action, creates a false impression of the amount of rationality (as defined) existing or possible in human affairs.

Now we may properly hold that the concept of rational action is placed at the center of administrative study and action. This is what it is about, so to speak. But the emphasis needs to be qualified — mellowed — by knowledge and appreciation of the nonrational. It is now generally agreed that earlier students of administration had a rationalist bias that led them to overestimate the potentialities of man (at least in the foreseeable future) for rational action.

Most of the streams of modern psychology emphasize — indeed perhaps overemphasize — the irrational component in human psychology: the role of the conditioned response, the emotive, the subconscious. Much of anthropology and sociology stresses complementary themes: the large amount of adaptive social behavior that is below the level of individual — and even group — conscious choice of goals and means to realize the goals. (The fact that goals are not chosen consciously does not mean that there are no goals in this behavior, nor that the goals are necessarily unimportant, nor even that they are any less true or meaningful than those consciously chosen. A baby responding to food stimuli, for example, is not choosing the goal of survival — but survival is usually thought a highly important goal. Actually, though such words as *conscious* and *unconscious* or *deliberate* and *adaptive* suggest two different realms of behavior, there is probably no sharp break, but rather varying levels of awareness of ends and means.)

The general picture that the nonrationalist conclusion of the psychologists, anthropologists, and sociologists (and others — the sources and manifestations of this mode of thought are many) present for the student of administration is this: An administrative organization has an internal environment and an external environment that are largely nonrational, at least so far as the formal goals of the administrative organization are concerned. People do not come into administrative organizations as pieces of putty, as units of abstract energy, nor as mere tools sharpened to some technical or professional purpose. They bring with them their whole cultural conditioning and their personal idiosyncrasies. Each is genetically unique, and all are members of institutions — families, churches, clubs, unions, and so forth — outside the administrative organization; and within the administrative organization they form into natural or adaptive groups of various kinds — friendships, cliques, car pools, and so forth — that flow across the lines of formal administrative organization, sometimes darkening sometimes lightening, and sometimes erasing these lines.

Students of administration have become increasingly aware of the nonrational factors that surround and condition administration. They have broadened the base of their study to include much information that was formerly either unavailable or ignored. The goal of rationality has not been abandoned. Rather, it has been put in a new perspective: to achieve rationality demands a respect for the large area of the nonrational and much knowledge of it. Partly this new perspective is but a more serious heeding of Bacon's maxim: "Nature to be commanded must be obeyed." (These nonrational factors are not to be understood as, by definition, working against formal organization goals, but rather, paradoxically, as phenomena which, properly understood, can often be directed toward the realization of organization goals. They are resources as well as liabilities. Thus personal rivalries can be channeled — as by an official contest — to help rather than hinder goal achievement.) Partly the new perspective is a philosophical or psychological reorientation, as implied in the word *respect*. Students of administration now know that they are not going to take heaven by storm, that is to say, quickly reduce human affairs to rule and chart. Some of them, even, without ceasing to desire and strive for more rationality than we have now achieved, are heard to say that complete rationality in human affairs is not the proper goal; that a world in which *all* is orderly and predictable, with no room for spontaneity, surprise, and emotional play, is an undesirable world.

2   The Public Bureaucracy*

J. W. Pfiffner
R. V. Presthus

The system of authority, men, offices, and methods that government uses to carry out its programs may be called the *bureaucracy*. Although the term is often used cynically, here it refers to a system of complex organization, made up of a vast number of technical and hierarchical roles, used to carry out policies usually made by others, and peculiarly suited for large-scale operations. Ideally, bureaucracy, which has existed since ancient times, demands from its members consistency, loyalty, and adaptability. Its major characteristics, both functional and dysfunctional, are the subject of this chapter.

* Reprinted and slightly abridged with permission of authors and publisher from J. W. Pfiffner and R. V. Presthus, *Public Administration*, Ronald Press, New York, 1967.

The Rise of Modern Bureaucracy

Modern bureaucracy developed hand in hand with the national state, which assumed many functions once carried out by religious orders. The first modern bureaucracy was probably the army, which replaced the transitory forces of feudal times in order to insure national survival. Mercantilism also encouraged bureaucracy as the early states embarked upon various public enterprises aimed at promoting industry and commerce.[1] The resulting mastery of detail by officials brought about one of the characteristics of public administration: the delegation of policy-making authority and discretion to the bureaucracy. Permanent subordinates of impermanent ministers assumed powers which made them indispensable. This feature of bureaucracy was well established by the seventeenth and eighteenth centuries. As a French scholar noted:

> The various ministers have accumulated for the century past so much detail in affairs of all kinds that it is impossible for them to attend to them directly. Thence a new kind of intermediary power has grown up between the ministers and the citizens . . . it is that of the clerks, persons absolutely unknown to the State, and who, however, speaking and writing in the name of ministers, have like them an absolute and irresistible power, and are even more than they sheltered from all investigation, since they are much less well known.[2]

Such developments meant that administration became more than merely a clerical function. Not only was the policy role of the administrator recognized, but also the fact that the best of plans require loyal and expert implementation.[3] When government's role was minimal and technology was primitive, the need for a competent bureaucracy was hardly felt. But the industrial state placed a premium on technical and organizational skill. As a result, traditional criticisms of bureaucracy are often irrelevant, although they may meet ideological needs.

Weber's Ideal-Type Construct

Bureaucracy differs from nation to nation, reflecting the values and institutions of the society it serves. Within a given society, moreover, bureaucracy is ambivalent, exhibiting both a will to power and growth and a resistance to change. One of the most helpful theoretical models for studying large-scale organization is the ideal-type concept of bureaucracy set down by Max

---

1 For the German example, see Thorstein Veblen, *Imperial Germany and the Industrial Revolution*, Macmillan, New York, 1946.

2 De Lucay, *Les Secrétaries. d'Etat depuis leur institution jusqu'à la mort de Louis XV*, Paris, 1881, p. 149, quoted and translated by Herman Finer in *The Theory and Practice of Modern Government*, Dial Press, New York, 1932, p. 1,234n.

3 One embryonic politician who recognized the expanding role of public administration was Woodrow Wilson; see his "The Study of Administration", Vol. 2, *Political Science Quarterly*, June 1887, pp. 197-222.

Weber, a German economist who wrote around the turn of the twentieth century.[4] However, his generalizations must be applied with caution. Drawn from Western Europe and ancient civilizations of China, Egypt, India, and Rome, where social mobility was limited and civil service entry and advancement were closely articulated with class and educational systems, Weber's inferences are most useful in appraising the rational and structural aspects of the American bureaucracy. But they fail to emphasize adequately its "informal" character and its highly political context, which reflect in turn the social and constitutional climate in which it developed. Although Weber's model is an effective research tool and a place from which one may start to analyze bureaucracy, it must therefore be qualified when applied to America.

Despite these qualifications, Weber is important for two reasons: he provided the first major theoretical analysis of twentieth-century large-scale organization; and he has had great influence on administrative thought and research in the United States.

It should be emphasized that Weber's was a construct of *formal* organization, and as such, parallels in many respects the integrationist model later referred to in our chapters on organization. Although it is impossible to consider Weber fully here, the generalizations that follow provide a rough outline of his bureaucratic model:

1. *Hierarchy.* Offices are organized on the hierarchical basis.

2. Bureaucracy is a term which applies to both public and private effort.

3. *Rationalized job structure.* There is a rational division of labor, and each position is accompanied by the legal authority necessary to accomplish the goals set.

4. *Formalization.* Acts, decisions, and rules are formulated and recorded in writing (red tape).

5. *Management separated from ownership.* There is a hired, professional administrative class.

6. There is no property right to office.

7. Special competence and training are required of the administrative class.

8. Members are selected competitively on the basis of competence.

9. *Legal flavor.* Weber's construct reflects the legalistic flavor attaching to administration in continental Europe. "Each office has a clearly defined sphere of competence in the legal sense."[5]

---

[4] Max Weber, *From Max Weber: Essays in Sociology* in H. H. Gerth and C. W. Mills (eds. and trans.), Oxford University Press, Fair Lawn, New Jersey, 1946; and *The Theory of Social and Economic Organization* in Talcott Parsons (ed. and trans.), Oxford University Press, Fair Lawn, New Jersey, 1947.

[5] Max Weber, *From Max Weber; Essays in Sociology, op. cit.,* p. 21.

Nature of Bureaucracy

Ideally, bureaucracy is the systematic organization of tasks and individuals into a pattern which can effectively attain the ends of group effort. Individual behavior is harnessed into productive channels by rules, sanctions, and exhortation. Everywhere a "maximum calculability" of rules is sought. Predictability, standardization, and loyalty are highly valued. A certain depersonalization follows in which regulations and precedents tend to become supreme and personal feelings are submerged. The discipline of the military and attending restrictions upon individualism are an illustration. While it is obviously impossible to achieve complete predictabilty (as our study of informal organization will reveal), a special virtue of bureaucracy is to minimize human irrationality.

Hierarchy

As seen earlier, the public bureaucracy is commonly defined as a closed hierarchical system in which, presumably, each person has a superior who directs his own efforts. The various layers are stratified according to authority, and ultimate control by those at the top is encouraged by a pyramidal structure. Formally, such is the case in most large-scale organizations. The error is in assuming that authority always follows the formal chain of command. Instead, we find various conflicting bases of authority at work.[6] Perhaps the most persistent challenger is specialization. Indeed, one of the few firm generalizations one can make about organizations is that tension will exist between authority based upon position and authority based upon skill.[7] Professionalization tends to aggravate this condition by focusing the loyalty of specialists on their national associations and their craft, rather than on the organization in which they work. Such professionals have been called "cosmopolitans," contrasted with "locals" who tend to remain loyal to their organizations.[8] Weber's assumption seems to have been that such conflicts would not occur, and that officials would conform nicely to hierarchical expectations. But not only does specialization now counter hierarchy, but the political milieu of our bureaucracy also encourages countervailing loci of influence and loyalty.

Technical Specialization

Specialization is another important condition of bureaucracy. We have seen that the origin of bureaucracy lies mainly in the need for technical skills.

---

[6] Robert Presthus, "Authority in Organizations" in S. Mailick and R. Van Ness, *Concepts and Issues in Administrative Behavior*, Prentice-Hall, Englewood Cliffs, New Jersey, 1962.
[7] This is the central theme in Victor A. Thompson, *Modern Organizations*, Knopf, New York, 1962.
[8] A. Gouldner, "Cosmopolitans and Locals: Toward an Analysis of Latent Social Roles", *Administrative Science Quarterly*, Vol. 2, December 1957 and March 1958, pp. 281-306, 403, 444.

Trained in a certain skill, performing it again and again, and viewing his position as a career, the official develops a high degree of proficiency and commitment. Specialization is reinforced by the fact that entry and advancement are based upon technical preparation and experience in a certain type of work. In both public and private enterprise, the demand for technical expertise continues unabated. Professional societies abound; vocabularies become intelligible only to the elect; and career training becomes increasingly specialized. Thus bureaucracy is both a cause and an effect of professionalization, bringing to routine matters greater precision, disinterest (the official's loyalty is assigned mainly to competent performance), and speed of operation. But specialization and the other attributes of bureaucracy have a paradoxical effect: They encourage introversion and a limited perspective which increases the inertia of big enterprises.

Framework of Law

Bureaucratic inflexibility is aggravated by the legal framework in which public officials work. Their conduct is bound up with the "rule of law," a principle brought to America from England, where it was developed as part of the long struggle against arbitrary government. The "rule of law" required that administrative actions affecting individual rights reflect precedent and legal sanction rather than arbitrary, personal discretion. To insure this, Congress has included in most of its legislation standards to guide the official in his relations with the citizen. The "rule of law," it must be said, does not mean that the state cannot deprive men of life, liberty, or property but only that such action must follow certain legal procedures. Thus the official must be able to justify every action by law or by administrative rules and orders created under statute law. In the area of administrative discretion the citizen has certain rights. Not only is he entitled to notice and hearing in regard to the matter which the state wishes to regulate, but he has the right of appeal against the administrative decision in a court of law.

It is often maintained that the attitudes of individuals reflect their work environment. Thus salesmen tend to be hail-fellow-well-met types, while research scientists often seem rather diffident. The public official is similarly conditioned by his environment. As the sociologist Robert Merton has shown, he will be oriented toward precedent; he will seek accountability through conformance with the law; he will lean toward inflexibility.[9] The administrator will be dependent upon his legal and financial aides, who can furnish a path through the maze of legal minutiae confronting him. The ludicrous ends to which this desire for accountability can lead are illustrated in a report of the first Hoover Commission. It was found that the cost of paying bills on purchase orders (half of which amounted to less than ten

---

[9] R. Merton, "Bureaucratic Structure and Personality" in Merton *et al.* (eds.), *Reader in Bureaucracy*, The Free Press, New York, 1953.

dollars) was more than the amount of the bill itself in nearly half of all cases.[10] Strict conformity to established procedures and legal regulations necessarily reduces dispatch and economy.

A Value System

Administrators are conditioned also by cultural values and the dominant opinions of their colleagues.[11] Generally they develop a value system which satisfactorily identifies their role with that of the organization, and in turn, the role of the latter with the values of society. Given the dominant free enterprise ethic of our society, public servants often develop feelings of insecurity based on the common view that they have, after all, "never met a payroll." It seems fair to say that the derogation of government is inevitably reflected in the marginal status of civil servants. The official's view of his role has been influenced in turn; he seeks morale through an emphasis on professional competence. The bureaucrat's existence is bound up with his specialist role and the proper exercise of it. Bureaucratic loyalty, for example, is less conferred upon a person — the supervisor or bureau chief — than upon impersonal functions. In theory, at least, the bureaucrat views himself as the objective instrument of popular will. At the same time, however, loyalty to certain abstractions such as the agency "mission," the political party, or the state may exist. Like other men, bureaucrats have political opinions which influence their decisions. In general, however, the public official exchanges professional expertise and competence for security and an assured income.

In European countries, the official receives psychic income in the form of social approval. The United States is almost unique in its lack of respect for public officials. There are several reasons for this, including the relative lack of class differentiation in America. The social distribution of power is important too. In England, for example, the higher civil service has long represented influential social groups.[12] Along with the military and politics, it has been among the most honored careers. Entry has been based upon costly educational preparation, which restricts the number of applicants while making for a system of "co-optation" in appointing candidates to the higher civil service. Co-optation (defined here as the control of entry by the members of a profession) is often a symptom of social stratification. In the United States, on the other hand, because of its wealth, the absence of a feudal tradition, and the frontier which provided unusual opportunity,

10 Commission on Organization of the Executive Branch of the Government, *The Organization and Management of Federal Supply Activities*, Government Printing Office, Washington, District of Columbia, 1948, note 2, pp. 26-27.

11 For an analysis of the values of federal officials, see L. Warner *et al*, *The Federal Executive*, Yale University Press, New Haven, Connecticut, 1963.

12 For a provocative historical analysis of the social basis and representative function of the British civil service, See J. Donald Kingsley, *Representative Bureaucracy*, Antioch Press, Yellow Springs, Ohio, 1944.

class lines have been more fluid and a business career has been more valued than one of public service.

The bureaucratic position involves an "office," frequently viewed as a life career, with a precise enumeration of duties. There is usually a distinction between the power exercised by the bureaucrat and his authority as a person. While deference may tranfer from office to social life, there is a complete separation of power; the bureaucrat away from his job has no more authority than anyone else. His authority is the authority of the impersonal "office" in which he works. Compensation is in the form of a fixed wage, preferably in money form. Ordinarily he has no other source of income. The "offices" are arranged in an hierarchical order insuring control over promotion, demotion, appointment, and removal. Fitness is generally determined by technical skill or academic attainment tested by examination and often requiring long periods of training. This is the general structure of bureaucracy which, as Weber points out, is the most efficient instrument of large-scale administration yet developed.

Criticisms of Bureaucracy

In our society, with its dominant values of free enterprise and its fear of centralized political power, the growth of a huge federal bureaucracy has brought many criticisms, even predictions of national decline, because of the assumed loss of individual freedom and initiative as government assumes more and more responsibility for insuring security. The remainder of the chapter will be concerned with the validity of such criticisms.

Criticisms of bureaucracy include the charge that bureaucracy is unresponsive to popular demands; that bureaucrats have a lust for power; and perhaps most important, that the bureaucracy is usurping the policymaking role which traditionally has been the prerogative of the legislative branch and the President.[13]

The critics of bureaucracy, it seems, proceed upon the Hobbesian assumption that men thirst for power, that power corrupts and power once delegated is impossible to control. The basic idea is often fear of government. Allied with this is a belief, of eighteenth-century liberal origin, that big government necessarily subverts individual political and civil liberties. On the other hand there is the "twentieth-century" liberal doctrine which, stemming from a happier view of the nature of man, would invest government with great power in the firm belief that public power alone can mitigate social and economic inequity. Of late, however, this group too has become more concerned with the dangers of big government, particularly in the area of civil liberties. Although these conflicting ideologies are not watertight, they represent roughly the dominant split in regard to the "proper" role of government.

[13] See, among others, Ludwig von Mises, *Bureaucracy*, Yale University Press, New Haven, Connecticut, 1944; Frederick Hayek, *Road to Serfdom*, University of Chicago Press, Chicago, 1944; and James Burnham, *The Managerial Revolution*, John Day, New York, 1941.

The Charge of Unresponsiveness

"Responsiveness" here refers to the speed and the attitude with which the bureaucracy reacts to changes in the political climate. The claim that the bureaucracy is unresponsive has some basis in fact. The factor of size is relevant, for bigness brings about standardized procedures which make change difficult. Face-to-face contacts are minimized, and when they occur, officials often seem unduly impersonal. This frustrates the human desire for personal recognition, if not for preference. Actually, the very attributes of bureaucracy that make for effectiveness and popular control tend to move toward extremes which destroy their initial advantage. Routine procedures breed inflexibility, while a passion for accountability fosters legalism and delay. The official becomes a specialist, intellectually isolated, oriented toward techniques rather than people, who may appear as vexing inconsistencies in an otherwise rational system.

The bureaucracy, moreover, is an institution with a certain self-sufficiency; it has its own hierarchy of values and its drives for status and power. Like other institutions, it resists change when change threatens its interests. The precedents and procedures, the "official secrets," the social values of individual officials, and the innate inflexibility of big organizations — all tend to slow down the reaction time of the bureaucracy. Thus it is not surprising that the civil service, which is often regarded as radical, is in fact often conservative. Many examples can be cited: the counterrevolutionary view of the German service under the Weimar Republic; the resistance of certain elements in the British civil service to Keynesian economic policy; the opposition of the old-line agencies to some New Deal programs. One suspects that, in the round, radicalism is hardly a flourishing quality among civil servants.

Despite this, the democratic civil service has been responsive to great changes in public policy during this century. It is this large context, rather than in the area of random individual contacts with reluctant officials, that responsiveness is meaningful. In both the United States and Britain the social programs of the New Deal and the Labour government were carried through. There was inevitably some resistance, but the protests of those who opposed the results of the programs suggest the extent to which change *was* effected. The political neutrality of the British civil service is surely exaggerated, but the British system of party government insures majority rule. In the United States, a much greater opportunity for official resistance exists, but here, too, the experience of the recent past indicates that the bureaucracy, like the Supreme Court, will follow the election returns.

The reconciliation of responsibility and the official's need for initiative is perhaps the basic problem of democratic administration. The expanding role of government has brought a greater need for top-notch personnel. The casual acceptance of indifferent performance and the uninformed criticism of government which have been part of our ideology are luxuries we can no longer afford. The solution may require more faith in the good intensions of government rather than the corrosive attitude that often exists. To strew the bureaucrat's path with every conceivable obstacle, seeking account- ability, while condemning him for failing to act decisively, is unfair. Private management has usually tried to get good men, make their authority and responsibility clear, and then leave them alone. We fail to follow this policy in government. Obviously, the final control must rest with elected representatives, but if the reaction time of the bureaucracy is to be quick- ened, there is a need for the positive attitude reflected, for example, in the policy of transferring hiring responsibility from the Civil Service Commis- sion to the line agencies.

The Will to Power

That there are power-hungry bureaucrats, no one can doubt. The struggles between the Army Corps of Engineers and the Bureau of Reclamation or between the Soil Conservation Service and the Extension Service furnish illustrations. But to assume that big government results from the personal ambition of officials is a great oversimplification. This view also under- estimates the final authority of Congress as keeper of the purse. The execu- tive branch has a big advantage in preparing the national budget, framing political issues, and presenting them to the country. But if government is to expand, large appropriations are needed, and these in the last analysis must come from Congress. Moreover, if Congress is now unable to control the executive budget because of inadequate staff aid, this too is a condition which the legislators could improve. In sum, it is population growth, urbanization, industrialization, interest-group demands, war, depression, and the threat of war that have brought big government.

Usurpation of Policy Determination

A more significant criticism of bureaucracy is the claim that too much policy determination has been wrested from the President and the Congress. This is a reasonable claim. In the past we have had a philosophical ideal which called for a nice distinction between policy and administration. This doctrine holds that "politics" and policy determination must be reserved to the legislature and chief executive and that the administrative branch must limit itself to carrying out policy. Democratic responsibility can be achieved only if the broad outlines of public policy are determined by a representative Congress. The appointed bureaucracy is obviously less respon- sible to the citizen and henceforth should have no part in determining what government should do. Like Aristotle's slave, the bureaucracy is merely an animated instrument, requiring the guidance of a rational master, the President and the legislature.

The extent to which such beliefs persist is suggested by the second

Hoover Commission, whose recommendations included a "clear delineation between career and noncareer posts. More noncareer executives are required at the departmental level to take over all political and partisan tasks, including work of that nature which many career executives now are forced to handle." Similarly, the words of Philip Young, former Chairman of the United States Civil Service Commission, indicate that the policy-administration distinction remains seductive. Regarding the personnel policy of the Eisenhower Administration. Young maintained, "We are making a clear distinction for the first time between the political appointment area and the career service area. We are providing an orderly, logical means of placing in policy-making positions persons who are sympathetic to the policies of the administration. At the same time, we are removing the career service as far as possible from political interference."

This thesis is tenable; it is good democratic theory. But it does not fit either the needs or the realities of government today.

The discrepancy arises because our public administration functions in a political and technical context. The separation-of-powers system, local election of congressmen, competition among bureaucrats for new programs, efforts of political parties to effect change once they achieve control of government, and the influence of big interest groups (which reflects the separation of powers and the localism of American politics) — all tend to make ours a highly political administrative system.[14] Zones of discretion that grow increasingly "political" as one ascends the hierarchy exist throughout civil service. The policeman chooses between a ticket and a reprimand; the foreign service officer "makes policy on the cables." The political nature of administration and the need for the delegation of legislative authority blur the line between policy making and the execution of policy; the technical character of government forces the amateur legislator to lean upon the expert official.

The regulatory commissions are illustrative. Congress was obliged to create expert bodies to handle the complicated task of regulating important economic interests. The general framework for such regulation was set down by Congress, but in carrying out that policy and meeting a bewildering variety of special conditions, considerable policy discretion had to be delegated to the commissions. In England, similarly, it has been shown that the administrative class exercises a sustained influence on policy. Indeed, some observers claim that only the most accomplished minister can avoid being unduly influenced by career officials.[15]

---

14 See, among others, "Unofficial Government: Pressure Groups and Lobbies," 319, *Annals of the American Academy of Political and Social Science*, September 1958.

15 "[T]he Government of Great Britain is in fact carried on, not by the Cabinet, nor even by the individual ministers, but by the Civil Service." Sydney and Beatrice Webb, *Constitution for the Socialist Commonwealth of Great Britain*, Longmans, Green, London, 1920, p. 67. See also Brian Chapman, *British Government Observed*, George Allen & Unwin, London, 1963.

Some Conclusions

In reviewing the principal criticism of bureacracy, it seems possible to temper the claim that the administrative machine is unresponsive to changing popular demands. While routine matters are often time-consuming and exasperating, in the vital area of broad policy change the bureaucracy is responsive. Within the past thirty years, minor social revolutions have been carried out under the New Deal in the United States and in Britain with the cooperation of the bureaucracy. The official apparatus is often legalistic and bound up in red tape; yet much of this comes from the passion for accountability which the public brings to government. Here, perhaps, a change in the external environment is the main requirement for improvement. That public servants sometimes have a lust for power, or at any rate for survival, is undoubtedly true. This is a universal attribute of men; but government service is probably a poor place to indulge it. Both the nature of our federal system and that of bureaucratic decision making by committee thwart vigorous action: power and responsibility are too broadly shared. The expansion of public power is largely due to depression, war, and world revolution rather than to aggressive officials.

That these officials now have a major role in policy determination cannot be denied. In the light of its implications for democratic control, this development is significant. In view of the political and technical nature of modern administration, however, it seems unrealistic to advocate that the official restrict himself to a purely advisory role. Delegation will continue; alternatives will present themselves; differences in value judgments will abound; and technical expertise will command respect. Perhaps more adequate control of administrative discretion is necessary, but this must be done without hamstringing public officials.

3   Premises of Public Administration: Past and Emerging*

Wallace S. Sayre

When the first textbooks in public administration appeared in the United States a little more than thirty years ago Leonard D. White's *Introduction to the Study of Public Administration* (Macmillan Co., 1926), and W. F. Willoughby's *Principles of Public Administration* (Johns Hopkins Press,

* Reprinted with permission of author and publisher from *Public Administration Review*, Vol. 18, Spring 1958, pp. 102-105.

1927), they were based upon premises and concepts about the executive branch and its administrative agencies which had been at least a half century in the making. The civil service reform movement beginning in the late 1860's and culminating in the Pendleton Act of 1883, Woodrow Wilson's essays on "Public Administration" in 1887, Goodnow's *Politics and Administration* in 1900 (Macmillan Co.), the work of the New York Bureau of Municipal Research and its counterparts throughout the country, the scientific management movement in industry, the reorganization movement (including the Taft Commission studies of 1910-12, the Illinois and New York reports of 1915), the city manager movement beginning in 1910, the Budget and Accounting Act of 1921, the Classification Act of 1923, the New York state governmental reorganizations under Governor Smith — all these, as well as other events and writings, helped to provide the raw materials for the syntheses attempted in the pioneer textbooks in public administration. These texts, in turn, not only provided the first effective teaching instruments for the new field of study; they also codified the premises, the concepts, and the data for the new public administration.

The Textbooks' Codification

The main elements of this codification of 1926-27 may be very briefly summarized:

1. The politics-administration dichotomy was assumed both as a self-evident truth and as a desirable goal; administration was perceived as a self-contained world of its own, with its own separate values, rules, and methods.
2. Organization theory was stated in "scientific management" terms; that is, it was seen largely as a problem in organization technology — the necessities of hierarchy, the uses of staff agencies, a limited span of control, subdivision of work by such "scientific" principles as purpose, process, place, or clientele.
3. The executive budget was emphasized as an instrument of rationality, of coordination, planning, and control.
4. Personnel management was stressed as an additional element of rationality (jobs were to be described "scientifically," employees were to be selected, paid, advanced by "scientific" methods).
5. A "neutral" or "impartial" career service was required to insure competence, expertise, rationality.
6. A body of administrative law was needed to prescribe standards of due process in administrative conduct.

In these pioneer texts the responsibility of administrative agencies to popular control was a value taken-for-granted; the responsiveness of administrators and bureaucrats was not seen as a problem because everyone then understood that politics and policy was separate from administration, which was concerned exclusively with the execution of assignments handed down from the realm of politics.

The events of the 1930's — depression, New Deal, the rise of Big Government — served at first to confirm the premises of the texts. The expansion of government, especially the great growth in the size, complexity, and discretionary power of administrative agencies, was regarded as making all the more relevant and urgent the tools of rationality which public administration offered to the practitioners in the new and expanded agencies of the executive branch. Many of the teachers and the students of public administration themselves became practitioners.

The *Report* of the President's Committee on Administrative Management and its literary companion-piece, the Gulick and Urwick *Papers on the Science of Administration* (Institute of Public Administration, Columbia University), both appearing in 1937, represent the high noon of orthodoxy in public administration theory in the United States. In the Gulick and Urwick *Papers* were brought together eleven essays constituting the classic statements then available in the United States and Europe, in business and public administration, of the elements believed to be embodied in *the science* of administration. (It is perhaps worth noting that of the ten authors only Gulick wrote as a political scientist.) The *Report* of the President's Committee, for its part, set forth in eloquent language the prescriptions of public administration made orthodox by the texts of 1926-27. The significant and impressive managerial changes in the executive branch of the national government which were made as a result of the *Report* strengthened the prestige of public administration as a body of precepts.

Post-War Dissent

But the high noon of orthodoxy had a brief hour of prominence. World War II interrupted the further development of public administration research and literature, and at the close of the war the resumption took the form of dissent and heterodoxy. Prewar orthodoxy, it is true, was reasserted in the *Reports* of the two Hoover Commissions, in most of the textbooks, and in the rash of post-war administrative surveys at state and local government levels. There was, however, a strong ferment of dissent in the monographic literature, in the journals, and elsewhere. The dissent took three main lines:

1. *The assault upon the politics-administration dichotomy.* This keystone of prewar orthodox public administration had always been viewed with some skepticism by a considerable number of political scientists (particularly by those mainly concerned with political theory or with the political process); to them, all administrative agencies and their staffs seemed to be involved in politics. This view was now to recruit strong support from within the public administration fraternity itself. The first textbook to appear after the war — Fritz Morstein Marx (editor), *The Elements of Pub-*

lic Administration (Prentice-Hall, 1946), with fourteen political scientists among its contributors — brought a new, if still mild, emphasis upon the involvement of administrators and administrative agencies in policy formation, in the use of discretionary power, and in the general political process. In 1949 Paul H. Appleby's influential monograph, *Policy and Administration* (University of Alabama Press), boldly and persuasively described administration as "the eighth political process." In 1950 the second post-war text — Herbert A. Simon, Donald W. Smithburg, and Victor A. Thompson, *Public Administration* (Alfred A. Knopf) — presented a systematic exposition of public administration as a political and group process. In 1952 the first casebook in public administration — significantly titled *Public Administration and Policy Development*, Harold Stein (editor), (Harcourt, Brace and Co.) — emphasized in each of its case studies the political role of the administrator; and, in the introductory essay, Harold Stein wrote incisively of "public administration as politics." These several illustrations serve to reveal the stages by which public administration as politics, as involved deeply in policy and values, was firmly established in the literature of public administration within a few years after the war. Even the most orthodox texts yielded some ground on the doctrine that politics and administration were separable.

2. *The assault upon the claims to science and to universal principles of administration.* The premises which pre-war public administration had borrowed primarily from scientific management were of course necessarily subjected to criticism by all those who were asserting that administration was a political process. These critics were soon joined by the students of the history and development of administrative theory. When, for example, Dwight Waldo published in 1948 his important study, *The Administrative State: A Study of the Political Theory of American Public Administration* (The Ronald Press), he demonstrated how value-loaded, how culture-bound, how political — in short, how "unscientific" — were the premises, the "principles," the logic, of orthodox public administration.

To these powerful critical voices there was soon added a third group: the prophets of a new science of administration. The outstanding representative of this school of thought has been Herbert Simon whose *Administrative Behavior: A Study of Decision-Making Processes in Administrative Organizations* (Macmillan Co., 1947) not only attacked the orthodox "principles" of public administration as being merely "proverbs" but also presented a new administrative science based upon the argument of logical-positivism that facts must be separated from values. For Simon, the orthodox politics-administration dichotomy was to be replaced by the new fact-value dichotomy.

These critics have successfully made their point. The claims to scientific principles and to their universal applicability have been placed on the defensive although they have not entirely disappeared from the literature of public administration. But the claims of a new science of administration have not been widely accepted.

3. *"Sociological" studies of bureaucracy.* Another stream of ideas and knowledge contributing to the post-war growth of dissent from orthodoxy has been the "sociological" study of the public bureaucracies as representing in themselves a form of political power. The primary impact of these studies has been upon the orthodox doctrines of the neutral career service. Philip Selznick's *TVA and the Grass Roots* (University of California Press, 1948), for example, revealed a career bureaucracy deeply involved in the political process, demonstrating that the creation and maintenance of a career bureaucracy is more a problem in values and politics than a problem of administrative science.

Emerging Reformulations

The post-war decade of dissent and heterodoxy has not yet revealed the clear outlines of an emerging new body of comprehensive doctrine. But perhaps we can anticipate some of the major components of the reformulation now in process. The premises around which the new consensus — perhaps to become a new orthodoxy — would seem to be forming, may be stated somewhat as follows:

1. Public administration doctrine and practice is inescapably culture-bound. It is also bound to more specific values: to varying conceptions of the general public interest, to particular interest-group values, to the values of a specific administrative organization or bureaucracy at a specific time.

2. Public administration is one of the major political processes. The exercise of discretionary powers, the making of value choices, is a characteristic and increasing function of administrators and bureaucrats; they are thus importantly engaged in politics.

3. Organization theory in public administration is a problem in political strategy; a choice of organization structure is a choice of which interest or which value will have preferred access or greater emphasis. Organization is, therefore, as Robert A. Dahl and Charles E. Lindblom suggests in *Politics, Economics and Welfare* (Harper & Bros., 1953), a determinant in bargaining.

4. Management techniques and processes have their costs as well as their benefits. Each new version has a high obsolescence rate, its initial contributions to rationality declining as it becomes the vested interest of its own specialist guardians and/or other groups with preferred access.

5. Public administration is ultimately a problem in political theory: the fundamental problem in a democracy is responsibility to popular control; the responsibility and responsiveness of the administrative agencies and the bureaucracies to the elected officials (the chief executives, the legislators) is of central importance in a government based increasingly on the exercise of discretionary power by the agencies of administration.

4 Government Bureaucrats Are Different*

James F. Guyot

At the sound of the word "bureaucrat" the man in the street will probably imagine some time-serving Post Office clerk or a power-hungry New Dealer. At the same time a sociologist will conjure up the "ideal type" of an official occupying a defined position within a large scale, rational organization (be it church, army, trade union, or telephone company), where he plays out his role according to prescribed rules and becomes more like those rules day by day. Perhaps it is a fault of our language that one word carries two such different meanings, yet there is a common referent. Both layman and academic would agree that a GS-9 Qualifications Rating Examiner in the U.S. Civil Service Commission is a "bureaucrat." But which is the more appropriate characterization? How might we distinguish government bureaucrats from their opposite numbers in the business world? Or are they both running the same race under different colors?

The Togetherness of Person and Position

Underneath a characterization of bureaucrats in terms of what kinds of positions they hold in what kinds of organizations lies the assumption that there exists a particularly appropriate relationship between an individual and his occupational position. Speculation on the nature of this relationship has led to the flowering of a number of interesting social theories such as Max Weber's delineation of the role of the "Protestant Ethic" in the development of capitalist institutions, the influence of class on consciousness in Marxian sociology, and Robert K. Merton's often quoted essay on "Bureaucratic Structure and Personality," which concludes that:

> . . . the bureaucratic structure exerts a constant pressure upon the official to be "methodical, prudent, disciplined." If the bureaucracy is to operate successfully, it must maintain a high degree of reliability of behavior. . . . Discipline can be effective only if the ideal patterns are buttressed by strong sentiments.[1]

Here the question arises, to what extent do occupational situations shape personality or to what extent do personality needs influence the selection and continuation in an occupation? Sociologists and psychologists tend to give different weights to occupational role and personality factors. Others give up the game and label the interaction of organizational and individual forces the "fusion process." Another set of theoretical questions has to do with the latitude of personal behavior that "fits" into what may be defined as a particular role. The present state of role theory is too unstable to pro-

---

* Reprinted and slightly abridged with permission of author and publisher from *Public Administration Review*, Vol. 22, December 1962, pp. 195-198, 201-202.
1 R. K. Merton *et al* (eds.), *Reader in Bureaucracy*, The Free Press, New York, 1952, p. 365.

vide much guidance here. Nevertheless, there is general agreement that some sort of a relationship does exist between personalities and occupational roles. From this it follows that significant differences or similarities in the character of bureaucratic roles in government agencies and large business organizations, should appear also in the personality characteristics of people playing comparable roles in these two structures.

Who Goes with Whom?

What motives propel a bureaucrat along his career in the federal government, and how are they different from those of his counterpart in a large business organization? What tells us more about the structure of a man's motives: knowing whether he works in a public or a private bureaucracy or knowing whether he is an engineer, an accountant, or a public relations man? Speaking concretely, does the personality of a production engineer in the Air Material Command run along lines somewhat similar to a budget assistant in the Office of Naval Research, or is it closer to the personality of a managing foreman at General Motors?

To answer this question and probe the reality behind the public and the sociological images of bureaucrats personality tests were given to comparable samples of 247 middle managers coming from several government departments and a range of large private firms.[2] To aid the comparison, these parallel samples are cross cut into five types of occupational roles similar to those used in the *Dictionary of Occupational Titles* and other research on occupations. The three motives measured by these tests — motivation for *Achievement*, for *Affiliation*, and for *Power* — are particularly relevant to the characteristics of these two images. *Achievement* motivation resembles loosely the "Protestant ethic," a desire to accomplish something as an end in itself, a concern with standards of performance. *Affiliation* motivation, on the other hand, as a concern with acceptance or rejection by others comes close to the "social ethic" which Whyte finds motivating the organization man. *Power* motivation is simply the desire to dominate or influence others and, as a crucial variable in any governmental system, its importance grows with the increasing effectiveness of the machinery of government.[3]

A Split Decision

Table 1 shows the average motive scores for matching the samples of governmental and business bureaucrats. Checking the position of our hypothetical production engineer in the Air Material Command, it can be seen

[2] The characteristics of these samples are discussed in the note at the end of this article.
[3] For discussion of the origins, measurement, and social significance of these motives see David C. McClelland, *et al, The Achievement Motive*, Appleton-Century-Crofts, New York, 1953, John W. Atkinson (ed.), *Motives in Fantasy, Action, and Society*, Van Nostrand, Princeton, New Jersey, 1958, and particularly McClelland's *The Achieving Society*, Van Nostrand, Princeton, New Jersey, 1961.

Table 1

Achievement, Affiliation and Power Motivation Scores by Sector and by Role for a Sample of Business and Federal Government Middle Managers

Occupational Roles	Cell Size Govt.	Cell Size Bus.	Achievement			Affiliation			Power		
			Govt.	Bus.	Av. for Role	Govt.	Bus.	Av. for Role	Govt.	Bus.	Av. for Role
Sales and Public Contact	8	21	6.00	7.467	6.738	14.71	18.79	16.75	19.42	16.72	18.07
General Management	33	30	8.758	5.233	6.995	17.90	20.02	18.96	15.41	14.33	14.87
Budget and Personnel	53	15	6.019	5.333	5.676	16.94	17.49	17.22	14.92	15.15	15.03
Science and Research Engineering	23	8	7.783	3.875	5.872	15.73	16.61	16.17	16.97	18.60	17.79
Production Engineering	30	26	7.00	5.385	6.193	15.91	22.74	19.33	15.18	15.18	15.18
Average for each Sector			7.112	5.460		16.24	19.13		16.38	16.00	

that in *Achievement* and *Affiliation* motivation he resembles his fellow government employees and is not much like his opposite number on the business side. In *Power* motivation, however, he seems closer to his business counterpart.

A statistical analysis of variance in the average motive scores finds these relationships true for the sample at large. *Achievement* motivation distinguishes significantly between government and business bureaucrats as a whole but not between different occupational roles encompassing both government and business middle managers. The same is true for *Affiliation* motivation, except that some of the variation can be attributed to a combination of role and sector factors. But, with *Power* motivation occupational roles are clearly distinguished while differences between business and government are not. In the first two motives there are fundamental differences between bureaucrats who work for the government and those who work for private business.[4]

Do these findings mean that the sociological image of bureaucracy is a mirage? Not at all. There are significant similarities along the lines of occupation in *Power* motivation and occupational roles bear some relation to differences in *Affiliation* motivation. Although occupational roles do not distinguish motivations across the board, some other organizational characteristic or combination of characteristics such as size of organization, degree of centralization, etc. might do so. Do these findings mean that the popular image is a true copy? We must look at the nature of the differences in motivation between government and business bureaucrats to answer this question.

Distinguishing Between Bureaucrats

Overall differences in motivation between government and business bureaucrats appear in Figure 1. Here the government bureaucrats show a higher level of *Achievement* motivation while the businessmen are higher in *Affiliation* motivation. This is quite the opposite from what an examination of American folklore would lead one to expect. Furthermore, the expected distinction in *Power* motivation is too small to be significant. How can we explain research results which fly in the face of widely if not altogether reasonably held beliefs, and what significance does this have for the role of government bureaucracy in the United States?

First of all, let us keep in mind the time and space dimensions of the samples from which these results were drawn. These are men who held middle management rank in large-scale government and business organizations during the late 1950's and who probably selected their particular bureaucratic career sometime before or shortly after World War II. The spread of the government sample does not include such stereotyped

---

[4] In *Achievement* motivation sector differences are significant with $P < .05$ in *Affiliation* motivation both sector and a combination of sector and role factors are significant with $P < .01$, while in *Power* motivation role factors are significant with $P < .05$.

departments as State and the Post Office but covers rather heavily the area of the defence agencies. Neither does the business sample cover all kinds of businesses but only those firms large enough and "progressive" enough to ship young men off for a year or so to high priced executive development programs. Taking account of these limitations for generalizations can be suggested to explain these results.

Figure 1

Relative levels of achievement, affiliation, and powers motivation in comparable samples of government and business bureaucrats[a]

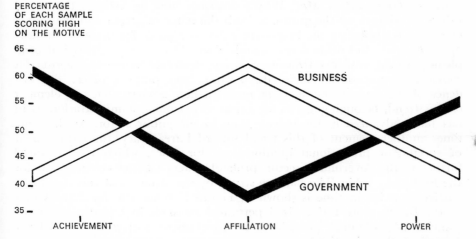

a In comparing samples of 147 government and 100 business bureaucrats, the differences in *Achievement* and *Affiliation* motivation are statistically significant ($X^2 = 8.70$, P < .02 and $X^2 = 5.47$, P < .04 respectively) while the difference in *Power* motivation is not. ($X^2 = 0.448$, P > .50).

1. The merit system has made at least some of the impact it was intended to make on the character of the civil service.
2. "Bureaucratic" recruitment to management positions draws more from the lower socio-economic groups than do the usual processes of business succession.
3. The money motive and the Protestant Ethic are not the same thing.
4. The civil service is no special preserve for the quest for power.

The Protestant Ethic, the Social Ethic and the Merit System

Perhaps the most general formal distinction in character between public and private bureaucracies lies in that bundle of personnel practices known as the "merit system." In theory, regularized and objective criteria rather than caprice and personal favor govern the selection, retention, and promotion of civil service employees while careers in the business world are shaped by a complex of factors among which favoritism and nepotism may play a significant role. If there really exists such a difference in the character of these two bureaucracies, then a prima facie case could be made for finding a higher level of *Achievement* motivation in one and a higher level of *Affiliation* motivation in the other just as they appear in Figure 1.[5]

Another factor contributing to a heavy concern for the affections of others on the part of rising junior executives would be the relatively longer apprenticeship to the "human relations approach" which business organizations, especially the progressive ones, have enjoyed.

In the *Organization Man* Whyte describes how he believes the Social Ethics or reliance on the group, as both the mode of action and the source of values, is displacing the Protestant Ethic as a guide for those on the way up in business and other large organizations. Here is a psychological complement to the bureaucratization of society described by the sociologists. Of course the sweep of any social trend varies from place to place. The evidence of the study in motivations reported here suggests that one element of this trend, belongingness as an aspect of personnel administration, is in fact more advanced in the private than in the public sector. At the same time, another element of this trend toward bureaucracy, the requirement of specific or professional qualifications for office, which has advanced further in the government sector, probably offers a better environment for the Protestant Ethic. The balance struck by the elements of this trend at a particular point in time is shown in Figure 1. What are the chances that in the future more rationalized personnel methods in business and more judicialized personnel procedures in government will push the balance toward another direction?

The Profit Motive and the Motivation to Achieve

Frequently the fundamental difference in character between business and government organizations is defined as the operation of the "profit motive" in one and its absence in the other. From this it follows that high *Achievement* motivation should be more characteristic of business than government. But, what role does the profit motive play in large-scale business organizations these days, and how congenial is the pursuit of money with the *Achievement* motive as defined in this research?

[5] Evidence of such a difference in the weight of personal advantage is hard to come by although there is general agreement that government has tranditionally led business in the use of objective selection techniques. Paul P. Van Riper, *History of the United States Civil Service*, Row, Peterson, New York, 1958, pp. 279-282. Sharper evidence in this direction comes from analysis of subsamples within the groups tested. One of the business groups shows a slight but not statistically significant relation between success in the organization (salary divided by age) and high affiliation motivation while John Hill has found in a selected government subsample a significant and *inverse* relation between success (GS grade divided by age) and high affiliation motivation. See Ch. 7 of McClelland, *op. cit.*

The middle manager in mid-century seems a far cry from the rational economic man or the lonely free enterpriser of an earlier era. It would be difficult to define what meaning "profits" carries with any but the very top level employees of many of today's large-scale, complex, business organizations. Probably, the closest approximation to "profits" as an operative incentive would be a sense of identification with the organization and its successes, which successes may be measured in terms of growth in size, developing and maintaining a reputation for craftsmanship and service, or technical leadership within its field, as well as a high rate of profits. Similarly, a government employee may measure the success of his particular agency in both concrete and more abstract ways — the launching of an earth satellite, the fair distribution of welfare benefits, or a high rate of returns in the collection of income tax.

But, assume that businessmen are fundamentally more concerned with making money for themselves and perhaps others, for they do bring in greater incomes than do government servants. This concern in itself is not enough to qualify them as devotees of the Protestant Ethic or the *Achievement* motive. Speaking of the Protestant Ethic, Weber points out that "the ideal type of capitalistic entrepreneur ... gets nothing out of his wealth for himself, except the irrational sense of having done his job well."[6] Experimental studies with the *Achievement* motive indicate that money is an effective stimulus for people high in the motive only when it is perceived as a measure of success. In fact a survey of the occupational values of college students distinguished the pursuit of money quite strongly from those values logically associated with the *Achievement* motive — creativity, originality, and the opportunity to use special abilities and aptitudes. Furthermore, the study found that "money and security, which have traditionally been considered polar opposites as occupational values, are, on the contrary psychologically close together."[7]

The profit motive in its mid-century form may not have been a great attraction for men with a lot of *Achievement* motivation. On the other hand, the challenge of the New Deal, coming at a time when many of today's middle managers were shaping their career images, may well have provided an incentive for such men to join the government service. If this was the pattern of the past, what can we say about the appeals of the government service in the 1960's? Is the prospect as dark as it was painted in Edward H. Litchfield's, "Apostasy of a Merit Man," at the Public Personnel Association's International Conference in 1960?[8] Does the enthusiastic response of the college generation to the Peace Corps mean that at least in certain areas government service offers the main challenge?

---

6 Max Weber, *The Protestant Ethic and the Spirit of Capitalism*, Talcott Parsons (trans.), Scribner's, New York, 1958, p. 71.

7 Morris Rosenberg *et al*, *Occupations and Values*, The Free Press, New York, 1957, pp. 5, 14.

8 *Public Personnel Review*, 24, 85-89, March-April 1961, pp. 85-89.

The Benevolent Leviathan

The popular image of the character of government employees mentioned at the beginning of this article is made up of two opposing elements 1) laziness and incompetence, and 2) malevolence and an attempt to control the lives of the citizens. If this article has shown that the first of these elements is not as characteristic as commonly thought, does that increase the threat posed by the second?

Certainly the "First Problem of Politics" in the democracies today is how to maintain effective citizen control over the growing apparatus of government. Not only the size and scope of government activity but improvements in social technology as well have brought about a concentration of power in the government bureaucracy which some fear may be able to pursue an autonomous course armed with its special information, expertise and indispensability. From time to time *Horrible Examples* of this possibility are drawn from the operations of the Department of Defense. Frequently solutions to this problem are sought in institutional controls working within the bureaucracy or through Congress and the courts.

On the psychological side the problem seems more ominous. Elaborating on the folk wisdom that "power is of an encroaching nature," Michels forged inevitably into his "iron law of oligarchy" when he demonstrated how in the German social revolutionary parties holding a position of power induces the official to displace the general goals of the organization in favor of his own power interests. Pessimists claim that the opportunity to tyrannize over their fellow men attracts the worst sort of people to public office in a welfare state. To what extent does the availability of the means to power draw out the motive for power, or how much hope is there that self-restraint may supplement the institutional checks placed on the autonomy of the bureaucrat?[9]

The research results reported in Figure 1 suggest that the opportunity to exercise power in a government bureau is no more enticing than it is in an executive suite in a business organization. Looking at those particular occupations which exercise power on the clientele of the organization we find that income tax collectors are lower than the average in *Power* motivation while salesmen are the highest of any group. Perhaps the existing institutional controls have placed such curbs on individual autonomy that the civil service is not an unusually attractive field for those absorbed in the pursuit of power. Here, a comparison with the motivations of men in the elective branch of the government could be interesting.

Image and Reality

In the age of the Welfare State and Competitive Coexistence special demands are placed on government. How well these demands are met depends in part on the image government servants hold for themselves and

---

[9] See R. Michels, *Political Parties*, The Free Press, New York, 1949.

the image of them held by those who deal extensively with them — congressmen; the business and academic communities; students, who are potential recruits to the government service; and citizens, who must ultimately sanction the behavior of government servants.

Empirical test of the popular and an academic image of the civil servant seems to show both images to be erroneous. The government bureaucrat of this study emerges as more energetic, less dependent, and no more power-hungry than his opposite number on the business side.

A Note on Methodology

Middle managers were selected for this study because, as C. Wright Mills suggests, "It is in the middle brackets of managers that bureaucratic procedures and styles are most in evidence," and it seemed worthwhile to compare two kinds of bureaucracy. At higher levels the government bureaucrat's special relation to Congress might reduce this comparability. Since the term "middle management" carries a variety of meanings, samples of businessmen were decided upon who had been selected for middle management development programs and government members of similar programs who ranged between grades GS-12 and GS-15. The two samples that resulted are well matched in age and education as shown in Table 2.

Table 2

Age and Education of the Samples of Business and
Federal Government Middle Managers

		Government	Business
Age	Range	29–46	27–42
	Average	37.8	35.3
Education	Attended College	92.5%	94.0%
	Advanced Degree	16.0%	9.0%
Total in Sample		147	100

The next question is, how representative are the samples? The fact that these people were chosen by their organization for executive development programs indicates at least that they are not misfits and, perhaps, that they are the ideal type of business and government bureaucrats. To the extent that these samples represent such a vanguard they may be quite unlike the average government or business middle manager. The "vanguard" aspect of the government sample is supported also by the heavy weighting given the currently significant Department of Defense (80.3% of the sample yet only 50% of total civilian government employment). To reflect some of the diversity of government the Treasury Department (8.8% of the sample) was included as one of the traditional agencies, the Department of H.E.W.

(7.5%) as one of the welfare agencies, and some men from research and intelligence agencies (3.4%) who happened to be attending the business training programs. While the diversity of business organizations would be even more difficult to represent in detail, the business sample moves in that direction by drawing from a variety of industrial and consumer goods industries and utilities throughout the nation.

To the extent that the size of a sample controls its breadth of representativeness, these samples of 100 business and 147 government middle managers are about as representative as samples of higher level bureaucrats such as Reinhold Dendix's 192 higher civil servants and W. E. Henry's over one hundred business executives. In this respect they may be less representative than the more than eight thousand big business leaders who answered Warner and Abegglen's questionnaire or the 400-member sample to be interviewed with T.A.T.'s in the Warner-Van Riper-Martin study of federal executives.

In time perspective the samples represent middle managers of the middle and late 1950's. Two groups of the business sample were tested by Professor McClelland of Harvard in the spring of 1957. Mr. David Berlew of the Social Relations Department at Harvard tested another group in the summer of 1958. The government sample was tested in the late fall of 1957 through the assistance of Mr. Chester A. Evans of the Department of the Navy, Mr. Joseph G. Colmen of the Department of the Air Force, Mrs. Elizabeth Mulholland of the Social Security Administration, and Mr. E. N. Montague of the Internal Revenue Service. While the assistance of these persons is gratefully acknowledged the analysis and interpretation of the results are the author's responsibility.

5   Challenge and Response: A Retrospective View of the Public Service of Canada*

J. E. Hodgetts

John Donne's comment that "no man is an island" applies with equal relevance to organizations created by man to serve his needs. Thus, the central proposition I hope to demonstrate by this excursion into the past is that our public service has been shaped to the environment in which it has had to operate and that changes in the environment bring about alterations in the public service.

* Reprinted with permission of author and publisher from *Canadian Public Administration*, Vol. 7, December 1964, pp. 409-421.

When the Founding Fathers met one hundred years ago they were seeking to grapple with the forces of change then confronting them. The result was a constitutional document that has proven surprisingly durable over the ensuing years. But constitutions are notably rigid, and it has been largely within the public services — local, provincial and federal — that we find the main evidences of adaptation to changing conditions and emergent social needs which have provided the necessary flexibility. I see no evidence for claiming that this administrative adaptation has followed any iron laws of administrative growth. We are here concerned with a most complex set of interacting forces in which the organization acted upon, i.e., the public service, is far from passive. While the public service bears the marks of environmental factors that press upon it, society also bears the imprint of the activities and enhanced authority of public servants.

In considering the environmental pressures that have set the goals and moulded the shape of the public service over our first century, we find that some have remained relatively unchanged. These we may describe as the constant or "the givens" with which the public service must live. They include the pervasive impact of our geographical setting, the constitutional framework, the legal base of administration and the political system. The elements of the environment subject to the greatest change and requiring the greatest flexibility of response from the public service have been economic, technological, cultural and philosophical factors. I should like to show briefly how each of these has contributed to the public service we know today.

The powerful persuasion of geography has been noted by Sir Ernest Barker in his examination of the growth of European public services. The large Egyptian bureaucracy, for example, he attributed to the Nile and the costly irrigation works required to harness it. England's insular position, on the other hand, delayed the emergence of the large centralized bureaucracies which grew up on the Continent largely to service the needs of standing armies. In Canada, for the better part of its first half century, geography dictated the major goals which the public service was to pursue. The Department of the Interior, the giant amongst early federal departments, was described as late as 1936 as "the barometer of Western conditions." The so called barometric departments were those concerned with opening up the west, encouraging its population and settlement and providing the water or rail transportation to serve as the linkage for these activities.

Not only did geography dictate the goals, it also imposed the conditions which governed the way in which the tasks of public servants had to be performed. If administrative apoplexy was to be avoided at the centre, public servants had to be widely dispersed: police and protective services, agents for immigration, for colonization and Indian affairs, fisheries overseers, customs collectors, surveyors and construction teams on railways and canals, spread often in isolated places across a continental domain.

New means of communication have alleviated the problems of communication and administration in remote outposts. But the harsh facts of our geography still exact a high price for preserving a union based on an artificial East-West axis against the counterpull of the geographically more natural North-South axis.

Thus, from the outset, geography forced Canada to adapt its services to dispersed operations. The subsequent expansion of welfare and regulatory activities necessitated the continuation of dispersed or area administration, governed now less by the limitations on our means of communication but more by the need to preserve a face-to-face relationship with individual citizens seeking benefits and services. Consequently a physical decentralization of the work force, which took root as a logical response to the challenge of administering across a continent, continues in being as a vital necessity to provide the flexible response to the contemporary state's positive welfare and regulatory functions. Decentralization is now as much dictated by the need to preserve democratic responsiveness of the administrative machine as it is a natural outcome of the original geographic challenge.

It is passing strange that this, perhaps the most obvious feature of our public service, has received so little formal analysis. It is one of a number of areas that warrant fuller discussion and study.

The second constant feature of the environment is the constitutional framework which was evolved one hundred years ago. It is no reflection on the Founding Fathers to claim that a division of labour between provinces and dominion made one hundred years ago is bound to become outmoded. Formal constitutional amendment has been infrequent and judicial interpretation has not always been in conformity with rapid changes in social philosophy, new needs, or revolutionary transformation in technology. Flexibility has been provided by the development of what the Rowell-Sirois Commission called "administrative expedients." These have ranged from the sporadic assembling of a diplomatic conference between dominion and provincial leaders, ministerial or official conferences for more limited purposes — often in conjunction with national interest groups (as happened, for example, in the case of labour and agriculture), formal agreements rather like treaties, joint advisory committees, the use of federal officers to perform provincial tasks (and vice versa), and the employment of federal funds to finance provincial programs.

At the outset, most of these expedients were not developed because potential conflict was restrained by the limited undertakings of public organizations at all levels. Beginning with fisheries and then moving into labour and industrial relations, on to health and welfare and the regulation of interprovincial trade, the respective jurisdictions began to touch, then overlap: inevitably friction was generated. The limitations on and unevenness of provincial revenues required action on a broader front. Thus, throughout the years, one can see the administrative response of the federal public service gathering momentum in distinct stages. First, it began to act as a centralized data collecting source; from statistics it went on to research; research results required dissemination and so we move to extensive publication (and some would say public relations); next came conditional grants that required "policing" by federal officials; ultimately certain programs came to be operated by the federal government.

Two factors contribute to the perpetuation and even the continued expansion of the federal public service in such areas. First, there is the natural reluctance to dismantle an organization by giving up these programs. The historic rationale has been that the provincial services were less than adequate for the task involved – an estimate that today bears hard critical examination. The other factor has been the inability of the tax-poor provinces to carry the burden of these new services. Once again, I would offer this entire area as a rewarding subject for fresh examination: we need full scale studies of provincial public services to begin with and of the administrative interrelations that have developed between provincial and federal public departments. Here, we must content ourselves with noting that the cumulative results of these developments have induced the federal government to assume fact-gathering, research, promotional and grant dispensing responsibilities that are quite different in kind from the more directly programme-oriented, operational jobs undertaken by the provinces. At the same time, these activities have introduced in unprecedented numbers new types of professional, scientific and technical personnel into the public service whose problems of adaptation to the traditional hierarchical organization have received far less study than they deserve.

The third fixed element of the environment is the legal foundation for public administration. At Confederation, the tension between executive and legislature built up during the previous period of colonial rule inclined the Canadian Parliament to adopt a more assertive attitude than the British Parliament towards the public service. The British North America Act bears signs of this attitude in the oft-invoked phrase tied to the few sections concerning the disposition of the public service "until the Parliament of Canada [or the provincial legislature] otherwise provides." The fact is that the Parliament of Canada has "otherwise provided" in much more detail than has ever been the case in the United Kingdom, the most outstanding testimonial being the Civil Service Act of 1868, which had its precursors in pre-Confederation times and continues to this day with its counterpart in every province. No such act, significantly, has ever been passed in Britain.

This is not the place to thread my way through a most complex maze. That it *is* a maze, I know, for in a personal effort to explore the legal foundations of public administration I found to my surprise that there were few available guides in this lonely enterprise. I do not propose to inflict the details of my explorations on you but I can at least state the problem and its implications for the public service.

The essential difficulty derives from the union of executive and legislative functions which we have inherited from Britain. That union creates what I might call a legal ambivalence from which it is hard to say whether the public service is directed by sovereign parliament or by the executive. Put in another way, the question is: are public servants employees of parliament or employees of the executive, standing in the place of the Crown?

That this is not an academic question can be readily demonstrated by indicating the problem of identifying the centres of authority for handling the organization and management of the public service. Parliament clearly must authorize the creation of a department, but the executive determines when the department shall begin to function. Moreover, since a new department involves a money bill and only the executive can initiate such a bill, one must assume that even the major organizational units are dictated by the executive, with rather automatic ratification by parliament. For more detailed re-organization, parliament has in effect devolved authority on the executive through the *Public Services Rearrangement and Transfer of Duties Act*. A glance at the organic acts for each department shows that parliament has made no effort to bind the executive's hands by stipulating a detailed organizational breakdown. Equally, the day-to-day organization-and-methods work has been left by parliament entirely to the discretion of departments or to other management bodies.

In the field of management, the dichotomy is much more evident and perplexing. First, there is the question, previously noted, of the apparently dual allegiance of the public servant. For all practical purposes, including appointment, classification, promotion, pay scales, and tenure, the civil servant appears to be a servant of the executive (which in practical terms might be logically extended to read a servant of the party in power). In the performance of his functions, he is responsible through the hierarchy to his minister. Yet many members of parliament, stressing the term "public" in public servant, claim to occupy the role of employer. When at the same time they claim the Civil Service Commission as their specially selected agency to perform this function on their behalf, further problems arise. Indeed the Civil Service Commission is perhaps the chief victim of this legal dualism, on the one hand being regarded as the peculiar instrument of parliament in its role of employer but on the other often sharing management functions with executive agencies, such as Treasury Board, which parliament in its indecision has divided between them. It is enough, perhaps, to add that the Pay Research Bureau of the Commission has at times been caught in the crossfire of this legal uncertainty and the current investigation of arbitration for federal public servants must also find some resolution of the problem.

This commentary on the legal basis of administration could be prolonged but I have perhaps said enough to support the conclusion that because the legal ambivalence of our system has not been confronted head on we have grown into a confused system of divided management responsibilities that is cumbersome to work and difficult to live with.

The fourth and final fixed feature of the environment is our political system or, more accurately, the conventions that have grown up around that system. The three elements of this system that have left the deepest imprints on the public service are the conventions surrounding cabinet-making, the doctrine of ministerial responsibility and, that handmaiden of the party system, patronage.

The well-known convention that cabinets must be so constructed as to represent significant regional, provincial, religious and ethnic groupings in a pluralistic community needs no elaboration. Its implications for the public service, though obvious, have scarcely ever been noted. Even in 1867, a cabinet of fourteen members was needed to meet all the claims for weighted representation. Critics at the time asked how it was that in the United States as compared to Canada "forty million instead of four were ably governed by an administration of seven members instead of fourteen." But the necessity of securing a representative cabinet overrode any objections. On the other hand, if the American model did not commend itself, neither did the British system of making a distinction between the cabinet and the much larger Ministry. The Canadian convention in short was and continues to be that all Ministers should be in the cabinet.

The rejection of both the American and British models had these consequences: (1) for nearly half a century we were overstocked with departments and the slow accretion of government duties could readily be absorbed within a relatively static group of portfolios; (2) but, when the duties of the state began to mount at an accelerated pace, we were left little room to manoeuvre. If more departments were created to embrace the new tasks and if all ministerial heads by convention had to be in the cabinet, that body would soon reach an unmanageable size. The alternative was to create a variety of non-departmental entities to undertake the newer tasks. The generous provision of departmental portfolios and their extremely elastic walls enabled us to absorb a great deal of this expansion and necessitated surprisingly few additions to the original departmental roster. But it has meant that some departments have come to embrace a variety of ill-assorted functions simply as a means of housing what otherwise might become administrative orphans. The consequent problems of co-ordination through the cabinet and other centralized agencies have been acute.

The practical restrictions on the number of departmental portfolios also account in part for the profusion and variety of non-departmental entities. The effort to seat them comfortably within the traditional framework of ministerial responsibility has led to an incoherent "second" public service that represents a piecemeal, haphazard response to the growing burden of state activities, even as it confuses the legislator and general citizen.

Indeed, the doctrine of ministerial responsibility is the second feature of the political setting whose implications for the public service need brief elaboration. The principle not only establishes a bridge across which most of the traffic between parliament and the public service is routed but, applied collectively to the cabinet, it ensures a unity of purpose and a coordination of direction at the top. Parliament benefits by being able to home in on one identifiable target; the public servant benefits because he does not have to debate publicly any challenge of his political overlords. His anonymity preserves the constitutional fiction of his political non-commitment and thus ensures his permanency in office whenever there is a change in the governing political party.

The benefits of the doctrine are obvious and desirable but a literal application in today's enlarged public service poses an impossible burden on the Minister. This was recognized on the administrative side at the very beginning by giving the Minister a permanent Deputy and on the legislative side, but much more recently, by giving him a Parliamentary Secretary. But the fact remains that there have been constant pressures that force the Minister into a "managing" rather than a "directing" role, thereby compelling Ministers in both their individual and collective capacities, to concern themselves with too much detail, at the expense of general coordinating and policy-making functions. The convention that the cabinet provides regional representation makes sense only if most matters are brought before cabinet. Thus, in contrast to England where statutes generally confer authority on individual Ministers, in Canada they more commonly confer powers on the Governor-in-Council, i.e., Ministers in their collective capacity. If to this we add the historic reliance on patronage, we can see why Ministers have been unable to extricate themselves from direct involvement in the details of management. Sir George Murray's succinct epitaph (written in 1912) accurately described a predicament that certainly existed until 1939. "Ministers," he concluded, "both have too much to do and try to do too much."

The significance of patronage, the third element of the political system to be examined here, is that the measures taken to eradicate it have left an enduring mark on the public service. A formal self-denying ordinance is necessary, at some time or another, if patronage is to be eliminated. In Britain, this was done by executive decree but in Canada, as has been noted, by statute, authorizing a Civil Service Commission to institute a rigorous regimen of controls. Over time the desired result was achieved of preventing the unfit from gaining admission to the public service; but for many years this negative approach dominated to the exclusion of more positive measures required to attract the best candidates available. The Civil Service Commission was given additional and comprehensive authority over most of the personnel management field. Thus the orientation toward control, generated by its primary function as patronage eliminator, tended (so to speak) to rub off on to the other management responsibilities that demanded a more positive, service-minded approach.

A somewhat parallel development occurred in the field of expenditure control in an effort to prevent peculation and patronage. When the Glassco Commission came to examine this situation, it found that departmental managers had been caught in the pincers of centralized agencies and have had to operate in that atmosphere of distrust which had been responsible in the first place for the imposition of such controls. It was the thesis of the Glassco Commission that, while the system had been a legitimate and logical response to the evils of patronage and dishonesty, the departments were, in the vernacular, "big boys now" and should be put more on their own mettle. The readjustments required to meet this thesis will make heavier calls on the initiative and ability of departmental managers and will require centralized agencies to think less in terms of negative control and more in positive terms of guidance, service and setting standards for the departments.

I may remind you at this stage that I distinguished at the beginning between the constant and variable elements of the environment that have helped mould our public service. Having touched on the constants, let me now turn to the variables, beginning with the economic setting.

Economic historians have familiarized us with the importance of staple products to Canada's economic growth and well being. The characteristic features of staples such as fish, fur, timber, minerals, wheat and pulpwood is that they are all extractive enterprises, based on the exploitation of a great wealth in natural resources requiring bulk transportation and access to markets abroad. Neither the exploitation, transportation or marketing of these staples has taken place within an Adam Smith type of economy. Government has been heavily committed from the outset to mapping out and making inventory of these resources; it has been deeply engaged as regulator, constructor and operator of transport systems by water, rail and air; it moved early into promotional activities — the first trade commissioner dates back to the 1880's as does the agricultural research station, and only slightly later do we find such services as forecasting facilities. Governments have even engineered the formation of economic interest groups such as the livestock producers and the pulpwood producers — presumably the better to deal with them. Today the major concern of at least one third of our federal departments is still with problems associated with the production, conservation, and transportation of and the trade in our main staple products.

This clear cut identification of the departments with staple products is only one example — though a most persistent one — of how the unique features of the Canadian economy have shaped the public service. As government has more and more been drawn into an operating and regulatory role, we find that the new responsibilities have largely devolved on non-departmental agencies. A point has now been reached where the number of people employed in these sectors of the public service is nearly as large as the number employed in the departmental system proper. It is not surprising that, in devising non-departmental forms, governments have looked to the private industrial or commercial concerns for their models. We are still struggling to find a solution to the problems of grafting the consequent collection of heterogeneous administrative entities on to the conventional departmental system with its tradition of ministerial responsibility. We are also still seeking for ways to bridge the gap between the personnel in the civil service proper and in the other portion excluded from it, to the end that there may be truly *one* public service. In short, the mixed economy, with its avoidance of outright governmental monopoly and its favoring of a system of economic parallelism in transport, communication and finance, has produced a corresponding organizational "mix" in the public service itself.

Nor does the impact of the world of private economic organization end here. It finds expression in a pervasive assumption that only a "business-man's approach" to the public service can produce efficiency. We find early expression of this philosophy in the attempt to levy appropriate charges for the services that governments provide specific groups of beneficiaries. And, in the report of the Glassco Commission, dozens of such services have been identified, accompanied by evidence that some pay their way, others are given free, some make a profit, others lose money. The Royal Commission's reminder that we need to set this part of our administrative house in order is merely a reiteration of the old plea to inject sound business principles into public administration. The Commission's recommendation that many of these services might well be contracted out to private concerns is not so much a free enterpriser's special pleading but a legitimate concern to help public organizations keep their attention focussed on their main job, subject to as few peripheral distractions as possible.

The major impact of the business man's approach is to be found in the contemporary reliance on private management consultant firms that are refinements on the early school of efficiency experts nourished at the beginning of this century by Taylor and his followers. We owe to this school the detailed classification plans which were inaugurated after World War I in the civil service. The modern consultant is in the main an offshoot of the accountant, though his advice now ranges from financial and accounting practices through paperwork and systems analyses to feasibility studies on computers. His main customer is government and one of his most lasting marks will be found in the reports of the Glassco Commission. We find here the accountant's concern for identifying "real" costs; the business-man's concern for relating revenues from services to the costs of providing them, the need to import the new techniques of systems analyses that have proven effective in private business. In brief, there is the assumption that the differences between private and public organization are not so substantial that practices proven successful in the private realm cannot be applied with equal effectiveness to the public organization. This is an assumption that in my view must constantly be tempered by the other environmental factors I have been discussing and to which private organizations need pay much less attention.

Turning from the economic setting to the impact of changing technology on the public service, we find a two-edged situation. In the broadest sense, changing techniques affect the substance of administrative activity — they alter the things that have to be done by administrators, by inducing the state either itself to sponsor the development of the techniques or else to grapple with the social and other problems posed by their widespread adoption. In the narrower sense, new techniques influence administrative procedures. We live in an age of gadgetry and public servants are no more immune to the charm of applying gadgets to their daily labours than are others in private organizations.

The Canadian public service has grown up during a century in which there have been more technological innovations than in all of man's past history. It was born in the steamboat and railway age, witnessed the emergence of telegraph and telephone, saw the origin and full onslaught of the internal combustion engine and, while still adjusting to these developments, has had to make its peace with the air age, the electronics revolution, the atom, and now outer space.

The incredible fertility of man, the innovating engineer and scientist, has left man, the social scientist, staggering for breath. The steamboat and railway brought the state into the centre of activity as owner, maintenance man and operator or regulator. The automobile age has left its most indelible imprint on provincial and local public services, as they have had to grapple with highway construction, traffic regulations, and all the social and economic problems of urban concentration that have sprung up in the wake of the automobile.

Jurisdiction over the air for transportation and communication purposes was settled in favour of the federal government in 1932 and the stage was set for a fresh crop of agencies and further adaptation of the public service to meet the challenges. From virtual monopolies of national services, designed to pioneer in these new fields, the state has gradually permitted the private sector to emerge as a full partner. Similarly, in responding to the nuclear revolution, the state has harnessed the conventional component by regulatory action but has assumed, itself, nearly the full burden of research and development. With the largest research resources and establishments in the country, the federal government's relationship with universities and the increasing importance of science in government now raise problems that we are only beginning to assess, let alone solve.

One should also observe that many technological changes have affected the means of communication and transportation. These have required such substantial capital investment that the state has had to become an active participant as developer and owner. The consequent fostering of an interdependent economy brought new regulatory problems, most of which had to be met on a national front. World-wide application of these techniques has shrunk the world and produced further problems of international trade and communication that also fall naturally on the shoulders of the federal government.

Apart from these broad repercussions of technological change, there are also the products which derive from the new technology and affect the procedures of the public service. One of the most important consequences of the age of gadgets is the ease with which paper can now be created and the resulting problems of record keeping, storage, filing and so on. Historically, the mechanics of paper management were characterized unflatteringly but accurately as the "donkey work" in the civil service. (There is more than a shadow of home truth in the classification of the first females in the British public service as "female typewriters.") Yet, as the Glassco Commission has emphasized, the new gadgets and procedures necessitate an upgrading of those concerned with the management of paper if the government is not, like the sorcerer's apprentice, to be drowned in a flood of its own creation. At this point we can confidently coin a neo-Parkinsonian Law: *the quantity of paper will rise to meet the capacity of the machines available for processing it.* It is still difficult to know how the electronics revolution will affect an organization where there is so much routine repetitive work that lends itself to automation. At the least, its wide-scale application will necessitate major re-training programs.

The high costs of the more versatile automatic data processing equipment imply that the new technology may force a reversal of the traditional pattern of dispersed and decentralized operations as work gets concentrated in a few large electronic machine shops. On the other hand, it may well be that centralized processing is quite compatible with — indeed, a genuine encouragement to — more effective decentralization, because the new machines can improve reporting and control techniques. It would be pure speculation to carry this line of inquiry further but, now we are in the throes of numbering the nation, it may not be too unrealistic to visualize our master cards going into the computer and slipping us anything from a birth certificate to an old age pension, a request for payment of back taxes to a passport. At the best we should see improved, though depersonalized, service to the public and the collation of new masses of data from which our social planners in the future should be able to make more confident and accurate predictions.

From this Orwellian world that is less fantastic than it seemed less than a decade ago, let us turn to the cultural setting. Canada is a middle power both in the figurative and literal sense, geographically positioned next door to the United States and still bound by tradition and sentiment to England. At good neighbour rallies, we extol the virtues of our undefended frontier, which on closer inspection is seen to bristle with defences, most of them of the Canadian government's own making. Tariffs and the all-Canadian railway were but the precursors of a host of other expressions of the do-it-yourself philosophy inspired by national pride and a reluctance to be beholden to our more powerful neighbour. The airplane and radio brought government monopolies as chosen instruments of national policy. The Canada Council was a far-too-modest answer to the American foundations, the proposal to re-direct the Canadian advertisers' dollars to Canadian publications and the BBG's prescription of a fifty-five per cent quota of "Canadian content" for broadcasting are all recent evidences of the same spirit.

If a number of the federal government's most important cultural activities have evolved in response to our defensive posture toward United States cultural penetration, it is equally true that the organization of the public service itself bears marks of our constant borrowing. Here, however, we have tended to gyrate between American practices and British tradition. Our Civil Service Act and the Civil Service Commission are more American than British in conception, intent and in the powers conferred; so, too, is our classification system. Our attempts to create a cadre of senior administrative officers and the abortive reports of such Royal Commissions as the Murray and Gordon Commissions show much clearer traces of the British pattern. The most recent reports from the Glassco Commission are an interesting amalgam of American management practices and British institutional devices, both adapted to the Canadian setting.

Apart from the significant and continuing pressure from these external cultural influences the Canadian public service has to face a unique indigenous cultural factor —the principle of bilingualism enshrined in the B.N.A. Act. The hyphenated premierships, the double-barrelled ministries and, more particularly, the rotating capitals that characterized the pre-Confederation public service reveal that the bicultural nature of the earlier union gave much blunter expression than we have since given to the concept. For nearly a century the federal public service has shown at times even a deliberate disregard of this cultural fact of life and is now an obvious target for the moderate nationalist as well as the extremist in French-speaking Canada. The problem goes deeper than a mere recognition of two official languages, for it extends to the whole cultural context and will not be easily ameliorated by well-intended gestures on the part of English-speaking groups. The situation is probably most acute at headquarters, particularly at the senior officer level. Working within an essentially unilingual communication system, bilingualism becomes a one-way street where the only person who needs to be bilingual is the French-speaking officer. That he is called upon to make his home in an alien cultural environment only adds to the difficulties. With the rapid industrialization and bureaucratization of the Province of Quebec, the opportunities for advancement in executive ranks are so enhanced that it will probably be increasingly difficult to make the Ottawa service attractive to French-speaking recruits. On the other hand, Canada, as an officially bilingual country, has a potentially important contribution to make in fulfilling obligations to the international community. This fact by itself should be additional incentive to mount a more effective campaign to bring the federal public service into line with the realities of its long and much neglected bicultural tradition.

I close with a brief reference to what might be called the philosophical pressures that have shaped the public service. I am referring here to the familiar transition from a laissez-faire to a collectivist philosophy which is a world-wide phenomenon. The repercussions on the public service have been obvious. The new expectations and demands for broader and better services have led to an enormous growth in the number of public servants and an increasing complexity and variety of administrative organizations. It is an expansion shared by all levels of government and by no means confined to the federal public service. The vast expansion in the scale of operations means that more and more attention must be devoted to the auxiliary or housekeeping services that exist simply to look after the "care and feeding" of the public bureaucracy. Problems of internal management, as the Glassco Commission reveals, assume much more significant proportions and older techniques of centralized control prove incapable of coping with the new situations or else, in trying to cope, bring irritation and frustration in their wake. Public services geared to a slower, steadier breathing rhythm find that each day now brings what appears to be a new crisis, until the realization dawns that these are not crises, but part of the speeded-up rhythm of our lives. No organization, let alone any public official, can cope for long with crisis administration unless interested in abnormal psychology and ready to become a patient of the psychiatrist. Current preoccupation with planning evidences an effort to meet the new problems of administrative change not on a crisis basis but as part of normal administrative life.

The collectivist philosophy has changed the scale, the pace, the very tone of administration. These are problems of which the working civil servant is aware. The general public probably goes on believing in its old stereotype of the public servant who, like the fountains in Trafalgar Square, "plays from ten until four." And it is the response of the general public that brings me to my final point. The shift from laissez-faire to collectivism has been accompanied by an unprecedented shift in the balance of real power, discretion and initiative — away from courts, legislatures and even cabinets to public servants. The shift is inescapable and necessary but the public cannot be blamed for suspecting that the "faceless" men, the establishment, the mandarins or what you will are up to no good, that their rights are being invaded even as they are ostensibly being served by public employees. It is from this sense of unease that the proposals for an Ombudsman, a public defender, emanate.

I have, perforce, had to use the technique of the quick-sketch artist to present this hasty, episodic perspective on our developing public services. I trust that if you stand far enough back the likeness is reasonably accurate in its general outlines and focus, even if many of the details need much more amplification, qualification or clarification.

6   Public Administration in Canada Today*

W. D. K. Kernaghan

The Growth of Bureaucracy

Improved management of the public's business at all levels of government in Canada is a prime determinant of this nation's capacity to realize its

* Condensed from W. D. K. Kernaghan, Vol. XI, September 1968, pp. 300-317. "Public Administration in Canada Today", *Canadian Public Administration*, to be published in 1968. This paper does not pretend to be an exhaustive survey of the status of the study and teaching of public administration in Canada. Rather, its purpose is to review briefly the state of the field on the tenth anniversary of the founding of Canada's professional journal *Canadian Public Administration*. The content of this essay is confined largely to the federal public service although data related to the other tiers of government will on occasion be used for comparative purposes.

political, social and economic goals. Skilful and highly motivated public personnel are crucial to achieving these objectives. To minimize the influence of public servants on policy making, on the provision of a striking variety of public services and on the enforcement of regulations is to close one's eyes before overwhelming evidence.

The lingering popular image of the bureaucracy as a passive instrument of political masters serves as a convenient fiction for the politician who desires recognition as an effective policy maker and the administrator who covets his anonymity. Yet students and practitioners of public administration have long acknowledged the participation of administrators in the policy-making process and the difficulty of maintaining any well-defined structural differentiation between policy making and policy implementation. In regard to the pervasive nature of policy making, R. G. Robertson, Clerk of the Privy Council and Secretary to the Cabinet, commented recently that "any civil servant above clerical or stenographic grades who has spent any substantial time in a job without contributing to some degree to the policy he administers should be fired".[2] Furthermore, he asserted, "the distinction is not between those who contribute to the 'making' of policy and those who do not — but between those who finally decide and those who try to carry the decided policy out, whether it is the policy they contributed to making, a caricature of it, or the very opposite".[3]

Senator Maurice Lamontagne, however, has made the provocative suggestion that the "twilight of the civil servants" is at hand. He has argued that the new centres of influence on policy making will be the intellectual community through "the rising number of Royal Commissions, task forces, advisory boards and councils"; the general public through its measured response to polls and motivation surveys; backbenchers through their increasing contributions in party caucus and in parliamentary committees; and the mass media through their control of communication.[4] This novel hypothesis remains to be proved but it points to a fruitful area for inquiry into the determinants of any given public policy. Even if the validity of the hypothesis is granted, however, effective influence may still remain with the administrators who will have less to say about *what should be done* but will continue to determine *how it should be done*.

The continuous expansion of government activities has also markedly altered the administrative process. New and challenging areas of concern have supplemented the increasingly complex task of fulfilling the traditional responsibilities for the conduct of external relations and national defence and for the administration of justice. The irreversible momentum of welfare state legislation has raised health, welfare and educational serv-

---

2 "The Canadian Parliament and Cabinet in the Face of Modern Demands". Unpublished manuscript of an address to the Nineteenth Annual Conference of the Institute of Public Administration of Canada, McMaster University, September 8, 1967, p. 2.

3 *Ibid.*

4 "The Influence of the Politician". Unpublished manuscript of an address to the Nineteenth Annual Conference of the Institute of Public Administration of Canada, McMaster University, September 8, 1967, pp. 11-22.

ices to unprecedented heights and has greatly extended the regulation of individual and group conduct in diverse areas of socio-economic life. Canadians are intimately and continuously affected by government policy on such fundamental matters as education, federal and provincial schemes for medical care, air and water pollution, and housing. The unavoidable interdependence of all levels of government in planning programs and allocating tax revenues to discharge these obligations raises intricate problems of political accommodation and administrative coordination. Priorities among competing public demands must be established and justified. Yet setting priorities is complicated further by regional disparities in needs. Some areas of the country enjoy ample housing but suffer severely from inadequate transportation or educational facilities. Increasingly large staffs of administrative and technical personnel must be recruited and trained to implement government programs to meet these needs. Indeed, approximately one out of every six members of the Canadian labour force is engaged in public employment.

Recent Developments

The satisfaction of public needs and the implementation of legislation depend on the capacity of the public services to operate in the most economical and efficient manner compatible with limitations imposed by politicians, judges, the news media and the public. Improvement in the public services rests largely on a spirited and continuing dialogue between civil servants and outside experts and upon a reciprocal exchange of advances in the art and the science of administration. In recent years, there has been accelerated interest, even excitement, among students and practitioners of public administration in Canada. Internal developments in the federal public service in particular have aroused public consciousness of the growing dynamism of both the study and the practice of public administration. The single most powerful stimulus to popular awareness of the need for administrative reform was the appointment in 1960 of the Royal Commission on Government Organization (the Glassco Commission) and the controversial proposals of the five-volume *Report* of the Commission released between September 1962 and February 1963.[5] The Commission's terms of reference called for the recommendation of changes in the management of government departments and agencies which "would best promote efficiency, economy and improved service in the despatch of public business". The recommendations of the *Report* were screened by the Bureau of Government Organization and approved by the Cabinet before the implementation of most of the central reforms began.

Two additional administrative developments have stimulated national interest in the federal public service. The Liberal Government has enacted legislation "to encourage bilingualism in the federal public service, as part of

[5] See Donald C. Rowat, "Canada's Royal Commission on Government Organization", *Public Administration* (U.K.), Vol. 41, Summer 1963, pp. 193-205.

its fundamental objective of promoting and strengthening national unity on the basis of the equality of rights and opportunities for both English- and French-speaking Canadians".[6] Then, in July 1967, following the 1960 *Report of the Preparatory Committee on Collective Bargaining in the Public Service*, the Public Service Staff Relations Act[7] established a system of collective bargaining and arbitration for a large proportion of Canada's public employees. Although it is premature to attempt any meaningful evaluation of these developments in bilingualism and collective bargaining, the central importance of these reforms for the future evolution of the public service cannot be denied. The debate over these progressive measures, coupled with noteworthy studies of provincial, municipal and regional governmental administration[8] has directed widespread attention to the potential benefits of inquiries into the management of the public services. In addition, revolutionary innovations in the United States civil service, particularly the service-wide application of the Planning-Programming-Budgeting System (PPBS) which originated in the Department of Defence, have encouraged extensive study and revision of the planning and budgetary process in Canada's public service.[9]

The Study of Public Administration [10]

Despite these indications of growth and change in the Canadian public services, Canadian public administration as a field of study has not yet come of age.[11] In view of the advanced stage of the discipline in the United States, and to a lesser degree in Great Britain, the paucity of literature on Canadian public administration is staggering.[12] In the United States, academic emphasis has turned from the structural and procedural features of public administration to the sociological and psychological aspects of the

6 *Debates* (Commons), April 6, 1966, p. 3,915.

7 *Statutes of Canada* (1966-1967), 14-15-16, Eliz. II, c. 72.

8 See, for example, Manitoba: Report of the Royal Commission on Local Government Organization and Finance, 1964; New Brunswick: Report of the Royal Commission on Finance and Municipal Taxation, 1963; Ontario: Report of the Royal Commission on Metropolitan Toronto, 1965; Ontario: Report of the Commission on Niagara Region Local Government Review, 1966; and Saskatchewan: Report of the Royal Commission on Government Administration, 1965.

9 See the Symposium on PPBS in *Public Administration Review*, Vol. 26, December, 1966, pp. 243-310. See also a succinct summary of Canadian developments in this area in *Debates* (Commons), October 10, 1967, pp. 2,933-2,936.

10 See Donald C. Rowat, "The Study of Public Administration in Canada", *Public Administration* (U.K.) Vol. 40, Autumn 1962, pp. 319-324.

11 For the purpose of this paper, the author accepts the very broad interpretation of "study" as embracing not only research contributions in the way of systematic analysis but also historical or contemporary accounts of administrative problems and processes.

12 An excellent bibliography of book-length and periodical literature in public administration at all levels of Canadian government is contained in the *Selected Lists of Current Materials on Canadian Public Administration* published between 1954 and 1965 by the Carleton University Library. Note also the lists of relevant new books and articles included in issues of the journal, *Canadian Public Administration*.

bureaucracy, whereas Canadian scholars have not yet adequately explored the first stage.

The Institute of Public Administration of Canada was founded in 1949. The publication of papers delivered at its annual conferences from then until the establishment in 1958 of the quarterly journal, *Canadian Public Administration*, served as the take-off point for more vigorous examination of selected aspects of public administration in Canada.

In the absence of a general textbook on Canadian public administration, students and teachers have been forced to read British and American works. The influence of American perspectives on public administration has been the more potent, however, and the content of Canadian instruction in public administration has tended to reflect American teaching. The descriptive and rather specialized Canadian works of Dawson[13] and of Cole[14] are dated now. Fortunately, in 1960 Hodgetts and Corbett compiled a useful collection of readings on Canadian public administration[15] which focuses on organization theory, administrative practice, personnel administration, and administrative powers and responsibilities.

Considerable research is being conducted in universities. Since 1962 *Canadian Public Administration* has published intermittently a list of graduate dissertations and theses, completed or in preparation, at Canadian, American and British universities dealing with questions of public policy and administration in Canada. Many of these scattered and unheralded writings have made an original, if rather specialized, contribution. From 1955 to 1967 the School of Public Administration at Carleton University alone directed the completion of 46 Masters' theses and 31 graduate and honours research essays.

Perhaps the best way to indicate the embryonic state of the discipline in Canada is to note that it is simpler to recount the studies that have been committed to paper than to indicate where the gaps lie. Happily, there is a growing number of scholars and professional administrators who are determined to do research. The Institute of Public Administration, for example, has initiated *The Confederation Series in Canadian Public Administration*. J. E. Hodgetts and J.-M. Martin have agreed to serve as general editors of the series and an advisory board of academics and public officials has been appointed. The Institute has proposed that during the next five years 12 volumes be prepared on contemporary issues and institutions of Canadian public administration at all levels of the public service. The completion of this project should provide new insights into the administrative process in Canada and a wealth of information for teachers and public servants. The long-awaited scholarly basis for the analysis of

---

13 R. MacGregor Dawson, *The Civil Service of Canada*, Oxford University Press, Toronto, 1929.

14 R. Taylor Cole, *The Canadian Bureaucracy*, Duke University Press, Durham, North Carolina, 1949.

15 J. E. Hodgetts and D. C. Corbett (eds.), *Canadian Public Administration*, Macmillan, Toronto, 1960.

the Canadian public services will have been laid. The volumes planned include an examination of the organization and machinery of government, personnel and financial administration, the management of human and physical resources, the administration of economic policy and the relations of the public services with the legislatures, the courts and the public.

Teachers of public administration in Canada who have been forced to rely almost exclusively on American case material might take note that a manual containing Canadian case studies initiated several years ago by Donald C. Rowat is now published by Carleton University's School of Public Administration under the editorship of A. M. Willms.[16] This case book provides the teacher with an opportunity to supplement lectures and seminars with discussion or re-enactment of actual administrative situations and decisions.

Aside from these materials, the documentation required by those interested in the systematic study of the structure and functions of the public service must be gleaned largely from reports of royal commissions,[17] Parliamentary debates, legislative committee reports and publications of departments and agencies. Many public servants devote a substantial portion of their time to researching and writing reports on issues peculiar to their own work. Despite the specialized nature of these studies, the researcher who gains access to a wide range of them may well be able to draw some general conclusions on problems of management. Willms, in furnishing a list of departmental studies of a broader scope, has commented that "in some instances generalizations have evolved, and at least one departmental group strives consciously to produce results generally applicable in its field".[18]

Unfortunately, the bulk of working papers prepared for royal commissions and many of the papers and reports of departmental and interdepartmental committees are accessible only to the most privileged researchers. There is increasing frustration among scholars over the Herculean task of gaining access to a variety of government documents indispensable to the verification of research hypotheses or to the mere accumulation of data about existing administrative institutions, problems and processes. Indeed, Rowat, in his persuasive analysis of administrative secrecy, concluded that in Canada, subject to reasonable limitations in the interest of national security or personal privacy, "the outright adoption of the principle of free access to government documents should be our ultimate objective".[19]

16 A. M. Willms (ed.), *Cases for Discussion in the Study of Public Administration*, Carleton University, Ottawa, 1967.

17 Willms has noted that of 44 royal commissions appointed by the federal government since 1945, 14 have touched on important features of Canadian public administration and six have centred exclusively on problems of management. See "The Administration of Research on Administration in the Government of Canada", *Canadian Public Administration*, Vol. 10, December 1967, p. 408.

18 *Ibid.*, p. 412.

19 Donald C. Rowat, "How Much Administrative Secrecy?", *Canadian Journal of Economics and Political Science*, Vol. 31, November 1965, p. 498.

Teaching Public Administration

Further research is essential to encourage Canadian university students to study public administration and to stimulate enthusiasm for a career in the public service. As a consequence of competition with many other fields, few Canadian departments of political science devote their resources primarily to teaching and studying public administration. Thirty of 44 universities recently surveyed[20] offered at least one undergraduate course in public administration and 11 of these provided graduate courses. In every case, the courses formed part of the program of departments of political science or political economy. Students are much less likely to be exposed to courses in provincial, local, regional or metropolitan government or urban politics or any combination of these subjects at Canadian universities. The survey showed that only 16 of the 44 universities offered undergraduate courses and only five made graduate work available in one or more of these subjects.

It is natural that the centre of federal administrative studies should be in Ottawa where the unique research opportunities and frequent exchanges between academics and administrators are invaluable. Under the directorship of R. O. MacFarlane, Carleton University's School of Public Administration, since its founding in 1953, has graduated more than 300 students. The school offers a varied program to full-time university students and to part-time students, most of whom are public employees. The program ranges from the undergraduate Certificate in Public Service Studies, through the Bachelor of Arts degree with honours in public administration, the graduate Diploma or the Master's degree in public administration, to public administration as one of the fields for a Ph.D. in political science. Increasingly specialized courses in personnel administration, government accounting and finance and administrative law are taught in the departments of political science, accounting and public law. In addition, Carleton University and the University of Ottawa conduct training courses in public administration for young career officers and senior public servants from countries overseas. These students are selected by their home governments and their financial support is borne by a number of sponsoring agencies and by Canada's External Aid Office which directs the overall training programs.[21] Outside Ottawa, the University of Saskatchewan at Regina has established a Faculty of Administration; and York University's Faculty of Administrative Studies, set up in 1966, proposes to inaugurate in 1968 programs leading to the Master's degree in public administration.

Long contends that "public administration is inevitably and deeply involved in the articulation of needs, the statement of problems and the formulation of policy alternatives. In these tasks it is concerned with equip-

---

20 This survey was based on an examination of courses listed in university calendars of all the major universities in Canada. The author readily admits the limitations to his findings resulting from the often misleading nature of course and program descriptions.

21 Since the academic year 1959-1960, Carleton University has provided these courses for 336 overseas students and the University of Ottawa has enrolled 53 students during its two-year-old program.

ping its practitioners to govern wisely".[22] The Canadian federal public service cannot guarantee the wisdom of its practitioners, but it does ensure that public servants have the opportunity to receive training in the concepts and techniques of administration.[23] The Public Service Commission of Canada, assisted by individual departments and agencies, offers extensive training and development programs not only to public servants in the Ottawa area but also to officials from federal field offices across the country.

The program offered by the Training and Development Services branch of the Commission for the 1967-1968 academic year is shown below:[24]

1. Introductory management courses in government administration
2. Middle management courses in government administration
3. Senior course in government administration (to be replaced by executive development program)
4. Advanced course in management development (Laval University, York University, University of Manitoba)
5. Personnel administration courses
   generalist (development)
   training (training officers)
   staff relations
   pay analysis
   classification and pay
6. Management analysis
7. Financial management
8. Material management
9. Management techniques
   work measurement
   forms management and design
   records management
   managing with networks
   electronic data processing
10. Short courses in management improvement
11. Senior coordinators and supervisors.

Items one to four are conducted by the Management Development Division and resemble very closely the general courses in public administration offered at the university undergraduate level but with a much more practical orientation. The difficulty of each program varies from introductory

---

[22] Norton E. Long, "Politicians for Hire — The Dilemma of Education and the Task of Research", *Public Administration Review*, Vol. 25, June 1965, p. 120.

[23] See Keith B. Callard, *Advanced Administrative Training in the Public Service*, University of Toronto Press, Toronto, 1958.

[24] Source: Public Service Commission of Canada, Staffing Branch, Training and Development Programs.

to senior courses. For example, the introductory management course is planned for young officers

> . . . to bring into focus the previous orientation and work experience and to develop from this an understanding of the broader aspects of government management. It will provide them with much information which can be put to use in their present jobs and at the same time instill in them a sense of involvement and participation beyond departmental bounds.[25]

The senior course in government administration, on the other hand,

> is a developmental course for senior government officials which reviews the application of present managerial concepts to public administration and which provides opportunity for study and observation of managerial policy and planning in federal and provincial governments and in crown corporations. . . . The Course is designed to broaden the participants' outlook on management and to help raise the level of their administrative and executive competence. It strives to foster excellence in officers charged with the management of public affairs.[26]

The introductory, middle and senior management programs require that participants live in residence at the public service training and development centres at Carleton Place or Kemptville near Ottawa. Incidental benefits by way of subsequent inter-departmental coordination on an informal basis result from the exchange of ideas and the development of friendships during these in-residence training sessions.

The remaining seven programs on the list are conducted in Ottawa by the Occupational Development and Training Division. They are more specialized and are intended to provide public servants with more detailed descriptions and analyses of narrower areas of management.

Finally, most departments and agencies supplement these external programs of the Commission with internal courses under the auspices of the departmental Training and Development Section. An internal program may include such subjects as supervisory development, letter writing, executive officer development, departmental orientation, effective oral communication and report writing.[27]

An uninformed public should be reassured by such a variety of in-service training and development programs for Canada's public servants. Moreover, the composition of many of these programs is continually recast to provide public employees with the conceptual and technological skills necessary to cope with the rapidly changing nature of the administrative process.

---

[25] Public Service Commission, Training and Development Service, Summary of Programs Conducted by Management Development Division, 1967.

[26] *Ibid.*

See also G. S. Follis, "The Senior Course in Public Administration", *Canadian Public Administration*, Vol. 8, March 1965, pp. 36-45.

[27] Source: Training and Development Programmes, Departmental Training and Development Section, Personnel and Organization, Department of Energy, Mines and Resources, 1967-1968, p. ii.

Prospects

That the study and teaching of public administration in Canada is beginning to flourish is cause for guarded optimism about accomplishments during the next decade. The status and the potential development of the subject may be assessed by an adaptation to the Canadian situation of concepts employed by Riggs in his celebrated studies of comparative public administration.[28] Riggs perceives three trends in the comparative study of public administration. The first shift in emphasis is from normative to empirical approaches. In Canada, the normative or problem-solving approach finds special application in view of such enduring issues of public policy as bilingualism and biculturalism, and federal-provincial financial relations. Yet, before problems can be solved or textbooks on Canadian public administration written, a solid base of empirical data on Canada's public services is required. The normative and empirical approaches now coexist in the Canadian context but there is an increasingly marked tendency to accumulate and analyze information for its own sake.

Within the empirical school, Riggs also notes a more gradual move from idiographic to nomothetic approaches. By idiographic, Riggs means "any approach which concentrates on the unique case – the historical episode or 'case study', the single agency or country, the biography or the 'culture area' ".[29] Unquestionably, Canadian studies are now in the idiographic stage of development. The dearth of historical accounts of our public service is slowly being remedied.[30] Reference has already been made to the scrutiny of individual government agencies and culture areas by the Royal Commission on Bilingualism and Biculturalism. It is remarkable, however, that Canadians have had so little opportunity to enjoy the biographical accounts or autobiographical reflections of some of the country's notable career officials. Nomothetic analysis complements the idiographic approach in that it "provides the theories, the conceptual schemes or criteria of relevance which – whether stated or not – guide the historian and area specialist in his selection of data".[31] For theoretical contributions of this nature, Canadian scholars have relied chiefly on American writings.

The final shift in emphasis observed by Riggs is from non-ecological to ecological approaches. The common practice of discussing administrative principles and procedures in Canada as if they were independent of historical, geographical, religious and social factors must be abandoned if Canadians are to understand the administrative system in relation to the total environment affecting its development. Nor is it sufficient merely to

---

28 F. W. Riggs, "Trends in the Comparative Study of Public Administration", *International Review of Administrative Sciences*, Vol. 27, 1962, pp. 9-15; and *Administration in Developing Countries*, Houghton Mifflin, Boston, 1964, pp. 399-429.

29 Riggs, "Trends in the Comparative Study of Public Administration", *op. cit.*, p. 11.

30 J. E. Hodgetts, *Pioneer Public Service: An Administrative History of the United Canadas, 1841-1867*, University of Toronto Press, Toronto, 1957; note also the important contributions to the administrative and governmental history of Canada in each issue of *Canadian Public Administration* during 1967.

31 Riggs, "Trends in the Comparative Study of Public Administration", *op. cit.*, p. 12.

set the administrative system in its environment, for as Riggs points out, "ecology implies not just a characterization of environment, but rather analysis of the patterns of interaction between the subject of study and its environment".[32]

Empirical and ecological studies other than those prepared for the Royal Commission on Bilingualism and Biculturalism, would greatly enhance the international reputation of the study of public administration in Canada and would be a valuable addition to the growing literature in comparative public administration. Nevertheless, the high cost of such field studies in the necessary depth may be prohibitive outside the framework of government-sponsored research.

Another method of analyzing the study of public administration in Canada would be to classify the field into political, managerial and socio-psychological categories. The treatment of public administration as part of the political process stimulates the political scientist to investigate such questions as the policy-making activities and ethical standards of public servants, legislative controls over the public service and the adjustment of demands for efficiency to demands for a public service representative of ethnic, linguistic and other special interests.[33]

Scholars and public officials disposed to examining the more practical operations of government are continuing to make significant contributions in such areas as personnel and financial management, material management and other managerial techniques. There is a special need for mathematicians and statisticians to assist in much of this practically-oriented research, particularly to promote innovations in the rapidly evolving managerial techniques of operations research and electronic data processing. The Treasury Board has already begun to meet this need through the recent creation of a new division within the Management Improvement Branch named SIMPAC (System of Integrated Management Planning and Control). The President of the Treasury Board, E. J. Benson, has explained that

> The SIMPAC division has been staffed with highly trained specialists in such management disciplines as computer technology, operations research, economics, accounting, and program budgeting.[34]

The socio-psychological aspects of the study of public administration involve a wide range of subjects including factors affecting decision making, styles of leadership and the effects on individual and group behaviour of interaction between the formal and informal elements of organization.

[32] *Ibid.*, p. 15.

[33] Donald V. Smiley has referred to the notable studies of "public policy devices and processes" since 1945 as "those of J. E. Hodgetts on public corporations and royal commissions, of Norman Ward on parliamentary control of public expenditures, of D. C. Rowat on the Ombudsman, and of Donald Smiley on federal grants-in-aid to the provinces". See "Contributions to Canadian Political Science since the Second World War", *Canadian Journal of Economics and Political Science*, Vol. 33, November 1967, pp. 569-580.

[34] *Debates* (Commons), October 10, 1967, p. 2,935.

Sociologists and psychologists could assist political scientists in these areas. Equipped with their sophisticated quantitative and methodological tools, they could examine traditional views on the nature of administrative functions in Canada and test hypotheses with more precise techniques of measurement.

Informed scholars and practitioners are conscious of the rapidly expanding and nebulous boundaries of the study of administration. The emphasis on the behavioural approach to the subject and its growing links with other social sciences have given an inter-disciplinary bent to inquiries into administrative systems. It is not surprising, therefore, that the design of curricula in public administration has become a frustrating task for the conscientious instructor. University and public-service courses which focus solely on the orthodox subject areas of organization, personnel management, financial management and administrative controls do not adequately cover the field. Despite the continuing controversy over the appropriate boundaries of the study of administration, little justification exists for the omission from course content of new insights into the traditional administrative functions of decision making, communication and leadership. A recently published book of readings on public administration in the United States[35] has arranged 54 essays into three course outlines allowing the instructor to employ the process of coordination, institutions and functions or behaviour as the focus of his teaching. Each course outline uses virtually the same readings in a different arrangement to allow for individual emphasis on the central issues of public administration.

Perhaps the most significant problem facing the teaching of public administration in the near future is its possible detachment from departments of political science. The limited evidence available in Canada suggests that in the creation of schools or faculties of administration or administrative studies intended to combine the study of private and public administration, the latter may be submerged, if not drowned, in the stream of courses on business administration and accounting.

The long-accepted standing of public administration as a sub-field of the study of politics and government has made it an integral part of the curriculum of political science departments at most Canadian universities. In 1954, Robson argued that

> Any tendency for public administration to break away from the parent discipline must ultimately weaken both political science as a whole and the study of public administration. It will weaken political science by removing the part of it which brings the teacher into closest relationship with the practical business of government. It will weaken the study of public administration by divorcing it from political theory and the principles of government which underlie political and administrative institutions.[36]

---

35 Robert T. Golembiewski, Frank Gibson and Geoffrey Y. Cornog (eds.), *Public Administration*, Rand McNally, Chicago, 1966.

36 W. A. Robson, *The University Teaching of Social Sciences: Political Science*, UNESCO, 1954, p. 47.

Perhaps developments have progressed to the point where some scholars would find the following statement a more persuasive argument:

> The greatest promise for study of public administration in the universities will be in association with the growth of an integrative, organizing, generic concept of administration. From the nucleus of general administrative studies, it may be possible to interrelate more meaningfully the study of administration to the various disciplines and professions. In the modern world, no clear line separates administration in government from the administrative processes of the total society. The organization of administrative studies in the university must ultimately correspond to this reality.[37]

No solution to this thorny problem is offered here nor is any simple remedy likely to be discovered. The question may in the long run be decided by a new breed of social scientists who tend to reject the significance of differences between public and private administration. This group has less enthusiasm for the political and the problem-solving orientations to public administration and more fervour for the development of new methodological tools and conceptual frameworks for the study of the "generic concept of administration".

It may be argued that the inter-disciplinary nature of administrative inquiry does not require the separation of public administration from political science. It does however, demand that instructors keep themselves informed of developments in other disciplines affecting the teaching and the practice of administration. Furthermore, it is essential that social scientists collaborate in their research efforts and incorporate the contributions of scholars in other disciplines. It is conceivable that such departments as those of economics, political science, psychology and sociology could jointly establish a school of administration under conditions allowing for disciplinary autonomy. Each department could offer courses on differing aspects of administration subject to overall coordination by a representative body. Certainly the concepts and techniques of public and private administration are identical in many respects and similar in others. Yet the distinguishing characteristics of the public services in their relations with legislatures, courts, pressure groups, the mass media and the general public cannot be disregarded.

Another problem is the division between political scientists who are practically oriented in their teaching and those who are theoretically oriented. Clearly, ready access to federal or provincial public officials and government documents makes it much simpler to illustrate administrative theory with Canadian materials. Moreover, it is easier to analyze governmental operations when teaching in Ottawa, Toronto or Quebec City than in Sudbury, Calgary or Sherbrooke. Academics in daily contact with civil servants and their current problems are naturally more disposed to

---

[37] Lynton K. Caldwell, "Public Administration and the Universities: A Half-Century of Development", *Public Administration Review*, Vol. 25, March 1965, p. 60.

practically-oriented teaching and to problem-solving research projects than their colleagues elsewhere. Perhaps the education of aspiring public servants could best be achieved through the establishing in Ottawa and certain provincial capitals of schools of public administration modelled on France's Ecole Nationale d'Administration or on the permanent staff college operated by the Canadian Armed Forces.

The Institute of Public Administration bears particular responsibility for the critical issues affecting the status of public administration in Canada today. The Institute may find it profitable to seek more members and more contributions to the journal from representatives of social disciplines other than political science. Then again, the establishment in Canada of a new journal comparable to the *Administrative Science Quarterly* in the United States may present a more rational alternative. The most knowledgeable and experienced members of the Institute must aggressively put their unique research and problem-solving abilities to work. Questions of inadequate literature, insufficient research funds, difficulty of access to government documents, new approaches to the study and teaching of public administration, and the need for contributions from fields other than political science will directly confront the Institute long before another 40 issues of *Canadian Public Administration* have lined the shelves of departmental offices and private libraries.

Chapter Two
Administrative Theory

The history of administrative thought is brief. The Cameralists, eighteenth century Prussian civil servants, were probably the first to consider administration worthy of study and research. Their concern with the theory of administration appears as an island in a sea of pragmatic unconcern. No further evidence of substantial interest in the philosophy or concepts of administration appears until more than a century later when the age of management was launched by Fayol, Taylor, Follett, Mayo and others.

This means that the substantive study of management is less than 70 years old. Yet students of management are already busily defining schools of administrative thought. With the assistance of philosophers, political scientists, economists and sociologists they are trying to trace patterns in the management theory maze in order to distinguish and compare the work of administrative theorists. Unfortunately, no generally acceptable model has yet emerged, though there is a consensus on the identity of the fathers of management theory.

The first three articles in this chapter discuss changes in administrative concepts during the last 50 years. V. Subramaniam summarizes the arguments of the classical and modern theorists and D. Woolf suggests a model to structure the discussion of administrative theory. R. A. Dahl explores the possibility of achieving a science of public administration and L. Urwick defends views of the school of scientific management. Finally, H. Diamond evaluates the influence of the behavioural sciences on administrative theory.

Volume 1 of B. Gross, *The Managing of Organizations* (Collier-Macmillan, Toronto, 1964) contains the most comprehensive review of administrative theory. Harwood F. Merrill has gathered a collection of speeches and articles by early management theorists in *Classics of Management* (American Management Association, New York, 1960).

Many of the more prominent contributions to administrative thought before World War II are also available:

C. I. Barnard, *Functions of the Executive*, Harvard University Press, Cambridge, Massachusetts, 1962.

H. Fayol, *General and Industrial Management,* Pitman, London, 1949.
M. P. Follett, *Dynamic Administration,* Harper, New York, 1942.
H. H. Gerth and C. W. Mills (eds. and trans.), *From Max Weber: Essays in Sociology,* Oxford (Galaxy Books), New York, 1958.
L. Gulick and L. Urwick, *Papers on the Science of Administration,* Institute of Public Administration, New York, 1937.
F. W. Taylor, *Scientific Management,* Dartmouth, Hanover, New Hampshire, 1912.
L. Urwick, *The Making of Scientific Management,* Management Publications Institute, London, 1951-1953.

The literature on contemporary administrative theory is immense.

7   The Classical Organization Theory and its Critics*

V. Subramaniam

The debate between the classical theory of organization (so christened by Simon) and modern organization theories was carried on in the post-war years in a rather curious manner. For our present purposes we may regard classical theory broadly as embracing the contributions of Taylor, Fayol, Mooney, Urwick and Gulick, culminating in the synthesis attempted by the last two.[1] The first frontal attack on this classical theory came from Simon

---

* Reprinted by permission of the editor and the author from *Public Administration* (U.K.), Vol. 44, Winter 1966, pp. 435-446.

[1] To be more precise, classical theory is regarded as being generally covered by the following standard works: L. Gulick and L. Urwick (eds.), *Papers on the Science of Administration,* 3rd ed., Institute of Public Administration, New York, 1954; James D. Mooney and A. C. Reiley, *Onward Industry,* Harper & Bros., New York, 1939; James D. Mooney, *The Principles of Organization,* 2nd ed., Harper & Row, New York, 1947; L. F. Urwick, *The Elements of Administration,* 2nd ed., Pitman, London, 1947; Henri Fayol, *General and Industrial Management,* Constance Storrs (trans.), Pitman, London, 1949. In the last two decades, classical theory and modern theory have been running in parallel streams. The former underpins most books on management and many articles in popular journals of business administration and management even while they are becoming more and more "decision" conscious and operations-research conscious. Modern theories of the sociological or decision-making school are discussed in academic journals and books. There have not been many occasions and places where they have met for discussion and debate. Simon's article, "Proverbs of Administration" did not provoke a reply till years later in Banfield's review of Simon's *Administrative Behaviour,* i.e. "Decision Making Schema", *Public Administration Review,* Vol. 17, p. 282. The next big debate was initiated by Pfiffner in *Public Administration Review,* Vol. 22, 1962. A more comprehensive review was made in a symposium in November 1962, see Harold Koontz, *Towards a Unified Theory of Management,* McGraw-Hill, New York and London, 1964.

in 1946, though the Hawthorne investigations had cast doubts much earlier on Taylor's simple assumption regarding the motivation of the worker solely through monetary rewards. Simon and March made further detailed criticisms in *Organizations* (chapter 2) in 1958 and others have since added their mite. The classical theorists on the other hand were rarely drawn into much direct controversy even while their influence in management education and consultancy reigned, unaffected by the advances of modern organization theories. Efforts have been recently made to bring the classical and modern theories together by highlighting some common ground (e.g. R. S. Parker) or through attempts at incorporating some research results of modern theories into the traditional apparatus of management consultants (e.g. Pfiffner). This paper attempts (i) to review the debate and reconciliation briefly, and (ii) to determine the place of classical theory in the university curriculum.

There is good reason for treating Simon's article, 'Proverbs of Administration' in *Public Administration Review* for Winter 1946, as the first comprehensive and serious criticism of the classical theory. The earlier criticisms were sporadic and piecemeal. Throughout the 1930's an agonizing reappraisal was going on in the field of public administration regarding the politics-administration dichotomy, but it did not seem to directly affect the formulations of classical theory, as this reappraisal was considered relevant only to 'public' administration.[2] Nor had the Hawthorne experiments made a real impact on administrative thinking, though they challenged Taylor's theory of motivation of the employee through bonuses. During these years the chief concern of that doyen of classical theorists, Urwick, was rather to fight the apathy of British managers and administrators to all administrative studies, than prepare for a serious theoretical controversy. Indeed, the first comprehensive formulation of classical theory was achieved in 1937 in *The Papers on the Science of Administration* by Gulick and Urwick, followed by a second more comprehensive reformulation by Urwick in the *Elements of Administration* in 1943. In neither work is Urwick particularly aware of the possibility of the findings of Mayo or the reflections of Mary Parker Follett constituting a point of departure for his critics;[3] on the contrary, one rather hears a note of triumph about the achievement of his attempted synthesis.

---

[2] Much of this reappraisal is surveyed in Dwight Waldo, *The Administrative State*, Ronald Press, New York, 1948. But this reappraisal was more concerned with such issues as the invalidity of the politics-administration dichotomy. In discussing values latent in the many 'scientific' approaches it became relevant to classical management theory, but management theorists paid little attention to this implication.

[3] In fact, Urwick edited together with Metcalfe, the papers of Mary Parker Follett, and his is perhaps the best short and straight forward account of the Hawthorne experiments (together with Brech) in *The Making of Scientific Management*, Pitman, London, 1951, Vol. 3.

The Two Strands of Criticism

Lack of Sophistication

Criticisms of the classical theory broadly fall into two classes, namely, (i) those which attack the inconsistencies, tautologies and lack of sophistication of the formulations of classical theorists — initiated mainly by Simon, and (ii) those which take issue with the pro-management bias of classical theory. We will take up the criticisms in that order for discussion.

Simon characterizes the 'principles' of administration of the classical theorists as mere proverbs; like proverbs they occur in pairs and for 'almost every principle one can find an equally plausible and acceptable contradictory principle'[4] leading to exactly opposite organizational recommendations. For example, according to the principle of span of control the number of subordinates whom a superior can efficiently supervise is limited to, say six. By adopting this in a large organization one would create more levels in the hierarchy than if a larger number, say twelve, was placed under each supervisor. At the same time there is a contradictory principle which enunciates that 'administrative efficiency is enhanced by keeping at a minimum the number of organizational levels through which a matter must pass.' It is obvious that whenever one seeks to increase efficiency according to the former principle it automatically decreases according to the latter, but there is nothing in the statement of these two principles to indicate which one is to be preferred on a given occasion or how the two considerations are to be balanced.[5] Simon goes on to show that all the other principles occur in such contradictory pairs. Thus the principle of unity of command is opposed by the principle of functional foremanship, and the principle of departmentalization by purpose is opposed by the principle of departmentalization by process.

In *Organizations* (chapter 2) Simon and March point out some more such failings:

1. Mooney does not make clear what he means by his five 'principles of administration; whether these five characteristics together define an organization or whether they are empirically observed in many organizations, or whether they are recommendations for the success of an organization.

2. The Taylorian researches about the best way to carry out manual jobs and the more elaborate time and motion studies of his followers are in the nature of techniques (rather than theory), and Taylor's hypothesis regarding the motivation of the worker through monetary rewards has been shown to be inadequate by the later researches of Mayo and his group.

3. Simon admits that Gulick's theory of departmentalization states in commonsense language a basic truth about the complex problem of allocating a given set of administrative activities among a given number of

---

4 *Public Administration Review*, Vol. 6, p. 53.
5 Simon develops this point more fully in his reply to Banfield. See "Decision making Schema: A Reply", *Public Administration Review*, Vol. 18, p. 61.

administrative units. But Gulick does not give any criteria to determine in advance the appropriateness of creating a process instead of a purpose organization at any level. He is not even aware that it is just impossible to prescribe criteria at a general level of analysis, because process similarities are discovered only by very detailed empirical investigation of the work done by thousands of employees, and a so-called purpose organization naively assumes that the total set of tasks to be accomplished is known in advance whereas it is a major function of the organization to elaborate these as it goes along.

4. In addition to the foregoing charges of commission, classical theorists, according to March and Simon, do not come to grips with the central problems of organization theory, namely conflict inside the organization between different sections and interests, the psychological limitations of a human (employee) in making decisions and carrying them out, and the continuous process of redefining the purposes of an organization.[6]

This writer would lay two further charges along the same lines. The first charge, of an artificial synthesis of classical theory, can be laid at the door of Urwick in particular. As Simon points out, part of the writings of classical theorists was highly repetitive and to that extent it was adequate just to declare this agreement within the happy family. Agreement was also easy even when somewhat different propositions were stated by different writers — if they were in vague non-quantitative terms. It became difficult, however, when the same term, such as staff, was used in somewhat different senses, and indeed Urwick's efforts to explain it in regard to the British Army, while starting probably as an attempt at reconciliation, ends up by highlighting the differences between his interpretation and Mooney's.[7] Of course, when a difference is strikingly plain, as is the one between the classical principle of unity of command and Taylor's principle of functional foremanship — of accepting several 'commanders' for one worker — a definite choice has to be made and in this case the former was chosen as overriding. But that was probably the only instance of a definite choice between two opposites. Synthesis is made possible in other cases through a benevolent accommodation without full comprehension of the basic differences — as for example of the conclusions of Mayo and Follett — as shown later in this paper.

The raison d'être of Urwick's synthesis, however, was to make intelligible and mutually relevant a number of loosely connected findings and observations about administration by other classical theorists, and his best efforts were directed towards this end. He does this in regard to Fayol's list of administrative functions and duties and Mooney's 'principles' through an extended use of the latter's device — of relating each principle to its process and each process to its effect. Each such process and effect give birth in

---

[6] J. G. March and H. Simon, *Organizations*, Wiley, New York and London, 1959, p. 33. Their words are here paraphrased into simpler English.

[7] L. F. Urwick, "Administration as a Technical Problem", *Papers on the Science of Administration*.

their turn to a principle, each followed by the relevant process and effect. This completes a master square of nine items in nine small squares. Three such master squares are constructed to encompass all the findings of Fayol and Mooney and to include even some observations of Taylor and Follett.[8] The result is an excellent aid to memory but a doubtful exercise in synthesis. Neither Mooney nor Urwick is clear about what they mean by the terms, principle, process and effect. Is a 'principle' a statement of a general cause-effect relation between two variables? Is a 'process' a manipulation of one of the variables to produce a desired change in the other? Does an 'effect' denote the actual attainment of this change by manipulating the first variable? These questions are never answered and indeed they seem to be avoided by the use of such phrases as a principle 'going into process' with whatever is termed a process and the process 'issuing into' whatever is called an effect. Besides this basic ambiguity, it is apparent that Mooney and Urwick are just too keen to fill all the small squares with some convenient phrase or other to make up a master square with the sacred nine little squares. For example, Mooney's original square has co-ordination listed thrice over as the principle of co-ordination, processive co-ordination and effective co-ordination and functionalism is listed similarly as determinative, applicative and interpretative functionalism. Urwick, when deriving two more master squares from Mooney, adds another instance of repetition with his principle of centralization, processive centralization and effective centralization.

Secondly, in elaborating the need, nature and limits of hierarchy, the classicalists have suffered from a similar lack of sophistication. Hierarchy and its ramifications such as unity of command are at the heart of classical theory and one would have expected something better from the classicalists, but their failure was in part due to sloppy scholarship and in part to their genuine confusion about the extent of a superior's authority over his subordinates. We shall deal with the second reason a little later in this paper. As an instance of the first we can point to Mooney's rather haphazard historical justification of hierarchical authority. Not satisfied with referring generally to the wide prevalence of authority relations and their wide acceptance in all forms of human effort, he must put together odd pieces of history about the Roman Empire and Papacy and what have you to buttress his case.[9] This mixing up of different forms of authority in one stew almost spoils his case. And yet, a rigorous case about the inevitability of oligarchy in organized human effort, and a clear distinction between different forms of authority had already been made well before Mooney started making his essays into history and sociology. Round the turn of the

---

8 *Ibid.*, p. 123, p. 125 and p. 128. See also L. F. Urwick, *The Elements of Administration*, *op. cit.*, pp. 120-1 for a consolidated diagram.

9 James D. Mooney goes to some pains to show the universal presence of authority in all collective human enterprise through his excursions into European history in *Onward Industry* as well as in *The Principles of Organization* — without trying to distinguish between different types of authority.

century the elitists such as Mosca and Pareto had already commented in detail on the existence of a 'ruling class' in all societies and in all ages. But Michels, who was more to 'our' point, went further and derived an iron law of oligarchy from a study of contemporary social-democratic parties in Europe.[10] He showed how in all human organizations with a goal, the few ultimately lead the many, because the old human weaknesses such as hero-worship and apathy combine with the new need for management by the intelligent few to take quick decisions for the many. Almost the same time, Max Weber drew distinctions between three types of authority, charismatic, traditional and bureaucratic. The classical theorists seemed to be altogether ignorant of these rich resources of advocacy, partly because they were too keenly interested in practical results, through refining actual practice. This rendered even the basic concept of their theory platitudinous and patchy. It was left to the post-war theorists of organizations to derive inspiration from Weber, and to build a more sophisticated academic theory of bureaucratic authority.

Classical theorists have not generally cared to answer in detail these charges concerning lack of sophistication, consistency, and precision. Their blanket reply, more often implicit in their attitudes, is that their approach is down-to-earth, yielding practical results in improving organizations and that the luxury of sophistication can wait.[11]

Pro-Management Bias

It is not difficult to establish a *prima facie* case concerning the pro-management bias of classical theorists, which is sometimes implicit and often explicit.

1. Thus even when they flaunt their practical achievements (in management consultancy) they are achievements *for* the manager. Rarely have they pressed any serious claim to study organization academically in a detached manner.

2. In regard to their personal backgrounds, the leading classical theorists were either successful top managers such as Fayol and Mooney or successful advisers to top management as Gulick and Urwick.

---

[10] The standard editions of the well-known works of these authors are referred to: namely, Gaetano Mosca, *The Ruling Class*, Hannah D. Kahn (trans.), McGraw-Hill, New York, 1939; Vilfredo Pareto, *The Mind and Society*, Arthur Livingstone (ed.), Cape, London, 1935; Roberto Michels, *Political Parties*, E. and C. Paul (trans.), The Free Press, New York, 1958; Max Weber, "Bureaucracy" in *Essays in Sociology*, H. H. Gerth and C. W. Mills (eds. and trans.), Routledge and Kegan Paul, London, 1947. It was unfortunate for the development of administrative theory that not only the sponsors of management studies but also university teachers of political science and public administration (such as Professor L. D. White) should have missed all this rich material till the forties — for one reason or another.

[11] E.g. Thomas L. Gardner, "First things First", *Public Administration Review*, Vol 22, p. 1,923.

3. The main part of their work (with the exception of Taylor's[12] work studies) was concerned with what the manager or administrator should know and do; Fayol wrote all about the functions of the administrator; Gulick's theories of departmentalization tell the top administrator how to build administrative units; and Mooney's principles and Urwick's elements are indeed written as compendia and guides for managers. Moreover, a general rule such as the natural limitations of the human span of attention applicable to *all* human beings, is discussed by these writers as the span of control of managers.

4. There is a clear emphasis too in classical theory on the superior-subordinate relationship, in the principle of unity of command, in its summary rejection of Taylor's functional foremanship and in the repeated mention of hierarchy or scalar process, authority and leadership. Urwick's emphasis on the drawing office approach in building up an organization is advice to the manager first to build a 'manageable' structure for himself and make the necessary human adjustments for the managed thereafter.

Classical theorists generally take this charge more seriously and contend that their position is deliberately caricatured by their critics and that many employee-oriented modern techniques have always formed part of their repertoire, as practical commonsense.[13] Aggressive defenders of classical theory thus claim to have anticipated, in practice and in common parlance, many of the worthwhile conclusions of modern theory such as employee participation and democratic leadership in decision making. The claim is often backdated with profuse quotations starting with the Bible to include every pithy observation by every historical leader of men on motivation, social cohesion and successful teamwork. Both the charge and counter-charge are out of focus in one regard. The critics often seem to imply that classicalists are oblivious to the needs and motives of the employee when they really mean that the classicalist vision is narrow. The latter naturally resent the implication while denying the charge.

Classical theory was after all fashioned from the turn of the century onwards and had escaped the crudities and cruelties of the owner-manager period of the early years of the Industrial Revolution and learnt the lessons. Even its earliest proponents, Taylor and Fayol, were already faced with the facts of worker's dissatisfaction and workers' organizations and the need for the worker's co-operation. The classicalist's sin was not really unawareness of the 'managed' part of the organization; rather did it consist in the confusing way they dealt with it in their theory, its inconsistencies and vagueness. Taylor accumulated a wealth of managerial self-pity at being misunderstood and projected it as pity for the misguided worker who did not understand his new methods. In the case of Urwick, with his British army background, the manager-managed relationship is enveloped by

12 Taylor's own major concern was with the operatives and foremen though the movement he fathered went on to study managers.
13 E.g. Merrill J. Collett, "Strategy versus Tactics as the Object of Research in Public Administration", *Public Administration Review*, Vol. 22, pp. 115-21.

paternalism, the paternalism of the commanding officer for his men.[14] In general, classicalists accept *ad hoc* dilutions of strict managerial authority without any precise accommodation of them in theory. This makes it possible for Urwick to claim Mayo and Mary Parker Follett as members of the classical company. The claim looks plausible partly because their work was contemporary with classical theory though not of it; partly because the picturesque, poetic language of Follett concealed its detonatory content, and partly because the researches of Mayo and his team were first launched to discover reasons for falling productivity. Indeed this approach — of using the results of research on the managed as an aid to better management — has given classical theory a new lease of life as management science. But more of this later.

Attempts at Reconciliation

Efforts have been made in recent years to bring the classical theory closer to modern theories. On the one hand, some writers on management use freely principles and propositions from both theories without acknowledging any need for an explanation or reconciliation of any conflict. The academic cannot possibly be satisfied with this flabby, eclectic approach and must recognize the conflict and attempt a reconciliation. Some do this by highlighting the common ground and others by showing up the complementary nature of both and the possibilities of fruitful collaboration. An example of the former method is provided by Parker's argument that the components of administration in the Simon model differ from those in the traditional, i.e. classical model, mainly in detail and terminology. This is illustrated by his comparative table given below.[15]

THE SIMON MODEL	A RATIONALIZED 'TRADITIONAL' MODEL
A. *Decisions* form a hierarchy of *ends* and *means*, i.e., means at each level are conditioned by ends at the next higher, or more general level (leading up to the ultimate 'purpose') and also by values, including:	I. *Planning* includes working out the *hierarchy of ends and means*; and establishing guiding and conditioning values of decision making.
1. values relevant to the ultimate purposes; and	
2. general values currently accepted as standards of behaviour by the community, the organization and the individual.	II. Organization means establishing and revising the *structure of horizontal and vertical specialization.*

---

14 L. F. Urwick, *Elements of Administration*, *op cit.*, p. 50.

15 R. S. Parker, "New Concepts of Administration — its Meaning and Purpose, *Public Administration* (Sydney), Vol. 21, p. 28.

THE SIMON MODEL	A RATIONALIZED 'TRADITIONAL' MODEL
B. The modes of organizational influence including:	III. Co-ordination and Control are the means of aiming at consistency of decisions with each other and with main purposes.
1. Specifying member's functions, thus narrowing the scope of their decisions (choices) to manageable limits, by means of	
(a) 'Horizontal specialization', allocating different functions to each;	IV. Motivation and morale are corresponding aspects of 'personnel' administration.
(b) 'Vertical specialization', i.e. allocating authority in a hierarchy of ends and means;	
(c) Setting other limits to members' choices, e.g. prescribing lines of policy, rules of procedure, etc.	V. Economy and efficiency are regarded as yardsticks for the leaders' use.
2. Establishing values, attitudes, and habits in members' minds, e.g.	
(a) Loyalties to leaders and identification with the organization and its purposes;	VI. Staffing (but wider than in Simon).
(b) Acceptance of efficiency as a value;	
(c) Providing advance information;	
(d) Training.	VII. Directing tends to be over-emphasized in this model — 'unity of command', military analogies, etc.
3. Imposing, by authority, decisions reached elsewhere in the organization.	
	VIII. Reporting singles out only one, formal kind of the communications that flow, in fact, in all directions.
C. Communications are needed throughout and beyond the organization to transmit all the above influences.	
D. Purposes, structure and activities of an organization at a given time represent a momentary equilibrium between the values and relative power of leaders, participants and other interested groups.	IX. 'Informal organization' (a contradiction in terms) is perhaps the nearest equivalent idea. Some of the more recent 'traditional' texts come nearer to Simon's notion with discussions of 'the power-politics of administration'.

This comparison does establish (i) that the things discussed by modern theorists with more sophistication are not basically different from the things dealt with by classical theorists in commonsense parlance, and (ii) that the latter's conclusions, if simple or imprecise, are not wholly false. In other words, it draws attention to the obvious but forgotten common ground between both schools, but it ignores the basic charges of lack of precision and sophistication in matters dealt with by the classicalists and their failure to deal with other things that matter. It is not likely to provoke much enthusiasm among classical theorists, who do not relish being saluted as superseded pioneers.

Pfiffner's plea to 'make social science operational' is an example of the second method of reconciliation.[16] He feels that several findings of modern social sciences (in the field of organizations) are both widely accepted and proven useful and suggests incorporating them in the traditional apparatus of management consultants – as techniques. His underlying assumption (which is more explicit in Parker's comparison) is that both stocks are compatible and his implied expectation is that it is possible ultimately to crossbreed from the 'practical' POSDCORB-minded[17] consultants and the academic modern organization theorists, a single but many-sided school. The immediate reception given to this suggestion by the former could not have been more hostile.[18] They suggested not only that they already had all that they needed, but that the additions were a useless luxury and might even prove treacherous. The immediate possibilities of a progressive evolution on the lines suggested by Pfiffner seemed rather slender and have not improved much since then. Thus the neo-classicalist management theorists, such as Koontz, and modernist critics of the classical theory, such as Simon, did not change their positions much at the end of a conference in 1962 in search of a 'unified theory of management'.[19]

The Teacher's Problem

A basic problem thus faces the university teacher of administration. He cannot ignore the existence and influence of the classical theory and exclude it from his curriculum. It is being widely taught by academics of the old school in the United States and the United Kingdom, and more vigorously to an increasing audience of students and administrators in developing countries to which they are seconded. With a few modifications it still forms the core of many management education courses and is widely used by management consultants in their daily work. The academic cannot ignore these facts of administrative life nor can he merge the classical theory offhand into the general body of modern organization theory. Such absorption may be the ultimate end of pioneering but unsophisticated formulations in most social sciences, but the classical theory still preserves a separate identity for reasons which we shall examine briefly.

The main reason is that it is regarded by many managers as 'the theory' which helped their predecessors to make some sense out of their growing organizations. These loyal men will keep it alive as the tried and tested

16 John M. Pfiffner, "Why not make Social Science Operational", *Public Administration Review*, Vol. 22, pp. 109-14.

17 POSDCORB, a term coined by Luther Gulick in 1937 to describe the major functions of a chief executive, stands for planning, organization, staffing, directing, coordinating, reporting and budgeting.

18 See the three articles following Pfiffner, *op cit.*

19 See Koontz, *Toward a Unified Theory of Management*, passim.

family doctor so long as it delivers some goods if not all. The classical theory seems to do this. How does it do it, in spite of its intellectual shortcomings?

It owes much of its success to its combination of 'practical' and 'theoretical' knowledge[20] in an unacademic way. The function of theory is mainly to provide a framework of 'abstracted' categories to classify concrete phenomena into and then to formulate propositions of a cause and effect type relating such categories or variables. Practical knowledge consists of acting in such a way as to 'use' one or more of such propositions so as to bring about a desired result. This can be done in two ways, either more consciously as a result of planned instruction and training or less consciously through a cultivation of skills and attitudes. The former is the way in established professions such as medicine or engineering, each with a large body of accumulated theoretical knowledge and an established mode of training. The latter is the way of arts where the body of accumulated theoretical knowledge is not large and training methods may be based on apprenticeship or may be purely experimental. In the former, the established mode of training itself has a clear structure which performs two separate and related functions, namely (i) of passing on the accumulated theoretical knowledge efficiently, in universities or technical institutions, and (ii) putting the student in successive conditioning postures in the laboratory, field and factory, wherein the knowledge is internalized and transformed into personal ability to apply it. In the case of arts, however, the distinct functions of discovering (research) and passing on (instruction) the knowledge are inextricably mixed up with the conditioning of the student to internalize it. Hence, the knowledge itself is stated in vague but suggestive language. The statements often do not amount to more than some refined proverbial wisdom and some useful tips on technique but their effect on the *receptive* student may be out of all proportion to the intellectual quality of the statements themselves.

The success of the classical theory with managers depends more on this suggestive potentiality and less on its intellectual content. Among the factors making up this potentiality two major ones may be identified. In the first place, it talks to managers in language familiar to them, using familiar terms such as staff and line, command and control or profits and productivity. Secondly it follows a flexible strategy which first treats things like organizational structure or personnel selection and training in such a way as to give the manager initial control, and then gracefully introduces the minimum modifications necessary to overcome destructive resistance from the managed. In other words, it offers to the manager a 'myth' which enthuses and invigorates him and simultaneously trains him to offer to the managed this myth as the first draft of a contract, negotiable in parts and at the margins. He is given a sense of purpose by the myth but also prepared to some extent to face reality. He is psychologically armed much

---

[20] Michael Oakeshott, *Rationalism in Politics and other Essays*, Methuen, London, 1962, pp. 7-11. I have taken the basic idea, but for the interpretation and all the additions I must bear the entire blame.

the same way the entrepreneur was (according to Max Weber) by the Protestant ethic.[21]

Essentially because of this implicit strategy the classical theory has survived and absorbed in its own way some new findings about the behaviour of the managed or the needs of the manager. A good example is the story of the ultimate absorption into most management text books of the Hawthorne findings. Mayo's group established the inevitability and importance of the formation of small groups of workers and their good and bad effects. In Likert's hands[22] the knowledge was transformed, after further experiments, into advice to the manager on how to 'manipulate' the groups for greater productivity. An even more interesting example is the slow incorporation of the less sophisticated aspects of the decision-making theories of Simon and his group in management literature. Thus recent text books in management include side by side with the POSDCORB stuff of classical theory some material on the 'use' of small work groups and on decision-making while other advanced books discuss the most recent control techniques within the framework of POSDCORB.[23] This development may ultimately result in a more sophisticated management theory which has cut off its classical umbilical cord but retains a liberal promanagement bias. But that day is not yet and till then, it would be proper for the university teacher to continue to discuss the classical theory in his curriculum (preferably in the words of its own proponents) as a contemporary influence.

8   The Management Theory Jungle Revisited*

Donald Austin Woolf

What is a Theory of Management?

The term, "theory" often seems to conjure up impressions of mystery and impracticality to managers and students of management alike. Indeed in discussions of theory, one sometimes gets the implication that people feel

21 Max Weber, *The Protestant Ethic and the Spirit of Capitalism* 7th imp., Talcott Parsons (trans.), George Allen & Unwin, London, 1965.

22 Rensis Likert, *New Patterns of Management*, McGraw-Hill, New York and London, 1961. Regarding the use of social sciences to help the manager, see Loren Baritz, *The Servants of Power*, Wesleyan University Press, Middletown, Connecticut, 1960.

23 A good example of this penetration of modern theories and their coexistence with the classical theory is the self-instruction pocket manual. At another level, Ernest Dale's *Management: Theory and Practice*, McGraw-Hill, New York and London, 1965, may be cited as an example of an attempt to discuss the old and new, e.g. chapter entitled "Taylor and Mayo. Who was right?"

* Reprinted with permission of author and publisher from *Advanced Management Journal*, Vol. 30, October 1965, pp. 6-15.

that a *theory* is impractical by definition. The phrase which frequently expresses this sentiment is, "Well, that may be all right in *theory*, but it will never work in *practice*." One of the reasons for this common belief is that some of our previously-held theories have been found unworkable; therefore, we are suspicious of the potential utility of present theory.

However, to generalize from prior unfortunate experience to the extent that *all* theory is rejected as a waste of time is to miss the point of having theory at all. A theory is an explanation of *why* something happens, and, sometimes, *how* something happens, as well as a statement of *what* happens. A good theory provides us with a reasonably reliable means of prediction. Because of this, there is by definition no such thing as a theory that is "all right" as a theory, but not "all right" in practice. If a theory is demonstrably unworkable in practice, then it ceases to have value as a theory.

A theory of management (and, by implication, organizations) should define *why* we have it, *what* it is, and *how* it works. Although management may exist in the absence of formal organization (e.g., management of personal finances) in the sense that some management activities such as planning may take place, we normally associate the practice and study of management with organizations. Therefore, the "why" of management can be answered, in part, by assessing the "why" of organizations.

The Origins of Organization and Management

Much of what we do is affected by organizations. Most of us work for organizations, secure our food and other essentials from organizations, enrich our leisure time through activities and the use of facilities provided by organizations, and rely on organizations for protection, regulation, and other governmental activities. We consider a complexity of interlocking organizational structures to be a prime characteristic of civilization, and those few remaining societies which are not characterized by this kind of development are referred to as "primitive."

Sometimes our experiences with organizations are not entirely satisfactory. A new product fails to function properly, a garment is not available in the proper size, or a government official informs us that our tax liability is greater than we thought it was. Our reactions may be fairly specific, in which case we may hypothesize solutions to the organizational problems which have contributed to our displeasure (although we rarely communicate these solutions — which may include the rapid demise of the organization or its offending member — to the organization or the individual involved). On the other hand, our reaction may be general, in which case we may hear sentiments expressed such as, e.g., "There's too much governmental interference with business," or "They just don't make things as good as they used to." In both cases, the assumption contributing to the adverse judgment is likely to be either (1) the organization is not achieving its logical purpose, i.e., its means are ineffective, or (2) the apparent goal of the organization is unacceptable, at least to us. If pursued to its logical conclusion, this line of inquiry may lead us to a consideration of what organizations-in-general are supposed to accomplish.

If we direct our attention to the nature and adequacy of goals of commercial organizations, the simple and obvious answer to our query is that their purpose is to make money. However, this answer is over-simple. In order to make money, they must get other people to spend it, and in order to get other people to spend it, these organizations must provide something that other people want.[1]

Moreover, the things which organizations provide for their clients must be either cheaper or more convenient than what they can provide for themselves (or than can be provided by another organization), or they may be things which cannot be provided without an organization. Examples of things which fall into the latter category include activities such as providing for national defense, building a skyscraper, or a band concert. In short, organizations provide goods and services which people want and these goods and services would be either more expensive, less convenient, or unavailable to people in the absence of organizations. Conversely, *organizations are created when people perceive a mutually desirable goal or goals which can be more effectively accomplished through cooperative action than without, and when the necessary resources are available to facilitate these goals.*[2]

These "necessary resources" include not only the economists's familiar land, labor, and capital, but also strategic factors such as time and influence. In order for organizational goals to be accomplished, resources have to be allocated in the amount and at the time needed. This process of allocation requires a dilineation of authority relationships, and task assignments. From a summary of the foregoing ideas we can propose a definition, viz., *organization refers to a group of people who have established patterns of authority, communications, and responsibility relating to the achievement of a common goal or goals.*

The determination of these assignments and relationships is not automatic. *The process of delineation of lines of authority, patterns of communication, and task assignment, as well as allocation of resources to achieve organizational goals is called management.* The central problem of constructing a theory of management and organization is to determine what authority is, how it ought to be distributed in the organization, the "best" patterns of communication, and the "best" allocation of resources to achieve organizational goals. In short, the purpose of management theory is not just to find a methodology that will work, but a method that will work better than any other.

It follows from the foregoing that if the organization cannot provide its service as cheaply and conveniently as people can provide it for themselves,

[1] Although the model being constructed here suggests a one-organization society, it is assumed that the clients of our hypothetical organization in turn obtained their money from other organizations, and that the clients, themselves, could be organizations.

[2] For a discussion of this and related matters, see Bronislaw Malinowski, *A Scientific Theory of Culture*, University of North Carolina Press, Chapel Hill, North Carolina, 1944, especially pp. 143-144.

the organization will not survive. Moreover, it has to provide its service about as well as other competing organizations for the same reason. Therefore, in addition to the general requirements of a theory, i.e., determining why something happens, what happens, and how it happens, a theory of management requires us to find out the best way for it to happen.

Two Approaches to Management Theory

Most theories of management found in recent textbooks and other writings in the field are eclectic, i.e. their component parts are drawn from a variety of sources and points of view. However, it is possible to isolate and identify a number of "schools" of thought which have been incorporated into current composite theory. Although there are a number of different ways of classifying the contributions made by various authors dealing with the subject, the analysis here is going to be in terms of the following:

1. Is the theory (or subsystem) primarily directed toward identification and solution of mechanical problems of internal structure and operation or is it directed toward the human problems of organizational members and clientele?
2. Is the theory essentially descriptive, and is it developed primarily through deductive reasoning, or is it primarily analytical incorporating inductive or experimental methodology?[3]

Generally speaking, most contemporary writers tend to use the dichotomy suggested by the first question, i.e. is the theory organization-centered or is it person-centered? Organization-centered theory is sometimes identified as the "principles of management" school, while person-centered theory is summarized under the title of "human relations." However, it is noteworthy that both schools of thought include early theorists who relied primarily on description, deduction, and the assumption of a number of postulates, or axioms. Both schools also include theorists whose contributions are much more experimentally oriented, and tend to exclude untested principles or beliefs.

   I. Organization-Centered Theory
      A. Descriptive, deductive
      B. Analytical, inductive, experimental
  II. Person-Centered Theory
      A. Descriptive, deductive
      B. Analytical, inductive, experimental

---

[3] This difference in approach may appear purely academic. Perhaps its importance may be illustrated by reference to the disparate findings, respectively, of Aristotle and Galileo about the behaviour of falling bodies. Aristotle, relying on description and deduction stated that heavier objects fall at a faster rate than comparatively lighter ones (which they do not); Galileo, who experimented with this phenomenon, found that objects (in this case of the same density, in the atmosphere) fall at the same rate, regardless of weight.

The Organization-Centered Approach: Descriptive Theory

Most of the early attempts to define management were primarily concerned with the more readily identifiable activities of managers, and with attributes of organizational structure which would facilitate the achievement of organizational goals. This kind of theory is constructed via two means. One method is to observe one or more "successful" organizations, and try to describe and classify the apparent activities which lead to this success. The other is to attempt to deduce or hypothesize the approprite logical solution to an organizational problem.

Perhaps the most prominent of the early writers of this school is Henri Fayol.[4] In general, his theory is descriptive rather than analytical, and tends toward the use of deductive reasoning rather than experimental evidence. Fayol's writing is consistent with the general pattern of most of those who have written since his time. He proposed essential activities of goal-setting (planning), determination of authority relationships and task assignment (organizing), and maintenance of communications (commanding, coordinating, and controlling) applied to functional areas of marketing, finance, controllership, technical problems (such as production, and security (safeguarding of property and persons).[5]

Although subsequent authors have proposed moderate variations in defining the activities and functions which are associated with the practice of management, the general approach has not been changed materially since Fayol's time.[6] After identifying the major activities and functions, the typical author utilizing this approach will propose "principles" for their

---

[4] See for example Henry Fayol, *General and Industrial Management*, Pitman, London, 1949. This pioneer in management conceived and practiced many of his ideas before the turn of the twentieth century; however, these ideas were not new by any means. Numerous examples of pre-Christian writings about management subjects may be found, such as Kautilya's *Arthasastra*, translated by T. N. Ramaswamy in *Essentials of Indian Statecraft*, Asia Publishing House, London, 1962; Plato's *Republic*, Modern Library, New York, 1941; and in the Old Testament. More recently, Gibbons' *Decline and Fall of the Roman Empire*, Modern Library, New York, n.d. and Niccolo Machiavelli's *The Prince*, Random House, New York, 1937, all treat with familiar management topics such as the chain of command, the span of control, and the specialization of labor.

[5] See Fayol, *op. cit.*, pp. 3-6. In the Storrs translation, the term "activities" is used to refer to both management action *and* functional areas such as finance, etc. More recent authors tend to use the term, "functions," to refer to both. Cf. Theo Haimann, *Professional Management*, Houghton-Mifflin, Boston, 1962. In the former work, management "functions" of planning, organizing, staffing, etc., are defined on pp. 35-38, while "functions" of production, sales, finance, and merchandising are discussed on pp. 101-196 and 147-154. Haimann uses the same term to describe the two different concepts on pp. 22-25, pp. 156-161, and 219 ff. For purposes of clarity and internal consistency, the present author will use "activities to denote planning, organizing, communicating, controlling, and related managerial actions, and the term "functions" to refer to finance, marketing, production, and similar operational requirements.

[6] Most texts today use the familiar planning, organizing, staffing, directing and controlling sequence of activities. See for example, Theo Haimann, *op. cit.*

proper execution, such principles being based on deductive logic and comparatively unsystematic observation.[7]

This approach is usually referred to as the "principles of management" school, and less frequently as the "management process"[8] or "administrative process" school.[9] The kinds of activities treated by the various authors utilizing this approach suggest that this theory is primarily directed toward the problems and practices of top management. However, managers also have the problem of making their plans operational, and need specific guides to action in addition to general principles. These specific guides have to be developed according to the needs of the particular individual enterprise. This kind of thinking resulted in the emergence of a more analytical school of theory, sometimes called "scientific management."

The Organization-Centered Approach: Analytical Methodology

At about the same time that Fayol was attempting to generalize from his managerial experience in order to construct some sort of theory of management, Frederick Taylor and a number of his contemporaries and associates attempted to apply some of the experimental methodology derived from the physical sciences to problems of management. Taylor's attention and findings are directed primarily toward the problems of production management rather than top management, and his proposals pertaining to managerial activities and organizational structure constitute more of a by-product of his work rather than the main object of it. However, a most important result of his work has been the inculcation of a healthy skepticism about the *status quo* on the part of many people in management positions, and the seeking of new uses for tools such as accounting, mathematics, and especially, motion and time study.

The experimental approach to the logistical problems of management came to be known as "Scientific Management," and consisted primarily of systematically varying the physical factors in a given situation in order to find the "one best way" of achieving the organizational objective. The factors with which exponents of this methodology experimented were obtained by splitting any process into irreducible parts or actions. This resulted in rather minute specialization of labor and a splitting of authority giving rise to a need for careful coordination as well as for improved methods of quality control. Although the research tools and methodology have been materially refined, the basic "principles" advocated by Taylor

---

7 The comparison implied here is with the methodology of Taylor, or with that of the experimentally-oriented behavioral scientists, some of whose works may be found in **Dorwin Cartwright** and **Alvin Zander** (eds.), *Group Dynamics*, 2nd ed., Row, Peterson, Evanston, Illinois, 1953.

8 See **William Newman** and **Charles Summer**, *The Process of Management*, Prentice-Hall, Englewood Cliffs, New Jersey, 1961.

9 **Edward H. Kitchfield**, "Notes on a General Theory of Administration", *Administrative Science Quarterly*, Vol. I, No. 1, June 1956, pp. 3-29.

and his followers have found current expression in the form of operations research and systems management.

Operations research consists in part of gathering information about organizational activities to facilitate decision-making. Systems management may refer to the systems utilized to provide operations research data (e.g., weekly sales reports), but usually is broader in scope, including the establishment of any periodic procedure designed to facilitate goal accomplishment. Operations research (usually abbreviated "OR") and systems management are not mutually exclusive, but tend to complement each other. For example, the recent advances made in the area of automatic data processing facilitate the obtaining of OR data as well as providing systems for keeping track of organizational resources.[10]

An Overview of the Organization-Centered Approach

In attempting to place in perspective the schools known, respectively, as management process and scientific management, in relation to each other, we have found that the former is primarily directed toward considerations of *why* something is done, and *what* is done, while the latter is more concerned with *how* it should be done. Both schools of thought point up a central problem of organizations, viz., that *when something is accomplished by a group of people rather than by a single person, methods or procedures ("systems") must be devised to accomplish what the single individual would have done had he been able to give his personal attention to the problem.*

For example, the single individual attempts to conserve his material resources. The executive in a large organization is charged with the responsibility of conserving organizational resources. However, he cannot be personally responsible for the receipt of accounts payable, nor for the delivery of purchased goods in the amount and quality ordered; therefore he must devise *systems* to insure that money and goods utilized for organizational purposes are not diverted to other uses, or wasted.

Also implied or explicitly stated by the exponents of organization-centered theory is the proposition that people inherently are not prone to serve the goals of organizations, i.e., that they are inclined to be lazy, and that subordinates are not intelligent enough to make substantial contributions even when their intentions are good. This is why "systems" become necessary and why authority must be from the top down, in this frame of reference.

In summary, the organization-centered approach is primarily directed toward questions of structure and process, and the optimum utilization of

10 Similar definitions of operations research and views on the relationship of OR to scientific management may be found in Richard A. Johnson, Fremont E. Kast and James E. Rosenzweig. *The Theory and Management of Systems*, McGraw-Hill, New York, 1963, pp. 216ff. Other similar views may be found in Herbert A. Simon, *The New Science of Management Decision*, 1st ed., Harper, New York, 1960, pp. 2-15; and C. West Churchman, Russell L. Ackoff and E. Leonard Arnoff, *Introduction to Operations Research*, Wiley, London, 1957, p. 18.

all available resources to achieve organizational goals. In this context labor is treated as a commodity or factor of production, a circumstance which was distressing to some contemporaries of Taylor and Fayol as well as to some current observers.

The Person-Centered Approach: Descriptive Theory

Following a rather thorough Congressional investigation of the prevailing modes of management just prior to World War I, at least one able exponent suggested that organizations generally should be more concerned with people than they had been.[11] The reasons *why* we should be more concerned with people were (and are) twofold, and are both moral and practical in nature. Firstly, our methods of operating organizations should be consistent with national goals and beliefs concerning enhancement and development of the individual.

Secondly, it was proposed that people whose environment provided this enhancement and development would be happier, and happy people would make greater contributions to the organization. However, popular acknowledgment and some acceptance of this view does not appear to have occurred until after the publishing of *Management and the Worker* and *The Functions of the Executive* in the late 1930's.[12] Of these latter two works, Barnard suggested that the way people feel about what they do *should* affect their propensity to cooperate with management, and Roethlisberger and Dickson showed that it *did*. These two works are also illustrative of the description-analysis dichotomy proposed here as a tool for analysis of existing management theory. Barnard, and, for that matter, Follett, are illustrative of the descriptive approach, utilizing stated assumptions, and developing their argument primarily through deductive logic.

Although the methods utilized in the Hawthorne experiments by Roethlisberger and Dickson are now considered comparatively primitive, this series of studies is illustrative of the analytical or experimental school, discussed below.

Person-centered theory, whether of a descriptive or an analytical nature, is usually called "human relations." The full impact of this approach was not felt until after World War II, when courses relating to this subject began to appear in the catalogues of colleges of business and appropriate texts were published.

Descriptive person-centered theory provides a number of fairly radical departures from organization-centered theory, particularly in the area of authority. In general, early theorists — whether speaking from the perspective of government, the Roman church, the military, or business — postu-

---

11 Henry C. Metcalf and Lyndall Urwick (eds.), *Dynamic Administration: The Collected Papers of Mary Parker Follett*, Harper, New York, 1942.

12 Fritz J. Roethlisberger and William J. Dickson, *Management and the Worker*, Harvard University Press, Cambridge, 1939.

lated that the proper and *de facto* locus of authority is at the top of the organizational hierarchy.

However, as popular sovereignty gained favor as a theory of government and Protestantism challenged the position held by the Roman church, so Follett, Barnard, and more recent writers such as Simon and McGregor proposed that the proper and *de facto* of authority — and, indeed the origin, in a sense — was at the base of the organization rather than at the top.[13] Within this context of reasoning, leadership ultimately depends upon at least minimal acceptance of authority on the part of the led, and organizational goals must be mutually acceptable rather than imposed from the top. However, both Barnard and Simon readily agree that the level of acceptance may only consist of indifference to a particular action rather than fervent agreement with it. In other words, subordinates normally do what is asked of them because it is not objectionable, rather than doing what is asked of them because they enjoy it.[14]

A second departure from earlier theory is the disagreement of person-centered theorists with the concept of "economic man," i.e., the dual concept of labor as a commodity or factor of production as well as the hypothesis that laborers are motivated primarily by personal economic gain. The dissenting view holds that the employer does *not* merely hire a hand (or an eye, a brain, or a foot); a whole human being is attached to the part needed for the job. Moreover, the needs of this human being are considerably broader in scope than is suggested by the concept of economic man, and the entire environment — not merely the economic environment — must be considered by the organization requiring his services.[15]

Many of the writings which may be associated with this school of thought tend to use the vocabulary and are addressed to the problems associated with the organization-centered approach, and particularly the descriptive branch of that approach. For example, the writings of Simon and those of Argyris are directed toward and critical of such ideas as the span of control, the specialization of labor, and the chain of command.[16] By contrast, *experimentalists* using the person-centered approach tend not to use the postulates of more traditional theory as a point of departure.[17]

In summary, exponents of the descriptive variety of person-centered theory postulate an ethical position, viz., that organizations ought to demonstrate more interest in workers as people (rather than as factors of production), and hypothesize that such interest will result in happier workers as

---

[13] Herbert A. Simon, *Administrative Behavior*, 2nd ed., Macmillan, New York, 1957; see also Douglas McGregor, *The Human Side of Enterprise*, McGraw-Hill, New York, 1960.

[14] Simon, *op. cit.*, p. 116.

[15] For a summary of this point of view, see Temple Burling, *You Can't Hire a Hand and Other Essays*, Extension Bulletin No. 2, New York State School of Industrial and Labor Relations, Council University, Ithaca, New York, n. d.

[16] Simon, *op. cit.*, Chapters 1 and 2; Chris Argyris, *Personality and Organization*, Harper & Bros., New York, 1957, Chapter 3.

[17] See Robert Tannenbaum, Irving R. Weschler and Fred Massarik, *Leadership and Organization*, McGraw-Hill, New York, 1961; particularly the Preface and Chapter 1.

well as more production. Correlated with this position is the proposal that authority ought to — and does logically — originate at the base of the organization rather than at the top. These positions have been challenged not only by firm adherents to organization-centered theory, but also by some experimentally-minded behavioural scientists.

The Person-Centered Approach: Analysis and Experimentation

Two central questions raised by the experimentalists may be summarized as follows:

1. Does the nature of the work environment, including administrative action, supervision, composition of the work group, task assignment, method of compensation, and other working conditions result in measurable differences in employee attitudes?
2. Do differences in employee attitudes result in differences in productivity?

The determination of answers to these questions requires the development of a taxonomy so that differences in the environment and differences in employee attitudes as well as in productivity can be identified and classified. In addition, methods of measurement of these differences must be developed. For the most part, behavioral scientists engaged in these kinds of research have not utilized the vocabulary of the more traditional schools of thought, but have borrowed mainly from the fields of psychology, anthropology, sociology, and psychiatry. As a result, their findings often do not relate directly to the more traditional "principles" of management and organization, but are supplementary to or different from these principles.

Generally speaking, findings of those in this school indicate that the nature of the work environment has a definite effect on employee attitudes. However, the evidence concerning the relationship between attitudes and productivity have been inconclusive.[18] More precisely, only about half of the studies demonstrate a positive relationship between favorable job attitudes and productivity, while the balance shows either no correlation or a negative relationship.

Research tools employed in this kind of research range from observation of existing work groups to the creation of experimental groups and the utilization of instruments designed to measure social interaction, attitudes, aptitudes, and abilities of group members, as well as the nature and frequency of communications. In some respects, the over-all point of view of the person-centered experimentalist is not substantially different from the organization-centered experimentalist. The major difference between these two schools is the object of research. In the case of the earlier school, repre-

---

[18] For a summary of research and findings on this point, see Frederick Herzbert et al, Job Attitudes, Psychological Service of Pittsburgh, Pittsburgh, 1957, Chs. 3 and 4.

sented by adherents to scientific management, the focus of attention is directed toward logistical problems of utilization of physical assets; the person-centered experimentalists are almost exclusively interested in the human problems of management.

An Overview of the Person-Centered Approach

If one attempted to summarize the view of the adherents of the person-centered approach toward the more traditional organization-centered approach in a single phrase, one would have to say that they are against it. This antagonism is reciprocated. It is for this reason that Peter Drucker has stated that, ". . . Human Relations is, at least in the form in which it exists thus far, primarily a negative contribution. It freed management from the domination of viciously wrong ideas; but it did not succeed in substituting new concepts."[19] Nevertheless, human relations (or the behavioral science approach) has had a substantial and lasting impact on management theory, not only as it is taught in the classroom, but as it appears in the journals and literature available to executives.[20] Although primarily confined to occasional books, texts and articles in the 1940's, the person-centered approach is now treated in most general texts in management and marketing, and articles utilizing this approach are now regularly found in almost every major management journal.

Among the differences between these two approaches is the fact that the older, organization-centered approach is more-or-less self-prescribing, i.e., it tells one in general or specific terms what to do, and sometimes, when and how to do it. Lacking this in some instances, it tells you how to find out what to do, when to do it, and how to do it. By contrast, the person-centered approach tends either to be primarily negative on the one hand, or fragmentary on the other. For this reason, the established community of organizations has not put into practice the "principles" of human relations, because the principles are either elusive or non-existent.

Moreover, most of the research of the person-centered exponents has been directed toward either small groups or individuals, and may be of little immediate practical use to the organization of more than, say, 10,000 persons. In addition, this approach is comparatively silent about many of the problems of management. It was stated previously in this paper that a good theory should explain a phenomenon in terms of what happens, why it happens, and how it happens. The person-centered approach, by definition, fails to do this for many of the necessary functions and activities of management. In other words, it will not tell you how to set up an assembly line, nor how to organize a retail establishment.

---

[19] Peter Drucker, *The Practice of Management*, Harper, New York, 1954, p. 278.

[20] Donald Austin Woolf, *Behavioral Science Research and the Practicing Administrator*, unpublished Ph.D. dissertation, Cornell University, Ithaca, New York, 1963.

An Overview of Management Theory

In assessing the various theories of management, a variety of things become apparent. Firstly, none of the theories are complete in themselves in that none explain all of the things that we observe about the behavior of people in organizations. For this reason, all have experienced varying degrees of ascendancy into the spotlight of attention, and then been assimilated, at least in part, into the body of existing theory. For the most part, the theory which has prevailed for at least most of this century has been the descriptive, organization-centered approach. One explanation of this observation might be that this kind of theory explains more of what goes on than any of the others. Moreover, it is sufficiently broad that it *can* assimilate the others. Thus, our current theory presents the broad form of the principles of management approach, with overtones of scientific management, operations research, and ethical as well as experimental varieties of human relations.

Interestingly enough, a truly "eclectic" theory has not emerged from the efforts of theorists working from comparatively divergent viewpoints. There appear to be at least two primary causes for this condition. Firstly, the assumptions of the theories regarding human behavior and the nature of man are virtually irreconcilable. Organization-centered theory treats people as subsidiary to the organization and comparable to other necessary resources and commodities, i.e., their behavior and needs will be modified to meet the needs of the organization. Moreover, the motives of people are probably suspect. By contrast, person-centered theorists start with people as the focal point, and propose modifying organizational structure and goals to meet human needs.

The second basic reason for the failure of an eclectic theory is that theorists writing from divergent viewpoints do not appear to use the same vocabulary or address themselves to the same questions. Indeed, their occasional apparent hostility to opposing viewpoints would seem to preclude their doing this. Therefore, until some agreement on these two vital issues is reached, management theory will continue to be a "jungle."

9 The Science of Public Administration: Three Problems*

Robert A. Dahl

The effort to create a science of public administration has often led to the formulation of universal laws or, more commonly, to the assertion that

* Reprinted and slightly abridged with permission of author and publisher from *Public Administration Review*, Vol. 7, Winter 1947, pp. 1-11.

such universal laws *could* be formulated for public administration.[1] In an attempt to make the science of public administration analogous to the natural sciences, the laws or putative laws are stripped of normative values, of the distortions caused by the incorrigible individual psyche, and of the presumably irrelevant effects of the cultural environment. It is often implied that "principles of public administration" have a universal validity independent not only of moral and political ends, but of the frequently nonconformist personality of the individual, and the social and cultural setting as well.

Perhaps the best known expression of this kind is that of W. F. Willoughby. Although he refused to commit himself as to the propriety of designating administration as a science, Willoughby nevertheless asserted that "in administration, there are certain fundamental principles of general application analogous to those characterizing any science. . . ."[2] A more recent statement, and evidently an equally influential one, is L. Urwick's contention that "there are certain principles which govern the association of human beings *for any purpose,* just as there are certain engineering principles which govern the building of a bridge."[3]

Others argue merely that it is possible to discover general principles of wide, although not necessarily of universal validity.[4] Surely this more modest assessment of the role of public administration as a study is not, as an abstract statement, open to controversy. Yet even the discovery of these more limited principles is handicapped by the three basic problems of values, the individual personality, and the social framework.

The first difficulty of constructing a science of public administration stems from the frequent impossibility of excluding normative considerations from the problems of public administration. Science as such is not concerned with the discovery or elucidation of normative vlaues; indeed, the doctrine is generally, if not quite universally, accepted that science *cannot* demonstrate moral values, that science cannot construct a bridge across the great gap from "is" to "ought." So long as the naturalistic fallacy is a stumbling block to philosophers, it must likewise impede the progress of social scientists.

Much could be gained if the clandestine smuggling of moral values into the social sciences could be converted into open and honest commerce.

---

1 See, for example, F. Merson, "Public Administration: A Science", *Public Administration,* Vol. 1, 1923, p. 220; B. W. Walker Watson, "The Elements of Public Administration, A Dogmatic Introduction", *Public Administration,* Vol. 10, 1932, p. 397; L. Gulick, "Science, Values and Public Administration", *Papers on the Science of Administration,* Gulick & Urwick, (eds.), Institute of Public Administration, 1937; Cyril Renwick, "Public Administration: Towards a Science", *The Australian Quarterly,* March 1944, p. 73.

2 W. F. Willoughby, *Principles of Public Administration,* The Brookings Institution, 1927, Preface, p. ix.

3 See n. 10, *infra,* for the full quotation and citation.

4 This I take to be Professor Leonard D. White's position. See his "The Meaning of Principles in Public Administration", *The Frontiers of Public Administration,* University of Chicago Press, Chicago, 1936, pp. 13-25.

Writers on public administration often assume that they are snugly insulated from the storms of clashing values; usually, however, they are most concerned with ends at the very moment that they profess to be least concerned with them. The doctrine of efficiency is a case in point; it runs like a half-visible thread through the fabric of public administration literature as a dominant goal of administration. Harvey Walker has stated that "the objective of administration is to secure the maximum beneficial result contemplated by the law with the minimum expenditure of the social resources."[5] The term "social resources" is sufficiently ambiguous to allow for almost any interpretation, but it suggests that the general concept involved is one of maximizing "output" and minimizing "cost." Likewise, many of the promised benefits of administrative reorganization in state governments are presumed to follow from proposed improvements in "efficiency in operation." And yet, as Charles Hyneman has so trenchantly observed, there are in a democratic society other criteria than simple efficiency in operation.[6]

Luther Gulick concedes that the goal of efficiency is limited by other values.

> In the science of administration, whether public or private, the basic "good" is efficiency. The fundamental objective of the science of administration is the accomplishment of the work in hand with the least expenditure of man-power and materials. Efficiency is thus axiom number one in the value scale of administration. This brings administration into apparent conflict with certain elements of the value scale of politics, whether we use that term in its scientific or in its popular sense. But both public administration and politics are branches of political science, so that we are in the end compelled to mitigate the pure concept of efficiency in the light of the value scale of politics and the social order.[7]

He concludes, nevertheless, "that these interferences with efficiency [do not] in any way eliminate efficiency as the fundamental value upon which the science of administration may be erected. They serve to condition and to complicate, but not to change the single ultimate test of value in administration."[8]

It is far from clear what Gulick means to imply in saying that "interferences with efficiency" caused by ultimate political values may "condition" and "complicate" but do not "change" the "single ultimate test" of efficiency as the goal of administration. Is efficiency the supreme goal not only of private administration, but also of public administration, as Gulick contends? If so, how can one say, as Gulick does, that "there are . . . highly inefficient arrangements like citizen boards and small local governments which *may* be necessary in a democracy as educational devices"? Why speak

---

5 Harvey Walker, *Public Administration*, Farrar & Rinehart, 1937, p. 8.

6 Charles Hyneman, "Administrative Reorganization," *The Journal of Politics*, Vol. 1, 1939, pp. 62-65.

7 L. Gulick, *op. cit.*, pp. 192-193.

8 *Ibid.*, p. 193.

of efficiency as the "single ultimate test of value in administration" if it is not ultimate at all — if, that is to say, in a conflict between efficiency and "the democratic dogma" (to use Gulick's expression) the latter must prevail? Must this dogma prevail only because it has greater political and social force behind it than the dogma of efficiency; or ought it to prevail because it has, in some sense, greater value? How can administrators and students of public administration discriminate between those parts of the democratic dogma that are so strategic they ought to prevail in any conflict with efficiency and those that are essentially subordinate, irrelevant, or even false intrusions into the democratic hypothesis? What *is* efficiency? Belsen and Dachau were "efficient" by one scale of values. And in any case, why is efficiency the ultimate test? According to what and whose scale of values is efficiency placed on the highest pedestal? Is not the worship of efficiency itself a particular expression of a special value judgment? Does it not stem from a mode of thinking and a special moral hypothesis resting on a sharp distinction between means and ends?

The basic problems of *public* administration as a discipline and as a potential science are much wider than the problems of mere *administration*. The necessarily wider preoccupation of a study of *public* administration, as contrasted with *private* administration, inevitably enmeshes the problems of public administration in the toils of ethical considerations. Thus the tangled question of the right of public employees to strike can scarcely be answered without a tacit normative assumption of some kind. A pragmatic answer is satisfactory only so long as no one raises the question of the "rights" involved. And to resolve the question of rights merely by reciting *legal* norms is to beg the whole issue; it is to confess that an answer to this vital problem of public personnel must be sought elsewhere than with students of public administration. Moreover, if one were content to rest one's case on legal rights, it would be impossible to reconcile in a single "science of public administration" the diverse legal and institutional aspects of the right to strike in France, Great Britain, and the United States.

One might justifiably contend that it is the function of a science of public administration, not to determine ends, but to devise the best means to the ends established by those agencies entrusted with the setting of social policy. The science of public administration, it might be argued, would be totally nonnormative, and its doctrines would apply with equal validity to any regime, democratic or totalitarian, once the ends were made clear. "Tell me what you wish to achieve," the public administration scientist might say, "and I will tell you what administrative means are best designed for your purposes." Yet even this view has difficulties, for in most societies, and particularly in democratic ones, ends are often in dispute; rarely are they clearly and unequivocally determined. Nor can ends and means ever be sharply distinguished, since ends determine means and often means ultimately determine ends.

The student of public administration cannot avoid a concern with ends. What he *ought* to avoid is the failure to make explicit the ends or values that form the groundwork of his doctrine. If purposes and normative considerations were consistently made plain, a net gain to the science of public administration would result. But to refuse to recognize that the study of public administration must be founded on some clarification of ends is to perpetuate the gobbledygook of science in the area of moral purposes.

A second major problem stems from the inescapable fact that a science of public administration must be a study of certain aspects of human behavior. To be sure, there are parts of public administration in which man's behavior can safely be ignored; perhaps it is possible to discuss the question of governmental accounting and auditing without much consideration of the behavior patterns of governmental accountants and auditors. But most problems of public administration revolve around human beings; and the study of public administration is therefore essentially a study of human beings as they have behaved, and as they may be expected or predicted to behave, under certain special circumstances. What marks off the field of public administration from psychology or sociology or political institutions is its concern with *human behavior in the area of services performed by governmental agencies*.[9] And yet many of the supposed laws of public administration and much of the claim to a science of public administration derive from assumptions about the nature of man that are scarcely tenable at this late date.

The field of organizational theory serves as an extreme example, for it is there particularly that the nature of man is often lost sight of in the interminable discussions over idealized and abstract organizational forms. In this development, writers on public administration have been heavily influenced by the rational character that capitalism has imposed on the organization of production, and have ignored the irrational qualities of man himself.

Capitalism, especially in its industrial form, was essentially an attempt to organize production along rational lines. In the organization of the productive process, the capitalistic entrepreneur sought to destroy the old restrictive practices and standards of feudalism and mercantilism; to rid the productive process of the inherited cluster of methods and technics that characterized the guilds and medieval craftsmen; in short, to organize production according to rational rather than traditional concepts. Combined with a new acquisitive ideal, this rational approach to production transformed not only the whole economic process but society itself. The rapid growth of mechanization, routine, and specialization of labor further

---

9 See Ernest Barker's excellent and useful distinctions between state, government, and administration, in *The Development of Public Services in Western Europe, 1660-1930,* Oxford University Press, 1944, p. 3. Administration "is the sum of persons and bodies who are engaged, under the direction of a government, in discharging the ordinary public services which must be rendered daily if the system of law and duties and rights is to be duly 'served.' Every right and duty implies a corresponding 'service'; and the more the State multiplies rights and duties, the more it multiplies the necessary services of its ministering officials." See also Leon Duguit, *Law in the Modern State,* B. W. Huebsch, 1919, Ch. 2.

increased the technically rational quality of capitalist production. It was perhaps inevitable that concepts should arise which subordinated individual vagaries and differences to the ordered requirements of the productive process; for it was this very subordination that the replacement of feudal and mercantilist institutions by capitalism had accomplished. The organization (though not the control) of production became the concern of the engineer; and because the restrictive practices authorized by tradition, the protective standards of the guilds, the benevolent regulations of a mercantilist monarchy, and even the non-acquisitive ideals of the individual had all been swept away, it was actually feasible to organize production without much regard for the varying individual personalities of those in the productive process. The productive process, which to the medieval craftsman was both a means and an end in itself, became wholly a means.

Ultimately, of course, men like Taylor provided an imposing theoretical basis for regarding function, based on a logical distribution and specialization of labor, as the true basis of organization. Men like Urwick modified and carried forward Taylor's work, and in the process have tremendously influenced writers on public administration. Urwick, so it must have appeared, provided a basis for a genuine science of administration. "There are principles," he wrote, "*which should govern arrangements for human association of any kind*. These principles can be studied as a technical question, *irrespective of the purpose of the enterprise, the personnel composing it, or any constitutional, political, or social theory underlying its creation*."[10] And again, "Whatever the motive underlying persistence in bad structure it is always more hurtful to the greatest number than good structure."[11]

Sweeping generalizations such as these gave promise of a set of "universal principles": i.e., a science. American students of public administration could not fail to be impressed.

Aside from the fact that Urwick ignored the whole question of ends, it is clear that he also presupposed (though he nowhere stated what sort of human personality he *did* presuppose) an essentially rational, amenable individual; he presupposed, that is to say, individuals who would accept logical organization and would not (for irrelevant and irrational reasons) rebel against it or silently supersede it with an informal organization better suited to their personality needs. Urwick must have supposed this. For if

---

[10] L. Urwick, "Organization as a Technical Problem", *Papers on the Science of Administration*, p. 49. (Italics added.) See also his "Executive Decentralisation with Functional Co-ordination", *Public Administration*, Vol. 13, 1935, p. 344, in which he sets forth "some axioms of organisation", among others that "there are certain principles which govern the association of human beings *for any purpose*, just as there are certain engineering principles which govern the building of a bridge. Such principles should take priority *of all traditional, personal or political considerations*. If they are not observed, co-operation between those concerned will be less effective than it should be in realising the purpose for which they have decided to co-operate. There will be waste of effort". (Italics added.) See also his criticisms of the "practical man fallacy", p. 346.
[11] *Ibid.*, p. 85.

there is a large measure of irrationality in human behavior, then an organizational structure formed on "logical" lines may in practice frustrate, anger, and embitter its personnel. By contrast, an organization not based on the logic of organizational principles may better utilize the peculiar and varying personalities of its members. Is there any evidence to suggest that in such a case the "logical" organization will achieve its purposes in some sense "better" or more efficiently than the organization that adapts personality needs to the purposes of the organization?[12] On what kind of evidence are we compelled to assume that the rationality of organizational structure will prevail over the irrationality of man?

Patently the contention that one system of organization is more rational than another, *and therefore better*, is valid only (a) if individuals are dominated by reason or (b) if they are so thoroughly dominated by the technical process (as on the assembly line, perhaps) that their individual preferences may safely be ignored. However much the latter assumption might apply to industry (a matter of considerable doubt), clearly it has little application to public administration, where technical processes are, on the whole, of quite subordinate importance. As for the first assumption, it has been discredited by all the findings of modern psychology. The science of organization had learned too much from industry and not enough from Freud. The more that writers on public administration have moved from the classroom to the administrator's office, the more Urwick's universal principles have receded.

Thus by a lengthy and circumspect route, man has been led through the back door and readmitted to respectability. It is convenient to exile man from the science of public administration; it is simpler to forget man and write with "scientific" precision than to remember him and be cursed with his maddening unpredictability. Yet his exclusion is certain to make the study of public administration sterile, unrewarding, and essentially unreal.

If there is ever to be a science of public administration it must derive from an understanding of man's behavior in the area marked off by the boundaries of public administration. This area, to be sure, can never be clearly separated from man's behavior in other fields; all the social sciences are interdependent and all are limited by the basic lack of understanding of man's motivations and responses. Yet the ground of peculiar concern for a prospective science of public administration is that broad region of

---

12 See John M. Gaus's excellent definitions: "Organization is the arrangement of personnel for facilitating the accomplishment of some agreed purpose through the allocation of functions and responsibilities. It is the relating of efforts and capacities of individuals and groups engaged upon a common task in such a way as to secure the desired objective with the least friction and the most satisfaction to those for whom the task is done and those engaged in the enterprise. . . . Since organization consists of people brought into a certain relationship because of a humanly evolved purpose, it is clear that it should be flexible rather than rigid. There will be constant readjustments necessary because of personalities and other natural forces and because of the unpredicted and unpredictable situations confronted in its operations." "A Theory of Organization in Public Administration", in *The Frontiers of Public Administration*, pp. 66-67.

services administered by the government; until the manifold motivations and actions in this broad region have been explored and rendered predictable, there can be no science of public administration.

Development of a science of public administration implies the development of a science of man in the area of services administered by the public. No such development can be brought about merely by the constantly reiterated assertion that public administration is already a science. We cannot achieve a science by creating in a mechanized "administrative man" a modern descendant of the eighteenth century's rational man, whose only existence is in books on public administration and whose only activity is strict obedience to "universal laws of the science of administration."

If we know precious little about "administrative man" as an individual, perhaps we know even less about him as a social animal. Yet we cannot afford to ignore the relationship between public administration and its social setting. There should be no reason for supposing that a principle of public administration has equal validity in every nation-state, or that successful public administration practices in one country will necessarily prove successful in a different social, economic, and political environment. A particular nation-state embodies the results of many historical episodes, traumas, failures, and successes which have in turn created peculiar habits, mores, institutionalized patterns of behaviour, *Weltanschauungen*, and even "national psychologies."[13] One cannot assume that public administration can escape the effects of this conditioning; or that it is somehow independent of and isolated from the culture or social setting in which it develops. At the same time, as value can be gained by a comparative study of government based upon a due respect for differences in the political, social, and economic environment of nation-states, so too the comparative study of public administration ought to be rewarding. Yet the comparative aspects of public administration have largely been ignored; and as long as the study of public administration is not comparative, claims for "a science of public administration" sound rather hollow. Conceivably there might be a science of American public administration and a science of British public administration and a science of French public administration; but can there be "a science of public administration" in the sense of a body of generalized principles independent of their peculiar national setting?

Today we stand in almost total ignorance of the relationship between "principles of public administration" and their general setting. Can it be safely affirmed, on the basis of existing knowledge of comparative public administration, that there are *any* principles independent of their special environment? These conclusions suggest themselves:

1. Generalizations derived from the operation of public administration in the environment of one nation-state cannot be universalized and applied

---

13 See the fragmentary but revealing discussion on national differences in *Human Nature and Enduring Peace*, Third Yearbook of the Society for the Psychological Study of Social Issues, Gardner Murphy, (ed.), Houghton Mifflin, Boston, Massachusetts, 1945.

to public administration in a different environment. A principle *may* be applicable in a different framework. But its applicability can be determined only after a study of that particular framework.

2. There can be no truly universal generalizations about public administration without a profound study of varying national and social characteristics impinging on public administration, to determine what aspects of public administration, if any, are truly independent of the national and social setting. Are there discoverable principles of *universal* validity, or are all principles valid only in terms of a special environment?

3. It follows that the study of public administration inevitably must become a much more broadly based discipline, resting not on a narrowly defined knowledge of techniques and processes, but rather extending to the varying historical, sociological, economic, and other conditioning factors that give public administration its peculiar stamp in each country.

The relation of public administration to its peculiar environment has not been altogether ignored.[14] Unhappily, however, comparative studies are all too infrequent; and at best they provide only the groundwork. We need many more studies of comparative administration before it will be possible to argue that there are any universal principles of public administration.

We are a long way from a science of public administration. No science of public administration is possible unless: (1) the place of normative values is made clear; (2) the nature of man in the area of public administration is better understood and his conduct is more predictable; and (3) there is a body of comparative studies from which it may be possible to discover principles and generalities that transcend national boundaries and peculiar historical experiences.

10 Public Administration and Business Management*

L. Urwick

Some ten years ago Professor Dahl in an article in the *Public Administration Review,* "The Science of Public Administration: Three Problems," took

---

14 See, for example, Walter Dorn, "The Prussian Bureaucracy in the Eighteenth Century", *Political Science Quarterly*, Vol. 46, 1931, pp. 403-423; and 47 *Ibid.*, 1932, pp. 75-94, 259-273; Fritz Morstein Marx, "Civil Service in Germany" in *Civil Service Abroad*, McGraw-Hill, New York, 1935; John M. Gaus, "American Society and Public Administration", *The Frontiers of Public Administration*, University of Chicago Press, Chicago, 1936.

---

* Reprinted with permission of author and publisher from *Public Administration Review*, Vol. 17, Spring 1957, pp. 77-82.

me very severely to task for the statement that "there are principles . . . which should govern arrangements for human association of any kind. These principles can be studied as a technical question, irrespective of the purpose of the enterprise, the personnel composing it, or any constitutional, political, or social theory underlying its creation."[1]

"Sweeping generalizations such as these," he commented, "gave promise of a set of 'universal principles': i.e. a science. American students of public administration could not fail to be impressed." He then proceeded to take me to task on the ground, *inter alia*, that I had "presupposed an essentially rational, amenable individual . . . who would accept logical organization . . . ." (p. 5)

Meaning of a "Science"

It is not my purpose here this afternoon to enter into debate with Professor Dahl. Though I must confess that some of his dicta at that time made me chuckle.

For instance, "Development of a science of public administration implies the development of a science of man in the area of services administered by the public." (p. 7) Why not just "a science of man"? Admittedly the genus *homo* was somewhat optimistically classified *sapiens*. But are his behavior and his habits really so frozen into the ice pack of his calling that we can detect no common rules, no human qualities and tendencies, that transcend these occupational categories? Is this suggestion more than the ancient alibi which so long handicapped the development of a body of knowledge about business management — "my business is different" — implying that the maker of soap had nothing to learn from the vendor of sausages. Are we really condemned to a biology of bureaucrats, a physiology of professors, and a psychopathology of politicians? Are these occupational distinctions valid?

The trouble, of course, centers round the phrase "a science." But is was Professor Dahl, not I, who stated that my "generalizations gave promise of a science." The article from which the quotations are drawn made no such claim. It was entitled, with intention, "Organization as a *Technical* Problem."

Personally I believe that an *exact* science of human social behavior is many centuries away. Individual psychology has been an inductive study for little more than half-a-century. Our knowledge of the biochemistry of the nervous system is as yet insufficient to provide an adequate physical foundation for an exact science of individual psychology. The prospects of a reliable group psychology are much more remote. Indeed it seems to me that altogether too much ink and paper are being expended on discussing

---

1 Robert A. Dahl, "The Science of Public Administration: Three Problems", *Public Administration Review*, Vol. 7, Winter 1947, p. 5, quoting from L. Urwick, "Organization as a Technical Problem" in L. Gulick and L. Urwick, (eds.), *Papers on the Science of Administration*, Institute of Public Administration, Columbia University Press, New York, 1937, p. 49.

whether this or that body of knowledge is or is not a science, as though there were no two meanings to the word.

A *"science"* can mean a body of knowledge like the knowledge found in the physical sciences. Or it can mean an organized body of knowledge of any kind. The argument about this ambiguity is at least half-a-century old. It started with the phrase "scientific management" adopted by Frederick Winslow Taylor, though with misgivings.

But that Taylor ever meant by the phrase that management is "a science" in the first sense is contrary to the record. He said precisely the opposite — "management is also destined to become more of an art."[2] And he also made it quite clear that in using the adjective "scientific" he merely intended to imply the possibility of an organized body of knowledge about the subject.[3]

There is a vast amount of human experience about all kinds of administrative and managerial problems. If we will organize it, measure it where we can, and generalize from it, we can build up a body of knowledge about managing which can be taught and learned. And that will be a much better plan than leaving people to learn merely by the accidents of practical apprenticeship and "trial and error." Before supporting too enthusiastically the old empirical method of learning, critics would be wise to remember that in the activity of managing the learner's errors are other peoples' trials.

What Taylor did say very definitely, however, and I think very rightly, was that the only way out of the conflict between employers and employed which has crystallized since the industrial revolution is for both sides (1) to recognize that they are engaged in a common activity and (2) to approach the problems created by that common activity in the scientific temper and spirit. That seems to me incontestable. We cannot live within a culture dominated and shaped by advances in our control over material things, advances which have placed a great strain on our capacity to cooperate with each other, without modifications in our political and social arrangements. And if we are to arrive at such changes without endless strife and confusion we must agree on a common mental approach to our problems. That it should be the same approach as has created the problems, the scientific approach, is merely an example of the traditional remedy for another form of excess "the hair of the dog."

A similar lack of semantic sophistication is found in the use of the word "principle." In the same article Professor Dahl refers to the "supposed laws of public administration." (p. 4) And it is obvious that he regards my "principles" not as provisional generalizations which have, so far, been found useful in practice, but as statements of an invariable relation between cause and effect. The same mistake was made by Professor Simon, in his chapter on "Some Problems of Administrative Theory," in his otherwise invaluable *Administrative Behavior.*[4]

[2] F. W. Taylor, "Shop Management" in *Scientific Management*, Harper & Bros., New York, 1947, p. 63.
[3] *Ibid.*, "Testimony", p. 41.
[4] Herbert A. Simon, *Administrative Behavior*, Macmillan, New York, 1947, Ch. 2.

I find it necessary to make the point because there is obviously a reaction under way, especially among academic people, against the proposition that there are very great similarities about the way human beings react to similar organizational and administrative arrangements whether in the public service, in business, or anywhere else. I am convinced that by the study of those similarities we can arrive at important generalizations which are of the greatest value both as a diagnostic instrument and as a guide to correcting difficulties encountered in practice.

A more hopeful note was sounded recently by Chancellor Edward Litchfield of the University of Pittsburgh:

> Actually our practice is years ahead of our thought. There is abundant evidence to demonstrate our unexpressed conviction that there is much that is common in administration. . . . The constant movement of executive personnel from business to government, from the military forces into large business, from both government and business into education, is emphatic testimony supporting our conviction . . . of an essential universality in the administrative process itself. Again, it is a commonplace to observe that management consulting firms find their knowledges and skills applicable in the department store, on the one hand, and in the government bureau or the university, on the other. . . . As theorists we have not yet established generalized concepts which keep pace with the facts of contemporary administration.[5]

Surely the discovery of such similarities and their use as a guide in our perplexities and confusions is a more hopeful and constructive task than endless logic-chopping directed to proving that a particular principle is not universal or that this or that presentation is not truly scientific. Criticism let there be in plenty. That is healthy and invigorating. But let the critics from the academic world remember that they are professionals in inky warfare. The practical man trying to describe his experiences and to generalize from them is not. They may well lose the advantage of that experience if they try to make the practical man compete with them on their own professional terms.

Personally, I infinitely prefer the homespun philosophy of the late Ortega y Gasset:

> . . . Life cannot wait until the sciences may have explained the universe scientifically. We cannot put off living until we are ready. The most salient characteristic of life is its coerciveness: it is always urgent, "here and now" without any possible postponement. . . . If the physicist had to *live* by the ideas of his science, you may rest assured he would not be so finicky as to wait for some other investigator to complete his research a century or so later. He would renounce the hope of a complete scientific solution, and fill in, with approximate or probable anticipations, what the rigorous corpus of physical doctrine lacks at present, and in part, always will lack.[6]

[5] Edward H. Litchfield, "Notes on a General Theory of Administration", *Administrative Science Quarterly*, Vol. 1, June 1956, pp. 8-9.
[6] José Ortega y Gasset, *Mission of the University*, trans. H. L. Nostrand, Princeton University Press, Princeton, New Jersey, 1944, p. 84. Italics added.

It is to such "approximate or probable anticipations" that I attach the title "principle." We use them all the time in our practical work as management consultants.

The Span of Control

Take, for instance, the principle described as "the span of control," about which there has been much verbal disputation on the ground that it is supposed to conflict with the principle of reducing administrative levels to a minimum. To be sure, when the doctor tells you not to eat too much your wife is apt to invoke the opposite principle and to tell you that you will make yourself ill if you starve yourself so. But that doesn't prove your doctor wrong.

Men have an appetite for power and self-importance, just as they have an appetite for good food. It is an appetite which feeds on having rows of subordinates waiting on their doormat. And where it is not restrained by recognition of the limits imposed by the span of control, there will always be some managers in every kind of undertaking driving their subordinates scatty and themselves into the ground by ignoring the human limitation of a restricted span of attention.

Literally hundreds of times in the course of professional practice our consultants have encountered cases of managers and foremen who were "falling down on the job" for no other reason save failure to recognize the importance of that principle. A simple adjustment, grouping up independent subordinate units or appointing an assistant who could take direct responsibility for half his too numerous brood, and both the man (they were often good men: merely ignorant) and the situation were saved.

And yet, only the other day, there was a young assistant professor from an American School of Business Administration arguing at great length in *Advanced Management* that the principle has no validity.[7] He even quoted a soldier who had admitted that in peacetime, and especially in Washington, the Army often neglects the principle because of personal ambitions, status hunting, and similar sinister motives, to prove that the principle had no application to business.

What I am pleading for is a more open-minded approach to the whole problem of administration, a more thorough exchange of experience and knowledge, a determination to hang, draw, and quarter the ancient fallacy that "my business is different."

I am also arguing that there is a vast fund of experience on which we all can and should draw. I am pleading with the academic people not to get in the light of that process of cross-infiltration of knowledge by verbal

7 Waino W. Suojanen, "The Span of Control — Fact or Fable", *Advanced Management Journal*, Vol. 20, November 1955, p. 5. See also L. Urwick, "The Manager's Span of Control", Harvard Business Review, Vol. 34, May-June 1956, p. 39, and "The Span of Control — Some Facts about the Fables", *Advanced Management Journal*, Vol. 21, November 1956, p. 5.

campaigns aimed at proving that this or that "possible or probable anticipation" is not "scientific." I am arguing on the same lines as my old and deeply-mourned friend Mary Parker Follett when she explained why she had transferred her attention and her researches from the field of government to the field of business management.

> . . . the principles of organization and administration which are discovered as best for business can be applied to government or international relations. Indeed, the solution of world problems must eventually be built up from all the little bits of experience wherever people are consciously trying to solve problems of relation. And this attempt is being made more consciously and deliberately in industry than anywhere else.[8]

The Clearinghouse Principle

Take another example of a principle which I have encountered practically both in business and in government. Let us call it the clearinghouse principle. "Communication" is currently somewhat of a "blessed word" in the study of management and of administration. We all know Chester Barnard's dictum that a chief executive is really the center of a system of communication.

If communication is important it is essential that the mechanics of the process should run smoothly and easily *and quickly*. On the other hand, we all believe in decentralization. And in any large complex of offices constituting the government of a country or the headquarters of a business, decentralization tends to run along functional lines. The heads of functional departments are often jealous of their authority and independence. They all manage their own communications with each other. The consequence is a sea anchor on routine communications. They take an inordinate time to pass from the desk of one official in one department to the desk of the addressee in another department. It follows that, since many communications are reasonably urgent, there is an excessive use of "special messengers."

I don't know how it is in Washington. It is so in Whitehall. There are more than 100 offices within two or three square miles each running its own post office to all the others. There is no clearinghouse. Any document which calls for an answer within, say, twenty-four hours tends to go by "special messenger." If the chief executive is really the center of a process of communication, there is one quite routine responsibility which he cannot, with safety, delegate away from his central control, the actual routine of communication. It is quite secondary in importance, but critical to effectiveness. Of course, in Whitehall there is at the executive level no chief, only a vestigial anachronism, a committee which never meets, called The Lords of the Treasury.

---

8 Henry C. Metcalf and L. Urwick (eds.), *Dynamic Administration*, Harper and Bros., New York, 1941, p. 19, quoting from a paper, "Leadership," by Mary Parker Follett, read to the Rowntree Oxford Conference, 1928.

The same clearinghouse principle indicates that, whether in business or in government, specialized advice and direction should never flow directly downward to lower echelons. If they do you are bound to get clashes about competence and authority between specialists and those with general responsibility at lower echelons. The specialist always expects the man with general responsibility to devote more time and attention to his "ewe lamb" than the "generalist" thinks either suitable or convenient. That's the way of specialists.

Specialized advice and direction should always move *upward* so that they can be incorporated in the "chain of command." I know the word "command" is not liked in this country. But the use of the term here merely implies a particular channel of communication. This has two advantages. It enables specialist requirements to be coordinated with the other demands on those responsible for lower echelons *before* instructions are issued. This saves much friction and subsequent recrimination. It also ensures that specialized communications are "authenticated" before reaching subordinates.

If this is done, however, it means that there is quite a large volume of "paper work" passing over the chief's desk. The number of specialists who have to be integrated in the overall plan tends to increase. The chief will have insufficient time to visit his subordinates. They will lose confidence in central direction and tend to kick at "paper" instructions.

The General Staff Relationship

This makes it virtually mandatory that in any large organization the chief should have an assistant or assistants in a "general staff" relation to himself. The *general* should be distinguished from the *special* staff relation. The special staff officer looks after and advises on his special function: the general staff assistant advises the chief and assists him with all *his*, the chief's, functions of direction. He is his *alter ego*. He should also relieve him of at least 90 per cent of his paper work. Paper work is really quite secondary at the level of the chief. His main function is personal leadership. If he is so desk bound with paper work that he has insufficient time for it, the organization will suffer.

The paper work, the records, are essential. Some men lie and all men die. The record becomes critical where these accidents occur. It is also essential in all large-scale organization because men change posts and forget. But it is only a record, an *aide memoire*. The big decisions get taken not on paper, but by individuals meeting face to face who trust each other. The paper is like the drains in a house: it carries off the waste matter of poor human relations. Far too many people in responsible positions try to live in their drains.

This general staff relationship is not very well understood in civil life. Many mistakes are being made in using it. It is a direction in which both business and the public services can learn from the experience of the combat services.[9] All these questions flow from an acceptance of the clear-inghouse principle. No chief can be an effective center of a system of communication unless he is equipped with the apparatus and the assistance which being such a center postulates.

The Need for a Chief Executive

In discussing the clearinghouse principle I have, of course, made an assumption that it is not generally accepted, though it is a part of the Constitution and of the general business practice of this country. That is that there must be in all organizations which aim to *do* something, rather than at deciding what is to be done, a chief executive.

This executive principle was clearly laid down by the President's Committee on Administrative Management in 1937:

> ... the foundations of effective management in public affairs, no less than in private, are well known. ... Stated in simple terms these canons of efficiency require the establishment of a responsible and effective chief executive as the center of energy, direction, and administrative management. ...[10]

It is F. W. Taylor's distinction between planning and performance carried to a higher level.

Fear of this principle is undoubtedly at the root of much of the confusion in the ordering of our affairs. It is felt to be undemocratic, arbitrary. The President's Committee on Administrative Management recognized this fear and gave the answer:

> It may be said that there is danger that management itself will grow too great and forget where it came from or what it is for — in the old and recurring insolence of office. [But] a weak administration can neither advance nor retreat successfully — it can merely muddle. Those who waver at the sight of needed power are false friends of modern democracy. ...[11]

If this principle, this distinction, between the legislative, the policy-making, and the executive function is clearly admitted the pattern begins to fall into shape. Because management today is nine-tenths a technical, a scientific job. The dream in many men's minds that it can be submitted to mechanisms of control modeled on those devised for political purposes is "a moonbeam from the larger lunacy." Attempts to impose such mechanisms are as crazy as the requirement that the captain of a ship should call a meeting of the crew every time he wished to change course. Such a

---

[9] For a fuller discussion of this question, see L. Urwick and Ernest Dale, *Profitably Using the General Staff Position in Business*, American Management Association, 1953, General Management Series No. 165.

[10] President's Committee on Administrative Management, *Report*, U.S. Government Printing Office, 1937, p. 3.

[11] *Ibid.*, p. 53.

requirement would not only greatly increase the hazards of the crew; it ignores completely the rights of another party to the transaction — the passengers, the consumers.

To say this in no way absolves the captain from his responsibility so to discharge the duties of his office that his leadership is acceptable to the members of the crew. Indeed that is the first of those duties.

Will Rationality Prevail?

Professor Dahl posed the rhetorical question "On what kind of evidence are we compelled to assume that the rationality of organizational structure will prevail over the irrationality of man?" We are not compelled to assume it. We can only hope that it will be so. For this hope we have two grounds:

1. Men when they engage in some common activity for a defined end prefer to "know where they are" and "what is expected of them." Rational organization tells them this. It does not leave the issue vague and at the mercy of those who are stronger or less scrupulous than their fellows. In other words, rational organization creates positions in which the necessary leadership can be developed and is expected. It is acceptable leadership which identifies the social sentiments and social living of those under authority with the purpose that authority was created to fulfill and the methods it adopts in doing so.

2. Men, where their lives are at stake, are usually fairly quick at grasping the realities of a situation. I have heard of ships' crews mutinying: I have yet to hear of a ship's crew electing a committee to do the steering. They know, being sailors, that safe steering isn't done that way.

In the same way we are assimilating, albeit all too slowly, the lesson that a civilization dependent on modern science and power-driven machinery for its material necessities must observe the imperatives underlying the design and utilization of these facilities if it is to avoid total disruption. To be sure, our old folkways and superstitions die hard. But we do learn. I doubt if there is a citizen in this country today who would try to make a stalled automobile start again by kissing its radiator or kicking its differential. He knows that he can only make the thing go by understanding how it works, or by finding someone else who does and trusting him.

We may not learn this simple lesson in time. In the words of an American thinker of the first order, Thorstein Veblen:

> History records more frequent and more spectacular instances of the triumph of imbecile institutions over life and culture than of peoples who have by the force of instinctive insight saved themselves alive out of a desperately precarious institutional situation, such, for instance, as now faces the peoples of Christendom.[12]

---

12 Thorstein Veblen, *The Instinct of Workmanship*, Macmillan, New York, 1914, p. 25.

It is not without significance that that somber passage was written two world wars away — in March, 1914.

11   Implications of the Behavioral Sciences for Management*

Harry Diamond

The behavioral sciences include the disciplines of anthropology, psychology, social psychology, and sociology. Research and findings in these areas have focused on systems of belief, attitudes, values, and other facets of the motivational complex, as well as the dynamics of communication, leadership, informal group norms, and the decision-making process at various levels in the organization. "It seems useful to define behavioralism by its essential orientation, which is toward the systematic study of human behavior. Behavioralism often asks: How do individuals or groups act, as contrasted with institutionalized expectations and conventional assumptions about their behavior?"[1]

There has been an awareness for some time that the formal organizational mechanism (organizational charts, lines of authority and responsibility, rules and regulations, downward communication, and various other formal organizational controls) reveals very little about human behavior in the organization. "All organizations have both manifest and latent functions. Manifest or public functions are the official, conventional modes of behavior and mission which partially motivate an organization and legitimate its existence. Latent private values include the drive for power, security, and survival. Behavioral research and theory are often concerned with the latent facet of analysis."[2]

The behavioral approach attempts to meet the need for understanding how and why an organization functions as it does. The orientation is obviously people. Managerial techniques to be successful must reflect a philosophy of attunement to people within and without the organization, sensitive to their norms, attitudes, values, and motivating forces. Within the organization, management is concerned with a maximization of human and physical resources to effectively fulfill agency goals, as well as providing

* Reprinted with permission of author and publisher from *Public Personnel Review*, Vol. 28, January 1967, pp. 26-30.
1 Robert Presthus, *Behavioral Approaches to Public Administration*, University of Alabama Press, 1965, p. 21.
2 *Ibid.*, p. 21.

the climate for individual growth and development. Research findings of the behavioral sciences indicate, for example, that an excess of detailed rules and regulations to meet every contingency, detailed supervision, stifles initiative and individual growth, and innovative solutions to problems, and promotes dependency.[3] In external operations, the police department's task would be greatly facilitated if the community had a high compliance-with-law attitude. An agency that enjoys a good measure of public confidence, respect, and support, generally has carried out its mission with overtones of sensitivity to community needs and problems.

Types of People in the Agency

To understand the behavior of personnel in an organization requires some insight into the different types of people in the agency. Herbert Simon[4] refers to the "administrative man" who does not wait for the perfect solution or decision. He cannot wait until all possible alternatives are in. In any complex problem there is an inherent skills and knowledge limitation. Robert Presthus[5] presents this perspective of types of people in the organization:

1. The upward mobile: he is a conformist and is opportunistic, obeys rules and enjoys working in the hierarchical climate with a view toward moving ahead.
2. The indifferent: he is apathetic and uninvolved, seeks satisfaction and fulfillment outside the job.
3. The ambivalent: the neurotic type, can't make up his mind.

Amitai Etzioni[6] views personnel in an organization as:

1. Alienative: negative involvement (somewhat similar to Presthus' indifferent type).
2. Calculative: emphasis on personal betterment primarily, and the organization secondarily.
3. Normative: this person is deeply committed and dedicated, with attitudes that have become internalized.

Chris Argyris[7] refers to two types of personnel in an organization:

1. Those who are achievement-oriented, who need a balanced tension (to meet challenging problems, solve them and go on to the next unprogrammed situation, forever traveling, never

---

3 Rensis Likert, *New Patterns of Management*, McGraw-Hill, New York, 1961.
4 Herbert Simon, *Administrative Behavior*, Macmillan, New York, 1961.
5 Robert Presthus, *The Organizational Society*, Knopf, New York, 1962.
6 Amitai Etzioni, *A Comparative Analysis of Complex Organizations*, The Free Press, New York, 1961.
7 Chris Argyris, *Interpersonal Competence and Organizational Effectiveness*, Dorsey, Homewood, Illinois, 1962.

to arrive). In this process, self-esteem and interpersonal competence are developed.

2. Those who prefer a role of dependency.

It is obvious, therefore, that individuals in an agency differ and will consequently react differently to forces that have an impact on them.

Forces on the Individual

Formal forces: Excessive hierarchical pressures with overly detailed rules and regulations may cause the achievement-oriented individual to become dependent and seek satisfaction and fulfillment outside the job, or resign. Formal pressures may result in short-term gains (initial compliance) but at the long-run expense of human resources.

Informal forces: Cliques, the informal group, peer groups all create an impact on the individual by shaping norms and attitudes.

Another force has been termed "congruency" by Chris Argyris[8]: Unintended consequences may follow when incongruences develop between individual needs and the organizational climate. For example, if the individual is a mature personality and needs challenging problem-solving opportunities, a repressive organizational atmosphere will develop an incongruency. Or, if the individual is dependency-oriented, a democratic or permissive organizational climate will also develop an incongruency in this case. In both of these situations, compensatory social defense structures are created, and psychological energy is diverted from organizational tasks and goals.

To place the impact of the behavioral sciences on organizational management in another perspective, it is useful to sketch briefly the evolution of three main schools of thought concerning management theory.

Metamorphosis of Management Theory

Theories of management have gone through three main stages during the past 60 years.[9]

The first stage has been referred to as the classical school. This stage focuses on: the individual as a passive instrument in the agency, the distribution of authority in a formal way, organizational blueprint and rules, and an impersonal rationality taken for granted. The organization was viewed as a machine, with emphasis on efficiency and economy.

The research and findings of the second stage (social science, behavioral school) reflected the impact of the psychological and sociological disciplines. During the decades (1940-1960) a large amount of evidence was accumulated revealing that people tend to support what they help to create, that demo-

---

[8] Chris Argyris, *Integrating the Individual and the Organization*, Wiley, New York, 1964.
[9] William G. Scott, "Organization Theory: An Overview and an Appraisal", *Organizations: Structure and Behavior*, Joseph A. Letterer, (ed.), Wiley, New York, 1963.

cratically run groups develop loyalty and cohesiveness, that strong identification with and commitment to decision making are generated by honest participation in the formulation of these decisions. Attunement to people in the agency transcended the earlier mechanistic view of organizational behavior (individual satisfaction and fulfillment often assumed more significance than material benefits). Rigid supervisory controls were seen as an impediment to individual growth and development which in turn could jeopardize the health and vitality of the agency.[10] Democratic management with a generalized supervision (trust, confidence, large areas of delegation) became a core rationale of the behavioralists.

"For the manager, creative growth is the product of policies and actions that focus on the growth potential of many individuals . . . too much concentrated power invites rigidity and a slowing down of innovation."[11] In other words, "the function of administration is to provide an environment in which the individual employee, of whatever rank, can function at or near the level of his talents, training, and experience."[12]

It has become apparent, however, that some of the behavioral science findings have been distorted. For example, concerning group behavior in the organization:[13]

STATEMENTS OF BEHAVIORAL SCIENTISTS	DISTORTIONS
1. Social determinants of behavior are important.	1. One's behavior is determined by his membership in social groups.
2. It is helpful to realize that a person's aspirations at work have many aspects; he seeks membership, self-esteem, economic security, prestige, etc.	2. Even incentive pay and other material benefits aren't of much importance any more.
3. Social behavior and individual satisfaction are related in some significant fashion to productivity.	3. You ought to give workers whatever they want. If they're happy, they'll produce more.
4. Social sub-systems in organizations exert much control over their members. Consequently administrative control is limited.	4. Nobody can really be a boss, only a follower. We should all be soft and tenderhearted.

The Systems Approach

The third stage (contemporary view of organization theory) has not excluded the classical and social science doctrines, but has added additional dimensions for a more complete analysis: the systems approach, and operations

---

10 Rensis Likert, *op. cit.*

11 Marshall E. Dimock, *A Philosophy of Administration*, Harper, New York, 1958, pp. 167-168.

12 Harry L. Case, "Gordon R. Clapp: The Role of Faith, Purposes and People in Administration", *Public Administration Review*, June 1964, p. 87.

13 James V. Clark, "Distortions of Behavioral Science", *Calif. Management Review*, Winter 1963, p. 7.

research. "The distinctive qualities of modern organization theory are its conception-analytical base, its reliance on empirical research data and, above all, its integrating nature. These qualities are framed in a philosophy which accepts the premise that the only meaningful way to study organization is to study it as a system. . . . . It treats organization as a system of mutually dependent variables. As a result, modern organization theory which accepts system analysis shifts the conceptual level of organization study above the classical and neo-classical (social science) theories."[14] William Scott identifies five parts of the organizational system:[15]

1. The individual (the personality structure replete with motives and attitudes).
2. The formal organization (the organizational structure or blueprint with its rules and regulations).
3. The informal organization (its influence on behavior and attitudes of members). The individual has expectations of satisfaction he hopes to derive from association with people on the job.
4. Status and role patterns (a fusion of the foregoing components of the organizational system that acts to keep the organization institutionally fit).
5. The physical setting (the work environment).

The systems approach is, therefore, useful in analyzing behavior in an organization by focusing on the interrelationship of the parts of the organizational system. Similarly, the systems method (identification of all interreacting components) is brought to bear on solving complex problems.

Organizations exist to solve problems. Due to the information and technological revolution, management has become increasingly dependent upon the advice of teams of experts representing the components of the problem. In problem situations where prior solutions or programs are not available or have been largely ineffective, the operations research approach provides the optimum answer. Ad hoc teams of experts from all relevant fields of knowledge (inside and outside the agency) are structured to provide the greatest number of communications interchanges to maximize creativity.[16]

It is obvious that systems analysis and the use of ad hoc teams of experts are geared toward "quality" solutions of problems rather than concentrating on democratic management. Herein lies a dilemma. How can broad acceptance and commitment to a program be developed in an organization, when "quality" solutions or policies have been superimposed with limited participation by members of the agency? Program development and implementation require a blend of quality, and acceptance by those carrying out the program. Yet, an emphasis on participation (to assure acceptance) is not

14 William G. Scott, op. cit., p. 19.

15 Ibid., pp. 19-20.

16 Warren G. Bennis, "Organizational Developments and the Fate of Bureaucracy", address given at the American Psychological Association, September 1964.

necessarily a criterion of the quality of a program arrived at in such a democratic fashion.[17]

Democratic management focuses on the willingness of people to implement a program that they helped to create. However, there are complex situations where a systems approach by an ad hoc team of experts is needed to produce the most effective (quality) program. Quality of the solution in such instances should be the primary consideration.[18] Implementation of the program is then sought by explanation and persuasion. The ideal is obviously the attainment of quality plus acceptance.

Toward the Future

Due to the information and technological revolution, management will become increasingly dependent upon ad hoc teams of experts (from within and without the organization) to provide effective programs (quality solutions to problems). The measure of such attainment is heavily dependent upon the degree of morale, the sense of accomplishment on the part of those rendering the service.

Dr. Robert Tannenbaurm, University of California at Los Angeles, Graduate School of Business Administration, in a recent talk, referred to the new frontier with respect to organizational values and methods. "If management conveys trust, it leads to a much greater willingness on the part of both individuals and groups to assume responsibility for their own behavior and decisions. . . . To meet the needs of the future, trends will be:

"From a mechanistic, formalistic view of organization to an organic, systems-oriented view.

"From linkages between individual units by organizational chart to linkages by organizational needs.

"From motivating individuals from the outside in, to motivating them from the inside out.

"From the use of formal authority to developing an atmosphere conducive to freedom, creativity, and growth.

"From telling people, to listening to them.

"From a primary concern with the isolated individual to a concern with teams.

"From inter-individual and group competition to collaboration.

"From maskmanship (hiding one's thoughts and feelings) to a more appropriate degree of openness.

"From a primary concern for the immediate utilization of individuals to a greater concern for their development."[19]

---

[17] Yehezkel Dror, "Muddling Through — Science or Inertia", *Public Administration Review*, September 1964.

[18] Harold J. Leavitt, "Unhuman Organization", *Harvard Business Review*, July-August, 1962.

[19] *Los Angeles Times*, May 16, 1966.

The challenge for management will be to generate internalized support within the organization for a "quality" program (often developed by teams of experts from within and without the agency) arrived at by systems analysis and operations research.

Organizational problems will be handled from the wide perspective of the totality of their interacting components (systems approach). Wider exposure to all fields of relevant knowledge (operations research) will afford mind-stretching, innovative programs to deal not only with the immediate problem at hand, but also its long-range implications, so that, hopefully, the same "brush fire" problems do not constantly flare up.

Chapter Three
Theories of Organization

Until the results of the Hawthorne studies were published in the late 1930's, the aspect of administrative study which received the most attention was the structure or organization of enterprise. Proponents of the school of scientific management started with organization perhaps because it appears easier to analyze the skeleton than to investigate the complexities of the muscles or the nervous system. Today the study of organization or structural analysis no longer enjoys priority. It has been replaced by the study of human behaviour in organizations. A glance at the titles of some of these behaviour studies would be misleading because many current publications deal almost entirely with human relations under the guise of organizational study. In fact, of course, while a study of organization requires a knowledge of human behaviour, the two are not synonymous.

In this chapter the first article is an early attempt to define organization. The second, by one of today's leading administrative theorists, outlines the trend in organizational thought on structural hierarchy for contemporary complex work units. The rest of this chapter is devoted to basic concepts of line and staff, span of control, support services, decentralization and coordination.

There is much available literature on organization. The early classic is still L. H. Gulick and L. Urwick *Papers on the Science of Administration* (New York Institute of Public Administration, 1937). Dwight Waldo's bibliographical essay, "Organization Theory: An Elephantine Problem" (*Public Administration Review*, Vol. 21, No. 4, Autumn 1961), is a wide survey as are R. T. Golembiewski's "Organization as a moral problem" (*Public Administration Review*, Vol. 22, No. 2, Spring 1962), and E. G. Koch's "Three Approaches to Organization" (*Harvard Business Review*, Vol. 39, No. 2, March-April 1961). One of the more comprehensive monographs is P. M. Blau and W. R. Scott, *Formal Organizations: A Comparative Approach* (Chandler, San Francisco, 1962). More specialized articles on various aspects of organization are

R. J. Baker, "The art of delegating", *Public Administration*, Vol. 43, No. 2, Summer 1965.

D. S. Brown, "Why Delegation Works and Why It Doesn't", *Personnel*, Vol. 44, No. 1, January 1967.

G. H. Caldwell, "Unity of Command", *Canadian Public Administration*, Vol. 7, No. 4, December 1964.

R. A. Dahl, "The validity of organizational theories", *Public Administration Review*, Vol. 7, No. 1, Winter 1947.

D. R. Daniel, "Team at the top", *Harvard Business Review*, Vol. 43, No. 2, March-April 1965.

C. A. Efferson, "In Defence of the Line-Staff Concept", *Personnel*, Vol. 43, No. 4, July-August 1966.

G. G. Fisch, "Stretching the span of management", *Harvard Business Review*, Vol. 41, No. 5, September-October 1963.

R. T. Golembiewski, "Specialist or Generalist: Structure as a Crucial Factor", *Public Administration Review*, Vol. 25, No. 2, June 1965.

H. Kaufman, "Organization theory and political theory", *American Political Science Review*, Vol. 58, No. 1, March 1964.

R. E. Park, "The span of control", *Advanced Management Journal*, Vol. 30, No. 4, October 1965.

R. A. Richards, "On administrative decentralization", *Public Administration* (Australia), Vol. 21, No. 1, March 1962.

M. N. Zald, "Decentralization — Myth vs. Reality", in R. T. Golembiewski (ed.), *Public Administration*, Rand McNally, Chicago, 1965.

12   What is Meant by Organization and its Principles*

James D. Mooney
Alan C. Reiley

Every human society, however primitive, must have something in common, and it is as a means for the furtherance or the protection of these common interests that formal organizations appear. If, however, we search beneath such formal organizations for their psychic fundaments, we find them in full operation even in acts and objectives where only one person is concerned. Thus we frequently speak of organizing one's self for a given purpose. . . .

---

* Reprinted with permission of authors and publisher from James D. Mooney and Alan C. Reiley, *Onward Industry! The Principles of Organization and Their Significance to Modern Industry*, Harper & Row, New York, 1931, pp. 9-11, 12-17.

The very act of walking implies . . . that the mind has defined its objective, the sentiment has affirmed it as a desirable objective, and that the will is moving toward the objective. . . . It is impossible to exclude the idea of an objective, and of a definitely organized movement to attain it, from any psychic act, however casual or inconsequential.

When two persons combine for a given purpose, we have the same psychic fundaments, plus the principle which must underlie all associated effort. Let us again employ the simplest illustration. Two men unite their strength to move some object which is too heavy or bulky to be moved by one. Here we have associated effort, which is synonymous with organization, and likewise coordination, the first principle which underlies all such effort.

This simple illustration indicates clearly the exact definition of organization. *Organization is the form of every human association for the attainment of a common purpose.* . . .

Organization has been termed the formal side of management; likewise the machinery of management, the channel through which the measures and policies of management become effective. There is truth in these descriptions, but not the whole truth. Again organization has been likened to the framework, the articulated skeleton of the business structure. Here again the simile is sound as far as it goes, but inadequate. It implies that organization refers only to the differentiation and definition of individual duties, as set forth in the familiar organization charts. But duties must relate to procedure, and it is here that we find the real dynamics of organization, the motive power through which it moves to its determined objective. Organization, therefore, refers to more than the frame or skeleton of the industrial edifice. It refers to the complete body, with all of its correlated functions. And it refers to these functions as they appear in action, the very pulse and heart beats, the circulation, the respiration, the vital movement, so to speak, of the organized unit. It refers to the coordination of all these movements as they combine and cooperate for the common purpose. This analogy between human group organization and the *biological organization* of the physical body has been noticed by several writers. . . .

If the sphere of organization is so all inclusive, how then are we to define administration and management? . . . Following the previous analogy, management is nothing less than the psychic principle itself. Management is the vital spark which actuates, directs and controls the plan and procedure of organization. With management enters the personal factor, without which nobody could be a living being with any directive toward a given purpose. The relation of management to organization is analogous to the relation of the psychic complex to the physical body. Our bodies are simply the means and the instrument through which the psychic force moves toward the attainment of its aims and desires. It is evident also that, in order to attain these objects, the body must be adequate to the performance of this instrumental function. This same instrumental adequacy is an absolute necessity in a business organization, and for the same reasons.

Through this analogy we may see clearly the importance of formal organization in the pursuit of business objectives, and the need for its broader and more intensive study.

This description of the true relation between organization and management also indicates exactly what is meant by system in organization. As organization relates to procedure, involving the inter-relation of duties as well as duties in themselves, so system may be defined as the technique of procedure.

The introduction of the word technique gives us another slant on the relation of management to organization. It would appear from what we have already written that organization is in some way subordinated to management. In a practical sense so it is, for the instrument must always appear subordinate to that of which it is the instrument, and, furthermore, one important duty of management is to provide its own instrument, which means to organize. Yet in another sense the relationship is reversed. If the building presupposes the builder, or organizer, the function of management also presupposes the building, or something to manage. Let us therefore compare these two things in terms of technique.

The technique of management, in its human relationships, can be best described as the technique of handling or managing people, which should be based on a deep and enlightened human understanding. The technique of organization may be described as that of relating specific duties or functions in a completely coordinated scheme. This statement of the difference between managing and organizing clearly shows their intimate relationship. It also shows, which is our present purpose, that the technique of organizing is anterior, in logical order, to that of management. It is true that a sound organizer may, because of temperamental human failings, be a poor manager, but on the other hand it is inconceivable that a poor organizer can ever make a good manager, if he has any real organizing work to do. The prime necessity in all organization is harmonious relationships based on integrated interests, and, to this end, the first essential is an integrated and harmonious relationship in the duties, considered in themselves. . . .

All history bears witness to the reality of that something we have called organizing genius, a genius which is truly creative, like the genius manifested in the higher realms of creative art. Indeed organizing is an art, which means that, like every art, it must have its own technique, which in turn must be based on principles. That the great organizers of history applied these principles unconsciously proves nothing except that their technique was not acquired; it was inherent in their genius. Nevertheless all experience proves that a technique can be acquired, and the more readily if its underlying principles are known. This does not mean that a knowledge of these principles will make everyone who knows them an efficient organizer. To know principles is one thing, and to apply them efficiently is another. Nevertheless it stands to reason that a knowledge of these principles must be the first step in the acquisition of a sound organizing technique.

The importance of such knowledge is evident in the problems that now confront modern industry, among which that of growth through organization is the most important. An industrial organization may achieve a certain limited size through the business acumen of some individual, the genius of an inventor or scientist, or the knowledge of tools and production technique of some engineer. To expand this organization beyond a limited size, however, requires some experience and knowledge of the sheer technique of organization, and how its principles must be applied in order to provide for the necessary growth. As an industrial organization grows in size, a knowledge of these principles becomes increasingly important, for two reasons. If these principles are not understood and properly applied the organization either becomes threatened with disintegration, or it develops an increasing inertia which constitutes in itself an obstacle to further growth. . . .

Far more conspicuous in the public eye, however, is the other side of the picture, furnished in the vastness of the leading units of modern industry. These institutions may be accounted for by that faculty we have called organizing genius; in fact this is the usual explanation. Nearly always, in these great institutions, there is some one individual whom popular belief identifies as the real architect and creator of the organized edifice. If we grant the soundness of this belief, then we cannot escape its implications, namely that industrial growth through organization must ever be dependent on that exceptional quality we call genius. The answer is that even organizing genius cannot create principles of organization; it can only apply them, and if these principles can be found and definitely identified then human qualities that fall far short of genius should be adequate for their efficient application.

13   Some Fundamentals of Organizational Design*

Herbert A. Simon

The Hierarchical Structure of Organization[1]

Large organizations are almost universally hierarchical in structure. That is to say, they are divided into units which are subdivided into smaller units, which are, in turn, subdivided, and so on. They are also generally

---

* Reprinted and slightly abridged with permission of author and publisher from Herbert A. Simon, *The Shape of Automation for Man and Management*, Harper & Row, New York, 1965.
1 The speculations of the following paragraphs are products of my joint work over recent years with Allen Newell.

hierarchical in imposing on this system of successive partitionings a pyramidal authority structure. However, for the moment, I should like to consider the departmentalization rather than the authority structure.

Hierarchical subdivision is not a characteristic that is peculiar to human organizations. It is common to virtually all complex systems of which we have knowledge.

Complex biological organisms are made up of subsystems — digestive, circulatory, and so on. These subsystems are composed of organs, organs of tissues, tissues of cells. The cell is, in turn, a hierarchically organized unit, with nucleus, cell wall, cytoplasm, and other subparts.

The complex systems of chemistry and physics reveal the same picture of wheels within wheels within wheels. A protein molecule — one of the organismic building blocks — is constructed out of simpler structures, the amino acids. The simplest molecules are composed of atoms, the atoms of so-called elementary particles. Even in cosmological structures, we find the same hierarchical pattern: galaxies, planetary systems, stars, and planets.

The near universality of hierarchy in the composition of complex systems suggest that there is something fundamental in this structural principle that goes beyond the peculiarities of human organization. I can suggest at least two reasons why complex systems should generally be hierarchical:

1. *Among possible systems of a given size and complexity, hierarchical systems, composed of subsystems, are the most likely to appear through evolutionary processes.* A metaphor will show why this is so. Suppose we have two watchmakers, each of whom is assembling watches of ten thousand parts. The watchmakers are interrupted, from time to time, by the telephone, and have to put down their work. Now watchmaker A finds that whenever he lays down a partially completed watch, it falls apart again, and when he returns to it, he has to start reassembling it from the beginning. Watchmaker B, however, has designed his watches in such a way that each watch is composed of ten subassemblies of one thousand parts each, the subassemblies being themselves stable components. The major subassemblies are composed, in turn, of ten stable subassemblies of one hundred parts each, and so on. Clearly, if interruptions are at all frequent, watchmaker B will assemble a great many watches before watchmaker A is able to complete a single one.

2. *Among systems of a given size and complexity, hierarchical systems require much less information transmission among their parts than do other types of systems.* As was pointed out many years ago, as the number of members of an organization grows, the number of *pairs* of members grows with the square (and the number of possible subsets of members even more rapidly). If each member, in order to act effectively, has to know in detail what each other member is doing, the total amount of information that has to be transmitted in the organization will grow at least proportionately with the square of its size. If the organization is subdivided into units, it may be possible to arrange matters so that an individual needs detailed information only about the behavior of individuals in his own unit, and

aggregative summary information about average behavior in other units. If this is so, and if the organization continues to subdivide into suborganizations by cell division as it grows in size, keeping the size of the lowest level subdivisions constant, the total amount of information that has to be transmitted will grow only slightly more than proportionately with size.

These two statements are, of course, only the grossest sorts of generalization. They would have to be modified in detail before they could be applied to specific organizational situations. They do provide, however, strong reasons for believing that almost any system of sufficient complexity would have to have the rooms-within-rooms structure that we observe in actual human organizations. The reasons for hierarchy go far beyond the need for unity of command or other considerations relating to authority.

The conclusion I draw from this analysis is that the automation of decision making, irrespective of how far it goes and in what directions it proceeds, is unlikely to obliterate the basically hierarchical structure of organizations. The decision-making process will still call for departmentalization and subdepartmentalization of responsibilities. There is some support for this prediction in the last decade's experience with computer programming. Whenever highly complex programs have been written — whether for scientific computing, business data processing, or heuristic problem solving — they have always turned out to have a clear-cut hierarchical structure. The over-all program is always subdivided into subprograms. In programs of any great complexity, the subprograms are further subdivided, and so on. Moreover, in some general sense, the higher level programs control or govern the behavior of the lower level programs, so that we find among these programs relations of authority among routines that are not dissimilar to those we are familiar with in human organizations.[2]

Since organizations are systems of behavior designed to enable humans and their machines to accomplish goals, organizational form must be a joint function of human characteristics and the nature of the task environment. It must reflect the capabilities and limitations of the people and tools that are to carry out the tasks. It must reflect the resistance and ductility of the materials to which the people and tools apply themselves. What I have been asserting, then, in the preceding paragraphs is that one of the near universal aspects of organizational form, hierarchy, reflects no very specific properties of man, but a very general one. An organization will tend to assume hierarchical form whenever the task environment is complex relative to the problem-solving and communicating powers of the organization members and their tools. Hierarchy is the adaptive form for finite intelligence to assume in the face of complexity.

The organizations of the future, then, will be hierarchies, no matter what the exact division of labor between men and computers. This is not

---

2 The exercise of authority by computer programs over others is not usually accompanied by affect. Routines do not resent or resist accepting orders from other routines.

to say that there will be no important differences between present and future organizations. Two points, in particular, will have to be reexamined at each stage of automation:

1. What are the optimal sizes of the building blocks in the hierarchy? Will they become larger or smaller? This is the question of centralization and decentralization.
2. What will be the relations among the building blocks? In particular, how far will traditional authority and accountability relations persist, and how far will they be modified? What will be the effect of automation upon subgoal formation and subgoal identification?

Size of the Building Blocks: Centralization and Decentralization

One of the major contemporary issues in organization design is the question of how centralized or decentralized the decision-making process will be — how much of the decision making should be done by the executives of the larger units, and how much should be delegated to lower levels. But centralizing and decentralizing are not genuine alternatives for organizing. The question is not whether we shall decentralize, but how far we shall decentralize. What we seek, again, is a golden mean: we want to find the proper level in the organization hierarchy — neither too high nor too low — for each important class of decisions.

Over the past twenty or more years there has been a movement toward decentralization in large American business organizations. This movement has probably been a sound development, but it does *not* signify that more decentralization is at all times and under all circumstances a good thing. It signifies that at a particular time in history, many American firms, which had experienced almost continuous long-term growth and diversification, discovered that they could operate more effectively if they brought together all the activities relating to individual products or groups of similar products and decentralized a great deal of decision making to the departments handling these products or product groups. At the very time this process was taking place there were many cross-currents of centralization in the same companies — centralization, for example, of industrial relations activities. There is no contradiction here. Different decisions need to be made in different organizational locations, and the best location for a class of decisions may change as circumstances change.

There are usually two pressures toward greater decentralization in a business organization. First, it may help bring the profit motive to bear on a larger group of executives by allowing profit goals to be established for individual subdivisions of the company. Second, it may simplify the decision-making process by separating out groups of related activities — production, engineering, marketing, and finance for particular products — and allowing decisions to be taken on these matters within the relevant organizational subdivisions. Advantages can be realized in either of these ways only if the units to which decision is delegated are natural subdivisions — if, in fact, the actions taken in one of them do not affect in too much detail or too strongly what happens in the others. Hierarchy always implies intrinsically some measure of decentralization. It always involves a balancing of the cost savings through direct local action against the losses through ignoring indirect consequences for the whole organization.

Organizational form, I said earlier, must be a joint function of the characteristics of humans and their tools and the nature of the task environment. When one or the other of these changes significantly, we may expect concurrent modifications to be required in organizational structure — for example, in the amount of centralization or decentralization that is desirable.

When the cable and the wireless were added to the world's techniques of communication, the organization of every nation's foreign office changed. The ambassador and minister, who had exercised broad, discretionary decision-making functions in the previous decentralized system, were now brought under much closer central control. The balance between the costs in time and money of communication with the center, and the advantages of coordination by the center had been radically altered.

The automation of important parts of business data-processing and decision-making activity, and the trend toward a much higher degree of structuring and programming of even the nonautomated part will radically alter the balance of advantage between centralization and decentralization. The main issue is not the economies of scale — not the question of whether a given data-processing job can better be done by one large computer at a central location or a number of smaller ones, geographically or departmentally decentralized. Rather, the main issue is how we shall take advantage of the greater analytic capacity, the larger ability to take into account the interrelations of things, that the new developments in decision making give us. A second issue is how we shall deal with the technological fact that the processing of information within a coordinated computing system is orders of magnitude faster than the input-output rates at which we can communicate from one such system to another, particularly where human links are involved.

Let us consider the first issue: the capacity of the decision-making system to handle intricate interrelations in a complex system. In many factories today, the extent to which the schedules of one department are coordinated in detail with the schedules of a second department, consuming, say, part of the output of the first, is limited by the computational complexity of the scheduling problem. Often the best we can do is to set up a reasonable scheduling scheme for each department and put a sizeable buffer inventory of semi-finished product between them to prevent fluctuations in the operation of the first from interfering with the operation of the second. We accept the cost of holding the inventory to avoid the cost of taking account of detailed scheduling interactions.

We pay large inventory costs, also, to permit factory and sales managements to make decisions in semi-independence of each other. The factory often stocks finished products so that it can deliver on demand to sales warehouses; the warehouses stock the same product so that the factory will have time to manufacture a new batch after an order is placed. Often, too, manufacturing and sales departments make their decisions on the basis of independent forecasts of orders.

With the development of operations research techniques for determining optimal production rates and inventory levels, and with the development of the technical means to maintain and adjust the data that are required, large savings are attainable through inventory reductions and the smoothing of production operations, but at the cost of centralizing to a greater extent than in the past the factory scheduling and warehouse ordering decisions. Since the source of the savings is in the coordination of the decisions, centralization is unavoidable if the savings are to be secured.

The mismatch — unlikely to be removed in the near future — between the kinds of records that humans produce readily and read readily and the kinds that automatic devices produce and read readily is a second technological factor pushing in the direction of centralization. Since processing steps in an automated data-processing system are executed in a thousandth or even millionth of a second, the whole system must be organized on a flow basis with infrequent intervention from outside. Intervention will take more and more the form of designing the system itself — programming — and less and less the form of participating in its minute-by-minute operation. Moreover, the parts of the system must mesh. Hence, the design of decision-making and data-processing systems will tend to be a relatively centralized function. It will be a little like ship design. There is no use in one group of experts producing the design for the hull, another the design for the power plant, a third the plans for the passenger quarters, and so on, unless great pains are taken at each step to see that all these parts will fit into a seaworthy ship.

It may be objected that the question of motivation has been overlooked in this whole discussion. If decision making is centralized how can the middle-level executive be induced to work hard and effectively? First, we should observe that the principle of decentralized profit-and-loss accounting has never been carried much below the level of product-group departments and cannot, in fact, be applied successfully to fragmented segments of highly interdependent activities. Second, we may question whether the conditions under which middle-management has in the past exercised its decision-making prerogatives were actually good conditions from a motivational standpoint.

Most existing decentralized organization structures have at least three weaknesses in motivating middle-management executives effectively. First, they encourage the formation of and loyalty to subgoals that are only partly parallel with the goals of the organization. Second, they require so much nonprogrammed problem solving in a setting of confusion that they do not provide the satisfactions which, we argued earlier, are valued by the true professional. Third, they realize none of the advantages, which by hindsight we find we have often gained in factory automation, of substituting machine-paced (or better, system-paced) for man-paced operation of the system.[3]

We can summarize the present discussion by saying that the new developments in decision making will tend to induce more centralization in decision-making activities at middle-management levels.

Authority and Responsibility

Let me draw a sketch of the factory manager's job today. How far it is a caricature, and how far a reasonably accurate portrait, I shall let you decide. What is the factory manager's authority? He can hire and fire. He can determine what shall be produced in his factory and how much. He can make minor improvements in equipment and recommend major ones. In doing all of these things, he is subject to all kinds of constraints and evaluations imposed by the rest of the organization. Moreover, the connection between what he decides and what actually happens in the factory is often highly tenuous. He proposes, and a complex administrative system disposes.

For what is the factory manager held accountable? He must keep his costs within the standards of the budget. He must not run out of items that are ordered. If he does, he must produce them in great haste. He must keep his inventory down. His men must not have accidents. And so on.

Subject to this whole range of conflicting pressures, controlling a complex system whose responses to instructions is often erratic and unpredictable, the environment of the typical middle-management executive — of which the factory manager is just one example — is not the kind of environment a psychologist would design to produce high motivation. The manager responds in understandable ways. He transmits to his subordinates the pressures imposed by his superiors — he becomes a work pusher, seeking to motivate by creating for his subordinates the same environment of pressure and constraint that he experiences. He and his subordinates become expediters, dealing with the pressure that is felt at the moment by getting out a particular order, fixing a particular disabled machine, following up a particular tardy supplier.

I do not want to elaborate the picture further. The important point is that the task of middle managers today is very much taken up with pace setting, with work pushing, and with expediting. As the automation and

---

[3] The general decline in the use of piece-rates is associated with the gradual spread of machine-paced operations through the factory with the advance of automation. In evaluating the human consequences of this development, we should not accept uncritically the common stereotypes that were incorporated so effectively in Charlie Chaplin's *Modern Times*. Frederick Taylor's sophisticated understanding of the relations between incentives and pace, expressed, for example, in his story of the pig-iron handler, is worth pondering.

rationalization of the decision-making process progress, these aspects of the managerial job are likely to recede in importance.

If a couple of terms are desired to characterize the direction of change we may expect in the manager's job, I would propose rationalization and impersonalization. In terms of subjective feel the manager will find himself dealing more than in the past with a well-structured system whose problems have to be diagnosed and corrected objectively and analytically, and less with unpredictable and sometimes recalcitrant people who have to be persuaded, prodded, rewarded, and cajoled. For some managers, important satisfactions derived in the past from interpersonal relations with others will be lost. For other managers, important satisfactions from a feeling of the adequacy of professional skills will be gained.

My guess, and it is only a guess, is that the gains in satisfaction from the change will overbalance the losses. I have two reasons for making this guess: first, because this seems to be the general experience in factory automation as it affects supervisors and managers; second, because the kinds of interpersonal relations called for in the new environment seem to me generally less frustrating and more wholesome than many of those we encounter in present-day supervisory relations. Man does not generally work well with his fellow man in relations saturated with authority and dependence, with control and subordination, even though these have been the predominant human relations in the past. He works much better when he is teamed with his fellow man in coping with an objective, understandable, external environment. That will be more and more his situation as the new techniques of decision making come into wide use.

A Final Sketch of the New Organization

Perhaps in the preceding paragraphs I have yielded to the temptation to paint a Utopian picture of the organization that the new decision-making techniques will create. If so, I have done so from an urge to calm the anxieties that are so often and so unnecessarily aroused by the stereotype of the robot. These anxieties are unnecessary because the existence in the world today of machines that think, and of theories that explain the processes of human thinking, subtracts not an inch, not a hair, from the stature of man. Man is always vulnerable when he rests his case for his worth and dignity on how he differs from the rest of the world, or on the special place he has in God's scheme or nature's. Man must rest his case on what he is. This is in no way changed when electronic systems can duplicate some of his functions or when some of the mystery of his processes of thought is taken away.

The changes I am predicting for the decision-making processes in organizations do not mean that workers and executives will find the organizations they will work in strange and unfamiliar. In concluding, I should like to emphasize the aspects in which the new organizations will much resemble those we know now.

1. Organizations will still be constructed in three layers: an underlying system of physical production and distribution processes, a layer of programmed (and probably largely automated) decision processes for governing the routine day-to-day operation of the physical system, and a layer of non-programmed decision processes (carried out in a man-machine system) for monitoring the first-level processes, redesigning them, and changing parameter values.

2. Organizations will still be hierarchical in form. The organization will be divided into major subparts, each of these into parts, and so on, in familiar forms of departmentalization. The exact bases for drawing departmental lines may change somewhat. Product divisions may become even more important than they are today, while the sharp lines of demarcation among purchasing, manufacturing, engineering, and sales are likely to fade.

But there is a more fundamental way in which the organizations of the future will appear to those in them very much like the organizations of today. Man is a problem-solving, skill-using, social animal. Once he has satisfied his hunger, two main kinds of experiences are significant to him. One of his deepest needs is to apply his skills, whatever they be, to challenging tasks — to feel the exhilaration of the well-struck ball or the well-solved problem. The other need is to find meaningful and warm relations with a few other human beings — to love and be loved, to share experience, to respect and be respected, to work in common tasks.

Particular characteristics of the physical environment and the task environment are significant to man only as they affect these needs. The scientist satisfies them in one environment, the artist in another; but they are the same needs. A good business novel or business biography is not about business. It is about love, hate, pride, craftsmanship, jealousy, comradeship, ambition, pleasure. These have been, and will continue to be man's central concerns.

The automation and rationalization of decision making will, to be sure, alter the climate of organizations in ways important to these human concerns. I have indicated what some of the changes may be. On balance, they seem to me changes that will make it easier rather than harder for the executive's daily work to be a significant and satisfying part of his life.

14   Line, Staff and Support Services

A. M. Willms

The words *line, staff* and *service* were coined to describe organization before administrative structures reached the size and complexity they have today.

They are used as nouns and adjectives to describe three different aspects of organization:

roles or functions
the people or groups who are filling these roles
the relationships between people and groups.

It is unfortunate that common usage includes all three of these aspects making their meaning imprecise and their use difficult. We shall attempt to outline the most common contemporary usage in Canadian government administration and point out the difficulties of ambiguous usage.

The *line* role contributes directly to achieving the objectives of the enterprise. The infantry private at the front with his superiors, the auto worker on the assembly line with his foreman, manager and vice-president, and the treasury department clerk and his supervisors are all working directly towards the objective of the enterprise. While also contributing to the objectives, the regimental cook, the public relations man and the construction company paymaster do so indirectly and are not "in the line". Line structure presupposes a normal scalar hierarchy of authority and responsibility that may have any number of levels. The people or groups which have this role or which are located in the normal hierarchy are often called line.

The *staff* role is to assist a manager by taking part in his activities in a subordinate capacity. It is mainly concerned with accumulating, arranging and disseminating facts and making recommendations. Traditionally the staff role carries no authority over line people and no responsibility for line functions. The staff role is often filled part time by line employees. There are normally only two levels in the staff hierarchy: the manager and the staff. When the number of staff people reporting to one manager increases and further levels of hierarchy are formed, then presumably there is a line hierarchy within the staff. This staff group would then have a staff role and a line relationship. From this description it is obvious that the use of the word "staff" to describe people or positions can be very confusing since it is commonly applied to people whose main role is that of staff but who may also have other roles in line or in service. In military use the term is often applied to people whose positions historically had a staff role but who today spend the major part of their time carrying out line functions, sometimes at a very senior level.

The word *service* probably came into use to help eliminate some of the difficulties in the use of the word "staff". The service role assists the operations of an enterprise, usually by fringe activities of a repetitive, specialized nature which are common to many units and levels of the enterprise. Support services may involve highly specialized professional skills such as the preparation of legal cases or they may be routine and repetitive such as messenger service. Normally services are rendered to several units of a department. The relationship within services is the normal line relationship, while the senior service supervisor generally acts part time in a staff role to senior management. In Canadian government the units that carry out the services to departments or agencies are known as administrative services, auxiliary services, departmental services or support services. Traditionally the following roles have been regarded as services in Canadian government administration:

Personnel services
Financial services
Purchasing and stores
Organization and methods
Information and public relations
Legal services
Office services and secretarial services
Engineering and maintenance services.[1]

It is often difficult to distinguish between the line role and staff or service roles, between direct contributions to the objectives of the enterprise and indirect, auxiliary, support or facilitative contributions. And it has been suggested that the staff and service concepts do not serve any useful purpose and could be eliminated.[2] It can be argued since all units of an enterprise are created to help achieve its objectives the distinction between line, staff and service is redundant and that organizational difficulties are sometimes caused by distinguishing between line and staff. Complaints from line that staff are usurping line authority are often founded on fact. Staff, with all the self-assurance of specialists who have the ear of the boss and a detailed knowledge of many parts of the operations sometimes tend to take over from line supervisors. On the other hand the line is often too suspicious of the motives of staff who depend on line people for much of their information. But eliminating the staff concept will not really eliminate the difficulty. There will still be friction between line supervisors and the specialists consulted or hired by management to assist in management details. The duties of an executive often exceed his capacity to carry them out because he does not have the time or the specialist knowledge required. He may not be able to delegate these extra duties to line subordinates because several subordinate units are closely involved and usually none should have priority knowledge or contacts which may constitute discrimination; furthermore, capable line subordinates are seldom available to carry out special duties. The executive must therefore turn to a special assistant or aide to fill the staff role. Whether these assistants are called staff or by any other name they will still tend to clash with line managers who have the responsibility to fulfil the objectives of the enterprise.

Services also create difficulties in the organization. Service people often see ways of making their own operations more efficient by wielding controls

1 Civil Service Commission, *Analysis of Organization in the Government of Canada*, Queen's Printer, Ottawa, 1964, pp. 282-291.
2 See G. G. Fisch, "Line-Staff is Obsolete", *Harvard Business Review*, Vol. 39, No. 5, September-October 1961, and O. G. Stahl, "The Network of Authority", *Public Administration Review*, Vol. 18, No. 1, Winter 1958 and Vol. 20, No. 1, Winter 1960.

over the line, particularly by insisting on detailed procedures which they have devised to make their own work easier and to increase efficiency. Line men will argue that the role of service is assistance and not control. But a measure of control is inherent in the specialist knowledge and skills of the services.

All this makes the line-staff-service controversy one of the big problems in organization. But eliminating the use of words which describe the line, staff or service role will not solve these problems, nor will the elimination of staff or service concepts be a satisfactory answer to most managers in large enterprises. The fact is that certain functions and roles must be performed and they will always be given some generic title. Furthermore these attempts to distinguish types of activity help to bring a rationale into the complex anthill of a large enterprise.

The line-staff-service concepts grew up in a period of simpler structure but they remain with us. The difficulty would be diminished by restricting these names to roles or activities and by avoiding their use for people, groups or positions. But this is a vain hope. The designations are so apt and so convenient that they are constantly on the manager's lips.

The separation of services from the normal departmental functions adds to the complexity of the organization and managers must carefully evaluate whether services need to be singled out and separated. The three main justifications for separate services are the skills and knowledge gained through specialization, the economy of having services performed on a large scale and the need for several units of a department to use common management tools, such as records. Economy considerations enter when the equipment or the skills required are costly, for example, computers or the professional skills of a doctor and when there is a chance that this equipment or these skills may not be employed full time by one branch alone. The burden of proof for separating a service from normal operations should always rest in the separation — separate only when necessary.[3]

Effective organization of support services is often difficult. A balance must be struck between the amount of independence that services should enjoy from their line customers to ensure flexibility and the extent to which they need to be controlled by line units to ensure adequate service. All too often the services gain virtual independence from line control and almost invariably the services set up controls over the line. Services personnel soon discover that they have a big stick; the power to refuse their services unless their requirements are met by line. Since the heads of the services usually act as staff advisers to senior managers, it is often easy to establish these controls.

Although controls by services often increase efficiency and economy, particularly in the short run, generally speaking this type of control is undesirable. The line manager must take responsibility for the department's work and production and he must be given as much freedom as possible

---

[3] W. H. Newman, *Administrative Action*, Prentice-Hall, Englewood Cliffs, New Jersey, 1963, Ch. 10.

to achieve his objectives. Control should be wielded by a service or staff unit only when there is no alternative. The services must always recognize that their role is to help line units, not handicap them.

The Glassco Commission emphasized this in setting up five "general principles which should govern the provision of administrative services by one organization to another".[4] Two of the five principles deal directly with control: "such arrangements must not impair the essential authority and responsibility of operating departments . . . service and control must be sharply differentiated. The suppliers of services should exercise no control over the users except within the strict limits of any responsibility for applying special considerations of public policy".[5]

It is undesirable for departmental services to exercise control over line. But we are still left with the problem of the amount of control those being served should have over their servicemen, and the related problem of the best location of services within the departmental structure.

The ideal solution to the problem will consider the nature of the services, the extent to which they are required by the line, the extent to which they must be shared by various units and the extent to which the services affect the quality and speed of the main departmental functions.

For services in which speed is of little moment but consistency and economy are important — as for example in most personnel services, management analysis, engineering, data processing, financial services or even in janitor services — the locations depicted in Diagrams 1 and 2 may be most suitable, since they leave the service in the complete control of the specialist. The supervisor normally supplies the service on request ensuring that the quality of services is up to specialist standards. Location as in Diagram 1 would apply when the product of the services is used interchangeably by a number of units of the department. If, for instance, Branches A, B, and C all use common records then those records must be equally accessible to all branches. If the services must be shared they can be divided according to work process or by function thus gaining the advantages of specialization. On the other hand, when each branch has its own requirements but quality of services is still the main criterion, then organization as shown in Diagram 2 may be applicable. Here the services are located in the branches but supervised by Administrative Services.

In government, departmental support services frequently are subject to regulations and controls set up by a central control agency such as the Civil Service Commission or the Treasury Board. This may mean that intelligent compliance with regulations becomes nearly as important as helping the department carry out its functions. To these support services, such as personnel, the quality of the service will usually be more important than speed and therefore they should probably be organized as in Diagrams 1 or 2.

---

4 Royal Commission on Government Organization, *Report*, Vol. 1, Queen's Printer, 1962, p. 58.

5 *Ibid.*, see also Vol. 2, pp. 15-16 and Vol. 5, p. 104.

DIAGRAM 1

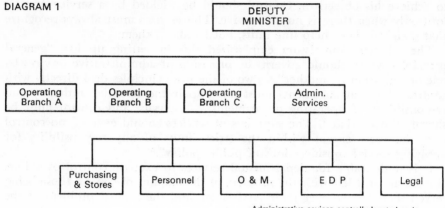

Administrative sevices centrally located and ·
controlled, services available to all Branches
as required.

DIAGRAM 2

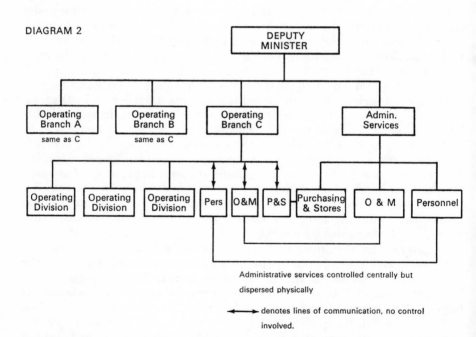

Administrative services controlled centrally but
dispersed physically

◀──▶ denotes lines of communication, no control
involved.

Most commonly however, speed of service and flexibility are the major considerations. The service must be quickly available and readily adjusted to meet the needs of the branches and divisions of the department. In these cases the organization as shown in Diagram 3 would be preferable. This leaves the services under the direct control of the line with only functional control, advice and assistance from the specialists in Administrative Services.

DIAGRAM 3

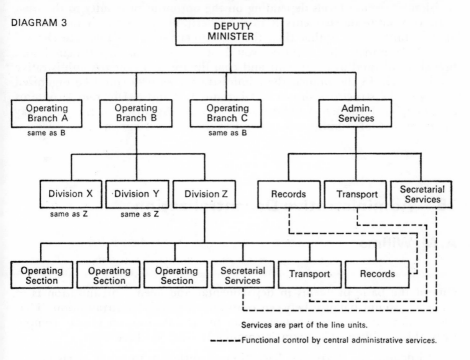

Services are part of the line units.

------Functional control by central administrative services.

DIAGRAM 4

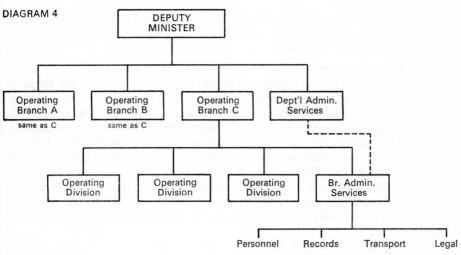

Departmental Administrative Services acts as adviser, consultant and co-ordinator.

These types of organization are usually suitable for services such as records, transport or secretarial services. The services may be available at the branch, division or section levels depending on the optimum proximity to the user.

In very large departments it may be desirable to establish the services at the branch level, rather than the department level. In this case Departmental Administrative Services would act as staff to departmental and branch heads and as consultant and coordinator to Branch Administrative Services. Within the branch the administrative services could be organized in any of the structures shown in Diagrams 1, 2 and 3. Diagram 4 contains an example of Branch Administrative Services organized in the same way as Departmental Administrative Services shown in Diagram 1.

15   Administrative Decentralization

A. M. Willms

One of the basic problems in departmental and agency organization is to achieve a sound balance between centralization and decentralization. That we are not always sure what we mean by decentralization greatly complicates this problem. The term is commonly used in three ways:

> to denote the degree of delegation of authority to lower levels of the agency
> to discuss the geographic dispersal of the units of an agency
> to describe the degree of control the line supervisors have over departmental services.

The first use is preferable and this meaning will be adopted in the essay. But because these three aspects of organization tend to overlap there is little hope of one concise usage throughout the government. Dispersal is not decentralization, but dispersal affects decentralization. Physically scattering an organization usually results in more delegation of decision making to sub-units. Otherwise work slows down, communication channels become overloaded and decisions may be made at headquarters that are unsuitable for local conditions. Thus whenever an enterprise is required to disperse, sound management will assess the amount of delegation that must accompany the dispersal. Similarly, when operations are taken from the field and reassembled in headquarters some change in centralization is usually required.

The amount of control line supervisors have over their own departmental support services is not a degree of centralization or decentralization. But within the support services the head may give his supervisors freedom to adapt their unit's services to the needs of the individual line unit which they serve. This is decentralization. Similarly a change in the structure of support services to effect dispersal is not decentralization. But this change usually coincides with an increase in the autonomy of the sub-units involved and this is decentralization. Thus the creation of a number of sub-registries is not in itself decentralization, nor is granting authority to line managers to control these sub-registries decentralization; but giving decision-making authority to each supervisor in charge of a sub-registry is decentralization.

Decentralization deals with the amount of delegation of authority within the enterprise. In a decentralized agency the authority to make decisions, to command resources and to demand results is localized as far down in the organization as possible. It implies the freedom of the supervisor and employee at lower levels to make decisions within clearly enunciated guidelines.

There is of course no ultimate in decentralization, nor is there any gauge for determining the ideal degree of decentralization. As in UP and DOWN there are many degrees, and also as in UP and DOWN the degree of decentralization will appear different to each viewer depending on his position in the structure. The organization will invariably appear more decentralized to the man at the top than to the man at the bottom. It is not unusual to find a manager of intermediate rank who feels that below him the agency is adequately decentralized while above him it is much too tightly controlled.

As an organization grows more decentralization becomes necessary. If this is not arranged then a state of "apoplexy at the center with anemia at the fringes" tends to prevail. Communications will become clogged, paperwork will prosper, cases requiring decisions will take weeks or months to process and employee morale will be low. The employees at the lower levels will be forced to play it safe and avoid decisions instead of taking responsibility. The severe penalty for over-centralization has been recognized and since World War II there has been a great tendency in both government and business to decentralize. But good decentralization is difficult to achieve. It is not enough merely to pass problems to subordinates with the injunction: "You solve this!" Nor is it feasible to "leave the subordinate alone to work out his problems", for this is abdication of responsibility and not delegation of authority. This irresponsible attitude of management has sometimes given decentralization a black eye. "We tried it, but it was no good" is an excuse for drawing the reins tighter and resuming the practice of having subordinates relay all problems to their supervisor.

Good decentralization is not federalization nor is it giving autonomy to lower units. Instead it demands a clear enunciation of policy. This entails more than just one elucidation of departmental objectives and the basic considerations to bring about their realization; it involves repeating this process for every branch, division or section in the agency. Of course the branch heads must formulate their own policies with their division heads, while division heads must enunciate policy with their section heads.

Sound decentralization requires adequate central control. Top management in a decentralized organization must ensure that the interests of the whole department remain the guide lines and that the interests of sub-units do not subvert the aims and objectives of the whole branch or the department. The controls exercised must, however, be limited. They must ensure that central aims are achieved and that central policy is the guide, but they must infringe as little as possible on the manner in which the aims are achieved. The best and easiest controls are those which can measure the quality and quantity of the department's operation. If the end results are satisfactory then the means should be questioned as little as possible. Unfortunately, in government administration, a mathematical evaluation of results is frequently not possible, therefore management control must take the form of less precise measures such as monthly reports of activities, occasional visits to sample the overall results and the atmosphere of the office, conferences to discuss problems, and management audits to make sample inspections of the processes of the unit.

Above all, decentralization requires delegation of authority and allocation of responsibility. It is not usually too difficult to allocate responsibility but it takes courage to delegate authority.

Delegation is dividing the right to make decisions and assigning part of this authority to a subordinate — in three steps. The first step is usually assessment of the subordinate's duties. Then the subordinate's ability to make commitments, to requisition resources and to make decisions must be recognized. It is easy to say that the authority granted must be adequate to allow successful performance of the duties assigned but opinions on what is adequate will often differ. When possible, supervisor and subordinate should consult to establish criteria. And the subordinate must agree to stay within decision-making policy guidelines to ensure the overall objective.

By transferring authority and responsibility to the subordinate the superior does not abdicate responsibility. He shares it. "The most important factor in delegation is the recognition of the fact that the management responsibility at higher levels is not discontinued by the act of delegation. It is not a question of being able to sit back and put feet on the desk because by delegation all responsibility has been given away . . . *the responsibilities of higher levels are altered, they are not* extinguished."[1]

Earlier when decentralization was rare, the *exceptions principle* was devised to clarify the interrelation of superior and subordinate, and to act as a guide for assessing the ideal limits of delegated authority. It states that:

the scope of authority must be outlined
for decisions outside this scope the information is passed to the
next higher level
for interpretations of the scope the next higher level is consulted.

---

[1] H. J. Kruisinga (ed.), *The Balance Between Centralization and Decentralization in Managerial Control*, H. E. S. Kroese, Leiden, 1964, p. 18.

In other words, decisions which are not clearly within the scope of the working level are passed upward.

Although there has been a general trend in industry toward decentralization since World War II, Canadian government administration has been slow to follow.[2] The reason usually given is that government administrators are closely accountable to the government and the people. A government manager may be asked to justify his conduct on any aspect of his management to a number of authorities whereas a manager in private industry is responsible to only one person or to a few people — the owners. It is further argued that the public requires consistent and uniform treatment, and an absolute adherence to principle while private owners can condone flexibility, opportunism and inconsistency in the interest of greater profits. This reasoning is not as valid as it first appears. It is not only the public that demands accountability. The private owner also requires strict accounting, he also has policies on which he insists and his accounting is often painfully exact since his business life depends on the calibre of management.

In the public service decentralization is often feared by the supervisor and the subordinate because it impairs that uniformity of decision and treatment which is deemed necessary for good government. Public servants claim that uniformity is essential for fairness to everyone. In fact, uniformity often has other motives. It constitutes a ready reason or excuse or justification: "We have always done it exactly in this manner" or "Branch X did exactly this yesterday" is usually ample justification for almost anything. Moreover, uniformity gives the appearance of justice having been done, while in fact there are very few problems that are identical and the same answer to similar problems is seldom the right answer. Lastly, uniformity is easy to enforce because the most junior clerk can recognize its virtue. There is no doubt that public servants must strive for consistency in their decisions and relations with the public. But the emphasis should be on decisions and actions consistent with governmental, departmental and branch policy — today's policy — rather than consistency with yesterday's transactions.

There are many other reasons for reluctance to delegate. The desire of executives to dominate and control is probably not the most common reason, but it does occur. It is sometimes necessary and laudable to run a taut ship, to have the impress of the character of the leader in the whole establishment, but with the constant growth in size and functions of government units this is becoming more difficult and less rewarding. Many supervisors are afraid that their subordinates will make too many mistakes; governmental scrutiny often rewards the supervisor who manages to keep his nose clean, even at the cost of inactivity, while it severely penalizes errors. Supervisors who are promoted to another level of management

---

[2] G. E. Morse, "Pendulum of Management Control" in *Harvard Business Review*, Vol. 43, No. 3, May-June 1965, argues that the pendulum of management decentralization is swinging back to centralization, but generally speaking management still subscribes to the merits of decentralization.

often carry with them the interests acquired at the last level and insist on carrying their new responsibilities without relinquishing the old. The fear of giving subordinates too much authority lest they show up the boss may sometimes also be a factor.

Occasionally a supervisor finds that he can get his subordinates to assume responsibility without the formality of giving them authority. This makes it all the easier to disclaim responsibility if something goes wrong. "It is always easy to tell when a manager is too small for his job — he gives his subordinates a great deal of responsibility but no authority, so that he can take the credit for the right decisions, and blame them for the wrong ones".[3]

In Canadian federal administration decentralization should require little justification. The size and diversity of the country demands specialized knowledge of local conditions to such a degree that it cannot be held by top management. The volume of communications necessary in centralized departments is obvious and some of the blame for the excess paperwork must lie in inadequate decentralization. The rapid growth of government functions in Canada makes much flexibility and trial-by-error management necessary and such experimentation can be done effectively at the lower levels.

It is true that improved methods of communication now available eliminate some of the disadvantages of centralization. And the advance in computer technology apparently offsets some of the advantages of decentralization. The amount of information now produced for decision making by computers often enables the top manager to make better decisions than his subordinate, but the decisions that warrant the use of computers are usually at the policy level and would seldom have been made at the working level anyway.

Adoption of automation will result in less dispersal of routine operations. For example, a machine can be installed in Ottawa to process income tax forms which were previously dealt with in Regina, or Edmonton or Halifax. The machine can deal with these forms much more quickly and adequately than local clerks and the complex machinery can be installed only at headquarters until the volume of business justifies a machine in each large taxation centre. The geographic concentration of operations will make central control easier and more expedient than in the dispersed state. As methods of communication improve and automation makes central decision making more attractive, field offices will tend to become merely service depots for local inquiries and complaints. This trend must be carefully watched for it could result in over-centralization with all the attendant disadvantages. Moreover, if local units are allowed to deteriorate the information fed into the computers will be inadequate and automated decision making will collapse.

Decentralization is valuable because delegation promotes initiative — there is no greater motivating factor. Initiative is a sensitive plant that requires plenty of encouragement. Also, there is no better method of train-

---

[3] S. Harris in the Ottawa *Citizen*, June 11, 1963.

ing a man for higher duties than by letting him make decisions at his own level. Centralization puts a premium on the weak men who obey orders and refer all difficulties to the boss, while decentralization tends to nourish the strong men who will be ready to challenge the adequacy of conditions. Decentralization tends to ease the burden of detail that weighs on senior managers and it gives them more time to devote to major problems. Senior managers are almost invariably in favour of decentralization but too frequently they cannot find the time to arrange it.

Coordination and Committees

Perhaps the biggest difficulty in the structure of government administration at Cabinet level is coordination. This top-level coordination is the responsibility of Cabinet and unless we can make Cabinet over into an effective government manager, coordination must be achieved by keeping the structure simple. In departments and agencies there are different considerations. Here we have full-time managers who are responsible for effective administration and good coordination does not present such a problem. Nevertheless, good coordination is necessary and will not be achieved without conscious effort.

The topic of coordination, like that of decentralization, is the subject of much confusion. Again it is a problem of meaning. Perhaps because of this, it is receiving less attention than it once did, and certainly less than it deserves.

There appear to be two basic meanings of coordination. The first, like efficiency, is a state or condition of management and not an activity of managers. In this sense, good coordination, like efficiency, is the result of sound management techniques. "Coordination is not a separate activity but a condition that should permeate all phases of administration", according to Newman.[4] Advocates of this definition maintain further that if the manager has to resort to special coordinating measures then his management is obviously inadequate. The second meaning of coordination is the traditional one that coordination is one of the basic *activities* of the manager along with planning, control, organizing and so on. By this definition, coordination is managerial activity aimed at integrating the operations of an enterprise, or the processes by which a manager develops an orderly pattern of group effort and secures unity of action. It is regulation and adjustment so that the actions of individual employees or groups will fit together as required. Proponents of this definition often contend that coordination is the most important activity of the manager.

Coordination by the manager is becoming more important as the complexity and specialization of operations increase. The Glassco Commission says: "It can be predicted with confidence that the need for coordination of federal action on a variety of overlapping patterns will become increas-

---

4 W. H. Newman, *Administrative Action*, Prentice-Hall, Englewood Cliffs, New Jersey, 1963, p. 415.

ingly urgent".[5] The complex, specialized activities of modern government can differ so much that they even have their own languages, therefore coordination requires considerable effort and ingenuity. The increasing interdependence of specialized units, such as the reliance of various parts of an enterprise on the automatic data processing unit, enhances the value of coordination. Today the manager is exhorted to rely less on control with its autocratic overtones and more on the motivation of employees. As this emphasis moves from boss-control to self-control of employees, coordination becomes mandatory.

We can divide the manager's coordinating activities into two: internal coordination within his own unit and external coordination with other units. Internal coordination is vertical, from the top down, while external coordination is horizontal. Both types of coordination ensure that the operations of units with similar activities do not clash, overlap or leave a gap. External coordination would be the coordination of the Royal Canadian Mounted Police and the Ontario Provincial Police, where no common control is available. The coordination between federal and provincial governments is entirely external since there is no common supervisor. In these examples there is external coordination between units that have no common control but external coordination can also take place within one enterprise where control exists.

The biggest enemy of coordination is a complex, unwieldy organization. The manager who has difficulty achieving good coordination should first study the structure of his unit. Numerous sub-units make coordination difficult. Organizing lower levels by function or purpose may be the source of problems and a unitary reorganization may solve them. Simplified organization normally means fewer but larger sub-units, with each unit being as self-sufficient as possible.

A manager who has difficulty coordinating may need to examine his communications. A great volume of communications, whether these be regulations and orders or merely information, can be self defeating. Employees can become immune to communications by the bucket. On the other hand the communications may be too infrequent, they may not reach the right people, or they may be confusing or inadequate.

Planning is a good place to begin internal coordination. Plans should be checked to ensure that they are consistent and that the objectives, procedures and timing are compatible. Also, the objectives of the department, the branch and division must be clearly stated and widely known, and easily understood policy statements must be readily available. Voluntary coordination is much more likely when everyone knows what is expected of him. And carefully thought-out routines which automatically provide good coordination can be employed.

If these built-in coordinating techniques are not sufficient then special measures are needed. Coordinating committees may have to be appointed

---

5 Royal Commission on Government Organization, *Report*, Vol. 5, Queen's Printer, 1963, p. 46.

and liaison or coordinating staff may be necessary. Periodic conferences will help provide coordination. They are often most effective if held informally.

External or horizontal coordination is more difficult than internal coordination because no one manager or body is responsible for this function. In Canada the need for external coordination is most obvious where the administrative activities of the federal and provincial governments overlap. The three devices which have been used most commonly to overcome these coordination problems are periodic conferences, unilateral provision of services and information and permanent liaison units which may be provided unilaterally or by common support.

The Glassco Commission acknowledged the need for more coordination in the federal service and pointed out that the most common method of coordination is appointing a committee. But it warned against the careless use and proliferation of committees.[6]

It has become fashionable to deride committees. They have been called "a group of men, each one unable to make the decision that nothing can be done", "an anonymous shield for weak managers to hide behind", "a refuge from the weariness of labor and a haven from the loneliness of thought" and it has been said that "committees exist to spread the blame". These criticisms are often the reaction to excessive use or misuse of committees and they may reflect an authoritarian manager's distaste for the democratic process.

It is true that committees are used to dilute responsibility and serve as a sounding board for an opinionated chairman, and they can be a complete waste of time. But the committee, a small group of people appointed for special activities which cannot be carried out as effectively by individuals or by a large assembly, can be a valuable administrative device. There is no easier or better way to effect coordination among interdependent units than by having responsible individuals from those units meet to exchange information and arrive at agreements. When coordination is required continuously a standing committee is usually the best answer. When a complex decision requires intensive study an *ad hoc* committee is often the best way of organizing the necessary discussion. If a variety of views from a number of groups needs to be represented over a period of time or if the manager feels it desirable to involve his subordinates in decisions so that they will identify their interests with those of the enterprise or if a decision requires continuing consultation with interested parties, then a committee is probably the answer. A group can produce more ideas in a short time than individuals working separately. Advertising agencies use committees for brainstorming purposes. A group can also explore and analyze ideas more effectively than individuals. For this reason universities use committees to assess theses of graduate students. A committee can also be used as a training ground for junior executives. Here they are exposed to the ideas and methods of senior people in the organization.

---

[6] *Op. cit.*, Vol. 5, p. 45.

There is the danger in committee work that those who are not interested, not involved in the matter to be discussed or not qualified, waste their own time and that of other members. The decorum of group meetings apparently requires that all members be permitted to have their say and meetings can be lengthy, useless, boring sessions which are expensive in terms of wasted time — committees are accused of keeping minutes and wasting hours. Moreover, it is true that divided responsibility is nobody's responsibility and committee decisions can be such as would not be made by a responsible individual. There is always danger that a committee decision is a compromise decision rather than a good decision. Weariness, boredom or the need to be agreeable may result in the surrender of the best-informed member to the more presumptuous or arrogant members.

It is expedient to avoid appointing a committee when a quick decision is needed, when qualified people are not available to serve on the committee or when precedent or discretion would require appointing members who would make little contribution. When executing an order or controlling an operation a committee is very seldom justifiable. These are tasks for an individual and not the business of committees. Whenever management appoints a committee it should first consider the cost. Is the information to be gathered, the opinions to be heard and the coordination involved likely to be worth the time to be spent? If not, then the answer is obvious.

On the other hand when a great diversity of information and opinion is necessary for education, motivation, coordination or training, then a committee may well be the answer. Having decided to appoint the committee the manager should make clear the aim, the functions and the terms of reference to ensure effectiveness. Sometimes it may be desirable for the committee to establish its aims and procedures. In this case the chairman must make sure that this is done at the first meeting.

Chapter Four
Canadian Government Organization

The structure of the Canadian public services is immensely complicated. Moreover, they appear to be thrown together in an unsystematic fashion. Any student searching for a rationale to explain the conglomeration of departments, corporations, boards, commissions and other agencies of the public service will be disappointed. The deeper he digs in his analysis the more incongruities he will find. The difficulties start at the top where there is an executive council which is both a board of directors and a management committee. Members of this executive are individually responsible for the conduct of very large divisions of the governmental structure — departments — but they must spend most of their time elsewhere. As a result, most of the responsibilities and functions usually assigned to top management are exercised by their deputies while other executive functions reside in control agencies. The administrative structure is subdivided into departments and various other units totalling more than 100 — no one knows just how many there are — a profusion which cannot be sorted into neat categories. Whether one approaches these uncounted agencies by study of their purpose or function, by analysis of budgetary controls as in the federal Financial Administration Act or by their relation to Cabinet or to a minister, there appears no logical or really useful classification that would include them all.

Canadian government organization seems to have evolved through haphazard adaptation of the British model to Canadian circumstances. The organization is to a great extent the result of trial and error processes in which there were few criteria to condemn any trials as errors. Apparently expedients were accepted because they served a temporary purpose and they then became permanent through vested interest, precedent or laziness. If a student of Canadian government made the deduction that this structure was entirely unplanned he would be jumping to conclusions, but it would be difficult to distinguish the results of such a random, aimless origin from the structure which now exists.

Despite the organization's appearance the machinery works. And judging from recent critical analyses by the Glassco Commission and others, it

141

works quite well. "The over-zealous application of organizational logic must not be permitted to damage a healthy, mature organism that, for all its apparent untidiness, is functioning with relative efficiency on the basis of subtle working conventions familiar to its members".[1] But a moderate application of logical analysis may still be profitable.

[1] Royal Commission on Government Organization, *Report*, Vol. 5, Queen's Printer, Ottawa, 1963, p. 26.

This chapter begins with a survey by Public Service Commission management analysts of the machinery of the federal executive followed by excerpts from the Royal Commission on Bilingualism and Biculturalism on the problem of two languages in the public services. The administration of federal-provincial relations is briefly discussed by Taylor Cole. Although government departments are the traditional form of basic government organization, many types of agencies — once described as "creatures of expediency designed to meet the special needs arising out of the complexity of government" — have evolved in the past 30 years. The largest of these is the crown corporation.

The first and fifth volumes of the Royal Commission on Government Organization *Report* are a prime source for material on the federal public service. Taylor Cole's *The Canadian Bureaucracy* (Duke University Press, Durham, North Carolina, 1949) is out of date but reflects the traditional setting. J. E. Hodgetts and D. C. Corbett (eds.), *Canadian Public Administration* (Macmillan, Toronto, 1960) was a step forward in Canadian literature but was published at the beginning of an era of great change in the public service. The annual reports of government departments and agencies are good research sources while the Queen's Printer's *Organization of the Government of Canada* (Ottawa, 1966) is a convenient reference book. The journal, *Canadian Public Administration*, now 10 years old, is an indispensable source for Canadian students. Other monographs and articles in this field are

C. A. Ashley and R. G. H. Smails, *Canadian Crown Corporations*, Macmillan, Toronto, 1965.

R. M. Dawson, *The Government of Canada*, University of Toronto Press, Toronto, 1963. The fourth edition of this book has seven fine chapters on the executive and the administration.

Institute of Public Administration of Canada, *Proceedings of Annual Conferences*, 1949-1958.

Norman Ward, *The Public Purse: A Study in Canadian Democracy*, University of Toronto Press, Toronto, 1962.

16   The Machinery of Government*

Constitutional and Political Factors

21. The Canadian people are the ultimate source of political power, but jurisdiction over government activities is divided in the British North America Act between the federal government and the provincial governments. At the federal level the political power of the people is delegated by them to their elected representatives in the House of Commons, and to the appointed representatives in the Senate. In practice, effective legislative power is usually held by the largest party in the House of Commons and this party, in turn, puts executive authority into the hands of a group of its members, the Cabinet, led by the Prime Minister.

22. Within the Cabinet there are a number of standing committees, one of which, the Treasury Board, provides a further pronounced authority level. Finally, executive authority over individual agencies or departments is divided among the ministers who form the Cabinet. Delegations and divisions of authority have therefore been made at several constitutional and political levels before the level of the senior appointed official is reached.

23. The minister is the linking-pin between legislative and executive authorities on the one hand and administrative authority on the other. No substantial alteration can be made in an agency's structure without the minister's consent; normally, such changes require his whole-hearted support. If this support is to be forthcoming, due weight must be given, in reviewing an agency's organization structure, to the minister's role at constitutional and political levels. The design of the structure must be in harmony with the demands inherent in this role.

24. Specifically, an organization plan should, whenever relevant:

(a) recognize the division of powers between the federal and provincial governments; in sensitive areas of jurisdiction even the appearance of federal overlapping into provincial fields must be avoided unless government policy on the subject is clear;

(b) recognize that the government exists to serve the people; recommendations that are administratively sound must also be acceptable to the segment of the population the agency has been set up to serve. In field organizations, in particular, it is sometimes necessary to modify organization principles to meet such a situation and to provide for local requirements;

(c) recognize that the minister concerned is one member of the Cabinet and that the functions of the agency, including the funds necessary for carrying them out, are often subject to balancing mechanisms within the Cabinet which supersede purely administrative considerations. Recommendations which

* Reprinted with permission of publisher from Civil Service Commission, *The Analysis of Organization in the Government of Canada*, Queen's Printer, Ottawa, 1964, pp. 13-18.

propose the extension of an agency's function into areas where other agencies have an interest, for instance, should be made only after the most careful exploration with the agencies concerned.

Statutes and Administrative Functions

25. If conditions were perfectly static and Parliament could provide in its laws for all possible eventualities, the terms of reference of any public administrator could be readily ascertained by consulting the statutes. However, because of the lack of precision in the statutes and because of changes in the social, political and physical characteristics of the country, situations arise constantly where the original intent of Parliament has to be interpreted more broadly or more narrowly, and the interpretation has to be related to the changed environment. The onus rests on the judiciary to ensure that the interpretations conform to the original intent, and upon Parliament to review and adapt its legislation to changing conditions.

26. While a law remains in force, and subject to the effect of clear, legal precedents, the administrator must adjust and direct the organization and resources under his direction towards the attainment of specific objectives. This he must do within the web of financial and other controls, and under the policy direction of the government, as expressed through his Minister who, in turn, must discharge a broad responsibility to Parliament.

27. The pursuit of specific objectives should be reflected in the functions of every organization, both in terms of its total operations, and in the activities of each of its components and sub-components down to the last individual.

28. No matter how broadly or narrowly the objectives are set forth in acts and regulations, they should be stated, they should be clear, and they should be traceable to the statutes.

29. In organization planning, it is vital to relate the objectives and functions for the following reasons:

(a) To assess the permanency and/or the changing nature of a function. For example, the payment of a statutory allowance, such as family allowances, is a more permanent function than the payment of a grant due to a particular catastrophe; similarly, the function of payment of family allowances has changed less than the collection of income tax, which is changed or adjusted almost year-by-year. Differences in permanency or stability should be reflected in the organization.

(b) To identify and classify main functions and sub-functions separately from support or ancillary functions, and to appreciate the relative significance of the support or ancillary functions in different contexts. A simple example is Purchasing which is the *main* function in the Department of Defence Production, a *major support* function in the Department of

Public Works, and a *minor* function in the Public Service Commission.

(c) To determine the relationships between functions. For example, the need to group or co-ordinate certain functions may be directly implied in statutes which set one function conditional upon or sequential to another.

(d) To appreciate the need for and the role of functions which are primarily related to policy formation rather than administration.

30. The participation of senior administrators in the formation of policy and the preparation of legislation is an accepted fact in modern government administration. In this role, the administrator can contribute purposefully only if he is fully and constantly aware of the relationships between the functions pursued by his organization and their legal basis, and is willing to strive constantly for the clarification in law of implied functions.

The Distribution of Functions among Departments and Agencies

31. The term "machinery of government" is commonly used to describe organization which is inter-agency as opposed to intra-agency. The aim is to achieve the best allocation of functions among agencies and to devise the appropriate mechanisms for co-ordinating functions of concern to two or more agencies.

32. Decisions as to how functions will be allocated to agencies are made by Cabinet. In deciding how functions will be grouped, or divided, the principles of basic organization (i.e., grouping functions with a common purpose, process, geographical area, or clientele) are taken into account. Even if only these principles were considered, the division of functions among agencies would not be easy and questions would arise of the following kind:

(a) Should Indians be provided with medical care by the Indian Affairs Branch (which is a grouping of functions for a clientele), *or*, should Indian Health Services be made a function of the Department of National Health and Welfare (which is, primarily, a grouping of functions by major process)?

(b) If, as is the case, the Department of National Health and Welfare is authorized and required to provide Indian Health Services, why then are Veterans' Treatment Services designated as a function of the Department of Veterans' Affairs?

33. These apparently contradictory applications of principle can be multiplied many times over in the machinery of government and give some indication of the intricacy of determining how functions should be assigned among agencies.

34. In addition to assessing the effect of the application of conflicting principles, the Cabinet may have to consider some or all of the following:

(a) a need to achieve a reasonable balance of the load of responsibility to be carried by Ministers and senior officials;

(b) a desire to highlight some aspect of public policy by giving a separate identity to the agency responsible for its execution;

(c) the effect and interplay of personalities, of which one is the tendency of functions to gravitate toward a "strong" minister;

(d) a desire to alter the size of the Cabinet either by consolidating agencies and reducing the number of ministers, or by breaking up agencies and creating additional portfolios;

(e) reports of Royal Commissions which sometimes recommend organizational changes in the functions they have been set up to examine; and

(f) representations by citizens and organizations with an interest in how a particular function should be allocated.

35. In studying the objectives and structure of an individual agency it is often useful, as a means of putting things in perspective, to examine its relationships with those agencies with which its activities are connected. This looking beyond the confines of a single agency will sometimes reveal problems which are beyond the power of that agency's head to resolve, and may require a study of co-ordinative mechanisms and overlapping objectives.

36. If the two or more agencies, in which problems of co-ordination and over-lapping are suspected or perceived, are responsible to the same Minister, one course of action is to have the deputy head of the agency under examination approach the Minister with a request that he authorize the extension of the organization study to embrace the additional agency or agencies. Thus, an examination of the Department of Veterans' Affairs could conceivably be broadened to include the Canadian Pension Commission or a study of the Department of Transport could encompass related agencies, such as the Air Transport Board.

37. Another kind of machinery of government study may arise with respect to the division and co-ordination of activities for which the responsibility is shared by "line" agencies and central service or control agencies. For example, personnel administration is shared with the Public Service Commission and the Treasury Board, financial administration with the Comptroller of the Treasury and the Treasury Board, construction and maintenance with the Department of Public Works, printing and duplicating with the Department of Public Printing and Stationery, the processing of statistics with the Dominion Bureau of Statistics, and so on. The allocation of duties within these functions, and the instruments of co-ordination where functions are shared, should be analyzed to remove duplication and to ensure that a proper balance is achieved between service and control.

38. Yet another kind of problem arises when conflicting principles are applicable to the same function. In the example given earlier concerning Indian Health Services and Veterans' Treatment Services, it was pointed out that the principle of major process was applied in allocating Indian Health Services to the Department of National Health and Welfare but that the principle of clientele was applied in putting Veterans' Treatment Services under the Department of Veterans' Affairs. The apparent inconsistency, however, is explainable. In the former instance, it was decided that the relatively small Indian Health Service would be more effective if it were associated with the medical specialists available in the Department of National Health and Welfare. Veterans' Treatment Services, on the other hand, are conducted on such a large scale that the employment of medical specialists by the Department of Veterans' Affairs could be justified. In this situation, the objective is integration with other veterans' services; ergo, the Treatment Services could reasonably be grouped with other services to the same clientele.

39. Certain functions are relatively self-contained and unique but are conducted on too small a scale to warrant separate identity as independent agencies; this situation leads to the creation of multi-purpose agencies. Such functions are normally divided among agencies with the aim of achieving a reasonable balance in the load of responsibility of ministers and agency heads. The problem with unique functions is to determine when they have grown to the point where they merit separate identity. In 1961 a new Department of Forestry was established because it was judged that federal activity in this field had grown to the point where it became necessary to amalgamate all related activities in a new and integrated department. Conceivably, government activities in the field of culture might grow to the point where the unification of the National Gallery, the National Museum and the National Library in an agency of national culture would be justified.

40. There are cases where a particular activity of government is conducted on a large scale but has so many facets that individual segments must be retained by various agencies. Oceanography, for instance, is vital or of major interest to the Fisheries Research Board, the Marine Sciences Branch of the Department of Mines and Technical Surveys, the Defence Research Board, the Royal Canadian Navy, the National Research Council, and the Department of Transport. Co-ordination of activities is achieved through the Canadian Committee on Oceanography on which the interested agencies and the universities are represented.

41. A further question with which "machinery of government" could be concerned would be the relative merits of traditional departments and crown corporations as instruments for the effective execution of public policy within a parliamentary democracy. A good knowledge of political theory, particularly that part of it which concerns responsibility to parliament, would be necessary for assessing machinery of government studies in this area.

17 Bilingualism and Biculturalism in the Public Services*

Language Rights

There are no constitutional provisions governing the language of public administration either at the federal level or within the provinces. Such federal or provincial legislation as there is on the subject is generally incidental or secondary. Also because the Constitution very properly states only the minimum linguistic requirements, it is entirely silent as to the language to be used in the actual conduct of government and administration. It does not provide for the linguistic composition of the civil service or guarantee the language rights of citizens in their various contacts with the state. It makes no provision for the protection of language rights in municipal government. In short, the Constitution does not ensure that the public affairs of any given jurisdiction (federal, provincial, or local) must be conducted in either language. It is not even clear from the B.N.A. Act who has jurisdiction over languages. The most casual reading of Canadian statutes soon discloses that language is dealt with in two interrelated ways: first of all, as a substantive head of legislation guaranteed in the Constitution to ensure cultural survival and evolution; secondly, as the object of incidental regulation in the course of the exercise of the various powers attributed by the B.N.A. Act to Parliament or to the provincial legislatures.

The following conclusions can be drawn from a careful examination of all pertinent Canadian and provincial statutes. As far as public notices are concerned, federal law generally does not require that they be published in both languages except in Quebec. The general practice of Quebec is to require bilingual publication of all notices of a general nature and even of many special notices. Similar rules apply in some municipalities to signs, labels, and required notice boards. In all other provinces the language is English. Except within the federal jurisdiction and in the province of Quebec, official forms and returns are required to be English but in Manitoba some employment records are to be kept in either English or French, according to the language of the employee. Ballots and other forms are normally bilingual only in Quebec.

When there are statutory linguistic requirements for government officials or professionals, such as river pilots or municipal councillors, the following situation was found: such federal laws as exist treat English and French almost equally, with a slight preference for English; in Quebec, both languages are generally on the same level; in all other provinces and territories, with almost no exception, English is the only qualifying language.

Finally, when the language of documents such as trade marks, negotiable instruments, and bills of lading is regulated, federal law places both languages on an equal level, at least in Quebec. Quebec itself requires the use of both languages. When there is no special law applying to them, in

---

* Reprinted and abridged with permission of publisher from the Royal Commission on Bilingualism and Biculturalism, *Report*, Vol. 1, Queen's Printer, Ottawa, 1967, pp. 54-113.

all provinces contracts and other private legal arrangements can be made in any language and will be enforced when proven. Persons who do not speak either English or French are not legally incapable.

Many governmental activities in Canada are governed by federal-provincial agreements. These agreements are executive acts rather than legislative enactments, though they sometimes find support in statutes. In other words, they normally take the form of agreements entered into with Ottawa by the various provincial governments. These agreements are numerous and deal with the whole spectrum of public administration. The Commission's investigation disclosed that all agreements with common-law provinces are negotiated, drawn up, and signed in the English language only. For Quebec, the practice varies considerably, not only from department to department, but within departments themselves.

The only province with which agreements are signed in French is Quebec. The other nine provinces never have signed the French text of a federal-provincial agreement. But not all agreements signed with Quebec are in French or even bilingual. Irrespective of the language of the ultimate text, the practice of federal agencies involved is to prepare the original draft in English only. But when bilingual texts are eventually signed, they seem to be treated as being of equal validity.

Canadian linguistic practices in signing international agreements are equally diversified. The final draft of all Canadian agreements is prepared by the Legal Division of the Department of External Affairs which also occasionally participates in negotiations. The Department has traditionally had the following rule: when Canada signs a treaty, at least one official text must be in either English or French. In January 1965, however, for the first time, Canada signed an agreement with a foreign country in both an English and a French version.

A comparison with Quebec practices is revealing. Our enquiries about agreements made by Quebec with other jurisdictions revealed that in most cases when Quebec had signed with English-speaking jurisdictions in Canada or abroad, its agreements were in English only. A French translation is prepared for the government's own files, but it is not official. Agreements with French-speaking jurisdictions tend to be in French.

Under the B.N.A. Act, municipalities fall within provincial jurisdiction. But section 133 does not refer to them and there are no constitutional language guarantees governing their operations. At the present time, all municipal corporations in Quebec are bilingual to some degree by virtue of purely provincial statutes. A certain degree of *de facto* bilingualism also prevails in some areas of New Brunswick and elsewhere in Canada.

At the time of our survey there did not appear to exist any specific legal impediment for a municipality anywhere in Canada, no matter how small its linguistic minority, to use also a minority language in the conduct of its affairs. Our investigations have in fact shown that some municipalities in New Brunswick use French to a considerable extent.

This brief survey of language rights in Canada reveals the wholly inadequate way in which present laws give effect to the concept of the country as an equal partnership between two linguistic communities. It is certainly true that language rights have been gradually recognized through the years and still continue to expand. But this evolution has been intermittent and has suffered numerous setbacks. There does not exist a fully developed linguistic régime expressing the bicultural character of the country as a whole and based on well defined and fully accepted legal rights.

Recommendations

We recommend that English and French be formally declared the official languages of the Parliament of Canada, of the federal courts, of the federal government, and of the federal administration.
This equality of the French and English languages must be complete and must apply also to all bodies and agencies deriving from Parliament and the federal government. It must be indisputable; otherwise we shall simply revert to the arguments of the past. The consequences of applying this principle at the federal level are substantial.

No Canadian, French-speaking or English-speaking, will feel that the language of his group is considered equal to the other official language if he does not find it used in such basic institutions as Parliament and the Supreme Court, in the statutes and important regulations governing his activities, and in all the documents of general interest that the central government issues. Both languages are used in these fields, but much more remains to be done.

Similarly, in its contacts with other countries, the federal government must assert the bilingual character of Canada, and this involves much more than our embassies. All departments and federal agencies dealing with foreign countries — such as External Affairs, Trade and Commerce, Industry, Manpower and Immigration, Labour, Finance, and National Defence; Air Canada, the CBC, and the National Film Board — must be able to do so in French and English.

The federal government constantly makes agreements with the provinces. At present, in the provinces with an English-speaking majority, the documents are drawn up in English only; agreements with Quebec are drawn up sometimes in both official languages, sometimes only in French, sometimes only in English. We do not feel this is proper, at least when important agreements are concerned. Either all agreements should be drawn up in both official languages or the policy should be to use, in all negotiations and drafting, the language of the provincial majority — that is, French for Quebec and English for the other provinces. Or, perhaps, in officially bilingual provinces, both should be used.

Other requirements are of a more immediate, practical nature. The administration in Ottawa must be able to communicate adequately with the public in both languages. All government publications, as well as forms and notices, must be simultaneously available in either language. Federal government offices and Crown corporations across the country must be able to deal with people in either French or English. For example, in the immigration and customs offices at all ports of entry, in important transportation terminals, on Canadian National's trains, and on Air Canada's airplanes — everywhere, even in the completely unilingual sections of the country, where there is contact with the travelling public — services should be available in both languages as a matter of course.

The federal government has at its disposal other means of recognizing the two official languages. It is in a position to use agreements and contracts negotiated with provinces, municipalities, and private organizations to require compliance with its own laws — for example, with respect to minimum wages. We think it should do the same in the field of bilingualism. These changes can be made without forcing a single citizen, Francophone or Anglophone, to learn the other official language. For the most part these changes will cost little.

We believe further that all the provinces should accept official bilingualism in their jurisdictions, though to degrees which in practice will vary according to the prevailing demographic conditions. Linguistic demography will be our guide.

Therefore **we recommend that the provinces of New Brunswick and Ontario themselves declare that they recognize English and French as official languages and that they accept the language régimes that such recognition entails.** Moreover, **we recommend that any province whose official-language minority reaches or exceeds 10 per cent declare that it recognizes French and English as official languages and that it accepts the language régime that such recognition entails.**

Any citizen of Quebec, Francophone or Anglophone, may deal with all provincial agencies or departments in either language. Most of the Quebec government's official publications and forms appear in both languages. Under the Municipal Code either French or English may be used in council meetings; all documents and records including by-laws may be in either language but their publication must be in both languages unless the minister of Municipal Affairs has granted an exemption. For larger municipalities governed by the Cities and Towns Act, each council may determine its own proceedings but public notices must be given in French and in English.

We cannot, however, draw absolute rules from Quebec practices because they have been evolving since the Conquest in 1760 and have been long accepted by custom. Furthermore, the conditions under which the minorities live, their size, and their general situation, as well as the prestige of the two languages, are not the same in Ontario, Quebec, and New Brunswick. In each province the proportion of bilingual people in both the majority groups differs greatly. However, despite the foreseeable regional variations, we propose to outline the minimum degree of recognition and services which a province will have to provide if it is to call itself officially bilingual. In principle the two languages must have completely equal status in all three provinces, even though we know that in practice English will occupy a larger place in New Brunswick and still larger in Ontario, while French will predominate in Quebec.

An officially bilingual province must first legalize the use of both English and French in the debates of its legislature. As well, the laws and principal regulations of that legislature must be published in both languages and the same must apply to its records, minutes, and journals.

Being an officially bilingual province entails establishing in the provincial administration certain services in the minority language as they are needed in the central provincial administrative offices and in branches located in bilingual regions. The dominant working language of the public service in New Brunswick and particularly in Ontario will still be the language of the majority, as it is in Quebec. But each bilingual province will have to grant its minority the right to deal with the government in the official-minority language and to receive an answer from the provincial offices in this language.

Under our conception of the future Canada, the other seven provinces will not have to adopt the kind of language régime we have outlined for Quebec, New Brunswick, and Ontario. This does not mean that they must be considered unilingual. They too must take steps based on the recognition that official-language minorities live within their borders. **We recommend that the provinces other than Quebec, New Brunswick, and Ontario declare that both English and French may be used in the debates in their legislatures and that these provinces provide appropriate services in French for their French-speaking minorities.**

All seven provinces have to take into account those localities where the minority is more heavily concentrated. To meet local situations, the provincial governments must equip themselves with a minimum of facilities in the second language, if only to communicate with certain local administrations. In many sectors a translation bureau will suffice; for the educational system much more will be needed. Obviously this question hardly arises in such a province as Newfoundland, where there were about 3,000 Canadians of French mother tongue (less than 1 per cent of the population) in 1961. The situation is more serious in Manitoba where the last census counted about 61,000 Francophones (7 per cent of the total population).

Up to this point we have focussed on language practices at the federal and provincial levels. These practices will apply to the whole country or to the provinces chiefly through the centralized services of these jurisdictions and through citizens' direct contact with federal and provincial legislative and administrative centres. However necessary and beneficial these reforms might be, wherever they could be instituted, they would not by themselves assure genuinely equal opportunities for both official languages. We must also provide for a set of language practices of federal and provincial jurisdictions within the communities they serve. We must set out language laws and practices for school boards and other municipal institutions.

Our aim is to encourage an active co-operation among all governments in providing services to the regional minority in its own language. The objective is not so much the recognition of a specific right as the linguistic reorientation of a number of institutions in the three levels of government. Their combined action will noticeably alter the living conditions of the minority in a defined area.

Consequently, we are going to propose the creation of "bilingual districts" — special areas within which a defined language régime would be established for federal, provincial, and local jurisdictions. These districts would be areas where the official-language minority is numerous enough to warrant the kind of linguistic reorientation we feel desirable. We will propose that they be defined essentially by regional clusters of the official-language minority. This geographic framework will thus be closely related to real language needs.

The bilingual district is neither a new jurisdiction nor, technically speaking, a new administrative structure. Rather it is designed to bring about linguistic co-operation in the services of existing governments. Our goal is to be just toward members of an official-language minority, without imposing too heavy obligations on the majority.

The actual creation of these districts and the precise definition of their boundaries would legally be the responsibility of provincial or federal authorities. The federal and interested provincial governments will have to agree on a common criterion for defining the boundaries of the bilingual districts. Therefore, **we recommend that bilingual districts be established throughout Canada and that negotiations between the federal government and the provincial government concerned define the exact limits of each bilingual district.**

We assume that this process will include consultations with local authorities. The importance of the role of local governments is continually increasing, especially in major urban centres. They are performing more and more functions and exercising more and more direct influence on the day-to-day life of their taxpayers; the success of many provincial measures will depend to a large degree on the extent of their collaboration. Therefore, those responsible at the federal and provincial levels must pay strict attention to these local aspects.

At the district level, only local governments have legislative functions. We believe that, in bilingual districts, municipal councils and other local government bodies should be required to permit either official language to be used in their deliberations. All by-laws and regulations should be recorded and printed in both official languages.

On the administrative level, the creation of bilingual districts will have important consequences. All federal and provincial offices located in a bilingual district will be so staffed that residents can communicate in either English or French, orally or in writing. This does not mean that all members of the staff must be bilingual — a certain number of bilingual employees will suffice to guarantee these services. Letters and inquiries will be answered in either language. Forms, notices, information sheets, and so on will be bilingual or available in either language. Signs will be bilingual (or possibly, in the case of road signs, non-lingual).

Local governments within a bilingual district should make all administrative services, written and oral, available in both official languages, in the way described in the preceding paragraphs. Priority should be given to personal services — those rendered by welfare officials, municipal hospital staffs, and police. But in due course French-speaking and English-speaking citizens can expect to be served in their own language and, whenever possible, by someone who understands their culture.

18   The Federal Bureaucracy and Federal-Provincial Relationships*

Taylor Cole

The federal bureaucracy has become increasingly involved in the complexities of the federal-provincial relationships. These involvements, usually embraced under the heading of cooperative federalism, have injected the federal bureaucracy into the institutional ties in the dynamic federal system. Three factors have, according to Donald V. Smiley, been responsible for the growth of this inter-governmental machinery and relationships.[1] They are: 1) the constitutional rigidities which prompted a search for flexibility through administrative arrangements; 2) the exercise of the powers possessed by the federal government to equalize the range and quality of the public services; and 3) the desire and capacity of administrators at varying levels of responsibility to "devise and implement collaboration arrangements." Whatever be the relative weight placed upon each of these explanations, there has developed a myriad and rapidly increasing number of committees and meetings which play a key part in these cooperative arrangements.

Three types of inter-governmental machinery, which have come into being, can be differentiated on the basis of the degree of the federal initiative in their establishment, the part played by federal officials in their operation, and the territorial areas which are involved. The one type of committee and meeting has come into being generally at federal initiative,

---

* Reprinted with permission of author and publisher from Taylor Cole, *The Canadian Bureaucracy and Federalism 1947-1965*, University of Denver Press, Denver, Colorado, 1966.

[1] Donald V. Smiley, "Public Administration and Canadian Federalism", *Canadian Public Administration*, Vol. 7, September 1964, pp. 372-373. Professor Smiley prefers to speak of "joint federalism" and "consultative federalism", rather than cooperative federalism.

finds its headquarters or secretariat as a rule in Ottawa, and involves functions in the federal-provincial area where federal and provincial governments usually have concurrent jurisdiction. These committees and meetings, that is, the formal as distinguished from the informal ones, were the subject of a study by K. W. Taylor, then Deputy Minister of Finance, in 1958.[2] At that time, he found some 67 "federal-provincial committees," 14 of which had broad and 50 narrow "terms of reference." These committees included 5 which were operating at the ministerial level, 13 at the deputy minister level, 18 at the director level, and 28 at the professional and technical level. Membership in 40 of these consisted of governmental personnel, whereas the membership of 24 included non-governmental personnel. The secretaries of all except half a dozen of these committees and meetings were federal officials.

Since Taylor made this pioneering study eight years ago the committee structure has become much more complex. Two closely cooperating centers of influence in Ottawa, the Prime Minister's Office and the Ministry of Finance, are heavily involved. The functions of the Federal-Provincial Relations Division in the Ministry of Finance, which was created in 1954, have grown in a number of ways in connection with the meetings of the Federal provincial conferences. The Assistant Deputy Minister, who heads this Division, is a key participant, and along with the Deputy Minister of Finance is active in the work of the Continuing Committee on Fiscal and Economic Matters of the Federal-Provincial Conference. These two officials also play key roles in the work of the Tax Structure Committee of the Federal-Provincial Conference. The Tax Structure Committee is composed of the federal and provincial ministers of finance, or their ministerial counterparts, and is preparing studies on which projections for tax sharing, equalization, and inter-governmental fiscal relationships for the period from 1967-1972 can be based. As previously indicated, the federal Cabinet has a special committee on federal-provincial relations whose special secretariat maintains liaison with the appropriate officials in the provinces and federal ministries. He prepares the agenda and attends the meetings of Federal-Provincial Conferences. Thus, important new machinery has been recently established or expanded in the office of the Prime Minister and Ministry of Finance to cope with the growing complexities of federal-provincial relations.

But perhaps more important has been the rapid expansion of the federal-provincial committees and meetings, and especially those dealing with professional and technical problems. By the end of 1964, the number of Federal-Provincial Conferences, committees, and other meetings had nearly doubled since 1957 to a total of 114.[3] Twenty of these were at the minis-

---

2 K. W. Taylor, "Co-ordination in Administration", in J. E. Hodgetts and D. C. Corbett, (eds.), *Canadian Public Administration*, Macmillan, Toronto, 1960, pp. 145-164 (including discussion by R. B. Bryce).

3 Data procured by the author from official sources indicate that the number will be increased in 1965.

terial level. Some 62, or approximately half of them, involved participation by all provinces, whereas the balance involved only the federal government and one or more provinces. The "authority" for the meetings ranged from decisions of Federal-Provincial Conferences, to federal statute, to federal Order-In-Council, to action by the Cabinet, to federal departmental "initiative," and, in a few cases, to "provincial sponsorship." The federal representation on the purely professional and technical conferences and meetings, as was to be expected, has been the heaviest from the Ministries of Health and Welfare, Agriculture, Forestry, and Labour. The importance of these meetings ranges from that of the Federal-Provincial Conferences[4] and its Tax Structure Committee to that of such "meetings" as those on Ownership of Beds of Pre-Confederation Harbours and on the Replacement of Swing Bridges and Canal Systems. Several of these meetings, such as the ones on Provincial Taxation of Joint Canada-United States Defence Projects and on Cultural Agreements with France and Belgium, have external affairs implications.

The contributions of the federal officials in providing much of the leadership, administrative direction, and implementation of decisions are recognized in many quarters. The personal testimony of participating officials in provincial capitals, including Quebec, is one bit of evidence. Competent students, such as Donald V. Smiley, conclude that the program specialists from the bureaucracy have removed certain types of decision-making from the political arena and have produced an impressive amount of non-controversial agreement.[5] The Glassco Commission found that there were no less than 16 federal departments and an equal number of agencies, which now "have some close and significant concern with matters in which provincial governments had common or related interests" and that "the points of intersecting interest" had multiplied.[6] It concluded that added responsibilities and staff should be given to the Division of Federal-Provincial Relations to advise in general regarding federal-provincial consultative and cooperative arrangements, and, specifically, regarding consultation, conditional grants, administrative delegation, and contracting services by one government for another.

Despite this accumulating evidence, the full appraisal of the role of the federal official in this rapidly growing network of federal-provincial committees and meetings must still be based somewhat on subjective evaluations, at least, until, as J. E. Hodgetts suggests, the need for more "full scale studies of provincial services ... and of the administrative interrelations

[4] The last meeting of the Federal-Provincial Conference was held in July 1965 to discuss proposals made by Prime Minister Pearson in the Speech from the Throne to Parliament in April 1965, and other matters suggested by the provinces.

[5] Smiley, *op. cit.*, pp. 378-379; see, by the same author, *Conditional Grants and Canadian Federalism*, Canadian Tax Foundation, Toronto, 1963, p. 38.

[6] Royal Commission on Government Organization, *Report*, Vol. 3, 1962, p. 124; see also A. R. Kear, "Co-operative Federalism: A Study of the Federal-Provincial Continuing Committee on Fiscal and Economic Matters", *Canadian Public Administration*, Vol. 6, March 1963, p. 56.

which have developed between provincial and federal public departments"[7] has been satisfied. Until that time, we shall not be able to evaluate the collaborative and competitive relationships and to compare the contributions of the federal-provincial meetings of the federal officials with those of the increasing number of able and active provincial officials who are participating.[8]

On the horizontal level, where the initiative has been taken by the provincial governments, where the emphasis is upon the provinces and inter-provincial relationships as such, and where the federal official is less in evidence, the growth of committees and meetings has also been rapid since World War II. In the first major study made of "inter-provincial co-operation" in 1958, Richard H. Leach found a surprisingly large number of professional and technical meetings and organizations which were composed partially or exclusively of public officials from the provinces.[9] The purely inter-provincial meetings have often invited federal officials as observers, or even as members, and the nature of their participation has depended upon the circumstances. There is no constitutional basis for inter-provincial cooperation as such, but its development has an important bearing on the contours of Canadian federalism.

Two recent examples of such meetings at quite different levels of participation have been the annual inter-provincial Premiers' conferences which were revived on the initiative of Quebec in 1960. One federal official was present at the first meeting in strictly an observer capacity. Again, the meeting of presidents or chairmen of civil service commissions was started in 1963, with Quebec again taking some initiative. A secretariat has been established for the exchange of information, and the annual meetings have been attended by commissioners and invited officials from the Public Service Commission in Ottawa. The province of Saskatchewan was reported in 1960 to be represented in some capacity in at least 75 organizations where inter-provincial cooperation was a matter of major concern, though, as J. H.

---

[7] J. E. Hodgetts, "Challenge and Response", *Canadian Public Administration*, Vol. 7, December 1964, p. 411.

[8] "My own impression", says one highly capable critic, "is that the increasing frequency and importance of federal-provincial meetings is bringing about a community of sorts... [through] Bryce, Kent, and especially Johnson from Ottawa, Morin from Quebec, Mac-Donald (newly-appointed Chief Economist from Ontario), Tansley from New Brunswick, and possibly Veitch from British Columbia." The new channels of communication between Ottawa and the provincial capitals, says another observer, are "between the civil services of both governments". This development can be explained in the case of Quebec by the rise of a "new group and mentality within the Quebec civil service [many of whom have come from the federal civil service] which corresponds more closely to the type of men and patterns of thinking in the Ottawa civil service". Peter Desbarats, *The State of Quebec*, McClelland and Stewart, Toronto, 1965, p. 134.

[9] Richard H. Leach, "Inter-provincial Co-operation: Neglected Aspects of Canadian Federalism", *Canadian Public Administration*, Vol. 2, June 1959, pp. 83-99. It is to be noted that the Province of Quebec has established a special Department of Federal-Provincial Relations.

Aitchison has pointed out, there was "federal representation" on nearly all of them.[10]

Looming on the horizon are the organizations which have a distinctive area orientation. Already many of the federal-provincial and inter-provincial committees and meetings are largely constituted of members from regional areas, such as the Maritimes, to deal with problems of coordination at regional levels.[11] The growth of municipal governments and of metropolitan areas has prompted discussion of three-tier and three-level federalism[12] and of a real division of powers.[13] Proposals for regional levels of government receive academic mention,[14] and the Glassco Commission was concerned with appraisals of future dispersion of operations.[15] Regional concerns receive special attention in the presentation of party and provincial government programs.[16]

Whatever be the direction and rapidity of these developments, federal-provincial, inter-provincial, or regional, the handiwork of the federal public employees is present in some capacity at nearly every stage. Their involvements give both added flexibility and additional strength to the complex of flexible and dynamic interrelationships which constitute the heart of the federal system in Canada.

---

[10] "Interprovincial Co-operation in Canada", in J. H. Aitchison (ed.), *The Political Process in Canada*, Toronto, 1963, esp. pp. 165-166.

[11] See, for example, Hon. Maurice Sauvé, "Problems of Regional Development in Canada", *Professional Public Service*, Vol. 43, October 1964, pp. 2-4.

[12] Note the criticism of the inadequacy of the "normal federal-provincial channels to serve the interests of municipal governments" in George S. Mooney, "The Canadian Federation of Mayors and Municipalities: Its Role and Functions", *Canadian Public Administration*, Vol. 3, March 1960, pp. 82-92, esp. pp. 86-87. This is not a new point of view.

[13] J. Stefan Dupré, "Applied Areal Analysis: The Case of Canada", in Arthur Maas (ed.), *Area and Power*, The Free Press, New York, 1959, pp. 89-109.

[14] Eric Beecroft, "Agenda for Regional Government", *Canadian Public Administration*, Vol. 5, June 1962, pp. 227-228.

[15] *Report, op. cit.*, Vol. 5, 1963, pp. 79ff.

[16] Note, for example, J. W. Pickersgill, *The Liberal Party*, McClelland and Stewart, Toronto, 1962, pp. 125-126. For a discussion of the matters being considered at the sixth Premiers' conference in Winnipeg in 1965, see *Winnipeg Free Press*, August 3, 1965, p. 1.

19   Crown Agencies

A. M. Willms

In the British political tradition cabinet ministers take complete responsibility for the actions of government departments, but a great part of government administration is carried out by non-departmental units called agencies which have varying amounts of ministerial surveillance.

Like many other governments the Canadian federal government has a wide range in the types of administrative units it uses to put its objectives and policies into practice. The Financial Administration Act of 1951, with subsequent amendments, divides these as follows:

Government departments	26
Departmental corporations	13
Agency corporations	15
Proprietary corporations	14
Designated as departments for purposes of this Act	46[1]

The Act classified government units for the purpose of clarifying their budgetary relations with the Treasury Board and with Parliament, and it uses both financial practices and agency functions to effect the classification. The definitions which result leave a lot of gaps and a great deal of overlapping; neither the definition nor the classification is satisfactory for purposes other than those of the Act. For instance, in the last category it leaves in one catch-all-class the commissions, royal commissions, boards, the Auditor General, the Chief Electoral Officer, the Privy Council Office, the National Library, and many others varying in structure, functions, methods and in almost every administrative feature. Nor is the list which the act presents exhaustive. It lists more than 100 units; the number varies from year to year; but this is not complete. It does not name agencies whose finances are regulated entirely by the creating statute such as the Bank of Canada, the Canadian Wheat Board or the Board of Grain Commissioners. Nor does it include those agencies which for budget purposes are closely affiliated to a government department such as the Dominion Bureau of Statistics, the Agricultural Prices Support Board or the Defence Research Board, or those agencies which have provincial as well as federal representation such as the Canadian Corporation for the 1967 World's Fair, the Eastern Rockies Forest Conservation Board and the Canadian Council of Resource Ministers.

There are a great number of types of units in the governmental administrative net with a wide range of functions, of organization and of procedures and no classification that is useful for purposes of discussion and study has been devised. But it is possible to distinguish departments from the assortment of corporations, boards, commissions and others which are generally labelled *agencies*. Some of the more obvious differences are

1. Departments are answerable directly to a Cabinet minister and that minister takes responsibility for their actions. Agencies usually have a minister designated to them through whom they report to Parliament but

---

1 Financial Administration Act, R.S. 1952 C. 116 as amended to September 1967, Schedules A, B, C and D.

the degree of supervision and accountability varies and is much smaller than that with departments. When questioned in Parliament on the activities or policies of an agency the minister who reports for that agency will frequently disclaim responsibility: "this is a matter involving an independent agency and I can answer only in so far as the agency sees fit to provide me with the information".[2]

2. Departments are all subject to the estimates system of budgeting, that is, revenues coming from the Crown must be spent exactly as directed by Parliament and Treasury Board, and receipts must be returned to the Receiver-General. Agencies vary widely in their budget practices.

3. The personnel of departments are generally recruited by the Public Service Commission and their promotion and transfer is closely supervised by the Commission. There have always been exceptions: departments have recruited their own day labour — prevailing-rate employees — and those in a few other categories such as postmasters in revenue post offices, ships crews and some employees of overseas offices have been exempt from the Commission's authority. Only a few of the agencies recruit through the Public Service Commission. Generally speaking they are responsible for their own personnel matters.

4. Departments have deputy ministers as the administrative heads while agencies vary widely in the nature of their management. Some have boards of directors, others have chairmen, commissioners, or directors.

It is also commonly accepted that a short-term purpose is to be served by an agency while the long-term, continuing functions more often rate the creation of a department. Thus the numerous wartime enterprises of the government took the form of agencies while the long-term function of caring for veterans was incorporated in a department. Royal commissions are a group that is obviously set up on an *ad hoc* basis. But many agencies are set up for the long-term, such as the CNR, CBC, and there have been departments such as Soldiers Civil Reestablishment created for a short-term function. It is also suggested that departments are set up to carry out functions that would not normally be tackled by private enterprise while agencies frequently compete with private business. This has a grain of truth but once again there are a number of exceptions; the Department of Public Works carries on activities commonly found in private business as do also Defence Production, Industry, Mines and Technical Surveys, and others.

We have seen that departments can be distinguished from the agencies. The departments are a group that has some semblance of uniformity in its ranks, but this cannot be said of the agencies. They are just about as diverse as can be, but even so we can discern a few classes among them. One type of agency that has a title and has been treated as a genre is the Crown Corporation. This group is described fully in the Glassco Commission *Report*[3]

---

[2] J. E. Hodgetts and D. C. Corbett (eds.), *Canadian Public Administration*, Macmillan, Toronto, 1960, p. 199.
[3] Royal Commission on Government Organization, *Report*, Vol. 5, Queen's Printer, Ottawa, 1963, pp. 58-75.

and its members are readily distinguishable because they are identified in the Financial Administration Act. The Crown Corporation can be defined as an institution operating a service of an economic or social character on behalf of the government, but it possesses most of the legal and commercial attributes of private enterprise. Though largely autonomous in management it is still responsible to the public and subject to some directions by the government.[4]

Crown corporations are created in two ways — by special statute or they are incorporated by order-in-council under the Companies Act. There are about a dozen of the latter and they form another distinguishable group known as Crown companies and carry the commercial designation "Limited" in their name. This little flourish is of course meaningless.

> (the corporate device) . . . provides a means by which a group of individuals, the shareholders can band together to create a legal personality, the corporation, the existence of which is unaffected by the withdrawal or even the death of individual shareholders, and toward which the financial obligations of the shareholders are limited to the share capital they have subscribed. None of these things is of any relevance to a government organization . . . It is inconceivable that a corporation could survive the extinction of its sole shareholder, the Government of Canada. It is equally inconceivable, in terms of political realities, that the government would ever claim a limited liability and permit the organization to be forced into liquidation by its creditors.[5]

The parliamentary authority for the creation of Crown companies is found in any one of a number of acts which give ministers the power to procure the incorporation of bodies for carrying out the purposes of the act. The Defence Production Act, the Research Act and others carry this proviso.

The Financial Administration Act has divided the Crown corporations into three classes. The departmental corporation "is a servant or agent of Her Majesty in right of Canada and is responsible for administrative, supervisory or regulatory services of a governmental nature".[6] Examples of this class are the National Research Council and the Unemployment Insurance Commission. The second class of Crown corporation is the agency corporation which is defined as "an agent of Her Majesty in right of Canada and is responsible for the management of trading or service operations on a quasi-commercial basis, or for the management of procurement, construction or disposal activities . . ."[7] Typical examples are the Crown Assets Disposal Corporation, Canadian Arsenals and the National Harbours Board. Lastly, there are the proprietary corporations, "any Crown corporation that (i) is responsible for the management of lending or financial operations, or for the management of commercial and industrial operations involving the

---

4 Paraphrased from W. Friedmann (ed.), *The Public Corporation*, Carswell, Toronto, 1954, p. 541.
5 Royal Commission on Government Organization, *op. cit.*, p. 69.
6 Financial Administration Act, Part VIII, para. 76.
7 *Ibid.*

production of or the dealing in goods and the supplying of services to the public, and (ii) is ordinarily required to conduct its operations without appropriations".[8] Examples are the CBC, Central Mortgage and Housing Corporation and Air Canada. The purpose of these definitions is to classify these agencies in their budgetary relations with Parliament and the government but there are also a few other distinguishing features in these groups. Thus no departmental corporations are created under the Companies Act while there are about half-a-dozen Crown companies in each of the agency and proprietary classes. No agency or proprietary corporations are subject to the Civil Service Act while one third of the departmental corporations are. All departmental and agency corporations are audited by the Auditor-General's staff while three proprietary corporations choose their own auditors. However, all Crown corporations are uniformly required to submit annual reports to their ministers.

Another form of government agency which can be distinguished is the royal commission. Royal commissions may be appointed by order-in-council under the authority of the Inquiries Act, and their function is usually to gather information on a specific topic which is of concern to the government.

Besides Crown corporations and royal commissions there is a whole host of other agencies ranging from the permanent quasi-judicial such as the Tax Appeal Board, to the *ad hoc* administrative, for example, the Bureau of Government Organization. There is no common pattern in the organization, staffing or procedures of these bodies.

The question inevitably arises: Why do these agencies exist? Does this diversity in government administration serve a purpose? The agencies have been defined as: "Those creatures of expediency designed to meet the special needs arising out of the complexity of government",[9] but why could not existing departments serve these special needs?

Dean Thomas McLeod has suggested that the agencies have been created because of popular misconceptions concerning the civil service. These include the belief that senior civil servants are more docile and less sensitive than their business counterparts, that departmental administration invariably attracts routine and red tape, and that political direction is interference motivated by ignorance, stupidity, venality, nepotism and graft.[10] There can be no doubt that one of the purposes in creating such agencies as the Canadian National Railways and the Canadian Broadcasting Corporation was to keep them from detailed political control and therefore from political interference. The history of the Inter-colonial Railways suggested to the government of Sir Robert Borden that the newly acquired government railways would be much better off with a management that would feel truly independent in the appointment of staff, the location of railway stations

---

[8] *Ibid.*

[9] L. C. Audette, Q.C., Chairman, Tariff Board, in a talk to Junior Administrative Officer Class 1954.

[10] Institute of Public Administration of Canada, *Proceedings*, University of Toronto Press, 1956, pp. 153 ff.

and other similar matters which had hitherto been subject to political patronage.[11] Today the departments are more adequately shielded than the agencies from patronage in appointments and contracts by those watch-dogs the Public Service Commission, the Treasury Board and the Auditor-General and following Sir Robert's logic the CNR should now become a department.

It is desirable to keep politically sensitive functions such as broadcasting, the redistribution of electoral seats, the investigations of commissions and quasi-judicial actions from the detailed supervision of government and such activities can profit from the political aloofness of an agency. It is much more difficult to justify the difference between departments and agencies in controls over personnel and financial management. There appears to be a general consensus that the facility of expeditious hiring, firing and promotion, the privilege of fixing salaries and allocating budgets without the triple check of the Public Service Commission, the Comptroller of the Treasury and Treasury Board has made agencies generally more effective than many departments and that it would be undesirable to hedge them about with the restrictions which departments have to accept. This leaves the uncomfortable question: If these detailed management controls lessen effectiveness why must departments suffer them?

Some of the agencies such as Polymer Rubber, Air Canada, Canadian National Railways, Eldorado, St. Lawrence Seaway and several others are organized to carry on activities in direct competition with private industry. Therefore they feel that they must be free to copy commercial practices in such areas as trade secrecy, legal accessibility, investment without detailed justification before a board of civil servants, business decisions based on business considerations rather than government policy and so on. Moreover, these agencies find that their dealings with other enterprises, such as contractors and suppliers are easier, and staff development and training is simpler when the organization resembles that of the other enterprises with which it is in daily contact.

Our federal constitution as interpreted by the courts does not permit the federal and provincial levels of government to share each others' functions or to delegate responsibilities one to the other. With ingenuity, the consequent inflexibility can be modified. Agencies can be staffed by personnel who are "coincidentally" acceptable to both governments. This would be difficult to do in a department. The National Battlefields Commission, the Halifax Relief Board, the Eastern Rockies Forest conservation Board and various marketing boards have proved efficacious in bridging this constitutional gap.

Agencies set up in the form of boards or commissions permit the representation of a diversity of interests as with the Board of Broadcast Governors or the representation of interested groups as in the labour and management representation in the Unemployment Insurance Commission.

11 *Debates* (Commons), May 15, 1918, p. 1,999; see also a statement of Sir Thomas White, p. 1,634.

Lastly, the agencies provide a device which helps to make distasteful political ideas acceptable to the Canadian public. Socialism or the nationalization of activities which are normally in the field of private enterprise is unpopular in Canada. The political parties advocating socialism have, as a rule, had fairly slim backing but our governments have found it expedient to put into practice many socialist ideas and when the government takes over the operation of such functions as the manufacture and distribution of electricity or the retailing of liquor it does this with devices which have little connection in the public mind with public ownership of enterprise. The agencies are acceptable politically because they are different. They are not identified with the civil service in the public mind and therefore are considered quite proper competitors with private enterprise.

We have noted that in the conglomeration of government agencies there is this common pattern: a tendency to independence from detailed ministerial control and a freedom from the restraints of the Public Service Commission and Treasury Board. Does this mean that agencies can be independent of government policy, that they can act irresponsibly without regard to government or Parliamentary supervision? Far from it. Both Parliament and Cabinet have a number of ways in which they can control the functions and actions of these agencies. These controls have not always been exercised but they do exist.

The cabinet appoints the directors or commissioners or board members who are the heads of the agencies. Usually it is the Cabinet collectively, the Governor-in-Council, which makes the appointments although sometimes individual ministers are charged with this responsibility. The heads may be appointed for a set period of time; three years, five years, seven years and 10 years are popular periods, although "during pleasure" is used in almost one third of the statutes. Most statutes of incorporation state that heads may be reappointed and none bar further terms of office. Some heads may be "removed for cause" while in other statutes this is not explicit. The experience of the Diefenbaker government with the dismissal of James Coyne from the post of Governor of the Bank of Canada will probably lead other governments to hesitate before attempting similar measures, but it is established that the government can dismiss as well as appoint the heads of agencies.

Another measure of control is exercised by the appointment of those as heads of an agency who are already responsible to the minister in another capacity. Thus senior public servants, such as the deputy minister, the assistant deputy minister, or other senior men in a department may serve as directors or board members of an agency and in at least 20 agencies civil servants are members of the board.

> In most cases the civil servants are drawn from departments having a particular interest in the operations of the agency concerned. They constitute, in effect, an interdepartmental committee advising the chief executive of the agency concerned. . . . It is one thing for ministers to disclaim responsibility for the affairs of undertakings having a board of

management with independent status; but it would seem to be quite a different matter when the board consists of or is controlled by permanent officials, each of whom is answerable to his own minister for his actions.[12]

Some provinces have gone one step further in that they have appointed ministers to the directorates of agencies. This practice seems to have been forestalled in the federal government by the declaration of the father of many agencies, Hon. C. D. Howe, that "the board will function very much better if no minister of the Crown is a member of it.".[13] Since political aloofness is one of the justifications for the existence of agencies it would be difficult to disagree with Howe.

In many agencies the power to make regulations is "subject to approval of the Governor-in-Council". This veto power of Cabinet is seldom used and in fact isolated incidents, such as the Coyne affair, indicate that neither the Cabinet nor the minister are always consulted or informed about the regulations that have been made even when the regulations are subject to approval of the Cabinet. But the control is available.

The minister through whom the agency reports to Parliament has a number of prerogatives in connection with that agency. Thus the Air Transport Board may issue licenses subject to the approval of the Minister of Transport, "subject to the directions of the Minister the Board shall from time to time make investigations and surveys", and "the Board shall make recommendations to the Minister and advise the Minister".[14] With two exceptions, all agencies report to Parliament through the minister and they are usually required by the founding statute to make an annual report to the minister who is required to table the report in the House.

Most agencies are subject to the provisions of the Financial Administration Act which invokes various financial controls. These controls vary from the whole gamut to which departments are subjected, as in departmental corporations, to the virtual financial autonomy of the proprietary corporations which must submit annual capital budgets but have full banking and borrowing freedom and, so long as no further revenue is required, can act independently except for the requirement to report to the minister as the shareholder. Agency corporations must submit both capital and operating budgets for ministerial approval. The extent of the minister's scrutiny will depend on the minister but is not likely to be in great depth. Most agencies are subject to audit by the Auditor-General which involves more than a purely accounting audit.

As well as being subject to Cabinet controls, the agencies are also responsible to Parliament in varying degrees. Two agencies, the Public Service Commission and the Auditor-General report directly to Parliament in their annual reports although in each case the responsible minister must table

---

12 Royal Commission on Government Organization, *op. cit.*, p. 63.
13 *Debates* (Commons), 1946, pp. 2,482-2,483 as quoted in Hodgetts and Corbett, *op. cit.*, p. 203.
14 Aeronautics Act, Part 11, R.S. 1952, Ch. 2, para. 12.

the report. The designation of each to a minister makes quite clear that these two agencies, contrary to popular opinion, are subject to some Cabinet supervision. In fact, both agencies have duties for which they are responsible to Cabinet or to individual members of the Cabinet. The Auditor-General has some responsibility to the Minister of Finance and must report to Cabinet through this minister[15] while the Public Service Commission must report directly to Cabinet as it desires or as Cabinet requires and must "perform such other duties and functions with reference to the public service as are assigned to it by the Governor in Council"[16] in addition to the primary duties listed in the Act. The Commission also has duties for which it is responsible to the Minister of Finance. In the main, however, these two agencies consider themselves responsible to Parliament and not to the government as incorporated in the Cabinet.

Members of Parliament may show their interest in the agencies by asking questions of the Minister through whom the agency reports and they will normally get the answer to their questions. Parliament can discuss the affairs of any agency in the general debates such as those which precede the budget debates and if the agency has to ask for Parliamentary appropriations then it expects a discussion of its affairs. The review of agency affairs by Parliamentary committees could be an effective control and Parliament can institute such an investigation at any time. The best known reviews have taken place in the meetings of the Public Accounts Committee.

The government does not lack control devices to measure and regulate the conduct of agencies. These controls are not always used and when exercised affect the general tenor of policy making and not the details of management.

---

[15] Financial Administration Act, 1951, para. 70(2).
[16] Civil Service Act, 1961, para. 6(8).

Chapter Five
Planning and Financing

Planning has been classed as one of the basic functions of the manager ever since Henri Fayol made his graphic analysis of the operations involved in business enterprise. On every list of management functions planning stands first for two reasons: it appears logically to precede all other action and it is the function which is most involved in every other function.

This chapter begins with a summary of the tenets of conventional wisdom on planning. Next government financing is presented from a political scientist's viewpoint and government budgeting as seen by the practitioner and expert. An outline of the current developments in program budgeting is followed by descriptions of the two main agencies involved in government budgeting: the Treasury Board and the Comptroller of the Treasury.

In government administration planning has been neglected. But in the last decade it has been recognized as one of the manager's key activities and, therefore, the worthwhile literature is recent. On the other hand, the material on budgeting and financing is more mature and there is more of it. The most comprehensive and authoritative study of Canadian government financing is Norman Ward's *The Public Purse* (University of Toronto Press, Toronto, 1951). A. E. Buck's *Financing Canadian Government* (Public Administration Service, Chicago, 1949) is out of date but has never been replaced. The annual Department of Finance *Estimates* and the two other annuals in this field: *The Public Accounts of Canada* and the Auditor General's *Report* are indispensable to a thorough study. The Royal Commission on Government Organization, *Report*, Vol. 1, sections 1 and 2, (the Glassco Commission) is a thorough critique with suggestions for improvements in financing. H. R. Balls, Comptroller of the Treasury, has written a number of articles including essays in this chapter and

"Financial Management in Government", *Canadian Chartered Accountant*, Vol. 72, No. 1, January 1958.

"The Public Accounts Committee", *Canadian Public Administration*, Vol. 6, No. 1, March 1963.

The publications of the Canadian Tax Foundation are useful and their annual, *The National Finances*, published by the Foundation in Toronto is a valuable reference. Other literature on planning and financing that may be interesting to students includes

Y. Dror, "The Planning Process", *International Review of Administrative Sciences*, Vol. 29, No. 1, 1963.

B. Gross, "National Planning: Findings and Fallacies", *Public Administration Review*, Vol. 25, No. 4, December 1965.

W. Z. Hirsch, "Toward Federal Program Budgeting", *Public Administration Review*, Vol. 26, No. 2, June 1966.

F. K. Levy *et al*, "The ABC's of the Critical Path Method", *Harvard Business Review*, Vol. 41, No. 5, September-October 1963.

R. D. MacLean, "An Examination of the Role of the Comptroller of the Treasury", *Canadian Public Administration*, Vol. 7, No. 1, March 1964.

R. S. Murdick, "Nature of Planning and Plans", *Advanced Management Journal*, Vol. 30, No. 4, October 1965.

D. Novick (ed.), *Program Budgeting*, Harvard University Press, Cambridge, Massachusetts, 1965.

Jacques Parizeau, "The Five-year Budget", *Canadian Public Administration*, Vol. 9, No. 2, June 1966.

S. C. Sager, "Parliamentary Control over Expenditure in the Fiscal Year 1957-1958", *Canadian Public Administration*, Vol. 4, No. 3, September 1961.

20   The Theory of Planning

A. M. Willms

Everyone plans but not everyone knows what planning is. Obviously some people and some institutions plan more than others and equally apparent is the need for more planning in some enterprises than in others. The Defence Research Board did some very detailed and involved planning to launch Allouettes I and II while the public servant who prides himself on his punctuality has a standing plan to get up on time, get ready quickly and catch the right bus to work. To those who plan unwittingly, planning is merely the deliberation which precedes action but to the thoughtful manager planning is not so simple. He has attempted to analyze the process of deliberation and has had little success; at least he has found few conclusions which assist him in his work.

Managerial or administrative planning is so complex — involving projections which are tentative, resource requirements which are difficult to assess, equipment and procedures which are to be used in unknown circumstances — that at first glance the process seems too makeshift and difficult for useful generalizations. The manager has been told that planning is one of his functions and he accepts the maxim that planning is necessary for successful administration; but he is often not clear what the actual benefits of planning are, nor is he certain which procedures will give him the most benefits.

Very little research has been done on planning. Even such a comprehensive survey of government administration as that by the Glassco Commission is satisfied with a reference to planning as a major function of management before escaping into a detailed study of budgeting. But the questions about planning which bother the manager cannot be answered without the information only a large study can gather and arrange. Today's ideas are largely the product of deduction with the basic premises gained from untried assumptions[1]. When practical data become available in quantity managers will be able to confirm by analysis the ideas we now broach as concepts or suggestions. It is a measure of the preponderance of art over science in management that we must be content with ideas which, though popular, may on practical testing turn out to be half truths or even myths.

The questions which management asks about planning are quite basic.

> Why plan? What determines the amount of planning? Are there limitations or diminishing returns in planning?
> How do we plan? Is a standard process of planning applicable; can comprehensive procedures be sketched which will be generally applicable or will procedures differ with different organizations? Is long-range planning essentially different from short-range planning? Which activities, functions, programs or projects most require long-range planning? How far into the future can planning profitably go?
> What is the optimum role of staff in planning?

We are not in a position to answer these questions, yet. We are not even certain the answers will turn out to be as vital to an adequate understanding of planning as the questions suggest. But they will be interesting and may well suggest further questions.

---

[1] B. Gross claims that between 1940 and 1960 "at least four hundred articles and two hundred books have been based largely, if not entirely, upon the empirical study of specific organizations". *The Managing of Organizations*, Vol. 1, Collier-Macmillan, Toronto, 1964, p. 23. But I have yet to discover a publication describing a comprehensive empirical study of administrative planning. As a result of President Johnson's order of August 25, 1965 and Bureau of the Budget Bulletin 66-3 dated October 12, 1965, United States bureaus have launched into a new Planning, Programing and Budgeting System which requires considerable study and experimentation. The Canadian Treasury Board is in the process of drawing up instructions and advice on planning for Canadian government departments and agencies. Management consultants have carried out four large studies of the management of four Canadian government departments. Evidently these contain material on planning but they are treated as confidential. Among others, the Canadian National Railways has initiated a study of its planning procedures.

Though we have more questions than answers in any discussion of planning there are a number of items of conventional wisdom which are generally found in textbooks. These include definitions of some of the terms, the traditional steps in the planning process, the reasons for planning, the limitations which determine the amount of planning and the roles of line and staff. These topics are covered in this article.

In the last few years management planning has been assisted by the development of PERT (Program Evaluation and Review Techniques) and CPM (Critical Path Method). And the manager's brightest hope for answers to his planning problems may be in these techniques. This stylized, cut-and-dried, cookbook approach may offer recipes for successful administrative planning.

While in the past the government manager has usually considered the preparation of estimates as synonymous with planning, there is now a strong movement to make budgeting auxiliary to both planning and control. The preparation of estimates should result from and follow the planning although realistic planners will keep in mind budget policy and budget limits. But planners should not set up a framework of estimates and then fit their activities into that framework. "A budget is a financial expression of a program plan."[2] A statement of resource requirements is merely one part of a plan.

Planning as a Management Function

Planning and control are very closely related and sometimes are almost inseparable in their practical application. Effective control is impossible without adequate planning and a part of planning is usually devoted to the definition of objectives which are the basis for control. On the other hand, the detail or extent of planning is often determined by the controls which the manager feels he needs.

In politics and economics planning has sometimes been equated with direction and control. Planning has even been regarded as synonymous with regulation. "What government plans, government enforces" has been the popular assumption for many years. This has resulted in some confusion. Men have argued bitterly against comprehensive planning when their arguments were really against the arbitrary attitudes which created an authoritarian environment to enforce the plans. F. A. Hayek, L. von Mises, H. Finer and others have conducted their vitriolic discussions on planning without once making the distinction between planning and dogmatic directions resulting from the plans.[3] What J. D. Millett has said of Hayek in this respect can be said of others: "Hayek at the least has done a grave disservice to the cause of administrative efficiency in government by

---

2 U.S. Bureau of the Budget Bulletin 66-3, *op. cit.*, p. 1.
3 F. A. Hayek, *The Road to Serfdom*, University of Chicago Press, Chicago, 1944; L. von Mises, *Planning for Freedom*, Libertarian Press, South Holland, Illinois, 1963; H. Finer, *Road to Reaction*, Quadrangle Books, Chicago, pb. ed., 1963.

his loose use of the term planning."[4] The political issue at stake in these writings is the desirability of detailed government regulation and control over economic activities of the nation and not the desirability of government planning.

Authoritarian governments have used the word "planning" in a wider sense than the one we normally use. This serves to mask the compulsory aspect of economic direction. It is not surprising to find this definition in a discussion of planning written by a Russian academic:

> By 'Planning' we mean the fullest and most rational *utilization* of all work and of all the material resources of the community, in the light of a scientific forecast of the trends of economic development and with strict observance of the laws of social development.[5]

If planning is the "utilization of all work and of all the material resources" small scope is left for other managerial functions. And since planning is the prerogative of central agencies in Russia, the latitude of the manager is greatly reduced by this definition.

Even Western students of administration have failed to make this critical distinction, as witness this definition by Dwight Waldo:

> Planning is the means by which the discipline of science applied to human affairs will enable man to incarnate his purposes. It is the inevitable link between means and ends. Moreover, it is in itself an inspiring ideal. For once it is realized that there is no natural harmony of nature, no Divine or other purpose hidden beneath the flux and chaos it becomes immoral to let poverty, ignorance, pestilence, and war continue if they *can be obliterated by a plan*.[6]

This definition includes in planning the functions of direction and control and while it is difficult to separate planning, direction and control in the manager's day-to-day work the distinction can and must be made, even though these functions like parts of anatomy do not operate without each other. In the planning process decisions are made and rationalizations and models are created to show which actions will be most profitable, and standards to measure success are suggested. But the application of the plans is a directing function and the measurement of success or failure is a concern of control.

Planning involves decision making. A complex of decisions is required from the manager when he makes an organized effort to anticipate future events as they may affect his objectives and when he outlines what must be done to achieve his goal. Dror calls them a "set" or "matrix of interdependent and sequential series of systematically related decisions".[7] Plan-

---

[4] J. D. Millett, *The Process and Organization of Government Planning*, Columbia University Press, New York, 1947, pp. 4-6.

[5] Y. Dror, "The Planning Process: A Facet Design", *International Review of Administrative Services*, Vol. 29, No. 1, March, 1963, p. 4. Italics added.

[6] *Ibid.*, p. 4. Italics added.

[7] *Ibid.*

ning not only involves decision making but also resembles decision making at its most complex.

The process of planning has customarily been broken down into five or six steps. These steps are not always distinguishable in the actual planning activity. They are hypothetical stages. But it is interesting to see how closely the new techniques of specialized operational planning follow them.

1. Aims and Policy

Each planning process must begin with clarification, determination or establishment of the aim or objective and of the policy that is to set the perimeter of action. This basic step needs considerable emphasis. It is by no means as obvious as one might think.

In Canadian government the word "policy" is often used to include both the objective and the means to secure it. But there is a distinction. The objective is a forecast of what is to be achieved while policy dictates the range of means to accomplish that aim. In setting up controls the objective is used to measure managerial success, while policy fixes the boundaries within which the manager must try to reach his objective. Too frequently in government administration the manager is measured by his success in staying within policy, much of it quite hazy, rather than by his achievement.

The government manager may find that his objectives are difficult to identify. They may be hidden in outdated legislation and departmental regulations concerned primarily with procedures rather than with achievement or he may find that his objectives are set by precedent, customs and unwritten policies. Usually he finds it much easier to raise questions, not to ask for a restatement of his aims, for if he does he may meet with evasion or even with hostility. It has been suggested that the manager in Canadian government requires extrasensory perception to determine which objectives and policies are acceptable both to his department and to his political masters. And yet most of the theorists agree that "a clear statement of purpose universally understood is the outstanding guarantee of effective administration"[8] and "the more unified and concrete the objective, the more efficient the planning and the administration of any enterprise".[9] "Top management must bear the responsibility for working out objectives . . . The finest organization brains and money can devise will never produce the desired result if the end is obscure".[10] P. Selznick says: "One type of

---

8 W. Newman, *Administrative Action*, Prentice-Hall, Englewood Cliffs, New Jersey, 1963, p. 19.

9 J. D. Millett, *op. cit.*, p. 41.

10 R. Falk, *The Business of Management*, Penguin Books, Baltimore, Maryland, 1962, p. 53. There are similar statements in U.S. General Services Administration, *Planning, Programming, Budgeting*, December 1965, p. 19, and in forthcoming literature from Canadian Treasury Board.

default is the failure to set goals".[11] If planning is to have a singleness of purpose, then its goal must be sharply defined. Without clear objectives and policy at the deputy minister's level it is difficult for the branches to coordinate their objectives and policy, and without this clarity from the branch director the division heads may find that their goals conflict or overlap. And so it goes, down through the hierarchy of the organization.

Millett, one of the authorities on government planning contends that policy making must precede planning and that it is an activity quite distinct from planning. He maintains that "policies make up the fundamental principles upon which governmental action — that is, government administration — is based. Policies fix the terms of reference within which plans are prepared. But policies are not plans. Rather, they are the basic framework for planning".[12] Millett is right so long as he speaks only of the role of Parliament and the Cabinet. These bodies make policy and they do no administrative planning for the departments. But at the administrative level, there is both policy making and planning. And they are not always divisible. Furthermore, the policy made by Cabinet and Parliament is not made unassisted. The administrators frequently inaugurate and usually develop policy. The myth that policy making is the prerogative of Cabinet and Parliament dies hard,[13] but it has never been more than a myth.

It is a truism to say that objectives and policy should be as precise as possible, but evidently it needs to be said. The U.S. Bureau of the Budget directs its agencies as follows:

> Express objectives and planned accomplishments wherever possible, in quantitative non-financial terms . . . In some programs, it may not be possible to obtain or develop adequate measures in quantitative physical terms such as these but it is important to do so wherever feasible. In any case, objectives and performance should be described in as specific and concrete terms as possible.[14]

2. Assessing Alternatives

Forecasting the future, discerning current trends, projecting and qualifying them, is all-important in economic planning. In administrative planning also the manager must constantly consider the future and the factors that will shape his actions. To do this realistically he must define the future for which he is planning — next year, five years hence or tomorrow. The assessment of future probabilities begins with an examination of present conditions and facilities.

> . . . knowledge of the existing situation is an essential part of planning. The job ahead is measured in terms of the difference between what we

11 P. Selznick, *Leadership in Administration*, Row and Peterson, Evanston, Illinois, 1957, pp. 25-26.
12 Millett, *op. cit.*, p. 12.
13 See, for example, *The Globe and Mail* editorial, December 23, 1965.
14 U.S. Bureau of the Budget, *op. cit.*, p. 6.

have and what we want . . . Planning almost never begins with nothing
. . . No planning can proceed very far without detailed knowledge of the
present position, whether it concerns an inventory of physical plant,
present conditions of soil erosion, current land use practices, or the
current record in providing educational facilities for American youth. The
planner must know what is as part of what should be.[15]

The collection and testing of information may be extensive. This is
sometimes labelled *operations research* which may involve feasibility studies,
statistical analyses, simulation experiments or any other aspects of operations research. Above all others, it is this step in planning which usually
justifies a special planning staff.

Once he understands existing conditions and future probabilities the
planner can outline the alternatives. This assessment should be made for
existing and continuing programs as well as for the new ones which have
not yet begun. Though a program may have been successful in the past,
changing conditions, techniques, equipment or personnel may dictate
changes in organization or procedures. Moreover, last year's planners may
not have noticed all the factors which are obvious a year later and the
additional information may help to make better judgements.

In complex planning the staff will probably explore and present alternatives at some length but they cannot make the final choice. This is the
manager's responsibility. He must decide on alternatives, to be followed in
planning.

3. Arranging for Necessary Resources

When the alternatives have been chosen the planner must assess the resources of manpower, equipment, materials and time required. These
requirements must be measured and steps must be taken to make sure that
they will be available as required.

Resource planning is easier for the civil servant than for his counterpart
in crown corporations or in the smaller enterprises in private business. The
public service is so large that special services have been set up to provide
most of the resources and to give advice. Thus the Public Service Commission recruits personnel and helps with their assessment. The manager
need not concern himself with the details of acquiring funds. He merely
requisitions what he needs from the Treasury Board in the estimates
process. Accommodation, complete with heating and caretaker facilities,
is provided by the Department of Public Works and the necessary equipment and raw materials are usually obtained through the Department of
Defence Production.

What the manager must do here is measure the cost of the necessary
resources. This will be a more detailed and accurate costing than that at
stage 2, and he can now confirm or change the cost assessments made in
the previous stages of planning.

---

15 Millett, *op. cit.*, pp. 45-46.

4. Outline of the Organization, Methods and Procedures

Normally, when plans are made for continuing or extending a program, the organization, the methods and procedures, the directives and controls required will have been under constant review and will not need much attention in current planning unless the analysis at stage 2 has shown that a new approach is needed. Even with a new program existing organization and procedures can often be taken over without too much change. But the planner should be certain that the current methods and facilities are adequate.

Some aspects of the methods and procedures which must be reviewed at this stage are time schedules, standards by which the results are to be measured, and the reporting or feedback techniques which will indicate to the manager what has been achieved and where there is a malfunction to be corrected.

5. The Plan

Finally, a conspectus containing all the main aspects of administration to be used in achieving the objectives constitutes THE PLAN. This will seldom be found under one cover or in one file, but the manager and his aides must have ready access to the various parts of the plan. The plan generally includes:

Statements of objectives and policy
Forecast of expectations which will affect the work of the enterprise
Outline of resources required including:
the estimates
inventories
establishment
Organization charts
Outlines of methods and procedures.

Not all planning is consummated in a plan. In fact, *most* planning in government administration does not reach this final stage. Gross tells the following story:

Many years ago a brilliant regional planner who had just received the first doctorate in planning given by the University of Chicago decided that he wanted to get some practical experience. Fortunately he was offered a position with the Tennessee Valley Authority then doing the outstanding regional planning in the world. Upon reporting to work, his first question was "May I see the plan?" The response was a big laugh. TVA officials were too busy planning and acting to have taken time out to put together any single comprehensive plan.[16]

16 B. M. Gross, "National Planning: Findings and Fallacies", *Public Administration Review*, December 1965.

Gross goes on to say that the plan rather than the aims of the enterprise may become the overriding objective of the planners. Pre-eminence of the plan may result in document orientation instead of action orientation and the existence of documents may result in inflexibility.

These are warnings which the manager-planner must heed but he will be a better manager if he has access to a plan, a concentrated source of information which can act as a guide and is a witness to the extent and success of his planning activities.

Plans are frequently categorized. They may, for example, be designated as *single-use, repeat, standing* or *stand-by*. The single-use plan is used once and then discarded. The repeat plan is virtually the same as a standing plan which is available whenever required. The distinction may be made that a standing plan is always available — as in a manual on methods and procedures — and is in constant use, while the repeat plan is dug out of the files at the manager's request and applied at his discretion. A stand-by plan may be either an alternative to a plan in use, ready to be used if the original is not satisfactory or it may be a provision for an emergency as are the stand-by plans of the Emergency Measures Organization or the Red Cross.[17]

Why Plan?

The need for planning is easily seen in everyday life. The family that starts out on a camping trip with no preparation or with inadequate knowledge may get into considerable difficulty. The young couple who set out to build a house without considering in detail the financial and other implications of house building and the size, shape and lay-out of the building they want could be very disappointed with the final results. The contractor who tackles a complex job without measuring his labour and resource requirements, and without budgeting for money, men, equipment and materials will not be in business very long.

The Glassco Commission states, "Good management of any enterprise, either in government or industry, requires sound planning"[18] and yet government departments have worked for many years with very little formal planning. There are several reasons for this apparent anomaly.

> First, the budget process in our government is elaborate and constitutes a form of planning. In fact, estimates preparation has often been considered to be departmental planning and the estimates have been called the plan.
>
> Second, the elaborate outside controls and the many routines which have grown up over the years act as guides to keep the operations of departments realistic and coordinated. Such fixed

---

[17] See also R. G. Murdick, "Nature of Planning and Plans", *Advanced Management Journal*, Vol. 30, October 1965, pp. 36-45.

[18] The Royal Commission on Government Organization, *Report*, Vol. 1, 1962, p. 96.

guide lines, especially in resource procurement, sometimes virtually constitute a standing plan.

Third, lacking clear objectives and standards against which achievement could be measured neither the department nor the public knows the extent of success or failure of the department's operations.

As in private enterprise government resources are scarce and they must be allocated to the uses in which they will give most satisfaction — including both political satisfaction and profits. Planning is necessary to reduce waste and produce maximum returns.

Through planning the manager can effect coordination. Action which has not been anticipated cannot be matched by appropriate support from different parts of an enterprise. Unplanned action in one branch can interfere with the achievement of other units of the department. Since government administration is complex and specialized, coordination is essential.

The only way to have controls in any enterprise is to set standards and to devise means of measuring the results. This is particularly true in government administration where the desired results or the standards needed for success are not self-evident. They must be laboriously defined and this definition is achieved by planning.

By studying future prospects a manager can often anticipate potential difficulties and thus be able to forestall or sidestep them if they materialize or failing that, have remedies handy. To drift into situations is to find oneself at the mercy of circumstances.

> Thus it happens in matters of state; for known afar off (which it is only given to the prudent man to do) the evils that are brewing, they are easily cured. But when for want of such knowledge, they are allowed to grow so everyone can recognize them, there is no longer any remedy to be found.[19]

Planning saves time and money. The systematic study of alternative courses of action and their costs allows the manager to select the most suitable. Knowledge of objectives and policies permits the supervisor and the worker to evolve the best methods and procedures. Lastly, planning is a basis for communication. It allows the superior to tell the subordinate what is expected of him and permits the latter to say what he can accomplish, thus providing a measure of his achievements against expectations. These are the obvious administrative reasons for planning.

Some Limitations to Planning

There is no doubt that government administration should have planning as its basic function, but how much planning shall we have? What criteria determine the amount of planning which is necessary, profitable or feasible?

---

[19] Machiavelli, *The Prince* (Modern Library, p. 11), quoted in W. Newman, *Administrative Action*, Prentice-Hall, Englewood Cliffs, New Jersey, 1963, p. 38.

We must wait until we have more information for definitive answers to these questions, but some ideas have emerged. We know for instance that planning is not easy in government administration because it is difficult to clarify and enunciate objectives and policy at the ministerial level. Administrative or operational policy and objectives must be derived from executive policy, and departmental policies grow out of ministerial policy. The administrator's planning is limited by the extent to which he can obtain a statement of objectives and policy from his political masters. Sometimes Cabinet or the minister may consider it politically inexpedient to define policy too precisely. At other times politicians are not available for consultation. It may happen that the minister's lack of interest in departmental management will make it difficult for administrators to get policy direction.

But none of these conditions is a valid excuse for the partial paralysis of a government department or agency. When political discretion dictates policy vagueness, senior administrators must still be advised; and if the policy is to go slow and steer by the wind they must plan accordingly. Since the minister often is preoccupied elsewhere the administrator must assume a share of the responsibility in policy formulation. He must advise the minister that policy direction is needed and offer help and advice in framing policy. Frequently he is familiar enough with the minister's ideas and wishes to be able to prepare policy directives for the minister's ratification.

Another very obvious limitation to planning in Canadian government administration is the lack of confidence in planning techniques by senior managers who have worked their way to the top without much formal administrative planning. While no senior manager would openly condemn planning, many have shown their distrust. And those managers who have conscientiously sought to use it have often had difficulty finding staff who know how to plan. At the moment the dearth of qualified staff is a serious limitation. Furthermore, the techniques of planning are still in a confused and elementary state, and while specialized techniques such as PERT and CPM are becoming popular they do not always fill the manager's needs.

In long-term planning a point may be reached where the forecasting is not accurate enough to justify peering farther into the future. There is an inverse relation between distance of projection and accuracy — the greater the time span the more chance for the unexpected — and reliability diminishes quickly. Sophisticated forecasting will help determine the amount of feasible planning.

The cost of planning, in time and resources, must be considered and compared to the results. But since we are not certain of the extent of the benefits gained by planning, an accurate mathematical assessment is possible in very few cases. Nevertheless, it would be safe to say that in all complex operations the benefits earned will outweigh the cost of better planning.

21   Parliamentary Control of Finance*

Norman Ward

Parliamentary Control of Finance, both in theory and as it works particularly in the United Kingdom, has been described with admirable lucidity by many well-known authorities,[1] and it is not the purpose of this introduction to do more than recapitulate the main principles, and the essentials of contemporary Canadian practice.

Underlying all the others are two principles, both of which have to be supported by a number of subsidiary principles and practices:

   (i) The executive should have no income which is not granted to it, or otherwise sanctioned, by Parliament.

   (ii) The executive should make no expenditures except those approved by Parliament, in ways approved by Parliament.

The observance of these principles would be impossible were it not for the existence of a variety of rules, customs, devices and institutions, in all of which principle and practice are impossible to separate, for the practices have meaning only because they are based on principles. Among these various rules, etc., the essential ones are[2]

1. There is a budget (using the word in its widest sense to mean, in effect, "a financial plan") which brings together all the government's financial needs in such a way as to give everyone concerned a clear, unified picture of what is involved.

2. The plan is prepared annually; that is, Parliament does not grant the executive permanent rights to spend money, but (with a few exceptions) requires it to obtain a fresh sanction to spend money each year, and for stated purposes. Money voted for a year, but not spent, lapses.

3. The preparation of the budget is an executive function, and so is the subsequent spending of public funds which are made available to the executive.

4. Parliament has the right to debate and criticize the budget fully, both as it affects past or current executive activities, and the executive's proposals for future spending.

---

* Reprinted with permission of author and publisher from Norman Ward, *The Public Purse*, University of Toronto Press, Toronto, 1955.

1 See e.g. Samuel H. Beer, *Treasury Control*, Oxford, 1956; Basil Chubb, *The Control of Public Expenditure*, Oxford, 1952; A. J. V. Durell, *The Principles and Practice of the System of Control over Parliamentary Grants*, London, 1917; Paul Einzig, *The Control of the Purse*, London, 1959; Sir Ivor Jennings, *Parliament*, 3rd ed., Cambridge, 1957; and *Cabinet Government*, 3rd ed., Cambridge, 1959; and references therein. The only comparable book on Canadian affairs is the *Audit Office Guide*, Queen's Printer, Ottawa, 1958, which is naturally written from a particular point of view. See also Lloyd D. Musolf, *Public Ownership and Accountability: The Canadian Experience*, Cambridge, Mass., 1959.

2 See W. C. Clark, "Financial Administration of the Government of Canada", *Canadian Journal of Economics and Political Science*, Vol. 4, 1938, p. 393.

5. The executive is responsible not only for all financial planning, but also for any changes made in it as a result of parliamentary discussion. (This principle is one of the essential differences between Canadian parliamentary and American congressional government.)

6. The executive must account fully to Parliament for its management of public funds, both receipts and expenditures.

7. An independent auditor, responsible only to Parliament, audits the accounts, and his reports are promptly made available to Parliament.

8. Finally, Parliament itself audits the accounts of both revenues and expenditures, in almost any way it chooses; parliamentary surveillance, that is, is as loose or rigid, or as selective or comprehensive, as Parliament desires.

These several principles and practices, as they are applied in Canada today, can be described in a remarkably few words, considering the enormous complexity of governmental operations. Each year the proposals for next year's expenditures begin in each department, where they are prepared, often with the assistance of officials from the Treasury Board staff, in accordance with rules and forms laid down originally by custom but more immediately in accordance with a manual provided by the Treasury Board. In each department the proposals work their way upward from lesser dignitaries to the minister, who may himself make some changes or additions to them. From the minister the proposals go to the Treasury Board, a financial subcommittee of the cabinet which has risen from modest beginnings to enjoy a more pervasive influence over the preparations of plans for spending money than any other part of the Dominion administration. When the proposals have been scrutinized by the Treasury Board, they go to the cabinet for final approval. The large document which receives the cabinet's approval is "the estimates".

The estimates, by now a detailed list of proposals to spend money, neatly divided off into several hundred separate items, or votes, are presented to Parliament nowadays as early in a session as possible. The executive alone can present estimates, and recommend the expenditure of the relevant money to Parliament, in the name of the Crown. Parliament passes each item in the estimates separately, and each item limits the executive to spending no more than the amount of money named in the vote, for the purpose described. Parliament approves each vote in one of its most celebrated committees of the whole House of Commons, the Committee of Supply; sometimes, nowadays, after some of the estimates have been scrutinized by one of several standing committees. In its other well-known committee of the whole, the Committee of Ways and Means, the House of Commons debates and approves the government's proposals for raising the money to be spent. Parliament subsequently passes, in the ordinary way, appropriation bills which legally make available to the executive the moneys listed in the estimates.

After Parliament has passed the estimates and the necessary legislation, the process of spending public money (which is actually a continuous process, the executive, as will be explained, starting to spend each year's money before Parliament has finished voting all of it) reverts to the executive, which has naturally been responsible for the passage of all relevant business through the House of Commons. The spending function is centralized in the Department of Finance: just as there is one vast fund, the consolidated revenue fund, into which all public money goes (with a few clearly defined exceptions mostly connected with the independent commissions and Crown corporations), all outgoing money (with similar exceptions) is effectively channelled through a single office for approval before it can legally be spent. The Comptroller of the Treasury, an official in the Department of Finance, is responsible for auditing all public expenditures *before* they are made, and none can legally be made without his certificate of approval; his task, in essence, is to ensure that all money is spent as Parliament said it should be, in no larger amounts and for no other purposes than Parliament has approved.

The Comptroller of the Treasury is obviously in a strategic position to keep the public accounts, and he does. The accounts, which are subjected to a post-audit (that is, *after* expenditures have been made) by the Auditor General on behalf of Parliament, are published with the Auditor General's report and, like the estimates, are promptly tabled in Parliament by the Minister of Finance. The fiscal year runs from April 1 to March 31, and the public accounts must, by law, be presented to Parliament by December 31 or, if Parliament is not in session, within fifteen days after it begins to sit.

What Parliament does with the public accounts and the Auditor General's report (which, though separate documents, were bound together from 1943 to 1960) is not laid down by any statute, and in Canada depends entirely on custom and, at any one time, the whims of members of Parliament. Ideally, the House of Commons, through a committee on public accounts, should thoroughly scrutinize the accounts and especially the Auditor General's report, and complete the cycle of parliamentary control by commenting thereon, and receiving replies, in some way, to its comments.

In one sense, it will be perceived, the process of spending public money begins and ends with the executive, which plans the expenditures, takes responsibility for piloting the plans through Parliament, and subsequently carries the plans out. In a more important sense, the process begins and ends with Parliament. Most of the steps followed by the executive would have no legal sanction if it were not for Parliament, and the last words on the spending process belong to Parliament's officer, the Auditor General, and ultimately to Parliament itself.

Parliamentary control of finance assumes a close liaison between the legislative and executive branches of government, and like any chain of command is no stronger than its weakest link. As the foregoing outline suggests, the Canadian system of control (which in its operation has been so unlike the British on which it is theoretically modelled that many apparently useful comparisons are in reality irrelevant) relies on a series of documents and practices, all of which have had to be developed, starting from an initial acceptance of the principles involved, and ending pragmatically with the invention of something satisfactory to Parliament. There are several points at which the process could break down if the required devices disappeared or were suddenly modified. The preparation of the original estimates in the departments, for instance, is now systematized, and closely watched by officers of the Treasury Board; the House of Commons, for most of its history, appears to have had a profound faith in the preparation of the estimates. Yet if the Department of Finance were to become inefficient or corrupt, or merely to return to the happy-go-lucky outlook which characterized public spending down to at least the 1920's, that part of parliamentary control which depends on the estimating process would be dangerously weakened, if not destroyed. Parliamentary control would clearly be weakened if all departments consistently over-estimated their requirements, and destroyed if the departments consistently spent more money than had been voted to them. The Comptroller of the Treasury, whose post was created in 1931, is obviously another officer with enormous responsibilities, and the necessity that the Minister of Finance be a man of both probity and ability need only be mentioned for its importance to become at once apparent.

On the parliamentary side, there are two major institutions (apart from the House of Commons itself) which have dominated the history of financial control: the Committee of Supply, or committee of the whole House, in which the expenditure of money is authorized in detail; and the Committee on Public Accounts, which is Parliament's own auditing committee, and thus becomes of significance after the appropriated money has been spent. Weaknesses in either of these devices are patently weaknesses in parliamentary control of finance, and the same is true of the Audit Office. Parliament needs, also, three major documents which must be not only accurate, but intelligible to laymen: the estimates, the public accounts, and the Auditor General's report. All three of these have at times presented serious problems, and on occasion they are still complained about by members, though now rarely.

22 The Budget and Its Function*

Herbert R. Balls

"The nineteenth century idea of a sound budgetary policy," wrote Paul Einzig, "was that its aim was to be simply to keep down expenditure, cover it with the aid of taxation, and, if possible, produce a revenue surplus for

* Reprinted with permission of author and publisher from *Cost and Management*, Vol. 41, October 1967, pp. 25-28.

the gradual reduction of the public debt."[1] Sir Courtenay Ilbert's description of the United Kingdom budget was an accurate description of the Canadian budget until the 1930s:

> Once in every year, usually soon after Easter, the chancellor of the exchequer makes his budget statement in the committee of ways and means. He reviews the finance of the past year, comparing estimated with actual results, and then estimates his requirements for the current or forthcoming year, and explains the mode in which he proposes to raise revenue for meeting them. In so doing he always tries to make as close an approximation as possible between estimated revenue and estimated expenditure. If the estimated revenue on the existing basis is more than sufficient to meet estimated expenditure, he may be in a position to remit or reduce taxes. If it is insufficient he may have to increase existing taxes or impose new taxes.[2]

In his budget speech, delivered in the House of Commons on May 1, 1936, the Minister of Finance, the Hon. Charles A. Dunning, accepted this doctrine as the ultimate, if not the immediate, aim of his policy. After stating that it would not be feasible to achieve a complete balancing of the budget immediately, he enunciated the government's budgetary and fiscal policy:

> What we can and must do is to make an immediate, appreciable approach to a balanced budget as the first step in a definite, positive program which will assure the attaining of our final objective within a limited period.[3]

Following World War II, with the firm intention of preventing any future recurrence of massive unemployment such as had occurred in the 1930s, the Canadian government, in 1945, issued a White Paper on Employment and Income. In it, the government adopted a "high and stable level of employment and income, . . ." as a major aim of government policy. Recognizing that such an aim could only be achieved if the government were prepared to run surpluses or deficits as the economy required, with a balanced budget only being achieved over a period of more than a year, it stated:

> The government will be prepared, in periods when unemployment threatens, to incur the deficits and increases in the national debt resulting from its employment and income policy, whether that policy in the circumstances is best applied through increased expenditures or reduced taxation. In periods of buoyant employment and income, budget plans will call for surpluses. The government's policy will be to keep the national debt within manageable proportions and maintain a proper balance in its budget over a period longer than a single year.[4]

1 Paul Einzig, *How Money is Managed*, Penguin Books, Baltimore, Maryland, 1954, p. 245.
2 Sir Courtenay Ilbert, *Parliament, Its History, Constitution and Practice*, Home University Library, no date, p. 105.
3 Budget Speech delivered by Hon. Chas. A. Dunning, Minister of Finance . . . in the House of Commons, May 1, 1936, p. 24.
4 *Employment and Income with Special Reference to the Initial Period of Reconstruction*, Ottawa, 1945.

The Keynesian revolution in economic thought in the depression years of the 1930s and during World War II had led to a change in the role of the budget in government finance, as reflected in these two statements made less than ten years apart. From a relatively simple process of adjusting income to outgo, it became an increasingly sophisticated system of planning and control, not only for government activities but for the economy as a whole. It is this dual system that I propose to describe.

System of Planning and Control

The federal budget is both a process and a document or, more accurately, a series of processes and documents. The budget processes are the procedures whereby the government's financial proposals for both revenue and expenditures are formulated, considered and ultimately laid before the House of Commons.[5] The budget speech is the culmination of that process, wherein the "whole range of the government's financial programs and policies is brought into a single focus. In presenting a report of the operations of the fiscal year just ended or ending, it marks the completion of one budgetary period. In setting out the financial plans and programs for the next fiscal year, it marks the commencement of the new budgetary period or cycle. It is thus, on the one hand, a backward-looking review in which the plans and expectations of the previous year are reviewed and compared with the actual outturn. On the other hand, it is a forward-looking survey or projection in which the hopes, plans and expectations for the ensuing year are developed. In this latter aspect, it is the culmination and crystallization of a continuing year-round process in which all the complex and often conflicting considerations that enter into the development of budgetary policy are resolved. On the one hand, the program requirements of the spending departments are under day-to-day scrutiny by departmental officials working in close cooperation with officials of the Treasury Board. On the other, the revenue potentialities of existing taxes, together with proposals for new taxes or for changes in existing taxes and tax machinery, are constantly reviewed by officials of the Departments of Finance and National Revenue in the light of representations received from interested individuals and groups and of goverment policy generally.

The Annual Estimates of Expenditure and the Budget Papers

The budget speech is the culmination of the budget process but, for a full appreciation of the government's budgetary program and its implications, it is necessary to give some attention to two other sets of documents. The first consists of the annual estimates of expenditure. The main estimates, which set out in considerable detail the government's basic expenditure program

---

5 A. Kenneth Eaton, *Essays on Taxation*, Canadian Tax Foundation, Toronto, 1966, p. 19 f. H. R. Balls, "Key Steps in Preparing the Budget", *The Canadian Chartered Accountant*, December 1956.

for the year, are tabled in the House of Commons by the president of the Treasury Board, usually in January or February, several weeks before the budget is brought down.

Inevitably, there are some requirements which cannot be foreseen or estimated accurately when the main estimates are under consideration. There are others which arise out of new legislation passed by Parliament or as a result of programs approved by the government after the content of the main estimates has been settled. Consequently, supplementary estimates are submitted to Parliament, usually several weeks before the summer adjournment or prorogation. Further supplementary estimates are introduced two or three weeks before the end of the fiscal year. These are to provide funds for programs, the requirements of which were under-estimated when the estimates were prepared some months before. They also authorize reimbursement to Crown corporations and various government accounts for deficits or losses sustained when these cannot be determined in time or accurately enough to be included in the main or supplementary estimates.

The second set of documents is the "budget papers." These have assumed greater significance since their introduction in 1939, and it is now customary for the Minister to table them for the information of Parliament a day or so before he delivers his budget speech. The budget papers consist of two parts: a general review of economic conditions for the preceding calendar year, with preliminary estimates of, and brief comments on, the more significant economic statistics or indicators; and a preliminary report on the government's accounts and financial operations for the fiscal year just ended or ending, with statements of revenues, expenditures, assets, liabilities, cash and debt transactions.

With the budget papers in the hands of members, it is no longer necessary for the Minister of Finance to review in detail in his budget speech the economic conditions prevailing in the country during the past year or to discuss at length the financial operations of the government during the preceding year. It is customary for him, however, to review briefly the international economic situation and major domestic economic developments.

A short section of the speech is usually devoted to a summary report on the government's accounts. The actual revenues and expenditures and surplus or deficit for the year are compared with the forecasts given in the budget speech of the preceding year. There are brief references to the government's non-budgetary transactions and the overall effect of budgetary and non-budgetary operations on the government's cash and debit position. The Minister then proceeds to give a forecast of the probable financial requirements for the year ahead. This takes into account the main estimates which are already before the House and makes allowances for supplementary and further supplementary estimates to come and the probable lapsing or underspending in some appropriations. Since 1964, it has also been customary to translate the budget into terms of the national economic accounts, into terms of its impact on the economy.

After calculating the budgetary surplus or deficit, the Minister outlines what he considers is the appropriate tax policy for the ensuing year. He announces his proposals for increases or reductions in taxes and customs tariffs. If no changes are proposed, all existing tax rates and customs tariffs remain in effect since it is unnecessary to re-enact the tax laws each year. If changes are proposed in commodity taxes or in the customs tariff, they are usually made effective immediately by having the revelant tax laws, when enacted, apply retroactively to the date of the speech. This prevents taxpayers from avoiding the effect of tax or tariff increases by heavy buying during the period between the budget speech and the enactment of the legislation.

At the close of his address, the Minister tables the formal resolutions for changes in existing tax rates and customs tariffs, giving notice of the amendments which the government intends to seek. In accordance with parliamentary procedure, these must precede the introduction of money bills.

Purposes of the Budget

The budget is a multi-purpose document, designed not only to facilitate the planning and control of government activities, but also the planning and control of the national economy. As a means of planning and controlling government activities, the budget presents:

1. an accounting or financial review of the government's own domestic economy;
2. a statement of the government's expenditure program for the ensuing year, and a forecast of government revenues available to finance that program; and
3. an analysis of the government's overall cash and borrowing requirements.

As an *accounting or financial review* of the government's own domestic economy, the budget is essentially a housekeeping report of the government's operations for the past fiscal year. In the budget speech and in the section of the budget papers dealing with the government's accounts, there are preliminary reports on the government's revenues and expenditures for the year and the resulting surplus or deficit; the principal changes in the government's assets and liabilities during the year; the cash available at the beginning of the fiscal year to pay the government's current obligations; the additional cash that was required to meet the needs of government during the fiscal year; and the steps that were taken to ensure that sufficient cash resources were available to meet those needs.

A second purpose of the budget is to present *a statement of the government's expenditure program* for the coming year *and a forecast of government revenues* on the basis of existing and proposed taxes and tax rates available to finance that program. The Minister of Finance usually devotes a considerable part of his budget speech to his tax proposals, but the expenditure estimates are also an integral part of the budget process.

The Expenditure Program

The expenditure program for the year is presented to the House when the main estimates are tabled, usually some weeks before budget day. Consequently, relatively little mention of prospective expenditures is made in the budget. The main estimates, however, contain, in considerable detail, the basic spending plans of the government. When these are placed before the House, they are usually accompanied by a statement from the president of the Treasury Board indicating the government's expenditure policy and the basic proposals contained in the estimates.

For the revenues, however, it is customary for the Minister of Finance to present a forecast of anticipated collections by each tax source on the basis of existing and proposed rates and in the light of the expected performance of the economy.

As *an analysis of the government's cash and borrowing requirements*, the budget presents a forecast of the probable financial needs for the ensuing year on both budgetary and non-budgetary account. In estimating the expenditure side of the budget, account is taken of the main estimates that are already before the House. Allowances are made for supplementary and further supplementary estimates to come and probable lapsing or underspending in some appropriations. On the revenue side, an estimate is made of the expected budgetary revenues on the basis of existing taxes and in the light of assumed economic conditions. This is adjusted to take account of the tax changes announced in the budget. Taking into consideration the estimated budgetary surplus or deficit so determined and the net extra-budgetary cash requirements for loans and other disbursements on the one hand, and net receipts from the various annuity, insurance and superannuation accounts and the repayment of loans on the other, an estimate is given of the net amount that is expected to be available for debt reduction or to be obtained by additional borrowing.

Budget Exerts Economic Influence

For many years, the planning and control of government activities constituted the main purpose of the annual budget presentation. However, as the operations of government expanded and as government revenues and expenditures became an ever-increasing proportion of the gross national product, the budget came to be recognized for the influence it could exert, by its sheer size, on the economy. Subsequently, it was found that the budget could be used deliberately to direct that influence to assist in achieving and maintaining the economic objectives of government policy.

As a system of planning and control for the economy, the budget fulfils three functions.

1. As an *economic review*, the budget is an economic weather report of the past year — primarily for Canada but also for the world economy generally and for those nations with which Canada and Canadians do business.

As a survey of the forces at work in the economy or in particular segments of the economy during the year, the budget speech and the budget papers present a wealth of pertinent information.

2. As *a forecast of the economic climate,* the budget indicates the conditions under which government and business may expect to operate during the coming year. This is customarily a short part of the budget speech. The usual practice is, after reviewing the state of the economy during the current year, to indicate the prospects for the coming year and the basis on which the budget policy and tax proposals are developed.

3. An important function of the budget speech is its role as *a statement of the fiscal, economic and tax policies of the government* in the light of all the foregoing considerations and of the government's proposals for tax changes. It is hard to overemphasize the importance of this aspect of the speech; to appreciate it fully, it would be necessary to read a budget speech and budget papers in their entirety.

23   The Program Budget: Planning and Control for the Public Sector*

P. L. Little
C. L. Mitchell

Elements of a Program Budget

"1. Definition of the 'program' (broad project) in terms of the specific results or outputs desired.

2. Identification of alternative methods.

3. Comparison of costs between methods.

4. Development of methods for appraising effectiveness in achieving desired results.

5. Organization of information for continuous comparison of results with costs.

6. Facilitation of revision of plans and programs."

To a student of business administration, this definition of program budgeting which appeared in a recent C.E.D. booklet[1] would appear to be little more than a collection of well-established management and control

* Reprinted with permission of authors and publisher from *Cost and Management,* Vol. 41, September 1967, pp. 22-26.
1 Committee for Economic Development, *Budgeting for National Objectives,* January 1966, p. 34.

principles. In the realm of government management, however, the application of sound cost-effective planning and control procedures to expenditure programs has lagged seriously behind the pace set by business. Hence the public administrator, unlike his colleague in the firm, is likely to regard program budgeting as being quite revolutionary.

Program budgeting is a concept born of necessity — the increasing necessity for greater effectiveness in government spending. Governments have grown spectacularly, and each year more projects compete for the public investment dollar. The aim of program budgeting is to ensure that competition does indeed take place, and that analytical tools are used in the design and control of expenditure programs to reveal the cheapest and *most effective* method of performing public functions.

The Development of the Program Budget

It is generally accepted that program budgeting, even though it is an ill-defined and over-defined concept, should be adopted by governments as soon as possible to ensure effective spending.

In this paper, the program budget will be examined from the viewpoint of a business administrator. It will be considered first as a planning device, and then as a control technique for (investment) activity in the public sector. If we are to appreciate fully the need for a program budget, we should first examine the traditional process of public budgeting. Since the U.S. federal government has pioneered the application of program budgeting, its practices have been used as our principal point of reference.

Weakness of Traditional Public Budgeting

The basic problem of current budgeting in the U.S. is that it is carried out exclusively "from the bottom up." Each year the executive agencies, sub-agencies and administrative sub-divisions submit estimates of their financial requirements up the line — eventually to the President's office where they are summarized into a budget. One weakness of this approach is that it encourages each sub-division to continue its traditional activities undisturbed while seeking to extend its operations. "Such self-interest should be controlled . . . agency activities should regularly be subjected to a searching review to see that they *conform with* broad national goals and basic governmental objectives."[2] At present this is not done: "Traditional scrutinization consists of reviewing proposed increases in objects of expenditures, with particular emphasis on personnel of various grades, supplies, etc."[3]

At first glance, criticizing any budgeting process because it is done "from the bottom up" would appear to be questionable. Any basic accounting text points out that the responsibility centre that incurs the expense should

---

2 *Ibid*, p. 27.
3 David Novick (ed.), *Program Budgeting: Program Analysis and the Federal Budget*, Harvard University Press, Cambridge, Massachusetts, 1965.

be responsible for budgeting it for the next period. But a basic text also tells us this: "... several members of top management should oversee the work of preparing the budget. This committee will *set the general guidelines* that the organization is to follow, coordinate the various budgets prepared by the organization units and resolve differences among them..."[4] In other words, (a) budgeting should take as its terms of reference a statement of objectives established on higher levels and (b) top management should pilot the many components of the final budget towards those objectives.

Because it is "spending-unit-oriented" rather than "broad-objective-oriented," the U.S. federal budget has many serious inadequacies as an overall basis for rational decision-making and as a planning-control device. The federal budget places too much emphasis on detail and too little on coordination between spending units. It lacks quantitative goals and expresses little interest in long-range planning. As a result, the budget is not helpful to the planner attempting to allocate scarce public resources among competing agencies or projects.

A New Planning Device

In a recent speech, President Johnson made a statement of purpose that seems to include all the essential components of good planning:

> Once in operation, (program budgeting) will enable us to:
> 1. Identify our national goals with precision and on a continuing basis.
> 2. Choose among those goals the ones which are most urgent.
> 3. Search for alternative means of reaching those goals most effectively and at the least cost.
> 4. Inform ourselves not merely on next year's costs but on the second, third, and subsequent years' costs of our programs.
> 5. Measure the performance of our programs to insure a dollar's worth of service for each dollar spent.[5]

When we get into the details of the program budget, we note that there are many characteristics which mark it revolutionary for government planning. The most basic feature is that it is predicated on activities or "programs" rather than on agencies. Ideally, the program budget will not take an individual government department as its basis of reference. Already, to some extent, programs are being budgeted and appraised on their own merit and on their effectiveness in promoting national goals or objectives (e.g., such as a large flood control project or a big educational expenditure). Except in rare cases, however, budgeting and appraisal have taken place historically within the limits of existing bureaus and departments. Hence it is the agency, and not the program, that is evaluated and for which appropriations are made. It is obvious that programs of different government

---

[4] R. N. Anthony, *Management Accounting: Text and Cases*, 3 ed., Irwin, Homewood, Illinois, 1964, p. 396.

[5] Committee for Economic Development, *Budgeting for National Objectives*, January 1966, p. 22.

agencies can, and do, overlap and interact. Until public expenditure activities are appraised on a very broad basis and the roles of the various agencies are laid down and coordinated, it is clear that "program" budgeting is not being effected.

This most fundamental characteristic of program budgeting is the essential framework from which many other planning factors spring. Initially, the range of the budget or expenditure period is tailored to the program. A program which will entail either benefits or expenditures for 25 years, for example, can be evaluated and hence, budgeted, for that period. We shall see later how the program budget, acting as a control device, attempts by periodic review to keep a program on budget throughout this planning range. To have a basis for planning beyond the traditional one-year budget is, of course, imperative. Today, in fact, most public projects do demand long lead times. It is ridiculous, for example, to appropriate funds for a hydro electric project each year of a six or seven-year construction period. Attention is focussed on the details of each year's expenses and the budget consists of little more than a statement (rather than a total plan) of such expenses and details.

What effective planning presupposes is a conscious attempt to lay out *total* expenditures and an effort to review and abide by such guidelines each year of the program.

The third characteristic of the program budget as a planning device is the emphasis it lays upon, first, broad national goals; and second, fairly specific objectives stated in quantitative terms. The latter, more definite, aims are set in conjunction with the former broader ones. Ideally, a proposed program is set up so as to contribute to some rather broad national purposes.

At this point, the program budget demands that a substantial set of *alternatives* be developed for achieving or at least aiming at the chosen goal. Searching and sophisticated techniques of quantitative analysis are used to reduce each alternative method, as much as possible, to common *numerical* terms. On the basis of cost-utility or cost-benefit comparisons, the most efficient and effective overall plan is chosen. Indeed, this "cost-effective" analysis must be applied to all components of the overall plan where *any* alternative method is possible. By thus "programming," the best way of spending public money can be determined. The "best" way might be that which achieves a quantitative goal at least cost, or that alternative which, at a standard cost, brings about the greatest benefit, again quantitatively measured.

It is difficult to describe the formal "raison-d'être" of a cost-effective approach to government planning. In a free society, the business firm has little difficulty in establishing precise, quantitative efficiency "yardsticks" to aim at and be measured by. Rare is the policy which cannot be examined against alternatives on the basis of return on investment or incremental profit/sales, etc. The competitive market supplies the corporate manager with a ready-made set of goals and costs, both of which are financial.

The government official, on the other hand, must find it very difficult to quantify his objectives, especially in financial terms. Not only are government goals more qualitative than quantitative in nature, but quite often the public sector is concerned with measures of prevention rather than with affirmative gains to the nation. For example, it is very difficult to compute the value of crime prevention, protection from disease, or military defence systems. More difficult again is the task of trading them off, one against the other, as program budgeting may require. It is entirely different from, say, computing the long-range return on investment that might result from building a shoe factory in Yellowknife.

This introduces us to the field of "value analysis," a practice for attaching financial value to benefits, both direct and indirect, accruing from an otherwise intangible investment program. This area will not be considered extensively here.[6] It should be noted, however, that realistic value analysis which purports to simulate market conditions and attach market prices for and to public investments, should obviously precede any serious attempt to use cost-effective program budgeting techniques.

A Potential Control Process

The planning and control processes of any organization are inextricably linked. Although program budgeting as a planning device has been well covered in the previous section, a separate examination of the concept as a control process may be useful.

The importance of gearing programs towards clearly-stated (and quantitatively-stated) goals has been emphasized. For the program budget, this is an essential step in planning. The effectiveness of the program budget hinges, however, on how well the budget is administered each year, i.e., how alert the control process is in evaluating progress and appraising results. Effective execution is no less important than effective planning.

The program budget adopts the corporate principles of flexible budgeting, frequent regular analysis and review of progress. Traditional U.S. federal budget practices involve merely the revision of estimates, during October, for the next nine months. Such revision, of course, relates only to the individual agency, not to the broader concept of a program or an objective.

It has been noted that analytical tools such as cost-benefit and capital budgeting techniques are an important part of the planning side of the program budget. As a control device, the program budget, again, gives far greater scope for the use of management science techniques to (1) design

---

[6] R. M. McKean, *Efficiency in Government Through Systems Analysis*, pp. 1-154, gives the reader an indication of the need for "value analysis" in measuring benefits to be derived from such public projects as hydro dams and flood control.

G. D. Quirin, *The Capital Expenditure Decision*, Irwin, Homewood, Illinois, and Toronto, 1967, Chapters 7 and 8, gives very good treatment of the problem of measuring "unmarketed benefits".

and operate an efficient information system and to (2) analyze critically data as they are reported.

Numerous techniques are presently used by business to deal with these two types of program management problems. The techniques include standard flexible budgeting practices, management accounting techniques, variance analysis, critical path method, PERT, Gantt charting and scheduling.

Incorporation of such methods into program review and execution is one of the most essential characteristics of the program budget. Whereas control amounted traditionally to mere yearly cost cutting, agency by agency, it is increasingly becoming the exact, scientific process that business has used for some time.

After a program has been executed, one element of control still remains — final performance evaluation. It is at this stage that control becomes planning again. The review should attempt to determine how valuable the contribution of each executive agency or program element was to the final program result and to the higher national objectives. A searching review should then be made to determine just how effective the type of program just completed has been in contributing to the agency's stated objectives. Review techniques such as this emphasize how greatly priorities can change over the course of a program. Identification of opportunities for revision in the future is the least that might be expected.

Finally, the program budget offers a reliable means of reviewing "executive performance." Governments can never aspire to the quality of control and executive evaluation made possible to business through responsibility accounting and "profit centres." The parameters of public spending do not lend themselves to such analysis. But, just as it should be possible to analyze quantitatively programs and components of programs in terms of contributions to objectives, it should also be possible to evaluate the men responsible. Advocates of program budgeting herald the opportunity it provides to compare agency performance, hence agency management, on the basis of objectives achieved in relation to dollars spent.

Implementation of Program Budgeting

Current Use

Although the term "program budget" is heard quite frequently today, the use of this concept is still most limited. Nor is this difficult to understand: the lead time for implementing such a revolutionary planning/control device in even one executive agency would be considerable. Moreover, traditionalists can be expected to buck the program budget relentlessly.

U.S. Department of Defence

The U.S. Department of Defence, headed since 1961 by Robert McNamara, has initiated and developed most of the characteristics of the program budget, both in the control and planning stages.

In the past, the secretary of defence prepared the budget first by bringing the overall expenditure into line with the administration's fiscal policy. He then divided the proposed appropriations among the three military departments, which were left to allocate funds as they desired. Understandably, each sought to garner a larger future share by concentrating on dramatic new weapons. The budget was projected for one year and was clearly not coordinated among the departments. No provision was made for relating the elements of the budget to overall planning.

Functional or mission-oriented budgeting is now the order of the day. "The new program budget procedures have two primary aims; first to permit analysis of total force structures for all of the services in terms of *common* missions or national objectives, second, to project the financial requirements of the proposed force structures over an extended period of years."[7] For example, the Navy's Polaris System is identified as an *element* of the Strategic Retaliatory Forces Program and now must *compete* for finances against other elements of the Strategic Forces such as Titan (Army) and Minuteman (Air Force). This is in contrast to the previous rationale which put Polaris, for example, in "competition" with other Navy programs only — each having *quite different objectives* (e.g., Sealift, Home Defence Forces, Retaliatory Forces). Moreover, examination is done today over a five-year horizon.

The U.S. Department of Defence has identified major programs under eight main headings (e.g., Strategic Retaliatory Forces) and each program is broken into hundreds of program elements (e.g., B-52 Fleet) and sub-elements. All costs (direct and indirect) associated with each element are allocated to it and the element is related to national security objectives. Program elements competing for inclusion in the same program are then traded off against each other on the basis of cost-utility or benefit-cost comparisons. The rationale of such analysis was described previously.

It has been the use of the program budget as a *control device* that has attracted publicity for McNamara and his department. In fact, the press and various authors seem to have equated the program budgeting of the Department of Defence with the employment of management science techniques to control costs. Program budgeting, however, can hardly be written off as simply a scientific means of cost control; McNamara's "control" takes in far more than expense cutting. *Efficiency* in this context is not necessarily foreign to the traditional practices of the U.S. Department of Defence nor, for that matter, to any government bureau. What is revolutionary though is the emphasis on *effectiveness*, i.e., the extent to which program *costs are bringing about well established goals*. As Robert Anthony puts it, "Effectiveness is always *related to* the organization's *goals*. Efficiency per se is not related to the goals. An efficient manager is one who does whatever he does with the lowest consumption of resources; but if what he does (i.e., his output) is an inadequate contribution to the accomplishment of the

---

7 David Novick, "Program Budgeting", *Program Analysis and the Federal Budget*, A Rand Corporation Sponsored Study, Washington, 1965, p. 203.

organization's goals, then he is ineffective."[8] Scientific techniques that apply to this type of "cost effectiveness" rather than to "cost control" are key components in the "McNamara Revolution" in its true sense.

An Imperative for Canada?

The reverberations of program budgeting have long since reached our national government in Ottawa. It is not strange that the publicity given the McNamara efforts has initiated some self-analysis on the part of Canadian government departments and agencies.

There is a very real danger that our government, while trying to emulate a most popular movement in the U.S., might be misunderstanding, misinterpreting, and grossly underselling the true precepts of program budgeting.

It is clearly the influence of the program budget that has inspired recent crusades to Ottawa by management consultants, chiefly of the operations research variety. They have been sounding off to a great extent on what they could and should be doing for public management. The consultant senses the pressure on our national government to update its operations and, at the same time, sees a lush market for himself. Another indication that our government realizes the need to catch up with private business techniques is the amount and type of staffing currently being done. One constantly hears that the Canadian government is, like McNamara, bringing along its own "whiz kids" in a wide range of technical areas.

Certainly no one can discredit the efforts of our government and many others to *increase efficiency* and improve methods through scientific techniques. It is unfortunate, however, that these efforts are often naively compared with the advanced thinking of U.S. program budgeters.

At present there seems to be little evidence that true program budgeting is seriously being considered in Canada. Our annual budget is written in terms of departments, not in terms of programs integrated to achieve long-term goals. Our budget is still a series of year-to-year appropriations and a "description of cost cutting" rather than an embodiment of a rational plan. Admittedly, the U.S. budget is still written up on this basis. The President, however, has committed himself to some form of program budget by 1969.

It will likely be a long time before Canada adopts or considers adopting a program budget as it is understood in the U.S. John Meyer[9] notes that "recognizing efficiency" as a goal might be the first step. I disagree. Efficiency, rather than effectiveness, is already a considerable goal of our government. More important would be an effort to appropriate funds in terms of specific goals and desired outputs instead of on any agency basis. Secondly, perhaps one of the most important imperatives of the program budget is to place the emphasis on identifying *alternative means of achieving the goal of a program.*

---

[8] R. N. Anthony, J. Dearden and R. F. Vancil, *Management Control Systems*, pp. 168-9.
[9] Novick, *op. cit.*, p. 18.

These are the two basic steps that we must look for in our government's budgetary process before we can say that program budgeting has started. Cost comparisons, appraisal, development of control techniques and the other measures we have examined can only *follow* these two basic characteristics.

24   The Treasury Board

A. A. Sterns

When on September 27, 1960, Her Majesty commissioned J. Grant Glassco, Robert Watson Sellar and F. Eugene Therrien to inquire into the government organization, and specifically directed the Commissioners "to report upon steps that may be taken for the purpose of improving efficiency and economy by alterations in the relations between government departments and agencies on the one hand and the Treasury Board . . . on the other,[1] a new era was opened up.

The Glassco Report first dealt with a "Plan for Management" in which it stressed that "the needs for effective management fall into two general categories: first, those associated with the administration of departmental operations; and second, those involved in the central direction and co-ordination of government activities as a whole".[2] It acknowledged that central management had been progressively delegated by the Cabinet to the Treasury Board, but it pointed out two handicaps under which the Board had laboured: first that the Ministers of the Board, especially the Minister of Finance as its Chairman, had heavy departmental responsibilities in addition to Board duties, and, second, that the 16,000 annual submissions to the Board contained mostly time-consuming routine matters.

The Glassco Commission came to the following conclusions:

> that the Treasury Board should be strengthened by having
> its own presiding Minister; the Minister of Finance should be
> relieved of this office but remain an *ex officio* member of the
> Board;
> that the Secretary of the Board should be elevated to
> a position equal to that of a deputy minister;
> that the Treasury Board staff be severed from that of
> the Department of Finance, and,
> that the Privy Council Office and Treasury Board

---

1 The Royal Commission on Government Organization, *Report*, Vol. 1, Queen's Printer, Ottawa, 1962, Preface.
2 *Ibid.*, p. 48.

Office should be physically joined — which would mean two deputy ministers within the Privy Council Office, the Clerk being concerned in main with policy, and the Secretary with the functions of administrative direction.[3]

In effect, the Commission designed the following plan of central authority:

GENERAL PLAN OF CENTRAL AUTHORITY

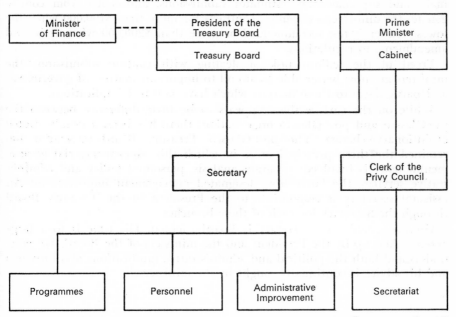

From 1962 to 1967, the recommendations of the Glassco Commission affecting the Treasury Board were carefully researched and evaluated. A committee made up of senior deputy ministers met regularly and made recommendations to the government. The amendments to the Financial Administration Act as proclaimed on October 1, 1966, reflect these recommendations: Section 3(2) creates a President of the Treasury Board; Section 4(2) gives the Secretary of the Treasury Board the rank of deputy minister and Section 4(3) creates the legal machinery to build up separate Treasury Board staff.

Constitutionally, the new organizational changes have made little difference. The Governor-in-Council still determines which of its powers are to be exercised by the Treasury Board. The Board continues to be simply a committee of the Council. True, there were discussions about making the Board an entity distinct in law but they were turned down by the Cabinet.

---

3 *Ibid.*, pp. 55-56.

Though the Treasury Board is a committee of Cabinet, it is very seldom that the Cabinet reverses decisions of the Board.

The reorganization did not change patterns in the weekly meetings of the Board but the agenda was cut down and routine matters no longer reach the ministers. Thus during the first quarter of 1968 only 209 of 1,869 departmental submissions were considered by meetings of the Board. The remainder were resolved by the staff. A Treasury Board manual lists 22 types of submissions which must be seen by the ministers. Among these are main and supplementary estimates submissions, allotments from contingencies for unforeseen expenses, contracts for more than $100,000 when the lowest tender is not recommended or more than $200,000 when it is, and amendments to regulations.

Freed of the tedious task of dealing with routine submissions the ministers are now better able to attend to important matters of government and particularly to those matters which have political implications.

While on the surface there appears to be little difference between the pre-Glassco and post-Glassco organization, there has been a deeply rooted evolutionary change. The post-Glassco Treasury Board secretariat has retained the three principal areas in which this supermanagerial governmental body is involved: program analysis, personnel policy and administrative services, the latter now designated management improvement. An assistant secretary is responsible to the President of the Treasury Board through the Secretary for each of these branches.

Unquestionably the Secretary is Board-oriented. His time is to a large extent taken up by the President and the ministers of the Board. He must understand both the political and administrative implications of all matters and his advice is continually sought by the ministers.

The Program Branch

The Board's program branch is responsible for program analysis in government departments, as well as estimates and supply procedures. Program analysis has been nothing more than program examination — an examination of new programs, their costing and an investigation of their incremental changes. Now new methods of planning, programing and budgeting — such as systems analysis, cost-benefit analysis and cost-effectiveness studies — are finding favour.

The program branch is organized on a functional basis, each division being headed by a director. There are five program divisions:

General government
Defence services
Economic measures and scientific research
Social measures and cultural services
Transportation, works and telecommunications.

Justifying the financial requirements of all government departments and fitting them into the whole budgetary picture is the most important function of the Treasury Board. If these requirements cannot be made to fit within the framework of government policies, the issues involved are referred to the Cabinet for decision.

The process begins with a program review, justification of departmental plans for a five-year period, to provide the Board with the information required to allocate resources among competing requirements of all departments. Emphasis is placed on the relationship of costs and benefits.

This is followed by the submission of the main estimates — a detailed submission relating activities to areas of responsibility and to specific resources required.

The timetable prescribed by the Board for these submissions and the submission for the Supplementary Estimates is as follows:

Year preceding
Estimates Year

March	Treasury Board letter calling for program review submission
May	Submission of program review
June	Treasury Board consideration of program review
August	Communication of targets for estimates year and letter calling for main estimates
November	Submission of main estimates
December	Treasury Board consideration of main estimates
February	Tabling of main estimates

Estimates Year

February	Letter calling for final supplementary estimates
March	Treasury Board consideration of final supplementary estimates
March	Tabling of final supplementary estimates

The estimates submissions are received from departments in books of multilithed material which explain in considerable detail, for analysis by the staff and for the information of the Board, the functions performed under the various votes and the reasons for proposed changes in function or scale. Explanations of costs in the various categories are also given. These books supply the information necessary to enable the Board's staff to detect substantial issues implicit in the program of each department. This usually leads to discussions with the departments to bring out the relative priorities of the various proposals.

Usually in December the Board holds a heavy schedule of meetings to consider the estimates. The Board is assisted by the Secretary and assistant secretaries and one or two members of the staff. A synoptic and analytical picture of departmental proposals, individually and collectively, is presented to the Board. At the direction of the Chairman, the Secretary or an assistant secretary first indicates the latest information on the economic prospects for the next year. When the estimates of individual departments are under consideration a similar approach is used in which new proposals and issues are presented in a balanced fashion.

It is customary for the minister whose estimates are being considered, together with one or two of his senior officials, to explain and, if necessary, defend the proposals. Having stated the facts and the issues, if any, the officials then step out of the picture and the discussion is conducted by the ministers. The officials remain on the sidelines to answer any further questions that may arise. While the amount of ground to be covered dictates a regular order of procedure, the atmosphere of these meetings is informal enough to ensure that all substantial issues are thoroughly thrashed out. Issues that are not resolved by the Board may be referred to the full Cabinet which in any event must approve the estimates as finally determined by the Board.

Traditionally, supplementary estimates are handled in much the same manner as the main estimates. They are restricted to emergency matters which could not have been foreseen when the main estimates were considered or which result from new decisions taken by the Cabinet or by Parliament. At the end of the year it is customary to bring down in the House what are called further supplementary estimates, or colloquially, final supplementary estimates, to cover errors that have emerged since the estimates were originally made — 18 months earlier. These final estimates do not purport to include anything involving changes of policy.

The preparation of the estimates for submission to Parliament is the function of the Estimates and Supply Procedures Division in the program branch. This division also prepares supply bills and studies the procedures involved in the estimates process. It is particularly concerned to see that the views of Parliament, as expressed by the Public Accounts Committee, are included in the method of estimates presentation.

In performing its three functions the Estimates and Supply Procedures Division exemplifies the process of consultation and coordination necessary in an effective Treasury Board. The Board organization cannot function without cross liaison at all levels. At one time or another virtually every program of the Government appears in Treasury Board submissions. Since the functions of the departments must not overlap or leave gaps coordination is as necessary as control and many programs have ramifications for departments other than those making the submissions. It is therefore standard practice among the staff to consult their colleagues working in related fields at all stages of their study of complex programs. Not only is this true within the staff of the Board, but also it applies with equal, but perhaps less frequent force, to liaison with the various divisions of the government departments and agencies.

The Personnel Policy Branch

The greatest changes in Treasury Board organization are those in the personnel policy branch. Both the new Public Service Employment Act and the amendments to the Financial Administration Act of March 1967 established new personnel duties for the Board. Section 7 of the Financial Administration Act added the complex problems of employer-employee relations to the Board's responsibilities. The various other responsibilities in personnel such as manpower requirements and utilization, training and development, classification of positions, pay determination, hours of work, leave, awards, discipline, physical working conditions, travel and other allowances, and so on, are listed in Section 7. It clarified powers of the Board *vis-à-vis* the new Public Service Employment Act and the new Public Service Act.

To create the proper staff support for the new duties five divisions have been created in the branch.

1. *Planning and Coordination Division*

For general liaison with personnel directors in departments, to promote appropriate patterns of organization and standards of staffing in departmental personnel units, promotion of effective personnel practices in departments and liaison with the Public Service Commission's personnel administration staffing unit.

2. *Manpower Division*

To develop policies and procedures for the management of the executive group, and to coordinate matters affecting that group; to develop policies on personnel data systems; to develop an information base for manpower requirement and resources combined with analysis of existing manpower and critical areas; to render advice regarding personnel research; to develop, implement and establish criteria and evaluation measures for staff training.

3. *Staff Relations Division*

To plan, coordinate for negotiations with assigned occupational groups, and coordinate bargaining policy and render advice relating to the interpretation and administration of collective bargaining agreements; to develop general policies governing the system of employer-employee relations and to coordinate activities relating to the certification process and to grievance procedures.

4. *Compensation and Conditions Division*

To plan and coordinate regarding compensation and conditions, giving particular attention to leave, hours, overtime, travel and employment of foreign service officers and officers employed in isolated posts.

5. *Classification Division*

To provide standard classification and pay structures, implementing a system of performance pay and development of policies for movement within pay ranges. Since all classifications are being reviewed as a result of the new legislation, this division is called the Bureau of Classification Revision.

The personnel policy branch is responsible for personnel establishment. In 1954 a process was begun by Cabinet directive whereby a system of committees was set up to examine and report on departmental staff requirements for the coming year. This process, known as establishment review, has now been discontinued and its function is absorbed within the estimates review procedures. The establishment control and reporting by departments and agencies is now guided by an *Establishment Manual*, compiled by the personnel policy branch. It sets forth clearly how the departments are affected by the procedures, how establishments are determined, as well as the methods of registration, control and amendment of establishments.

The Management Improvement Branch

This new branch was created by the implementation of recommendations by the Glassco Commission. The branch not only absorbed the administrative services division but has a new role.

The Glassco Commission criticized the Treasury Board's assumption of direct management responsibilities which properly belong to departments. To guide, advise and strengthen departmental management, the branch has organized itself into four principal divisions.

1. *Management Improvement Policy*

Advises and sets policy on data processing, material management, office machinery and equipment, productivity, paperwork, machinery of government, technical services, operations research, operational audit and regional administrative operations.

2. *Contracts Division*

This division is not only responsible for the development and implementation of policy governing the practices of departments' procurement, real property transactions and other related matters, but is involved in the appraisal of submissions to the Board in such matters.

3. *SIMPAC Division*

This new division has been created to implement a System of Integrated Management Planning and Control. The purposes are very similar to those embracing planning, programing and budgeting systems. SIMPAC is staffed by highly paid specialists, trained in systems analysis, cost benefit analysis, cost effectiveness analysis and other sophisticated quantitative methods. The SIMPAC division necessarily has close liaison through the program branch with the departments.

4. *Research Division*

To conduct research on methods and techniques designed to improve management and to act as a clearinghouse for ideas.

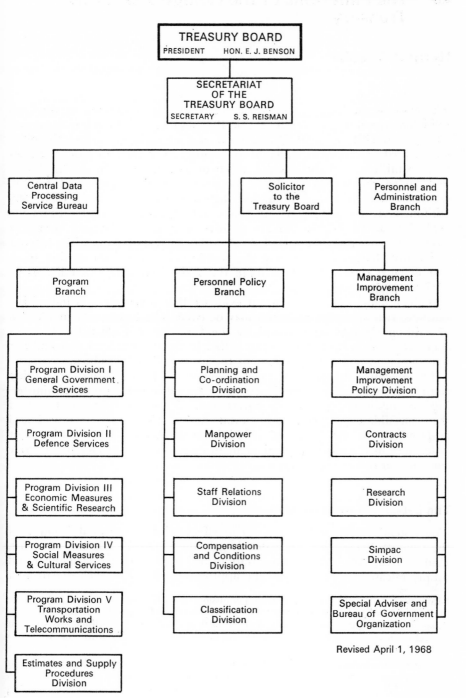

TREASURY BOARD
PRESIDENT   HON. E. J. BENSON

SECRETARIAT
OF THE
TREASURY BOARD
SECRETARY   S. S. REISMAN

Central Data
Processing
Service Bureau

Solicitor
to the
Treasury Board

Personnel and
Administration
Branch

Program
Branch

Personnel Policy
Branch

Management
Improvement
Branch

Program Division I
General Government
Services

Planning and
Co-ordination
Division

Management
Improvement
Policy Division

Program Division II
Defence Services

Manpower
Division

Contracts
Division

Program Division III
Economic Measures
& Scientific Research

Staff Relations
Division

Research
Division

Program Division IV
Social Measures
& Cultural Services

Compensation
and Conditions
Division

Simpac
Division

Program Division V
Transportation
Works and
Telecommunications

Classification
Division

Special Adviser and
Bureau of Government
Organization

Estimates and Supply
Procedures
Division

Revised April 1, 1968

25 The Functions of the Comptroller of the Treasury*

Herbert R. Balls

The office of the Comptroller of the Treasury was established by the Consolidated Revenue and Audit Act of 1931 and came into active operation on April 1, 1932. In 1931-32, the fiscal year immediately before the office was created, government expenditures amounted to $450 million, revenues to $335 million, and there was a deficit of $115 million. In the fiscal year that ended on March 31, 1959, budgetary revenues were $4¾ billion, expenditures were $5⅓ billion, and there was a deficit of more than $600 million, revenues being fourteen times and expenditures twelve times the 1931-32 total. In 1958-59 old age security and family allowance payments were each more than the total federal outlay 27 years before, while interest and other charges for servicing the public debt were $200 million more and defence costs more than three times the aggregate expenditures in 1931-32.

If these figures are not sufficient evidence that government is indeed big business, two more sets of figures may be cited. The first is that in 1958-59, 57 million cheques were issued by the Comptroller's office for amounts aggregating $8 billion. The second is that in that year federal expenditures were equal to about 16 per cent of the gross national product.

These figures demonstrate the vital need for financial and accounting control procedures in their highest and most advanced state in administering the public finances of the government of Canada. The enactment of the Consolidated Revenue and Audit Act of 1931, and its repeal and replacement by the Financial Administration Act of 1951, mark major milestones in the effort of parliament to establish and consolidate effective control over public expenditures.

The Letter of Credit System

The system of expenditure control in effect prior to the establishment of the Comptroller's office was based largely on a system of letters of credit. Under this system,[1] when appropriations had been voted by Parliament and supply released by the Crown, the appropriate official of each department

* Reprinted and slightly abridged with permission of author and publisher from "Issue Control and Pre-Audit for Authority: The Functions of the Comptroller of the Treasury", *Canadian Public Administration*, Vol. 3, June 1960, pp. 118-130. The editors have updated this selection to take account of amendments to the Financial Administration Act up to 1968.

[1] For a more complete description of the letter of credit system see "The Development of Government Expenditure Control: the Issue and Audit Phases" by the author in *Canadian Journal of Economics and Political Science*, Vol. 10, No. 4, November 1944, pp. 464-475.

applied to the Minister of Finance for authority to spend part of the monies granted by Parliament for the departmental services. These applications were referred to the Auditor General who authorized the issue of a letter of credit, which was prepared in the Department of Finance, signed by the Minister of Finance and countersigned by the Auditor General. It was addressed to a bank which had public monies on deposit and authorized it to pay all cheques drawn upon it by the authorized signing officers up to the amount of credit.

Upon receipt of the letter of credit the chief accountant or other responsible officer of the department presented it to the bank and proceeded to issue cheques and disburse the monies thus made available. Each month statements of all payments under each letter of credit were prepared in duplicate. One copy together with the supporting vouchers and paid cheques was sent to the Auditor General and the other to the Minister of Finance. In the Audit Office the cheque lists were compared with the vouchers, and if satisfied as to the accuracy of the statement, the authenticity of the documents and the authority for the payments, the Auditor General would ask the Minister of Finance to reimburse the bank for advances made by it under the letter of credit by issuing a cheque in its favour drawn on one of the Receiver General's bank accounts.

The Act of 1951 made significant changes in the existing system. It introduced far-reaching provisions for the financial control and accountability of Crown corporations, provided for the first time a sound basis for stores and inventory accounting and control, extended the authority and clarified the role of the Treasury Board, and relieved the Auditor General of any responsibility for auditing expenditures before payment. However, it made little change in the basic duties of the Comptroller, except to broaden his authority in some respects and to place on a statutory basis certain functions which he had assumed over the years.

Most of the principles underlying Canadian parliamentary control over the public treasury are given statutory expression in the British North America Act and the Financial Administration Act. The British North America Act established a consolidated revenue fund into which all public money must be paid and which was to be appropriated for the public service of Canada by the Parliament of Canada. This is reaffirmed by section 24 of the Financial Administration Act, which provides that no payment shall be made out of the fund except with the authority of Parliament. Under section 25 all estimates of expenditure submitted to Parliament must be for services coming in course of payment during the fiscal year, and under section 26 a warrant of the Governor General is required for the release of supply before a payment out of the consolidated revenue fund may be made. The basic requirement is that expenditures must not exceed the amounts voted annually by Parliament and released by warrant of the Queen's representative, but certain expenditures such as those for family allowances, old age security, subsidies and tax rental payments to provinces, interest and other public debt charges, the salaries of judges and the Auditor General, and a limited number of other expenditures which parliament has agreed should not be subject to annual review and debate are made under the authority of what are known as "statutory" appropriations. The latter appropriations, which may continue from year to year without lapsing, authorize payments out of the Consolidated Revenue Fund for specified purposes and for such definite or indefinite amounts, and during such period of time as parliament may prescribe. However, the authority for by far the greater part of all public expenditures is contained in the annual appropriation acts which cover the period from April 1, in one year, to March 31, in the next. Consequently, for these expenditures new authority must be sought annually.

This principle of "annuality" is confirmed by section 35 of the Financial Administration Act which provides that the unexpended portion of an appropriation granted for a fiscal year shall lapse at the end of that year except that payments properly applicable to the year may be made for thirty days thereafter.

Status and Powers of the Comptroller

Appointed as an officer of the Department of Finance and with a salary fixed by the Governor in Council, the Comptroller holds office during good behaviour but is removable for misbehaviour, incapacity, inability, or failure to perform his duties properly, or for other cause. To give some assurance against arbitrary dismissal the Act provides that any order in council providing for the removal of the Comptroller from office and the documents relating thereto shall be laid before parliament within fifteen days after it is made or if parliament is not in session within fifteen days after the commencement of the next ensuing session. Provision is made for the Governor in Council to appoint a person to act as Comptroller during the illness, incapacity or other absence of the Comptroller, or during a vacancy in the office.

To enable the Comptroller to perform his duties the Act gives him free access "at all convenient times" to all files, documents and other records relating to the accounts of each department and entitles him to request and receive from members of the public service such information, reports and explanations as he considers necessary for the proper performance of his duties. He may station in any department any person employed in his office to enable him to carry out his duties more effectively and the department must provide the necessary office accommodation. To ensure that departmental security requirements are observed the Comptroller must require every person employed in his office who is to examine the accounts of a department to comply with any security requirements applicable to, and to take any oath of secrecy required to be taken by, persons employed in that department. He may also suspend from the performance of his duties any person employed in his office.

The System of Expenditure Control

The principal function of the Comptroller is to ensure that the financial decisions of parliament, the Governor in Council, the Treasury Board and ministers are enforced. For this purpose, the Comptroller operates a centralized accounting and disbursement system which enables him to maintain a complete record of parliamentary appropriations, the commitments against them, and the disbursements chargeable to them.

Under Part III of the Financial Administration Act, no charge may be made against an appropriation except on the requisition of the minister of the department for which the appropriation was made or of a person authorized by him in writing and no payment may be made for the performance of work or the supply of goods whether under contract or not unless the deputy minister or some other officer authorized by the minister certifies that the work has been performed or the material supplied and the price charged is according to contract or if not specified in the contract is reasonable. Where a payment is to be made before completion of the work or delivery of the goods, a certificate is required that the payment is in accordance with the contract.

All departmental requisitions for payment must be submitted to the Comptroller in such form and accompanied by such documents and certified in such manner as he may require. The Comptroller may reject a requisition if he is of the opinion that the payment

1. would not be a lawful charge against the appropriation,
2. would result in an expenditure in excess of the appropriation, or
3. would reduce the balance of the appropriation so that it would not be sufficient to meet the commitments charged against it.

Moreover, where a cost audit of a contract is required and the Comptroller reports that in his opinion certain costs or charges claimed by the contractor should not be allowed, these costs or charges may not be allowed to the contractor unless the Treasury Board otherwise directs.

The Comptroller may refer to the Treasury Board any departmental requisition on which he desires the direction of the Board and the Board may order that payment be made or refused. If he declines to make payment, disallows an item in an account, or refuses to give a certificate required by the Act, the minister of the department concerned may report the circumstances to the Treasury Board and the Board may confirm or overrule the Comptroller and give such directions as are necessary to carry out its decision.

Although appropriations for the administrative and other expenses of the Houses and Library of Parliament are technically grants to the Crown, and are subject to the same controls as are applicable to departments of government generally, the Treasury Board is not considered an appropriate body to deal with cases where the Comptroller questions the legality of proposed charges to votes for these bodies. Accordingly, the Financial

Administration Act provides that whenever the Comptroller is of the opinion that a doubt exists as to the legality or otherwise of a proposed charge to an appropriation provided for the expenses of the Senate, House of Commons or Library of Parliament he must, through the President of the Treasury Board, draw the matter to the attention of the appropriate Speaker, or in the case of the Library of Parliament, to the Speakers jointly, who shall obtain a decision

> in accordance with such procedure as may from time to time be prescribed by the Senate or the House of Commons, as the case may be, or in the case of the Library of Parliament, by the Senate or the House of Commons

and the Comptroller is required to act in accordance with the decision thus obtained.

Disbursements

Control of issue or payment is one of the Comptroller's prime statutory duties. All payments under appropriations are made under his direction and control by cheque drawn on the account of the Receiver General or by other instrument in such form and authenticated in such manner as the Treasury Board directs.

In practice, most payments in Canadian dollars are made by drafts on the Receiver General and not by cheques drawn on one of his bank accounts. However, for payments in sterling or United States dollars, cheques are drawn directly on bank accounts maintained by the Receiver General in London or New York. Formerly these drafts were cleared daily by the banks, usually through their main Ottawa branches, to the Cheque Adjustment Branch[2] and were reimbursed by cheques drawn on the Receiver General's account with the Bank of Canada. However, in May 1957, a change was made in this procedure whereby the banks, instead of transmitting the cheques paid by them to Ottawa for reimbursement, now deliver them to agencies of the Bank of Canada which are located at Halifax, Saint John, Montreal, Ottawa, Toronto, Winnipeg, Regina, Calgary and Vancouver, and are reimbursed promptly. Under the new system, the agencies send the cheques to the Bank of Canada at Ottawa, which, in turn, delivers them to the Cheque Adjustment Branch where they are examined and reconciled with the Comptroller's statements of cheques issued and are then retained until they are microfilmed and destroyed in accordance with regulations made by the Treasury Board on the recommendation of the Minister of Finance with the approval of the Auditor General.

In some circumstances it is desirable to have payments originate in local departmental offices or in other places where the Comptroller has

---

[2] The Branch, formerly a separate branch of the Department of Finance, was placed under the direction of the Comptroller on February 1, 1960.

no representative and where it would be uneconomical to establish a district treasury office. In such cases, other methods of payment have been authorized by the Treasury Board.

Most departmental offices have modest imprest or petty cash accounts out of which small local payments may be made, the accounts being replenished by the Comptroller on the presentation and audit of the supporting invoices. Some local offices are authorized to operate departmental banking accounts from which payments are made by cheques drawn by authorized departmental signing officers. These are placed in funds initially by advances out of the Consolidated Revenue Fund and are reimbursed by the Comptroller on the receipt and audit by him of the invoices and paid cheques.

Again, in a few cases where large numbers of payments must originate in many scattered local offices (as in the case of unemployment insurance benefits) or in processing plants (as in the case of hog premium payments) where there is no representative of the Comptroller, the Treasury Board has agreed that payments may be made by warrants drawn on the Comptroller by designated departmental officers or other authorized persons. For example, unemployment insurance benefits are paid by the local offices of the Unemployment Insurance Commission by warrants. These are presented by the payees to the banks which cash them and, in turn, present them for redemption to any one of the five district treasury offices servicing the Unemployment Insurance Commission, which are located at Moncton, Montreal, Toronto, Winnipeg and Vancouver, and they are reimbursed by Comptroller's cheque drawn on the Receiver General.

Commitments

The foregoing statutory duties of the Comptroller are essentially for the purpose of controlling cash transactions. However, other provisions of the Act are intended to ensure that there are commitment and other controls operating well in advance of the actual disbursement of cash.

At the beginning of each fiscal year, each department is required to divide its appropriations into allotments in the form detailed in the estimates or in such other form as the Treasury Board may approve and to submit them to the Board through the Comptroller. While appropriation limits must not be exceeded, the need for some flexibility is recognized and transfers between allotments within votes are permitted if approved by the Treasury Board.

To avoid over-spending appropriations, the Comptroller's representatives record and control all commitments due to come in course of payment within a year for which parliament has been asked to provide appropriations. Under section 30 of the Act, no contract may be entered into or has any force or effect unless the Comptroller has certified that there are unencumbered funds available in the appropriation or in an item included in the estimates before the House of Commons to discharge any commitment under the contract coming in course of payment during the fiscal year in which the contract is entered into.

There is an exception to this requirement which provides that where the Comptroller is satisfied that an agreement was entered into to defray an immediate expense that through accident to public property or other emergency was necessary to protect the property, or provide for the emergency, he may issue his certificate accordingly, whereupon the agreement is exempt from the operation of section 30 of the Act from the time the agreement was entered into.

Some appropriations, notably those for the defence services, contain a limitation upon the power of the executive to incur liabilities or commitments that will mature for payment in future years. However, these carry with them an implication, but no more than an implication, that parliament will vote monies when needed to meet any commitments incurred within the stipulated amounts. Generally, however, there are no statutory limits upon the commitments that may be incurred for payments in future years, but through the Treasury Board and the Comptroller's representatives the government maintains a careful control over these for it must be prepared when the time comes to make payment to ask parliament for appropriations for the monies required and to justify its requests. Technically, each contractual commitment is subject to parliament providing funds, but in practice the government limits its commitments to those which have been specifically authorized by the so-called "statutory" appropriations and those for which it is confident parliament will provide the necessary funds in subsequent annual appropriations.

To enable to Comptroller to give the necessary certificate as to the availability of funds he maintains a record of all commitments chargeable to each appropriation, and to facilitate this every contract involving the payment of money by Her Majesty must be submitted to him as soon as it is made or entered into unless he certifies that he does not require it.

Accounting

The control and audit of departmental appropriations, commitments and disbursements, and the maintenance of the necessary accounting records for these purposes, are the Comptroller's major functions but these are not his only areas of interest and responsibility. Section 63 (1) of the Financial Administration Act requires the Minister of Finance to cause accounts to be kept to show

1. the expenditures made under and commitments chargeable against each appropriation,
2. the revenues of Canada, and
3. the other payments into and out of the Consolidated Revenue Fund.

Section 63 (2) provides that the Minister subject to regulations of the Treasury Board

1. shall cause accounts to be kept to show such of the assets and direct and contingent liabilities of Canada, and
2. may establish such reserves with respect to the assets and liabilities

as in his opinion are required to give a true and fair view of the financial position of Canada. In practice these accounts recording transactions relating to revenues, assets and liabilities, as well as to expenditures, are maintained in the office of the Comptroller.

Although the main purpose of these accounts is to control expenditures and to ensure that parliamentary and executive directions governing the disbursement of public monies are observed they are also used by the Comptroller and his representatives to assist those who are responsible for administration in formulating policy and generally in carrying out their duties. Both for the Minister of Finance, the Treasury Board and the other central executive control agencies of the Government on the one hand and for departments and administrative bodies on the other, treasury officers record information and produce cash and budgetary forecasts, analytical statements and financial statistics to be used as tools of management and in other ways assist ministers and departmental officers by providing advice and guidance for the formulation and execution of financial and accounting policy.

In addition to furnishing advisory services to departmental administrators there are other ways in which treasury officers serve departments notably in regard to the management of revenues and stores.

With regard to revenues, the collecting department is responsible for its own revenues but the Financial Administration Act provides that on the request of a minister and with the approval of the Treasury Board the Comptroller may provide accounting and other services in connection with the collection and accounting of public money for a department and may examine the collecting and accounting practices applied in a department and report to the minister of the department.

With respect to stores, under the Financial Administration Act the administering department is responsible primarily for the management of stores, the maintenance of adequate records of stores and materials under its jurisdiction, and for the constitution periodically of boards of survey to examine the state of the stores under the management of the department and to recommend the deletion from inventory of any stores or materials that are or that have been obsolete or unserviceable or lost or destroyed. Such deletions, however, may be made only on the direction of the minister of the department with the approval of the Treasury Board and a statement of all such deletions must be included annually in the *Public Accounts*. Although stores are primarily a departmental responsibility, when Parliament authorizes the establishment of a revolving fund for the purpose of acquiring and managing stores, the financial accounts are kept by the Comptroller. Moreover, under section 61 of the Financial Administration Act, he may examine records, accounts and procedures respecting stores and materials of a department and report thereon to the minister of the department or to the President of the Treasury Board.

Financial Reporting

Financial reporting also plays an important role in government, but a distinction must be made between accountability or stewardship reports for proprietors and shareholders represented by parliament and the public on the one hand, and reports for management represented by the executive on the other.

The principal published financial report from the standpoint of accountability or stewardship is the annual *Public Accounts* which is prepared in the Comptroller's office. Each year, on or before December 31, or if parliament is not then in session within fifteen days after the commencement of the next ensuing session, the *Public Accounts* must be laid before the House of Commons by the Minister of Finance. This volume contains a survey of the financial transactions of the fiscal year, statements of the revenues and expenditures for the year and of the assets and direct and contingent liabilities of Canada as at the end of the year, together with such other accounts and information as are considered necessary to show the financial transactions and financial position of Canada, or which are required by law to be reported in the *Public Accounts*. In recent years it has been the practice to publish the financial statements of all Crown corporations, and the auditors' reports thereon, in a separate volume of the *Public Accounts*.

In addition, monthly and annual statements of budgetary and non-budgetary financial transactions, and of the government's cash and debt position, which are also prepared by the Comptroller, are published in the Canada Gazette. The Minister of Finance's annual budget speech, together with the budget papers containing a preliminary survey of the government's accounts for the year just ended or ending, presents another source of information regarding the government's financial operations.

In addition to these stewardship or accountability reports, there are also a number of management reports produced for the information and guidance of ministers, deputy ministers and the senior administrative and executive officers. In most departments reliance is placed on the Comptroller and his representatives who, in addition to their control activities, provide services and financial advice to management in regard to the revenue as well as the expenditure transactions of the department.

For the Department of Finance a number of statements and reports are prepared which are used for broad policy making and management purposes. These include daily statements of receipts and disbursements for the government as a whole, and of the Receiver General bank balances and monthly statements of revenue, expenditures and assets and liabilities. Special purpose statements are prepared from time to time to meet special needs, the most important of which are the periodic forecasts of the government's cash requirements.

Pre-audit and Post-audit

The audit of financial transactions is an essential element in the control of governmental finances, but a distinction must be made between pre-audit on behalf of the executive and post-audit on behalf of the legislature.

Parliamentary control of expenditure is exercised primarily by determining how the public revenues are to be spent. This phase of the control cycle ends with the appropriation of money or the voting of supply to the Crown. However, legislative interest does not terminate at this point and there are statutory provisions requiring those who are responsible for spending public monies to make an accounting to parliament, and for the Auditor General, as a servant of parliament, to examine the accounts to ascertain whether the expenditures conform with the parliamentary grants. Under section 70 of the Financial Administration Act the Auditor General is required *inter alia* to call attention to every case in which he has observed that an appropriation was exceeded or was applied to a purpose, or in a manner, not authorized by parliament, or an expenditure was not authorized, or was improperly vouched or certified.

In essence, the Auditor General's post-audit is an examination after payment for the purpose of reporting to the House of Commons whether the accounts have been faithfully and properly kept, whether the money has been spent for the purposes for which it was appropriated, and whether the expenditures have been made as authorized. It is, for the most part, a test audit, is based on statutory requirements, custom, convention and commercial practices and is essentially for the purpose of reporting, for the Auditor General has no power of disallowance.

The pre-audit or examination of expenditures before payment is primarily for the protection of the executive and is carried out by the Comptroller of the Treasury as part of his statutory duties under the Financial Administration Act. In this case the audit is usually a complete one hundred percent audit and is associated with the control of issue or payment. The Comptroller, unlike the Auditor General, has a power of disallowance, and may refuse to make a payment if in his opinion there is no authority for it or if it is improper in any way, but a disallowance by the Comptroller is subject to appeal to the Treasury Board, which may sustain or overrule him.

In concluding this survey of the Canadian system of expenditure control and audit and of the powers and duties of the Comptroller of the Treasury, it remains to be noted that in at least one respect the office of Comptroller is unique. In the United Kingdom and in most of the Commonwealth countries the functions of issue control and post audit are the responsibility of the one official — usually the Comptroller and Auditor General. In Canada since 1932 the two functions have been separated and Parliament has allotted to the Comptroller, as an officer of the executive, full responsibility for controlling issues or payments out of the Consolidated Revenue Fund, and has made the Auditor General, as a legislative officer, responsible for carrying out an independent audit after payment and reporting to the legislature the results of his examinations.

This division of responsibility for issue on the one hand and audit on the other constitutes a basic departure from United Kingdom practices where custom and constitutional theory have decreed that issue control and audit must be in the hands of an officer responsible only to the legislature. However, in seeking to ensure that the executive is able to supervise effectively the expenditures for which it is responsible, the Parliament of Canada has not surrendered its sovereignty nor has executive accountability been sacrificed. Indeed the executive is now answerable not only to the questions of Parliament but also to the criticisms and comments of an informed Auditor General whose reports are available to the House of Commons.

Chapter Six
Control in Administration

Unfortunately the topic of control has acquired a connotation of unpleasantness in the vocabulary of management. It is linked with the arbitrary, authoritarian manner of the typical manager-owner of the nineteenth and early twentieth centuries. It has a ring of coercion that apparently is in sharp contrast to the human relations orientation now found in many of the schools of administration. This stigma has contributed to neglect of this topic in recent literature on public administration. Current material is found mainly in the writings on business management and even there it is remarkably thin.

The first item in this chapter identifies control in its roles within social institutions and particularly in business. The next article looks at control in Canadian government administration and the last paper discusses a major aspect of control: the search for efficiency.

Current business textbooks have the most adequate discussions of the control concept. Notable among these works are

William Newman, *Administrative Action*, Prentice Hall, Englewood Cliffs, New Jersey, 1963, Chapters 24 to 26.

H. Koontz and C. J. O'Donnell, *Principles of Management*, McGraw-Hill, Toronto, 1964, Chs. 28 to 31.

D. McFarland, *Management: Principle and Practices*, Macmillan, New York, 1964, Ch. 18.

G. N. Currie's essay, "Efficiency vs. Service in Public Administration" (*Canadian Public Administration*, Vol. 7, No. 2, June 1964) with commentary by O. M. Solandt is virtually an addendum to the Glassco Commission *Report*. It stresses the need for control in the Canadian public service. One aspect of control is dealt with thoroughly in W. E. Leonard's *The Management Audit* (Prentice Hall, Englewood Cliffs, New Jersey, 1962). The U.S. Bureau of the Budget has produced a booklet describing detailed studies of productivity measurement in four U.S. government agencies: *Measuring Productivity of Federal Government Organizations* (U.S. Government Printing Office, Washington, D.C., 1964). Rensis Likert has contributed two noteworthy articles entitled: "Making Cost Control Work" (Harvard Business Review, Vol. 41, No. 6, November-December 1963) and "Measuring Organizational Performance" (Harvard Business Review, Vol. 36, No. 2, March-April 1958).

There are many descriptions of technical aspects of control, such as work measurement, but all-in-all this area of management is sadly in need of further research.

26   Controls, Control and Management*

Peter F. Drucker

Section I

In the grammar of social institutions the word *"controls"* is not the plural of the word "control." Not only do more "controls" not necessarily give more "control" — the two words, in the context of social institutions have different meanings altogether. The synonyms for "controls" are measurement and information. The synonym for "control" is direction. "Controls" pertain to means, "control" to an end. "Controls" deal with facts, that is with events of the past. "Control" deals with expectations, that is with the future. "Controls" are analytical and operational, concerned with what was and is. "Control" is normative, concerned with what ought to be, with significance rather than with meaning.

We are rapidly acquiring great capacity to design "controls" in social institutions, based on a great improvement in techniques, especially in the application of logical and mathematical tools to events of this social universe, and in the ability to process and analyze large masses of data very fast. What does this mean for "control?" Specifically what are the requirements for these greatly improved "controls" to give better "control" to management? For, in the task of a manager, "controls" are purely a means to an end; the end is "control."

That here is a problem, ordinary language and its use makes abundantly clear. The man in a business who is charged with producing the "controls" is the "controller." But most, if not all executives, including most controllers themselves, would consider it gross misuse and abuse of controllership were this "controller" to use his "controls" to exercise "control" in the business. This, they would argue would actually make the business be "out of control" altogether.

---

* Reprinted with permission of author and publisher from C. P. Bonini *et al, Management Controls*, McGraw-Hill, New York, 1964.

The reasons for this apparent paradox lie in the complexity, both of human beings and of the social task. I do not intend to go into metaphysics, nor is this necessary. I am willing to grant that both the human being and society are actually completely determined. But there are so many determinants, and their form and impact are so varied, that, at least on the microcosmic level on which we operate — and on which even the basic policy decisions of great powers are being made — there is so much complexity as to result in a genuine "uncertainty principle" insofar as the relationship between "controls" and "control" is concerned. A genuine feed-back is not possible.

If we deal with a human being in a social institution, "controls" must become personal motivation to lead to "control." Instead of a mechanical system, the control system in a human-social situation is a volitional system. That we know very little about the will is not even the central point. A translation is required before the information by the "controls" can become ground of action — the translation of one kind of information into another which we call *perception*.

In the social institution itself there is a second complexity, a second "uncertainty principle." It is almost impossible to pre-figure the responses appropriate to a certain event in a social situation. We can, and do, build a control into a machine which slows down the turning speed whenever it exceeds a certain figure. And we can do this either by mechanical means or by instrumentation which shows a human operator what the turning speed is, and which gives him the specific, unambiguous instruction to turn the speed down when the indicator reaches a certain point. But a control reading "profits are falling" does not indicate, with any degree of probability, the response "raise prices" let alone by how much; the control — reading "sales are falling" does not indicate the response "cut prices," and so on. There is not only a large — a very large — number of other equally probable responses — so large that it is usually not even possible to identify them in advance. There is no indication in the event itself which of these responses is even possible, let alone appropriate, not to mention its being right. The event itself may not even be meaningful. But even if it is, it is by no means certain what it means. And the probability of its being meaningful is a much more important datum than the event itself — and one which is almost never to be discerned by analyzing the event.

In other words what is needed in the social situation is a decision based on assumptions — and essentially assumptions not in respect to the recorded event but in respect to the future, that is expectations which know no probability but can only be judged according to plausibility. For there are no "facts" in the future in a social universe in which periodicity — at least on our minuscule scale — cannot be assumed, must indeed rather be considered quite unlikely.

There are at least parts of such a situation which resemble the phenomena of the physical universe. We can in other words "simulate," that is, pretend that we deal with physical events rather than with social events. And such "simulation" is indeed highly fruitful as we have learned these last ten years or so. But we should never forget the fact that this is "simulation" — and therefore something completely different from the symbolic representation of reality which the physicist's formula represents. It is always based on assumptions regarding volition, perception and expectations which need constant re-appraisal.

Section II

Does this mean that "controls" are unimportant? Does it mean that they are misleading? The opposite actually follows. Precisely because we deal with such a complex subject, we need control very badly. And precisely because we find ourselves in constant uncertainty as managers in such a situation, "controls" tend to have tremendous impact. In fact both the need and the impact are so great that the wrong "controls" can be exceedingly misleading and dangerous. It is, therefore, important today when our capacity to design and to manipulate controls is increasing so fast, to think through what controls in a social institution and in particular in the business enterprise have to be and have to do, and also what they cannot be and must not attempt to do.

There are four major characteristics of "controls" in business enterprise — two pertain to all social institutions and reflect the fact that business enterprise is a social institution. One of these characteristics pertains to institutions within a society of which business enterprise is one. And the fourth and last one is specifically a characteristic of business enterprise as an economic institution.

1. When we measure the rate of fall of a stone, we are totally outside the event itself. By measuring we do not change the event; and measuring the event does not change us, the observers.

Measuring is both objective and neutral.

In a wide range of natural phenomena, however, especially on the microcosmic level, the act of measuring interferes with the event measured — whether the events are nuclear, microbiological or psychological. The observer in these events becomes a part of the situation. Measurement is still objective but no longer neutral.

In a perceptual situation of complexity, that is in any social situation of the kind we deal with in business enterprise, the act of measurement is, however, neither objective nor neutral. It is subjective and of necessity biased. It changes both the event and the observer. For it changes the perception of the observer — if it does not altogether create his perception. Events in the social situation acquire value by the fact that they are being singled out for the attention of being measured. No matter how "scientific" we are, the fact that this or that set of phenomena is singled out for being "controlled," signals that it is being considered to be important. Everybody who ever watched the introduction of a budget system has seen this happen. For a long time — in many companies forever — realizing the budget figures becomes more important than what the budget is supposed to measure, namely economic performance. This goes often so far that managers, upon their first exposure to a budget system, deliberately hold back sales and cut back profits rather than be guilty of "not making the budget." It takes years of experience and a very intelligent budget director to restore the balance. And there is any number of otherwise perfectly normal research directors who act on the conviction that it is a greater crime to get research results for less than the budgeted amount than not getting any research results at all while spending all the "proper" budget money.

"Controls" in a social institution, in other words, are goal-setting and value-setting. They are not "objective." They are of necessity moral. The only way to avoid this is to flood the executive with so many "controls" that entire system becomes meaningless, becomes mere "noise." From that point of view maybe the gross abuse of our new data processing capacity, namely as a tool for grinding out huge quantities of totally meaningless data — the abuse of which every early computer user is guilty — is a blessing after all. But it is hardly the right way to use our capacity to provide "controls." This must start out with the realization that "controls" create vision. That is they both affect the events measured and the observer. They endow events not only with meaning but with value.

And this means that the basic question is not "How do we control?" But "What do we measure in our control system." That we can quantify something is no reason at all for measuring it. The question is: "Is this what a manager should consider important?" "Is this what a manager's attention should be focused on?" "Is this a true statement of the basic realities of the enterprise?" "Is this the proper focus for "control," that is for effective direction with maximum economy of effort?"

If these questions are not being asked in designing "controls," we will end up by making business essentially uncontrolled — for then we will simply have no remedy except to proliferate control information to the point where it does not register at all.

2. Because "controls" have such an impact it is not only important that we select the right ones: to enable controls to give right vision and to become the ground for effective action, the measurement must also be appropriate. That is it must present the events measured in structurally true form. Formal validity is not enough.

Grievances coming out of a work force are commonly reported as "five grievances per thousand employees per month." This is formally valid. But is it structurally valid? Or is it misdirection?

The impression this report conveys is first that grievances are distributed throughout the work force in a random matter. They follow, the report seems to say, a U-shaped Gaussian distribution. And secondly — a conclusion from the first impression — they are a minor problem especially if we deal with five grievances per thousand employees per month.

It is almost certain, however, that this, while formally valid, completely mis-represents and mis-informs, let alone mis-directs. Grievances are a social event. Physical nature knows no such phenomena. And social events are almost never distributed in the "normal distribution" we find in the physical world. The "normal distribution" of social events is almost always exponential — with the hyperbola the typical curve. In other words, the great majority of departments in the plant, employing ninety-five per cent of the work force, normally does not even have a single grievance during one year. But in one department, employing only a handful of men, we have a heavy incidence of grievances — so that the "five per thousand" may well mean (and in the actual example from which I took these figures, did mean) a major grievance per man per year. If this department is then the final assembly through which all the production has to pass, and if the workers in this department go out on strike when their grievances are being neglected by a management which has been misled by its own "controls," the impact can be shattering. In the case I quoted it bankrupted the company which is no longer in existence.

Similarly 90 per cent of the volume of a business is usually represented by 2 to 5 per cent of the number of its products. But 90 per cent of the orders by number cover, typically, only 4 or 5 per cent of the volume — but account for 90 per cent and more of the costs. And so it goes. A modern strategic bomber may have a million parts. But 90 per cent of its cost is represented by a very small number of parts, maybe fifty or so — and so is 90 per cent of the upkeep it needs though, unfortunately, the 90 per cent of the dollars and the 90 per cent of the upkeep-needs rarely comprise the same parts.

Practically all the innovations in a research laboratory, no matter how large, come out of the work of a very small percentage of the research people. And invariably, 80 per cent of a company's distributors move, at best, 20 per cent of its output, while 10 per cent or fewer of the distributors move two-thirds to three quarters of total sales.

This, unfortunately, very few managers know. The traditional information systems, especially accounting, conceal rather than highlight this fact. (In particular the allocation of overhead tends to obscure the "normal distribution" of economic and social phenomena).

At the same time knowledge of this fact and understanding of it are pre-requisites for effective control. For control is above all a principle of economy. It means allocation of efforts where they can produce the most results with the minimum of energy. This means allocation of efforts to the small number of phenomena which in any social situation account for the great bulk of results.

Without controls that bring out sharply what the real structure of events is, the manager not only lacks knowledge. He cannot, normally expect to do the right thing. On the contrary, all the weight of the daily work pushes him towards allocating energies and resources in proportion to the *number* of events. There is a constant drift towards putting energies and resources where they can have the least results, that is on the vast number of phenomena which, together, account for practically no effects.

Any sales organization I have ever seen, has the bulk of its salesmen — and especially the good men — working on the 90 per cent of the customers who, together, buy 10 per cent of the output, or on the 90 per cent of products by number which, together produce 10 per cent of the company's revenue and markets, and so on. Any technical service force — one of the most expensive and most valuable resources of a company — in the absence of the right information regarding market structure and customers, will put its best men on the smallest and least valuable accounts, if only because these are the people who have the least technical competence themselves and therefore seem to need technical help the most. In fact this constant drift towards the irrelevant and unproductive is so great, and the weight behind it so heavy, that a "controls" system which did nothing but focus attention on the central events — the events which under normal probability statistics are not seen at all — would give any manager a great deal more control and very much better performance and results than the most elaborate simulation and quantification can possibly produce.

To bring out the structure of economic and social events should be a major contribution of our new approaches to "controls." We now have the logical and mathematic tools available for the job. Indeed it is in this area that the new methods have been most productive. Of course not everything there is to be measured, conforms to the "normal distribution" of social events. After all we also deal with physical events in business enterprise. And one of the most important and least understood areas of operation are those where events following the "normal distribution" of the physical universe have to be coupled with events following the "normal distribution" of the social universe, for instance, where we have to bring together the physical flow of materials through a plant with an order pattern.

Here in other words is an area of very great contribution. But the new tools and methods will not make this contribution, will indeed miss their greatest opportunity, unless it is realized that how we measure is as important as what we measure — and that the question: "What is the proper measurement and the proper scale" is infinitely more important in social events than it is in the physical universe — precisely because perception is an integral part of the events themselves.

3. The third characteristic important for the design and use of controls in business enterprise is that business is an institution of society. It exists to contribute to economy, society and individual. In consequence *results* in business exist only on the outside — in economy, in society and with the customer. It is the customer only who creates a "profit". Everything inside a business, manufacturing, marketing, research and so on, creates only costs, is only a "cost center."

In other words the "managerial" area is concerned with costs alone. *Results are always entrepreneurial.*

Yet we do not have adequate, let alone reliable information regarding the "outside." They are not only by far the hardest to get — to the point where no organization for the acquisition and collection of meaningful outside information could really be set up — the job is much too big. Above all we simply lack the necessary entrepreneurial concepts. The job itself has never been thought through — at least not so far. And the century of patient analysis of managerial, inside phenomena, events and data, the century of patient, skillful work on the individual operations and tasks within the business, has no counterpart in respect to the entrepreneurial job.

To put it differently, we can easily record and therefore quantify efficiency, that is, efforts. We have very few instruments to record and quantify effects, that is, the outside. But even the most efficient buggy whip manufacturer would no longer be in business. It is of little value to have the most efficient engineering department if it designs the wrong product. The Cuban subsidiaries of U.S. companies were by far the best run and, apparently, the most profitable — let alone the least "troublesome" — of all U.S. operations in Latin America. And it mattered little, I daresay, during the period of IBM's great expansion in the last ten or fifteen years how "efficient" its operations were; it's basic entrepreneurial idea was the right, the effective one.

It is not only that the outside, the area of results, is much less accessible than the inside. It is at the same time much more remote as well. The central problem of the executive in the large organization is his — necessary — insulation from the outside. This applies to the President of the United States as well as to the President of United States Steel. What today's organization therefore needs, above all, are synthetic sense organs for the outside. If modern "controls" are to make a contribution, it would be above all here.

Yet this is exactly the area where we do not put to work the new technology of control. We tend — as people with a new tool kit always do — to go to work where it is easy. These are the inside, the managerial events. We should, however, go to work where we can make the greatest contribution. On the outside, we cannot indeed hope to come up with anything of such beautiful precision as a Queuing Theory inventory system. But we may come up with something which (unlike some fancy inventory systems I have seen) is actually useful and may even be used. In other words a new approach, a new technology, a new set of tools should always be put to work on the difficult rather than the easy, on the things the old tools could not do at all rather than on the things they did passably well. It should give new power rather than be frittered away on improvements. And unless we use the new approaches for an understanding and ordering of the outside, the entrepreneurial world of business enterprise — even though all we can produce there for the time being are insights rather than quantitative statements — we are not going to make the new technology truly useful. We are going to abuse it for the gratification of the technician's virtuosity rather than for the satisfaction of an urgent need of business and society.

4. Finally, in terms of specifications for effective quantitative controls, we should look at business enterprise as something separate, that is as business as a meaningful sphere of human action by itself. As such it presents a unique appearance to people interested in controls and control. Business, unlike all natural and mechanical systems, exhibits a wide range of events and results that are of profound importance and yet cannot easily be quantified within any meaningful system of measurement. But business, also, unlike any other social system, has a wide range of events and results which can be quantified. Business is the only system we know which has both quantifiable and non-quantifiable results and events, both equally important.

This gives business a unique opportunity for controls, but also a unique problem.

Any experienced executive knows companies or industries which are bound for extinction because they cannot attract or hold able people. This, every experienced executive also knows, is a more important fact about a company or an industry than last year's profit statement. Any logical positivist who was to tell an executive that this statement, being incapable of unambiguous definition is a "non-statement" dealing with a "non-problem," would be quickly — and correctly — dismissed as an ass. Yet the statement cannot be defined clearly let alone "quantified." It is anything but "intangible;" it is very "tangible" indeed (as anyone ever having to do with such a business quickly finds out.) It is just "non-measurable." And the results, while exceedingly measurable, will not show up for a decade.

But business also has measurable and quantifiable results of true meaning and significance. These are all those that have to do with past economic performance. For these can be expressed in terms of the very peculiar measurement of the economic sphere, money.

This does not mean that these are "tangibles." Indeed most of the things we can measure by money are so totally "intangible" — take depreciation for instance — that they outdo any Platonic Idea in that nothing corresponds to them in any reality whatever. But they are measurable.

That they are abstractions the "management scientist" with his background in physics or engineering often has to learn the hard way. Far too few management scientists for instance realize that practically every single definition of accounting is based on assumptions of high metaphysical content — and that any accountant worth his salt, can convert any profit figure into a loss figure, or vice versa, if given control of the accounting definitions, all unquestionably, "within the limits of proper accounting practice."

This does not alter the fact that there are important measurable events. And then, to say it again, there are equally important events that cannot be measured.

To this comes the fact that the measurable results are things that happened, they are in the past. There are no "facts" about the future. To this comes secondly that the measurable events are primarily inside events rather than outside events. The important developments on the outside, the things which determine that the buggy whip industry disappears and that IBM becomes a big business — let alone that Cuban subsidiaries of American companies are confiscated — are not measurable until it is too late to have "control."

A balance between the measurable and the non-measurable is therefore a central and constant problem of management. In many ways it is *the problem* of management and the true decision area.

Measurements which do not spell out the assumptions in respect to the non-measurable that are being made — as parameters if you please or in any other form — misdirect therefore. They actually misinform. Yet the more we can quantify the truly measurable areas, the greater the temptation to put all out emphasis on those — the greater, therefore, the danger that what looks like better "controls" will actually mean less "control" if not a business out of control altogether.

Section III

There is one more important thing to be said. There is a fundamental, incurable, basic limitation to "controls" in a "social institution." This lies in the fact that a "social institution" is both a true entity and a complete fiction. As an entity it has purposes of its own, a performance of its own, results of its own — and a survival of its own. These are the areas of which we have been speaking so far. But a social institution is comprised of persons, each with his own purpose, his own ambitions, his own ideas, his own needs. No matter how "totalitarian" the institution, it has to satisfy the ambitions and needs of its members, and do so in their capacity as individuals but through institutional rewards and punishments, incentives and deterrents. The expression of this may be quantifiable — such as a raise in salary. But the system itself is not quantitative in character and cannot be quantified.

Yet here is the real "control" of the institution, that is the ground of behavior and the cause of action. People act as they are being rewarded or punished. For this, to them, rightly, is the true expression of the values of the institution and of its true, as against its professed, purpose and role. Employment selection and promotion decisions are the real "controls." In the employment selection an institution decides what kind of people it wants altogether. In the promotion decisions it makes operational its true and actual values and its real performance standards. A company that tells its foremen that the job is human relations but which then promotes the foreman who best does his paper work, makes it very clear to even the dumbest man in the shop that it wants paper work rather than human relations. And it will get paper work.

A system of "controls" which is not in conformity with this true, this only effective, this ultimate "control" of the organization which lies in its people-decisions, will therefore at best be ineffectual — as most are. At worst it will cause never-ending conflict and will push the organization out of control. Unfortunately this is only too often the situation where economically focused controls are imposed upon a research organization which professes dedication to "scientific values." Either promotions are then being made according to economic criteria — which violates the profession of the research group. Or promotions are being made according to scientific criteria — which destroys the credibility and acceptance of the economic "controls."

In designing "controls" for a business one therefore has to understand and analyze the actual "control" of the business, its personnel decisions especially in respect to promotion. Otherwise one designs a system of "controls" which does not lead to "control." One secondly has to think through the actual "control" system, the personnel decisions, to see whether it really is in agreement with the true needs of the business. Otherwise there is no economic performance.

But finally one has to realize that even the most powerful "instrument board" complete with Computers, Operations Research, and Simulations is secondary to the invisible, qualitative control of any human organization, its systems of rewards and punishments, of values and taboos — as it expresses itself in the ultimate decision, the personnel decision.

The new controls technology has tremendous scope and power. There is tremendous need for new and better controls, and especially for controls that are quantitative and therefore not just matters of "opinion." But the new "controls" have this power and satisfy this need, precisely because they are not "objective," are not "neutral," precisely because they change both the events they record and observe and the men to whom they report and whom they inform. What is needed therefore for those who are the designers of these "controls" is an attitude very different from that of the physical scientist or the instrument maker. Theirs is much greater power — but also much greater limitation. They have to know that they can do much less — and have to know what they cannot do. But they also have to know that what they can do means much more — and have to impose on themselves the responsibility appropriate to this power.

27 Control in Government Administration

A. M. Willms

Under the hierarchical organization now prevalent in administration, control is indispensable. It enters every phase of management and becomes more vital as decentralization and delegation become more popular and more inevitable. Through control the manager can exercise directing, restraining or governing influence over the actions of subordinates but much more important, control enables the manager to measure achievement in the various parts of his program and to adjust and replan as necessary. Control is not used primarily to allocate responsibility or to allot blame — though sometimes these are side effects of control — it is set up to ensure effective achievement of objectives.

In administration, control is usually understood to have three functions:

> control sets standards or performance indicators to measure achievement
> control checks results or measures achievement
> control takes corrective or remedial action as required.

Currie, speaking to the Institute of Public Administration, defined control in management:

> By control I mean the process of measuring performance in relation to cost or expenditure of time, materials, space or some other asset, then comparing that performance against some standard which we know to be fair and reasonable and finally taking action to correct deficiencies where these are identified. This process of measurement and control is *constructive* in that it aids managers to improve their operations.[1]

Currie suggests substituting the word "monitor" for the word "control" and in view of the connotations which crowd the latter this might be a good idea, at least in theory. In fact it probably would not work since managers have been using the word control for a long time and they are not likely to change.

In management control is usually concerned with three aspects of the objective-achieving process:

> productivity, effectiveness and efficiency
> legality
> morality.

That is, the manager wants to achieve his objective as efficiently as possible, without transgressing the law and without violating codes.

Control Sets Standards

Setting standards can be one of the most difficult of the technical exercises in management. While it is possible and comparatively easy to set standards for manufacturing activities where countable units are produced, it is not easy when the activities involved have intangible results which do not lend themselves to quick, precise measurement. It is difficult, for example, to set standards to assess the achievements of an embassy or a

---

[1] G. N. Currie, "Efficiency vs. Service in Public Administration", *Canadian Public Administration*, Vol. 7, No. 2, June 1964, p. 167. Italics added.

consulate and it is almost equally difficult to devise a gauge to judge the work of a management analysis unit. But many attempts have been made to define both quantity and quality of achievement and undoubtedly much more will be done.

There are *physical standards* based on operational measures which can be applied fairly easily, especially at the lower levels of an enterprise. The physical units may be words per minute by a typist or typesetter; they may be units of output per hour, day or week, they may be man-hours or man-days per unit of output or some other tangible quantity. Physical standards can measure quality as well as quantity — the number of errors per page of type, the number of rejects in production and so on.

The technique most frequently used to set up physical standards is called *work measurement*. This is simply "a means of establishing what a fair day's work should be".[2] It is especially effective in routine duties where a large volume of highly repetitive operations occur. Work measurement uses a number of specialized skills such as technical estimating, work sampling, time studies or the application of predetermined time data. The benefits of work measurement to a manager can be many. These mathe-matical standards may help him to:

establish the optimum size of his work force and justify increases
   or decreases in staff
forecast the duration and cost of jobs in which human resources
   play a large role
evaluate the performance of workers
evaluate techniques or equipment
establish training needs.

They are the basis for all incentive pay schemes.

Employees dislike detailed control and that is the main drawback to using work measurement. Also, these skills may be misapplied. Work measurement began under a cloud. It was used by the efficiency experts in the first two decades of this century as a device to make employees work harder and in some instances became so odious that the United States Congress was moved to attach a rider to defence budgets that no stop watches be used in arsenals. On the other hand, if management has the confidence of its employees, explains carefully the purpose and applica-tion of work measurement, enlists employee participation to help set standards and if incentives are related to improved productivity, then work measurement can become an effective motivator.

There are *money* or *dollar standards* arising from the budget which can be imposed on the budget or which can be used apart from the budget.

Cost standard. Here is a relatively simple and obvious standard which can be most effective. It may involve computing the costs per unit produced or per hour of service rendered or, more frequently in government, it may

---

2 Civil Service Commission, "An Introduction to Work Measurement", September 1963, p. 4.

entail defining the cost of branches, divisions and sections per month or week of operation. The cost of an operation does not in itself constitute a measure of efficiency or effectiveness. It is only half of the efficiency equation. But the use of cost standards may induce employees to become cost conscious, and eventually become efficiency conscious. If costs are defined and credit is given for reduction of costs an attitude is created which may engender efficiency consciousness.

Revenue standards are only applicable to a few parts of the government service — where the government produces goods or services at a direct cost to the user — but where applicable they should be used. The Queen's Printer must have a standard when pricing books and Air Canada has a standard to determine the price of an airplane ticket.

Capital standards are used by departmental or agency comptrollers to calculate the ratio of net return to capital investment or to determine optimum inventories in relation to storage costs, turnover and so on.

There are other dollar standards. Many are designed to meet special needs.

Physical standards and money standards can be calculated mathematically but *program standards* are more informal and far less precise. Program standards are usually a loose comparison of the project's expectations with its success. They are now receiving much attention in United States government administration[3] and this is the type of standard which the Treasury Board of the Canadian federal government hopes to apply to departmental programs.

In recent years a skill has been developed which can assist in setting program standards — benefit-cost analysis. Benefit-cost analysis is primarily a tool of the economists but it is also being used to assess and measure program or project feasibility. Its advocates define a project as "an undertaking whose benefits and costs are identifiable and whose feasibility can be determined in technical terms".[4]

However, there are simpler ways of devising program standards. Historical comparison is widespread: what this unit achieved last year and the year before is compared to what it has achieved this year with allowances for changes in personnel, in the budget and so on. The achievement of one unit may be compared to that of another if the two are similar in size and objective. Project standards can be based on a comparison of performance and cost in government projects with similar projects contracted out to business. Many government departments and agencies can use contracting as an effective device to set up control standards.

Intangible standards are quite common in government management and are sometimes the only standards available for measuring performance. Frequently these standards are used unconsciously and a manager should be aware he is using measures which usually require qualification or careful analysis. This includes such vague indications, or straws in the wind, as

---

3 See, for example, U.S. Bureau of the Budget Bulletin, Vol. 66, No. 3, October 1965.
4 W. R. D. Sewell *et al, Guide to Benefit-Cost Analysis*, Queen's Printer, Ottawa, 1965.

complaints or approbation from customers or the public generally. Snap judgements are sometimes based entirely on the more obvious indications of attitude or morale gleaned from one visit to a field office. The opinions of outsiders who have frequent dealings with an enterprise are inevitably used as a standard. These intangible standards can be misleading but they are in common use.

In the public service the prevalent objection to control is that because of the nature of the work, standards are difficult to design and any standards devised for the public service must have so many qualifications that they become meaningless. Currie had a reply to these objections:

> The professional manager starts with the proposition that all things can be controlled. He believes that there is some criterion or measurement which can be applied to evaluate the results. If the manager started with the opposite philosophy, he would end up with no control. He would fail to manage and would be defeated. As managers we must guard against negative thinking and approach every activity with the conviction that there is some means of control and that the challenge is to find the most appropriate one.[5]

Some axioms about standards have evolved over the years and the manager does well to heed them. First, standards should be set up, as much as possible, with the participation of those to whom they will be applied. When it is not possible to have the employees participate they should at least be consulted and advised. They should know how the standards were chosen, what purpose they will serve and how they will be applied. Today this participation by staff is almost *sine qua non*; standards can be a bar to better performance when applied arbitrarily.

It follows then that standards should not be hidden in the manager's desk in a file marked "Confidential". They should be readily available to all affected. It also follows that standards should be as simple as possible so that each employee can understand them.

Standards should be permissive and flexible rather than rigid in their application. One of the best known standards is par in golf. There is no attempt to make all golf players shoot par and no sanctions are used against those who do not rise to the standard. Everyone admits that because of many and varying circumstances some players have a bigger handicap than others. All this assumes of course that the players strive to play the game as it should be played.

Measuring Results

Having set up standards, the next essential is to know how to use them to measure what has been achieved.

There are a number of techniques which are specially designed to measure progress. One of these frequently used in the last few years is

---

[5] Currie, *op. cit.*, p. 168.

called *management audit* or *operational audit*. Actually only the name has recently become popular. The process has been used much longer under such names as inspections, inspection services or visits. Management audit is an assessment of the effectiveness of an enterprise or a unit of that enterprise. Its object is to reveal defects, irregularities or weaknesses and to assist in improvement. Most large enterprises now have specialists to do this. They are usually thoroughly familiar with many aspects of management. They must be able to begin an audit of one aspect of management and when necessary follow it through into other spheres of management as the enquiry proceeds. For this reason auditors are often recruited from the ranks of management analysts. They have no direct responsibility for the achievements of the unit which they assess.

Another means that management has to measure results are *reports* that are normally demanded of subordinate units. These may be daily, weekly, monthly or annual reports or they may be required at the completion of various stages of a program or project. The reports may be in detail on *pro forma* or they may merely indicate that a certain stage in the project plan has been reached.

Research on the content and methods of reporting can be summarized briefly.[6] Most enterprises require too many reports. Moreover, reports that were originally required for one time or for one purpose continue to appear after their initial use has been accomplished. Managers do not hesitate to ask for reports when they feel these will be useful but they seldom think to turn off the tap when the flow is no longer required. Consequently head offices often receive a profusion of reports which may be only marginally useful, which could have been summarized or abbreviated and which often are costly to prepare.

Reports must serve a purpose. Very frequently the supervisor of the reporting unit and the manager who receives the reports will find that both profit from succinct reports designed to give the most specific summary of the activities of the reporting unit. This report often begins with a *pro forma*. Concise information is required in a form which makes possible comparison with other reports and the report ends with a narrative qualifying the form's contents.

Personnel ratings as they have traditionally been used in Canadian government administration have not been a measure of achievement but the newly introduced *performance reviews* should be eminently useful. In fact, the theory of performance review is almost an ideal portrait of control as applied to individuals. The employee and his supervisor jointly set up aims or objectives and standards of work, and periodically both are reviewed.

Generally speaking the manager must have a method for measuring the

---

[6] The Royal Commission on Government Organization, *Report*, Vol. 1, 1962. This is a brief synopsis of considerable study by members of the Commission staff. For records management training purposes the United States National Archives has done much work on reporting. This is reflected in training literature in use there.

achievement of his units. As much as possible the method should be applied jointly by supervisor and subordinate. The allocation of blame or praise should be incidental and as far as possible the cause for failure rather than the responsibility for failure should be sought.

Remedial Action

The third step in effective control is correcting weaknesses or adjusting plans as necessary.

Remedial action can employ any or all areas of management. It will frequently involve a change in planning, it can include reorganization, or changes in methods, procedures, equipment, staff or accommodation. Sometimes remedial action will entail special training for all employees and it may include disciplinary measures.

Control has been unpopular with government management for a number of reasons. As Mary Parker Follett pointed out many years ago, it is a human characteristic to reject control unless the law of the situation demands it.[7] It must be obvious to the employee on whom the controls are imposed that they are necessary. He will then be more willing to accept them. In business, particularly in smaller firms, it is obvious to even the lowliest clerk that controls generate profits and that the firm must have profits to survive. But in government this is not so. The average public servant assumes that resources are available to fill all demands and so the need to measure productivity is not at all obvious to him. Furthermore, control has frequently been misused. Sometimes it has been instituted merely as a gesture and the measurement has been applied to picayune details of methods and procedures rather than to achievements. The inspection teams which operate in many government departments have not been capable of measuring results. They have exercised their meagre talents in checking personnel attendance, the state of the records or the condition of stationery stores.

Efficiency and Effectiveness

Efficiency and effectiveness are two words which are frequently used in describing the success or failure of an enterprise. Efficiency is a measure of performance: it is a ratio of accomplishment over cost, or output over input, while effectiveness is a measure of the achievement of the objectives of an enterprise.

It is ironic that efficiency, a word which lends itself to perhaps the most precise definition in the manager's glossary, is in Simon's phrase: "... almost certainly one of the most abused words in the dictionary of administra-

---

[7] L. Gulick and L. Urwick (eds.), *Papers on the Science of Administration*, Institute of Public Administration, New York, 1937, p. 161.

tion".[8] Efficiency is a measure of the performance in an enterprise which is based on both productivity and cost, and it can best be expressed as a ratio:

$$\frac{\text{Measure of production}}{\text{Measure of resources used}} = \text{measure of efficiency;}$$

or in government administration it might be more accurate to say:

$$\frac{\text{maximum production}}{\text{given resources}} = \text{best efficiency.}$$

Other ratios that are used to indicate efficiency are:

$$\frac{\text{Benefits}}{\text{Cost}} \quad \text{or} \quad \frac{\text{Output}}{\text{Input}}$$

In a community concerned with traffic safety the measure of efficiency would be the steps taken to ensure safety — for example the man-hours devoted by the police to traffic patrol, the number of children on school patrols, the number of pedestrian crosswalks installed — in relation to the cost of these steps. The measure of effectiveness, on the other hand, would probably be the reduction in accidents or injuries compared to last year.

Obviously effectiveness cannot be measured unless the objectives of an enterprise are clearly spelled out and, conversely, it is a clear indication that the objectives of a department or agency are adequately defined when effectiveness can be measured. Most government enterprises have not yet reached this stage. Fortunately there is a strong correlation between efficiency and effectiveness — high efficiency in performance usually means success in achieving objectives.

It is true that the achievement of great efficiency in the mathematical sense is not always desirable. Often it is better for the manager to accept less efficiency and short term effectiveness, and retain customer support or reduce efficiency to keep the community happy. These are non-mathematical judgements which the manager must make but they do not alter his basic definition of efficiency. Consideration of efficiency always "dictates that choice of alternatives which produces the largest result for a given application of resources"[9] or demands the greatest productivity with minimum resources.

Efficiency can often be specified as either short-run or long-run. In government management it is the short-run which is most frequently used as a yardstick. Even short-run efficiency is often quite difficult to measure and long-run efficiency is frequently impossible to assess.

To find the best means of achieving optimum efficiency is difficult and perplexing, but before the manager tackles that problem he has other questions to ponder. First he must decide what role efficiency shall play in his scale of values as manager. This question was answered quite confidently by Luther Gulick:

[8] H. A. Simon, D. W. Smithburg and V. A. Thompson, *Public Administration*, Knopf, New York, 1959, p. 490.
[9] *Ibid.*

> In the science of administration whether public or private the basic 'good'
> is efficiency. The fundamental objective of the science of administration
> is the accomplishment of the work in hand with the least expenditure of
> manpower and materials. Efficiency is thus axiom number one in the value
> scale of administration.[10]

His dictum is probably still valid for private enterprise but there is considerable doubt that it is applicable in government administration. While the businessman today avows responsibility for the welfare of his employees, his customers and his community as well as to the owners of the business there is no doubt where his first allegiance lies. In government administration this is not so clear cut. The political acceptability of the service or of the rate of production is just as important to the public servant as maximum efficiency. There is no doubt that the standard most acceptable to the public is frequently not the most efficient. The public servant must give as much priority to the wants and wishes of his customers as to his bosses because indirectly his customers usually are also his bosses.

The public administrator's top manager, the minister to whom he is responsible or to whom he reports, is not usually concerned primarily with efficiency. He is more closely concerned with the welfare of his constituents, his party, his fellow parliamentarians and the country. Therefore the first criterion for success in public service management will be something other than efficiency.

Furthermore, government organization has not been set up to maximize efficiency. When we accept the thesis that the ratio of efficiency is made up of the numerator (production) and the denominator (resources) we also establish that both parts of the ratio must be the concern of one manager. Neither part of the ratio can be manipulated without affecting the whole. In government however we have tended to divide the responsibility. The concern for the resources has been allocated to the supreme controller, the Treasury Board, while the departmental manager has been expected to concern himself with production and productivity. Therefore, if the manager thinks he can increase his production by $2x$ units if given an increment of x resources, this discovery will be useless to him. The body which controls the resources is not concerned with productivity and since it is the supreme body, the yardstick in administration tends to be resource consumption rather than production. This is in sharp contrast to the fact that, generally speaking, greater efficiency is usually achieved by increasing productivity and seldom by reducing resources. Here we have a dilemma. We have deliberately promoted resource-orientation knowing full well that for greater efficiency our managers should be production-oriented.

It is often difficult to find suitable units with which to measure the two parts of the efficiency ratio and especially the numerator in the ratio. The productivity of public servants is frequently intangible.

Despite these difficulties efficiency is sought and the public servant will at least improve his public image by striving to attain it.

---

[10] Gulick and Urwick, *op. cit.*, p. 192.

28   Efficiency in Government and Business*

A. W. Johnson

The Royal Commission on Government Organization — the Glassco Commission — has aroused an unusual interest in efficiency in government. For some, its reports — frequently unread — have confirmed a long-standing suspicion that governments always have been, and always will be, inefficient. For others the Commission's reports hold out a new hope that business-like methods can and will be introduced into government. For still others the reports reveal once again a profound misunderstanding on the part of businessmen as to the processes of parliamentary government, and confirm once more the need for continuing organization and methods studies within government. For a few — the management consultants — the reports and the public interest which they have aroused create a sort of happy hunting ground where new commissions and new studies can be proposed with confidence — all of them requiring the specialized skills of the management consultant.

However heterogeneous the responses to the Glassco Commission's work, anyone who is interested in perfecting the processes of government will welcome warmly this new-found interest in government administration.

Having said this, I find myself wanting to sound a note of caution about the premises which seem to underlie the discussions of the Glassco reports, and indeed the reports themselves.

First, there seems to me to be abroad an assumption that "everyone knows what efficiency means." It is simply a matter of good organization, of effective management practices, of streamlined procedures, and the like. But is this all that there is to efficient government, to effective government? Are there not other dimensions to "efficiency" which are equally important to, if not more important than, the purely administrative or management aspect?

Second, the proposition seems to have been accepted, without too much critical scrutiny, that the methods by which efficiency is achieved in business are equally applicable in government — or very nearly so. There is a science of administration, in other words, which can be employed with equal effectiveness in business or in government. But is it true that the "efficiency techniques" of business are entirely applicable in government — or at least in all phases of government? Can efficiency in the public services be achieved simply by perfecting the "horizontal" processes — organization, financial management, personnel management, and the like? Or are there large areas of public administration where new "efficiency techniques" must

* Reprinted and slightly abridged with permission of author and publisher from *Canadian Public Administration*, Vol. 6, No. 3, September 1963, pp. 245-260. This paper was presented to meetings of the Victoria, Vancouver, Edmonton, Hamilton and Halifax Regional Groups of the Institute of Public Administration of Canada.

be evolved, or the conventional ones substantially adapted if the unique program problems of the public services are to be evaluated effectively?

Third, I find myself wondering, if governments are less efficient than they might and should be — and surely all of us will acknowledge that they are — why is this so? Is it enough to say that organization is defective, or that procedural practices are deficient, and they should be remedied? Or should we stop to consider whether there is in the civil service a sufficient "efficiency motivation" — a motivation upon which we can build so as to ensure a *continuing* concern for effective operation? Or must we reconcile ourselves to the need for periodic royal commissions which will shake up the public services on these occasions, only to be followed by intervals of decline and decay? This sometimes seems to be the assumption which underlies the public discussions of the Glassco reports.

These are the questions which I want to consider. Please notice that I am not pretending to analyze the Glassco Commission reports, nor to analyze the analyses that have been made of them. Instead, what I am trying to do is to question whether we really have thought through what we mean by efficiency in government, whether we really know the methods by which it can be achieved, and whether we have considered carefully enough the source of efficiency motives in government — if any.

What is Efficiency?

My first question is what do we mean when we talk of efficiency? The conventional notion is clear enough: it simply means reducing administrative expenses, eliminating waste and extravagance, and speeding up service to the public. This is what I am inclined to call "administrative efficiency."

The notion of "administrative efficiency" first was developed, as we all know, in private business — specifically, in manufacturing enterprises. Its pioneers — Henri Fayol and Frederick W. Taylor — were seeking to increase productivity, to maximize production, and they sought to do so by improving work arrangements. Given the production of a certain commodity, given sometimes the present technology, how could an enterprise best divide and order the processes of manufacture in order to maximize output and minimize inputs? The techniques they used now are well known: product simplification and standardization, production planning and control, proper division of work, the use of management improvement techniques, staff training and the development of happy staff relations, performance analysis and control, and the rest.

I do not want to elaborate on these techniques of "administrative efficiency" right now — that will come later. My present purpose is to point out the premises upon which "administrative efficiency" is based: this kind of efficiency takes for granted the policy decisions which created the manufacturing enterprise in the first place. "Administrative efficiency" *assumes* that the right product is being produced; it *assumes* that the market for the product exists or can be developed; it *assumes* that the plant is properly located; and frequently it *assumes* that the technology of production being used is the appropriate technology.

But notice that if the wrong policy decisions had been made in the first place — if the plant were poorly located or the market were insufficient — not all the administrative efficiency in the world would compensate for these errors in decision-making. There is, in short, another kind of efficiency which is of a higher order than "administrative efficiency," and that is "policy efficiency" — the making of the right policy decisions.

In manufacturing enterprise the components of "policy efficiency" — though it is not called that — are well known. Economic studies precede a decision to manufacture a new product — studies both of the potential market for the product, and of the manufacturing processes which will have to be developed. Feasibility studies determine the economics of the enterprise — studies which forecast the sales revenues and all of the costs of production: capital, labour, raw materials, transportation, and so on. Plant location studies compare the economics of alternative plant locations, given the differentials between the wage costs, transportation costs, and power costs of different areas. Financial analysis determines how much of the capital can be interest-bearing and how much must be equity capital in order that costs might be minimized, while at the same time retaining control in the hands of the sponsors of the enterprise. "Policy efficiency," in short, is what the economists call proper resource allocation.

The same distinction between "administrative efficiency" and "policy efficiency" can be made in government. "Administrative efficiency" — what the Glassco Commission concerned itself with primarily — consists of good organization, efficient procedures, effective financial control, proper inventory control, appropriate paperwork and systems management, and the rest. "Policy efficiency," on the other hand, is a matter of making the right policy decisions, of selecting the appropriate programs in order to achieve the government's objectives.

Let me give a few examples. If a highway is properly located, given the trends in population distribution, travel patterns and the rest, the taxpayers will be saved enormous sums of money in their travel costs. If welfare programs are constructed so as to return people to the active labour force, the social aid bill which the taxpayers bear will be significantly reduced. If treatment programs in mental hospitals are calculated to return patients to the community the number of mental institutions required will be controlled. If education programs produce the kind of trained labour force which the economy requires, the numbers of unemployed will be reduced. On a more sophisticated level still, if a proper balance is achieved between monetary policy, fiscal policy and trade policy, the rate of growth of the economy will be increased, and the cost to the community of unemployment will be reduced.

Here once again, the economies of "policy efficiency" greatly outweigh the savings which can be achieved by "administrative efficiency." One bad policy decision — for example, the construction of an uneconomic railway or road — will cost the taxpayer more than can possibly be saved by better control over the purchase of underwear for the armed forces.

It is important, in other words, not to be misled when we talk about efficiency. "Administrative efficiency" unquestionably is important, but let no one think that it is the only kind of efficiency, or even that it is the most important kind.

Now let me build into this framework a third kind of efficiency — "service efficiency." This is an obscure phrase, I know, but it is the only one I can think of to describe "effectiveness" as opposed to "efficiency."

All of us are familiar, I am sure, with the conflict which sometimes exists between administrative economies on the one hand, and the provision of better service to the public on the other. Let me give some examples. It is almost always possible to achieve economies of scale through the centralization of services, such as health and welfare. But the effect of doing so is to make the services less accessible to the public. It is always possible to enforce safety programs more efficiently by giving the safety inspectors more power, or by making the regulations more explicit; but the effect is to subject the citizen to requirements that are sometimes impractical, if not downright hostile to his freedom of action. It is frequently possible to streamline financial processes by reducing some of the controls over departmental spending, but to do so may be to reduce parliamentary control over the government and the civil service.

I acknowledge that I have collected under this heading of "service efficiency" a heterogeneous group of public service objectives, including service to the public, responsiveness to public opinion, and the preservation of parliamentary control. But my point, I hope, is clear: efficiency in government must be measured not in economic terms alone, Equally, indeed more important, it must be measured in terms of the effectiveness with which it provides public services within the context of constitutional government. Public services must be readily and equally accessible to all citizens. They must be close enough to the citizen, in fact, that he can exert an influence upon them — adapting them to the needs of the community as the needs of the community change. The regulatory functions of the state must be discharged not for the sole purpose of protecting people and their property, but also with the purpose of preserving to the maximum extent possible the rights of the citizens being regulated. All public services must be provided and financed in such a way that the cabinet remains in control of the bureaucracy and that parliament remains in control of both. The prime measure of efficiency in government, I am arguing, is whether the government provides the public services the public wants and where it wants them, and whether the public services provided and the public servants who provide them remain firmly in the control of the public's representatives.

Let me make one more point about "service efficiency." In business this kind of efficiency is less distinguishable from "policy efficiency" and "administrative efficiency" than it is in government. If an enterprise fails to provide what the public wants, or fails to respond to shifts in consumer tastes, an economic penalty sooner or later must be paid. Sales will decline. So "service efficiency" in business is looked upon in economic terms. In government, however, the penalty for inefficiency in service is a political or a constitutional one: the government is defeated or constitutional processes are eroded, or both. And only a fairly perceptive observer will see the relationship — perhaps I should say the conflict — between "administrative efficiency" and "service efficiency."

My first observation, then, is this: it is a mistake to judge efficiency only in administrative terms. It would be possible to have the slickest and the most streamlined government in the world, and yet to have public policies which resulted in a gross misallocation of resources, or public services which were quite incompatible with the objectives of constitutional democracy. I am not suggesting by any means that we should ignore administrative efficiency: quite the contrary, it is one of our primary goals. But I do suggest that as public servants we have a responsibility to look to the broader kinds of efficiency as well — "policy efficiency" and "service efficiency" — if we are to serve the public well.

Efficiency Methods

If I have identified correctly the several kinds of efficiency in government, the next question is whether we know how to achieve them. It is usually assumed — I suspect that the Glassco Commission assumed — that the methods by which business achieves efficiency are equally applicable in government. This may be so. But if, on the other hand, a different approach is required in government, or a substantial adaptation of business methods is needed, we will be misled if we simply try to transplant into the public service the "efficiency techniques" of private business. At best we will have done an incomplete job.

It is in the field of "administrative efficiency," of course, that the approach of private business is best known. The goal, as we all know, is to maximize output and to minimize expense. This means that each factor of production — labour, equipment, and so on — must be identified, and its contribution to production — its productivity — must be measured. If the productivity of a given factor, labour for example, can be increased, then the cost per unit of production will be reduced. If on the other hand, the productivity of a given factor of production has reached its limit, management may seek to substitute a cheaper production factor — equipment in place of labour, for example.

The key to this approach is measurability: you must be able to measure the inputs — man-hours, equipment hours and so on — and you must be able to measure the outputs — units of commodity produced. Having done this it becomes possible to establish a "standard" as to the quantity of inputs required in order to produce a given unit of output. The standard may be the average of previous levels of productivity, or it may be a target level established through controlled production experiments. In either event these standards are applied to the manufacturing process, and the various factors of production are expected to perform at the target levels.

There are, of course, techniques for raising productivity to the standards which have been set, or for raising the standards themselves. These include greater specialization in the manufacturing processes, production planning and control, improvements in organization and coordination, the simplification of work processes through work study and measurement, staff training and so on.

These techniques were developed specifically for manufacturing operations, but they have been adapted to office operations. This has been possible wherever inputs and outputs have both been found to be measurable. Production planning and control takes the form of planning and controlling paper operations and paper flows. Work simplification takes the form of analyzing what is "added" at each stage of the office procedure, and of eliminating steps which are found to be unnecessary. Staff training and development and space layout studies both are applied much as they are in manufacturing operations. And office equipment — notably, today, data-processing equipment — is substituted for labour where it is found to be a cheaper "input" than are clerical man-hours.

These techniques have been found to be applicable in many office operations, but by no means in all. Wherever the output is diffuse, or does not lend itself to precise measurement, it is unlikely that these conventional efficiency techniques can be used. This is true not only in the production of office services but in the production of other services as well — legal, medical and personal services, to name a few. The point to be noted is that business itself has found it difficult, sometimes impossible, to apply the efficiency techniques of commodity-producing industries to industries which produce services. And this is nearly always where the output does not lend itself to precise measurement. We should no more expect to be able to apply the "efficiency techniques" of commodity-producing industries to government than we are able to apply them to other service industries. Some government services, such as large-scale paperwork operations, road building, the production and sale of electric power, and sewer and water systems, lend themselves to these "efficiency techniques." But a great many do not.

Consider some of the services which governments provide: public health nursing, primary and secondary schools, agricultural extension, social work services, and psychiatric research, to name a few. In each case the work inputs are measurable enough: staff time, differentiated between different classes of workers, materials used, equipment employed, travel expenses, telephone expenses, and so on.

But the output of these employees — the ultimate output — is extremely difficult to measure. This is partly because it is inherently difficult to identify and to measure, and partly because the results become apparent only several years after the services have been rendered. Here are some examples. The results of the child health clinics conducted by public health nurses become apparent only in the morbidity and mortality statistics of the future. The results of the education given in primary and secondary schools are felt only when the children involved have become active members of the labour force — and then it is difficult to compare what is with what might have been had the schooling not been given. The agricultural education given farmers by "Ag Reps" becomes evident years later in higher and more stable crop production, but even then it is difficult to establish a clear causal relationship. The effect of social workers' efforts may never be known statistically; all we know is that certain families or young people or offenders have become active and productive members of the community. The relationship between psychiatric research and more effective treatment of the mentally ill becomes known, and even measurable statistically, but the lag between the cause and the effect is very substantial indeed.

Obviously we cannot expect to measure real output at the time the service is given and sometimes we may never be able to do so (though I think we should try much harder than we do). All we can hope to do is to measure the units of service given — and even here the exercise is sometimes futile (for example in primary and secondary education). But it *is* possible in some branches of government to measure the units of service that are provided — the number of clinics held by the public health nurse or the number of farm equipment demonstrations given by the agricultural representative — and where this is possible the conventional "efficiency techniques" may be adapted to the needs of the public service.

My point, then, is this: the methods used by business to achieve "administrative efficiency" may be used directly by governments only in a few areas of public service. If we are to develop "efficiency techniques" for the rest of the service we must adapt and innovate to a very considerable extent.

"Policy Efficiency"

The same holds true of "policy efficiency." Business administration schools have developed a considerable body of knowledge as to how manufacturing enterprises can achieve "policy efficiency" — they teach market analysis, plant location analysis, alternative forms of industry organization, including horizontal and vertical integration, the strategy of competition and so on. But none of this is useful to us in the public service.

What *is* useful, however, are the underlying methods being used by businessmen. What I am talking about now — or trying to — is the use of scientific method, of rational planning. There is, of course, a lot of guesswork in the policy decisions of boards of directors, but the forward-looking firm seeks to reduce the guesswork to a minimum. The elements in decision-making are analysed and measured statistically wherever possible: market trends, changes in consumer tastes, whether involuntary or induced, trends in costs, trends in technology, the behaviour of competitors, and so on. And alternative courses for achieving a given objective are examined before a decision is made. To take a simple example, the productive capacity of an industry is expanded only after markets have been analyzed, after alternative plant locations have been examined, after alternative methods of production have been explored, and so on.

There are areas of government where the same analytical processes can easily be employed. Road location by departments of highways is a good example: public servants study traffic patterns and road-use trends, and then, using the benefit-cost analysis approach, determine the optimum location and design of a highway. This sort of approach is quite common in the engineering phases of government work — though I suspect that the public is quite unaware of the use of these planning techniques.

It is more difficult to apply such planning techniques in the area of social policies, though some advances have been made. It is in this area, however, where there is the greatest room for innovation and adaptation.

Let me give you some examples. Governments have assumed responsibility for the community's costs of hospitalization and, to a substantial extent, for the costs of nursing home care for the aged and the disabled. Having done so, they inevitably confront demands for enlarged facilities, as hospital utilization rises and as the population of the aged and disabled increases. Two courses are open to the government. One is to meet the demand, locating the facilities as rationally as possible, using population studies as a guide. The other is to determine whether alternative forms of care are possible or preferable. Are there disabilities for which preventive or even earlier treatment would reduce the incidence of institutionalization? Is it possible to embark upon rehabilitation programs which would reduce the length of stay in institutions, thus increasing the "turnover" in public institutions — to put it crudely? Is it possible to provide home-care services which would be less costly than institutionalization?

In other words, the objective is to care for the sick and the disabled, and the problem is not necessarily one of providing more capital facilities. The economic and social costs might be lower if alternative methods of prevention, treatment and rehabilitation, were adopted.

To make policy decisions such as these — and all of us could give many more examples — is to achieve efficiency in government of the highest order. But to do so requires a highly imaginative and a very skilful public service — to say nothing of the cabinets and parliaments involved. Clearly "policy efficiency" in government is not a matter simply of adopting the techniques of business "policy efficiency": we in government must evolve our own techniques. Moreover, we will have saved pennies and lost dollars for the taxpayer if we preoccupy ourselves solely with "administrative efficiency."

Efficiency Incentives

My first two points, then, are these: efficiency in public administration has more dimensions than just one, and it will not be achieved simply by adopting the conventional "efficiency techniques." Public servants must concern themselves with all three kinds of efficiency — "policy," "administrative," and "service" — and they must do more than merely copy the "efficiency techniques" of business. They must adapt them and develop new ones.

My third question now comes into focus: are there in the public service sufficient incentives to efficiency? Is there the "will" to find the "way" to efficiency in government? The most melancholy part of public attitudes about the public service, is the assumption that there are not. We who are civil servants are, of course, inclined to dispute this, occasionally by rather pontifical pronouncements about our dedication to public service, and about our personal motivations — which we conceive to be of the highest order.

Now, I am not disputing these motivations, nor am I deriding them. They are most important. But I think the public would be relieved if they could see something more substantial, something less personal, perhaps even something less "chancy" than individual dedication.

The question that occurs to all of us, I'm sure, is why the efficiency motivation of business is so readily accepted as being sufficient, and how it really operates. I am referring, of course, to the profit motive. Can we assume with confidence that the profit motive operates automatically in industry? If so, how is it made effective — how is it "institutionalized"? If we had the answers to these questions we might have some clues as to where to look in the civil service for equivalent or alternative efficiency motivations.

It is probably fair to say that the profit motive in business influences primarily the owners of an enterprise, and top management staff whose effectiveness is judged largely by the profit and loss statement. And undoubtedly this motivation has a very real influence in the quest by these people for "policy efficiency."

But "administrative efficiency" cannot be achieved by top management alone: in the final analysis it can be only the product of the efforts of employees who are far removed from the direct benefits of greater productivity. It is the middle management people, the foremen and supervisors, indeed the workmen themselves, who must be relied upon to introduce new procedures and methods, to improve space layout, to speed up work flows, and so on. Yet these people rarely, if ever, see a profit and loss statement, and a good many of them would be unable to interpret one if they did see it. Moreover, even if they were able to read financial statements it would be most difficult for them to discern a clear and direct relationship between "administrative efficiency," higher productivity, and greater personal rewards. The effects of collective bargaining are more likely to be perceptible, even to foremen and supervisors.

What top management must do, then, is somehow to communicate at least to middle-management levels a "drive for efficiency." In some enterprises this is attempted by profit-sharing schemes. If this device were very common in private business, one might conclude that top management had in this way been able to make the profit motive operate among superintendents, supervisors, and foremen. The efficiency motivation even at these levels would then be the profit motive. But unless I am mistaken, it is a fact that profit sharing schemes are not that common in large-scale business enterprises.

What then is the " efficiency motivation"? How does top management instill in a large corporation the desire for efficiency — a desire which may flow from the profit motive but which is capable of existing by itself? I have the impression that what happens in a well-run corporation is that a sort of "efficiency value" is developed, and that this comes to be subscribed to by an important number of middle-management employees. The whole structure of rewards and penalties is designed to promote the efficient worker and the effective supervisor; and middle management people know that their success will be measured by the productivity of their departments. So efficiency, of and by itself, becomes the objective of the successful superintendent or foreman.

It would be idyllic to believe that this condition is produced with ease, or that it is common in all large-scale enterprises. In point of fact, businessmen themselves are not prepared to rely upon this approach alone. In addition to relating their system of rewards and penalties to employee-productivity — to the extent that their union contracts permit — business managers employ special teams whose job it is constantly to seek out improvements in organization and procedures. Work flow analysis, the examination of production processes, and all of the techniques of business engineering are used by these units to try to cut expenses and increase productivity. In smaller enterprises the services of management consultants may be used for the same end. To the extent that the "efficiency value" has been accepted by middle management people they will welcome the work of the systems analysts; to the extent that it hasn't the "time and motion boys" will be resented.

This oversimplification of the institutionalization of an "efficiency motivation" in private corporations is not meant to exalt business efficiency. Anyone who has had any experience in or association with corporate enterprise knows that there is room for improvement in business administration as well as in public administration. But my point is this: it is not a perception of the relationship between "administrative efficiency" and profits which drives middle management people or efficiency experts; it is the desire to prove their own ability to increase productivity. This is not to say that this "drive" has no relationship to the profit motive; it is merely to say that it can motivate people who are not themselves impelled by a desire for higher profits.

This being so, it seems to me reasonable to suppose that the same kind of efficiency motivation can exist in the public service, provided there is a will on the part of governments and senior public servants to create and to develop it. Since governments are not impelled by a profit motive, the question is whether there are other impulses that will cause them to instill in the public service an "efficiency value."

I suggest that there are. First, it is well known that inefficiency in government, whether manifested by indolent civil servants, or obstructive red-tape, or sheer incompetence, is quick to engage public criticism. And nothing can be more damaging, politically, to governments. Even if the public were docile, or immune to inefficiency in public administration, you can be sure that parliamentary oppositions would do their best to make people aware of the deficiencies of government bureaucracy. Certainly it has been my experience that ministers of the Crown react rather quickly to the complaints of citizens or of the opposition that they have encountered slothfulness, or rudeness, or inefficiency on the part of the public service. It is the ministers and their parliamentary supporters, after all, who pay the penalty for public dissatisfaction — just as it is the shareholders and the managers who are the losers when profits decline.

There is another reason, too, that ministers and senior public servants are impelled to take an interest in efficiency. All of us have learned that it isn't easy to enlarge our appropriations for the purpose of improving or expanding the programs for which we are responsible. Treasury boards and finance committees are notoriously difficult in these matters. But if we can demonstrate economies in some part of our department, the men on the treasury benches are more favourably disposed to an increase in the allotment for another part of the department. Moreover, the competition for funds is keen enough when budgets are being formulated that treasury board officials will often be told when departments feel that others are being profligate in their spending.

There is, in short, a constant competition for scarce resources in government — just as there is in the private sector of the economy — and finance officials like officials of operating departments are keenly aware of this fact. It has been my experience that this, in combination with the concern to avert public criticism, operates effectively to create in senior civil servants a real concern for efficiency.

I have said nothing about the "service motivation" which operates in government. It is all too easy to sound pompous or righteous in doing so. But I nevertheless believe it to be true that the great majority of cabinet ministers and senior civil servants are in the public service because of a concern that government should meet the social and economic needs of the community. And because of this motivation they are just as concerned about efficiency in public administration as businessmen are about efficiency in business administration. The question is whether they succeed in communicating their concern to the middle management levels of the civil service.

The techniques that senior public servants use to instill a concern for efficiency in their division heads and supervisors are the same that private management employ. First, promotion through the higher ranks of the civil service is based, so far as I can discern, upon demonstrated ability. This, like the system of rewards used in private business tends to focus the attention of middle management people upon efficiency and effectiveness. What is often misleading, I think, is the fact that efficiency assumes different forms in the public service; the result is that it is not readily recognizable to people who are accustomed to the patterns of efficiency in business.

Second, governments, like businesses, have established special agencies for the purpose of ensuring that departments do in fact organize their work effectively. Shortly after the second World War, Organization and Methods units were established in the Government of Canada and the Government of Saskatchewan, and since then Organization and Methods units, and the use of management consultants, have proliferated in federal departments, in provincial governments, and in municipal governments. These agencies operate in much the same manner as do their counterparts in industry.

Special Problems in Public Administration

I am arguing, in short, that the methods by which an "efficiency motivation" is institutionalized in the civil service are not too dissimilar from those used in private business. Having said this, I think it is fair to observe that there are special problems which must be overcome in government.

First, some governments, notably the Government of Canada, are such large organizations, and are so scattered geographically, that extra efforts are required to make the "efficiency motivation" operative. In a sense large governments should be compared with a national railway system rather than with a compact and homogeneous industrial enterprise.

Second, departmentalization in government is fundamentally different than it is in business. Each agency of the public service tends to operate a group of programs which are differentiated clearly from those of other agencies, with the result that a single approach to efficiency becomes impossible. Moreover, because of the principle of individual ministerial responsibility, it is more difficult to impose a central or unified approach to the management of the differentiated affairs of the several departments. The result is that it is possible to find some departments that are operated more efficiently than others. And it is not always easy for the cabinet to impose "efficiency requirements" on the weaker departments; certainly not as easy as it is for the management of a private business to do with respect to recalcitrant divisions of a relatively monolithic corporate enterprise.

Third, there is more frequently in government a conflict between "service efficiency" and "administrative efficiency." I was alluding to this when I spoke of the principle of individual ministerial responsibility. Greater "administrative efficiency" is sometimes possible, but only at the cost of diluting or modifying the arrangements of constitutional government. A cabinet is not a monolithic structure, any more than Canada is a homogeneous nation. And if individual ministers, like distinctive cultures in our nation, display a highly individual approach to the management of their affairs, it is not an easy matter, nor is it always proper, to impose a single or a unified approach. Similarly, a prime measure of success in government is whether parliamentary control is preserved and maintained. There is no doubt in my mind that financial processes in government could be streamlined if parliament's annual appropriation control were abandoned. But "service efficiency" — the preservation of parliamentary control — must take precedence.

Special difficulties are encountered also in achieving "policy efficiency." It seems to me reasonable to suppose that some government programs become obsolete during the passage of time, and that superior policies could be evolved for achieving the same ends. But the plain truth is, or so it seems to me, that there are strong, built-in pressures from the electorate to retain almost any public program which you might care to mention. Equally, new policies undoubtedly are adopted which are not the most efficient way of achieving a goal — indeed the goal itself may be questionable. I'm sure, for example, that most of us could select as illustrations some of Canada's tax laws; measures which are incredibly difficult to administer, but the results of which seem not to justify the effort involved. Yet each of these was built into the tax laws to meet the pressures of some part of the electorate.

It is not for me, as a civil servant, to identify more specifically than this alleged examples of "policy inefficiency." I content myself with the assertion that such inefficiencies, if they do exist, are the product largely of the political process in Canada. And if in fact we are getting the kind of government which we vote for, it is simply a contradiction in terms to suggest that these policy aberrations are in fact inefficiency. They may be inefficient ways of achieving an objective, or the objective itself may be inefficient in economic terms. But as long as the policies involved are the product of democratic processes they are legitimate in themselves — they are the product of "service efficiency."

Chapter Seven
Decision Making and Communicating

P. F. Drucker's paper on "The Effective Decision", which introduces the vast topic of decision making in this chapter, treats decision making in the deductive-logical manner that has established the conventional wisdom about this activity in the last two decades. By contrast, H. A. Simon, whose excerpt follows Drucker's, treats "decision making as synonymous with managing" unperturbed by the attendant problems in definition. The growth in analytical tools for managerial decision making is mentioned by Simon and is discussed by Ronayne under the title of operations research. The problems of communication are then discussed, followed by an excerpt from the Glassco Commission's comments on information services in Canadian government administration.

The topics of decision making and communication can be expanded to include most of man's socio-political activities and hence the literature available is vast and disparate. It is found in almost every field of psychology, sociology and economics as well as in political science and administration. An American bibliography of decision making for 1945-1957 — P. Wasserman and F. S. Silander, *Decision making: An Annotated Bibliography* (Cornell University Press, Ithica, New York, 1958) — contains more than 400 entries while its *Supplement* (Cornell University Press, Ithica, New York, 1964) for 1958-1963, has more than 600 entries. It is a formidable task to select the more significant items from this agglomeration.

H. A. Simon's *Administrative Behavior: A Study of Decision Making Processes in Administrative Organization* (Macmillan, New York, 1961) is the second edition of the book which in 1945 first introduced the idea of decision making as the "common conceptual roof under which both economic man and administrative man can live". Chapter 10 of J. C. Charlesworth (ed.), *Contemporary Political Analysis* (The Free Press, New York, 1967), "The Theory of Decision Making" sets decision making in a political science methodological context while Chapters 14 and 15 examine communications in a similar manner. Y. Dror and others present a series of articles on administrative decision making in *Public Administration Review*, Vol. 24, No. 3, September 1964. Other notable contributions are

American Management Association, *Effective Communication On the Job*, New York, 1963.

C. A. Milton, "Group vs. Individual Problem Solving and Decision Making", *Canadian Public Administration*, Vol. 8, No. 3, September, 1965.

J. M. Pfiffner, "Administrative Rationality", *Public Administration Review*, Vol. 20, No. 3, Summer 1960.

F. J. Roethlisberger, "The Administrator's Skill: Communication", *Harvard Business Review*, Vol. 31, No. 6, November-December 1953.

J. T. Dorsey, "A Communication Model for Administration", *Administrative Science Quarterly*, Vol. 2, No. 3, December 1957.

C. R. Rogers, "Barriers and Gateways to Communication", *Harvard Business Review*, Vol. 30, No. 4, July-August 1952.

E. Walton, "Motivation to Communicate", *Personnel Administration*, Vol. 25, No. 2, March-April 1962.

E. Walton, "A Study of Organizational Communication Systems", *Personnel Administration*, Vol. 26, No. 3, May-June 1963.

29   The Effective Decision*

Peter F. Drucker

Effective executives do not make a great many decisions. They concentrate on what is important. They try to make the few important decisions on the highest level of conceptual understanding. They try to find the constants in a situation, to think through what is strategic and generic rather than to "solve problems." They are, therefore, not overly impressed by speed in decision making; rather, they consider virtuosity in manipulating a great many variables a symptom of sloppy thinking. They want to know what the decision is all about and what the underlying realities are which it has to satisfy. They want impact rather than technique. And they want to be sound rather than clever.

Effective executives know when a decision has to be based on principle and when it should be made pragmatically, on the merits of the case. They know the trickiest decision is that between the right and the wrong compromise, and they have learned to tell one from the other. They know that the most time-consuming step in the process is not making the decision but putting it into effect. Unless a decision has "degenerated into work," it is not a decision; it is at best a good intention. This means that, while

* Reprinted with permission of author and publisher from *Harvard Business Review*, Vol. 45, January-February 1967, pp. 92-98.

the effective decision itself is based on the highest level of conceptual under-standing, the action commitment should be as close as possible to the capacities of the people who have to carry it out. Above all, effective execu-tives know that decision making has its own systematic process and its own clearly defined elements.

Sequential Steps

The elements do not by themselves "make" the decisions. Indeed, every decision is a risk-taking judgment. But unless these elements are the stepping-stones of the executive's decision process, he will not arrive at a right, and certainly not at an effective, decision. Therefore, in this article I shall describe the sequence of steps involved in the decision-making process. There are six such steps:

1. *The classification of the problem.* Is it generic? Is it exceptional and unique? Or is it the first manifestation of a new genus for which a rule has yet to be developed?
2. *The definition of the problem.* What are we dealing with?
3. *The specifications which the answer to the problem must satisfy.* What are the "boundary conditions"?
4. *The decision as to what is "right" rather than what is accept-able, in order to meet the boundary conditions.* What will fully satisfy the specifications *before* attention is given to the com-promises, adaptations, and concessions needed to make the deci-sion acceptable?
5. *The building into the decision of the action to carry it out.* What does the action commitment have to be? Who has to know about it?
6. *The feedback which tests the validity and effectiveness of the decision against the actual course of events.* How is the decision being carried out? Are the assumptions on which it is based appropriate or obsolete?

Let us take a look at each of these individual elements.

The Classification

The effective decision maker asks: Is this a symptom of a fundamental dis-order or a stray event? The generic always has to be answered through a rule, a principle. But the truly exceptional event can only be handled as such and as it comes.

Strictly speaking, the executive might distinguish among four, rather than between two, different types of occurrences.

First, there is the truly generic event, of which the individual occurrence is only a symptom. Most of the "problems" that come up in the course of the executive's work are of this nature. Inventory decisions in a business, for instance, are not "decisions." They are adaptations. The problem is generic. This is even more likely to be true of occurrences within manufacturing organizations. For example, a product control and engineering group will typically handle many hundreds of problems in the course of a month. Yet, whenever these are analyzed, the great majority prove to be just symptoms — and manifestations — of underlying basic situations. The individual process control engineer or production engineer who works in one part of the plant usually cannot see this. He might have a few problems each month with the couplings in the pipes that carry steam or hot liquids, and that's all.

Only when the total workload of the group over several months is analyzed does the generic problem appear. Then it is seen that temperatures or pressures have become too great for the existing equipment and that the couplings holding the various lines together need to be redesigned for greater loads. Until this analysis is done, process control will spend a tremendous amount of time fixing leaks without ever getting control of the situation.

The second type of occurrence is the problem which, while a unique event for the individual institution, is actually generic. The company that receives an offer to merge from another, larger one, will never receive such an offer again if it accepts. This is a nonrecurrent situation as far as the individual company, its board of directors, and its management are concerned. But it is, of course, a generic situation which occurs all the time. Thinking through whether to accept or to reject the offer requires some general rules. For these, however, the executive has to look to the experience of others.

Next there is the truly exceptional event that the executive must distinguish. The huge power failure that plunged into darkness the whole of Northeastern North America from the St. Lawrence to Washington in November 1965 was, according to first explanations, a truly exceptional situation. So was the thalidomide tragedy which led to the birth of so many deformed babies in the early 1960's. The probability of either of these events occurring, we were told, was one in ten million or one in a hundred million, and concatenations of these events were as unlikely ever to recur again as it is unlikely, for instance, for the chair on which I sit to disintegrate into its constituent atoms.

Truly unique events are rare, however. Whenever one appears, the decision maker has to ask: Is this a true exception or only the first manifestation of a new genus? And this — the early manifestation of a new generic problem — is the fourth and last category of events with which the precision process deals. We know now that both the Northeastern power failure and the thalidomide tragedy were only the first occurrences of what, under conditions of modern power technology or of modern pharmacology, are likely to become fairly frequent occurrences unless generic solutions are found.

All events but the truly unique require a generic solution. They require a rule, a policy, or a principle. Once the right principle has been developed, all manifestations of the same generic situation can be handled pragmatically — that is, by adaptation of the rule to the concrete circumstances of the case. Truly unique events, however, must be treated individually. The executive cannot develop rules for the exceptional.

The effective decision maker spends time determining with which of the four different types of the above situations he is dealing. He knows that he will make the wrong decision if he classifies the situation incorrectly.

By far the most common mistake of the decision maker is to treat a generic situation as if it were a series of unique events — that is, to be pragmatic when lacking the generic understanding and principle. The inevitable result is frustration and futility. This was clearly shown, I think, by the failure of most of the policies, both domestic and foreign, of the Kennedy Administration. For all the brilliance of its members, the Administration achieved fundamentally only one success, and that was in the Cuban missile crisis. Otherwise, it achieved practically nothing. The main reason was surely what its members called "pragmatism" — namely, the Administration's refusal to develop rules and principles, and its insistence on treating everything "on its merits." Yet it was clear to everyone, including the members of the Administration, that the basic assumptions on which its policies rested — the valid assumptions of the immediate postwar years — had become increasingly unrealistic in international, as well as in domestic, affairs in the 1960's.

Equally common is the mistake of treating a new event as if it were just another example of the old problem to which, therefore, the old rules should be applied. This was the error that snowballed the local power failure on the New York-Ontario border into the great Northeastern blackout. The power engineers, especially in New York City, applied the right rule for a normal overload. Yet their own instruments had signaled that something quite extraordinary was going on which called for exceptional, rather than standard, countermeasures.

By contrast, the one great triumph of President Kennedy in the Cuban missile crisis rested on acceptance of the challenge to think through an extraordinary, exceptional occurrence. As soon as he accepted this, his own tremendous resources of intelligence and courage effectively came into play.

The Definition

Once a problem has been classified as generic or unique, it is usually fairly easy to define. "What is this all about?" "What is pertinent here?" "What is the key to this situation?" Questions such as these are familiar. But only the truly effective decision makers are aware that the danger in this step is not the wrong definition, it is the plausible but incomplete one. For example: the American automobile industry held to a plausible but incomplete definition of the problem of automotive safety. It was this lack of awareness — far more than any reluctance to spend money on safety engineering — that eventually, in 1966, brought the industry under sudden and sharp Congressional attack for its unsafe cars and then left the industry totally bewildered by the attack. It simply is not true that the industry has paid scant attention to safety.

On the contrary, it has worked hard at safer highway engineering and at driver training, believing these to be the major areas for concern. That accidents are caused by unsafe roads and unsafe drivers is plausible enough. Indeed, all other agencies concerned with automotive safety, from the highway police to the high schools, picked the same targets for their campaigns. These campaigns have produced results. The number of accidents on highways built for safety has been greatly lessened. Similarly, safety-trained drivers have been involved in far fewer accidents.

But although the ratio of accidents per thousand cars or per thousand miles driven has been going down, the total number of accidents and the severity of them have kept creeping up. It should therefore have become clear long ago that something would have to be done about the small but significant probability that accidents will occur despite safety laws and safety training.

This means that future safety campaigns will have to be supplemented by engineering to make accidents themselves less dangerous. Whereas cars have been engineered to be safe when used correctly, they will also have to be engineered for safety when used incorrectly.

There is only one safeguard against becoming the prisoner of an incomplete definition: check it again and again against *all* the observable facts, and throw out a definition the moment it fails to encompass any of them.

The effective decision maker always tests for signs that something is atypical or something unusual is happening. He always asks: Does the definition explain the observed events, and does it explain all of them? He always writes out what the definition is expected to make happen — for instance, make automobile accidents disappear — and then tests regularly to see if this really happens. Finally, he goes back and thinks the problem through again whenever he sees something atypical, when he finds phenomena his explanation does not really explain, or when the course of events deviates, even in details, from his expectations.

These are in essence the rules Hippocrates laid down for medical diagnosis well over 2,000 years ago. They are the rules for scientific observation first formulated by Aristotle and then reaffirmed by Galileo 300 years ago. These, in other words, are old, well-known, time-tested rules, which an executive can learn and apply systematically.

The Specifications

The next major element in the decision process is defining clear specifications as to what the decision has to accomplish. What are the objectives the decision has to reach? What are the minimum goals it has to attain? What are the conditions it has to satisfy? In science these are known as "boundary conditions." A decision, to be effective, needs to satisfy the boundary conditions. "Can our needs be satisfied," Alfred P. Sloan, Jr. presumably asked himself when he took command of General Motors in 1922, "by removing the autonomy of our division heads?" His answer was clearly in the negative. The boundary conditions of his problem demanded strength and responsibility in the chief operating positions. This was needed as much as unity and control at the center. Everyone before Sloan had seen the problem as one of personalities — to be solved through a struggle for power from which one man would emerge victorious. The boundary conditions, Sloan realized, demanded a solution to a constitutional problem — to be solved through a new structure: decentralization which balanced local autonomy of operations with central control of direction and policy.

A decision that does not satisfy the boundary conditions is worse than one which wrongly defines the problem. It is all but impossible to salvage the decision that starts with the right premises but stops short of the right conclusions. Furthermore, clear thinking about the boundary conditions is needed to know when a decision has to be abandoned. The most common cause of failure in a decision lies not in its being wrong initially. Rather, it is a subsequent shift in the goals — the specifications — which makes the prior right decision suddenly inappropriate. And unless the decision maker has kept the boundary conditions clear, so as to make possible the immediate replacement of the outflanked decision with a new and appropriate policy, he may not even notice that things have changed. For example, Franklin D. Roosevelt was bitterly attacked for his switch from conservative candidate in 1932 to radical President in 1933. But it wasn't Roosevelt who changed. The sudden economic collapse which occurred between the summer of 1932 and the spring of 1933 changed the specifications. A policy appropriate to the goal of national economic recovery — which a conservative economic policy might have been — was no longer appropriate when, with the Bank Holiday, the goal had to become political and social cohesion. When the boundary conditions changed, Roosevelt immediately substituted a political objective (reform) for his former economic one (recovery).

Above all, clear thinking about the boundary conditions is needed to identify the most dangerous of all possible decisions: the one in which the specifications that have to be satisfied are essentially incompatible. In other words, this is the decision that might — just might — work if nothing whatever goes wrong. A classic case is President Kennedy's Bay of Pigs decision. One specification was clearly Castro's overthrow. The other was to make it appear that the invasion was a "spontaneous" uprising of the Cubans. But these two specifications would have been compatible with each other only if an immediate island-wide uprising against Castro would have completely paralyzed the Cuban army. And while this was not impossible, it clearly was not probable in such a tightly controlled police state.

Decisions of this sort are usually called "gambles." But actually they arise from something much less rational than a gamble — namely, a hope against hope that two (or more) clearly incompatible specifications can be fulfilled simultaneously. This is hoping for a miracle; and the trouble with miracles is not that they happen so rarely, but that they are, alas, singularly unreliable.

Everyone can make the wrong decision. In fact, everyone will sometimes make a wrong decision. But no executive needs to make a decision which, on the face of it, seems to make sense but, in reality, falls short of satisfying the boundary conditions.

The Decision

The effective executive has to start out with what is "right" rather than what is acceptable precisely because he always has to compromise in the end. But if he does not know what will satisfy the boundary conditions, the decision maker cannot distinguish between the right compromise and the wrong compromise — and may end up by making the wrong compromise. I was taught this when I started in 1944 on my first big consulting assignment. It was a study of the management structure and policies of General Motors Corporation. Alfred P. Sloan, Jr., who was then chairman and chief executive officer of the company, called me to his office at the start of my assignment and said: "I shall not tell you what to study, what to write, or what conclusions to come to. This is your task. My only instruction to you is to put down what you think is right as you see it. Don't you worry about our reaction. Don't you worry about whether we will like this or dislike that. And don't you, above all, concern yourself with the compromises that might be needed to make your conclusions acceptable. There is not one executive in this company who does not know how to make every single conceivable compromise without any help from you. But he can't make the *right* compromise unless you first tell him what right is."

The effective executive knows that there are two different kinds of compromise. One is expressed in the old proverb: "Half a loaf is better than no bread." The other, in the story of the Judgment of Solomon, is clearly based on the realization that "half a baby is worse than no baby at all." In the first instance, the boundary conditions are still being satisfied. The purpose of bread is to provide food, and half a loaf is still food. Half a baby, however, does not satisfy the boundary conditions. For half a baby is not half a living and growing child.

It is a waste of time to worry about what will be acceptable and what the decision maker should or should not say so as not to evoke resistance. (The things one worries about seldom happen, while objections and difficulties no one thought about may suddenly turn out to be almost insurmountable obstacles.) In other words, the decision maker gains nothing by starting out with the question: "What is acceptable?" For in the process of answering it, he usually gives away the important things and loses any chance to come up with an effective — let alone the right — answer.

The Action

Converting the decision into action is the fifth major element in the decision process. While thinking through the boundary conditions is the most difficult step in decision making, converting the decision into effective action is usually the most time-consuming one. Yet a decision will not become effective unless the action commitments have been built into it from the start. In fact, no decision has been made unless carrying it out in specific steps has become someone's work assignment and responsibility. Until then, it is only a good intention.

The flaw in so many policy statements, especially those of business, is that they contain no action commitment — to carry them out is no one's specific work and responsibility. Small wonder then that the people in the organization tend to view such statements cynically, if not as declarations of what top management is really *not* going to do.

Converting a decision into action requires answering several distinct questions: Who has to know of this decision? What action has to be taken? Who is to take it? What does the action have to be so that the people who have to do it *can* do it? The first and the last of these questions are too often overlooked — with dire results. A story that has become a legend among operations researchers illustrates the importance of the question, "Who has to know?" A major manufacturer of industrial equipment decided several years ago to discontinue one of its models that had for years been standard equipment on a line of machine tools, many of which were still in use. It was, therefore, decided to sell the model to present owners of the old equipment for another three years as a replacement, and then to stop making and selling it. Orders for this particular model had been going down for a good many years. But they shot up immediately as customers reordered against the day when the model would no longer be available. No one had, however, asked, "Who needs to know of this decision?"

Consequently, nobody informed the purchasing clerk who was in charge of buying the parts from which the model itself was being assembled. His instructions were to buy parts in a given ratio to current sales — and the instructions remained unchanged.

Thus, when the time came to discontinue further production of the model, the company had in its warehouse enough parts for another 8 to 10 years of production, parts that had to be written off at a considerable loss.

The action must also be appropriate to the capacities of the people who have to carry it out. A large U.S. chemical company found itself, in recent years, with fairly large amounts of blocked currency in two West African countries. To protect this money, top management decided to invest it locally in businesses which (a) would contribute to the local economy, (b) would not require imports from abroad, and (c) would if successful be the kind that could be sold to local investors if and when currency remittances became possible again. To establish these businesses, the company developed a simple chemical process to preserve a tropical fruit — a staple crop in both countries — which, up until then, had suffered serious spoilage in transit to its Western markets.

The business was a success in both countries. But in one country the local manager set the business up in such a manner that it required highly skilled and technically trained management of a kind not easily available in West Africa. In the other country the local manager thought through the capacities of the people who would eventually have to run the business. Consequently, he worked hard at making both the process and the business simple, and at staffing his operation from the start with local nationals right up to the top management level.

A few years later it became possible again to transfer currency from these two countries. But, though the business flourished, no buyer could be found for it in the first country. No one available locally had the necessary managerial and technical skills to run it, and so the business had to be liquidated at a loss. In the other country so many local entrepreneurs were eager to buy the business that the company repatriated its original investment with a substantial profit.

The chemical process and the business built on it were essentially the same in both places. But in the first country no one had asked: "What kind of people do we have available to make this decision effective? And what can they do?" As a result, the decision itself became frustrated.

This action commitment becomes doubly important when people have to change their behavior, habits, or attitudes if a decision is to become effective. Here, the executive must make sure not only that the responsibility for the action is clearly assigned, but that the people assigned are capable of carrying it out. Thus the decision maker has to make sure that the measurements, the standards for accomplishment, and the incentives of those charged with the action responsibility are changed simultaneously. Otherwise, the organization people will get caught in a paralyzing internal emotional conflict. Consider these two examples.

When Theodore Vail was president of the Bell Telephone System 60 years ago, he decided that the business of the Bell System was service. This decision explains in large part why the United States (and Canada) has today an investor-owned, rather than a nationalized, telephone system. Yet this policy statement might have remained a dead letter if Vail had not at the same time designed yardsticks of service performance and introduced these as a means to measure, and ultimately to reward, managerial performance. The Bell managers of that time were used to being measured by the profitability (or at least by the cost) of their units. The new yardsticks resulted in the rapid acceptance of the new objectives.

In sharp contrast is the recent failure of a brilliant chairman and chief executive to make effective a new organization structure and new objectives in an old, large, and proud U.S. company. Everyone agreed that the changes were needed. The company, after many years as leader of its industry, showed definite signs of aging. In many markets newer, smaller, and more aggressive competitors were outflanking it. But contrary to the action required to gain acceptance for the new ideas, the chairman — in order to placate the opposition — promoted prominent spokesmen of the old school into the most visible and highest salaried positions — in particular into three new executive vice presidencies. This meant only one thing to the people in the company: "They don't really mean it." If the greatest rewards are given for behavior contrary to that which the new course of action requires, then everyone will conclude that this is what the people at the top really want and are going to reward.

Only the most effective executive can do what Vail did — build the execution of his decision into the decision itself. But every executive can think through what action commitments a specific decision requires, what work assignments follow from it, and what people are available to carry it out.

The Feedback

Finally, information monitoring and reporting have to be built into the decision to provide continuous testing, against actual events, of the expectations that underlie the decisions. Decisions are made by men. Men are fallible; at best, their works do not last long. Even the best decision has a high probability of being wrong. Even the most effective one eventually becomes obsolete.

This surely needs no documentation. And every executive always builds organized feedback — reports, figures, studies — into his decision to monitor and report on it. Yet far too many decisions fail to achieve their anticipated results, or indeed ever to become effective, despite all these feedback reports. Just as the view from the Matterhorn cannot be visualized by studying a map of Switzerland (one abstraction), a decision cannot be fully and accurately evaluated by studying a report. That is because reports are of necessity abstractions.

Effective decision makers know this and follow a rule which the military developed long ago. The commander who makes a decision does not depend on reports to see how it is being carried out. He — or one of his aides — goes and looks. The reason is not that effective decision makers (or effective commanders) distrust their subordinates. Rather, the reason is that they learned the hard way to distrust abstract "communications."

With the coming of the computer this feedback element will become even more important, for the decision maker will in all likelihood be even further removed from the scene of action. Unless he accepts, as a matter of course, that he had better go out and look at the scene of action, he will be increasingly divorced from reality. All a computer can handle is abstractions. And abstractions can be relied on only if they are constantly checked against concrete results. Otherwise, they are certain to mislead.

To go and look is also the best, if not the only way, for an executive to test whether the assumptions on which his decision has been made are still valid or whether they are becoming obsolete and need to be thought through again. And the executive always has to expect the assumptions to become obsolete sooner or later. Reality never stands still very long.

Failure to go out and look is the typical reason for persisting in a course of action long after it has ceased to be appropriate or even rational. This is true for business decisions as well as for governmental policies. It explains in large measure the failure of Stalin's cold war policy in Europe, but also the inability of the United States to adjust its policies to the realities of a Europe restored to prosperity and economic growth, and the failure of the British to accept, until too late, the reality of the European Common Market. Moreover, in any business I know, failure to go out and look at customers and markets, at competitors and their products, is also a major reason for poor, ineffectual, and wrong decisions.

The decision maker needs organized information for feedback. He needs reports and figures. But unless he builds his feedback around direct exposure to reality — unless he disciplines himself to go out and look — he condemns himself to a sterile dogmatism.

Concluding Note

Decision making is only one of the tasks of an executive. It usually takes but a small fraction of his time. But to make the important decisions is the *specific* executive task. Only an executive makes such decisions.

An *effective* executive makes these decisions as a systematic process with clearly defined elements and in a distinct sequence of steps. Indeed, to be expected (by virtue of position or knowledge) to make decisions that have significant and positive impact on the entire organization, its performance, and its results characterizes the effective executive.

30   The Executive as Decision Maker*

Herbert A. Simon

What part does decision making play in managing? I shall find it convenient to take mild liberties with the English language by using "decision making" as though it were synonymous with "managing."

What is our mental image of a decision maker? Is he a brooding man on horseback who suddenly rouses himself from thought and issues an order to a subordinate? Is he a happy-go-lucky fellow, a coin poised on his thumbnail, ready to risk his action on the toss? Is he an alert, gray-haired

*Reprinted with permission of author and publisher from Herbert A. Simon, *The Shape of Automation*, Harper & Row, New York, 1965.

businessman, sitting at the board of directors' table with his associates, caught at the moment of saying "aye" or "nay"? Is he a bespectacled gentleman, bent over a docket of papers, his pen hovering over the line marked (X)?

All of these images have a significant point in common. In them, the decision maker is a man at the moment of choice, ready to plant his foot on one or another of the routes that lead from the crossroads. All the images falsify decision by focusing on its final moment. All of them ignore the whole lengthy, complex process of alerting, exploring, and analyzing that precedes that final moment.

Intelligence, Design and Choice in Decision Making

In treating decision making as synonymous with managing, I shall be referring not merely to the final act of choice among alternatives, but rather to the whole process of decision. Decision making comprises three principal phases: finding occasions for making a decision; finding possible courses of action; and choosing among courses of action. These three activities account for quite different fractions of the time budgets of executives. The fractions vary greatly from one organization level to another and from one executive to another, but we can make some generalizations about them even from casual observation. Executives spend a large fraction of their time surveying the economic, technical, political, and social environment to identify new conditions that call for new actions. They probably spend an even larger fraction of their time, individually or with their associates, seeking to invent, design, and develop possible courses of action for handling situations where a decision is needed. They spend a small fraction of their time in choosing among alternative actions already developed to meet an identified problem and already analysed for their consequences. The three fractions, added together, account for most of what executives do.[1]

The first phase of the decision-making process — searching the environment for conditions calling for decision — I shall call *intelligence* activity (borrowing the military meaning of intelligence). The second phase — inventing, developing, and analysing possible courses of action — I shall call *design* activity. The third phase — selecting a particular course of action from those available — I shall call *choice* activity.

Let me illustrate these three phases of decision. In the past five years, many companies have reorganized their accounting and other data processing activities in order to make use of large electronic computers. How has this come about? Computers first became available commercially in the early 1950s. Although, in some vague and general sense, company managements were aware that computers existed, few managements had investigated their possible applications with any thoroughness before about 1955.

---

[1] The way in which these activities take shape within an organization is described in some detail in James G. March and Herbert A. Simon, *Organizations*, Wiley, New York, 1958, Chaps. 6 and 7.

For most companies, the use of computers required no decision before that time because it hadn't been placed on the agenda.[2]

The intelligence activity preceding the introduction of computers tended to come about in one of two ways. Some companies — for example, in the aircraft and atomic energy industries — were burdened with enormously complex computations for engineering design. Because efficiency in computations was a constant problem, and because the design departments were staffed with engineers who could understand, at least in general, the technology of computers, awareness of computers and their potentialities came early to these companies. After computers were already in extensive use for design calculations, businesses with a large number-processing load — insurance companies, accounting departments in large firms, banks — discovered these new devices and began to consider seriously their introduction.

Once it was recognized that computers might have a place in modern business, a major design task had to be carried out in each company before they could be introduced. It is now a commonplace that payrolls can be prepared by computers. Programs in both the general and computer senses for doing this are relatively easy to design in any given situation.[3] To develop the first computer programs for preparing payroll, however, was a major research and development project. Few companies having carried their investigations of computers to the point where they had definite plans for their use, failed to install them. Commitment to the new course of action took place gradually as the intelligence and design phases of the decision were going on. The final choice was, in many instances, almost *pro forma*.

Generally speaking, intelligence activity precedes design, and design activity precedes choice. The cycle of phases is, however, far more complex than this sequence suggests. Each phase in making a particular decision is itself a complex decision-making process. The design phase, for example, may call for new intelligence activities; problems at any given level generate subproblems that, in turn, have their intelligence, design, and choice phases, and so on. There are wheels within wheels within wheels. Nevertheless, the three large phases are often clearly discernible as the organizational decision process unfolds. They are closely related to the stages in problem solving first described by John Dewey:

> What is the problem?
> What are the alternatives?
> Which alternative is best?[4]

---

2 Richard M. Cyert, Herbert A. Simon, and Donald B. Trow, "Observation of a Business Decision", *Journal of Business*, Vol. 29, 1956, pp. 237-248.

3 For a good discussion on the use of the computer for such purposes, see Robert H. Gregory and Richard L. Van Horn, *Automatic Data-Processing Systems*, Wadsworth, San Francisco, 1960.

4 John Dewey, *How We Think*, Heath, New York, 1910, Ch. 8.

It may be objected that I have ignored the task of carrying out decisions. I shall merely observe by the way that seeing that decisions are executed is again decision-making activity. A broad policy decision creates a new condition for the organization's executives that calls for the design and choice of a course of action for executing the policy. Executing policy, then, is indistinguishable from making more detailed policy. For this reason, I shall feel justified in taking my pattern for decision making as a paradigm for most executive activity.

Developing Decision-Making Skills

It is an obvious step from the premise that managing is decision making to the conclusion that the important skills for an executive are decision-making skills. It is generally believed that good decision makers, like good athletes, are born, not made. The belief is about as true in the one case as it is in the other.

That human beings come into the world endowed unequally with biological potential for athletic prowess is undeniable. They also come endowed unequally with intelligence, cheerfulness, and many other characteristics and potentialities. To a limited extent, we can measure some aspects of that endowment — height, weight, perhaps intelligence. Whenever we make such measurements and compare them with adult performance, we obtain significant, but low, correlations. A man who is not a natural athlete is unlikely to run the four-minute mile; but many men who are natural athletes have never come close to that goal. A man who is not "naturally" intelligent is unlikely to star in science; but many intelligent scientists are not stars.

A good athlete is born when a man with some natural endowment, by dint of practice, learning, and experience develops that natural endowment into a mature skill. A good executive is born when a man with some natural endowment (intelligence and some capacity for interacting with his fellow men) by dint of practice, learning, and experience develops his endowment into a mature skill. The skills involved in intelligence, design, and choosing activities are as learnable and trainable as the skills involved in driving, recovering, and putting a golf ball. I hope to indicate some of the things a modern executive needs to learn about decision making.

Executive Responsibility for Organizational Decision Making

The executive's job involves not only making decisions himself, but also seeing that the organization, or part of an organization, that he directs makes decisions effectively. The vast bulk of the decision-making activity for which he is responsible is not his personal activity, but the activity of his subordinates.

Nowadays, with the advent of computers, we can think of information as something almost tangible; strings of symbols which, like strips of steel or plastic ribbons, can be processed — changed from one form to another. We can think of white-collar organizations as factories for processing information. The executive is the factory manager, with all the usual responsibilities for maintaining the factory operation, getting it back into operation when it breaks down, and proposing and carrying through improvements in its design.

There is no reason to expect that a man who has acquired a fairly high level of personal skill in decision-making activity will have a correspondingly high skill in designing efficient decision-making systems. To imagine that there is such a connection is like supposing that a man who is a good weight lifter can therefore design cranes. The skills of designing and maintaining the modern decision-making systems we call organizations are less intuitive skills. Hence, they are even more susceptible to training than the skills of personal decision making.

Programmed and Nonprogrammed Decisions

In discussing how executives now make decisions, and how they will make them in the future, let us distinguish two polar types of decisions. I shall call them *programmed decisions* and *nonprogrammed decisions*, respectively. Having christened them, I hasten to add that they are not really distinct types, but a whole continuum, with highly programmed decisions at one end of that continuum and highly unprogrammed decisions at the other end. We can find decisions of all shades of gray along the continuum, and I use the terms programmed and nonprogrammed simply as labels for the black and white of the range.[5]

Decisions are programmed to the extent that they are repetitive and routine, to the extent that a definite procedure has been worked out for handling them so that they don't have to be treated *de novo* each time they occur. The obvious reason why programmed decisions tend to be repetitive, and vice versa, is that if a particular problem recurs often enough, a routine procedure will usually be worked out for solving it. Numerous examples of programmed decisions in organizations will occur to you: pricing ordinary customers' orders; determining salary payments to employees who have been ill; reordering office supplies.

Decisions are nonprogrammed to the extent that they are novel, unstructured, and consequential. There is no cut-and-dried method for handling the problem because it hasn't arisen before, or because its precise nature and structure are elusive or complex, or because it is so important that it deserves a custom-tailored treatment. General Eisenhower's D-Day decision is a good example of a nonprogrammed decision. Remember, we are considering not merely the final act of ordering the attack, but the whole complex of intelligence and design activities that preceded it. Many of the components of the decisions were programmed — by standard techniques

---

[5] See March and Simon, *op. cit.*, pp. 139-142 and 177-180 for further discussion of these types of decisions. The labels used there are slightly different.

for military planning—but before these components could be designed they had to be provided with a broader framework of military and political policy.

I have borrowed the term program from the computer trade, and intend it in the sense in which it is used there. A *program* is a detailed prescription or strategy that governs the sequence of responses of a system to a complex task environment. Most of the programs that govern organizational response are not as detailed or as precise as computer programs. However, they all have the same intent: to permit an adaptive response of the system to the situation.

In what sense, then, can we say that the response of a system to a situation is nonprogrammed? Surely something determines the response. That something, that collection of rules of procedure, is by definition a program. By nonprogrammed I mean a response where the system has no specific procedures to deal with situations like the one at hand, but must fall back on whatever *general* capacity it has for intelligent, adaptive, problem-oriented action. In addition to his specific skills and specific knowledge, man has some general problem-solving capacities. Given almost any kind of situation, no matter how novel or perplexing, he can begin to reason about it in terms of ends and means.

This general problem-solving equipment is not always effective. Men often fail to solve problems, or they reach unsatisfactory solutions. But man is seldom completely helpless in a new situation. He possesses general problem-solving equipment which, however inefficient, fills some of the gaps in his special problem-solving skills. And organizations, as collections of men, have some of this same general adaptive capacity.

The cost of using general-purpose programs to solve problems is usually high. It is advantageous to reserve these programs for situations that are truly novel, where no alternative programs are available. If any particular class of situations recurs often enough, a special-purpose program can be developed which gives better solutions and gives them more cheaply than the general problem-solving apparatus.

My reason for distinguishing between programmed and nonprogrammed decisions is that different techniques are used for handling the programmed and the nonprogrammed aspects of our decision making. The distinction, then, will be a convenient one for classifying these techniques. I shall use it for that purpose, hoping that the reader will remind himself from time to time that the world is mostly gray with only a few spots of pure black or white.

The four-fold table below will provide a map of the territory I propose to cover. In the northern half of the map are some techniques related to programmed decision making, in the southern half, some techniques related to nonprogrammed decision making. In the western half of the map I placed the classical techniques used in decision making—the kit of tools that has been used by executives and organizations from the time of the earliest recorded history up to the present generation. In the eastern half of the map I placed the new techniques of decision making — tools that have been forged largely since World War II, and that are only now coming into extensive use in management in this country. I shall proceed across the map from west to east, and from north to south, taking up, in order, the north-west and the south-west quadrants (section B), the north-east quadrant (section C), and the south-east quadrant (section D).

I can warn you now to what conclusion this journey is going to lead. We are in the midst of a major revolution in the art or science — whichever you prefer to call it — of management and organization. I shall try to describe the nature of this revolution and, in my final chapter, to discuss its implications.

Traditional Decision-Making Methods

Let us examine the western half of our map of decision-making techniques (Fig. I). This half represents methods that have been widely understood and applied in human organizations at least from the time of the building of the pyramids. In painting with a broad brush, I may convey the impression that there was no progress in organizational matters during the course of three millennia. I do not believe this to be true, and I do not intend to imply it. But the progress that was made did not enlarge the repertory of basic mechanisms to which I shall refer.

We shall consider, in turn, techniques for making programmed decisions and techniques for making nonprogrammed decisions.

Traditional Techniques for Programmed Decisions

"Man," says William James, "is born with a tendency to do more things than he has ready-made arrangements for in his nerve centres. Most of the performances of other animals are automatic. But in him the number of them is so enormous, that most of them must be the fruit of painful study. If practice did not make perfect, nor habit economize the expense of nervous and muscular energy, he would therefore be in a sorry plight.[6]

Habit is the most general, the most pervasive, of all techniques for making programmed decisions. The collective memories of organization members are vast encyclopedias of factual knowledge, habitual skills, and operating procedures. The large costs associated with bringing new members into organizations are principally costs of providing the new members, through formal training and experience, with the repertoire of skills and other habits they need in their jobs. Partly, the organization provides these habits; partly, it acquires them by selecting new employees who have already learned them in the educational and training institutions that society maintains.

---

6 William James, *The Principles of Psychology*, Henry Holt, New York, 1890 or Dover, New York, 1950, Vol. 1, p. 113.

FIGURE I. TRADITIONAL AND MODERN TECHNIQUES OF DECISION MAKING

TYPES OF DECISIONS	DECISION-MAKING TECHNIQUES	
	Traditional	*Modern*
Programmed: Routine, repetitive decisions Organization develops specific processes for handling them	1. Habit 2. Clerical routine: Standard operating procedures 3. Organization structure: Common expectations A system of subgoals Well-defined informational channels	1. Operations Research: Mathematical analysis Models Computer simulation 2. Electronic data processing
Nonprogrammed: One-shot, ill-structured novel, policy decisions Handled by general problem-solving processes	1. Judgment, intuition, and creativity 2. Rules of thumb 3. Selection and training of executives	Heuristic problem-solving technique applied to: (a) training human decision makers (b) constructing heuristic computer programs

Closely related to habits are standard operating procedures. The only difference between habits and standard operating procedures is that the former have become internalized — recorded in the central nervous system — while the latter begin as formal, written, recorded programs. Standard operating procedures provide a means for indoctrinating new members into the habitual patterns of organizational behaviour, a means for reminding old members of patterns that any one member uses so infrequently that they never become completely habitual, and a means for bringing habitual patterns out into the open where they can be examined, modified, and improved.

Organization structure, over and above standard operating procedures, is itself a partial specification of decision-making programs. The organization structure establishes a common set of presuppositions and expectations as to which members of the organization are responsible for which classes of decisions; it establishes a structure of subgoals to serve as criteria of choice in various parts of the organization; and it establishes intelligence responsibilities in particular organization units for scrutinizing specific parts of the organization's environment and for communicating events requiring attention to appropriate decision points.

In the past, the improvement of programmed decision making in organizations has focused largely upon these techniques: upon improving the knowledge, skills, and habits of individual employees by means of training programs and planned tours of duty; upon developing better standard operating procedures and securing adherence to them; and upon modifying the structure of the organization itself, the division of labor, the subgoal structure, the allocation of responsibilities.

Mankind has possessed for many centuries an impressive collection of techniques for developing and maintaining predictable programmed responses in an organization to those problems posed by its environment that are relatively repetitive and well-structured. The history of the development of these techniques has never been written — much of it is undoubtedly buried in prehistory — but one can point to particular periods of innovation. The scientific management movement, and particularly the development of standard methods for performing repetitive work, is one of the most recent of these.

Traditional Techniques for Nonprogrammed Decisions

When we turn to the area of nonprogrammed decisions, we have much less to point to in the way of specific, describable techniques. When we ask how executives in organizations make nonprogrammed decisions, we are generally told that they "exercise judgment," and that this judgment depends, in some undefined way, upon experience, insight, and intuition. If the decision we are inquiring about was a particularly difficult one, or one that yielded especially impressive results, we may be told that creativity was required.

There is a scene in *Le Malade Imaginaire* in which the physician is asked why opium puts people to sleep. "Because it possesses a dormitive faculty," he replies triumphantly. To name a phenomenon is not to explain it. Saying that nonprogrammed decisions are made by exercising judgment *names* that phenomenon but does not explain it. It doesn't help the man who lacks judgment (i.e., who doesn't make decisions well) to acquire it.

Making programmed decisions depends on relatively simple psychological processes that are somewhat understood, at least at the practical level. These include habit, memory, simple manipulations of things and symbols. Making nonprogrammed decisions depends on psychological processes that, until recently, have not been understood at all. Because we have not understood them, our theories about nonprogrammed decision making have been rather empty and our practical advice only moderately helpful.

One thing we have known about nonprogrammed decision making is that it can be improved somewhat by training in orderly thinking. In addition to the very specific habits one can acquire for doing very specific things, one can acquire the habit — when confronted with a vague and difficult situation — of asking, "What is the problem?" We can even construct rather generalized operating procedures for decision making. The military "estimate of the situation" — a checklist of things to consider in analysing a military decision problem — is an example of such an operating procedure.

There is nothing wrong with such aids to decision making except that they don't go nearly far enough. They graduate the decision maker from nursery school to kindergarten, perhaps, but they don't carry his education much further.

How then do executives discharge their responsibilities for seeing that decision making in their organizations, nonprogrammed as well as programmed, is of high quality? Let me propose an analogy. If you have a job to do, and you don't have the time or the skill to design and produce just the right tool to do it, you look around among the tools you have or can get at the hardware store and select the best one you can find. We haven't known very much about how to improve human decision-making skills, but we observe that some people have these skills much better developed than others. Hence, we rely on selection as our principal technique for improving complex decision-making skills in organizations.

Even our selection techniques are not nearly as adequate as we should like. To some limited extent we have found out how to assess human qualities by formal testing. In the main, however, we select a good decision maker for an organizational position by looking for a man who has done a pretty good job of decision making in some other organizational position that is almost equally taxing. This is a simple-minded approach to the problem, but it is the only moderately successful one that we know.

We supplement our selection techniques with two kinds of training: the professional training in basic principles that generally precedes entrance into organizational life, and the training through experience and planned job rotation that the organization itself can provide. Man is a learning animal. If he is subjected to a sequence of problem situations of progressively greater difficulty and of difficulty appropriate to the level of skill he has attained, he will usually show an increasing capacity to handle the problems well. For problems of a nonprogrammed sort neither he nor we know from whence the improvement comes. The processes of learning have been as mysterious as the processes of problem solving. But improvement there is. We are thus able, in a crude way, to use training and planned experience as a means for improving nonprogrammed decision making in organizations.

Appropriate design of the organization structure is important for nonprogrammed, as it is for programmed, decision making. An important principle of organization design that has emerged over the years has been called facetiously "Gresham's Law of Planning." It states that programmed activity tends to drive out nonprogrammed activity. If an executive has a job that involves a mixture of programmed and nonprogrammed decision-making responsibilities, the former will come to be emphasized at the expense of the latter. The organizational implication of Gresham's Law is that special provision must be made for nonprogrammed decision making by creating specific organizational responsibilities and organizational units to take care of it. The various kinds of staff units that are so characteristic of large-scale modern organizations are mostly units specialized in particular aspects of the more complex nonprogrammed decision-making tasks. Market research units and research departments, to cite some examples, specialize in the intelligence phase of decision making; planning departments and product development departments specialize in the design phase. The creation of organizational units to carry on these activities allocates brainpower to nonprogrammed thought, and provides some minimal assurance that such thought will occur in the organization.

In summary, we have not had, in the past, adequate knowledge of the processes that are involved in decision making in complex situations. Human thinking, problem solving, and learning have been mysterious processes which we have labeled but not explained. Lacking an understanding of these processes, we have had to resort to gross techniques for improving nonprogrammed decision making: selection of men who have demonstrated their capacity for it; further development of their powers through professional training and planned experience; protection of nonprogrammed activity from the pressure of repetitive activity by establishing specialized organizational units to carry it on. We cannot say that these traditional techniques have failed — decisions do get made daily in organizations. Neither can we say that we might not do very much better in the future as our knowledge of the decision-making process grows.

New Techniques for Programmed Decision Making

World War II brought large numbers of scientists trained in the use of mathematical tools into contact for the first time with operational and managerial problems. Designers of military aircraft could not plan aircraft armament without making assumptions about the formations in which the planes would be flown and the strategy of their commitment to action. Mathematical economists responsible for material allocation had to come to grips with complex logistics systems. The need for solving these problems, coupled with the tools of quantitative analysis that the scientists and econometricians brought with them, have produced some new approaches to management decision making that are of fundamental importance.[7]

Operations Research

Many people — notably some of the pioneer operations researchers themselves — have tried to define operations research. The net result is usually to identify it with scientific method or straight thinking applied to management problems, and to imply that it is something that can be done only by natural scientists. Definitions of this kind, unintentionally imperialistic, raise the hackles of those identified with the earlier phrase "scientific management," who had thought that clear, scientific thinking is what they had always been doing. Except in matter of degree (e.g., the operations researchers tend to use rather high-powered mathematics), it is not clear that operations research embodies any philosophy different from that of scientific management. Charles Babbage and Frederick Taylor will have to be made, retroactively, charter members of the operations research societies.

A more understandable and defensible definition of operations research is a sociological one. Operations research is a movement that, emerging out of the military needs of World War II, has brought the decision-making problems of management within the range of interests of large numbers of natural scientists and, particularly, of mathematicians and statisticians.[8] The operations researchers soon joined forces with mathematical economists who had come into the same area — to the mutual benefit of both groups. And by now there has been widespread fraternization between these exponents of the "new" scientific management and men trained in the earlier traditions of scientific management and industrial engineering. No meaningful line can be drawn any more to demarcate operations research from scientific management or scientific management from management science.[9]

---

[7] See Fig. I, eastern half.

[8] Some standard works on operations research by leading members of the group are C. West Churchman, Russell L. Ackoff, and E. Leonard Arnoff, *Introduction to Operations Research*, Wiley, New York, 1957; and Philip M. Morse and George E. Kimball, *Methods of Operations Research*, Wiley, New York, 1951. The Operations Research Society of America publishes the journal *Operations Research*.

[9] The term "management science" was the trademark invented by the quantitatively oriented social scientists, primarily econometricians, who entered this area and who initially distinguished themselves from the operations researchers. The Institute of Management Sciences was organized in 1954. Its journal is the quarterly *Management Science*.

Along with some mathematical tools, which I shall discuss presently, operations research brought into management decision making a point of view called the systems approach. The systems approach is no easier to define than operations research for it is a set of attitudes and a frame of mind rather than a definite and explicit theory. At its vaguest, it means looking at the whole problem — again, hardly a novel idea, and not always a very helpful one. Somewhat more concretely, it means designing the components of a system and making individual decisions within it in the light of the implication of these decisions for the system as a whole.[10] We now know a *little* about how this might be done:

1. Economic analysis has something to say about rational behavior in complex systems of interacting elements, and particularly about the conditions under which the choices that are optimal for subsystems will or will not be optimal for a system as a whole. Economic analysis also has a great deal to say about the price system as a possible mechanism for decentralizing decision making.[11]

2. Mathematical techniques have been developed and adapted by engineers and economists for analysing the dynamic behavior of complex systems. Under the labels of servo-mechanism theory and cybernetics, such techniques underwent rapid development at about the time of World War II. They have considerable usefulness in the design of dynamic systems.[12]

Systems design is such a modish, if not faddish, word at the moment that I don't want to exaggerate the amount of well-understood technique that stands behind it. Nevertheless, it is fair to say that we can approach the design and analysis of large dynamic systems today with a good deal more sophistication that we could ten years ago.

The Mathematical Tools

Operations research progressed from the talking to the action stage by finding tools with which to solve concrete managerial problems. Among the tools, some of them relatively new, some of them already known to statisticians, mathematicians, or economists were linear programming, dynamic programming, game theory, and probability theory. Behind each of these formidable terms lies a mathematical model for a range of management problems. Linear programming, for example, can be used to provide a mathematical model for the operations of a gasoline refinery, or a commercial cattle-feed manufacturing operation. Dynamic programming can be used as a model for many inventory and production planning

10 See Churchman *et al*, *op. cit.*, pp. 109-111.
11 See Tjalling C. Koopmans (ed.), *Activity Analysis of Production and Allocation*, Wiley, New York, 1951.
12 The word cybernetics was first used by Norbert Wiener in *Cybernetics*, Wiley, New York, 1948, p. 19. A good exposition of these techniques may be found in Arnold Tustin, *The Mechanism of Economic Systems*, Harvard University Press, Cambridge, Massachusetts, 1953.

situations. Game theory models have been used to represent marketing problems. Probability models have been used in a wide variety of contexts — they have been, perhaps, the most versatile of all.

Whatever the specific mathematical tool, the general recipe for using it in management decision making is something like this:[13]

1. Construct a *mathematical model* that satisfies the conditions of the tool to be used and which, at the same time, mirrors the important factors in the management situation to be analysed.
2. Define the *criterion function*, the measure that is to be used for comparing the relative merits of various possible courses of action.
3. Obtain *empirical estimates* of the numerical parameters in the model that specify the particular, concrete situation to which it is to be applied.
4. Carry through the mathematical process of finding the course of action which, for the specified parameter values, maximizes the criterion function.

In any decision-making situation where we apply this recipe successfully, we have, in fact, constructed a *program* for the organization's decisions. We have either annexed some decisions that had been judgmental to the area of programmed decision making,[14] or we have replaced a rule-of-thumb program with a more sophisticated program that guarantees us optimal decisions — optimal, that is, within the framework of the mathematical model.

But certain conditions must be satisfied in order to apply this recipe to a class of decision problems. First, it must be possible to define mathematical variables that represent the important aspects of the situation. In particular, a quantitative criterion function must be defined. If the problem area is so hopelessly qualitative that it cannot be described even approximately in terms of such variables, the approach fails. Second, the model will call for certain parameters of its structure to be estimated before it can be applied in a particular situation. Hence, it is necessary that there be ways of making actual numerical estimates of these parameters — of sufficient accuracy for the practical task at hand. Third, the specification of the model must fit the mathematical tools to be used. If certain kinds of nonlinearities are absolutely crucial to an accurate description of the situation, linear programming simply won't work — it is a tool adapted to mathematical systems that are, in a certain sense, linear. Fourth, the problem must be small enough that the calculations can be carried out in reasonable time and at a reasonable cost.

Some relatively simple management problems — for example, many problems of factory scheduling — turn out to be far too large for even such

---

[13] See Churchman *et al*, *op. cit.*, Ch. V.
[14] Thus, operations research, in addition to providing techniques for programmed decisions, also expands their boundaries.

a powerful tool as linear programming. It is easy for the operations research enthusiast to underestimate the stringency of these conditions. This leads to an ailment that might be called mathematician's aphasia. The victim abstracts the original problem until the mathematical intractabilities have been removed (and all semblance to reality lost), solves the new simplified problem, and then pretends that this was the problem he wanted to solve all along. He expects the manager to be so dazzled by the beauty of the mathematical results that he will not remember that his practical operating problem has not been handled.

It is just as easy for the traditionalist to overestimate the stringency of the conditions. For the operations research approach to work, nothing has to be exact — it just has to be close enough to give better results than could be obtained by common sense without the mathematics. Furthermore, it is dangerous to assume that something is essentially qualitative and not reducible to mathematical form until an applied mathematician has had a try at it. For example, I have often been told that "you can't place a dollar value on a lost order from inventory runout." But why, the answer goes, can't you estimate the penalty cost of taking emergency action to *avoid* losing the order — shipping, for example, by air express? Thus, many things that seem intangible can be reduced, for management decision-making purposes, to dollars and cents.

But we need not spin out these generalities. Mathematical techniques are now being applied in a large number of situations. In many of these situations, when mathematical techniques were first proposed there was much head shaking and muttering about judgment. The area of application is large. It is growing. But there is no indication that it will cover the whole of management decision making.

Enter the Computer

It was an historical accident with large consequences that the same war which spawned operations research saw also the birth of the modern digital computer as a practical device.[15] The computer was conceived as a device for exploring by numerical analysis the properties of mathematical systems too large or too complex to be treated by known analytic methods. The systems of differential equations that were arising in aerodynamics, meteorology, and the design of nuclear reactors were obvious candidates for this treatment. It was soon realized that even larger problems were generated by the linear programming and dynamic programming models of management decision problems. Whatever the conceptual power of the mathematical models that have been used in operations research, their actual use in practical schemes for decision making hinged on the fortuitous arrival on the scene of the computer.

While computers were initially conceived as devices for doing arithmetic

---

15 A general book on the history of the development of computers and on their use by management is John A. Postley, *Computers and People*, McGraw-Hill, New York, 1960.

on problems that had first been cast in a mathematical form having known solution procedures, it gradually became clear that there were other ways of using them. If a model or simulation of a situation could be programmed for a computer, the behavior of the system could then be studied simply by having the computer imitate it and without solving, in the traditional sense, the mathematical equations themselves. In putting it this way, I make simulation sound like a simpler and more powerful technique than it really is. In general, we would need to simulate the behavior of the system not under a single set of conditions but over a whole range of conditions. Having simulated it, we would need some procedure for evaluating the results — for deciding whether the system behavior was satisfactory or not. Finally, before we could simulate the behavior, we would have to estimate accurately enough the structure of the system — simulation techniques do not at all reduce the burden of providing numerical estimates.

In spite of these limitations and difficulties, simulation has enabled an airline to determine how many reserve aircraft it should keep on hand, has been used to study highway congestion, has led to improvement in inventory control procedures for a huge warehousing operation, and has accomplished many other difficult tasks.

Of course, the bread-and-butter applications of computers to business decision making have had little to do with either mathematical models or simulation. They have had to do with automating a whole host of routine and repetitive data-processing activities that had for many years been highly programmed but not nearly so completely automated. Through this development, large-scale data processing is becoming a factory operation, an operation that exceeds in degree of automation all but a very few manufacturing processes.

The Revolution in Programmed Decision Making

The revolution in programmed decision making has by no means reached its limits, but we can now see its shape. The rapidity of change stems partly from the fact that there has been not a single innovation but several related innovations, all of which contribute to it.

1. The electronic computer is bringing about, with unexpected speed, a high level of automation in the routine, programmed decision making and data processing that were formerly the province of clerks.

2. The area of programmed decision making is being rapidly extended as we find ways to apply the tools of operations research to types of decisions that have up to now been regarded as judgmental — particularly, but not exclusively, middle-management decisions in the area of manufacturing and warehousing.

3. The computer has extended the capability of the mathematical techniques to problems far too large to be handled by less automatic computing devices, and has further extended the range of programmable decisions by contributing the new technique of simulation.

4. Companies are just beginning to discover ways of bringing together the first two of these developments: of combining the mathematical techniques for making decisions about aggregative middle-management variables with the data-processing techniques for implementing these decisions in detail at clerical levels.

Out of the combination of these four developments there is emerging the new picture of the data-processing factory for manufacturing, in a highly mechanized way, the organization's programmed decisions — just as the physical processing factory manufactures its products in a manner that becomes increasingly mechanized. The automated factory of the future will operate on the basis of programmed decisions produced in the automated office beside it.

31   Operations Research Can Help Public Administrators in Decision-Making*

Maurice F. Ronayne

There's a Need

Many public administrators today in the world still employ Eighteenth Century management tools to assist them in making Twentieth Century decisions. This is indeed unfortunate, especially since we are now living in an era which treats space exploration as an almost-common thing. Public administrators like their counterparts in business must have the right kind of intelligence to make decisions upon. But . . . they are often frustrated with the vague and incomplete character of the data given to them, which they must utilize to shape life and death policy decisions.

Documentation may often be disjointed . . . sometimes non-existent . . . often badly selected in the first place. Even statistics will show holes through which a herd of bull elephants could be driven. But far worse than all these faults is the deplorable lack of "toughness of mind" to attempt to make more reliable, more valid, and more scientific . . . the public official's job of drafting policy and making decisions.

Owing to the complex nature of modern-day affairs on one hand, and to the rapid expansion of all facets of the field of administration, both public and private, not only is it more difficult to determine clearly what decisions must be taken, but decisions made today are more far-reaching and more irrevocable in their consequences than ever before in history.

* Reprinted with permission of author and publisher from *International Review of Administrative Sciences*, Vol. 29, No. 3, 1963, pp. 227-234.

But one tool, slowly but surely establishing itself as an aid to public administrators, and which offers tremendous promise as a method for obtaining better decision-making capabilities, is Operations Research. . . .

History

Operations Research, or "OR" in its abbreviated version, has really been around for some time. But it usually has gone by different names. For example, the use of management games or of simulation techniques, important OR tools, can be traced back to 1872 when the British Army began practicing War Games!

During World War I, inventor Thomas Edison practiced OR. He collected statistics on anti-submarine warfare, developed ideas on sweep-widths for visual search, and applied operational gaming in connection with shipping across the English Channel. Unfortunately, Edison's ideas were too advanced, and most ended up gathering dust in British Admiralty files.

Twenty years later OR became active again when English scientists such as Sir Henry Tizard and colleagues began to work closely with the military to perfect a device to help England defend itself against the Luftwaffe.

Teamwork paid off with radar, making it possible for RAF Spitfires to know where to fly to engage the enemy. All saving time and precious petrol . . . and above all, Britain!

Later Americans began using OR techniques. Teams of top-drawer scientific researchers with military people pooled disciplines drawn from the life and natural sciences, and mathematics, to resolve problems ranging from the correct placing of "GI" soldier washtubs for cleaning messkits and expediting long chowlines, to picking the optimal number of armed escorts needed for ship convoys without having too little or too much protection against enemy U-boats.

Remarkably enough, through OR analyses, Dr. Glen Camp found out that the real problem was *not* Undersea Welfare, but Overseas Transport! Top-priority emphasis shifted from methods of killing enemy subs to finding different ways of increasing cargo delivered overseas, right in the teeth of even more deadly enemy sub offensives.

OR's capability to often identify the *real* problem rather than the *apparent* one, is one of its most important attributes.

A Few Explanatory Remarks

Operations Research strives to identify the optimal solution and policy in relation to the total organization. This is perhaps the *key characteristic* of OR. It utilizes scientific techniques to provide Management with a quantitative basis for decision-making.

Most often the OR expert will make a mathematical model of a system, connecting to it the certainties and uncertainties in any situation in order to measure and assign relative success rankings to possible solutions. These mathematical models describe the activity under review, and, upon the form of these models, propose alternative solutions to management problems.

Public administrators thus equipped can then make decisions on a rational basis, well aware of the effect that this solution will have on various parts of the organization, but carrying out the decision so that the best interests of the entire organization can be served.

OR is much like a branch of applied sciences. It analyzes facts or complex situations in varied fields, always endeavoring to help the administrator to minimize his resorting to hit-or-miss methods in arriving at decisions, in order to encourage him to base his acts to the fullest extent on the reality of cold, hard facts.

In mathematical terms, this approach narrows down to the general form of an OR model where:

$$E = f(x_i, y_j)$$

Effectiveness (E) of a system is a function (f) of variables that are subject to control (x_i) and variables not subject to it (y_j).

What's in OR for the Public Administrator

Operations Research can help the public administrator to (1) select the best alternatives in a specific problem to yield the best decisions or policies, (2) develop methodologies for making various types of optimum decisions, and, (3) educate others to review systematically all possible alternatives to come up with methods for yielding the best decision.

OR operates best when there are:

A large number of controlled variables . . . Using mathematical techniques OR easily works with large numbers of strategic possibilities and states of nature.

A small number of relevant uncontrolled variables . . . Operations Research methods identify unknown, but important variables.

Relevant measurable variables and good data . . . OR often provides the necessary problem-solving analysis to relate important variables to one another, to the outcome, and to the payoff measure.

Past relationships extending into the future . . . Mathematical methods can frequently be devised to search for innumerable payoff measures for purposes of applying decision criteria.

One typical problem subject to an OR payoff might be the motor-pool supervisor who wants to know how long it would take for two different brands of tires to wear out on his vehicles. He may decide to get a sample of twelve of each kind and put them on his vehicles . . . all at the same time. As tires wear out, he jots these facts down.

But . . . is his approach a valid one? How sure is he that the tires are each truly representative of the two manufacturer's products? Maybe one batch was older than the other? How were the vehicles used? Each under similar conditions? These and many other questions must be answered, if the supervisor wants to reach a meaningful conclusion as to which kind of tires to purchase.

This then, is the type of problem the administrator can apply OR to, for best results. It is a tool which helps administration to tie together all parts of any problem into a neat package, so that most effects and implications will be measured, and all costs and tangible benefits fully evaluated.

OR provides Figures, *not* Fancies . . .

Basic OR Techniques

Mathematics and statistics help OR resolve difficult problems. These two disciplines underline the basic OR tool applications.

The general picture of Operations Research shows it composed of several techniques, useful either singly or in combination. Queuing, Monte Carlo, Simulation, Game Theory, and Linear Programming are the most commonly applied techniques. Here is a description of their characteristics:

Queuing. Developed in the early 1900's by Erlang, an engineer with the Copenhagen Telephone Company, it relies heavily on the use of statistical probability theory as do most OR techniques.

The essential ingredients of queuing include (1) customers, (2) gate or service point, (3) input process, (4) queue discipline, and (5) a service mechanism. An analysis must be made also of (a) waiting time of customers, (b) number of customers in the waiting line, and (c) ratio of waiting time to service time.

Queuing works to reduce waiting time of the customer, number of customers in line, and ratio of waiting-time to service time. It also minimizes costs of the service agency by serving as many customers as possible, with the least number of facilities. This reduces idle facilities, inventory, and manpower.

In capsule form . . . *Service Rate should = Average Rate of Customer Arrivals, recognizing that such arrivals may fluctuate considerably.*

Past experience is analyzed, whenever available, to determine the distribution of random variations, of customer arrivals, orders, paper work flow, trucks, breakdowns, etc. Then, data are converted to probabilities.

Analyzing the random input itself is fundamental to solving a queuing problem. Although the "smoothing" of service times will reduce the congestion in queuing, *the real solution lies in getting better controls over the input* so as to get close to the desired input norm.

Monte Carlo. Uses random sampling to graphically simulate the process being analyzed. Essentially it is a trial-and-error method of repeated calculations to discover the best solution. When a large number of variables is present with inter-relationships too complex to be handled by straightforward analytical methods, it is especially useful. This technique, particularly relevant to any problem invoking probability theory, best applies when there is no past history on expected happenings. A good example is a queuing problem when the number and time of expected arrivals are completely unknown.

Simulation. Here the model need not have the same physical appearance as the actual system under analysis, but it must resemble it in ways such as the authority and responsibility patterns, the communications network, and the laws and conventions that actually exist.

In reality, the model is an abstraction. It simply duplicates a situation under investigation. No model is the real world! It only possesses what the analyst believes to be the important and pertinent aspects of the original. To get down to brass tacks . . . a model is neither true nor false; either it applies to a certain situation or it does not represent reality. When determining the possible benefit of a mathematical model, one must consider first not only the accuracy inherent in the model itself, but also the necessity to provide this exactness at all!

Game Theory. Concerns itself with the optimal choice of strategies in a competitive situation. Originally introduced by Emile Borel, but more fully developed by mathematician John Von Neumann and economist Oskar Morgenstern to describe competitive economic behavior. Game Theory came about from the study of simple two-man games (for example, coin tossing) with the especial characteristic that one player keeps what the other loses.

Later, Game Theory was applied to far more complex competitive situations with more players capable of providing a strategy of play that could reduce a player's overall loss. This technique also provides for the possibility that "opponents" are bluffing or using a games-theory approach.

To sum up, Game Theory is a mathematical method of picking out the best strategies in situations where people are in conflict. Each person is able to exercise control over some aspects of the game while other aspects are in control of competitors. One person alone can determine the final results of a "game" just as in any regular game of chance. Usually, however, recommended decisions rest more on a strategy of minimizing one's risks rather than maximizing one's goals.

A typical application might be to find out which one among two competing manufacturers, each offering a similar product, will be able to win control over a business market.

Linear Programming. Extremely useful in areas where restrictions on the use of resources make it very difficult to carry out each activity as if it were the only one performed. Linear Programming assumes a linear or straight-line relationship among variables. It only asks that the limits of variation be fairly well defined. Arithmetical computations are simple, but since they are most often used to handle a complex situation with many variables, the volume of computations is usually extensive, and often calls for an electronic computer. Probability plays *no part* in normal Linear

Programming, the theory behind the computational routines being that of matrix algebra.

Typical applications may be Inventory Planning, an Improved Product Mix, or an Assignment of Skilled Technicians to repair items as they arrive.

Electronic Computers and OR

A computer's tremendous speed enables it to simulate conditions impossible to study at first hand. Examples include War Games, a flight of a space ship, or the "trying out" of combinations of new engines, transmission, axles and tires for cars of the future.

One Detroit motor executive recently figured that some of the computations made to pinpoint where squeaks were most likely to develop in an automobile would have taken until 2061 A.D. if an electronic computer and OR hadn't been applied.

A Typical OR Application

OR methodologies, backed up with an electronic computer, can work together to solve this problem dealing with the unloading capabilities of a seaport. An optimal situation would provide for sufficient available berths, few ships kept waiting to dock, and berths filled most of the time.

A computer can simulate this problem. Program steps which a computer must answer include: "Is a berth free?", "If yes, is there a ship ready to dock?", "If so, is the tide favorable?", "If all the answers are affirmative, how long will the ship take to dock?".

Other variable factors are involved. Vessels of different tonnage differ in their unloading times. Even with a given tonnage the type of cargo affects the unloading time. Personnel problems present trouble too: "Will there be enough men ready in time to unload the boat?", "How many men do we have to have on the payroll at berths of different sizes to be sure that the right number of men will be able to unload the ship?", "How can the right number of men be placed at the dock?", "What are the risks of not getting enough men . . . or, of being any specific number short?", "How many will probably be sick or on vacation?"

If no data are handy to show the detailed effect of these factors, one can assume that there exist frequency distributions of ships handled in varying tonnage ranges and of unloading times achieved in each range. The Monte Carlo method can then be applied to simulate these variations by random-sampling. Coupled with the use of this tool would be the application of Queuing technique to data compiled by Monte Carloing.

Starting from some arbitrary set of conditions with a given number of berths, this model can be run indefinitely on a computer to produce berth-utilization and ship-queuing times after each month's simulated operation.

The model, once constructed, can be run repeatedly to try the effects of different numbers of berths. From these data, the administrator can then select the optimal course of action.

The Difference Between Systems Analysis and OR

Basically, the OR Analyst *translates observations into quantitative elements of an abstract mathematical model and then manipulates this model to arrive at an optimal solution.*

Straight systems analysis differs from Operations Research in the fact that OR uses a highly quantitative, often mathematical approach to a problem, which digs below the surface and accepts few conclusions till specific effects can be traced back to clear-cut causes.

An OR man leans heavily on symbolic logic drawn from the scientific disciplines, most often constructing a mathematical model to represent a system. The systems and procedures man usually does not have the habit of mind for applied research as the OR expert has, but instead gravitates naturally towards more empirical formulas. And, most unfortunately, through no fault of his own, the systems man so often becomes over-burdened with administrative work or compelled to engage in "fire-fighting", that he has little time to analyze the material available, and falls back on improvisations and "quickie" solutions.

Usually the OR man can work without interruption on his problems. Solitude permits him the luxury of applying his scientific techniques to the fullest on the highly unusual problems he's been assigned to do in the first place!

But . . . an especially valuable partnership can be formed between the OR man and the Systems Analyst. Techniques may not be the same, but they're *supplementary!* When your OR man comes down from his "Ivory Tower" to try out his esoteric formulas, the systems man with his two feet solidly on the ground with his overall knowledge of organization structure, administrative systems, and data processing flow, can not only contribute to the OR man's work, but also help to evaluate it, and when it is okayed, effectively implement the OR recommendations.

OR Limitations

1. *Mathematical Models.* Models at best are only an *approximation* of real life. Accuracy of the model may be compromised by possible inaccuracies in source data used to set up the model, and by deliberate approximations made during research.

2. *Intangible Factors.* It is extremely hard to measure important factors as goodwill, human behavior, moral values, human ethics. . . .

3. *Time.* OR investigations have to have research over long periods of time which makes it ineffective in solving day-to-day operating problems.

4. *High Costs.* Problem-solving must be limited to only those in which foreseeable gains over costs make it an attractive choice over other analysis techniques. Other problems within its scope must be left out.

5. *De-Humanization.* OR disregards any individuality and uniqueness among people, completely ignoring the humanistic approach to administration which has grown tremendously in popularity within recent years.

6. *Lack of Data.* Many organizations do not have available the data so vital to many OR formulas, nor can data always be successfully simulated.

7. *Basic Research.* OR men to grow, must not spend all their time on "bits and pieces". They require time for almost completely undirected research . . . a fact of scientific life that not all organizations can afford.

8. *Sub-Optimization.* There is the problem that the research will become so minute and so precise that the broad systems concept of the organization will be forgotten. It's not easy to locate the right level to optimize at, i.e. to meet the requirement to optimize at a level appropriate to the problem.

Some Problem Areas

To avoid frustration and a sense of complete futility, any OR man hoping to succeed in applying his bag-of-tricks must be alert to possible sources of hostility to his work. Above all, he must be a salesman *par excellence* to get around these organizational roadblocks.

1. *Different Management Philosophies.* Here the OR man must learn to cope with two types of philosophies, both of them at variance with his own *modus operandi.* There is *old-fashioned intuition* philosophy or the "fly-by-the-seat-of-your-pants" routine still held by many executives who possess complete indifference to all new-fangled management methods. Then, there is the *human relations* approach of getting things done through people by making their working environment as comfortable as possible.

2. *Communications.* Few public administrators have more than an elementary knowledge of mathematics and for many of them OR terminology is "Greek to them"! OR folks, to succeed must learn to sell their ideas in language which the layman grasps. Too much lingo, OR style, and many an administrator will peg the speaker as too theoretical!

3. *OR Man's Puff.* Any quackery by an OR man that his tool of management is a panacea for all of an administrator's ills will bring a very acid response from most executives. Too many colleagues have been "burnt" already by overly ambitious OR'ers who have failed to produce after making outlandish claims!

4. *Naïvety.* Unfamiliarity of OR practitioners with public administration practices leads to duplication of approaches already available and needless clashes with existing professions. OR men fresh from stints in military services often fail to realize that the same depth in data availability in the Military is not often the case for civilian government agencies. Others fail to cope with intangible factors of the human stripe. Many times

it becomes a case of "fools rushing in where brave men fear to tread". All OR men must spend the necessary time to know as much about their organization and work environment as they can.

How to get an OR Program Started

Most organizations begin with a team of two or three persons, and, as the work becomes accepted, increase the size of the team. A few worthwhile rules the public administrator can use in directing a new program are:

1. Make a modest start with a one- or two-man team.

2. Have the OR'ers work on short-range projects at first that can show immediate successful results.

3. Don't worry at the beginning about having OR report directly to the director of the organization — an echelon or two below the director won't hurt at the start.

4. Hitch your OR star to a going concern whenever possible such as the Controller or the Systems, or Industrial Engineering Department.

5. Be a little modest on putting yourself on record as to what OR can do for the organization. Then you don't have to apologize later for unfulfilled promises!

6. Don't try to overwhelm senior officials by having your OR experts display all their wares in the first application, unless needed. Only use those tools that will do the job in the simplest way.

7. Keep the OR people informed at all times of what the intentions of your superiors are . . . first, what they want to know, and secondly, what their goals are. . . .

Locating the Right Kind of Savvy

Who are the Operations Researchers?

Some are professional engineers, but mathematicians and statisticians play a prominent part in OR. Next in importance are physical and biological scientists. Economists, and sometimes psychologists, participate in OR studies.

The common-bond has been a background in research, for this experience seems to be the most useful for operations research, probably because these disciplines draw heavily upon theoretical constructs or models.

An operations researcher worth his salt must exercise competence over a wide-range of scientific disciplines. In mathematics, for example, he would have to be on top of probability theory, statistics, calculus, and differential equations.

After picking an OR leader, the public administrator should back him up with individuals thoroughly acquainted with all phases of organizational operations, even assigning one of the systems and procedures experts to work with him. This kind of team-mix stresses a much-needed practical approach rather than a theoretical one.

An OR candidate should have these qualifications:

1. Fairly mature, with possibly five or more years of professional experience in his fields of training.

2. Ambition and an appetite for OR work.

3. A broad-gauge viewpoint of things.

4. Better-than-average mathematical skill, and the ability to show results in quantitative form.

5. Ability to establish rapport, or to be at ease, with those with whom he works and to convince them that he knows what he is doing.

6. Forcefulness and clarity in expressing himself in writing or in speech, in order to "sell the ideas".

7. Resourcefulness to work independently and with a minimal amount of support.

8. Willingness to go anywhere at any time, and to do anything ethical.

9. And, *imagination* — perhaps *the most desirable attribute* needed in an OR expert.

Positioning OR in the Organization

Most staff functions feel that they're big and important enough to report directly to the senior official of the organization. A few do!

But with OR, the trend in government is for this function to report to the director or perhaps deputy director of an organization.

It's not absolutely necessary to have your own OR group report to the organization director. What is important is that the function has (1) a sponsor or "a friend in court", and (2) a position in the hierarchy to allow it to have ready access to the data which will enable it to look at problems in their full dimensions.

It is very essential that the OR function reports sufficiently high enough in the organization so that its status lends it enough backing and prestige, so that it can investigate problems and collect data across functional lines with a minimal amount of bureaucratic interference.

How to organize for an OR Study

Before an OR study is even begun, a feasibility study should be made to decide whether or not to apply Operations Research techniques at *all!*

Senior officials should make this determination based on facts gathered by personnel other than OR experts. Systems and procedures analysts can be most helpful. This approach will serve as a safeguard against using expensive OR techniques to solve problems which can be worked out utilizing less complex and expensive methods.

Of course, the main difficulty in the solution of any problem is its *identification*. However, once identified, a task force can begin to work on its final solution.

Perhaps the best OR team combination consists of personnel from different specialized fields in the sciences with no set pattern of representation or specific methodology to be used. It is here that the use of systems analysts as team members can help to expand the team's knowledge of the intimate operations of various components of the organization.

For example, it was slow progress for one OR team from Johns Hopkins University, which was making a study of the operations of a Baltimore hospital, until it added a systems man to the team. The final report stated that "No other single administrative step has done more to aid the initial efforts of the research group".

Digging for the Facts

When an OR man analyzes a system he asks these basic questions:

1. Is the present system necessary?
2. Can it be improved?
3. What will future needs be?
4. Of the available alternative systems, which will fit needs now and in the future?

Selling the OR Proposals

One word of warning. — A public administrator should never let the OR men get so wrapped up in their trade jargon that their reports read something like Einstein's Theory on Relativity. For example, one recent report submitted to senior officers of a government department read:

> We don't recommend using a Second-Degree Parabolic Function as it tends to curve too much and becomes highly volatile . . . and especially dangerous when extrapolated too far.

What this meant in Plain English was simply that while a certain trend is all right for a five-quarter forecast, it becomes highly suspect when used to predict events far into the future.

Public administrators would like answers in easy-to-understand layman's language to cover these main points:

1. How specific is the plan of action?
2. To what degree is the certainty of the outcome?
3. Can a decision favoring the recommended course of action be reversed without any loss whatever?
4. How permanent will the solution be?
5. Can the recommendation be used again, or in other similar problem areas?

OR reports, if written skillfully, present conclusions which should be self-evident. They should be written *for* the administrator rather than *to* him.

The Pluses of OR

OR today has already been accepted by many private business organizations as an important management tool. Around the world OR in private industry is being utilized for such applications as (1) locating the optimal path of flight for jets for Swissair in order to cut fuel consumption costs; (2) the minimum amount of life insurance for which a patient need not take a costly medical examination . . . being worked out for a Zurich firm; (3) the problem of mathematically describing and solving the transportation needs of Vienna; (4) in a Duisburg, West German, steel plant, the finding of the optimal sizes of iron sheets according to consumer demand so as to minimize waste because of cutting; and (5) in Munich, for Siemens, a manufacturer of electrical appliances, the use of OR-computer techniques to schedule delivery of hundreds of thousands of electronic parts to customers.

With each passing day, public administrators find more and more applications for OR. Not so long ago, the United States Department of the Navy used OR techniques to assign medical interns. Until OR, interns were often assigned to locations not always in attune with their original choices. OR techniques enabled Navy to allocate medical interns to at least one of the five hospitals to which they requested to be assigned. Highest ranking interns received billets to hospitals high on their selection list. As a result, over-all morale was greatly improved in this critically short field of occupational skills.

Federal agencies in the United States such as the National Bureau of Standards and the National Capital Transportation Agency have applied OR to resolving traffic transportation problems. Also, the Department of Agriculture has begun employing OR techniques to resolve personnel management problems.

Finis

The public administrator has the responsibility of recognizing the kind of problems which can be solved by OR. With this knowledge he can delegate to specialists the work of solving these problems more effectively. And — if he doesn't understand OR right now — then he should begin learning about OR as soon as he can.

In his position as an official of the organization the public administrator must explain to those who have the responsibility for Operations Research practices, what the objective is and what must be known in order to realize it.

It's up to the public administrator to give his specialists the maximum amount of information about the direction in which his own thoughts are moving and what is in the back of his mind. On the basis of these details the OR workers can then plan their work with complete scientific and technical detachment. If confidence and frankness do not exist between the public administrator and his OR staff, any work done will be hobbled from the start.

Final responsibility for decision-making cannot be delegated to anyone by the public administrator. Final responsibility for results remains with him. And that's the way it should be. No matter how extensively the data provided by OR analysis, few policy decisions can ever be made without the application of experienced judgment. OR simply provides a quantitative basis to narrow the range of intuition that the public administrator would otherwise have to fall back on for his decision-making.

With OR, decisions rely on Facts — not Fancies. . . . It's time for OR to take its rightful place as an important tool of management for the public administrator to use to make him a more effective decision-maker.

32   Communications*

Felix A. Nigro

Communications has been defined as "that process whereby one person makes his ideas and feelings known to another."[1] However, experience has shown time and time again that more is required than the desire to communicate. One must be able to adjust to situations and personalities. Any organization relies on at least a fair degree of harmonious interaction among its employees in order to achieve its objectives, and, wherever there is friction, there will be a block at that point in the communications network. Yet, even when people enjoy good working relations, successful communication is not easy. Also needed is the ability to make one's thoughts entirely clear to the other person, and for this to be possible, the individual's own thinking must be absolutely clear. Vague instructions reflect cloudy thinking; "If an executive cannot shape up in his own mind a clear concept of policies, objectives, programs, and organization structure, and cannot produce a clear picture in the minds of others, he is seriously handicapped."[2]

* Slightly abridged with permission of the author and publisher from Felix A. Nigro, *Modern Public Administration*, Harper and Row, New York, 1965, pp. 188-207.
1 Lawrence A. Appley, *Management in Action*, American Management Association, New York, 1956, p. 182.
2 *Ibid.*, p. 186.

Decisions must be explained properly to those who are to put them into effect. The individual may know exactly what he wants to say but is unable to express himself clearly. Yet, if a sound decision is communicated poorly, the desired results will not be obtained. Decisions themselves are based on communications received from different sources, and subordinates present their recommendations and progress reports to their superiors in the form of communications, both written and oral. In written communications, the individual may use the wrong words or employ expressions that cloud his real meaning, and similar confusion results from lack of clarity in oral communications. Sometimes, too, a cause of the difficulty is failure on the part of one or both of the communicators to listen properly. All of these aspects are vital in the decisionmaking process discussed previously, and for this reason, it is frequently stated that communications and decisionmaking are inseparable.

Further, power in the organization is measured by the respect commanded by an official's communications. Since communication is basically interaction, study of the communications pattern in an organization will reveal the role of each of the participants:

> Let us suppose that a man is foreman in a factory, and that we are watching him at work. What do we see and hear? We watch him, perhaps, overseeing a battery of punch presses, going from one man to another as they tend the machines, answering their questions and showing them, if they have made mistakes, where they have gone wrong. We see him also at his desk making out records. That is, we see that he has a certain kind of job, that he carries on certain activities. We see also that he deals with certain men in the plant and not with others. He goes to certain men and talks to them; others come to his desk and talk to him. He gets his orders from a boss and passes on the orders to members of his own department. That is, he communicates or, as we shall say . . . interacts with certain persons and not with others, and this communication from person to person often takes place in a certain order — for instance, from the boss to the foreman and then from the foreman to the workers — so that we can say . . . that the foreman occupies a position in a chain of communications.[3]

Types of Communications

From the standpoint of the direction in which communications flow, three types can be distinguished: (1) downward; (2) upward; and (3) lateral. Let us discuss each of these in turn.

Downward Communication

Downward communication refers to the directives and other messages which originate with the officials at the top of the organization and are

---

[3] George C. Homans, *The Human Group*, Harcourt, Brace, and World, New York, 1950, pp. 11-12.

transmitted down through the hierarchy — through the intervening levels of supervision — until they reach the lowest-ranking worker in the chain. The traditional approach to administration concentrated on this kind of communication and pretty much ignored the other two. It was assumed that the management was in a position to make decisions which were in the best interests of the workers. Once made, these decisions could be "dropped in the chute," so to speak, and be expected to slide smoothly down the hierarchy. If any hitch developed in the implementation of the decisions at any point in this downward chain, it was attributed to the shortcomings of the workers concerned. Furthermore, top management held the ultimate authority, so it could invoke means to force compliance with its instructions.

The Hawthorne experiments showed that downward communication was not so simple. Management could not make decisions which would be accepted at lower levels without first encouraging upward communication, that is the transmission of information and opinions by the workers up the same hierarchy, in other words, travelling the reverse route. In large organizations, downward communication is difficult enough to begin with, because orders must descend through numerous intermediate levels before the point of execution is reached. Misunderstandings can easily occur when instructions pass through so many people. If little upward communication exists, the difficulties are multiplied, because the orders themselves are apt to be unrealistic and to meet with worker resistance.

Upward Communication

Many years have passed since the Hawthorne experiments, but few organizations have been able to develop really effective systems of upward communication — that is, messages that are passed from the lower levels of the hierarchy up to the management. Earl Planty and William Machaver identify a number of barriers to upward communication:

1. Physical distance or inaccessibility
2. Dilution or distortion at each level
3. The attitude of the supervisor
4. The inferior status of the subordinate
5. Tradition.[4]

Workers separated by great distances from the source of authority at the top of the organization have difficulty in communicating upward. A field worker, for example, may have relatively infrequent contact with the head of the field office. The latter in turn may have only limited opportunity to see, and therefore to express his ideas fully to his superiors at headquarters. The same is true even when all the workers are located in the same area. The larger the organization, the greater the number of links in the super-

[4] See Earl Planty and William Machaver, "Upward Communications: A Project in Executive Development," *Personnel*, Vol. 28, No. 4, January, 1952, pp. 304-317.

visory chain, and the principle of "following channels" requires that no link in this chain be bypassed; everyone must deal through his immediate chief. It is not surprising, then, that few messages that are voluntarily initiated by the lowest worker ever travel upward until they finally reach the desk of the top executive. Reports required by the top management must traverse this route, but they do not have the spontaneity that ideally should characterize the system of upward communication.

As information is passed up the hierarchy, it is subject to a filtering process at each level. Some of this is deliberate; a good deal is unconscious. The picture of operations as described by a subordinate may not square with the superior's conception of the situation, particularly when the subordinate reports that some things are not going well at all. "Problems" are disturbing, and a typically human reaction is to refuse to believe that they exist or are as serious as they are painted to be. (Good news ascends the hierarchy much more easily than bad news.) The tendency is to "edit" the reports to present a brighter picture. An agency head can sometimes appear to be unbelievably blind as to what is really going on in his agency; yet based on the reports he gets everything *is* fine: these reports simply do not present him with all the facts. Consequently, the upwards reporting system is often of very limited value in locating trouble spots in the agency's operations.

The executive represents to the subordinate someone who wields power and could damage the subordinate's prospects for advancement. This creates a communications block, for the subordinate is wary even though the superior may urge him to be frank. Subordinates who, for one reason or another, feel secure in their positions tend to express themselves the most frankly to their superiors. The subordinate is handicapped at the outset of any upward communication, because he is not free to break in on the superior and intrude on his time. If the chief has something on his mind, he can, at any time, ask the subordinate to see him as soon as possible. In a sense, he controls their time; they in no sense control his. They must, rather, petition an audience with him. There are usually several who want to see the chief at the same time, and he is very busy as it is satisfying the other demands on his time.

Upward communication is in a very important sense "unnatural." It is like rowing upstream, against the current. Downward communication has the great force of tradition behind it. There is nothing at all unusual about communications originating at the top of the hierarchy and being routed downward. By contrast, upward communication is unconventional. In most organizations, it is not established procedure for the employees spontaneously to direct upward any large numbers of communications. The employee who attempts to do so may even take a risk. Further, the management that genuinely wants to encourage upward communication will have difficulty because the upward route will generally have been used so rarely in the past that the employees will remain reluctant to use it.

Management can embark on a program to stimulate upward communication. The management should not expect such communication to be spontaneous with the employees, nor is it enough simply to tell the workers that upward communication is desirable. Most of the employees will require clear evidence that the management really is interested in their opinions. Since an important change is being made in the worker's accustomed role, he understandably needs help and encouragement in making the shift from mere cog to full participant in the aims of the organization. Some workers may be so used to playing an insignificant role that they have become quite indifferent to the future of the organization. Thus, the management must change the whole outlook of these workers if it is to succeed in getting them to participate in any system of upward communication.

Superior officers should follow a consistent policy of listening to their subordinates. This may involve adapting to a willingness to face bad news. The management should encourage its supervisors to do this, and the example set by the agency head in this respect will normally have a great influence on the other executives. If he encourages communications from below, and accepts even negative reports, his key assistants are likely to do the same with their subordinates.

The most unfriendly atmosphere for upward communication is one in which the management seems to isolate itself, keeping information to itself and considering many matters "confidential" and not to be revealed outside the inner circle. A management which practices such limited downward communication automatically inhibits upward communication, and, in effect, builds a wall between itself and the rest of the organization. For subordinates to initiate upward communication in such an atmosphere would be almost tantamount to defiance. Fortunately, such an attitude by the management is now considered old fashioned and tends to be the exception rather than the rule.

The supervisor should exercise care in selecting his "communicators" — that is, those who provide him with information — and make sure that these communicators are not merely "reflectors" of what he is predisposed to seeing. Some executives make a point of surrounding themselves with at least one or two "no" men in a conscious effort to avoid the "conspiracy of smoothness". For example, Attorney-General Robert Kennedy acted as a "communicator" in his brother's Cabinet. Some newspaper reports indicated that as the President's brother the Attorney-General was able to be far more blunt with the Chief Executive than any other member of the administration, and this bluntness may explain why the late President depended so much on his younger brother.

The superior officer should also strive to correct those of his personal habits which prevent the subordinate from speaking to him freely. Again, the superior must first be aware of these mannerisms, and humans are typically blind when it comes to personal failings. Yet some self-prompting is possible once the supervisor has become aware of these tendencies and has really decided to encourage the subordinate. It should be pointed out here that superior officers frequently feel a compulsion to demonstrate their superiority to their subordinates. With some, this is a protective device; if they *appear* to know more than their subordinates, they can feel they are living up to their official roles in the organization. Other supervisors are vain and would in any case treat their subordinates with condescension. While the supervisor must never forget his responsibilities as a superior officer, his position hardly means that he is always better apprized of all the facts than is the subordinate. Once the supervisor recognizes that his subordinates are likely to possess information that he does not, he is much more apt to encourage subordinates to communicate with him freely.

Another common mistake is for the superior to state his own position before he listens to the subordinate, rather than inviting the subordinate to give his opinions on the particular problem. There may be no intention on the part of the superior to force his views on the subordinate, but the latter is quickly placed in a difficult position: he must agree with the boss. Few people will want to challenge the chief so openly. Encouraging one's subordinates to express their views holds another advantage. Some workers prefer to leave all decisions to someone else in order to avoid the responsibility. Such an attitude generally serves to impair the caliber of the individual's work, which ultimately reflects on the supervisor, as well as adds to his load of decisionmaking. If however, the supervisor encourages free expression of ideas from his subordinates, he is likely to lead this sort of individual to develop his capacity for greater responsibility. The supervisor will never succeed in this if he merely asks his subordinates for reactions to his own ideas.

Where it is indicated and feasible, the superior officer should *use* the information given to him by his subordinates. Nothing is more destructive of free expression — and of upward communication — than the chief's failure to act upon the ideas and problems reported to him. The subordinates are led to believe that they are wasting their time, and may even wish that the superior had not gone through the formality of listening. The purpose of communication is to achieve organizational objectives. Action at some point is essential if subordinates are to continue to feel motivated in contributing to these objectives by communicating significant information to their superiors.

Lateral Communication

Lateral communication is that which takes place among workers of the same level in the hierarchy, or among individuals of different levels who are not in a superior-subordinate relationship. Lateral relationships will frequently go from one agency to another, and are not restricted to intra-agency relationships. We use the term *lateral* instead of *horizontal* in order to be able to include *all* across-the-organization contacts.

Traditional organization theory is based on the organization chart and the system of *scalar* authority it depicts. The scalar principle means that the different positions of authority are shown in descending order of importance. The limitations of the chart give the clue to the inadequacies of traditional theory, as is so well revealed in the following statement:

> The relation between the scheme of activities and the scheme of inter-action in an organization is usually represented by the familiar organization chart, which shows the organization divided into departments and subdepartments, the various officers and subofficers occupying boxes, connected by lines to show which persons are subordinates to what other ones. Every such chart is too neat; it tells what the channels of inter-action ought to be but not always what they are. The pyramid-type chart is particularly misleading because it shows only the interaction between superiors and subordinates, the kind of interaction that we shall call, following Barnard, *scalar*. It does not show the interaction that goes on between two or more persons at about the same level of the organization, for instance, between two department heads. . . .
> This kind of interaction we shall call lateral interaction, though we must remember that there are borderline cases where the distinction between scalar and lateral interaction disappears. The conventional organization chart represents the scalar but not the lateral interaction. *If it were not for the unhappy association with predatory spiders, the facts would be much better represented by a web, the top leader at the center, spokes radiating from him, and concentric circles linking the spokes. Interaction takes place along the concentric circles as well as along the spokes.*[5]

Lateral communication is of great importance in assuring coordination of organizational objectives. The members of the organization should work together as a cohesive unit, but, if they are to do so, they must communicate their plans and intentions to one another clearly. Traditional organization theory has emphasized coordination through command; that is, through the downward communications of the superior. As Thompson explains: "each person's behavior is considered to be determined by the commands of his superior. If every superior is able to give integrated, rationally consistent commands, the organization will automatically be a coordinated system of behavior."[6] The fallacy in this reasoning is that the superior officer is not in a position to give subordinates these "integrated, rationally consistent commands."[7] The subordinates are likely to know the details of operations in their bailiwicks better than he can be expected to know them. Thompson continues:

> Specialization has long outrun human ability to coordinate in this fashion. Not only is the person in the command position increasingly dependent upon subordinates for the interpretation of incoming data and the initiation of activities, but interdependencies far beyond command jurisdictions have developed. Consequently, most coordination is programmed, built into routines.[8]

---

[5] Homans, *op. cit.*, pp. 104-105. Italics ours.
[6] Victor A. Thompson, *Modern Organization*, Knopf, New York, 1961, p. 181.
[7] *Ibid.*
[8] *Ibid.*, p. 183.

The concept of coordination by command is basically authoritarian in nature: The way to get the subordinates to work together is to order them to do so; if they fail to obey, punitive corrective measures should be taken. Overlooked is the fact that there are serious limits to the coordination which can be imposed on the employees from above. Such coordination tends to be nominal, simply because it is forced on the worker, and, at best, he only grudgingly complies. Real teamplay is characterized by spontaneity. The individual wants to cooperate because he derives *personal* satisfaction from functioning as a member of the team.

In modern organizations, decisionmaking is not monopolized by just a few top people. Management depends on the specialized skills and knowledge of its subordinates and modern administrations recognize this. Today, they invite workers to participate in the decisionmaking process. Logically, this requires the encouragement of both upward and lateral communication. The wise superior finds it advantageous to encourage his subordinates, not only to express their ideas to him freely, but also to settle as many problems as possible among themselves. If they are to cooperate in this manner, they must obviously be in close contact with one another.

Obstacles

Just as in the case of upward communication, the lateral pattern of interaction presents its difficulties. In some respects, effective lateral communication is even more difficult to achieve. In upward communication, the subordinate must adjust to only one person — his immediate supervisor. In lateral communication, workers must deal with several coworkers, and any one department head must try to work together harmoniously with all other department heads; he must also develop effective working relationships with department heads and other officials of outside agencies.

The very division of an organization into specialized parts creates barriers to lateral communication and coordination. Specialists typically develop strong loyalties, not to the organization as a whole, but to their own areas of interest. The tendency is for them to regard members of other specialized groups as threats to their own positions in the organization. The members of each specialized group think its function is the most important in the agency. Furthermore, specialized professions have their peculiar frames of reference and technical language. The members of each can communicate among themselves effectively, but they frequently have difficulty grasping the point of view of outsiders.

Horizontal cliques also provide the clue to much of the difficulty in lateral communications. Besides the frictions between specialists, there are rivalries and consequent tensions between the different organization units. Departments compete with other departments for bigger appropriations and more prominent roles in the total government program. Similarly, within any one department, the bureaus and other subdivisions fight for special status. The rival organization units eye one another with suspicion and sometimes with considerable hostility. Instead of freely exchanging information on operating plans, they may try to keep one another in the dark. Deviousness, instead of open discussion of mutual problems, may characterize the conversations between their respective personnel. The principal officials in each department may play their cards close to their chests, always afraid of being out-maneuvered by the other party.

The very complexity of modern organization also creates difficulties, just as it does in the case of downward and upward communications. The more persons an official must consult, both within and outside the agency, the more complicated the process of lateral communication becomes. Often he is uncertain as to whom he should consult, because the lines of responsibility within the agency are not that clearly defined. If he must check with another agency, his problem becomes even more difficult, for he may be unfamiliar with the work assignments of the officials in that agency. Valuable time is lost before he can identify the particular individual with whom he should deal. Furthermore, both in intra- and interagency contacts, physical separation may delay and impede communications, as is illustrated in communications between widely separated field offices. Merely looking at the organization chart of a large public agency will give some idea of the complexities of lateral communication. Although the interaction between the numerous departments, divisions, and organization units is not shown on the chart, the very number of these horizontally placed units suggests the intricate pattern of interrelationships necessary for efficient operation. Naturally, the red tape increases as documents and other communications are directed laterally from points inside and outside the agency.

A further difficulty arises from the fact that the person initiating a lateral communication usually cannot exert the same pressure as can a supervisor on his own subordinates. In dealing with coequals, representatives of other agencies, or even the subordinates of others, the official must usually rely on persuasion. This may mean far more delay in lateral than in downward communication, where the traditional flow of authority does give the communication at least some ring of urgency.

Improving Lateral Communication

The first step in developing efficient communications is to build a sound organization structure and to make clear everybody's responsibilities. As to achieving coordination, George F. Gant stresses what he calls "unity by agency objective."[9] By this he means that employees at all levels will work together better if the leaders of the agency clearly explain the importance of the agency program and of their own particular contributions to it. Many different techniques can be employed in this effort, but obviously a very superior quality of leadership is required if the employees throughout

[9] George F. Gant, "Unity and Specialization in Administration," in Felix A. Nigro (ed.), *Public Administration, Readings and Documents*, Holt, Rinehart and Winston, New York, 1951, pp. 126-135.

the agency are to be induced to work together as a team. Furthermore, there may be important limits to the degree to which any individual may be expected to identify with the organization with which he works. Thompson writes:

> Although some individuals undoubtedly give considerable loyalty to their bread-and-butter organization, it is only one loyalty among many. If the organization becomes the only object of one's loyalty, then the organization becomes a totalitarian state. Most people probably give their first or primary loyalty to their primary groups — the family, the informal work group, etc. The sharing of values and reality perceptions throughout the larger organization is, therefore, an illusion.[10]

One need not wholly agree with Thompson, but there must be some realization of the limitations to employee identification with organizational goals. Yet professional ties improve communication in grant-in-aid and other intergovernmental programs. Individuals within the same profession can get along well, despite the fact that they are of different governmental levels, due to their professional loyalties.

Apart from vocational specialization, there is another important way in which the members of modern organizations are specialized; they are "socially specialized," that is, they have become specialized in working with one another. In efforts to improve lateral communication, it must be recognized that it takes a good deal of time before individuals can become specialized in this way:

> We understand people easily through our experience with them, which teaches us their special use of words, the meaning of intonation and gestures, whether they are matter of fact or emotional, given to exaggeration or understatement, are reticent or voluble, and many other subtle characteristics of communication. Without the confidence that accompanies this kind of understanding, reticence, hesitation, indecision, delay, error, and panic ensue.
> "Know your people" is nearly as important as "know your language" in the communication upon which organized effort depends. The difficulty of communication on matters of concrete action between individuals who have not known each other is a matter of common experience, but its importance with respect to organization seems to be forgotten because the organizations we know have, in fact, developed usually through long periods. At a given time nearly everyone has habitual relationships with most of those with whom he needs to communicate regularly.[11]

The agency head naturally wants his subordinates to cooperate and to pull together; yet it takes a real effort to get even the heads of organization units to work together properly. Above all, the agency head must be aware of the probable existence of at least some sensitive relationships between them. With this awareness, he is in a much better position to

---

10 Thompson, *op. cit.*, p. 185.
11 Chester I. Barnard, "Education for Executives," in Robert Dubin (ed.), *Human Relations in Administration*, Prentice-Hall, Englewood Cliffs, N.J., 1961, p. 20.

induce coordinated efforts. The staff conference is frequently mentioned as a valuable tool for achieving coordination, yet the experienced executive knows that some of his subordinates may come to these meetings determined to conceal their real thoughts and plans from the others. He will also be well aware that some of the positions taken may be reactions to certain individuals and their personalities, rather than to the objective situation. Subordinate A may react negatively to suggestions made by subordinate B simply because it is B who makes them. If C were to make them, his reaction might be different. Thus, if the executive is to be successful in improving lateral communication, he must first be effective in improving the interpersonal relationships among his subordinates. Unless he understands his role in this way, the kinds of communications he evokes from them will likely consist of mere words unsupported by any real desire to cooperate. Surface appearances of harmony may be maintained during the conference — polite words may be exchanged — but, as a coordinating device, the meeting will have been a failure. Obviously, there are limits to what the executive can do to promote better personal relationships between his subordinates. It is a certainty, however, that he will have very little success unless he is first able to interpret accurately the feelings behind the communications they initiate, both when in a staff conference or when conferring with him individually.[12]

Informal Communications

The formal communications network will always be supplemented by an informal one. If clearances are difficult to obtain through the formal channels, contact can be made informally with a friend who can expedite things. The "grapevine" can damage the organization by carrying ugly gossip and false information, but it also can play a constructive role. Valuable information that an individual will normally not be willing to communicate through the official channels is often transmitted to superior officers very rapidly through the grapevine. For instance, John Jones may be unhappy about a certain condition in his office, but he is not inclined to "jump" channels and complain to the management. He expresses himself freely to his friends, one or more of whom may have an "in" with the top officials in the agency. They informally communicate John Jones' dissatisfactions, whereupon management can look into a situation of which it had not been aware. Thus, the friendship ties characteristic of the informal organization remove some of the communication blocks in upward communication. They perform the same function in facilitating lateral and even downward communication: the superior officer may want to give a subordinate personal advice, but he feels that his official capacity does not

12 An excellent treatment of this problem is Warren H. Schmidt and Robert Tannenbaum, "The Management of Differences," in Tannenbaum, Weschler, and Massarik (eds.), *Leadership and Organization: A Behavioural Science Approach*, McGraw-Hill, New York, 1961, pp. 101-118.

permit it. He talks freely to another employee who is in a position to pass the advice on to the person concerned. Obviously, considerable skill must be developed in utilizing these informal channels if the desired results are to be obtained. The dangers are great, because information which is fed into the gossip mill can easily be distorted and do more harm than good.

Eugene Walton observes that the "organization's informal communications network begins to hum whenever the formal channels are silent or ambiguous on subjects of importance to its members."[13] This indicates that the management stands to profit from knowing what kind of information is being transmitted through the grapevine. Walton has investigated the means by which employees learn of significant organization developments. In cases where the employees have heard about these developments mostly through the grapevine, there is a clear indication that the official channels were not functioning as efficiently as they should have been. Of course, no matter how good the formal system of communications, the grapevine will still exist, but it should not have to do the job of advising employees of management policies. This is the responsibility of the formal organization.

In closing this chapter, the following words of Herbert A. Simon are very much to the point:

> No step in the administrative process is more generally ignored, or more poorly performed, than the task of communicating decisions. All too often, plans are "ordered" into effect without any consideration of the manner in which they can be brought to influence the behavior of the individual members of the group. Procedural manuals are promulgated without follow-up to determine whether the contents of the manuals are used by the individuals to guide their decisions. Organization plans are drawn on paper, although the members of the organization are ignorant of the plan that purports to describe their relationships.[14]

33 Information Services in Canadian Government*

Information activities in the public service range from the reporting of policies, events and discoveries to the promotion of ideas and images. Every department and agency engages in some of these activities, whether or not they are formally recognized in the organization structure, and in a literal sense the information function is carried on at all levels from the minister

[13] Eugene Walton, "How Efficient is the Grapevine?" *Personnel*, Vol. 38, No. 2, March-April, 1961, p. 45.
[14] Herbert A. Simon, *Administrative Behavior*, Macmillan, New York, 1957, p. 108.

* Reprinted with permission of publisher from The Royal Commission on Government Organization, *Report*, Vol. 3, Queen's Printer, Ottawa, 1962, pp. 63-72.

and deputy minister to the switchboard operator. The nature of the task and the weight attached to it vary according to the purposes of the department or agency, and in each case some techniques and media of communication are more suitable than others.

In its broadest sense, the provision of information to the public is an integral part of the day-to-day working relations between all levels of the federal government and the Canadian public. The development of special machinery within the government to prepare and disseminate information was gradual, and generally occurred in recent years, although shortly after the Department of Mines was established in 1907 an Editorial and Information Division began to edit and publicize the scientific and other official reports of the Department. Three years later the Department of Agriculture, which had been issuing bulletins for farmers since 1887, created a Publications Branch. A decade later, the new Department of National Health established a Publicity and Statistics Division to enlighten the public on such matters as maternal and child welfare, and the dangers, incidence and treatment of various diseases.

In the ensuing years, a number of circumstances have combined to influence more systematic treatment of the information function. First, the growing range and complexity of government operations have accentuated public demands for information about government policies and programmes. Second, the increasing involvement of government in the economic life of the country has included a growing emphasis on promoting improved methods in the development and utilization of Canadian resources. Third, an increasing sense of national sovereignty and at the same time of interdependence in world affairs has created a growing concern with the projection abroad of Canadian viewpoints and aspirations. Fourth, the development of mass communications, especially radio, film and television, created a need for new kinds of specialists. Finally, the evolution of public relations techniques in industry has suggested, rightly or wrongly, the adaptation of these techniques to government purposes.

As in so many other matters, World War II had a catalytic effect on the development of specialized information services in the government. The machinery then established was designed for wartime needs — to explain and enlist public support for the war effort. To a degree, it was a propaganda effort with a special department headed by a minister assigned the task, and was dismantled at the end of hostilities. But the wartime experience left a lasting impression on political leaders and administrators and during the next few years most departments and agencies which had not already established information services did so.

However, the specialized services still account for only a part — and probably the lesser part — of the information activities of the government. Because the information function exists at every point of contact between the machinery of government and the public, it is bound to remain diffuse and unspecialized, with dimensions not susceptible of statistical measurement.

Services to the Public

The dissemination of information as a service to the Canadian public is either the sole or principal reason for the existence of some departments and agencies and is an explicit or essential corollary to the operations of others. The purpose may be to develop and propagate a body of knowledge of benefit to the public at large, or to promote efficiency, economy or market opportunities in a particular industry.

One of the most striking examples is the Dominion Bureau of Statistics which has a statutory obligation to publish. The Bureau may, in fact, be regarded in its entirety as a specialized information service. Proper distribution and service to users are not merely routine activities incidental to the preparation of statistics; they are essential to the effective fulfilment of the purposes of the organization. The same may be said of the Meteorological Service of the Department of Transport, whose weather reports are undoubtedly the most widely disseminated of all government information — and the most consistently and widely read.

The extension of knowledge is, of course, the purpose of all scientific research in government. Even where the objective is to facilitate or improve government operations, civil or defence, results are likely to be of wider interest. A project undertaken for defence purposes, for example, may fail in its objective but, nevertheless, establish a scientific principle or engineering technique that can be applied to improve a manufacturing process serving civilian needs. In the application of knowledge, two and two often add up to more than four and, what may appear to be unrelated or insignificant facts may provide the missing links in a development of benefit to the country. It is therefore essential that within reasonable limitations of security there be a free flow of the results of research both to other units of government and to the public at large. There may also be justification for the dissemination of research information that the federal government itself has not produced or sponsored, if this information is not otherwise readily available to potential beneficiaries in Canada.

The need to publish scientific findings is reinforced by the importance attached to publication by scientists themselves. In order to recruit research workers, the government must provide an attractive working milieu, which normally provides opportunities for developing professional recognition by the publication of scientific and technical papers. But such papers may be intelligible only to other scientists; therefore it may often serve a national purpose to have these supplemented by interpretative publication in terms the layman can understand.

These considerations apply generally to all government research, and are well illustrated in the National Research Council, which undertakes or sponsors pure and applied scientific research over a wide field. The principal work of its Information Branch is to act, on a national basis, as a clearing house for all types of scientific and technical information. The Branch consists of a library, a Technical Information Service and a Public Relations Office, with liaison offices in London, England, and Washington, D.C. The library serves as a national science library, accessible to all research workers, and working contacts are maintained and information exchanged with similar libraries around the world. The Technical Information Service studies Canadian and foreign scientific publications, both official and unofficial, adapting and editing whatever may be needed for publication in Canada, and maintains a directory of all Canadian undertakings making use of scientific and technical research information. Contact with the non-technical press is maintained through the Public Relations Office, which is responsible for publicizing the work of the Council in lay terms, facilitating access to people and information by newsmen and specialist writers, and arranging for public, radio and television appearances by research workers and other members of the organization.

Because much of the scientific work of the Defence Research Board is governed by security restrictions, its directorate of Scientific Information Service is designed to deal with classified material. However, digests are issued monthly of unclassified accessions to the document collection of the Board, and these are available to other departments and agencies. The Directorate collaborates with a Public Relations Officer, who deals with the press and other non-technical external contacts.

All departments concerned with the development and conservation of resources engage in extensive scientific programmes which, to be of value, must be complemented by effective information services. These departments include Agriculture, Fisheries, Forestry, and Mines and Technical Surveys.

Side by side with scientific research in the resources departments are programmes of consumer education and market promotion which are equally dependent on the dissemination of knowledge and ideas. In the Department of Fisheries, for example, its Information and Consumer Service encourages conservation practices among commercial and sport fishermen; publicizes the need for improved processing and marketing standards; promotes increased consumption of fish and fish products; and seeks to develop in the minds of the public a better understanding of fisheries as a natural resource. Similar aims are pursued by the Information Services of the Department of Agriculture.

A number of other departments undertake programmes designed to promote changes in the business practices and buying habits of the Canadian public or in standards of health and housing. The Information Division of the Department of Labour, for example, spends more than $500,000 a year in advertising and promotion, with its major campaigns being associated with winter works programme and vocational training, in both of which the provinces participate. The Unemployment Insurance Commission is also engaged in promotional activities supporting the winter works programme.

The Department of National Health and Welfare, among other things, co-operates with provincial authorities to protect and improve public health. The propagation of knowledge and sound practice to promote health and hygiene is the responsibility of the Health Services Directorate, and it is this which receives most attention and effort from the Information Services Division of the Department.

The Central Mortgage and Housing Corporation is, by statute, responsible for the promotion of good housing design and construction, and for making available educational material with respect to all aspects of housing in Canada, including the problems of city growth and renewal. The National Gallery promotes interest in art throughout Canada and in Canadian art abroad.

Thus, in many departments and agencies the provision of information as a service to the public is a primary or statutory responsibility. The purposes are widely assorted but the information activities have several characteristics in common. First, the information task is, in whole or in part, integral to a principal function of the department and may not be treated as an incidental activity. Second, there is no automatic standard by which to determine the quantity of information which should be distributed. Effective control is therefore imperative in order to maintain a proper balance of effort both within the organization and throughout the government.

Enlisting Public Support

In certain situations, operations of government can be assisted and their value enhanced when public co-operation is enlisted. In these cases, a properly directed information programme proves to be an invaluable aid to the economy and efficiency of government.

A perennial operational problem is the economical handling of peak loads either at particular times of day or in particular seasons of the year. A typical example is the flood of work imposed on the Taxation Division of the Department of National Revenue by reason of the April 30th deadline for filing income-tax returns. Since 1950 the Division has undertaken annual advertising and publicity campaigns to encourage early filing. The average cost has been between $30,000 and $40,000 a year and the response has been excellent; more economical work planning has been possible and the number of penalties imposed for late filing has been reduced substantially.

The Post Office faces a daily operational peak around five o'clock in the afternoon, and an overload of staggering dimensions before Christmas. The public can ease these burdens by mailing early in the day every day and posting Christmas mail early in December. Moreover, sorting operations at all times are facilitated when zone numbers form part of the address on mail for the larger cities. The Post Office conducts publicity campaigns to encourage the public to adopt these practices, and savings in direct operational expenditure far exceed the cost of advertising and other publicity.

This is not the total extent of Post Office effort in educating the public in the proper use of postal services. Lectures, posters, pamphlets, television filmstrips and radio broadcasts are all used to induce people to package and address mail properly. Nevertheless, every year as many as 50,000 parcels are so badly addressed or packed as to make delivery or return equally impossible, and up to $60,000 in cash may be retrieved annually from letters which give no clue to the identity or whereabouts of either addressee or sender.

Public co-operation of a different sort must be sought in staffing the public service. Several departments and agencies find it necessary to stimulate recruiting by general publicity about career opportunities, conditions of work, and other special benefits, quite apart from the direct advertising for specific vacancies.

The Department of National Defence is chief among these, because of the reliance on voluntary enlistment for the Armed Forces. In 1960-61, recruiting expenditures of the three Services approximated $1,300,000, excluding the pay and allowances of those engaged in the work; of this amount, $365,000 was paid for advertising, the balance being spent on the preparation and distribution of promotional material. Recruiting is the responsibility of the Manning Directorate in each Service, and advertising for this purpose is controlled by the Tri-Service Recruiting Advertising Committee. Service public relations activities assist indirectly in the promotion of recruiting, but separate budgets and chains of command are maintained for each function.

The Public Service Commission does most advertising for staff required by departments. Total promotional expenditures in 1960-61, excluding staff time and printing costs, are recorded as $268,000. In addition, a number of organizations regard the stimulation of interest among potential recruits as an important purpose to be served by their information programmes; this is especially true among departments requiring substantial numbers of scientific and technical personnel.

The Public Right to be Informed

Knowledge of government activities is a public right, and indeed a necessity; but the growing size and diversity of government make the satisfaction of this need more and more difficult. The machinery and processes of government are therefore taking increasingly into account the public demand to be informed.

Responsiveness

At the very least, this requires a responsiveness to requests for information and explanations. First and foremost, the needs of Parliament must be satisfied, both accurately and promptly. This is, of course, of overriding concern to ministers, who look to their departments for the data to meet the need. Every department furnishes material for replies to parliamentary questions and for ministerial statements both in Parliament and on other public occasions. In addition, with few exceptions, departments and agencies are obliged by law to make a formal report to Parliament each year.

Increasingly, the traditional parliamentary concern with the operations of the public service is being supplemented by manifestations of public interest through other channels, and especially through the media of mass communications. At the direct level, the public is ill-disposed to official procrastination in providing desired information. This is especially applicable to information about taxes. So far as the Royal Commission is concerned, there is too much evidence of frustration encountered by Canadian businessmen seeking information on which trading decisions depend. The classification of goods for import duty may determine the profitability of a venture, and inordinate delays in obtaining advance appraisal for duty may be costly to the businessman.

Publicity

The character and extent of the effort required to provide an adequate response to inquiries can be gauged with reasonable accuracy by the nature and volume of the requests themselves. However, when departments take the initiative in publicizing their operations, the proper limits of their information activity become debatable.

The provision of services to the public entails some obligation to make those services known to the public, even where they are free of charge; the money spent to make them available would be a total loss were they not used. This applies to such establishments as the National Gallery and the various museums maintained by the government. In this connection, the National Museum, in sharp contrast to the other branches of the Department of Northern Affairs and National Resources, appears to be little publicized.

Government publicity may also be required for services of a quite different nature which are available, in cash or in kind, to particular sections of the citizenry, often on a contingent basis. For instance, the benefits available to veterans and their dependants are regulated by several statutes of a complex nature, and the Department of Veterans Affairs is under an obligation to give comprehensive publicity.

In parallel with the need to publicize the rights of the citizen and the services that are available to him, the government is under an obligation to give adequate publicity to the restrictions and obligations imposed on the public by law. The judicial principle that ignorance of the law is no defence does not absolve the government from the duty of making the law reasonably plain to those affected.

Special considerations apply to the publicity activities of deciding tribunals. As a general rule, these tribunals observe the traditional reticence of the judiciary when out of court. But it is the invariable practice of the higher courts to give a reasoned exposition in support of a judgment, a practice that should properly be followed more consistently by administrative tribunals when the matter is one of public interest. Even more imperative is the need for the reasons for a decision, if published at all, to be released at the same time as the decision itself — not as a defensive afterthought consequent to public criticism. Regulatory tribunals should also be under obligation to publicize policy decisions so that those adversely affected may initiate timely action for remedy.

Beyond these special obligations, as departments go on to publicize their activities more generally, on the basis of newsworthiness, they enter an area of activity which is both ill-defined and controversial.

Every department and agency generates news, some more than others, and most try to work closely with the press and broadcasting media to provide timely and usable material in suitable form. Spot news of national interest does not arise every day, but in some government operations there is an almost continuous flow of routine news of interest to particular occupational groups or geographical areas. Government construction and procurement, for instance, have an effect on the national economy and often have a significant impact on the prosperity of a particular neighbourhood. This local importance is reflected in the volume of parliamentary questions and inquiries from the press and public about the letting and progress of contracts.

There is, however, a distinction — not always easy to draw — between releasing news and "telling the Department's story". What must be borne in mind is that all government activity has at least a modicum of political significance. Consequently, the publicizing of a department may be an excursion into the realm of political controversy.

The danger need not be overstated. It is not a matter of the deliberate misuse of the information process to manipulate public opinion for political purposes. Even if this were tried — and there is no evidence that it has been — the attempt would founder on the independence of the news media and the safeguards inherent in the political process itself. But short of this remote threat of crude and probably self-defeating efforts at political manipulation, government publicity may involve less fundamental but more subtle dangers.

There is no fixed line between exposition and argument, between publicity and propaganda. What is news to one man is propaganda to another. A news release, pamphlet or film about a missile installation, fall-out shelters, the treatment of offenders or the education of Indian children may be only a bare and even dull recital of fact but still seem argumentative and provocative to some of the public. It would be absurd to conclude that publicity should be given to government activities only by the political leaders, but certain other conclusions may be drawn.

First, general government publicity should be strictly factual and as far as possible objective. Apart from the special areas of promotional information, as defined elsewhere in this chapter, the task of information services is to inform rather than to persuade. Moreover, publicity should take the form of source material rather than be aimed directly at the public. Experienced information officers make a preliminary judgment as to newsworthiness and ensure that publicity material is released in clear and coherent form; but the ultimate decision as to what is news and how it should be presented must be left to the media. Elaborate presentations by film, book or feature and human interest stories may be good publicity on the part of private organizations, but cannot always be regarded as legitimate forms of general publicity by the government.

Second, there should be restraint and balance in volume; even when information is objective in character, sheer volume can transform it into propaganda and an excessive and undiscriminating flood of material defeats its purpose. Aggressive efforts to capture public attention constitute, regardless of intent, attempts to win public support. When this occurs, government information services become active participants in the political process.

Third, an important distinction should be drawn between material which genuinely informs and that which is calculated only to impress; the latter has no place in the information activities of government. It is tempting to issue news stories, pictures or films depicting weapons, laboratories and engineering works as marvels of the age — begging the question of their function and worth.

The philosophy of the public relations man promoting the interests of an industry is that everything which brings the company's name to the attention of the public in a not unfavourable context is advantageous. The very fact of being known is important for business reasons and so the job of publicizing may include a continuing effort to secure maximum publicity. Your Commissioners do not subscribe to the view that similar approaches are permissible in government. Keeping the mass media supplied with a flood of so-called news releases is not a function of a department. What is offered for publication should meet the test of being necessary in the execution of programmes of a department. The public is entitled to expect that public duties are competently performed, and the taxpayers' money should not be spent to impress people with the quality of performance. Thus the objective of being "well and favourably known", so legitimate in competitive business, forms no part of public information policies of departments.

Your Commissioners are satisfied that the current publicity effort in government is honest and well-intentioned. Whether it is entirely proper is doubtful, but to the question "how much is proper?" no clear answer can be given. Official reticence should not be carried to the point of un-responsiveness and indifference to the public's right to be informed. The vagueness of the other limit has already been indicated.

Whatever may be the proper limit to publicity by any individual organization, the examination made of current activities reveals a lack of balance among the departments and, in particular, between the civilian departments and the Department of National Defence.

The only civil departments having information staffs of some magnitude are those charged with providing information as a service to the public. These departments are more active in the dissemination of general publicity than are those without specific promotional functions; but, in general, their publicity activities are also restrained. The Armed Forces, on the other hand, overshadow the civilian organizations in the size of their information services. In May, 1962, these were manned by 67 Service officers, 67 other ranks and 56 civilians. By way of comparison, the Department of Transport had only five information officers although its operations affect the safety and convenience of all modes of transportation in Canada — by rail, in the air or on the water.

In part, the publicity activities of the Armed Forces are an indirect form of stimulus to recruiting although, as noted above, direct recruiting activities are substantial. It is clear that the principal aim of the Services' information programmes is to win public approbation, and "public relations" is consistently used in preference to "information" in describing both their work and staffs employed.

The activities of the three Service directorates of public relations were assessed by a check of output in a two-week period in November and December 1961. It revealed:

68 press releases, including 10 "major stories".
7 news-feature releases.
More than 2,500 photographic prints distributed.
More than 100 radio, television and film assignments completed, ranging from news clips to 15-minute film and television features.
More than 700 radio tapes and 500 television tapes produced and distributed.

So far as is known, this particular two-week period was in no way exceptional. In your Commissioners' view, this output is disturbing because of its volume and intensity and also for the high proportion of material offered not as source material but as a finished product to be carried by the media.

Chapter Eight
Human Relations and Leadership

Since human relations and leadership permeate the entire field of administration, they are included in any discussion of the diverse functions of management. But the pervasive nature of human relations and leadership makes it extremely difficult to extract them, for study purposes, from such closely interrelated administrative functions as coordination, control, decision making, communication and personnel administration.

The readings in this chapter demonstrate that effective leadership depends largely upon the extent to which the manager has mastered the principles and techniques of human relations. The leader's success or failure lies in his capacity to influence the behaviour of his subordinates to achieve the purposes of the organization.

The perspective of this chapter is from the top; that is, human relations are studied from the viewpoint of the manager rather than from that of the employee.

Literature on human relations is so vast that it is difficult to single out items for special attention. The following contemporary monographs are representative:

J. A. C. Brown, *The Social Psychology of Industry*, Penguin Books, Baltimore, Maryland, 1963.
Keith Davis, *Human Relations at Work*, McGraw-Hill, New York, 1962.
R. Dubin *et al*, *Leadership and Productivity*, Chandler, San Francisco, 1965.
S. W. Gellerman, *Motivation and Productivity*, American Management Association, New York, 1963.
F. Herzberg and Others, *The Motivation to Work*, Wiley, New York, 1959.
D. M. McGregor, *The Human Side of Enterprise*, McGraw-Hill, New York, 1960.

Articles in periodicals are so numerous that little purpose is served in singling out individual contributions. A look at the files of the following journals will prove particularly fruitful:

Administrative Science Quarterly,
Harvard Business Review,
Personnel Administration,
Personnel Psychology,
Public Administration Review.

34   Organization as a Problem in Human Relations*

J. D. Millett

Organization for public service is people working together for a common purpose. People working together create a reaction system, a behavior pattern of individual and group relationships. Organization is supposed to establish relationships among people in terms of work assignments, duties, and responsibilities. But organization does more than this. It provides opportunities and limitations, it encourages ambitions and frustrates the role some individuals believe they should achieve. In spite of political and technical considerations, organization quickly becomes also a problem in human relations.

Much of the literature about organization today tends to regard all organizational problems as problems in human relations.[1]

As one reads the great body of literature in monographs and articles which has now accumulated on this subject of personal and social behavior in formal organization, the more one is at a loss to extract from it some definite and positive theory of organization. For all the "scientific" orientation of the authors, they find themselves restricted to a single means of collecting their data and to a single point of view in analyzing their material.[2] Whether they utilize the depth interview or the questionnaire, and no matter how carefully constructed the sample, these investigators are still confronted with the subjective reactions of individuals to their social environment. These reactions may be important raw data, and certainly they are not to be considered as unimportant to administrators. But at best it is difficult to construct a positive theory of organization upon the basis of such data and their analysis.[3]

From the available literature and from various discussions, I am disposed to set forth six propositions which I believe represent the fundamental

* Reprinted with permission of author and publisher from J. D. Millett, *Organization for the Public Service*, Van Nostrand, Toronto, 1966, pp. 102-129.

[1] Cf. Rensis Lickert, *New Patterns of Management*, McGraw-Hill, New York, 1961; Robert Tannenbaum, Irving R. Weschler, and Fred Massarik, *Leadership and Organization: A Behavioral Science Approach*, McGraw-Hill, New York, 1961; Robert Presthus, *Behavioral Approaches to Public Administration*, University of Alabama Press, University, Alabama, 1965; Harold J. Leavitt, *Managerial Psychology*, The University of Chicago Press, Chicago, 1958.

[2] Cf. James C. Charlesworth (ed.), *The Limits of Behavioralism in Political Science*, The American Academy of Political and Social Science, Philadelphia, 1962; and *Strengthening the Behavioral Sciences*, a statement by the Behavioral Sciences Subpanel of the Life Sciences Panel, President's Science Advisory Committee, U.S. Government Printing Office, Washington, D.C., 1962.

[3] In addition to the books already cited, I would mention here: James G. March and Herbert A. Simon, *Organizations*, Wiley, New York, 1958; Maison Haire (ed.), *Modern Organization Theory*, Wiley, New York, 1959; and Thomas G. Spates, *Human Values Where People Work*, Harper and Bros., New York, 1960.

ideas which have been presented by various writers who accept the behavioral approach to organizational problems. If I do any injustice to these writers, it is entirely unintentional. But as I have noted, it is not easy to build a consistent set of ideas from their observations. We shall consider each of these in order.

1. *Regardless of the formal structure of organization in an administrative agency, there tends to develop an informal structure of personal relations among individuals in an agency. These informal relations become an important factor in the internal power structure.*

The process of selecting foremen, supervisors, and managers may not always bring to the formal positions of authority in an organization the natural born leaders of a group. Moreover, the number of positions of authority in an organization may be limited. Others with leadership ability may have to find their opportunity in informal rather than formal authority. In some instances the informal leader may be physically stronger, mentally superior, or more imaginative than the formal leader. In other instances the informal leader may more nearly represent the aspirations and anxieties of the group than the formal leader. Sometimes the formal leader is thought of as alien to the group, as obligated for his position and welfare to his superiors rather than to the group he is supposed to lead. Such a situation may undermine the capacity for accomplishment of the formal leader.

The importance of informal organization, however, does not lie exclusively in the potential conflict of natural and selected leaders. Informal relationships among persons in an organization may develop without necessarily involving a contest for influence or power. Much of the success of cooperative effort among various groups in an organization depends upon the personal and friendly relations which may spring up among various individuals. Within any large, formal organization there are specified channels of communication and coordination. At best it takes time to utilize these specified channels, and at their worst resorting to the prescribed procedures of information and instruction may result in a failure to get a needed task accomplished at the proper time.

Furthermore, much education of personnel is accomplished through informal communication. Professional individuals working in many different organizations may meet periodically in professional societies. Administrators and managers are often brought together in various associations. Sometimes, community relations build friendships among people in different groups or organizations. The result of all these various kinds of relationships may be to promote personal predispositions for certain people to work together in common administrative situations. Or individuals learn informally about improvements in work processes or about solutions to similar problems and are thus encouraged to undertake changes in their own group.

In my own experience these informal relationships have been of great importance in expediting and improving the work of an administrative organization. In the Army in World War II it was a great help to know a staff officer in another echelon and to be able to talk with him informally about a developing situation or about the meaning of some order. In the federal government it always helps to know someone in the budget bureau or on the White House staff. In state government, it is always worthwhile to build personal relationships with someone on the governor's staff, or on the staff of other executives. In the university world, various meetings of presidents, deans, and faculty members are most important in promoting an exchange of experience and ideas, to the mutual benefit of all concerned.

There is another aspect to informal organization. It can promote the rapid circulation of rumors, the misinterpretation of events, the "advance tip" on forthcoming action. There are persons in an organization who satisfy their desire for attention and recognition by dispensing "hot" information. There are others who interpret events in personal terms, as aimed at their own security. Such individuals must share their anxieties and seek to draw some comfort for their own misery by encouraging the anxieties of others. And there are always those who seek to build their own importance and to promote their own future career by passing along vital information to others outside the regular timetable or outside the regular channels of communication.

No administrator or manager can ever afford to ignore the realities of informal organization and its accompanying informal channels of communication. Sometimes it is possible to construct or reconstruct organization in terms of the informal relationships which have developed. Sometimes it is possible to try out ideas, to launch "trial balloons," through informal channels of organization just to observe the reactions which they arouse. Sometimes it is possible to exhort persons to new efforts through informal channels rather than through organizational commands.

Moreover, it is important for the administrator and manager to be prepared to meet the demands which informal relationships in an organization may create. Certainly false rumor can be very destructive of morale and work effort. The "hot-tip" can be lessened in its impact by prompt issuance of instructions and decisions. The intrigue of individuals can be neutralized by formal consultation.

The existence of informal organization must be admitted, however, and careful efforts made to counteract its tendencies if formal organization is to remain purposeful and effective. This is one lesson from the observation of human relations in administration.

2. *Authority in an organization is vested in groups and in leaders of groups in order to define the scope of action and of discretion entrusted to them. Such authority tends to be effective if it is legitimate and if its exercise is generally acceptable to those affected by it.*

Students of human behavior in organization are generally much interested in the phenomenon of authority. They point out that organization, among other attributes, is an allocation of authority. They then seek to observe the conditions, manifestations, and limitations of authority. If anything, these students seem to be more intrigued by the abuses and limitations of authority in an organization than they are in its uses and accomplishments.

Max Weber emphasized the factor of legitimacy in the exercise of authority, and this has received a considerable degree of discussion among American students of bureaucracy. Legitimacy implies only that normal or accustomed processes of career advancement shall lead a person to a position of authority. In any society, and within any unit of an organization of that society, there will be a generally accepted method of selection for those who occupy positions of authority. Whether the system of selection be by popular election, by board appointment, or by appointment of a superior with or without the assistance of a competitive examination, the arrangement is expected to observe traditional and expected modes of procedure. This very fact of custom may do much to establish the legitimacy of authority.

In addition, it must be noted that an element of rationality in the selection process is usually important. Rationality may have to do with educational background, with experience and professional achievement, with longevity or seniority. Organizations — that is, people in an organization — expect those placed in authority to have the qualifications appropriate to their particular enterprise. Persons in an organization tend often to resent the parvenue, the "Johnny-come-lately," the outsider, the inexperienced, the person with an inappropriate or different background. These elements of hostility can be overcome, and there are circumstances in any organization when the outsider and the newcomer may be highly desirable in order to patch over internal quarrels or to promote innovation in goals or programs. Nonetheless, an organization expects those who exercise authority to have the appropriate background of experience, age, and reputation for the position they occupy.

Acceptance of authority is more than a matter of legitimacy. It is even more a matter of ability and compatibility. Authority means leadership. The task of authority in an organization is not to hamper work output or to diminish cooperative effort. Rather, it is to advance the realization of the goals of the group. This entails leadership, with all of its concomitant characteristics of personal capacity. At the same time, authority means the embodiment of group aspirations and accomplishments. Authority expresses group goals and identifies itself with group welfare. In other words, authority becomes acceptable because it is compatible with group endeavor.

This word "authority" is another one in the lexicon of public affairs with an unfortunate connotation. To many individuals, authority means restrictions and obstacles in the way of action. Authority suggests someone alien to an "in-group" who seeks to impose his will upon a recalcitrant majority. For this very reason students of administration prefer to talk about leadership, about management, about facilitative and supportive endeavor which assists the group in realizing its goals.

Chester A. Barnard, president of the New Jersey Bell Telephone Company and later of the Rockefeller Foundation, wrote that the essence of the executive function was not to issue orders which would be disobeyed.[4] On the one hand, this was a counsel of communication, emphasizing the importance of careful preparation in discussion and planning before any important directive was issued. On the other hand, the observation was also a warning about the limitations of authority in an organization. The administrator is bound by the expectations of the group, and to depart substantially from those expectations is to invite disobedience, open or covert. Authority is not to be used lightly, capriciously, or selfishly. Even in an autocratic or despotic society there remains the weapon of assassination, or of suicide.

Leadership is undoubtedly a matter of ability: intellectual, physical, technical, and courageous. Leadership is tested by results, not by words. Action rather than reflection is the expected role of the leader. Authority becomes a means to leadership, not a substitute for it. The position of the administrator, manager, supervisor, or foreman exists to make group action effective in the accomplishment of stated goals. Authority is intended to assist the leader. His authority means little except for a general purpose.

Acceptance of authority by the group in turn rests in large measure upon this accomplishment. Assuming commitment to the purpose of an enterprise inculcated by various inducements, we may expect a group to react favorably to authority when it senses that desired goals are being realized. This is not to suggest, however, that objectives can be separated from methods. Leadership and authority become acceptable to a group when methods as well as goals represent prevailing attitudes and values.

Authority is inherent in administrative organization. The alternative is a group of co-equal workers who determine each for himself when to work, what to work on, and how to work. In highly unstructured circumstances, as in research projects or in education, such procedure may have its advantages. In many situations this kind of individual autonomy of enterprise is wasteful, expensive, and even purposeless. Authority then becomes essential to make certain that group effort does lead to intended goals.

3. *When persons work together purposefully, they should have a commitment to the goals of the enterprise, believe those goals to be important and worthwhile, and desire actively to see those goals achieved.*

In discussions of why people are willing to work together in formal organization, there is general agreement that most people are disposed by their basic drives to cooperate with one another. The family is a great socializing force in life. It is when family life breaks down that many individuals lose this disposition to work harmoniously with others. It is perhaps no accident that some of the great artists of any society are also the least socially inclined. On the other hand, the work of a technological society cannot be accomplished by individualists. Our species cannot be perpetuated except by a minimum social unit, the family. In addition, many other aspects of our lives — the satisfaction of our material wants,

---

4 Chester A. Barnard, *The Functions of the Executive*, Harvard University Press, Cambridge, Massachusetts, 1938.

the preservation of life and property, even the inspiration of our spiritual welfare — depend upon social units or institutions of various kinds: economic, governmental, religious.

Education is another great socializing force in our lives. We learn our culture and our traditions and are introduced to the world of ideas by the efforts of others: teachers, authors, and all those who communicate with us in different ways. This learning process tends to inculcate respect for others and to emphasize the contribution of our forbearers to our well-being. As our learning progresses, we come to understand our debt to those of outstanding ability who design, develop, and manage the intellectual and social achievements of our day.

When it comes time for us to engage in our own vocational and professional activity, we find our opportunities for satisfying endeavor most often in the company of others. We have acquired specialized abilities or we find only specialized tasks for our labor. With few exceptions, we thus become associated with others in varying degrees of close interrelationship in order to carry on our productive effort.

A disposition to cooperative activity is then one of the foremost characteristics of most people in our society. Perhaps our society has gone too far in its stress upon conformity and in its production of the organization man, as some critics contend; perhaps our society has need for special effort to encourage and cultivate the creative imagination of certain persons, as some enthusiasts proclaim. It still seems accurate to observe that there is a disposition toward cooperative activity in our society. We even "brainstorm" new ideas in cooperation one with another!

An administrative organization brings together persons with a basic disposition to work together. The organization must develop this particular disposition into a commitment to the purpose of the enterprise, including a determination to realize the avowed production goals of the group effort. In some enterprises, this commitment to purpose may be of a low order of intensity. In other endeavors, much conscious effort may be devoted to promotion of this commitment to purpose.

There are various methods of promoting this sense of identification of the individual with the purposes of the group. The three such methods which receive mention in most discussions are education and training, communication, and participation.

Any organization which is comprised largely of personnel who have a common professional or semi-professional status is necessarily one with a very real commitment to purpose. This is the case with a public health, public welfare, hospital, military, engineering, police and fire protection, forestry, public school, and public college or university agency. The principal personnel will usually have a common professional education, including indoctrination in the ethics of the profession. There may be an extensive in-service training program, intended to advance the professional capacities of the staff. A more or less definite structure of career ranks and job assignments will further encourage a common point of view. Some of the staff may be given an opportunity to further their educational background with advanced or graduate education. All of these factors tend to build a cohesive group with a sense of common identity and common purpose.

The word "communication" is much employed today in the lexicon of organization and management. In its broadest sense, communication means a shared understanding of a shared purpose. A wide variety of media of communication is available in any organization today. Most of these will be employed in most large-scale enterprises, since it is difficult to be certain that any one medium will be effective in reaching the intended audience. But communication is primarily a matter of content, and the sincerity and objective purpose of many instructions will often be suspect. This is especially likely to be the case where statement of purpose and actual performance appear to be considerably different.

Communication, we are continually reminded, is not a one-way street. Many administrators are likely to think of communication as the issuance of orders, directives, and instructions. Communication is also a matter of obtaining information, and analyzing its importance or significance correctly. We are often told that in a hierarchical organization communication from top to bottom, or from the center outward to the fringes of the enterprise, tends to be critical; while communication from below toward the center tends to be complimentary. This tendency may indeed be quite prevalent in many organizations, and it is one of the dangers which an alert management will seek to avoid.

Any consideration of the role of communication necessarily brings into focus also the matter of participation. If communication is to be a two-way street in an organization, then various persons and groups must be invited to participate in the decision-making process. One reason why suggestion systems have become popular in so many organizations today is the role of such a system in creating an attitude of individual participation in the enterprise. All groups or persons in an organization want to feel that their ideas are given some consideration. They want to know also that their experience in doing the work assigned to them is understood by their supervisors, and has been taken into account in the decisions which are made. Frequent contact between work groups and management is important in creating this sense of participation.

Just as many persons today are inclined to think that our technological society has become too complex and too large for the individual to have any influence in its direction, so many persons in their particular work organizations feel that the enterprise has become too impersonal, too bureaucratic, to have any interest in them individually. This kind of attitude is fatal to a sense of participation, and can be alleviated or eliminated only by the greatest effort. Of course, participation means just that. Individuals cannot be invited to participate in the consideration of problems of the enterprise and then have their suggestions ignored. Management may not always be able to adopt the proposals which various persons and groups suggest. And management must often choose a course of action among different proposals made by component groups in the enterprise. Nonetheless, it is possible to create an environment in which participation does become a meaningful process.

In any event, the objectives of an organization can be effectively realized through its human resources only if all or most persons in the enterprise loyally and fully accept the purposes desired to be accomplished. Whether such commitment be called esprit de corps or high morale or personal dedication, its existence in an organization is vital and its perpetuation must be continually cultivated.

4. *Organizational accomplishment depends upon recognition given to the achievements of individuals and groups within the enterprise.*

The rewards of service in an organization are many. Compensation is but one form of reward, and it is not always the most important. Trade unions in their efforts at collective bargaining in industry have tended to emphasize the adequacy of wage rates, although working conditions have received their share of attention as have pension and welfare plans in recent years. Yet most persons who have studied large-scale organization believe that wages are only a part of the rewards which individuals seek from their service.

First of all, most individuals want the satisfaction of worthwhile work. They expect the job they do to be important to others, to provide a product or a service beneficial to all users. There is limited, if any, satisfaction in made work or marginal activity in the scheme of human betterment. To be sure, there are the robbers, the cheats, the law-breakers for whom this general motivation is non-operative. Yet even in some of these cases there is a sense of providing people with a need, even when the service is illegal, as in gambling. But most persons in our society want to feel that they are involved in meeting an essential requirement of man for his life, his liberty, and his pursuit of happiness.

Secondly, most persons are concerned to have their individual contribution to human welfare properly recognized in terms of community prestige and status. It is not enough for any person to have his own inherent, personal sense of satisfaction in the work he does. This personal sense of satisfaction usually needs the reinforcement of external approbation. The individual wants the community in which he lives to demonstrate its appreciation of the work he does. This is one reason why we have so many "days" and "weeks" in the year designated as the occasion to recognize the contribution which various groups make to our existence and betterment.

Thirdly, individuals and groups in an enterprise want to be appreciated within the organization where they work. This appreciation may be demonstrated in many ways, from bonus payments for extra performance and buttons for length of service to titles, promotions, and new offices. It is a joking matter to some persons in an organization to observe the little "gimmicks" of status, whether these be the organization dinner, the provision of a rug on the office floor, or the redecoration of an office. Yet all of these perhaps somewhat contrived tokens of appreciation are helpful in providing a basic satisfaction to individuals for the work they may have rendered devotedly over a considerable period of time.

In the fourth place, most persons want and expect a degree of security in their work. This is one of the most troublesome of present-day problems in most organizations. Technological change is eliminating some jobs and modifying the nature of others. Many individuals are not needed to perform the same work they have undertaken in the past, and sometimes they lack the ability or inclination themselves to adapt to new work requirements. Yet when an organization can no longer utilize his services, the individual will tend to believe that the importance of his past contribution was not appreciated and that he is threatened with dismissal without any personal consideration. Moreover, when persons see this apparent lack of consideration evident toward others, they will begin to develop their own sense of insecurity in the job they perform. When a job is insecure, then satisfaction in its performance and recognition of service rendered become meaningless.

A number of years ago a well-known research study was undertaken at the Hawthorne plant of Western Electric Company in order to find out something about the impact of personal relations upon group performance.[5] The result of this research seemed to demonstrate that group productivity increased with group stability in composition, with group identification, with group satisfaction in the job performed, and with evident appreciation of the group. Later, the results of this research were questioned, and the term "Hawthorne effect" began to enter the vocabulary of students of human relations. It was pointed out that by making a particular group of production workers the object of study, especially by a university research project, the group suddenly gained a new importance, a new status for themselves among fellow workers. The very impact of being the subject of special study gave an impetus to the group to improve its output. It is ironic that special attention coming from research in human relations may in itself stimulate workers to a new sense of worth and of external appreciation. The "Hawthorne effect" simply points out how vital recognition is to individual and group effort.

5. *Many individuals in an organization become accustomed to the structural arrangements and the standardized procedure for operation and find satisfaction in continuation of accepted work methods.*

Desire for change is not an ordinary characteristic of persons and groups who comprise an administrative organization. Rather, many individuals find security for themselves in routine which has been long established. Such persons become "set in their ways," or inflexible, in the face of changing circumstances. These individuals are reluctant to admit the need

---

5 F. J. Roethlisberger and W. J. Dickson, *Management and the Worker*, Harvard University Press, Cambridge, Massachusetts, 1939. See also Elton Mayo, *The Social Problems of an Industrial Civilization*, Harvard University Graduate School of Business Administration, Boston, 1945.

for different work methods to meet different circumstances. They are usually convinced that old ways are the best ways.

This kind of fearful or hostile attitude toward change is frequently described as inherent in bureaucracy. Certainly, such an attitude is likely to rise in any agency which continues to perform the same kind of work for a long time. It is difficult for such an organization to take on new tasks, to meet new challenges, or to develop new techniques of operation.

It is easy to identify this fear of change in social units, and particularly in administrative organizations. It is much less simple to prescribe any method for dealing successfully with such attitudes. We shall explore some of these methods in the next section.

It is important here to observe that this attitude in defense of accustomed procedure is by no means unusual in an organizational environment. Rather, we must recognize that such an attitude is understandable enough. Many persons, as we have suggested, find their individual job security in accustomed arrangements and procedures for carrying on their expected work. Any proposed change in these arrangements or procedures creates basic anxieties for the individual. He becomes uncertain whether he can do the new work which he may be called upon to perform. He is fearful he will not be so important as before, will not have the same status or the same influence in the organization.

These anxieties and insecurities of individuals in an organization are likely to be compounded with age. Although it is not always or necessarily the case, it seems fair to observe that older people tend especially to be suspicious and even fearful of change. This is particularly the case with persons who have had some success or recognition in an organization. When they find younger people coming along in the organization with new ideas and methods, they tend to distrust such "new-fangled" proposals and even to be highly critical of them.

It is interesting to find that many business organizations are tending to lower the retirement age for their top executives simply because they fear that older men will be too inflexible to consider new product lines, new production or other techniques, or necessary adjustments to a changing business setting. As life expectancy advances and older people become more numerous in our society, we may be developing a larger segment of our society which fears social change of any kind.

In the public service, where the retirement age may be set at 70 in many instances, there is a particular likelihood that administrative organizations will become difficult to change in their work habits and procedures. This danger is not imaginary. Many illustrations will occur to almost everyone who has had any extensive experience in or with the public service.

It is easy to sympathize with the personal concerns of individuals which lead to this inflexibility in the routine of public service. And it is readily evident that attitudes fearful of change must be handled by administrators and others with care. A major concern with the need for change can be frustrated by the deep-seated anxieties and hostilities of many persons in an organization.

6. *The acceptance of change in an organizational environment depends upon careful preparation, upon a crisis which demands immediate action, or upon recognition of self-interest.*

Because so many administrators have learned from experience about the difficulties which beset attempts to change organizational structure and work methods, a good deal of attention has been given to the strategy of change. From this concern has emerged some agreement about the circumstances and conditions under which change can be realized.

It is possible, of course, for an administrator simply to decide that some fundamental changes are needed in an enterprise, to surround himself with a group of associates of like mind, and to proceed to demand that certain changes in organization and procedures be immediately introduced. Perhaps it is possible to adopt such a procedure in private enterprise. It is quite another matter to attempt such a process of change in the public service.

The public service is different. The great majority of personnel will be career or merit-selected individuals. They cannot usually be dismissed from their tasks without observance of a careful procedure designed to safeguard the interests of the individual employee. Furthermore, the component groups in a public agency are likely to have their friends in the various political or legislative or executive echelons of government. Protests and even outright misrepresentation of the facts of a situation can be launched through political channels and through media of mass communication. Such opposition can often defeat the best laid plans for organizational change.

I have had firsthand experience with efforts at organizational change which encountered just this kind of difficulty. And I may add that the opposition was successful and the proposed changes in organizational structure were not accomplished. The political climate became hostile to change, and nothing could be done under these circumstances. There is no need here to recite the details of this experience, although it taught a lesson which will not be forgotten. And I have witnessed other experiences of a similar nature. In the public service, there is little point in trying almost single-handedly to carry out major organizational changes in a short period of time. One will not usually achieve any lasting results in this way.

A first element of strategy in organizational change in the public service is careful and even lengthy preparation. Such preparation begins with extensive discussion and consideration of problem areas. Associates and colleagues in an organization are invited to make suggestions about how to meet some particular need. If legislation is needed, then discussion must include key legislative leaders who may be involved in the necessary action upon any proposals. If the change is likely to arouse animosity from important interest groups, then it is useful to involve some of the leaders of such groups in consideration of the situation.

It is often helpful, I have found, to bring in outside consultants in this process of considering organizational change. One reason perhaps why management consulting firms have become such an important factor today is because they can and do contribute substantially to organizational and procedural change. Many key individuals in an organization distrust proposals for change from a colleague. They see such proposals in personal terms, as a method of aggrandizement by the person recommending a change, a method of rising to new status and power within the organization. The outside consultant is free from this limitation. He is apparently not a competitor in the power struggle which is characteristic of any and all organizations. Accordingly, the consultant is "objective," is inclined to consider various proposals on their merits and not in terms of personalities. There is more to the whole matter of utilizing the outside management consultant than this brief statement might suggest. But use of the outside consultant is an important strategic move in the preparation for organizational change.

It is often necessary to postpone action on organizational change until key individuals internally can be taken care of, through retirement, transfer to some other agency, or assignment to some other position. Delay may be part of the wisdom of careful preparation for change.

Usually over a period of time, if organizational difficulties are apparent and if failures of job accomplishment become evident, some change will be possible. And decline in output or in ability to keep up with the job load is objective evidence of the need for change. Neither supervisors or managers nor an organization as a whole can stand against poor performance. Change is expected under such circumstances. Rising costs of an enterprise, especially if costs mount more rapidly than output of goods or services, may also point to internal problems. But it is not always possible to find such concrete evidence of failure. Then external criticism may provide the reason for some adjustment in organizational structure. Certainly criticism cannot be ignored, especially if it has considerable political backing.

There is a second factor in the strategy of organizational change. This is crisis. When a critical state of affairs occurs in national security, in the economy, in financing, in competition, in the load of an enterprise, then organizational change is often imperative. A far-reaching reorganization of the Department of War, postponed from World War I, suddenly became possible and feasible after Pearl Harbor and was duly made effective on March 9, 1942. The depression of 1929 brought about various changes in governmental administrative activities at the federal, state, and local level. I have seen a decline in the tax revenues of local and state governments create an atmosphere conducive to extensive organizational changes. A sudden increase in work load, such as the great influx of veteran students returning to college and university campuses after 1945, may provide a crisis in which great changes become imperative.

In a sense, technology gives rise to crisis. The Russian launching of

Sputnik in 1957 suddenly provided the impetus which literally made it possible for our own space research and development in the United States to get "off the ground." This was an illustration of both technology and international competition at work. Technology may operate in various ways to bring about change. We have not begun yet to comprehend or imagine the organizational changes which may be wrought in many agencies of government through the computer.

There is perhaps another factor which works for organizational change, the factor of self-interest. If a substantial number of persons in an organization perceive that change may be individually advantageous to them, then the demand for change, or at least acquiescence in change, will not be too difficult to encourage. One reason why organizations tend to favor expansion of their work load is because of the newer supervisory and management positions which may be created. Thus, promotions and higher levels of compensation become available in the organization. Probably no development is so painful in any organization as contraction.

Change in an organization is not automatic. It must be planned. Moreover, such planning must give careful attention to the strategy of organizational change. It is not enough for a group of organizational analysts and a few top administrators in an agency to decide that organizational change is desirable. The political and the human relations aspects must also be taken into account. The strategy of organizational change is as important as the substance.

Conclusion

As I have suggested earlier, the technical structure of an organization is a system of internal power. The factor or phenomenon of power is present in the structure of working units, supervisory hierarchy, and top-management direction and planning. A structure of power, or of authority, will also give rise to a conflict or struggle for power on the part of individuals and of groups. The struggle for power in an organization is also the story of human behavior within the organization.[6]

Human behavior in an organizational context seems to be primarily a reaction pattern. This behavior pattern, in its concern for informal relationships, acceptance of authority, commitment to goals, status, reward, and security, constitutes human response to a structure of work specialization

---

[6] The factor or characteristic of a power struggle within bureaucracy has been given special emphasis in the recent volume of a French behavioral scientist. See Michel Crozier, *The Bureaucratic Phenomenon*, The University of Chicago Press, Chicago, 1964. Crozier identifies such characteristics of the French bureaucratic "pattern" as isolation of the hierarchy, individual equality within each status group, and fear of face-to-face relationships among the various individuals and groups of the organization. These observations appear to reflect peculiarly a French cultural tradition and pattern, as the author himself asserts. Accordingly, except as his observations underline cultural differences and suggest cultural contrasts among bureaucracies, Crozier does not present a behavioral theory applicable to the American setting.

and work units, supervisory hierarchy, and top-management. The behavior pattern is understandable only in the context of the organizational structure itself, and of the broad cultural and institutional background of this structure.

Some individuals in a society are probably more inclined than others to seek power to influence or direct the behavior of their fellows. Not all persons in an organizational structure are necessarily seeking power or authority, but almost all persons in an organization will react in one way or another to their work environment. The behavioral scientists seek to discover the universals in this reaction pattern.

There is a unique element, however, to this reaction pattern in the public service which again serves to differentiate organization for public service from other organizational circumstances in our society. In our country our political system encourages influential members of the hierarchy and even groups of employees (through unions or civil service associations) to seek redress of grievances, imagined or otherwise, through political channels. Thus, concern on the part of individuals or groups who believe their status and security to be threatened, their recognition and rewards to be inadequate, or the authority to which they are subject to be hostile or burdensome, may find expression in political criticism. Individuals and groups may seek out sympathetic legislators to voice their complaints or find an informal channel in the chief executive's entourage as a means for exerting some pressure upon an offending administrator. Behind these complaints and pressures are the threat of political retaliation for failure to adjust grievances: retaliation in the form of reappointments not made or confirmed, promotions denied, appropriations reduced, restrictive legislation enacted.

The administrator in the public service must always bear in mind that the reaction pattern of the personnel of the organization not only may affect production and work effectiveness but also may result in political embarrassment for himself and the whole enterprise.

35   Leadership*

Felix A. Nigro

Frequently the complaint is heard that an organization "lacks leadership." What is meant is that action of some sort should have been taken, but no one assumed the initiative in trying to get others to see the need for action,

* Reprinted with permission of author and publisher from F. A. Nigro, *Modern Public Administration*, Harper & Row, New York, 1965, pp. 252-280.

and thus nothing was accomplished. In other cases, the criticism is that the organization does not have "good leadership." Decisions are made and action taken, but those responsible for persuading others to accept their ideas led them in the wrong direction. These statements reveal both the *nature* and the importance of leadership. The essence of leadership is influencing the actions of others. Where the attempt to exercise such influence is not even made, there is a default of leadership. Where the attempt is made and others are persuaded to agree to certain action but the anticipated results do not materialize, the consequences may be serious for the organization.

Approaches to Leadership

The Trait Approach

Not too long ago even learned, as distinguished from popular, discussions of leadership had a certain mystic quality. The leader was conceived of as someone blessed with certain qualities which made it relatively easy for him to bend others to his will. Nobody was really sure of the exact complement of leader personality traits, but it was generally assumed that many of these characteristics were inherited. Today most social scientists are convinced that the trait approach to leadership is fallacious, because those conducting research on the qualities of leaders have been unable to agree on what those qualities are. In 1940, one scholar compiled a long list of traits which were identified in one or more studies as distinguishing characteristics of leaders as opposed to nonleaders. Only about five percent of these traits, however, were common to four or more of the studies. Such a low percentage of agreement could hardly substantiate the claim that leaders basically have the same personality characteristics. Examination of the research conducted since 1940 has shown the same lack of consistency in the findings on leadership qualities.[1] Cartwright and Zander summarize the present state of knowledge as follows:

> On the whole, investigators in this field are coming to the conclusion that, while certain minimal abilities are required of all leaders, these are also widely distributed among non-leaders as well. Furthermore, the traits of the leader which are necessary and effective in one group or situation may be quite different from those of another leader in a different setting. This conclusion, if adequately substantiated, would imply that the selection of leaders must consider a man's suitability for the type of functions he is to perform in a given situation and it would raise questions about the desirability of formal arrangements which maintain the responsibilities of leadership in the same person regardless of the changing task of the group and the changing requirements upon leaders.[2]

[1] Dorwin Cartwright and Alvin Zander (eds.), *Group Dynamics, Research and Theory*, 2nd ed., Harper & Row, New York, 1960, p. 490.
[2] *Ibid.*, p. 491. See also Robert G. Wall and Hugh Hawkins, "Requisites of Effective Leadership", *Personnel*, Vol. 39, No. 3, May-June 1962, pp. 21-28.

The Situation Approach

Accordingly, most writers now support this situational approach, although actually it is not new. Long before the term "situational approach" came into usage, Mary Parker Follett was calling attention to the emergence in American life of "leadership by function." In the late 1920s, this wise lady, whose writings are classics in management literature, gave several lectures on leadership.[3] In these lectures, she noted that in scientifically managed organizations three types of leadership could be distinguished: the leadership of position, of personality, and of function. There was nothing new about the first two, because they represented the accepted views on leadership. The man holding a position which gave him formal authority over others obviously could make himself a leader. If he had a forceful personality, he could do this much more easily. This kind of individual combined the leadership of position with that of personality.

Something was absent, however, in such a conception of leadership. It failed to take into account the possibility that some persons, in fact quite a few in modern specialized organizations, exercised leadership because of their expert knowledge. The organization depended on them to give sound technical advice to their superiors. In many situations these experts actually did the "leading," because others were influenced by their judgments. Miss Follett stressed that "we have people giving what are practically orders to those of higher rank. The balance of stores clerk, as he is called in some places, will tell the man in charge of purchasing when to act. The dispatch clerk can give 'orders' even to the superintendent. The leadership of function is inherent in the job and as such is respected by the president of the plant." She noted that "the man possessing the knowledge demanded by a certain situation tends in the best managed businesses, and other things being equal, to become the leader at that moment."[4]

A distinction must be made between *formal* and *effective* authority. Formal authority is the basis for what Miss Follett called leadership of position. Sometimes someone in a position of formal authority is unable to persuade others to accept his ideas. He lacks effective authority. The explanation for this may very well be that he does not possess "the knowledge demanded by the situation." In any event not all effective authority is concentrated in the hands of a few persons at the top of the organization. Subordinates frequently exercise effective authority because they "know best" about a particular operation.

It should be made clear that Miss Follett did not consider that the leadership of function and the leadership of personality could not be combined in the same person. Nor did she deny that personality played a very large part in leadership. She did believe, however, that leadership of func-

---

[3] See Mary Parker Follett, "Some Discrepancies in Leadership Theory and Practice", in Henry C. Metcalfe and L. Urwick (eds.), *Dynamic Administration*, Harper & Row, New York, 1940, pp. 270-294. See also in this same collection of her papers the essay, "Leader and Expert", pp. 247-269.

[4] *Ibid.*, p. 277.

tion was becoming more important than leadership of personality. She felt that the success of an organization depended a good deal on its being "sufficiently flexible to allow the leadership of function to operate fully — to allow the men with the knowledge and the technique to control the situation."[5] Miss Follett makes an interesting point about Joan of Arc. This great woman possessed leadership of personality because of the "ardour of her conviction and power to make others share that conviction." Yet it is also related that "no trained artillery captain could excel Joan of Arc in the placement of guns."[6]

What are some of the other factors which affect the requirements for leadership, apart from expertise in a particular subject matter field? A change in the nature of the situation which confronts the group may call for a different kind of leader. The pilot in a bomber crew may be an excellent leader while the plane is in flight, but prove a very poor one if it crashes "and the crew is faced with the task of surviving or finding its way to safety."[7] The qualities needed to keep the crew working together efficiently in the air are not necessarily the same as those required when the men are afoot in a desperate situation for which advance planning was not possible. Similarly, the kind of activity influences the leadership requirements. The competent head of a public agency might be unsuited for a leadership role in a church group, yet a minor employee in the same public agency might be admirably equipped to lead the church group. Within the church, one person might be excellent for work with preschool children, another for youth activities, and so on. Thus, the characteristics of the followers obviously constitute an important variable in the situation. It takes one kind of person to lead a labor gang, another to direct professional activities. Within the professional ranks, supervisors lacking certain formal qualifications deemed essential by the subordinates, will prove ineffectual; a dean without the Ph.D. will not command the respect of many of the university professors. If the leadership assignment requires conciliation of various groups, the individual's personal background can eliminate him from consideration, as in an international agency, where the person's nationality might make him unacceptable to one or more parties to a dispute. These are only a few of the ways in which the situation can vary, thus altering the requirements for leadership. Readers of this book will probably be able to supply other examples.

Human Motivation and Leadership

Before discussing in specific terms the kinds of leadership techniques which should be used in given circumstances, it is advisable to make a brief exposition of some of the theories as to human motivation. Depending on their concepts of worker motivation, one person may select one leadership

---

5 *Ibid.*, p. 278.
6 *Ibid.*, p. 172.
7 Cartwright and Zander, *op. cit.*, p. 495.

pattern, another may choose a very different one. Anyone who seeks to lead others must be concerned with such questions as: What are the desires of people who work in organizations? what do they want from the management and its representatives? how do they want their superiors to treat them? what causes them to respect or not to respect the management? what are the needs of human personality anyway? As we shall see, we have various theories but no agreement on the answers to these questions.

Different Theories of Motivation

Without any pretense of being exhaustive in the treatment of this profound subject, we will present here the opinions of three outstanding young scholars: Chris Argyris, Robert Dubin, and Robert Presthus. Illustrating the common interest in this subject of researchers in many different disciplines, Argyris is on the staff of the Yale University Labor and Management Center, Dubin is a sociologist, and Presthus a political scientist.

The Views of Chris Argyris

In one of his earlier writings, *Personality Fundamentals for Administrators*, Argyris makes a thorough review of the findings of the psychologists on human personality. Summarizing these findings, he states:

> At this time we can say, therefore, that man in his need-fulfilling behavior is to some extent:
> like all other men
> like some other men
> like no other men.[8]

Argyris explains that man is like *all* other men "because some of his personality is derived from common biological roots," because "he experiences both gratifications and deprivations," and because he must adjust to the "traditionally defined expectations of the culture." Man is like *some* other men, because "he shares common experiences with his own work group, social class, sporting club, or other cultural organizations." The social pressures exercised by the groups with which he associates function to make him like the other members of these same groups. Man is *unlike any other* man, because he has his "own personal, private way of seeing and experiencing the world," and because "he behaves, feels, thinks in certain patterns which are unique to himself."

Based on his studies of the development of the human personality, Argyris believes that "people, in our culture, develop from a state of high dependence on others as an infant, to a state of independence, and finally, to a state of interdependence in their society as an adult," and that the individual enters the world of work just when he feels a strong desire to

---

8 Chris Argyris, *Personality Fundamentals for Administrators*, Labor and Management Center, Yale University, New Haven, Connecticut, 1953, pp. 10-12.

be self-reliant and to obtain the free expression of his personality. He wants to have something to say about the work situation, not simply to be the passive agent of others. He wants to be able to express his "needs, sentiments, and personal goals."[9]

The tragedy is that most modern organizations require the worker to be passive and dependent upon the management's wishes. In Argyris' opinion, it is the immature, not the mature, person who can find happiness in the modern organizations, because they are built upon the basis of scientific-management concepts which require the adjustment of the worker to the job, not the other way around. The worker is regarded pretty much as a tool of production, to be manipulated as the management sees best. The scientific-management point of view takes into account "primarily the physical and biological properties of man," and in many respects is even "diametrically opposed to the development of a healthy personality in our culture."[10] Argyris believes that most workers today are permitted "little control over their work-a-day world. [The] developmental processes and end result of the individual and organization are, at crucial points, fundamentally different and even antagonistic."[11] The individual seeks "self-actualization," that is, to be able to satisfy the needs of his personality, whereas the management is obsessed with trying to make the worker behave rationally. It even assumes that "individual differences in the human personality may be ignored by transferring more skill and thought to machines."[12] The task specialization of scientific management permits the individual to use only a fraction of his abilities. New work procedures based on even greater specialization, which management hails as a great improvement, make the workers feel even more frustrated. They find their role in the organization narrowed even more.

Argyris' analysis is disturbing, because he places the responsibility for this situation on the very nature of modern organization. It is not that the managers are responsible because of the mistakes they make in dealing with the employees, although such mistakes do make matters worse. It is that the typical organization is so constructed as to require that the employees be submissive and dependent, rather than active and interested participants. What, then, if anything, can be done to correct this situation?

Argyris does believe that something can be done. The organization might be altered in certain ways so that the personality of the worker can obtain "greater self-actualization on the job." Agreed, no attempt should be made to change the organization so that it meets the personal requirements of each and every worker. Formal organization as such is not "bad." Twisting it to meet the whims of every worker would produce chaos or at least a situation in which self-actualization could not take place in an orderly way.

---

9 *Ibid.*, pp. 46-47.
10 *Ibid.*, p. 46.
11 *Ibid.*, p. 48.
12 Chris Argyris, "Personal vs. Organizational Goals", in Robert Dubin (ed.), *Human Relations in Administration*, Prentice-Hall, Englewood Cliffs, New Jersey, 1961, p. 72.

The worker can be given more to say without weakening the formal organization; in fact, this will strengthen it. The leader should not assume that, simply because the formal organization shows him at the top, he can make all the decisions for the workers without consulting them first. He should allow them to be real participants in the organization and give them some measure of control over their work environment.[13]

In general, Argyris believes that modern organizations should be altered so as to permit the individual to express his personality and play an active, rather than a passive, role in the work situation. Sometimes this need is referred to as "job enlargement," that is, building up the job so as to make it more satisfying to the worker. Argyris does not present a blueprint to follow in any program of job enlargement; this will depend on the organization and the particular situation. He is mostly concerned with calling attention to the conflict between formal organization and the individual's need for self-actualization. He makes clear that fundamental modifications, not mere tinkering, are needed if the formal organization is to be adapted to meet human needs and replace worker apathy with real involvement.

The Views of Robert Dubin

Dubin does not deny the individual's need for self-actualization; he questions, rather, whether people in general look to their jobs to provide it. He believes that all too often the assumption is erroneously made that the individual seeks a maximum of satisfaction from *all* the organizations in which he participates. This mistaken assumption leads to the view that man is the captive of his employing organization, because it denies him these satisfactions. The trouble with this theory is that it ascribes desires to the workers that many of them do not have. They are not that much interested in what the work situation can do for their personality fulfillment needs. Indeed, Dubin believes that probably for the majority of workers, including some management personnel, the job is not a central life interest. He thinks that it is in the voluntary kind of activity that most individuals look for their greatest satisfactions. They are much more interested in their after-hours' activities as members of clubs and other social groups. Far from feeling tyrannized by the work situation, they tolerate it and even perform efficiently despite their general apathy. So long as the management makes clear what is expected of them and provides the requisite financial incentive, they can be counted on to do satisfactory work. This, to Dubin, is the "magic of social organization — the ability to sustain required behaviors even when the institution is not central to the actors' interests."[14] Dubin's view, then, is that most workers simply are not in the unhappy situation portrayed by Argyris and others. They never really become so involved in their jobs as to experience the frustrations they are supposed to have.

---

[13] Argyris, *Personality Fundamentals for Administrators, op. cit.,* pp. 46-49.
[14] Robert Dubin, "Persons and Organization", in *Human Relations in Administration,* Prentice-Hall, Englewood Cliffs, New Jersey, 1961, p. 80.

It must be made clear, however, that Dubin does not deny that some people do make work a central life interest. Any activity, whether it be required — such as working for one's livelihood — or voluntary — such as participation in a church group — can become an individual's most absorbing interest. Dubin's point is, rather, that the most absorbing interest does not have to be the work situation, and that probably for most people it is not. Accordingly, looking at our society as a whole, he finds, "nothing about the organization of productive work, or the supervision of people while doing it, that is so antithetical to human personality needs as to result only in frustration and disappointment."[15]

If Dubin is correct, "job enlargement" in many cases may not be necessary. Why try to make the job more interesting to someone who basically seeks his satisfactions elsewhere? Since there are limits anyway to making more interesting the narrow kind of assignment that has evolved through specialization, such efforts can easily boomerang. The leader should understand worker apathy for what it is and not expect total involvement in their job by the majority of the workers. After all, he has the "magic of social organization" on his side. On the other hand, Dubin's analysis does not mean that the management need not concern itself with making *any* of the jobs challenging, apart from the financial inducements. While the great bulk of the production line and clerical personnel may not be concerned on this score, those in professional and executive jobs often are. The professional typically is absorbed in his specialty and reacts as a distinctive individual with definite needs which he feels the organization should satisfy. The executive, whether the junior just starting or the senior man seeking to cement his position, is typically concerned with the image of himself as a "success." For him to feel that he is such a "success" or on the road to becoming one, he looks to the organization to satisfy his psychological needs.

The Views of Robert Presthus

As to Presthus, he bases his interpretations on the interpersonal theory of psychiatry of Harry Stack Sullivan, according to which the human personality develops mainly as the result of social interaction. The individual's personality forms in definite ways as he reacts to the pressures of those with whom he comes in contact. From childhood on, he seeks to release tension by deferring to certain "authority figures," such as parents, teachers, and, in later years, the supervisor in a work situation. The cause of the tension is anxiety: he is anxious to obtain the approval of these authority figures. Presthus quotes Sullivan as saying: "I believe it fairly safe to say that anybody and everybody devotes much of his lifetime, and a great deal of his energy . . . to avoiding more anxiety than he already has, and, if possible, to getting rid of some of this anxiety."[16]

---

[15] *Ibid.*, p. 79.

[16] Robert Presthus, *The Organizational Society*, Knopf, New York, 1962, p. 104.

Argyris posits an individual who wants to be independent, rather than dependent on others. The culmination of personality development is that the mature person does not relish having to defer to authority figures. He wants to be able to behave like an adult, not an infant. Presthus passes no judgments on what is "adult" or "childlike" behavior, but simply accepts Sullivan's theory and is thus led to believe that many adults accept a status of dependency on their superiors as a means of relieving their anxieties. Presthus does not challenge the view that, to be effective, the superior's authority must be accepted by the subordinate; what he does question is the implication that the subordinate has much choice in the matter. As he sees it, the subordinate must relieve his anxiety tensions by bowing to the wishes of his superior officer, just as all through his life he has sought inward peace by yielding to other authority figures.

Some Other Views of Motivation

Others besides Presthus have stressed how some workers seek a status of dependency on their superiors as a means of relieving their tensions. Robert N. McMurry believes that the banking industry prefers the passive type individual who can be expected to conform in every way with his superiors' concepts of how he should behave. The preferred kind of addition to the staff is often someone who as a child was never completely weaned emotionally from overprotective parents. Sometimes he is someone who grew up in a "loveless and threatening environment [and] never dared to become self-reliant."[17] When he enters the world of work and gets a job where he is expected to accept responsibility, he is terrified:

> On reaching late adolescence or adulthood, he suddenly finds himself isolated from those who formerly provided love and reassurance. The prospect of facing a strange, formidable, and threatening world alone overwhelms him with anxiety.
>
> Some young people react to shock by becoming mentally ill; they become schizophrenic or make use of some other flight mechanism, for example, narcotic addiction. Most, however, respond by seeking to regain the lost security of childhood. They look for parental surrogates among persons who have power, strength, and authority and attempt to establish the same type of relationship — attachment, dependence, and submission — which they enjoyed with their parents. In most cases they earned the support and approbation of the latter by being "good" boys and girls, industrious, conscientious, and docile. As employees they repeat their childhood behavior pattern; they become the "good soldiers," the loyal, conscientious workers.[18]

Such persons, McMurry believes, react very well to the authoritarian kind of supervision practiced in some banks. They are relieved to be in a position

---

[17] Robert N. McMurry, "Recruitment, Dependency, and Morale in the Banking Industry", *Administrative Science Quarterly*, Vol. 3, No. 1, June 1958, pp. 92-93.
[18] *Ibid.*

where they need take no risks and can depend on others to worry about what should be done. In fact, in McMurry's opinion, they make excellent employees in such a setting, because they "personify bourgeois, copybook virtues."

McMurry describes a conformist type of individual especially desired by some banks to suit their conception of the "right type" of employee. In other situations, however, there is no attempt to employ the submissive type of person only. The employing organization wants individuals with initiative, but the employee, for one reason or another, lapses into a passive state.

Harry Levinson of the Industrial Health Division of the Menninger Foundation calls attention to the "male menopause." He is referring here to the period of middle age which for many men is one of "acute psychological loss" and thus really a "change of life." At 45, a man realizes that very likely he has fewer years ahead of him than behind him. Usually he must realistically anticipate that in all probability he will remain in much the same economic and social position for the rest of his life as he occupies in middle age. Levinson writes:

> Given the long period of dependency on parents in our culture, everyone struggles with the wish to become independent versus the pleasure of remaining dependent. This is particularly the struggle of the adolescent. When one becomes an adult he asserts his independence, but few of us can altogether give up our wishes to be dependent. When one feels less an adult, his dependent wishes come more to the surface. But, since he is in fact physically an adult, it is difficult for him to face the existence of such wishes.[19]

Some executives at this stage in their life build a "psychological cocoon" about themselves. They lose their old fight and fall into a rut. They fear younger men as threats to themselves and may even refuse to train them. Instead of continuing as assets to the organization, they become a drag on it. Levinson explains that these are not aberrations of weak individuals but common experiences of men who have reached middle age. Understanding this, the management can deal sympathetically with executives who suddenly seem to have lost their vitality and, by providing them with new challenges, it can help them regain their confidence.

Implications for Leadership

The reader, however, may likely raise the query, "Where has this analysis of theories of human motivation taken us? Is it not inconclusive, in view of the differences of opinion between such writers as Argyris, Dubin, and Presthus?" First, let it be made clear that the basic purpose was to indicate the complexity of the problem of human motivation. A subject which has

---

[19] Harry Levinson, "The Executive's Anxious Age", Management Forum, *Public Administration News*, Vol. 12, No. 3, American Society for Public Administration, Chicago, August 1962.

so many ramifications cannot honestly be painted as relatively simple. It would be marvellous to be able to say, categorically, what all or most members of any organization can be expected to want in terms of leadership behavior by their superiors. It would simplify matters enormously if Argyris, Dubin, Presthus, and all the others espoused identical theories. The fact, however, is that they do not. From one standpoint, it is well that they do emphasize different needs of the human personality. People are different; no one person is exactly like another. All kinds of people will be found in any one organization: Some may feel the strong yearnings for independence described by Argyris and experience the frustrations he believes inevitable in modern organizations; others may be dominated by strong feelings of dependency, as depicted by Presthus and McMurry. Some may lapse into temporary feelings of dependency, as during the male menopause, while some may not care particularly about their experiences during the workday, as emphasized by Dubin; they may experience their joys and miseries after hours.

Actually, Argyris, Dubin, and Presthus do not claim that their theories apply to all individuals. Argyris admits that some workers have no desire to feel independent. Such workers, he states, must be classified as "not mature." He does not attempt to tell us what proportion of the working population is "mature" or "immature" in these terms[20] for the simple reason that he cannot. No statistical measures are available of the psychological make-up of millions of workers. Furthermore, as indicated, no one can predict exactly how many "mature" and "immature" workers will be found in any one organization. Similarly, Dubin does not say that all individuals look for their satisfactions off the job; and at no point does Presthus say that all employees feel the same strong urge to satisfy their anxiety tensions by deferring to the authority of others. The point, rather, is that each has a general theory of human motivation, which amounts to no more than an expectation as to what may probably be found in dealing with large numbers of workers. None denies that the supervisor must adapt his leadership pattern in accordance with the kinds of subordinates he has under him. Treatment that satisfies one employee may offend another. General theories are helpful, but they can never relieve the supervisor of the need to understand the variations in human personalities.

Leadership Style

Usually three types of leadership styles or patterns are identified: authoritarian, democratic, and laissez-faire. Because democracy is so important a value to Americans, it will disturb some people that democracy may not be feasible with some work groups and in some work situations. Therefore, it is advisable to make clear at once in any discussion of leadership style that, as Golembiewski states, "the research literature does not consistently

---

[20] Argyris, *Personality Fundamentals for Administrators, op. cit.*, pp. 47-48.

support any one leadership style."[21] On the other hand, while Pfiffner and Sherwood also recognize this to be so, their analysis is that "most of the research has seemed to support the desirability of moving toward the democratic type."[22] At this point, it seems wise to refer to some of these research studies.

Research Findings on Leadership

One of the most famous of these experiments was conducted with a group of ten-year-old boys at the University of Iowa in the late 1930s.[23] Four adult leaders were "trained to proficiency" in the three different leadership styles, authoritarian, democratic, and laissez-faire. The specific leadership behavior under each style is shown in Figure 1. Each of these adult leaders was assigned to direct the activities of a boys' club consisting of five boys who met after school to engage in hobby activities. The boys in each of the four groups were roughly similar in terms of social and economic background and mental, physical, and personality characteristics. The adult leaders were shifted every six weeks from one club to another, and every time they switched to a new group they changed to a different leadership style. All the boys' clubs met in the same places and carried out the same activities under the same conditions. During these meetings, observers were present to study the boys' behavior in detail. The boys themselves were later interviewed to determine their reaction to each leadership style. Home visits were also made to the parents to discover what the impact of each leadership pattern had been on the boys' conduct at home.

The basic findings were as follows:

1. Under laissez-faire supervision, the boys proved less efficient. Furthermore, they did not like the club activities as much as when they were treated democratically. They did less work and poorer work than when under democratic supervision. The complete freedom they had under laissez-faire conditions led them to play more than when under either democratic or authoritarian supervision.

2. If efficiency is evaluated both in terms of work production and social satisfactions, democracy was clearly superior to both laissez-faire and autocracy. The boys worked as efficiently under authoritarian as they did under democratic supervision, but they enjoyed themselves more under democracy.

21 Robert T. Golembiewski, "Three Styles of Leadership and Their Uses", Personnel, Vol. 38, No. 4, July-August 1961, p. 35. See also Erwin S. Stanton ,"Which Approach to Management — Democratic, Authoritarian or . . .?", Personnel Administration, Vol. 25, No. 2, March-April 1962, pp. 44-47.

22 John M. Pfiffner and Frank P. Sherwood, Administrative Organization, Prentice-Hall, Englewood Cliffs, New Jersey, 1960, p. 364.

23 The description of these experiments which follows is from Ralph White and Ronald Lippitt, "Leader Behavior and Member Reaction in Three 'Social Climates' " in Cartwright and Zander, op. cit., pp. 527-553.

Authoritarian	Democratic	Laissez-faire
1. All determination of policy by the leader	1. All policies a matter of group discussion and decision, encouraged and assisted by the leader	1. Complete freedom for group or individual decision, with a minimum of leader participation
2. Techniques and activity steps dictated by the authority, one at a time, so that future steps were always uncertain to a large degree	2. Activity perspective gained during discussion period. General steps to group goal sketched, and when technical advice was needed, the leader suggested two or more alternative procedures from which choice could be made	2. Various materials supplied by the leader, who made it clear that he would supply information when asked. He took no other part in work discussion
3. The leader usually dictated the particular work task and work companion of each member	3. The members were free to work with whomever they chose, and the division of tasks was left up to the group	3. Complete nonparticipation of the leader
4. The dominator tended to be "personal" in his praise and criticism of the work of each member; remained aloof from active group participation except when demonstrating	4. The leader was "objective" or "factminded" in his praise and criticism, and tried to be a regular group member in spirit without doing too much of the work	4. Infrequent spontaneous comments on member activities unless questioned, and no attempt to appraise or regulate the course of events

Figure 1. Characteristics of the three treatment variables. From Ralph White and Ronald Lippitt, "Leader Behavior and Member Reaction in Three 'Social Climates'" in D. Cartwright and A. Zander (eds.), *Group Dynamics, Research and Theory*, Harper & Row, New York, 1960, p. 528.

3. There was a significant difference in the boys' behavior when a democratic, as contrasted with a dictatorial, adult leader temporarily left the room. The boys in democracy kept right on working, but those under iron rule "stopped working as if glad to be relieved of a task which they 'had' to do." Work production went down precipitously during leader-out periods under autocracy whereas the decline was only slight under democracy.

4. The boys showed more originality and creative thinking under democracy than under either laissez-faire or autocracy, for "there was a larger amount of creative thinking about the work in progress than in autocracy, and it was more sustained and practical than in laissez-faire."[24]

---

[24] *Ibid.*, p. 541.

5. Autocracy can create much hostility and aggression, including aggression against scapegoats. "Dominating ascendance," meaning imperious treatment of one boy by another, illustrated by such language as "shut up," took place much more often in the autocratically managed groups. Real hostility between the boys and aggressive demands for attention were also more characteristic of the autocratic groups. Destruction of work materials and property was not unusual when the meetings of the autocratic groups ended, but it did not take place at all in the democratic groups.

As to scapegoat behavior, it was evidenced in the autocratic, but not in the democratic, groups. Held down by the adult leader when he was playing the authoritarian role, the boys vented their spleen on some innocent member of the group. They took out on him their accumulated resentments against the adult leader. They could not openly defy the leader, so they directed their "aggressions" against other club members who had done nothing to them.

Upon return to democratic or laissez-faire treatment after autocracy, the boys sometimes released their "bottled-up tensions." The change to relative freedom after repressive control resulted in their breaking loose and engaging in much aggressive behavior, with the democratic adult leader now the scapegoat. The boys appeared to say to themselves, "Aha! *Now* I can do what I've been wanting to do in this club!"[25] After a couple of days, however, the "thrill of new-found freedom" wore off and the boys again exhibited the "spontaneous interest" characteristic of democracy.

6. There was more group-mindedness and friendliness in democracy. The pronoun "we" was used much more often in the democratic than in the autocratic groups. The kinds of remarks made by the boys in the democratic groups indicated the existence of greater group cohesion than under autocracy. "Friendly playfulness" was more pronounced, and there was a greater readiness to share group property.

A number of studies made with adult workers have also shown that democratic supervision produces better results. Frequently cited are those of the Institute for Social Research of the University of Michigan. The major finding was that work output was directly correlated with the amount of freedom the supervisor gave the worker. A comparison was made between the production achieved by groups of clerical workers functioning under "close" or "general" supervision. Close supervision meant that the supervisor "watched" the subordinates and checked constantly on how they were carrying out their tasks. Under general supervision, the supervisor put the workers on their own and employed an honor system. It was found that production was highest in work units headed by supervisors who practiced general supervision. Furthermore, the high supervisors, in terms of production, in most cases themselves received general, rather than close, direction from their own superiors. Finally, the high supervisors were generally content to leave the detailed performance of the work to their

---

25 *Ibid.*, p. 545.

subordinates, and to concentrate on their supervisory responsibilities. In this respect, they were "people-oriented." The low supervisors tended to neglect their supervisory responsibilities and to spend too much time actually trying to do a share of the production job themselves. Accordingly, they were considered to be "work-oriented."[26]

Later studies at Michigan and elsewhere, however, showed that employee-centered behavior by the supervisor did not necessarily result in increased production. They showed that "all kinds of combinations may occur — high morale and low production, low morale and low production, high morale and high production — which indicates the lack of any fixed and clear-cut relationship."[27] For this reason, Golembiewski argues that it is a mistake to try to answer the question, "Which kind of leadership should we use?" The really pertinent question he feels is, "Which kind of leadership *when?*"[28]

Selecting the Appropriate Leadership Style

Robert Tannenbaum and Warren H. Schmidt take up this problem in a most stimulating essay.[29] Their analysis is particularly valuable because they organize it around the central question of decisionmaking. Figure 2 reproduces a continuum which they have prepared showing the range of possible leadership behavior available to the manager. They explain each of the "behavior points" shown on the bottom line of the continuum as follows:

1. *The manager makes the decision and announces it.* Here the executive gives his subordinates no opportunity to participate directly in the decisionmaking process. He decides what the problem is, determines the possible courses of action, selects one of them, and then tells the subordinates to carry it out. In making his decision, he may or may not take into account how the employees will react to it. He may or may not use coercion in getting them to do as he says.

2. *The manager "sells" his decision.* There is no difference between this and 1., except that the manager does try to persuade the subordinates to accept the decision. He recognizes that some employees may not like the decision and may try to resist it, so he is careful to make clear what they will gain by accepting it. Note that the area of authority exercised by the manager remains large.

3. *The manager presents his ideas and invites questions.* The difference between this and 2. is that the manager gives the subordinates the opportunity to explore with him the implications of the decision. Instead of simply explaining why they should accept it, he invites them to ask questions, and he takes the time to go into some detail about "his thinking and his intentions." At this point on the continuum, the "area of freedom for subordinates" begins to look significant.

26 Daniel Katz, Nathan Maccoby, and Nancy C. Morse, *Productivity, Supervision, and Morale in an Office Situation*, Survey Research Center, Institute for Social Research, Ann Arbor, Michigan, 1950.

27 Pfiffner and Sherwood, *op. cit.*, p. 415.

28 Golembiewski, *op. cit.*, p. 35.

29 Robert Tannenbaum and Warren H. Schmidt, "How to Choose a Leadership Pattern", *Harvard Business Review*, Vol. 36, No. 2, March-April 1958, pp. 95-101.

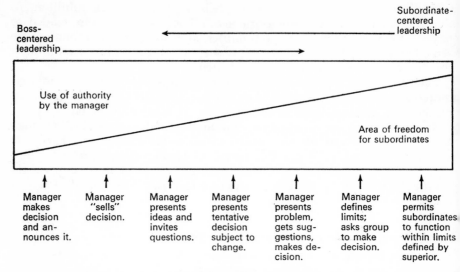

Figure 2. Continuum of Leadership Behavior. From Robert Tannenbaum and Warren H. Schmidt, "How to Choose a Leadership Pattern", *Harvard Business Review*, Vol. 36, No. 2, March-April 1958, p. 96.

4. *The manager presents a tentative decision subject to change.* Here for the first time, the subordinates are allowed to have some influence on the decision. The executive retains responsibility for identifying the problem and developing a proposed solution, but only on a tentative basis. Before making a final decision, he asks the subordinates to give their frank reactions, but he also makes clear that he is retaining the right to decide the question as he sees fit.

5. *The manager presents the problem, gets suggestions, and then makes his decision.* In 1. through 4. above, the manager in every case makes the decision himself, although in 4. it is a tentative one. In 5., he asks the subordinates for their opinions before he makes any decision, final or tentative. He respects their knowledge of operating problems and knows that they may be able to suggest solutions that would not occur to him. After evaluating their ideas, as well as his own, he "selects the solution that he regards as most promising."

6. *The manager defines the limits and requests the group to make a decision.* Here the manager delegates to the subordinates the authority to make a certain decision. He states exactly what the problem is and makes clear the restrictions on what the employees can decide. As a hypothetical example, the manager tells the subordinates that a new parking lot will be built for the use of the employees. A ceiling figure of $100,000 for the construction costs has been fixed. So long as this figure is not exceeded, the group can decide to build whatever kind of lot it wants, an underground one or a surface one with multilevel facilities. The management may not like the employees' decision but will accept it within the financial limit.

7. *The manager permits the group to make decisions within prescribed limits.* The difference between 6. and 7. is that in 7. a general grant of decisionmaking power is made, not limited to any one problem. The example given is of teams

of managers or engineers whose responsibility is not only to identify problems but also to decide what to do about them. The only limits on what the group can do are those specified by the official to whom the team leader reports. This leader may or may not himself participate in the making of the decision. If he does, he has no more authority than any other team member. He commits himself in advance to support whatever decision the group makes.[30]

Under 6 and 7, the subordinates' "area of freedom" widens greatly. The question remains, however, as to which of the leadership behaviors shown on the continuum is appropriate at a particular time. Tannenbaum and Schmidt identify three sets of factors which bear upon this question:

Forces in the manager
Forces in the subordinates
Forces in the situation.[31]

Forces in the Manager

By "forces in the manager" Tannenbaum and Schmidt mean his own preferences, based on his past history and experiences. Is he the type who strongly believes that people should participate in decisions which affect them as individuals? Or is he someone who has long been convinced that the supervisor must stoically assume the burden of making the decisions himself because he is paid to do so? How much confidence does he have in other people in general and in his present subordinates in particular? Some managers are so constituted that they become uneasy if there appears to be an element of risk and uncertainty in the operations they supervise. This kind of executive is better off if he frankly acknowledges to himself that he is not the person to make delegations of authority as broad as those shown on behavior points 6. and 7. of the continuum.

Forces in the Subordinates

"Forces in the subordinates" refers to the expectations of the employees as to how the supervisor should behave in his relations with them. It also means the personality requirements of each individual in the group as these bear upon the question of the kind of direction he responds to best. The executive can allow greater freedom to subordinates under the following conditions:

1. The subordinates have relatively high needs for independence.
2. They *want* to assume responsibility, rather than to avoid it.
3. They have a "relatively high tolerance for ambiguity," meaning they would rather receive broad instructions than to be tied down by clear-cut instructions.
4. They are interested in the problem and believe that it is important.

---

30 *Ibid.*, p. 97.
31 *Ibid.*, p. 98.

5. They understand the goals of the organization and identify with them.
6. They have the necessary knowledge and experience to be able to deal with the problem.
7. They are accustomed to sharing in decisionmaking. This is what they expect and are prepared for, rather than being denied such a role.[32]

If these conditions do not exist, there may be no alternative to running "a one-man show." Depending on his assessment of these factors, the executive may on one occasion decide to make the decisions himself, on another to let the subordinates participate. If the manager has the respect of the subordinates, they will understand why in the one case he brings them in and in the other he does not.

Forces in the Situation

"Forces in the situation" refers to the "critical environmental pressures" which surround the manager, stemming from "the organization, the work group, the nature of the problem, and the pressures of time."[33]

As to the organization, it has values and traditions which condition the manager's behavior. Someone newly appointed from the outside "quickly discovers that certain kinds of behavior are approved while others are not." There is a great compulsion for him to select that kind of behavior on the continuum which conforms to his superiors' concepts of how he should conduct himself. Sometimes this is referred to as the "management climate" in the agency; in other words, the lower ranking executives tend to imitate the behavior of the higher ones. The latter are a very important part of the "situation."

Other organizational factors influencing the extent of employee participation are: the size of the organization units; their geographical distribution; and whether or not information about work plans must be kept confidential. In a very large and dispersed organization, it may be impossible to have as much employee participation as the management would like. If the activity is one involving the national security, work plans and other information obviously cannot be communicated as freely to the employees.

"Group effectiveness" is another consideration. Before he gives a problem to the work group to solve, the manager must be convinced that it is equal to the task. Has the group functioned effectively in the past? Does it seem confident of its ability to cope with this kind of assignment?

The "nature of the problem" also sets limits on the extent to which the manager can safely delegate. Perhaps the problem is one with which the work group is not familiar, so he must handle it himself. There is no virtue in asking any one subordinate or a group of workers to take on responsibilities they are not ready to assume. Yet the executive wants to

---

[32] *Ibid.*, p. 99.
[33] *Ibid.*, p. 100.

be sure that he is making full use of the special knowledges and abilities of his staff. Tannenbaum and Schmidt suggest that the manager should ask himself, "Have I heard the ideas of everyone who has the necessary knowledge to make a significant contribution to the solution of this problem?" If he asks this question and answers it honestly, he is more likely to select the most appropriate leadership pattern.

"Pressure of time," meaning the need to act quickly, may force the manager to make the decision himself, without consulting with his subordinates. Leisurely consideration of every problem is not possible in the swift-moving environment of government. The manager does not by any means have full control of his time schedule; his own supervisors set deadlines for him. Unforeseen situations arise which make it necessary for him to make the best decision possible in a very short period of time. Under such circumstances, all he can do is consult with as many subordinates as possible, assuming that he even has time to do this.

The great value of the preceding analysis is that it makes clear the different considerations which should influence the decision as to leadership style. If the "boss-centered" type is used on occasion, this does not mean that the managers in question must be tyrants at heart. Of course, some may have such tendencies, evidenced by their use of "boss-centered" leadership even when it is not necessary. The point is that the manager should use the leadership pattern which is called for by the particular situation.

36   Managerial Facades*

Robert R. Blake
Jane S. Mouton

The word facade *as used in architecture means the* front *of a building. The very use of the word usually denotes a special architectural treatment. A second meaning of* facade *is "a false, superficial, or artificial appearance or effect." A building may have a false front to hide what exists behind it. This concept is useful for the understanding of managerial behavior. A managerial facade is made up of some manipulative practices quite different from those identified under the Managerial Grid.*

---

* Reprinted with permission of authors and publisher from *Advanced Management Journal*, Vol. 31, July 1966, pp. 30-37.

What is the Managerial Grid?

The Managerial Grid is an intellectual framework of ways that men manage. It is used to summarize management practices and compare them with behavioral science theories. For managers who have found it hard to understand these findings and apply them to their own behavior as they try to solve some of their companies' problems, it has become a means for understanding and using behavioral science to increase personal and managerial effectiveness.

The Grid identifies five kinds of managerial behavior based on two key variables, concern for output and concern for people. The Grid's vertical axis represents concern for people: the horizontal, concern for production. (See Exhibit 1.)

The lower left corner of the Grid shows the 1,1 style of indifference, representing the least possible concern for either production or people. The 1,9 upper left corner is "soft" management and reflects the greatest possible concern for people but the least for production. At the opposite lower right hand corner is the "harsh" 9,1 style, where concern for production is high and concern for people is at a minimum. The 5,5 style in the center represents the "middle-of-the-road" management that seeks a balance to get some production while not upsetting people. In the upper right corner is the 9,9 style, which represents the maximum of concern for production and people, an integration of people into the productive purposes of the organization.

A study of the Grid by managers provides them with a language system to describe their own managerial styles, those of others, and those of the organization as a whole as well as a framework of ideas for increasing the effectiveness of managerial practices and attitudes. With this framework, a man or an organization can strive to revise practices and procedures so as to achieve a 9,9 climate within the organization.[1]

A managerial facade is not as direct as 1,9, 9,1, or 5,5. Like the front of a building, it too is a cover for the real approach. It obscures the true intentions of the manager. A managerial facade conceals deception, intrigue, or trickery. A manager who builds a facade is trying to achieve by some roundabout way something which is not directly available or something which he believes he could not attain if he revealed his true intent or directly confronted the issues at stake.

It is difficult to interpret his purpose. His approach is manipulative. Many authors such as Machiavelli,[2] Carnegie,[3] Odiorne,[4] and Jennings[5] have described ways and means of building such facades.

---

[1] Robert R. Blake and Jane S. Mouton, *The Managerial Grid*, Gulf, Houston, Texas, 1964.

[2] C. Sforza, *The Living Thoughts of Machiavelli*, Fawcett, New York, 1958.

[3] D. Carnegie, *How to Win Friends and Influence People*, Pocketbooks, New York, 1958.

[4] G. S. Odiorne, *How Managers Make Things Happen*, Prentice-Hall, Englewood Cliffs, New Jersey, 1961.

[5] E. M. Jennings, *An Anatomy of Leadership*, Harper, New York, 1962.

EXHIBIT 1
THE MANAGERIAL GRID

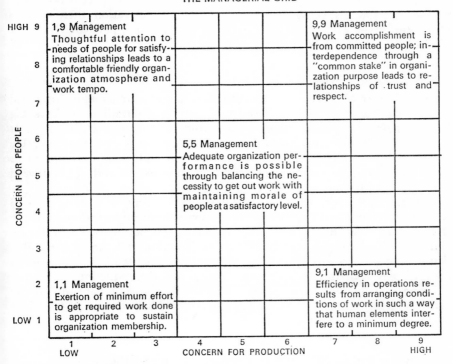

What Makes a Facade

The aim of a *facade* is mastery over persons and situations. The manager who covers his aim with a facade is distinguished from those who function according to well founded managerial assumptions by two signs. He is always striving for power. He has the capacity to exercise it. On the other hand, he can show little in the way of productive accomplishment.

Hidden Motivations

A characteristic of all managers who operate under facades is that they avoid revealing the "contents of the mind." Why does such a manager act in this way? If he were open and above board, others could understand him, and his false front would show. There are many ways to throw a cloak over one's intentions. The facade builder may simply avoid revealing his intentions by not initiating discussions that invite probing. He then will not be questioned about his motives.

Or he may withhold his reaction to a situation by seeming not to notice it. He may in speaking simply toss others' opinions back to them in such a way that they do not notice that he is not revealing his own opinions or attitudes. He may react to a question with a counterquestion to reflect a probe. Or he may react in half-truths which may be interpreted according to the interpreter's view. The facade builder's motivation then appears quite legitimate. Finally, he may resort to outright lies, particularly in the kind of situation in which they cannot be checked.

A Positive Reputation

Mere avoidance of revealing one's intentions is not quite enough. Successful facades are based on a positive front. A positive reputation can be a big help to a facade builder when he is trying to maintain a deception. It causes his intentions to appear quite different from what they are. He throws up a smoke screen to obscure his true ambition. He appears to have integrity since most other people do not see behind this outward appearance and sense what he really is.

Writers since Machiavelli have suggested how a reputation may be used to control, master, and dominate. Reputation is built on virtue, good deeds, and support of popular causes. Toward this end, a person works to bestow honor on all who excel. He identifies himself with excellence. It is possible that a person's very act of working for social movements which are admired because they contribute to human dignity and the reduction of human suffering may in fact be a facade. Whether it is or not depends on the person's intent. It is often hard to tell from surface behavior whether actions are motivated by good intentions.

Motivating and Controlling the Performance of Others

The facade builder knows that he can influence others by showing interest and using praise, or negatively, criticizing and using punishment.

Praise

From Machiavelli to Carnegie the uniform recommendation is, "Be lavish with praise." Compliments feed a person's pride. The person who feels praiseworthy likes and admires the person extending the praise. Praise whether or not earned or deserved can buy influence. The facade builder must be discriminating; he must not go too far. But how far is too far? Machiavelli, Carnegie, and Odiorne all point to the dangers of flattery. Flattery is praise that can boomerang. The facade builder, to maintain his own illusions, avoids the falseness of flattering others and is careful not to be led astray by flattery from others.

Concern for Others

A more subtle way of influencing than direct praise is concern for other persons' needs and opinions.[6] The importance of demonstrating an interest

---

[6] C. Sforza, *op. cit.*

in others, even to the point of learning and using their names, can hardly be overestimated. There are many recipes for doing so. Be a good listener. Get others to talk about themselves. Never tell a person he is wrong. Avoid arguments. The facade builder does not want to be disliked by others. He is sympathetic to their ideas and opinions. As a statesman said, "I make it a point to find out what a person is interested in so that I can ask intelligent questions and get him to talk. Then, not only is he put into a positive frame of mind, but it makes him feel important. Because he is friendly to me, he is more likely to buy what I want him to later on."

When all of these actions are well founded, the behavior can be judged as legitimate concern for others. When the aim is to gain a personal advantage which is unknown or perceived as something else, however, the characteristics of a facade are present.

Criticism

The direct use of criticism is dangerous, something to be avoided. As Carnegie says, "Even though one feels critical and criticism is justified, it should be avoided." Carnegie explains why:

> When dealing with people, let us remember that we are not dealing with creatures of logic. We are dealing with creatures of emotion, creatures bristling with prejudices and motivated by pride and vanity . . . and criticism is a dangerous spark — a spark that is likely to cause an explosion in the powder keg of pride . . .

His suggestion is that criticism is much too dangerous for a person to play with if he wants to win friends and influence. By avoiding criticism entirely, he can evade the negative reaction so often associated with it. This act of deception is of no consequence.

Punishment

The facade builder never is seen as the direct agent of punishment if he can help it. He can mete out punishment indirectly by delegating the responsibility for dispensing it. His goal is to appear innocent of the circumstances, the decision to punish, and the severity of the punishment. Henry Ford is said to have been lavish in his praise for performance, but to have employed a "hatchetman" to do his dirty work in the punishment department.[7]

Decision Making and Problem Solving

It is in the areas of decision making and problem solving that clues are found to managerial behavior. The ways a person develops and maintains convictions and deals with conflict are most revealing.

---

[7] E. M. Jennings, *op. cit.*

Convictions

A facade builder expresses his convictions in a special way to maintain maneuverability. He may use anonymous authorities or public opinion as sources supporting his beliefs. He never puts forth his convictions firmly enough to be proven wrong or stands behind them firmly enough to be seen as obstinate. He always keeps other avenues open so he can shift his course without being seen as having taken a wrong one, but rather be proved wise. While he may have to sacrifice a possible opportunity to make a contribution for being absolutely right, the losses from being quite wrong are avoided.

Conflict

The facade builder does not avoid conflict. This might make him seem cowardly. He uses conflict to gain his own purposes. He wages only limited offensive battles, avoiding direct conflict where he is vulnerable. As one manager said, "It is better to ask for a simple change and to go one step at a time than to try to go the whole hog and stir up resistance, resentment, and open conflict."

The facade builder turns conflict among others to his advantage. He keeps a neutral position only until those in conflict are clearly identified. Once the issues are drawn, the facade builder enters the conflict and throws his weight to the stronger protagonist. When he throws his weight in with the victor, the victor in turn is obligated for the help received. Had the facade builder maintained his neutrality, both the victor and the vanquished would have known that his support had not been forthcoming, and support withheld might have made a difference. Furthermore, should fate turn against the victor, the vanquished would have had no reason to feel obligated toward someone who had failed to be counted anyway.

The facade builder keeps the significance of conflict clearly in mind and fights to win his own decision, though he cleverly avoids seeming to relish a fight. He tries to avoid impatience, anger, and temper, remains calm and rational. It is the long haul win that counts and being able to win over the loser as an ally.[8] When his subordinates are in conflict, however, the facade builder provides an opportunity for direct confrontation, and he serves as the unbiased mediator, a fountainhead of justice. His subordinates increase their respect for him as a fair administrator.

Initiative and Perseverance

The facade builder demonstrates initiative. He sticks to his guns until he succeeds. He acts quickly when he sees an advantage to be gained. He demonstrates interest in other persons but does not become sentimentally

---

[8] G. S. Odiorne, *op. cit.*

involved. He is able to use others and to make alliances which he quickly sets aside as the occasion demands. He is not easily thrown by obstacles, is unlikely to have conflicting motives. If one action does not succeed, he tries another tack. Nor is he daunted by difficulty, by the hardness of a task, or by stress from the outside. He responds to information new to him and opportunities that might give him more leverage. He is not likely to be bound inwardly by authority and tradition since these could put obstacles in his path. When it is to his advantage, however, he upholds the *status quo*.

Compromise

The facade builder is not reluctant to commit himself to a compromise position, even if he has reservations about the matter in question. He recognizes compromise as a maneuver, a tactical accommodation. Compromise undercuts resistance because it appears to be "reasonableness." One facade builder said, "I compromise so I can go underground with my true purpose, and then later I come up again and about the third time around I win."

Advice and Counsel

The facade builder seeks advice and counsel for personal gain or loss in influence over other persons.

Receiving Advice and Counsel

Although the facade builder tries to make others feel important through praise and approval, he does not court favors by asking unneeded advice from others. This would make him seem weak. He also believes that accepting unsolicited advice would create an obligation to the advisor. Beyond that, the "smart" manager knows what is going on without having to be told. So the facade builder arranges for acceptance of advice only when he solicits it, thus avoiding any obligation to the giver. The information he gleans is more likely to be accurate than unsolicited advice because the advice-giver can then be kept uninformed of how much the facade builder really knows.

A facade builder must choose trustworthy subordinates if he wants candid advice. He makes it known that honesty is expected and rewarded. To test the loyalty of a subordinate, he showers him with authority. Then he observes how the authority is used. If the subordinate uses the authority in the facade builder's interest rather than his own, his apparent trustworthiness is corroborated. If he turns it to his own selfish gains, the facade builder can assume that he is an unreliable subordinate.

Giving Advice and Counsel

If a facade builder counsels another and the action suggested fails, the frustration associated with such failure invites criticism and his judgment has proved unreliable. On the other hand, if he counsels action that succeeds, he may be commended. The reward for counseling success, according to Machiavelli[9], is rarely as great as the consequences of counseling an action that fails. The facade builder learns to be wary of giving advice.

Making Use of the System

A facade builder has to keep in close touch with what is going on in the organization system and still hold on to responsibility for making the key decisions. He must make these decisions alone. This is an indispensable part of achieving control and domination over others. The facade builder has subtle ways of keeping this decision-making responsibility through deliberate use of the organizational system.

Incomplete Delegation

The facade builder finds incomplete delegation an ideal way of maintaining control and yet appearing to provide independence for his subordinates. He leaves jurisdictional boundaries a bit fuzzy or arranges overlapping responsibilities. In both cases the uncertainty about who is free to act under his authority causes a subordinate balancing act. No subordinate has enough authority to make a decision by himself. Nor does the facade builder provide quite enough information to permit decisions under the authority that is delegated. There is just enough information to make subordinates feel informed. But the incomplete delegation methods make it necessary for decisions to be made from above. Subordinates must seek the help of the facade builder, thus increasing his control.

If the facade builder is skillful in using these strategies, the troubles of his subordinates in striving to reach decisions seem to be traceable to the "system," *not* the administration of it. To support his facade, the facade builder has achieved continuous flow of upward communication and the retention of decision making power.

One-to-One Supervision and Managing Cliques

Another way in which a facade builder insures his control is by operating one-to-one. He avoids situations where others freely exchange ideas and information and makes information needed by subordinates available only through himself. Nor does he neglect to give attention to cliques, the grapevine, and other informal organization elements. With a thorough

---

9 C. Sforza, *op. cit.*

knowledge of the membership of cliques, he is able to tap the grapevine at strategic spots. He may influence key members of cliques and others will follow their lead. He often consults these key members before a decision to reduce resistance from clique members.

Pseudo Team Action

The facade builder sees any informal group as an important and useful unit. Meetings, for example, enable him to exert his influence on a whole group simultaneously, a convenient unit for the advancement of his interests.[10] He finds knowledge of power tactics and group dynamics an indispensable tool of his trade. He is not himself a "team man" but participates in groups to his own advantage, making clear that responsibility for any major high risk innovation is that of the group.

He sponsors minor changes that can be construed as tests of ability and that will probably be successful. He welcomes group interaction as a means to pick others' brains. In fact, he especially likes brainstorming because it is relatively easy for him to take credit for the ideas of others without ever being forced into the negative position of discarding someone's ideas or being committed to any action which represents group problem solving. He is a clever idea hitchhiker. He can present the good ideas of others as if they were his own.

Group interaction for getting a problem solved is viewed with distrust by the facade builder. Where team action is seen as appropriate, his goal is to provide an *appearance* of it. One way he makes sure that no real interaction takes place is this: the facade builder talks with each person who will participate in the group before it assembles. He feels out each person's position so as to achieve commitment on the course of action he has planned well in advance. Then he can more easily exert his influence and achieve a uniform opinion without open debate or deliberation.

If possible, he forms the group from among his allies. He prefers not to risk bringing together persons whose views are likely to differ from his or from one another's. He is agreeable to having a thorough group discussion over minor issues, but he is likely to prevent any discussion of major ones. Those he will reserve for unilateral decision making. Because few persons have developed the skills of team action, the clever facade builder finds a "group" an easy match.

One facade builder has described a useful way to keep control over others and to make certain of getting his own way under the guise of team action. "To keep one part of the organization from achieving more influence than other parts (which would reduce my own power), I keep problems in a fluid state even beyond the point where a decision could be made. This is done by keeping the situation open under the guise of not making the premature unworkable decision or testing all possible alternatives for

---

[10] E. M. Jennings, *op. cit.*

taking a step. The stronger faction thus becomes weakened, the weaker faction is not hurt, and when I finally make the decision, everyone is relieved and ready to go my way so as to get some action."

A Matter of Ethics

What lies behind the building and maintaining of a managerial facade? One consideration is ethics. The facade builder has no value of mutual trust in its own right. Still in all, he believes that the appearance of trustfulness is important. By creating the impression of trust as a basis for his relationships with others, he is readily able to achieve some of his personal goals. On the plane of social ethics, he takes shortcuts to achieve an end not governed by commonly accepted rules for maintaining social morality.

Another reason why a person builds a facade is that by doing so he is hiding the trickery that he is using to gain objectives which he could not achieve through honest ability-based performance. The end justifies the means.

A third reason for such behavior is that the underlying cause of it is hidden even from the person himself. He literally does not know that he is putting up a front. Not only is he deceiving others, he also is deceiving himself. Psychiatrists have described tricks of the mind in which a person's motivations are unclear to himself, he cannot identify them or describe them to others, and if he is directly confronted with his own self-deceptions, he denies them. Examples of these tricks are seen by psychiatrists in rationalization, projection, justification, and compensation.

Summary

In summary, a person who seeks control and mastery over others may adopt a personal managerial facade. Whatever strategy such a person uses, the goal is the same — to insure that true aims are perceived quite differently and much more positively than they in fact are. The person who is building or maintaining a facade will seize the opportunity to influence events and people and to control and dominate them. Such influence can far outweigh a person's true contribution or real ability.

Since his strategies for taking advantage of opportune situations and the weaknesses of others are of a wide variety, it is often difficult to pinpoint the facade builder unless one is able to track his every activity over a period of time.

For the manager who suspects that someone in his working situation is in fact a facade builder, understanding of the reasons for actions which are common in such cases may help the person involved to realize that, to some at least, his facade may be showing.

37 The Human Side of Enterprise*

Douglas M. McGregor

It has become trite to say that the most significant developments of the next quarter century will take place not in the physical but in the social sciences, that industry — the economic organ of society — has the fundamental know-how to utilize physical science and technology for the material benefit of mankind, and that we must now learn how to utilize the social sciences to make our human organizations truly effective.

Many people agree in principle with such statements; but so far they represent a pious hope — and little else. Consider with me, if you will, something of what may be involved when we attempt to transform the hope into reality.

Let me begin with an analogy. A quarter century ago basic conceptions of the nature of matter and energy had changed profoundly from what they had been since Newton's time. The physical scientists were persuaded that under proper conditions new and hitherto unimagined sources of energy could be made available to mankind.

We know what has happened since then. First came the bomb. Then, during the past decade, have come many other attempts to exploit these scientific discoveries — some successful, some not.

The point of my analogy, however, is that the application of theory in this field is a slow and costly matter. We expect it always to be thus. No one is impatient with the scientist because he cannot tell industry how to build a simple, cheap, all-purpose source of atomic energy today. That it will take at least another decade and the investment of billions of dollars to achieve results which are economically competitive with present sources of power is understood and accepted.

It is transparently pretentious to suggest any *direct* similarity between the developments in the physical sciences leading to the harnessing of atomic energy and potential developments in the social sciences. Nevertheless, the analogy is not as absurd as it might appear to be at first glance.

To a lesser degree, and in a much more tentative fashion, we are in a position in the social sciences today like that of the physical sciences with respect to atomic energy in the thirties. We know that past conceptions of the nature of man are inadequate and in many ways incorrect. We are becoming quite certain that, under proper conditions, unimagined resources of creative human energy could become available within the organizational setting.

We cannot tell industrial management how to apply this new knowledge in simple, economic ways. We know it will require years of exploration,

* Reprinted from *Leadership and Motivation* by Douglas McGregor by permission of the MIT Press, Cambridge, Massachusetts. Copyright 1966 by the Massachusetts Institute of Technology. First printed in *Adventure in Thought and Action*: Proceedings of the Fifth Annual Convocation of the School of Industrial Management, MIT, April 9, 1967.

much costly development research, and a substantial amount of creative imagination on the part of management to discover how to apply this growing knowledge to the organization of human effort in industry.

May I ask that you keep this analogy in mind — overdrawn and pretentious though it may be — as a framework for what I have to say this morning.

Management's Task: Conventional View

The conventional conception of management's task in harnessing human energy to organizational requirements can be stated broadly in terms of three propositions. In order to avoid the complications introduced by a label, I shall call this set of propositions "Theory X":

1. Management is responsible for organizing the elements of productive enterprise — money, materials, equipment, people — in the interest of economic ends.
2. With respect to people, this is a process of directing their efforts, motivating them, controlling their actions, modifying their behavior to fit the needs of the organization.
3. Without this active intervention by management, people would be passive — even resistant — to organizational needs. They must therefore be persuaded, rewarded, punished, controlled — their activities must be directed. This is management's task — in managing subordinate managers or workers. We often sum it up by saying that management consists of getting things done through other people.

Behind this conventional theory there are several additional beliefs — less explicit, but widespread:
4. The average man is by nature indolent — he works as little as possible.
5. He lacks ambition, dislikes responsibility, prefers to be led.
6. He is inherently self-centered, indifferent to organizational needs.
7. He is by nature resistant to change.
8. He is gullible, not very bright, the ready dupe of the charlatan and the demagogue.

The human side of economic enterprise today is fashioned from propositions and beliefs such as these. Conventional organization structures, managerial policies, practices, and programs reflect these assumptions.

In accomplishing its task — with these assumptions as guides — management has conceived of a range of possibilities between two extremes.

The Hard or the Soft Approach?

At one extreme, management can be "hard" or "strong." The methods for directing behavior involve coercion and threat (usually disguised), close supervision, tight controls over behavior. At the other extreme, management can be "soft" or "weak." The methods for directing behavior involve being permissive, satisfying people's demands, achieving harmony. Then they will be tractable, accept direction.

This range has been fairly completely explored during the past half century, and management has learned some things from the exploration. There are difficulties in the "hard" approach. Force breeds counterforces: restriction of output, antagonism, militant unionism, subtle but effective sabotage of management objectives. This approach is especially difficult during times of full employment.

There are also difficulties in the "soft" approach. It leads frequently to the abdication of management — to harmony, perhaps, but to indifferent performance. People take advantage of the soft approach. They continually expect more, but they give less and less.

Currently, the popular theme is "firm but fair." This is an attempt to gain the advantages of both the hard and the soft approaches. It is reminiscent of Teddy Roosevelt's "speak softly and carry a big stick."

Is the Conventional View Correct?

The findings which are beginning to emerge from the social sciences challenge this whole set of beliefs about man and human nature and about the task of management. The evidence is far from conclusive, certainly, but it is suggestive. It comes from the laboratory, the clinic, the schoolroom, the home, and even to a limited extent from industry itself.

The social scientist does not deny that human behavior in industrial organization today is approximately what management perceives it to be. He has, in fact, observed it and studied it fairly extensively. But he is pretty sure that this behavior is *not* a consequence of man's inherent nature. It is a consequence rather of the nature of industrial organizations, of management philosophy, policy, and practice. The conventional approach of Theory X is based on mistaken notions of what is cause and what is effect.

"Well," you ask, "what then is the *true* nature of man? What evidence leads the social scientist to deny what is obvious?" And, if I am not mistaken, you are also thinking, "Tell me — simply, and without a lot of scientific verbiage — what you think you know that is so unusual. Give me — without a lot of intellectual claptrap and theoretical nonsense — some practical ideas which will enable me to improve the situation in my organization. And remember, I'm faced with increasing costs and narrowing profit margins. I want proof that such ideas won't result simply in new and costly human relations frills. I want practical results, and I want them now."

If these are your wishes, you are going to be disappointed. Such requests can no more be met by the social scientist today than could comparable ones with respect to atomic energy be met by the physicist fifteen years ago. I can, however, indicate a few of the reasons for asserting that conventional assumptions about the human side of enterprise are inadequate. And I can suggest — tentatively — some of the propositions that will comprise a more adequate theory of the management of people. The magnitude of the task that confronts us will then, I think, be apparent.

Perhaps the best way to indicate why the conventional approach of management is inadequate is to consider the subject of motivation. In discussing this subject I will draw heavily on the work of my colleague, Abraham Maslow of Brandeis University. His is the most fruitful approach I know. Naturally, what I have to say will be overgeneralized and will ignore important qualifications. In the time at our disposal, this is inevitable.

Physiological and Safety Needs

Man is a wanting animal — as soon as one of his needs is satisfied, another appears in its place. This process is unending. It continues from birth to death.

Man's needs are organized in a series of levels — a hierarchy of importance. At the lowest level, but preeminent in importance when they are thwarted, are his physiological needs. Man lives by bread alone, when there is no bread. Unless the circumstances are unusual, his needs for love, for status, for recognition are inoperative when his stomach has been empty for a while. But when he eats regularly and adequately, hunger ceases to be an important need. The sated man has hunger only in the sense that a full bottle has emptiness. The same is true of the other physiological needs of man — for rest, exercise, shelter, protection from the elements.

A satisfied need is not a motivator of behavior! This is a fact of profound significance. It is a fact which is regularly ignored in the conventional approach to the management of people. I shall return to it later. For the moment, one example will make my point. Consider your own need for air. Except as you are deprived of it, it has no appreciable motivating effect upon your behavior.

When the physiological needs are reasonably satisfied, needs at the next higher level begin to dominate man's behavior — to motivate him. These are called safety needs. They are needs for protection against danger, threat, deprivation. Some people mistakenly refer to these as needs for security. However, unless man is in a dependent relationship where he fears arbitrary deprivation, he does not demand security. The need is for the "fairest possible break." When he is confident of this, he is more than willing to take risks. But when he feels threatened or dependent, his greatest need is for guarantees, for protection, for security.

The fact needs little emphasis that since every industrial employee is in a dependent relationship, safety needs may assume considerable importance. Arbitrary management actions, behavior which arouses uncertainty with respect to continued employment or which reflects favoritism or discrimination, unpredictable administration of policy — these can be powerful motivators of the safety needs in the employment relationship *at every level* from worker to vice president.

Social Needs

When man's physiological needs are satisfied and he is no longer fearful about his physical welfare, his social needs become important motivators of his behavior — for belonging, for association, for acceptance by his fellows, for giving and receiving friendship and love.

Management knows today of the existence of these needs, but it often assumes quite wrongly that they represent a threat to the organization. Many studies have demonstrated that the tightly knit, cohesive work group may, under proper conditions, be far more effective than an equal number of separate individuals in achieving organizational goals.

Yet management, fearing group hostility to its own objectives, often goes to considerable lengths to control and direct human efforts in ways that are inimical to the natural "groupiness" of human beings. When man's social needs — and perhaps his safety needs, too — are thus thwarted, he behaves in ways which tend to defeat organizational objectives. He becomes resistant, antagonistic, uncooperative. But this behavior is a consequence, not a cause.

Ego Needs

Above the social needs — in the sense that they do not become motivators until lower needs are reasonably satisfied — are the needs of greatest significance to management and to man himself. They are the egoistic needs, and they are of two kinds:

1. Those needs that relate to one's self-esteem — needs for self-confidence, for independence, for achievement, for competence, for knowledge.
2. Those needs that relate to one's reputation — needs for status, for recognition, for appreciation, for the deserved respect of one's fellows.

Unlike the lower needs, these are rarely satisfied: man seeks indefinitely for more satisfaction of these needs once they have become important to him. But they do not appear in any significant way until physiological, safety, and social needs are all reasonably satisfied.

The typical industrial organization offers few opportunities for the satisfaction of these egoistic needs to people at lower levels in the hierarchy. The conventional methods of organizing work, particularly in mass production industries, give little heed to these aspects of human motivation. If the practices of scientific management were deliberately calculated to thwart these needs — which, of course, they are not — they could hardly accomplish this purpose better than they do.

Self-Fulfillment Needs

Finally — a capstone, as it were, on the hierarchy of man's needs — there are what we may call the needs for self-fulfillment. These are the needs for realizing one's own potentialities, for continued self-development, for being creative in the broadest sense of that term.

It is clear that the conditions of modern life give only limited opportunity for these relatively weak needs to obtain expression. The deprivation most people experience with respect to other lower-level needs diverts their energies into the struggle to satisfy *those* needs, and the needs for self-fulfillment remain dormant.

Now, briefly, a few general comments about motivation:

We recognize readily enough that a man suffering from a severe dietary deficiency is sick. The deprivation of physiological needs has behavioral consequences. The same is true — although less well recognized — of deprivation of higher-level needs. The man whose needs for safety, association, independence, or status are thwarted is sick just as surely as is he who has rickets. And his sickness will have behavioral consequences. We will be mistaken if we attribute his resultant passivity, his hostility, his refusal to accept responsibility to his inherent "human nature." These forms of behavior are *symptoms* of illness — of deprivation of his social and egoistic needs.

The man whose lower-level needs are satisfied is not motivated to satisfy those needs any longer. For practical purposes they exist no longer. (Remember my point about your need for air.) Management often asks, "Why aren't people more productive? We pay good wages, provide good working conditions, have excellent fringe benefits and steady employment. Yet people do not seem to be willing to put forth more than minimum effort."

The fact that management has provided for these physiological and safety needs has shifted the motivational emphasis to the social and perhaps to the egoistic needs. Unless there are opportunities *at work* to satisfy these higher-level needs, people will be deprived; and their behavior will reflect this deprivation. Under such conditions, if management continues to focus its attention on physiological needs, its efforts are bound to be ineffective.

People *will* make insistent demands for more money under these conditions. It becomes more important than ever to buy the material goods and services which can provide limited satisfaction of the thwarted needs. Although money has only limited value in satisfying many higher-level needs, it can become the focus of interest if it is the *only* means available.

The Carrot and Stick Approach

The carrot and stick theory of motivation (like Newtonian physical theory) works reasonably well under certain circumstances. The *means* for satisfying man's physiological and (within limits) his safety needs can be provided or withheld by management. Employment itself is such a means, and so are wages, working conditions, and benefits. By these means the individual can be controlled so long as he is struggling for subsistence. Man lives for bread alone when there is no bread.

But the carrot and stick theory does not work at all once man has reached an adequate subsistence level and is motivated primarily by higher needs. Management cannot provide a man with self-respect, or with the respect of his fellows, or with the satisfaction of needs for self-fulfillment. It can create conditions such that he is encouraged and enabled to seek such satisfactions *for himself,* or it can thwart him by failing to create those conditions.

But this creation of conditions is not "control." It is not a good device for directing behavior. And so management finds itself in an odd position. The high standard of living created by our modern technological know-how provides quite adequately for the satisfaction of physiological and safety needs. The only significant exception is where management practices have not created confidence in a "fair break" — and thus where safety needs are thwarted. But by making possible the satisfaction of low-level needs, management has deprived itself of the ability to use as motivators the devices on which conventional theory has taught it to rely — rewards, promises, incentives, or threats and other coercive devices.

Neither Hard Nor Soft

The philosophy of management by direction and control — *regardless of whether it is hard or soft* — is inadequate to motivate because the human needs on which this approach relies are today unimportant motivators of behavior. Direction and control are essentially useless in motivating people whose important needs are social and egoistic. Both the hard and the soft approach fail today because they are simply irrelevant to the situation.

People, deprived of opportunities to satisfy at work the needs which are now important to them, behave exactly as we might predict — with indolence, passivity, resistance to change, lack of responsibility, willingness to follow the demagogue, unreasonable demands for economic benefits. It would seem that we are caught in a web of our own weaving.

In summary, then, of these comments about motivation:

Management by direction and control — whether implemented with the hard, the soft, or the firm but fair approach — fails under today's conditions to provide effective motivation of human effort toward organizational objectives. It fails because direction and control are useless methods of motivating people whose physiological and safety needs are reasonably satisfied and whose social, egoistic, and self-fulfillment needs are predominant.

For these and many other reasons, we require a different theory of the task of managing people based on more adequate assumptions about human nature and human motivation. I am going to be so bold as to suggest the broad dimensions of such a theory. Call it "Theory Y," if you will.

1. Management is responsible for organizing the elements of productive enterprise — money, materials, equipment, people — in the interest of economic ends.

2. People are *not* by nature passive or resistant to organizational needs. They have become so as a result of experience in organizations.
3. The motivation, the potential for development, the capacity for assuming responsibility, the readiness to direct behavior toward organizational goals are all present in people. Management does not put them there. It is a responsibility of management to make it possible for people to recognize and develop these human characteristics for themselves.
4. The essential task of management is to arrange organizational conditions and methods of operation so that people can achieve their own goals *best* by directing *their own* efforts toward organizational objectives.

This is a process primarily of creating opportunities, releasing potential, removing obstacles, encouraging growth, providing guidance. It is what Peter Drucker has called "management by objectives" in contrast to "management by control."

And I hasten to add that it does *not* involve the abdication of management, the absence of leadership, the lowering of standards, or the other characteristics usually associated with the "soft" approach under Theory X. Much on the contrary. It is no more possible to create an organization today which will be a fully effective application of this theory than it was to build an atomic power plant in 1945. There are many formidable obstacles to overcome.

Some Difficulties

The conditions imposed by conventional organization theory and by the approach of scientific management for the past half century have tied men to limited jobs which do not utilize their capabilities, have discouraged the acceptance of responsibility, have encouraged passivity, have eliminated meaning from work. Man's habits, attitudes, expectations — his whole conception of membership in an industrial organization — have been conditioned by his experience under these circumstances. Change in the direction of Theory Y will be slow, and it will require extensive modification of the attitudes of management and workers alike.

People today are accustomed to being directed, manipulated, controlled in industrial organizations and to finding satisfaction for their social, egoistic, and self-fulfillment needs away from the job. This is true of much of management as well as of workers. Genuine "industrial citizenship" — to borrow again a term from Drucker — is a remote and unrealistic idea, the meaning of which has not even been considered by most members of industrial organizations.

Another way of saying this is that Theory X places exclusive reliance upon external control of human behavior, while Theory Y relies heavily on self-control and self-direction. It is worth noting that this difference is the difference between treating people as children and treating them as mature adults. After generations of the former, we cannot expect to shift to the latter overnight.

Before we are overwhelmed by the obstacles, let us remember that the application of theory is always slow. Progress is usually achieved in small steps.

Consider with me a few innovative ideas which are entirely consistent with Theory Y and which are today being applied with some success:

Decentralization and Delegation

These are ways of freeing people from the too-close control of conventional organization, giving them a degree of freedom to direct their own activities, to assume responsibility, and, importantly, to satisfy their egoistic needs. In this connection, the flat organization of Sears, Roebuck and Company provides an interesting example. It forces "management by objectives" since it enlarges the number of people reporting to a manager until he cannot direct and control them in the conventional manner.

Job Enlargement

This concept, pioneered by I.B.M. and Detroit Edison, is quite consistent with Theory Y. It encourages the acceptance of responsibility at the bottom of the organization; it provides opportunities for satisfying social and egoistic needs. In fact, the reorganization of work at the factory level offers one of the more challenging opportunities for innovation consistent with Theory Y. The studies by A. T. M. Wilson and his associates of British coal mining and Indian textile manufacture have added appreciably to our understanding of work organization. Moreover, the economic and psychological results achieved by this work have been substantial.

Participation and Consultative Management

Under proper conditions these results provide encouragement to people to direct their creative energies toward organizational objectives, give them some voice in decisions that affect them, provide significant opportunities for the satisfaction of social and egoistic needs. I need only mention the Scanlon Plan as the outstanding embodiment of these ideas in practice.

The not infrequent failure of such ideas as these to work as well as expected is often attributable to the fact that a management has "bought the idea" but applied it within the framework of Theory X and its assumptions.

Delegation is not an effective way of exercising management by control. Participation becomes a farce when it is applied as a sales gimmick or a device for kidding people into thinking they are important. Only the management that has confidence in human capacities and is itself directed toward organizational objectives rather than toward the preservation of personal power can grasp the implications of this emerging theory. Such management will find and apply successfully other innovative ideas as we move slowly toward the full implementation of a theory like Y.

Performance Appraisal

Before I stop, let me mention one other practical application of Theory Y which — while still highly tentative — may well have important consequences. This has to do with performance appraisal within the ranks of management. Even a cursory examination of conventional programs of performance appraisal will reveal how completely consistent they are with Theory X. In fact, most such programs tend to treat the individual as though he were a product under inspection on the assembly line.

Take the typical plan: substitute "product" for "subordinate being appraised," substitute "inspector" for "superior making the appraisal," substitute "rework" for "training or development," and, except for the attributes being judged, the human appraisal process will be virtually indistinguishable from the product inspection process.

A few companies — among them General Mills, Ansul Chemical, and General Electric — have been experimenting with approaches which involve the individual in setting "targets" or objectives *for himself* and in a *self*-evaluation of performance semi-annually or annually. Of course, the superior plays an important leadership role in this process — one, in fact, which demands substantially more competence than the conventional approach. The role is, however, considerably more congenial to many managers than the role of "judge" or "inspector" which is forced upon them by conventional performance. Above all, the individual is encouraged to take a greater responsibility for planning and appraising his own contribution to organizational objectives; and the accompanying effects on egoistic and self-fulfiillment needs are substantial. This approach to performance appraisal represents one more innovative idea being explored by a few managements who are moving toward the implementation of Theory Y.

And now I am back where I began. I share the belief that we could realize substantial improvements in the effectiveness of industrial organizations during the next decade or two. Moreover, I believe the social sciences can contribute much to such developments. We are only beginning to grasp the implications of the growing body of knowledge in these fields. But if this conviction is to become a reality instead of a pious hope, we will need to view the process much as we view the process of releasing the energy of the atom for constructive human ends — as a slow, costly, sometimes discouraging approach toward a goal which would seem to many to be quite unrealistic.

The ingenuity and the perseverance of industrial management in the pursuit of economic ends have changed many scientific and technological dreams into commonplace realities. It is now becoming clear that the application of these same talents to the human side of enterprise will not only enhance substantially these materialistic achievements but will bring us one step closer to "the good society." Shall we get on with the job?

Chapter Nine
Personnel Administration

Of all the areas of public administration, personnel administration has developed most rapidly in the last two decades. It has risen from the clerical function of preparing staff requisitions and documenting personnel data in government departments and agencies to the senior staff advisory function on human relations and departmental services requiring the application of sophisticated techniques. In central staffing agencies this change has not been so marked but even there the most superficial assessment shows the tremendous increase in scope and complexity of the personnel functions.

The first selection in this chapter traces both the recent history of personnel administration in the federal government service and the scope of this field today; there is no other comprehensive, published work on contemporary Canadian personnel practice. The most useful general textbooks on personnel administration are American. P. Pigors and C. A. Myers, *Personnel Administration* (McGraw-Hill, Toronto, 1965) and P. Pigors *et al, Management and Human Resources: Readings in Personnel Administration* (McGraw-Hill, Toronto, 1964), constitute a comprehensive treatment. G. Strauss and L. R. Sayles, *Personnel — The Human Problem of Management* (Prentice-Hall, Englewood Cliffs, New Jersey, 1967), is another text.

Collective bargaining in the government milieu is a perfect example of a personnel activity that has expanded and changed beyond all recognition in the last few years. Two items in this chapter outline the significance and meaning of the new staff relations legislation. Again there is no other comprehensive treatment of current Canadian government staff relations, theories and practices. S. Frankel in *Staff Relations in the Civil Service — The Canadian Experience* (McGill University Press, Montreal, 1962), traces the background of employer-employee relations while the *Report of the Preparatory Committee on Collective Bargaining* (Queen's Printer, Ottawa, 1965), is a closely reasoned justification for present practices.

The recruiting and development of government managers for the future is the theme of the last selection.

Other specialized readings in personnel administration, particularly those dealing with business, are numerous. The Canadian student of public personnel administration will find two periodicals very useful:

Personnel Administration published bimonthly by the Society for Personnel Administration in Washington, D.C. and *Public Personnel Review*, the quarterly journal of the Public Personnel Association, Chicago.

"A Basic Bibliography in Public Personnel Administration" is found in *Public Personnel Review*, Vol. 22, No. 4, October 1961. Other suggested readings include:

J. C. Best, "Management and Staff Relations in the Public Service", *Canadian Public Administration*, Vol. 4, 1961, pp. 168-176.
Civil Service Commission, *Personnel administration in the public service; a review of civil service legislation*, Queen's Printer, Ottawa, 1959.
The Royal Commission on Government Organization, *Report*, Vol. 1, Queen's Printer, Ottawa, 1962, Section 3.
John J. Carson, "Equipping Men for Career Growth in the Public Service", *Public Administration Review*, Vol. 23, No. 1, March 1963.
S. J. Frankel, "Staff Relations in the Public Service: The ghost of sovereignty", *Canadian Public Administration*, Vol. 2, No. 2, June 1959, pp. 65-76.
Louis L. Friedland, "Fair Employment Practices in the Public Service", *Public Personnel Review*, Vol. 23, No. 2, April 1962.
R. W. Jones, "The Merit System, Politics and Political Maturity: A federal review", *Public Personnel Review*, Vol. 25, No. 1, January 1964, pp. 28-34.
Frederick C. Mosher, "Careers and Career Services in the Public Service", *Public Personnel Review*, Vol. 24, No. 1, January 1963.
George W. Noble, "Labour Relations in Canadian Municipalities, *Public Personnel Review*, Vol. 22, No. 4, October 1961.
M. Z. Prives, "Career and Promotion in the Federal Civil Service of Canada,", *Canadian Public Administration*, Vol. 3, No. 2, June 1960, pp. 179-190.
Kenneth O. Warner, *Management Relations with Organized Public Employees*, Public Personnel Association, Chicago, 1963.

38   Personnel Administration in the Federal Public Service

R. H. Dowdell

I. The Personnel Function in Management

The management of an organization is the body of executive and supervisory personnel responsible for defining its objectives, framing its policies and directing the activities of its work force. Management's resources include time, material and people (money may be considered either as a resource in itself or the ability to acquire resources). These resources must be efficiently and effectively employed if management is to achieve its objectives.

Because they behave according to the laws of physics and chemistry, management's material resources possess qualities which are either known or immediately discoverable and their behaviour is predictable Such is not the case with people. Despite the recent discoveries in the behavioural sciences, much remains unknown about the qualities of *homo sapien*, and his behaviour cannot be so reliably predicted, in the work situation or anywhere else. In a sense, the human resources of an organization are not "resources" at all, for all organized social activity is maintained to meet human needs and purposes, and the organization's employees are, in some measure, part of the reason for its existence.

A number of developments have made the task of "people management" in organizations progressively more complicated.

1. The business enterprise or government department of the nineteenth century characteristically employed a few score or at most a few hundred people. The owner-manager, or the minister, hired many of his staff personally and knew a good deal about their backgrounds and personal idiosyncracies. The predominant feature of modern organizations is their large scale. Government departments are classed as small if they employ less than 2,000 to 3,000 people. More than half of the civilian public service in the federal government is employed in two departments — Post Office (45,000) and National Defence (40,000). Two others account for over 30,000 more — Transport and Agriculture. For most employees, whether in the private or public sector, personal relationships are limited to a small fragment of the enterprise. They are separated by many layers of hierarchy from top management, which comes to depend on rules and procedures instead of face-to-face contact in daily activity. The quality of large organizations that Weber described as "rationalism" results in decisions which are based on policies and regulations rather than on personnel knowledge and the recognition of individual needs. There are now more than 200,000 people at work in the federal public service. Their wages and salaries total more than $100,000,000 annually.[1] Every year these figures increase, with a regularity that has become a major source of social and political concern. How can the public be certain that all of these people are really needed, and are working with optimum effectiveness? These questions derive from the large scale of government employment, and are addressed to some of the biggest problems in modern public personnel management.

2. In the last 40 years, scientists and managers have systemically studied people at work. Frederick W. Taylor and Frank B. Gilbreth — the founders of "scientific management" — proved that the attention given to improving the *way* a man works pays off handsomely in productivity. But their belief

---

[1] See Table 2.

TABLE 1
Growth of the Federal Civil Service[1]
1912-1952

Year	Employees[2]
1912	20,016
1916	29,219
1920	47,133
1924	38,062
1928	41,243
1932	44,008
1936	41,132
1940	49,739
1944	112,658
1948	118,370
1952	131,646

[1] *Canada Year Book*, 1927, p. 1013, 1946, p. 1141, 1954, p. 93.
[2] Includes only permanent and temporary employees subject to the Civil Service Act. Statistical series maintained after 1952 include all federal government employees.

TABLE 2
Monthly Federal Government Employment and Payrolls
(May 31, 1967)

	Employed	Payroll
		thousands of dollars
Departments	219,577	102,196
(e.g. Agriculture, National Defence)	10,621	
Departmental Corporations		5,602
(e.g. National Research Council, R.C.M.P.)		
Agency, Corporations	9,496	4,964
(e.g. Crown Assets Disposal, National Capital Commission)		
Proprietary Corporations	133,706	72,542
(e.g. CNR, Air Canada, CBC, Polymer)		
Other Agencies	10,057	4,846
(e.g. Bank of Canada, Canadian Wheat Board)		
	383,457	190,150
Corresponding figures:		
May 1966	360,565	$166,923
April 1964	335,552	137,767
April 1959	329,882	107,824

Source: Canada, Dominion Bureau of Statistics, *Federal Government Employment and Payrolls*. Published monthly. See reports for the months indicated.

in piece-rate incentives was based on the wrong assumptions about *why* people work, and the kinds of satisfactions they derive from it. Motivating forces of a quite different sort came to light in the studies of group influence and communication techniques at the Hawthorne, Illinois, works of the Northern Electric Company. The "Hawthorne studies" set the tone for the "human relations" school, pioneered by F. J. Roethlisberger and Elton Mayo. More recently, men like Rensis Likert, Douglas McGregor, Abram Maslow and Frederick Herzberg — to mention only a few — are doing what the physical scientists have done in connection with materiel resources: investigating the properties and other characteristics of people so that they can be employed more effectively and in a way that makes work a more meaningful human experience.

3. Knowledge in itself would do little to improve the management of people at work were it not for a change in the attitudes of the community at large. Since early in this century, society has expressed an increasing concern for human welfare, including the treatment accorded by employers. The law gives employees powerful leverage in pursuit of their own interests by recognizing their right to form associations and by requiring management to negotiate wages and working conditions with them. A management that is harsh, neglectful or indifferent may eventually find itself in violation of other laws on safe working conditions, minimum wages, and employment benefits. In addition, the community can apply economic or political sanctions to an employer who is considered to be guilty of unfair management practices.

4. The typical working man of the 1960's is more highly educated than his father was, and he has a more acute sense of social awareness. In addition to bargaining about wages and working conditions, he is beginning to demand, through his union, a voice in other aspects of management. Productive technology and plant location, for example, have widespread effects on the community, and labour has frequently challenged management's traditional right to make unilateral decisions in these and other matters. So strong is this trend that little credence can be given any longer to the concept of "sacred management prerogatives". The history of labour-management relations makes it clear that yesterday's management prerogatives are circumscribed in today's union contract, and those that management regards as inviolate now, may be on the bargaining tables tomorrow.

5. Continuing high levels of economic activity have made labour scarce and expensive. Fringe benefits, transferable pension rights and guaranteed annual wages add up to a substantial management investment in each employee, whether he continues to be productively employed or not. Increasingly complex technology demands skills which cannot be produced entirely through pre-employment education and management is consequently faced with high costs of training after the worker gets on the job. Frequent changes in technology would mean even higher training costs if management did not build on the skilled and experienced staff it already has.

> When a new computer installation is staffed with retrained employees we have found it to have a far greater chance of success than one staffed by new hires. Aside from the obvious morale advantages the reason for this is really quite simple. It is usually easier to train someone in computer techniques than it is to teach a man your business.[2]

Is is generally accepted in the private sector that competitive success depends more on the quality of people employed by an organization than on technological innovation. The latter will provide at best a temporary advantage which is likely to be overcome by competitors whereas a more competent work force, in particular a creative and capable management group, will be a continuing source of innovation.

Personnel Management and Personnel Administration

Personnel management is that part of management activity which concentrates on making effective use of people in achieving the organization's objectives. For the above reasons personnel management now requires the application of knowledge and skills which supervisors cannot be expected to acquire in addition to mastering the technical side of their jobs. Many aspects of management have become the concern of specialists — finance, law and public relations — and personnel management is no exception. "Personnel administration" is the term applied to the activities of specialists who assist management in the exercise of its personnel functions. These activities can be subsumed under three headings.

Advice. Personnel administrators counsel management on the development and application of personnel policies, and the resolution of problems. They do this in the light of legal requirements imposed by the community and the knowledge about the way people function at work. In this latter respect, their role is analogous to that of the engineer in the physical sciences — they form the link between research and application.

Service. Certain personnel activities which require specialized knowledge and skill are often carried out by personnel administrators as a service to or on behalf of management. The employment office, for example, conducts selective recruitment and tests candidates for basic qualifications, thereby relieving supervisors of the need to interview all but a few candidates to fill a position. Analysts write job descriptions for use in manpower planning, recruitment and training, and they identify and describe factors of significance in the job which are used in establishing wage and salary levels for individual positions.

Control. There are two kinds of control. One involves telling a person what he can or cannot do, and applying sanctions to enforce compliance. The other has come into prominence as a result of developments in cybernetics, and involves monitoring or feedback. This second form of control

---

[2] M. J. Rauseo, "Training Implications of Automated Personnel Systems", *Office Administration*, October 1967.

is the function by which an organization derives information from its own activities, analyzes it, and determines the need for changes. The personnel administrator has a control function in this sense. He *informs* management, for example, about the number and kind of grievances or accidents that are occurring, the incidents of illnesses among individuals or groups of people, and the frequency and causes of labour turnover (particularly resignations and dismissals). And he *advises* management on changes in policy and practices which will bring about improvements.

The proper relationship of personnel administration to management is summed up by describing the personnel officer's work as a staff function. He directs no one but his own subordinates. He advises members of management on policies and practices required for effective personnel management, and he assists them in dealing with specific problems. He may provide services for them, such as the employment office and the central administration of benefit programs. He can and should act as the senior executive's spokesman in dealing with lower levels of management, and as his eyes and ears in ensuring that the approved policies are carried out. This role requires that he be a person of considerable influence. But he must nevertheless respect the right of managers at lower levels to disagree with him and go to the senior executive for a decision. They are not going over his head, for he does not stand between them and the head of the organization. Should he attempt to do so, his influence will be short-lived, for he will have destroyed relationships without which he cannot do his job.

The Influence of the Political Environment

Despite broad and growing similarities, personnel management in the public service is different in many ways from its counterpart in the private sector. One of the principal differences can be identified at the highest level in government organization. In the public service, the concept of management must include the political heads of departments — i.e. the ministers of the Crown. It is commonly thought that the deputy minister — the senior appointed official under the minister — is the top management official in the department, but reference to any of the Acts of Parliament establishing government departments will dispel this notion. For example, section 22(1) of the Government Organization Act (1966) reads as follows:

> "The Minister of Forestry and Rural Development holds office during pleasure and has the management and direction of the Department of Forestry and Rural Development".

If the Minister is a manager, he is also a politician. Indeed, perhaps first and foremost a politician, for he will not remain a minister for long unless he can get elected to Parliament, be re-elected whenever the occasion demands, and exercise considerable political skill in executing his portion of the government's program.

In a commercial enterprise, the product or service must be produced at a profit. In the long run, there must be prospects of a reasonable rate of return on investment to bring the business into being and ensure its continued existence. The profit criterion is at once an important motive underlying plans, policies and decisions, and a yardstick against which their effectiveness can be assessed. Personnel directors in the private sector are in general agreement that one of their chief objectives is to contribute to their firms' profitability.

The pervasive characteristic of the public service is political rather than commercial. The administrator in the public service implements public policies and programs which have been shaped by political forces. His superiors are politicians — leaders of a political party or coalition which obtained, if not a majority, at least the largest number of seats in the House of Commons because it convinced the electorate it had the best program and was best qualified to carry it out. These elected executives will tend to do the things likely to ensure their re-election and to avoid doing things which jeopardize it. The public service is subject to their direction and accountable to them. They in turn are accountable to Parliament for the conduct of the public service and not the least of the senior public servant's concerns is to avoid embarrassing his minister. Thus the political criterion is to the public service what the profit criterion is to industry — the thread which runs through the decisionmaking process, and the standard against which these decisions must ultimately be weighed. That is not to say that every action must be calculated for the political advantage of the party in power any more than every action in business must be calculated to maximize profit. Short-run disadvantages must sometimes be borne and there are many actions whose political consequences are too remote to affect decisions significantly. But in the long-run top management of the public service must on balance redound to the credit of the party in power and in the short-run, actions which may produce adverse political consequences must be avoided as much as possible.

If these considerations are true of management generally in the public service, they are equally true of personnel management in particular. In a commercial organization, personnel policies and actions are evaluated by the profit criterion. The political criterion, however, is a nebulous thing at best and less susceptible to objective estimate. It is more likely to be applied by evaluating the sum of immediate consequences arising out of policies and actions. There is a temptation to regard each personnel action as an opportunity to secure a return of political advantage and to avoid those which are politically dangerous. For example, before the reform of the Canadian Public Service it was generally accepted that the party in power would use its power of appointment to secure or reward political support and the opponents of reform argued that a government must be able to depend on the loyalty of those who administer its policies.

Whatever may be said in theory for personnel practices based on short or long-term political advantage, the results were generally unfortunate

Although political appointees were sometimes people of great ability (MacKenzie King got his start in the public service as a patronage appointee) it was generally true that their qualifications for the job in question were a secondary consideration and frequently even minimum standards of ability were disregarded altogether. Security of tenure was uncertain and few political appointees tended to regard the public service as a career. The inevitable result was a low standard of competence and a poor quality of service to the public. At a time when government activity was highly circumscribed by today's standards, this situation could be tolerated. However, as the activities of the government began to expand, it became more and more necessary to employ people with the highest possible level of technical and administrative ability. To achieve this, methods of appointment and conditions of employment had to be changed.

The Merit Principle and Merit Systems

The merit principle which has replaced the patronage system as one of the cornerstones of personnel policy in the public service is an attempt to abandon political considerations altogether in managing the human resources of the public service. The significance of this policy may not be readily appreciated. To take politics out of public personnel management is to run counter to the very nature of the public service as an organization established to pursue political objectives. However necessary such a course may be, it generates stresses which are comparable to the psychological effects of repression. The political character of the public service which is denied outward expression in personnel management is nonetheless at the root of many of its problems, and accounts for many of its inconsistencies and shortcomings. One of the criteria by which public personnel management must be judged is its ability to cope with this dualism in its own character.

The merit principle is really two interrelated principles:
1. Canadian citizens should have a reasonable opportunity to be considered for employment in the public service
2. Selections must be based exclusively on merit, or fitness to do the job.

These principles are among the most important goals of policy in public personnel management. The merit *system* is the mechanism in use at any given time by which these goals are achieved. The merit principle has become, and should remain, a relatively stable part of our public ethic, although like all ethical tenets it may suffer somewhat in practice. A merit system is an administrative device which can and should be adapted to changing circumstances.

II. The Organization of Public Personnel Administration

The relationships involved in the development and implementation of personnel policy in the Canadian public service have been compared to a triangle, comprising the Treasury Board, the departments and the Public Service Commission. The first two are part of the management structure whereas the third is not. Yet the Commission has had a prominent — indeed until recently the pre-eminent — role in this three-way partnership. How this came about and how the Commission's role has waxed and waned relative to that of management is one of the key elements in the evolution of public personnel policy.

Canada inherited from its colonial antecedents a tradition under which offices in the civil government went to supporters of the party in power. Under the patronage system a change of government was usually followed by the dismissal of partisans of the opposition. Additional posts were created where necessary to provide for the faithful. Appointments were made with more regard for political loyalty than competence. Levels of salary which did not attract the able remained unchanged for more than a generation. The tenure of more than one position, and sub-contracting a position at a lower rate of pay, were commonplace.

The Civil Service Commission: Agent of Reform

Despite these conditions, the first attempts at reform were feeble. A Civil Service Commission responsible directly to Parliament was established in 1908, but its jurisdiction and the system of competitive examination which it inaugurated applied only to positions in Ottawa. During World War I, continued political mismanagement brought the service to a state of near-chaos.

The reforms introduced by the Union Government in 1917 were a drastic remedy for the serious conditions. In one sweep, virtually all the authority of management in personnel administration was stripped away and vested in the Civil Service Commission. The Commission's authority was exclusive in all matters regarding recruitment, selection, promotion, transfer, and the classification of positions. The organization of departments was subject to its scrutiny, even though final approval remained the prerogative of the Governor-in-Council. Pay scales could be changed only in accordance with the Commission's recommendations. Even disciplinary actions such as suspension and demotion were subject to its veto.

Despite the frequent creation of exempt classes and agencies, the personnel system instituted under the Civil Service Act of 1918 continued substantially intact, if not unquestioned, for nearly 50 years. But by the mid-1950's, centralized personnel administration began to break down under its own weight. Cumbersome staffing procedures could not respond quickly enough to secure scarce talent in a continually tight employment market. The system of across-the-board salary increases was a sluggish, undifferentiated, and often inaccurate attempt to maintain a competitive position in the labour market, and to retain staff in the face of attractive opportunities in the prosperous private sector. An increasingly professionalized management *cadre* in departments fretted under the restrictions imposed on them.

Modernizing the Civil Service

In 1958, the Commission published a report entitled *Personnel Administration in the Public Service*[3] in response to a request from the Prime Minister for an enquiry into its own role in the machinery of government. The report recommended a return to the unified service of 1918 by extending the jurisdiction of a modernized Civil Service Act to most of the civilian service. No change was proposed in the basic concepts of the merit principle or the competitive system of selection, but there were many changes designed to streamline their administration. The Commission would retain its exclusive authority in staffing, but be permitted to delegate it to departments. Classification would remain with the Commission, but its role in matters of organization and establishment control would be on a purely consultative basis. It should continue to initiate recommendations on salary and other conditions of employment, but only after presiding over management-staff consultations as a neutral third party. This proposal was made in lieu of any form of collective bargaining for which the civil service was not considered to be ready at that time.

The Commission's report of 1958 was the first step in a process of change whose pace and scope has continued to grow and which shows no sign of slackening. Though many of its recommendations were ignored, the report was the basis for a new Civil Service Act in 1961. This Act did much to modernize procedures, but it did not extend the Commission's jurisdiction to excluded portions of the public service.

The Civil Service Act of 1961 had scarcely been proclaimed in force when other changes of a broader and more profound character were precipitated. The Royal Commission on Government Organization, which had been appointed in 1959, began to publish its recommendations in 1962. The basic theme of the Glassco *Report* is summed up in these excerpts:

> Above all, departments should, within clearly defined terms of reference, be fully accountable for the organization and execution of their programmes, and enjoy powers commensurate with their accountability. They must be subject to controls designed to protect those general interests of government which transcend departmental interests. But every department should be free of external controls which have no such broad purpose.[4]
>
> These proposals for re-allocation of authority and responsibility in the field of manpower management are designed to secure effective use of human resources in the public service. They do so by placing responsibility and the necessary degree of authority to discharge it in the hands of the government's operating management, the only place where the

---

3 Civil Service Commission, *Personnel Administration in the Public Service*, Queen's Printer, Ottawa, 1958.

4 The Royal Commission on Government Organization, *Report*, Vol. 1, Queen's Printer, Ottawa, 1962, p. 51.

necessary links can be forged between people and programmes, between performance and objectives.[5]

Under these basic principles, the Glassco *Report* took serious exception to much of the Commission's operating role in personnel administration and to the authority vested in this non-management agency to control many important personnel functions. Conceding that the public service, unlike the private employer, is open to the pressure of improper influence on appointments, the *Report* recommended that "the Commission should continue to certify all initial appointments to the service, to ensure that selection has been made in accordance with proper standards".[6] But recruitment and selection should be a management responsibility. A common recruiting service provided by the Commission would facilitate an orderly approach to the labour market in many classes, especially those at intermediate and junior levels, but it should be the responsibility of the Treasury Board to determine the extent of that service. Departments should be authorized to recruit their own personnel above a salary of about $5,200, and to make promotions and transfers within guidelines established by the Treasury Board.

These recommendations oversimplified a number of complex problems. How, for example, could the Commission certify to the propriety of a selection in which it had no part? A central recruitment service might be desirable for occupations common to many parts of the public service, but departments which are the sole employer in an occupation (e.g. veterinarians, letter carriers and air traffic controllers) are in a better position to meet their own staffing needs. Many such classes had salaries below $5,200, and would come within the Commission's jurisdiction. No arbitrary salary level could adequately define the jurisdiction of the departments and the central recruiting agency.

When civil service personnel legislation was next amended it was the rearrangement of authorities required to implement collective bargaining more than the Glassco recommendations which influenced the measures that were passed. In 1966, Parliament passed three pieces of legislation which were proclaimed in force in March, 1967:

1. the Public Service Employment Act (replacing the Civil Service Act)
2. amendments to the Financial Administration Act
3. the Public Service Staff Relations Act.

All three had a bearing on the future role of the Commission. The first established a Public Service Commission to regulate staffing in the portion of the public service over which the former Civil Service Commission had jurisdiction. In addition, prevailing rate employees and ships' crews, previously exempt, were brought under the Act and provision was made to

---

[5] *Ibid.*, p. 300.
[6] *Ibid.*, p. 321.

extend it by Order-in-Council to other parts of the service. The amendments to the Financial Administration Act transferred responsibility for position classification to the Treasury Board. The Public Service Staff Relations Act included terms which made the new Public Service Staff Relations Board responsible for pay research and for hearing grievances on disciplinary matters which were previously the subject of appeals to the Commission.

Service or Control?

The legislative changes of 1967 brought about much of what Glassco had recommended regarding the role of the Commission. Only staffing remains as a statutory responsibility. Its training and management consulting services could as readily be provided to departments by the Treasury Board and it is by no means certain that they will not eventually be transferred there. The Commission's appellate function is limited to matters arising out of the administration of the merit system in promotions and transfers, and to cases in which an employee's release from the service is recommended for incompetence or inability to perform his duties. Pay rates and other conditions of employment, previously recommended by the Commission, will be established unilaterally by the Treasury Board until collective agreements are negotiated for the various occupational groups.

Despite these changes, the Public Service Commission is not the service agency advocated by Glassco. By law it retains exclusive jurisdiction in the recruitment, selection, promotion and transfer of employees in agencies which are subject to the Public Service Employment Act. Although it may delegate its authority, it retains final responsibility and the power to prescribe policies, standards and procedures. It can revoke appointments which it deems to have been improperly made and it can withdraw delegated authority if departments do not properly exercise it. In short, the Commission provides a staffing service, but not one which departments have any choice about using. It does so in order that it may control staffing in the public service. Control is the objective — service is only the means.

The Alternative to Control

If the Commission remains mainly a control agency, it is because other methods have not been used to ensure that improper pressures do not influence staffing. Yet other methods are available. In financial administration, reform was accomplished without removing management's operating authority. The Auditor General, like the Public Service Commission, is responsible directly to Parliament and hence is outside the management structure in the public service. Unlike the Commission, however, he has no authority except to determine, after the fact, whether funds have been spent in accordance with the authority voted by Parliament and whether adequate measures have been taken to account for revenues and to safeguard public property. His only means of exerting influence are his annual report to Parliament and the day-to-day consultations between his staff and departmental officers. Nevertheless, these influences have proven to be very powerful indeed.

In the United States, many state public service commissions have a watch-dog function similar to the Auditor General's. Authority in all personnel matters is vested in management. The Commission has access to records and the authority to conduct hearings, and is required to report to the legislature on the administration of the merit system. Sometimes it is also required to review personnel regulations before they are enacted and to hear appeals from employees against alleged improper recruitment and selection. In these circumstances the Commission can remain independent, non-political and above all influential, without displacing management in some of its most important functions.

This alternative to the present division of authority between management and the Public Service Commission has never been seriously considered in Canada. Personnel administration is still organized as though political patronage were the main obstacle to efficiency in the public service – as indeed it was before the reform of 1918. Today, the major problem in personnel management is the effective utilization of a work force that numbers over 200,000 employees and continues to increase by about three per cent each year. The continuing division of authority between the Commission and the Treasury Board makes manpower management more difficult and less effective despite the best efforts and intentions of the parties involved. It is time to ask whether the price exacted for present methods of protection against patronage is too high.

ORGANIZATION STRUCTURE OF THE PUBLIC SERVICE COMMISSION

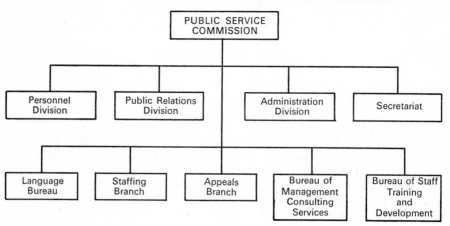

Central Management: The Treasury Board

The federal Cabinet has a number of committees through which it seeks to expedite the conduct of government business. The most important of these is the Treasury Board. The Board was established in 1867 and for many years it was concerned exclusively with financial management, reviewing departmental statements of income and expenditure, and estimates of future spending. For most of its existence it had little to do with personnel management directly, even during the period of reform which was inaugurated by the Civil Service Act of 1918.

During the depression of the 1930's, an acutely cost-conscious government gave the Board the power to restrict the increase of, and if necessary to abolish, permanent civil service positions, to curtail promotions and to reduce salaries. These controls were carried over into World War II, and new ones were introduced — among them a virtual freeze on the reclassification of positions. Restrictions on the creation of permanent positions were continued and many civil servants spent the better part of their career as "temporaries", denied pension rights and certain other benefits of permanent employment. During the war many new government agencies were established under legislation which exempted them from the personnel regime of the Civil Service Act. The Board stepped in to prescribe working conditions and salary schedules for many such agencies and gradually was drawn into broader questions of personnel regulation.

By the end of the war, the Board had firmly established a major role in public personnel management. But it was preoccupied with the financial implications of decisions on personnel matters and sought to keep costs to a minimum by retaining decision-making authority in a myriad of trivial administrative matters. Trapped by its own devices into dealing with literally hundreds of departmental recommendations each week, the Board and its staff had little time to devote to planning, the review of policy, or establishing criteria for effective management in the public service.

The Glassco Royal Commission on Government Organization made the Treasury Board one of the chief targets for criticism in its initial *Report*. The Board was criticized for excessive concern with administrative details, for a narrow emphasis on financial control and for failing to exert leadership in the management of the public service. Among the Commission's most important recommendations was the separation of the Board from the Department of Finance and the creation of a separate Cabinet post — President of the Treasury Board. The *Report* also recommended an organization structure for the Board's staff to include, under a Secretary of deputy minister rank, three divisions dealing with the review of government programs, personnel policy and management improvement.

In 1963 all federal political parties committed themselves to support a form of collective bargaining in the public service. When the Public Service Staff Relations Act was passed in 1967, the Treasury Board became the employer for most of the public service. In keeping with its new responsibility for negotiating and implementing collective agreements, the Board was also given the responsibility for position classification in the service — a function previously administered by the Public Service Commission.

The Board is now clearly identified as the central management agency in the public service. The Personnel Policy Branch, headed by an Assistant Secretary, was completely reorganized in 1966 as part of the reconstitution recommended by Glassco. It is responsible for "all aspects of personnel policy affecting the civilian Public Service (except those reserved to the Public Service Commission under the provisions of the Public Service Employment Act) and is also heavily involved in the review of personnel policy proposals affecting the Canadian Forces and the R.C.M.P. The Branch has five Divisions, one concerned with planning and coordination, one with manpower utilization, one with classification and salary administration, one with compensation and conditions, one with staff relations".[7]

In keeping with the policy of disengagement from detail, the Branch has made substantial progress in developing policy guidelines within which decision-making authority is being delegated to departments. Most important of all, it has assumed an effective management role in areas of personnel policy which, until recently, were largely ignored or left by default to the Public Service Commission: notably, training policy, manpower planning, and staff development.

Personnel Administration in the Departments

The removal of most of the responsibility in personnel matters from management obviated a role for personnel specialists in departments for many years. Deputy ministers had little authority in personnel management and accordingly accepted little responsibility for it. Their departments were small enough during the 1920's and 1930's that they could take an active personal role in many appointments, promotions and classification matters. The personnel specialist's role developed around the clerical activities in payroll, leave and attendance left behind when accounting services were centralized under the Comptroller of the Treasury in 1931.

During World War II many thousands of temporary employees had to be recruited under conditions of an acute labour shortage and had to be trained in duties which reflected new functions of government. Departments found it necessary to assign senior people to carry out the recruitment, organization and training of this greatly expanded work force. In 1946 the Royal Commission on Administrative Classes of the Public Service, under the chairmanship of Walter Gordon, criticized the generally rudimentary machinery for the administration of departmental personnel matters and recommended "the appointment in every department of an experienced and properly qualified personnel officer with adequate rank and power" as the means of promoting general efficiency, improving staff

---

[7] J. D. Love, Assistant Secretary (Personnel), Treasury Board, in a speech to the Ottawa Branch of the Public Personnel Association, October 17, 1967.

ORGANIZATION STRUCTURE OF THE PERSONNEL POLICY BRANCH

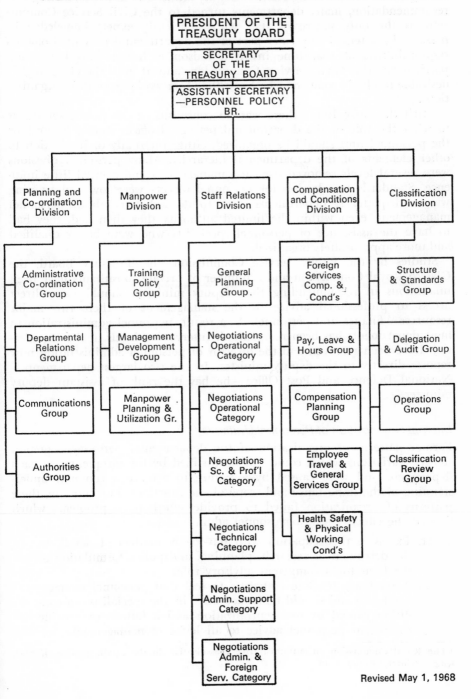

Revised May 1, 1968

management and affording relief to deputy ministers.[8] In implementing this recommendation, many departments turned to the Civil Service Commission as the only source of staff with sufficiently expert knowledge in personnel matters. The greater part of the departmental personnel officer's responsibilities at that time involved liaison with the central agencies, particularly the Civil Service Commission and it was therefore highly desirable to obtain someone who knew the inner workings of these organizations.

Until the early 1960's there was no consensus in the public service as to what the role of the departmental personnel officer should be or how the personnel unit should be organized, either internally or in relation to other elements of the departmental hierarchy. Many personnel divisions were several levels removed from top management and exerted little influence. Standards of selection for personnel officers were low and training was inadequate. If departments were to do a better job of personnel management, even within the limited authority they then had, they had to have the assistance of personnel specialists who were better qualified and more appropriately organized.

Studies by the Public Service Commission, the Treasury Board, the Glassco Royal Commission and a number of private consultants have been unanimous in recommending that deputy ministers should have direct access to professional advice in the management of their two major resources — finance and personnel. As a result, personnel administration in most departments has been reorganized. Intervening levels in the organization have been removed and the director of personnel administration now reports directly to the deputy minister. In the two largest departments — National Defence and Post Office — he has the rank of assistant deputy minister.

Internal Organization of Personnel Units

Former patterns of organization of the departmental personnel function showed variations which could not be justified by the uniqueness of each department and were caused by a failure to achieve a common understanding of the importance and scope of the functions. Furthermore, these patterns of organization failed to provide solutions to problems which limited the effectiveness of personnel administration:

1. Excessive preoccupation with day-to-day matters of detail, to the detriment of research, planning, and policy formulation as the basis for a competent advisory role
2. A tendency for line managers to feel that personnel management will and should be looked after by the specialists — a condition caused by over-centralization and a failure to provide competent personnel advice to all levels of management

[8] The Royal Commission on Administrative Classification in the Public Service, *Report*, King's Printer, Ottawa, 1946.

3. Stunted development of important areas of personnel administration, such as health, safety, staff relations and employee communications.

The organization of most personnel divisions now follows a pattern developed by Chairman of the Public Service Commission J. J. Carson, previously the head of the Glassco task force study of personnel management. The Carson Model is based on an important premise — that almost all day-to-day personnel administration be conducted by officers responsible to their branch directors or field unit heads. The central personnel unit in the department should be responsible for the functional guidance of these officers whose role would be to advise line officers closest to the problems. In this way the central unit would be free to concentrate on the development and evaluation of policy, while line officers would have advice more directly available to them in the fulfillment of their responsibilities for personnel management.

A MODEL ORGANIZATION PLAN FOR DEPARTMENTAL PERSONNEL UNITS

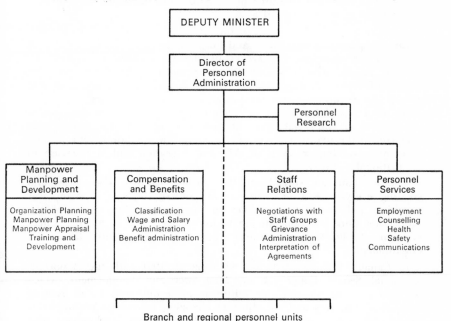

III. Manpower Planning and Staffing

In the first two decades of this century the patronage system was the chief obstacle to efficiency in the public service and hence the chief target of reform measures. In the personnel revolution of the 1960's, the focus of concern has shifted to the broader question of efficient use of manpower.

The continuing increase in the number of public servants has prompted many explanations, ranging from the never-ending demand for government services to Parkinson's observation that the increase of officialdom proceeds under immutable laws which have nothing whatever to do with the services required of the organization.[9]

The growing concern of politicians, economists and public administrators about employment levels in the public service is only one aspect of a much more complex problem described by J. D. Love, Assistant Secretary of the Treasury Board:

> For an explanation of the widespread current interest in manpower planning, one has to go back to the end of World War II, when patterns of thought in most industrialized countries were heavily influenced by fears that the postwar period would be plagued by a return of the type of unemployment that had characterized the 1930's. Within these patterns of thought, concern with anticipated problems of labour surplus left little room for concepts based on more optimistic assumptions. Blinkers fashioned by the Great Depression made it difficult for men to see manpower as a potentially scarce resource in an expanding peacetime society. And the blinkers were slow to fall away.
>
> It was only in the latter part of the 1950's that a basic shift in outlook began to appear, as economists and businessmen and men in public life began to appreciate the implications of what Galbraith was eventually to describe as the Affluent Society. They began to realize that, under the impact of an expanding demand for goods and services at home and abroad, the requirement for manpower would continue to grow, pressing hard against available resources. They began to realize also that, under the impact of industrial diversification and technological change, the character of the requirement would be altered in significant ways, placing a premium on higher levels of skill and education and an increase in occupational mobility.
>
> The new outlook spread rapidly, crossing national boundaries and creating everywhere a new interest in positive concepts of manpower planning and positive approaches to manpower policy. Some of the pioneering work was done in the United States, some in Europe, where creation of the Common Market provided an especially favourable environment.
>
> In Canada, the big break-through came in 1961 with the Report of a Special Senate Committee on Manpower and Employment, which sounded a strong warning that failure to make optimum use of existing manpower resources and to adjust to changing manpower requirements would place severe restrictions on national growth and development. The theme was picked up and given more concrete expression by the Economic Council of Canada, whose first Chairman, Dr. John Deutsch, had been a key witness before the Senate Committee. And, in 1965, with the creation of a new Department of Manpower and Immigration, it was imbedded in Government policy.

---

9 C. N. Parkinson, *Parkinson's Law and Other Studies in Administration*, Houghton Mifflin, Boston, Massachusetts, 1957.

Similar developments have occurred elsewhere, until now it can be said, without fear of exaggeration, that policies designed to achieve more effective use of manpower resources are a major concern of governments throughout the world.

Not surprisingly, these developments have created a climate conducive to manpower planning in private corporations and public services. Indeed, the recent emphasis on manpower as a national resource has served to stimulate and give greater status to the personnel function generally.

The tie-in has been very marked in the Public Service of Canada where, as you know, the whole approach to personnel management has been thoroughly re-worked in the past five years. Much of the stimulus for our programme of reform came from the decision of the Government to introduce a full-scale system of collective bargaining, but the foundation was clearly laid by the recommendations of the Royal Commission on Government Organization. . . . There is no doubt that both the Report of the Royal Commission and the manner in which it was received were influenced by the work of the Senate Committee on Manpower, whose findings were made public during the period when the Glassco investigators were at work. There is also no doubt that continuing support for the programme since that time has been due in part to the emphasis placed on more effective manpower utilization by the Economic Council of Canada and, of course, by the Government of Canada itself. A Government committed to a national manpower policy could hardly fail to concern itself with the quality of personnel management in its own Public Service.[10]

Determining Manpower Needs

Until the early 1950's, government departments sought the approval of the Treasury Board to employ additional staff whenever the need became evident. Beginning in 1954, the Board inaugurated an annual "establishment review" and departments were required to forecast their requirements as much as six months prior to the beginning of the fiscal year. The review consisted of a series of meetings between departmental and Treasury Board officials, and tended to deal almost exclusively with proposed additions to the staff complement, rather than with the total use of manpower in relation to program priorities. Often the discussions weltered in minutiae and ended in a compromise between what the department considered essential and the Board's staff considered reasonable, with neither party having much objective evidence to support its position.

In an effort to reduce its control of details, so much criticized by the Glassco Commission, the Board began in 1963 to set manpower ceilings within which each department could add to or adjust its establishment as it saw fit. At the same time it introduced a requirement for five-year

10 J. D. Love, Assistant Secretary (Personnel), Treasury Board, in a speech to the International Conference of the Public Personnel Association, Vancouver and Victoria, October 1967.

forecast of departmental program plans and the financial and manpower resources required to meet them. The techniques of program planning and resource forecasting are still imperfect in many ways, but the new approach has the advantage of focusing on program planning as a total entity and projecting plans over a longer period. It increases the likelihood that outmoded activities and low priority programs which absorb manpower without contributing proportionally to the achievement of objectives will be scrutinized more frequently and more closely. And it has made managers at all levels more acutely conscious of the phenomenon of manpower increase and the need to contain it.

Manpower Utilization

The total size of the public service work force is a function of many factors, including the programs to which various departments and agencies are committed, the tools and techniques they employ, and — by no means least — the extent to which the abilities of each employee are fully utilized. The aphorism calling for "the right man in the right job at the right time" summarizes, if it oversimplifies, the objectives of manpower utilization. People are not static. They have both a capacity and an aspiration for personal growth and development.[11] Every organization has a responsibility to itself and to the people it employs to foster that development in directions that are mutually advantageous. To achieve this, carefully planned career programs must be developed.

Career planning can be described in many ways, but its fundamentals include:

> a careful and detailed forecast of the organization's future manpower requirements, by occupation and level — the longer the forecast period, the more lead-time the organization has to plan effectively for meeting these needs
>
> an assessment of each employee's ability and motivation to increase his performance capacity in a way which will meet the organization's manpower needs
>
> a plan of development for each employee, including formal training and on-the-job experience which is varied and progressively challenging recognition of achievement.

All of these elements have been deficient in the traditional approach to career progression in the public service. Jobs have tended to be defined in terms of activities the employee is to perform, rather than what he is expected to achieve — i.e., procedures rather than objectives. Management has been highly centralized and managers have exercised close and detailed control on how the job is done, assuming that in this way the achievement

---

11 F. Herzberg, *Work and the Nature of Man*, World Publishing, Cleveland, Ohio, 1966, p. 56.

of results will take care of itself. Recognition of achievement has been largely undifferentiated except through promotion, because in-grade merit increases have been fixed in amount (usually very small) and frequency (annual or semi-annual), and have become so much a vested right that the denial of an increase was until recently grounds for appeal to the Public Service Commission.

The merit system — i.e., the administrative method by which the merit principle is implemented — has been synonymous with the advertised competitive examinations for filling positions. The competitive method is time-consuming and unwieldy at best, and the marked tendency to confine promotion competitions to a single department or branch has created barriers to the mobility and development of talented people. Information on the performance and abilities of candidates has been so unreliable and incomplete that the choice of a successful candidate has rested heavily upon the impression made in a single interview. The strong emphasis on current qualifications for the position under competition has made it difficult for management to consider long-term needs, such as the appointment of a person with less immediate ability but with greater potential. Planned career assignments are difficult under a system which relies on the sometimes unpredictable outcome of competitions to determine who will be appointed. Left to his own resources in finding opportunities for advancement through the competitive system, an employee has had to consider the immediate opportunity rather than vague future prospects which management has lacked the means to bring to fruition.

Despite these handicaps many capable people have found satisfying and rewarding careers in the public service, but there has also been a great waste of talented people who resigned in frustration and a great deal of latent ability which is only partly utilized. Consequently public administrators have sought a system of staffing and manpower development which can reconcile the needs and interests of both management and the employee. In recent years that search has borne fruit in staffing methods which are breaking away from the traditional competitive method and techniques of manpower planning and development which are more imaginative in concept and broader in their application.

Manpower Inventories

Most organizations devote a great deal of effort to updating their physical inventories and have developed elaborate administrative techniques for this. Yet few have given more than passing attention to their more costly and potentially much more valuable human assets.

In its simplest terms, a manpower inventory is a systematic way of recording the knowledge, experience, capabilities and interests of an organization's work force. It normally contains three kinds of data:

1. "tombstone" or basic identification — name, age, sex, and so on

2. quantitative data on length and type of education, training and experience
3. qualitative assessments on how well the employee has performed, his strengths and shortcomings, and his interest in and potential for development.

The third category is essentially a matter of judgement, and must be based on an appraisal of the employee. If a manpower inventory is to be effective, it must be updated with periodical reappraisals at intervals sufficiently frequent to keep the information valid for decisionmaking.

Manpower inventories can be compiled for an occupation within a department or for occupations that cut across the public service. They can include an entire occupation or only a segment of it. They can be limited to people in the occupation or they can include people in other occupations who, on the basis of appraisal, can be considered as prospects. The tombstone and quantitative information can be recorded for mechanized retrieval where the numbers of employees in the occupation make this desirable to speed up the identification of employees who fall within specified parameters. The two most important requirements of an inventory are that it be

1. complete — that is, contain all of the people in the occupation or the defined occupational segment, and
2. current — processes must be carefully worked out to ensure that the information is kept up to date.

Once it is established, an inventory can be much more satisfactory than the advertised competition as a means of identifying candidates for promotion or transfer. Its many advantages include:

speed — there is no need to post notices and wait a month or so before being able to evaluate candidates, employees with appropriate basic qualifications (education, training and experience) can be identified in a search that may take a few hours, or as little as a few minutes with automation
completeness — all employees in the inventory are automatically subject to consideration and there is no danger of missing a good prospect who did not see the poster
validity — systematic appraisals provide a much more complete and accurate source of information than is otherwise available on a candidate's performance and qualifications.

The initial identification of candidates with basic qualifications is followed by a further screening based on the appraisal reports. A small group of candidates can then be interviewed. If the staffing legislation provides for the right to appeal the resulting selection, that right is available in the same manner as if a competition had been held. All employees in the inventory can be notified of the results and given the right of appeal, or it can be limited to the segment from which the selection was made (e.g., for a Financial Administration 8 position, the inventory segment might be levels 6 and 7).

Staffing by the manpower inventory and appraisal method is not appointment without competition. In a sense it is competition without advertisement. It is a new merit system which guarantees more effective and more complete adherence to the basic elements of the merit principle — opportunity to be considered and an objective assessment of qualifications.

Delegation of Staffing

Although the Glassco recommendations on the staffing role of the Public Service Commission have not been accepted as government policy, the Commission has accepted the merits of decentralizing its authority both to its own regional offices and to departments. Under a plan recently introduced, the Canada Manpower Centres will assume much of the Commission's role in the recruitment and basic testing of candidates. Departments will be delegated the authority to make selections from among the candidates referred to them by the Manpower Centre, which will have a role in relation to public employment very similar to the service it provides to the private sector. Under a phased plan beginning with clerical, stenographic and blue collar occupations in 1968, the Commission's staffing role will be largely decentralized by 1970. It will continue to administer programs to select university and technological institute graduates, in shortage occupations and in certain other key classes such as the executive category. For the remainder, its role will be limited to establishing policies, standards and procedures and auditing the exercise of delegation.

Improvements in Career Planning

Manpower inventories have been established or are in the process of being established for most of the occupational groups in the administrative and foreign service category, and studies are under way to apply similar methods in the scientific and professional, and technical categories. These techniques can facilitate staff development and career planning, but other important measures must also be taken. Some of these have been incorporated in recent legislative and procedural changes in the public service.

1. The right of employees to appeal the lateral movement of another employee from one position to another at the same salary level was eliminated in the Public Service Employment Act of 1967. This removed a formidable barrier to the mobility of the work force.

2. In certain occupations, notably personnel and financial administration, it is now accepted that the stage on which an employee's career role will be played is service-wide and the tendency to limit careers to a single department is being overcome.

3. Career-planning guidelines are being established on a trial basis for certain occupations and the lessons learned will enable improvements to be made when similar guidelines are developed for other occupations. These guidelines endeavour to balance management and employee interests under a rational staffing policy which permits planned assignments, varied experience, periodical consideration for promotion, and a reduction of raiding between departments.

4. Manpower planning and development is now recognized as a sub-specialization of the personnel function and provision for its exercise is being made in the organization of the Treasury Board and departments. This function includes organization planning, the analysis of manpower requirements, employee evaluation, and training and development.

5. Long-term staff development programs such as the recently announced Career Assignment Program are being introduced. These programs include formal training and planned work assignments lasting several years, requiring the assumption of responsibility and the achievement of results fully commensurate with the employee's salary level. They are primarily a departmental responsibility within policy guidelines set by central management. And they use the facilities of the Public Service Commission to supplement departmental training resources and to effect interdepartmental assignments.

6. Financial barriers to interregional mobility are being reduced by compensating employees for some of the cost of buying and selling homes, and for incidental expenses which were not previously admissible under the travel and removal regulations.

7. Rules governing in-grade salary increases have been altered in a number of classes to permit more appropriate recognition of superior performance. Instead of the one-increase-a-year which became virtually automatic, deputy ministers can now grant increases of varying amounts, depending on the calibre of an officer's work in relation to that of his peers. Performance pay budgets have been designed in such a way that larger increases for the best performers must be balanced by smaller increases or none at all for others. Varying forms of performance pay are now applicable in the executive category, the upper two or three levels of the administrative and foreign service category, and in the research scientist class. Similar plans will probably be instituted for other scientific and professional classes, and perhaps also for lower levels in the administrative and foreign service category.

Training

Training is the process through which an employee acquires the knowledge, skills and attitudes required to make him fully effective in doing his job. Along with other techniques, such as planned work assignments, it is one of the elements in his development toward positions of greater responsibility. The public service has a particularly great demand for training of all kinds. It employs a greater variety of occupational skills than any other organization, including many that are unique to government. Like all employers, it must cope with rapid technological change. And the service it provides to the public is subject to frequent change, sometimes on short notice, because of the introduction of new government programs.

Training activities in the public service are so extensive and varied that a book could be devoted to their cataloguing. For example, in addition to the induction, skill, supervisory and management training found in all larger organizations, government must train *ab initio* in a number of highly complex fields such as air traffic control and meteorology. It must adapt basic professional skills in engineering and accounting to unique job requirements in purchasing and contract administration. As the largest employer of physical, biological and social scientists in the country, it sponsors post-graduate education for several hundred employees each year. In recent years it has undertaken the massive task of training thousands of employees to serve the public in both official languages.

The Treasury Board is responsible for training policy in the public service and for determining the resources to be allocated for this purpose. Most training programs are administered by the departments. The Public Service Commission interprets its mandate in staffing to include all measures required to meet the needs of the service for qualified personnel. Its Training and Development Branch conducts courses in administrative and managerial skills which are common to all departments and will assist them in developing training programs of their own.

Their is no overt conflict between the role of management and the Commission in training and staff development. But neither is there any necessity for the Commission to supplement its role as the guardian of the merit principle in this way. In this, as in other fields of personnel administration, the present division of authority and responsibility bears continued and critical examination.

IV. Wage and Salary Administration

One of the most important factors in building morale and efficiency in the public service is an orderly, systematic method of pay determination which ensures the taxpayer a fair return for the money he spends on government services and the employee an equitable income in return for the work he does. Of all the iniquitous results of the patronage system, none was more offensive to the sense of justice than the wide variations in salaries paid for similar work. The Royal Commission of 1907 reported differences of as much as 300 per cent between the salaries of different employees doing substantially the same job.[12] These anomalies were often less the result of overt political interference than the almost complete lack of a system for determining the worth of duties performed.

---

12 The Royal Commission on the Civil Service, *Report*, King's Printer, Ottawa, 1907.

Hard on the heels of the legislative reforms in the Civil Service Act of 1918, the government contracted with an American management consulting firm — Arthur Young and Company — to establish a job classification plan which was made the law of the land by an amendment to the Civil Service Act in 1919. The new classification plan was a triumph of the scientific management school. Detailed specifications and qualification requirements were written for literally hundreds of different jobs and each class was given its own set of pay scales. Job summaries were written for each class, and in theory at least, whenever a vacancy arose, recruitment to fill it was simply a matter of printing these standard duties and qualifications in an advertisement. Standard jobs, standard qualifications, standard pay scales and standard within-grade increases — this classification plan sought to master laxity by rigidity. But every job and every employee did not conform to the blueprint and the subsequent history of the classification plan records the ever-increasing complications which arose in an attempt to accommodate the growing number of exceptions.

Because the Civil Service Commission had already been cast as the agency of reform in the civil service it was also given responsibility for administering the classification plan. In this respect Canada followed the example of the United States rather than that of the United Kingdom where the Treasury has always had the primary responsibility for pay determination, including the classification plan.

Reform of the Classification System

The classification plan of 1919 contained a different grade structure and pay plan for every definable occupation, and was complicated enough even when it was introduced. It became more complex each year as changes were introduced to meet new or different conditions. Within a few years, there were more than 2,200 classes and in 1929 a royal commission recommended the scheme be simplified. However, retrenchment during the 1930's and the administrative priorities of World War II prevented action. Another royal commission[13] noted in 1946 that the number of classes had risen to 3,700, excluding the hourly-paid classes. There was some reduction in the next decade but as recently as 1964 there were 2,400 classes and grades with approximately 320 different salary ranges. There are a further 1,250 job titles covering the hourly-paid groups.

Reform of the classification system was forced by the government's commitment to introduce a form of collective bargaining. Pay rates are attached to the classification plan and administration of the plan in turn affects average pay levels, and therefore the entire pay structure. There could be no rational bargaining about pay rates until the occupational content of the various classes was made more consistent. Consequently, the government's Preparatory Committee on Collective Bargaining not only set a

13 The Royal Commission on the Administrative Classification, *op. cit.*, p. 14.

high priority on a reform of the classification system, but also recommended certain principles on which the reforms should be based.[14] These principles were accepted by the government and in 1965 the Civil Service Commission established the Bureau of Classification Revision to apply them in a complete overhaul of the classification system. Conversion to the new classification plan is expected to be completed by the end of 1968.

The Objectives of Reform

1. To establish a system in which pay rates and associated conditions of work could respond flexibly to competitive pressures from outside the service, while preserving as far as possible important relativities within the service, requires a structure of many parts which may move independently of each other.
2. The plan should be as simple as possible, to facilitate comprehension and ease of communication in collective bargaining.
3. It should permit different approaches to personnel administration for different types of employees.
4. The plan should facilitate rather than impede career planning and personal development.
5. Provision should be made for strong incentives to superior performance, and in particular, should facilitate the introduction of salary administration arrangements comparable to those of the Research Scientist and Senior Officer classes, where they are considered appropriate.
6. The system should be designed to permit extensive delegation of operational authority to departments.

The Preparatory Committee proposed that grouping jobs be approached on two levels. The first is the occupational category — a broad series of divisions characterized by similarity of educational requirements and the need for common approaches in classification, pay and other conditions of employment. The second is the occupational group — each one a category segment composed of employees with similar skills performing similar kinds of work and wherever possible bearing a relationship to an identifiable labour market outside the service.

The following diagram illustrates the structure of occupational categories and groups:

The Bureau of Classification Revision has so far identified and defined 72 occupational groups.

Each category must be examined to develop a classification and pay structure, and classification standards, suited to the needs of each group within it. In the classes developed to date there has been a significant improvement in the clarity of standards. This has been achieved in part

[14] Report of the Preparatory Committee on Collective Bargaining, Queen's Printer, Ottawa, 1965, pp. 12-14.

by a reduction in the number of grade levels, with the result that differences in grade characteristics can be more clearly described.

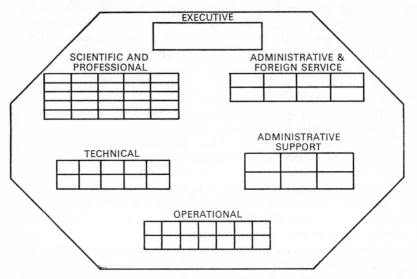

After considerable research the Bureau concluded that the grade-description method of job evaluation was best suited to the needs of many public service classes, mainly because it is the least complex to apply when suitable standards have been developed. However there are a number of occupations, of which the Administrative Support category contains several, composed of too many different jobs to permit identification in this way. Consequently, a modified form of the point-rating system[15] has been developed. This marks the first time that methods of job evaluation other than grade description have been applied in the federal public service.

Amendments to the Financial Administration Act passed in 1966 transferred responsibility for administering the classification system from the Public Services Commission to the Treasury Board. This step was an essential concomitant of collective bargaining. The agency which bargains for management must be in a position to implement agreements and its authority must therefore include the classification system which exercises a significant influence on pay levels in the service. However, the Treasury Board intends to keep its operating role in classification to a minimum. The new classification plan is being designed to facilitate delegation. As conversion to the new occupational groups progresses, decision-making authority is being delegated to departments. The Board's role will be to establish policy and standards, and audit departmental decisions. It will retain a decision-making role only in a few of the most senior classes.

---

[15] For detailed descriptions of the various methods of job evaluation, including point rating, see J. L. Otis and R. H. Leukhart, *Job Evaluation*, 2nd ed., Prentice-Hall, Englewood Cliffs, New Jersey, 1954.

39 The Introduction of Collective Bargaining in the Federal Public Service*

L. B. Pearson

That it is expedient to introduce a measure to provide for the establishment of a system of collective bargaining applicable to employees in the public service of Canada and for the resolution of disputes that may arise in the negotiation or conclusion of collective agreements applicable to such employees; to establish a process for the presentation of grievances of employees arising in connection with their employment and to establish a system for the adjudication of grievances of employees; to provide for the establishment of a board, to be known as the Public Service Staff Relations Board, which shall be responsible for the administration of the said measure and to provide further for the constitution and appointment of such other authorities, officers and employees as are required in connection with the administration of the said measure.

The object of this resolution is to make possible the introduction of legislation which will in its turn make possible the introduction into the public service of Canada of an appropriate system of collective bargaining.

The principle that public servants should have an opportunity to participate in such a system has, I believe, widespread support in the Canadian community. It is a principle which I think I can say is accepted by all parties represented in this House. It is our hope that the legislation which embodies this principle and which, if this resolution carries, will be placed before hon. members for their consideration and ultimate approval, will prove to be an effective instrument for the regulation of employer-employee relationships in the public service.

The legislation forecast in this resolution will rightly be regarded as a measure of very great significance in the history of the public service. For those who have customarily been identified as servants of the Crown, that is, servants of the people and whose terms and conditions of employment have been determined by Parliament or by the government of the day, this legislation will provide the right to participate in a process of joint determination of the terms and conditions of their employment. This is a process which is rooted in the concept of equity and equality between the government as employer and organizations representing its employees. Such a change will call for major adjustments in established processes and procedures and in the traditional attitude of all those who are concerned.

The legislation proposed by this resolution has been long in preparation - properly so, I believe, in view of its far-reaching implications and importance. The preparatory committee on collective bargaining under the distinguished chairmanship of a great Canadian public servant, Mr.

Excerpts from a Statement of the Prime Minister, the Rt. Hon. L. B. Pearson, in the House of Commons, April 25, 1966, pp. 4,242-4,244.

Arnold Heeney, was established in August of 1963. This committee of senior officials was asked by the government to prepare for the introduction into the public service of an appropriate form of collective bargaining and arbitration, and in doing so to examine the need for reforms in the system of classification and pay applying to civil servants and prevailing-rate employees. Supported by a staff of very competent experts, the preparatory committee met regularly during a two-year period. In the course of its deliberations it received briefs from and consulted with interested employee organizations. It also consulted a number of distinguished persons from the universities, from industry and from provincial and municipal governments. Its report to the government, made in June of last year, was tabled almost immediately and is, of course, available to hon. members.

The proposals contained in the preparatory committee's report which relate to the reforms in the classification system were welcomed by the government and after discussion with the Civil Service Commission the were approved. A program to convert all positions in the civil service to the new plan of classification was immediately undertaken and is expected to be completed next year. The reforms in the system of classification are of great importance to the successful introduction of a system of collective bargaining, since it is intended that the groupings established by the classification system will constitute the basis of the collective bargaining relationship.

The statutory reforms in the administration of the public service which are contemplated in this legislative program are, in the view of the government, no less significant than the reforms instituted by the Civil Service Act of 1918 which in essence constituted the beginning of our civil service as we know it today. It is the government's hope and expectation that the changes which will be brought about by this legislation, if it meets Parliamentary approval, will ensure that the public service of Canada in the years to come will have the administrative capacity and flexibility to adjust to the changing demands of the Canadian community which it serves.

It has been and is now, a civil service unexcelled in any country in the world and equalled by few. I hope that the changes now proposed will help to maintain that proud position.

When the report of the Royal Commission on Government Organization was first published, that is, the Glassco Commission, its stress on managerial authority was seen in some quarters as a threat to the traditional security of civil servants. The proposal to transfer a significant measure of authority from the independent Civil Service Commission to the Treasury Board and to departmental management was regarded at the time with some apprehension by employee organizations and by others.

It was argued that, if much of the traditional protection afforded employees by the involvement of the Commission in the determination of pay and the regulation of other conditions of employment were to be removed, employees themselves should be given the right to protect their own interest through appropriate collective bargaining procedures comparable with those available to employees in the private sector of the community. The argument was an impressive and persuasive one, and it has done much to establish the environment in which the new legislation was considered by the government.

In developing this new legislation the government has had certain general objectives in mind: First, to protect the public interest; second, to respond in an understanding and responsible manner to the aims and aspirations of its organized employees; third, to preserve the capacity of the public service to function efficiently in serving the people of Canada; and fourth, to respect the principles underlying industrial relations law and practice in Canada. In their evaluation of proposals made by the government I am sure members of the house will want to keep all these objectives very much in mind.

40   The Public Service Staff Relations Act*

The passing of the Public Service Staff Relations Act marks a momentous step forward in employer-employee relations in the public service of the federal government of Canada. It was introduced to the House of Commons in April 1966 by the Prime Minister; received first reading on April 25, second reading May 31 and was then referred to a special joint committee. The committee studied the act in 48 meetings and heard 47 witnesses, and finally reported back with a number of suggestions for amendments on February 3, 1967. The Bill received its third reading in the House on February 17, was passed on third reading by the Senate February 23 and received royal assent the same day. It became effective by proclamation of the Governor-in-Council on March 17, 1967.

The Act extends bargaining rights to almost all employees of the Canadian public service except managerial employees and persons serving management in a confidential capacity. A regulatory board to be known as the Public Service Staff Relations Board is provided. Its duties include defining bargaining agents and investigating complaints of infringement on statutory rights.

Initially, bargaining units in a large part of the public service are to be defined so as to correspond with the occupational groups drawn up by the Civil Service Commission. The Treasury Board represents the employer in bargaining, but agencies such as the National Research Council are desig-

---

* Based on *Current Reports on Legislation Affecting Labour*, prepared by the Department of Labour, June 27, 1966 and March 8, 1967.

nated as separate employers. Agreements reached will be binding on the parties.

The Bill has two options for settling disputes. One provides for recourse to binding arbitration. The other outlines a procedure requiring a conciliation board and permits strike action, except by employees whose services are considered essential to the safety or security of the public. A public service arbitration tribunal will be established to decide disputes over contracts being negotiated by employees accepting binding arbitration.

The Act provides for grievance processes throughout the public service. The Act also allows for third-party adjudication of grievances relating to the interpretation or application of a collective agreement or an arbitral award or disciplinary action resulting in discharge, suspension or financial penalty.

Application

The new legislation extends bargaining rights to all public servants except managerial employees. It does not apply to employees of crown corporations such as the CBC and CNR — these employees are now covered by the Industrial Relations and Disputes Investigation Act — nor does it apply to members of the armed forces and the Royal Canadian Mounted Police. The following other groups are also excluded: employees of the Public Service Staff Relations Board; persons appointed by the Governor-in-Council under the authority of an Act of Parliament; persons whose compensation consists of fees or is based on the amount of revenue collected; persons hired on a casual or temporary basis unless employed for six months or more; and persons who are not required to work more than one-third of the normal period for employees doing similar work. The managerial exclusions include: persons with executive duties in relation to the development and administration of government programs; legal officers of the Department of Justice; officers who represent and act for the employer in collective bargaining or in the processing of grievances; persons employed in positions confidential to the Governor General, Ministers of the Crown, deputy heads and chief executive officers, Judges of the Supreme Court or other persons excluded from the bargaining units.

Basic Rights and Prohibitions

The Act affirms the right of public servants to belong to an employee organization of their own choosing and to participate in its lawful activities. Certain management rights are, however, preserved. The new legislation does not affect the right of the employer to determine the organization of the Public Service, to group and classify positions, and to assign duties to employees.

Like legislation governing industrial relations in the private sector, the Act contains a number of prohibitions designed to protect the integrity of the collective bargaining relationship. It forbids any person employed in a managerial capacity to participate in or interfere with the formation or administration of an employee organization. No government official can refuse to employ nor can he discharge any person or otherwise discriminate against him in regard to employment or any term or condition of employment because he is a member of an employee organization or is exercising his statutory rights. Using discrimination and intimidation to influence membership in an employee organization is prohibited. An employee organzation, on its part, is forbidden to solicit membership during working hours except with the consent of the employer.

Public Service Staff Relations Board

The responsibility for administering the new system of collective bargaining is vested in the Public Service Staff Relations Board. Appointed by the Governor-in-Council, the Staff Relations Board is composed of a chairman, a vice-chairman and four to eight other members equally representative of the employer and the employees.

The duties and powers of the Staff Relations Board are similar to those of the labour relations boards that regulate labour-management relations in the private sector. It defines bargaining units, certifies bargaining agents and investigates complaints of alleged infringement of rights granted by the statute. The Board is authorized to decide issues affecting the establishment of bargaining units and the certification of bargaining agents. It is given broad authority to make regulations covering such matters as: time limits for filing notices and other documents; evidence of membership in an employee organization; rules of procedure for its own hearings and for hearings of the Arbitration Tribunal and those of an adjudicator; and other matters related to the exercise of its duties.

The Board may investigate complaints. This includes not only complaints that the employer or an employee organization had committed a prohibited act, but also complaints of failure to implement an arbitral award or to implement the decision of an adjudicator, or to comply with regulations respecting grievances. If the Board finds the complaint valid, it may make an order directing the person concerned to take such action as it considers appropriate, within a specified time. If the required action is not taken, the Board must send a copy of its order, together with a report of the circumstances and all relevant documents, to the responsible minister who is required to lay them before Parliament.

When determining a certification issue or hearing a complaint, the Board has the same powers as a superior court of record. It can compel the attendance of witnesses, to administer oaths, to receive sworn evidence and to order documents be produced. It also has virtually complete discretion in the kind of evidence received. The Board may also require the posting of notices and may inspect premises, subject to any security provisions.

Collective Bargaining and Collective Agreements

Under the Act, an employee organization certified by the Public Service Staff Relations Board enjoys the exclusive right to bargain collectively on behalf of employees in the unit concerned and to enter into a collective agreement on their behalf.

Initially, bargaining units are to be defined in such a way as to correspond with the occupational groups in the new classification structure developed and implemented by the Civil Service Commission. Under the Act, the Public Service Commission is authorized to specify and define the occupational groups within the occupational categories established.

An employee organization seeking recognition as the exclusive bargaining agent of a group of government employees must apply to the Public Service Staff Relations Board for certification in the manner prescribed in the regulations.

To be eligible for certification, an employee organization must supply proof of having as members in good standing a majority of the employees in the proposed bargaining unit. The type of evidence required would be left to the Board which has discretionary power to make such inquiries as it deems necessary or to direct a representation vote. In addition to having a majority, an organization applying for certification must meet certain other tests. It must be free from employer influence and must not discriminate against employees on racial or religious grounds. An organization will not be certified if it receives from any members who are employees of the federal government any contributions to a political party or requires such payments as a condition of membership or makes payments to a political party on their behalf. As well as meeting these requirements, a council of employee organizations seeking certification must satisfy the Board that appropriate legal and administrative arrangements have been made for the discharge of any obligations resulting from certification.

Once certified, an employee organization has the exclusive right to bargain for the unit of employees designated in the certificate until its certification is revoked. It has also the right to represent employees in the unit whenever a grievance relating to the application or interpretation of a collective agreement or an arbitral award is referred to adjudication. Should one organization through certification replace another, the successor organization is bound by any existing collective agreement or arbitral award. It may, however, terminate the agreement or award upon two months' notice given within one month of certification.

Provision is made in the Act for the revocation of certificates. If a collective agreement or arbitral award is in force, any person claiming to represent a majority of employees in a unit may, within the prescribed period, apply to the Board for a declaration that the certified bargaining agent no longer represents the majority of the employees. Upon receipt of such an application, the Board may take a representation vote. If satisfied that a majority of the employees no longer wish to be represented by the incumbent organization it will revoke the certification, in which case the agreement or award is void, unless another employee organization is substituted as bargaining agent. A certificate can also be revoked for fraud or if a bargaining agent ceases to act as such or if it engages in political activities or discriminates against employees contrary to the Act.

As in the private sector, bargaining procedures would begin with the giving of a notice to bargain. The notice may be given at any time in the first instance or, where a collective agreement or arbitral award is in force, within the last two months of its term. In either event, bargaining would have to begin within 20 days of the notice unless the parties agreed to an extension.

For most of the public service, the interests of the employer in bargaining will be represented by the Treasury Board. Provision is made, however, for the designation as separate employers of such agencies as the National Research Council and the National Film Board.

Where a notice has been given the employer may not, except in accordance with an agreement, alter any term or condition of employment that could be included in an agreement until an agreement has been concluded or until arbitration proceedings or the conciliation board stage has been completed, depending on the method chosen to settle the dispute.

Some limitation is placed on the subject-matter of collective agreements. No agreement can provide for any changes in terms or conditions of employment that would require legislative implementation (other than an appropriation act). Nor can it deal with such matters as superannuation, death benefits and accident compensation, because these are regulated by other statutes.

If difficulties are encountered conciliation services will be made available by the chairman of the Board on request of either party. A conciliator would be required to report within 14 days or within such longer period as might be fixed by the chairman.

Agreements entered into would be binding on the employer, the bargaining agent and on the employees in the unit concerned. Subject to an appropriation by Parliament, they would have to be implemented within the period specified in the agreement or, if no period was specified, within 90 days from the date of execution or within such longer period as might be fixed by the Board on the application of either party. The minimum term for a collective agreement is one year. No collective agreement can be entered into on behalf of a bargaining unit until six months after the employees in that unit become eligible for bargaining.

Arbitration

An independent arbitration tribunal to be known as the Public Service Arbitration Tribunal will be established to decide disputes referred to arbitration. The Tribunal will consist of a chairman appointed by the Governor-in-Council on the recommendation of the Board and two panels of other members chosen by the Board. One panel will consist of three representatives of the employer and the other will consist of three representatives of the employees. On the recommendation of the Board one or more alternate chairmen may be appointed. For any one dispute the tribunal will consist of the chairman of the Arbitration Tribunal and two members selected by the chairman of the Staff Relations Board, one from the panel of employer representatives and one from the panel representing the employees.

Arbitration proceedings may be started by giving a notice to the chairman of the Staff Relations Board. With the notice the party must include its proposals as well as a copy of any collective agreement entered into by the parties. A copy of this notice will be sent to the other party which will have seven days in which to advise the chairman of any additional matters it wishes arbitrated. The chairman of the Public Service Staff Relations Board is required to select members of the arbitration tribunal within 14 days after notice and the tribunal must consider the matter immediately.

Certain criteria are laid down in the Act to guide the Arbitration Tribunal. It must take the following factors into account:

1. the needs of the public service for qualified employees
2. the conditions of employment in similar occupations outside the public service, including such geographic, industrial or other variations as the Arbitration Tribunal may consider relevant
3. the need to maintain appropriate relationships in the conditions of employment between different grade levels within an occupation and between occupations in the public service.
4. the need to establish terms and conditions of employment that are fair and reasonable in relation to the qualifications required, the work performed, the responsibility assumed and the nature of the services rendered
5. any other factor that appears to be relevant to the matter in dispute.

Some limitations are placed on the subject-matter of arbitral awards. An arbitral award may deal with rates of pay, hours of work, leave entitlements, standards of discipline and related matters. It may not contain provisions requiring legislative implementation (other than by way of an appropriation act), nor can it deal with the standards, procedures or processes governing the appointment, appraisal, promotion, demotion, transfer, lay-off or release of employees.

An award would be binding on the employer, the bargaining agent and on the employees in the unit concerned, effective from the date on which it was rendered or such later date as the Arbitration Tribunal might fix. A provision could be retroactive but not before the date on which notice to bargain was given. Subject to the passing of any necessary appropriation act, an award would have to be implemented within 90 days from the date on which it became binding or within such longer period as the Board might decide on application of either party.

Conciliation Boards

The second method of resolving disputes is comparable to that in the Industrial Relations and Disputes Investigation Act. It provides for the appointment of a conciliation board and permits strike action in prescribed circumstances.

If a conciliator fails to bring about a settlement, the chairman of the Public Service Staff Relations Board would appoint a conciliation board on the request of either party. After consultation with each of the parties, the chairman could, however, decide not to appoint a conciliation board if he believed that it would not serve to bring about a settlement. The chairman also has discretionary power to establish a conciliation board whenever he thinks it might assist the parties in reaching agreement.

However, a conciliation board will not be established until the employees whose services are considered necessary in the interests of the safety and security of the public have been designated. The minister said that such a requirement was necessary because there were many areas where public servants provided services, which if withdrawn, could endanger individuals in the community; as examples he named prison security, air traffic control and hospital care. The initial designation of such employees is made by the employer who is required to submit a statement to the Board and the bargaining agent within 20 days after notice to bargain is given. If objections are raised by the bargaining agent, the Public Service Staff Relations Board will make the final determination, after giving the parties an opportunity to make representations.

The conciliation board would be the usual representative-type board composed of a representative of each of the parties and a chairman chosen by the other two members. If the required nominations are not made within the prescribed time, the chairman of the Public Service Staff Relations Board would appoint the member or chairman as the case might be.

The conciliation board is required to report within 14 days or within such longer period as might be agreed upon by the parties or determined by the chairman of the Staff Relations Board. There are restrictions on the subject-matter of conciliation board reports similar to those imposed on arbitral awards.

Strikes

The right to strike is restricted to employees in bargaining units that have rejected arbitration and have selected the alternate method of resolving disputes. As previously noted, designated employees in such a unit whose services are considered necessary in the interests of the safety or security of the public are forbidden to strike.

A strike during the term of an agreement is prohibited. If no collective agreement is in force, strike action is forbidden until seven days after the receipt of the report of the conciliation board or after the chairman of the Staff Relations Board has notified the parties that he is not going to appoint a conciliation board.

Upon application, the Board may issue a declaration that a strike is lawful or unlawful. An employee who engages in a strike contrary to the Act is liable to a fine of up to $100, and an officer of an employee organization who authorizes such a strike, may be fined up to $300. An employee organization that authorizes or engages in an illegal strike is liable to a fine of up to $150 for each day the strike continues. No prosecution may be instituted without the consent of the Board.

Grievance Procedures

The grievance provisions in the Act are intended to remove what the Prime Minister described as the "irritants in the relationship between individual employees and those who represent the government as employer". They provide for the establishment of grievance processes throughout the public service and for third-party adjudication of unresolved grievances relating to the interpretation or application of an award or agreement or disciplinary action resulting in discharge, suspension or financial penalty.

The grievance processes have a broader coverage than the bargaining provisions. They apply to managerial employees and to persons not included in a bargaining unit as well as to employees represented by a bargaining agent.

An employee who feels himself aggrieved by the interpretation or application of a provision of a statute, regulation, bylaw, direction or other instrument issued by the employer, dealing with terms and conditions of employment or a provision of a collective agreement or an arbitral award or as a result of any other occurrence or matter affecting his terms and conditions of employment for which no other means of redress is available under any other federal law, has the right to present the grievance up to the final level of the grievance process. Certain restrictions apply to an employee in a unit represented by a certified bargaining agent. Such an employee cannot present any grievance concerning the application or interpretation of a provision of a collective agreement or an arbitral award unless he has the approval of the bargaining agent and is represented by it during the proceedings.

The details of the grievance processes are to be set out in regulations of the Board.

A staff of permanent adjudicators is to be appointed to hear grievances. They will be appointed by the Governor-in-Council on the recommendation of the Board for a term of five years. One, to be designated as chief adjudicator, will administer the system of grievance adjudication, subject to regulations of the Board.

Under the proposed system of adjudication, a grievance would normally be heard by an adjudicator selected by the chief adjudicator unless an adjudicator is named in an applicable collective agreement. If no adjudicator is named in an agreement, the grievor may request that the matter be referred to a board of adjudication in which case a board would be established unless the employer raised objections within the prescribed time. A board of adjudication will be composed of three members, a nominee of each party and an adjudicator who would be chairman. The decision of an adjudicator or a board of adjudication will be final.

41 The Need for Executive Development— What it Takes to be a Good Executive*

Peter F. Drucker

I think all of you know that there is probably no other development in American management that has ever moved ahead so very rapidly as the interest and concern with executive development. Fifteen years ago when I first became interested in this, there was, to my knowledge, only one company in this country which did anything in this field, Sears Roebuck. They were in an extremely unusual situation, and considered their program an emergency program to meet the problems created by explosive expansion. About nine or ten years ago when I first tried to study this program, there was not one single line in print that dealt with it. Today, as you all know, we have produced a couple of libraries on this subject, and every company I know is doing something in the field, or is at least talking about what they should be doing.

I have never seen anything move so fast and become so generally accepted as executive development. Yet, frankly, I am not particularly happy when I look around at my friendly managements, at my clients, and look at the literature. I am not happy because I can't help but feel that this may very well turn out not to be a sound, solid basic development, but one of those management fads which we seem to go in for once in a while with a great blaring of bugles and waving of banners, only to march up the aisle and to march down again.

It seems to me that we are concentrating, as we so often do, on particular

* Reprinted with permission of author and publisher from *Advanced Management Journal*, Vol. 29, No. 1, January 1964, pp. 83-87.

gadgets, on methods, and are in danger of forgetting what we are doing and why. It seems to me, above all, that a great many managements rush into executive development as something that must be good because the other fellow does it; or because SAM and other management organizations talk about it. And such managements rush into executive development in many cases, I believe, in the wrong way, by thinking that this is a technique for which you hire yourself a technician, pay him as little as you can get him for, and then leave it to him.

I am, therefore, not talking about methods and techniques because you are going to hear others talk about them. There are people in this room and people on our speakers' list who are much better qualified than I. I shall try to remind you of why we should be doing executive development, what its reasons are, what its objectives should be, and some of the things one should keep in mind in order to have a program that is sound.

Let me say I believe that there are few things which are so important, not only to the individual business but to the country, as a sound executive development program to meet the problem of, where do tomorrow's executives come from? Now when you talk to management people about executive development and why they are interested in it, they rightly and understandably begin with the needs of their own company. Frankly I don't think that is the starting point. I think there is one aspect of the concern for tomorrow's management which we, in management, tend to forget, but which may very well be as important as the contribution to our own business and to American management in general.

The question of tomorrow's management is, above all, a concern of our society. Let me put it bluntly — we have reached a point where we simply will not be able to tolerate as a country, as a Society, as a government, the danger that any one of our major companies will decline or collapse because it has not made adequate provisions for management succession.

Unless we in management anticipate this responsibility and can prove to society that we can take care of this problem, we are bound to get government regulation. This is one of the areas in which an industrial society will be left to private enterprise only if private enterprise can convince the public that it is doing a job and is recognizing its responsibility.

Let me say that the public is not interested in who is going to be president or vice-president of your big corporations. It does have a vital interest in there being adequate provision that it will be somebody who is properly qualified and properly trained to whom this enterprise can be entrusted. I think that, beyond the needs of the individual enterprise, will be a social demand and social pressure, resulting in government action if it appears that a large corporation would be left without adequate management.

There is also another aspect of public interest in this whole area. It is quite obvious that for most of our citizens, the corporation is the place in which, and to which they look for the fulfillment of their aspirations, their hopes, and the basic beliefs and promises of our society. This simply says that this is a business society in which business has become the dominant and central institution, and the community for the majority of our people. This is an employee society, and we all know that.

Understanding and Acceptance

This means that increasingly people will look to the corporation and will say, "Are its approach and methods in the election of executives, within shouting distance of the things we in this country believe, we in this country were promised?" Above all, does business practice the belief in equal opportunities which it preaches? The place where this question will be raised, and is being raised, is in the election of tomorrow's executives. Any executive development program which formulates its aim and objectives purely in providing the company with enough men tomorrow to fill the vacancies caused by expansion is going to do only half the job, and maybe not the most important part.

There is a basic problem that any management development program *must* be attacking — it is giving as many men as possible as many opportunities as they deserve. The program must be focused on the fullest utilization of the citizens whose careers we decide in management.

This means simply, and it is not so easy and simple to do it, that it isn't sufficient to say, "I have provided for all the vacancies which will come up tomorrow. I know who is going to move in." The question is not only, "Have you really looked to find the best people, or have you just been satisfied if you found someone that will do the job?"

The question is also, "Have you developed your whole program in such a manner that to the people in your company this is a rational, a just, a fair and understood approach?" That, believe me, is one area where a good many management programs, I know, are woefully weak. They are not even understood, let alone accepted as rational by the vice-presidents, certainly not by the people who are being measured, selected, appraised and looked at. They are not sufficiently aware of the fact that the management development program is only a technical name for that system by which we, in this country, will fulfill our basic political and social promises to the great majority of our citizens.

No management development program should be completely ignorant or unaware of these social and political occasions, as if you dealt not with people who look to the company for the fulfillment of basic citizenship problems. No management handling executive development as if it is a packaging problem is going to last or is going to help the organization. It might give you very good executives, but it will demoralize the organization and will, on top of that, do a great deal of harm to our free economy and our business system.

Don't forget that when you say executive development, you talk about people and citizens, and not about tools. Don't forget that for a moment, because you can only do yourself, company and country a great deal of harm.

Participation

The next point I would like to raise is — forgetting what goes on outside our business — what do we want management development for in your business? What do we want management development to do for the business? The first answer is one which I hear far too rarely. We need management development for the simple reason that in an industrial economy, the management in power today simply cannot make proper, responsible and right decisions. It can only make guesses and depend on tomorrow's management to bail them out. Our basic management decisions — and that is true even for the corner cigar store — are 15-year decisions, whether they are on capital investment, on product development, on building an organization, on building a distributive system — every one of them is a long-range decision.

My consulting work is exclusively with top management problems, and I have yet to sit down with a client and discuss any decision, that will really come to fruition within 18 months. Five years is a fairly short-range decision. May I say that this is a characteristic of an industrial system, and perhaps it is an outstanding characteristic.

Now, our friends in the Armed Forces, have known that for a long time, and hence their emphasis on the training of tomorrow's leaders. Management decisions made today which do not expressly or explicitly carry a provision for tomorrow's management are not really decisions. Just ask the question: could any management have made the right decisions on a ten-year basis in 1937? It wasn't only the depression that was not foreseen. It was something less likely than a depression, the beginning of a period of the most rapid technological change. Any economist would have told you this could not have happened. Could any management in 1937 have foreseen that we would have a major war? That, I think, could be foreseen, but who could have anticipated the greatest peace-time boom we have ever seen.

Is there any reason to believe that decisions on plant expansion, product development, research, marketing, personnel, labor matters, which we make today, are any more likely to be based on a correct appraisal of the future? I don't see why anybody in management would assume that he can predict the future today when it is quite obvious that it can't be predicted.

Therefore, responsible management decisions can only be made if you have the people participating that will carry out the decisions.

Fortune this month has a very interesting study of the large corporations which shows that only one out of nine of the presidents and vice-presidents of our largest corporations are under 50 — and that, I think, is fairly typical. That, incidently, is probably as it should be. I have a horror of boy scouts in high places.

That simply means that the people who make the decisions today won't be around tomorrow. They are busy bailing out of the decisions of the previous people. That means that you must have a commitment to tomorrow's management or else your decisions are baseless. That also means that those people who will have to bail out the decisions tomorrow — let them be in on the other decisions so that they know what they are going to have to live with.

It means that your management development program should, above all, try to bring your second and third team into top management thinking, into at least a spectator role, for the simple reason that what goes on today will be their job, their problem, their headache tomorrow. That is the main function of a management development program.

Problem of Specialization

Let me say one more thing about how management develops. It is quite obvious — and incidently let me say it is quite natural — that a business does not automatically produce natural leaders. No institution has ever done that. There is no reason for criticism or for breast beating or even for amazement, that the business in many important respects, not only fails to train and to test a young man for leadership positions, but in many respects develops him in the wrong direction. This is a very normal problem. If you look at the Catholic Church, which has certainly one of the most successful records of management, there is no doubt at all that being a Parish Priest is about the worst preparation that there could be for a bishop. It emphasizes all the wrong things. There is no doubt that if you look at the command positions in the Air Force the training of a fighter pilot emphasizes all the wrong qualifications for a command position.

Yet, where else would leaders come from? There is no doubt, in other words, that every single institution has had the problem that the demands made on the young executives were exactly, in many important aspects, the opposite of the things that are needed for the command and leadership positions.

So we need not be perturbed by the fact that business is no different. But if you look at it, what are the most obvious problems? Well, the most obvious problems are, first, that our industrial and business strength rests upon specialization, so that in a man's formative years, there is a tremendous premium on his becoming more and more specialized. Maybe we overdo it, but let me say that no attempt to emphasize the generalization at the lower and middle levels of management will be more than a very minor offset, because in the job of a man's formative years, until he is about 35 or so, inevitably the emphasis will be on his becoming really and thoroughly competent in one special function.

Testing the Man

There is another problem. All of us are familiar with it. It is a much bigger problem than specialization, namely that we don't really know a thing about the man's ability to make decisions and to run the business until he is tested under actual conditions. Dry runs are not a sufficient test. I don't know whether you have heard of the once-popular parlor game of running a fictitious stock market account. A girls' school class in economics and finance always does that. Place the stock market on paper. I have yet to hear of anyone who always took a loss! They always came out right! It is easy to see why.

For that same reason, no appraisal of a man, no attempt to find people, no performance in a job can possibly be a real test of what a man will do, how he will do when he is on his own and has to make the decisions and has to take the responsibility.

Therefore, we have a real problem of testing people in actual, not in simulated battle conditions, but at a time when their failure won't mean danger to the entire organization.

Organization Aspects

Those are our major problems, and let me say it is quite clear that they cannot be lifted by a program of executive development alone. They are as much organizational problems as they are problems of developing individuals, for an executive development program which does not start out with the realization that maybe you have to make major changes will degenerate into a program that tries to cover up cracks in the foundation by putting a nicely colored wall paper over a six-inch crack, hoping not only to keep out the draft, but to keep the structure going. Realize the basic crack is the crack of the organizational structure, and that you cannot develop men against the flaws of the entire organization structure in which they live.

If your organization is of such a nature that it accentuates the difficulties which business has naturally developed, no executive development program will do any good. It will create a great deal of false hopes and a great deal of frustration, and it will be as effective as putting wall paper over the cracks in masonry. So don't just look at this program of people. This program has to be equally focused on the organization, or else it isn't going to do any good.

You cannot assume that the present organization is right. It might be or it might not be. How do you know without looking at it? — which incidently means that this is not just a problem for a technical specialist, though you may need one in large corporations. This is a problem for top management.

Character and Integrity

Finally, and this is the last thing I want to say, the reason why I am really unhappy, frankly, about how much I see going on, is that there is so much talk about skilled knowledge, intelligence, but very little realization to realize that the important qualities in a manager are character and integrity. You and I know it. As a matter of fact, I think that distinguishes a child from a grown man. Until you learn that intelligence is a drug on the market, and about the most useless commodity there is, if there is nothing else in the man, unless you realize that character is not only always more important, but will in an amazing majority of cases win out — until and unless you realize that, you haven't grown up. You are still a sophomore, because that is what we mean by sophomoric. Most managements do not realize when we talk of management, we do not primarily talk of the intellectual gift. We talk primarily of character and integrity, which are very hard things to measure. When you sit down with two or three of your company associates, and you talk about "Jimmy Jones down there," you may have grave doubts about his ability, but I think you have very little doubt about his character.

You know all this, and yet we don't recognize sufficiently that we are looking for people of character and integrity to discharge this tremendous managerial function, this key function of our society, a new function, and the one on which our society stands or falls.

The importance of character and integrity in management cannot be stressed too much. Top management is not merely responsible for identifying these traits. More important it is responsible for preserving the character and integrity of the individual. I would say that the first responsibility of management is not to destroy character and integrity, but to maintain and develop these traits. To me the sign of a really successful organization is its ability to bring out of its members more than they really possess. That may sound queer until you realize that the truly successful institutions in history have accomplished precisely this.

Conclusion

In conclusion, let me say that I am critical, not because I doubt the value of executive development, I am critical because I have a very deep understanding of its importance. To me executive development is the product of two major changes. First, over the last 40 years, we in this country have developed a new basic social order, a step in the evolution of the race, I think, in many respects as great as the one that occurred from animal to man. The development of management is a tremendous step. The development of a society in which there is a management function is an equally tremendous step. I think in retrospect it will appeal to the historian 200 or 300 years hence as a great revolution of our times.

The second reason why I believe that this is important is that the emergence of management also means that business has come of age, that it has become a social institution that will and can survive. It has emerged as a new way of organizing people to basic social ends for the greater good of society and of the individual. This simply means that, as an institution, business has the same problem every institution has, which is that foremost question, "Who will be our leaders tomorrow?" We are not overdoing executive development; we are probably still under-concerned with it, but we are not perhaps sufficiently aware that we are not talking about technical functions, but if I may manhandle a biological metaphor, we are talking about the basic reproductive functions of this new organism we created, modern business.

This is not purely a matter of technique. This is a matter of objectivity, of principle and of greater clarity, what we are doing and why. This is perhaps a central management principle and function, because our business, our business societies and our American system are only as strong as the ability, the competence and integrity of the people who will take over where we will stop, who will be our managers of tomorrow.

Chapter Ten
Administrative Responsibility

Virtually every text book of readings on public administration assigns at least one chapter to an analysis of the ever-expanding powers and influence of public servants, and the means of confining the administrators' domain within reasonable bounds. During the 1930's and 1940's, the enormous publicity and legal controversy surrounding the warnings of Lord Hewart in Great Britain and Dean Roscoe Pound in the United States against the growing legislative and judicial powers of the bureaucracy led to popular overemphasis on the threat of bureaucratic tyranny. Nevertheless, the necessity for delegation of quasi-legislative and quasi-judicial authority to public servants is now acknowledged by all but the most reactionary students of law and administration.

Different countries have experienced varying degrees of success in their attempts to develop institutions and techniques of control to ensure the responsible behaviour of public officials. The first few essays of this chapter describe the structure and processes of delegated powers and judicial review in Canada. An argument is also presented for the adaptation of the Scandinavian institution of the Ombudsman to Canada as a new method of guarding against administrative abuse of discretionary powers.

Efforts to place restraints on bureaucratic authority directly affect relationships between the government and the public but a multitude of other connections and conflicts also arise between public officials and those they serve or regulate. The readings explore the influence of public servants in the policy-making process and assess their relations with legislators, the press and the general public. An examination of the political rights of Canada's government employees is followed by a plea for easier access to government documents on the part of representatives of the public, the communication media and the academic community.

Space limitations have precluded a discussion of the complex subject of administrative law. However, two comprehensive general studies are

S. A. De Smith, *Judicial Review of Administrative Action*, Stevens, London, 1959.

H. W. Wade, *Administrative Law*, 2nd ed., Oxford University Press, London, 1967.

A Canadian overview is provided by John Willis in "Administrative Law in Canada", *The Canadian Bar Review*, Vol. 39, No. 2, May 1961.
Although the number of books, articles and government documents on the powers and responsibilities of public servants is legion, there are certain works which deserve special mention because they have become classics in the field. In regard to the growth of administrative powers, these are

G. H. Hewart, *The New Despotism*, Ernest Benn, London, 1929.

Great Britain, Committee on Ministers' Powers, *Report*, His Majesty's Stationery Office, London, 1932.

Great Britain, Committee on Administrative Tribunals and Enquiries, *Report*, Her Majesty's Stationery Office, London, 1957.

The views of Dean Pound are summarized in *Administrative Law: Its Growth, Procedure, and Significance*, University of Pittsburgh Press, Pittsburgh, Pennsylvania, 1942.
In the area of administrative responsibility note especially:

Paul H. Appleby, *Morality and Administration in Democratic Government*, Louisiana State University Press, Baton Rouge, Louisiana, 1952.

C. S. Hyneman, *Bureaucracy in a Democracy*, Harper, New York, 1950.

Carl J. Friedrich, "Public Policy and the Nature of Administrative Responsibility" in Carl J. Friedrich and E. S. Mason (eds.), *Public Policy*, Vol. 1, Harvard University Press, Cambridge, Massachussetts, 1940.

Herman Finer, "Administrative Responsibility in Democratic Government", *Public Administration Review*, Vol. 1, No. 4, Summer 1941.

Reference should be made also to such significant works as

S. A. De Smith, *Judicial Review of Administrative Action*, Stevens, London, 1959.

J. E. Kersell, *Parliamentary Supervision of Delegated Legislation; the United Kingdom, Australia, New Zealand and Canada*, Stevens, London, 1960.

Walter Gellhorn, *Ombudsman and Others: Citizens' Protectors in Nine Countries*, Harvard University Press, Cambridge, Massachusetts, 1966.

J. D. Millett, *Government and Public Administration: The Quest for Responsible Performance*, McGraw-Hill, New York, 1959.

Donald C. Rowat, *The Ombudsman*, University of Toronto Press, Toronto, 1965.

Glendon Schubert, *The Public Interest: A Critique of the Theory of a Political Concept*, The Free Press, New York, 1960.

42   Subordinate Legislation*

Elmer A. Driedger

I. Nature of Subordinate Legislation

A statute, or an Act of Parliament, may be defined as the written will of a sovereign legislative body, solemnly expressed according to the forms necessary to constitute it the law of the territory over which that legislative body has jurisdiction.[1] A statute is a law. We know, however, that there are other written laws in the form of statutes that were not enacted by a sovereign legislative authority. Thus, there are laws made by the executive, that is to say, by the Governor General in Council or by a minister; there are laws made by municipal authorities, and by other bodies, as, for example, the National Harbours Board, the National Capital Commission.

These laws that are not enacted by a sovereign legislature are nevertheless made under the authority of a statute. Unless authorized by statute, neither the executive nor any other authority has the power to make laws.[2] In the *Chemicals Reference*[3] Chief Justice Duff said that "every order in council, every regulation, every rule, every order, whether emanating immediately from His Excellency the Governor General in Council or from some subordinate agency, derives its legal force solely from . . . [an] Act of Parliament", and, quoting from *The Zamora*, he said that "All such instruments derive their authority from the statute which creates the power, and not from the executive body by which they are made."

These subsidiary laws are known by a variety of expressions — regulations, rules, orders, by-laws, ordinances — or, collectively, as subordinate legislation or delegated legislation. These expressions do not have precise or generally accepted meanings.

The term "regulation" is usually understood to be a subsidiary law of general application, whereas an "order" is usually regarded as a particular direction in a special case.[4] The term "order" is also used to describe the act or instrument that establishes rules or regulations, as, for example, an Order in Council. The term "regulation" is sometimes used to describe the whole instrument, and sometimes only to describe a provision thereof. The expression "rule" is usually applied to procedural regulations, as, for example, rules of court. These three expressions — regulations, rules, orders — are to some extent interchangeable, and one sometimes finds in one sentence power to make "orders, rules and regulations," with no clue as to what the difference is.

---

* Reprinted and abridged with permission of author and publisher from *The Canadian Bar Review*, Vol. 38, No. 1, March 1960, pp. 1-34.
1 Bouvier's Law Dictionary, 3rd rev. 3129.
2 *The Zamora*, [1916] 2 A.C. 77, *The Case of the Proclamations*, (1611), 12 Co. R. 74, 77 E.R. 1352.
3 *Chemicals Reference* [1943] S.C.R. 1, at p. 13.
4 Attorney General for Alberta v. Huggard Assets, [1953] A.C. 420.

A law made by a municipal authority is usually called a "by-law" or an "ordinance". The expression "by-law" is also applied to rules made by a corporation for its internal management, but in this sense it is not "law". The expression "ordinance" is also applied to the enactments of a nonsovereign legislative body, as, for example, the Council of the Northwest Territories or the Yukon Territory. The enactments of colonial legislatures are sometimes called "ordinances" and in early English history the term "ordinance" was applied to a document that issued from Parliament but differed from a statute in that the latter had the assent of the Sovereign, the Lords and the Commons — the three estates — whereas the former had the assent of only two estates.[5]

Subordinate legislation may roughly be divided into two classes. First, there are laws made by the executive or by some body or person that is subject to some degree of control by the executive. Into this category would fall regulations made by the Governor in Council, by-laws of the National Harbours Board, regulations of the National Capital Commission. Secondly, there are enactments by independent or quasi-independent local governments. They derive their powers from the legislature but are not directly responsible to the executive. As we shall see later, these two classes of legislation have to some extent received different treatment by the courts. Both classes constitute law, and are usually enforced by sanctions. Rules of court may perhaps be considered a third category. They are usually made, not be the legislative or executive authority, but by the judiciary, and the sanction for breach of the rules is not usually fine or imprisonment.

Not all instruments issued under statutory authority are included in the expression "subordinate legislation". A statute may confer power to exercise legislative, judicial or ministerial powers. We are not concerned here with the judicial or ministerial, but only with those instruments that are of a legislative character. The dividing line between these classes of powers may be thin or obscure, and any further discussion thereon falls more properly within the scope of administrative law.

It is not intended here to adopt any precise definitions, but, for the sake of convenience, all subordinate legislation will be included in the term "regulations"; where it is necessary to make a distinction, laws enacted by municipal authorities will be referred to as "by-laws", and regulations governing matters of procedure will be referred to as "rules".

All subordinate legislation constitutes law. Is it the same as a statute? In *The Queen* v. *Walker*[6] Lush J. said that "an order made under a power given in a statute is the same thing as if the statute enacted what the order directs or forbids". But it does not follow that a regulation is a statute. In *The King* v. *Singer*[7] the Supreme Court of Canada decided expressly that a regulation was not an Act of Parliament.

---

[5] *Craies on Statute Law*, 5th ed. 1952, p. 50.
[6] (1875), E.R. 10 Q.B. 355.
[7] [1941] S.C.R. 111.

II. The Challenge of Subordinate Legislation

In the United Kingdom an Act of Parliament cannot be questioned. Whatever it says, it is the law. In a federal state such as Canada, however, where legislative jurisdiction is divided between different legislative bodies, the validity of a statute can be challenged on the ground that the enacting legislature exceeded its constitutional authority. However, if a legislature in Canada acted within its constitutional powers, then the statute cannot be questioned.[8] Notwithstanding that a regulation may for some purposes be regarded as a statute, there is one important difference. The courts can question the validity of subordinate legislation on the ground that the authority conferred by the Act was exceeded. The principle is the same as that applicable to statutes in a federal jurisdiction. If the statute confers the power, the regulation is valid; if the statute has not conferred the power, then the regulation is *ultra vires*.

In some statutes there is a provision to the effect that the regulations or rules made thereunder "shall be of the same effect as if they were contained" in the Act itself. This language was considered by the House of Lords in the case of *Institute of Patent Agents* v. *Lockwood*.[9] Herschell L.C. concluded that this clause prevented the courts from considering the validity of the regulation. Lord Watson agreed, but Lord Morris held that the clause applied only to rules that were validly made; if valid, they then had the same effect as the Act, that is to say, they constituted a law. The point came up again in *Minister of Health* v. *The King* (on the Prosecution of Yaffe)[10] and this time the House of Lords did not consider itself precluded from considering the validity of a regulation of this character. In *MacCharles* v. *Jones*[11] the Manitoba Court of Appeal followed the *Yaffe* case and held that the court could question the validity of rules that were declared by the legislature to "have effect as if embodied in and as part of" the Act under which they were made.

A provision that a regulation is to have the same effect as if enacted in the Act is not common in modern Acts of the Parliament of Canada. There was a provision like this in the former Food and Drugs Act[12] and it was regarded as having some significance there. That statute conferred authority to make regulations, but did not expressly confer authority to prescribe penalties for breach of a regulation. The statute itself prescribed a penalty only for breach of a provision of the Act. The provision that the regulations should have the "same force and effect as if embodied in this Act" was regarded as incorporating the regulations into the Act for the purpose of making the penalty section applicable to a breach of the regulations. On the other hand, in *Willingdale* v. *Norris*[13] it was held that a provision

---

8 *The King* v. *Irwin*, [1926] Ex. C.R. 127.
9 [1894] A.C. 347.
10 [1931] A.C. 494.
11 [1939] 1 W.W.R. 133 (Man. C.A.).
12 R.S.C., 1952, c. 123, s. 3(2).
13 [1909] 1 K.B. 57.

in an Act prescribing a penalty for breach of the Act extended also to a regulation.

Whether regulations are or are not the same thing as a statute, it is clear that they are subordinate to the statute under which they are made, and if there is any conflict between them, the statute prevails.[14]

Parliament can, of course, by appropriate language, oust the jurisdiction of the courts to enquire into the validity of subordinate legislation. Thus, in *Ex Parte Ringer*[15] the court held that the order was not subject to review by the courts. A provision of this kind is unusual, and I am not aware of any provision like this in the statutes of Canada.

III. Grounds on Which Regulations May be Challenged

The validity of subordinate legislation has been challenged in the courts on many different grounds with varying success. The following seem to be the principal grounds that have been put forward.

(a) Repeal of Authorizing Act

If an authorizing statute is repealed then, apart from any special statutory provisions, the regulations made under the statute also are repealed.[16] The Interpretation Act, however, provides that where an Act is repealed and other provisions are substituted, all regulations made under the repealed Act continue good and valid, in so far as they are not inconsistent with the substituted Act or enactment, until they are annulled and others made in their stead.[17] In *Regina* v. *Konowalchuk*[18] the question arose whether an order continued in force after repeal of the statute under which it was made and the enactment of a similar provision, but somewhat wider in scope. The court held that the order under the repealed statute was inconsistent with the new statute and was therefore not in force. In some cases the new Act provides expressly for continuation of regulations made under the repealed Act.[19]

(b) The Authorizing Statute is Ultra Vires

Obviously a valid regulation cannot be founded on an invalid statute. Regulations based on a statute that has been declared by the courts to be *ultra vires* must be regarded as a nullity. This was expressly decided in the case of *In Re Beck Estate*.[20]

---

14 *Belanger* v. *The King, supra,* footnote 13; *Institute of Patent Agents* v. *Lockwood, supra,* footnote 12.
15 (1909), 25 T.L.R. 718.
16 *Blakey & Company, Limited* v. *The King,* [1935] Ex. C.R. 223.
17 R.S.C., 1952, c. 158, s. 20; R.S.O., 1950, c. 184, s. 15.
18 (1955), 112 C.C.C. 19.
19 Broadcasting Act., S.C., 1958, c. 22, s. 37.
20 [1939] 1 W.W.R. 208 (B.C. C.A.).

(c) Constitution of Subordinate Authority

If a statute authorizes a designated subordinate authority to make a regulation, it follows logically that if the authority is not properly constituted, then the power conferred by the statute cannot be exercised. This point is not likely to arise where power is conferred on a Minister of the Crown or on the Governor General in Council, but it has arisen where power to make regulations was conferred on a number of persons. In *Rex* v. *Hatskin*[21] this point was considered by the Manitoba Court of Appeal. The case was therefore not conclusive, but it does illustrate how the point might arise.

(d) Conditions Precedent

If the statute prescribes conditions precedent to the exercise of the power, then it follows that the conditions must be satisfied before the power exists.

(i) Consultation

A statute sometimes requires a regulation-making authority to consult with some other person or organization before making a regulation. A provision like this is perhaps more common in the United Kingdom than it is in Canada. A recent example of this in Canadian statutes is subsection (2) of section 11 of the Broadcasting Act,[22] which requires the Board to give notice in the Canada Gazette of its intention to make or annul a regulation that affects licensees and to afford licensees an opportunity of making representations to the Board with respect thereto. If a statute requires an authority to consult with some other person or persons before it makes a regulation, then it must necessarily follow that the regulation is invalid if the authority does not so consult.

(ii) Jurisdictional Facts

If a statutory power is to be exercised only in prescribed circumstances, it follows logically that there is no jurisdiction to exercise this power unless those circumstances do exist. Who decides whether the circumstances exist? If it is the courts, then the validity of a regulation can be challenged in the courts on the ground that there was no jurisdiction to make the regulation. If, on the other hand, it is the regulation-making authority, then the validity of the regulation may not be challenged on this ground. One of the clearest statements of this principle, applicable to all statutory powers, be they "legislative", "ministerial", "judicial" or "administrative", is to be found in the judgment of Lord Esher in *The Queen* v. *The Commissioners for Special Purposes of the Income Tax*.[23]

---

21 [1936] 2 W.W.R. 321 (Man. C.A.).
22 *Supra*, footnote 19.
23 (1888), 21 Q.B.D. 313, at p. 319.

Statutes conferring legislative power, however, do not usually authorize the power to be exercised "whenever" certain facts exist. Rather, they provide that an authority may make regulations whenever "he is satisfied" that certain facts exist, or whenever, "by reason of" certain facts he deems it necessary to do so. The effect of language of this kind has been considered by the courts.

In *Thorneloe & Clarkson, Ltd.* v. *Board of Trade*[24] the Board of Trade was authorized to establish by order a development council for any industry but the order was not to be made unless the board or minister concerned was satisfied that the establishment was desired by a substantial number of persons engaged in that industry. It was held that it was for the Minister or the board to assess on grounds they thought fit whether the requirement had been fulfilled.

It has been held in some cases that an express statement of facts is not necessary. For example, in *Jones* v. *Robson*[25] the court considered the Coal Mines Regulation Act which provided that "a Secretary of State on being satisfied that any explosive is or is likely to become dangerous may, by order . . . prohibit the use thereof in any mine". It was held that the fact that a Secretary of State made an order was sufficient evidence that he was so satisfied.[26]

If on the face of a regulation it is apparent that the regulation-making authority was not satisfied as to the existence of certain facts as required by the statute, the regulation would presumably be *ultra vires*.[27]

(iii) Necessity for the Exercise of Legislative Power

Where power is given to make "such regulations" as the subordinate authority "by reason of" certain facts "deems necessary" the question also arises whether the courts will strike down the regulations on the ground that they were not necessary. It would seem not. Thus, in *Rex* v. *Comptroller General of Patents, Ex Parte Bayer Products Limited*,[28] Scott L.J. said ". . . the effect of the words 'as appears to him to be necessary or expedient' is to give to His Majesty in Council a complete discretion to decide what regulations are necessary for the purposes named in the subsection. That being so, it is not open to His Majesty's courts to investigate the question whether or not the making of any particular regulation was in fact necessary or expedient for the specified purposes".[29]

In the *Chemicals Reference*[30] the Supreme Court of Canada considered the War Measures Act. Chief Justice Duff said that "when Regulations

---

24 [1950] 2 All E.R. 245.
25 [1901] Q.B. 673.
26 See also *Liversidge* v. *Anderson*; *Pugsley* v. *Garson* (1922), 50 N.B.R. 414.
27 See the remark of Clauson L.J. in *Rex* v. *Comptroller General of Patents, Ex Parte Bayer Products Limited*, [1941] 2 K.B. 306, at p. 316.
28 *Ibid.*
29 *Ibid.*, at pp. 311, 312.
30 *Supra*, footnote 3.

have been passed by the Governor in Council in professed fulfilment of his statutory duty, I cannot agree that it is competent to any court to canvass the considerations which have, or may have, led him to deem such Regulations necessary or advisable for the transcendent objects set forth".[31]

(e) Conditions Subsequent

(i) Publication

A statute takes effect upon Royal Assent, unless some other date for the coming into force of the statute is provided.[32] Subordinate legislation does not receive Royal Assent, so presumably a regulation takes effect from the moment it is made. However, in *Johnson* v. *Sargant & Sons*[33] an order was made on May 16th, 1917 and was published on May 17th. Mr. Justice Bailhache said "in the absence of authority upon the point, I am unable to hold that this Order came into operation before it was known, and . . . it was not known until the morning of May 17th."[34] This decision was followed in British Columbia in the case of *Rex* v. *Ross*.[35] The legal basis for these decisions is not clear. Other acts of the executive under statutory powers — appointments, for example — are also by order, and there is no doubt they are effective at once even though they were made without publicity. Why should regulations be any different? Sometimes a bill receives three readings in both Houses of Parliament and Royal Assent in one day or even a few hours, so that in fact its passage may not have had any publicity.

The Regulations Act[36] provides for the publication of regulations in the Canada Gazette and makes provision also for tabling a regulation before Parliament. The Act does not prescribe a commencement date. Section 5, however, says that a regulation is not invalid by reason only that it was not published in the Canada Gazette, but goes on to provide that no person may be convicted for an offence under a regulation that was not published unless the regulation was exempt from publication or it is proved that before the date of the alleged contravention reasonable steps had been taken for the purpose of bringing the purport of the regulation to the notice of the public or the persons likely to be affected by it, or of the person charged.[37] There is at least an implication in the Regulations Act that a regulation made under an Act of Parliament of Canada comes into force when it is made, but if it contains penalty provisions its full operation may be dependent on publication.

---

31 *Ibid.*, at p. 12.
32 Interpretation Act, *supra*, footnote 17, s. 7.
33 [1918] 1 K.B. 101.
34 *Ibid.*, at p. 103.
35 [1945] 1 W.W.R. 590 (B.C.).
36 R.S.C., 1952, c. 235.
37 For a discussion of similar provisions in United Kingdom legislation see *Simmonds* v. *Newell*, [1953] 1 W.L.R. 826 and *R.* v. *Sheer Metalcraft Ltd.*, [1954] 1 Q.B. 586.

(ii) Laying Before Parliament

Statutes sometimes provide that regulations should be laid before Parliament, and there is a general provision in section 7 of the Regulations Act to this effect. It would seem that failure to lay a regulation before Parliament does not affect its validity.[38]

In the United Kingdom provision is frequently made for parliamentary control of delegated legislation.[39] Regulations, or drafts, are required to be laid before Parliament. In some cases, the regulations have no effect or cease to have effect unless approved by Resolution, and in other cases the regulations may be annulled by Resolution. Apart from a few exceptional cases, there is no similar machinery in Canada, at least in the federal field.

(f) Implied Restrictions

Is the exercise of legislative power subject to implied restrictions? In other words, can the language conferring the power be taken at face value, or must it be read subject to some implied restrictions or limitations?

(i) Good Faith

All statutory powers must be employed in good faith for the purposes for which they are given.[40] A court of law may intervene if "powers entrusted for one purpose are deliberately used with the design of achieving another, itself unauthorized or actually forbidden".[41] The right to intervene, however, is more theoretical than real, and it would seem that bad faith must appear on the face of the regulation before the courts would hold it invalid on this ground.

In *Rex* v. *Comptroller General of Patents* Lord Justice Clauson said "if on reading an Order in Council making a regulation, it seems in fact that it did not appear to be necessary or expedient for the relevant purposes to make the regulations, I agree that, on the face of the Order, it would be inoperative".

(ii) Reasonableness

By-laws of corporations and local governments may be quashed by the courts on the ground that they are unreasonable. The leading case on the subject is *Kruse* v. *Johnson*. Lord Russell explained this unreasonableness as follows: "If, for instance, they were found to be partial and unequal in their operation as between different classes; if they were manifestly

---

38 *Bailey* v. *Williamson* (1873), L.R. 8 Q.B. 118.
39 See *Craies on Statute Law*, *op. cit.*, *supra*, p. 277; Griffith and Street, *Principles of Administrative Law*, 2nd ed., 1957, p. 126 *et seqq*.
40 Per C.J. Duff in the *Chemicals* case, *supra*, footnote 3, at p. 13. See also *Liversidge* v. *Anderson*.
41 Per Lord Radcliffe in *A. G. for Canada* v. *Hallet & Carey Ltd.*

unjust; if they disclosed bad faith; if they involved such oppressive or gratuitous interference with the rights of those subject to them as could find no justification in the minds of reasonable men, the Court might well say, 'Parliament never intended to give authority to make such rules; they are unreasonable and *ultra vires*' ".[42] And in a Canadian case, *City of Montreal* v. *Beauvais*,[43] J. Duff said "The by-law in question is also impugned as unreasonable and oppressive. To establish this contention in any sense *germane* to the question of the validity of the by-law it was necessary that the respondents should make it appear either that it was not passed in good faith in the exercise of the powers conferred by the statute or that it is so unreasonable, unfair or oppressive as to be upon any fair construction an abuse of those powers."

It would appear that the "unreasonableness" is something less than bad faith. If, for example, a statute gave to a local authority power to regulate the hours during which shops may remain open, a by-law providing that all shopkeepers with red hair should close their shops at six p.m., while other shops could remain open, would probably be *ultra vires* on the ground that it was not made in good faith. The enactment of such a by-law would be an attempt to exercise the powers for wrong purposes. On the other hand, if the by-law provided that all shops must close at noon every day during the week, this might be held to be *ultra vires* on the ground that it was an unreasonable exercise of the power. The distinction between the two may be only a matter of degree. The difference would appear to be that in the case of bad faith the by-law does not fall within the words of the statute and therefore the legislature did not confer the power; in the latter case, the by-law comes within the words of the Act, but it is such an unreasonable exercise of the power that Parliament must be presumed not to have conferred it.

(iii) Taxation

There would seem to be a presumption against the imposition of taxation.

In the *King* v. *Wright*[44] the Special War Revenue Act imposed a five per cent tax on automobiles manufactured in or imported into Canada, payable by the importer or manufacturer. Under a power to make "such regulations as he deems necessary or advisable for carrying out the provisions" of the Act the Minister made a regulation that when a manufacturer of a body mounts it on a chassis belonging to a customer, the tax should be computed on the combined price of the body and the chassis. The regulation was held invalid on the ground that "the regulation . . . cannot extend the application of the statute so as to impose a liability not otherwise imposed, and if it purports to do so it is to that extent ineffective."[45]

---

42 *Ibid.*, at pp. 99-100.
43 (1910), 42 S.C.R. 211, at p. 216.
44 (1927), 59 N.S.R. 443.
45 See also *The King* v. *National Fish Co. Ltd.*

(iv) Existing Rights

The validity of regulations has been challenged, and in some cases successfully, on the ground that they interfered with existing rights or that they were contrary to common law, statute law or fundamental justice.

Thus, in *Chester v. Bateson*[46] the court held the regulations *ultra vires*. J. Darling said "the regulation as framed forbids the owner of the property access to all legal tribunals in regard to this matter. This might, of course, legally be done by Act of Parliament; but I think this extreme disability can be inflicted only by direct enactment of the Legislature itself, and that so grave an invasion of the rights of all subjects was not intended by the Legislature to be accomplished by a departmental order".[47] Avory J. said "Nothing less than express words in the statute taking away the right of the King's subjects of access to the courts of justice would authorize or justify it".[48]

(v) Discrimination

In the case of *Ernest v. Commissioner of Metropolitan Police*[49] Defence Regulations prohibiting a person who is not a natural-born British subject from using any name other than that by which he was ordinarily known before the war were challenged. A naturalized British subject was convicted for using Ernest instead of Ernst. On appeal, he urged that the regulation was invalid because it took away his right to call himself by any name he pleased, and because it discriminated between naturalized and natural-born British subjects. Mr. Justice Darling said that the regulation was valid and that it was no objection to its legality that it discriminated between one class and another.

(vi) Sub-delegation

Can a subordinate legislative authority delegate his powers to another? In *Attorney General of Canada v. Brent*[50] authority to sub-delegate was denied.

On the other hand, in the *Chemicals Reference* the Supreme Court held that the Governor in Council could, under the War Measures Act, delegate to subordinate agencies the power to make rules and orders, and refused to read any limitations into the general words of the authorizing statute.

The result would appear to be that there is no rule or presumption for or against sub-delegation, and that in each case it is a question of interpretation of the language of the particular statute.

---

46 [1920] 1 K.B. 829.
47 *Ibid.*, at p. 833.
48 *Ibid.*, at p. 836.
49 (1919), 35 T.L.R. 512.
50 [1956] S.C.R. 318.

(g) Extent of Power

Thus far it has been assumed that the words of the statute were in themselves wide enough to confer the power to make the impugned regulation, and I have considered whether they must be read subject to some limitation. There still remains the question, to be decided in all cases, whether the statute has conferred the power.

The problem is to ascertain whether a regulation falls within the authority conferred by the Act. If not, it is *ultra vires*. How is this to be ascertained? There is little difficulty where the Act expressly confers power to make the specific regulations. Thus, if the statute authorizes the making of regulations imposing fees, prescribing licences, prohibiting transactions, there can be little scope for argument that a regulation doing those very things is *ultra vires*. Neither is there much difficulty where the regulation is contrary to some provision in the Act. Thus, in the case of *Belanger* v. *The King*[51] a regulation under the Railway Act was held ineffective to the extent that it conflicted with the empowering statute.

Difficulties arise where the power is not specifically conferred, and it becomes necessary to resort to general rules or principles of interpretation. Thus, in the *Lockwood* case[52] power to prescribe fees was not specifically conferred and it was necessary for the court to examine the statute as a whole to see whether Parliament contemplated that the regulation-making authority had power to impose fees.

The problem then of ascertaining whether a particular regulation is authorized by the statute under which it purports to be made is essentially one of statutory interpretation, and all the rules and principles of statutory interpretation as established by the courts may be applied. It is not intended to discuss here those rules and principles or their application.

(h) Terms of the Power

The lawyer's technique is to cite legal precedents for his propositions, and in attacking or supporting a regulation, he wants to refer to legal decisions, but, if they fail to answer the question of validity, what then? Is there anything else to which we can turn? There is, and it is almost too obvious to mention. But it is often overlooked. Having exhausted our store of legal precedent, why not look at the statute itself, and try to find out what the words mean, without worrying too much about what a judge may have said a long time ago, perhaps even in another country, about another statute. Can we find a clue to the extent or scope of a legislative power by looking closely at the words by which the power is conferred?

Many different forms may be used to authorize a subordinate authority to make laws, and a great variety is to be found in the statutes.

---

[51] (1916), 54 S.C.R. 265.
[52] *Supra*, footnote 9.

(i) General Forms

The form most commonly used now to confer a general power is:

> The Governor in Council may make regulations for carrying out the purposes and provisions of this Act.

As I have stated, it is doubtful whether the foregoing form would authorize anything more than purely procedural or administrative regulations.

The following examples, although in different words, probably have the same effect.

> For carrying the purposes and provisions of this Act into effect.
> Providing for the effective carrying out of the provisions of this Act.
> For carrying out the provisions of this Act according to their true intent and meaning.
> To give effect to the provisions of this Act.
> For the better execution of this Act.

Sometimes authority is conferred to make regulations *not inconsistent with* the Act. These words would seem to be unnecessary. It has been shown that it is not permissible to make regulations contrary to or inconsistent with the Act itself.

Sometimes the authority is to make *such regulations as are necessary* for carrying out the Act. It is doubtful that the words *as are necessary* add anything. In their absence, the courts would no doubt strike down a regulation they thought unnecessary. In either case, the courts would presumably be the judges of necessity.

A wider authority is conferred if a subjective test of necessity is prescribed. Thus, power may be conferred on the Governor in Council to make *such regulations as he deems necessary (advisable, expedient) for carrying out the purposes* of the Act. In such a case, as pointed out above,[53] the regulation-making authority is the sole judge of necessity and the courts will not question his decision, except possibly if bad faith were established. There is, therefore, a vast difference between the two following examples in the extent of the power conferred:

> May make such regulations *as may be necessary* for carrying out the provisions of this Act.
> May make such regulations *as he deems necessary* for carrying out the provisions of this Act.

(ii) Purposes

In the foregoing examples the limits of the authority conferred are set by the purposes of the Act, which, in turn, must be gathered from the terms of the Act. There is no statement of express purpose.

---

[53] *Rex* v. *Comptroller General of Patents, supra*, footnote 27 and *Berney* v. *Attorney General*.

Authority to make regulations may be conferred by defining a particular purpose:

> The Governor in Council may make regulations for the control and regulation of air navigation over Canada and the territorial waters of Canada.
> For the purpose of preventing the spreading of contagious or infectious diseases among animals.
> For the proper management and regulation of the sea-coast and inland fisheries.
> For regulating the export and import of agricultural products.

These examples constitute a wider authority than the general forms previously considered. In the case of a statute with power to make regulations for the better carrying out of the provisions thereof, Parliament has given at least partial effect to a legislative purpose by the enactment of the main principles of law essential to the implementation of that purpose, and has left it to others to fill in the details. But where Parliament authorizes regulations for a stated purpose, the regulation-making authority has a free hand to establish, not only the details, but also the main principles. The entire law is therefore to be left to the decision of subordinates. So long as the law is within the stated purpose, it cannot be challenged.

Even greater authority is conferred by authorizing a delegate to make such regulations *as he deems necessary* for a stated purpose. We recall the remarks of the Chief Justice of Canada in the *Chemicals Reference*[54] approved by the Judicial Committee of the Privy Council in the *Hallet & Carey case*[55] when he said that he could not agree that it was competent to any court to canvass the considerations which had, or might have, led the Governor in Council to deem the regulations necessary or advisable for the objects set forth; that the words of the War Measures Act were too plain for dispute — the measures authorized were such as the Governor General in Council (not the courts) deemed necessary or advisable.

A statement of purposes may be introduced by expressions such as *for, for the purpose of, in order to, etc.*

(iii) Subjects

Authority to make regulations may be conferred by assigning a subject-matter of legislation:

> May make regulations respecting the use, operation and supply of transport and storage facilities.
> May make regulations with respect to the export and import of animals.
> Relating to the construction and operation of factories.
> In relation to explosives.

---

54 *Supra*, footnote 3.
55 *Supra*, footnote 47, [1952] A.C. 427, at p. 445.

This again is a wide authority, embracing any regulation for any purpose coming within the defined subject. A subject-matter of regulation may be assigned by expressions like, *respecting, with respect to, in relation to, relating to, etc.*

Outstanding examples of the grant of legislative power with reference to subjects are to be found in sections 91 and 92 of the British North America Act. Power to make laws in relation to bankruptcy, for example, is complete power.

(iv) Specific Powers

Authority to make regulations is frequently conferred, not by defining a legislative purpose or subject-matter, but by conferring power to make a specific regulation. There is an important distinction between the two forms. For example, authority to make regulations:

> For the purpose of restricting or prohibiting the export of agricultural products.

sets forth the objective that may be attained by regulations. Any regulation having for its purpose the restriction or prohibition of exports would come within the powers conferred. Thus, regulations could provide for a multitude of ancillary or related matters.

On the other hand, authority to make regulations,

> Prohibiting or restricting the export of agricultural products,

is more restrictive. This is not a statement of objectives, but only a definition of a specific power — to prohibit or restrict. The language of the statute is in reality a description of the content of the particular regulation it authorizes. It would be open to doubt whether a regulation, for example, requiring dealers to make returns showing stocks on hand would be valid. Such a regulation might well be necessary *for the purpose of* restricting export, but it could hardly be described as a regulation that *restricts* export.

The distinction between purposes or subjects, on the one hand, and specific powers on the other, is also relevant in relation to sub-delegation. For example, if a minister had power to make regulations *respecting tariffs and tolls* he could probably authorize some other person to fix a tariff or toll; such a regulation would clearly be one *respecting* tariffs and tolls. But if the minister's authority is to make regulations *prescribing tariffs and tolls* then the minister must himself prescribe, because he is the only one who possesses the power. A regulation purporting to confer this power on another is not a regulation prescribing tariffs and tolls. Expressions commonly used to introduce specific powers are *prescribing, fixing, determining, prohibiting, requiring, establishing.*

In all but the simplest cases it is usual to include an omnibus provision, either before or after an enumeration of specific purposes, subjects or powers.

Where an enumeration follows the omnibus provision, it is usual to provide that the enumeration is not to be construed as restrictive.

Authority to make regulations is usually set out in tabular form. The tabulation may set out purposes only, subjects only, specific powers only, or may be a mixture of these various classes of authority. If the enumerations are all of one class, the governing participle or preposition is usually found in the general words preceding the enumeration:

May make regulations for the purpose of
   (a) ....
   (b) ....
May make regulations respecting
   (a) ....
   (b) ....

But where there is a mixture of classes, the governing participle, preposition or phrase is placed within each enumeration:

May make regulations
   (a) in relation to ....
   (b) for the purpose of ....
   (c) respecting ....
   (d) prescribing ....
   (e) determining ....

There may also be a fusion of the forms in which authority is conferred. Thus, the International River Improvements Act, provides in section 3 that:[56]

The Governor in Council may, for the purpose of developing and utilizing the water resources of Canada in the national interest, make regulations
   (a) respecting the construction, operation and maintenance of international river improvements;

The *purposes* for which orders and regulations may be made under the War Measures Act are "the security, defence, peace, order and welfare of Canada". The enumeration — which Lord Radcliffe called "powers", but which I have called "subjects" in the analysis suggested earlier — is but an enumeration of specific matters "for greater certainty" in relation to which orders and regulations may be made. In the words of Lord Radcliffe "They do not extend the purposes already defined, for they are directed to explaining what can be done, not the object for which things may be done".

In the 1945 Act, however, the enumeration is one of purposes, and the authority is to make such orders and regulations as the Governor in Council deems necessary or advisable for the enumerated purposes. Any regulation, therefore, is within the terms of the statute if it is for those purposes, and it is not necessary that the particular regulation should be specifically described in the statute.

---

[56] S.C., 1955, c. 47.

In considering whether a regulation is valid, it is important of course to examine legal principles and legal precedents. But in considering the nature and scope of a statutory power one must not overlook the words of the statute or the principles of language.

43 Appeals Against Administrative Decisions: The Function of Judicial Review*

H. J. Lawford

What is the function of judicial review of administration actions? Clearly, the courts must ensure that the law is obeyed by the administrators. As Professor Bernard Schwartz has recently said, "The judicial function is . . . one of control: we can expect judicial review to check — not to supplant — administrative action. The province of the judge is to confine the administrator within the bounds of legality, not to determine for himself the wisdom of challenged administrative action."[1]

Because of the sheer volume of administrative decision-making, the courts could not hope to supplant the administrative tribunals. Appeal Boards established by the Canadian Pension Commission alone considered some 1725 cases during a single fiscal year; the work of Appeal Boards represents only a small percentage of decisions given by the Commission.[2] Although the total number of tribunals in Canada is unknown, the Committee on the Organization of Government in Ontario found 84 provincial tribunals in that province alone.[3] A survey in Great Britain in 1959 showed about 2,000 administrative tribunals there.[4]

But if it is virtually impossible to imagine the courts replacing the administrative tribunals, there nonetheless remains the problem of distinguishing judicial review which properly determines the legality of administrative action from judicial interference with the formulation of policy. J. A. G. Griffith, Reader in English Law at the University of

* Reprinted and slightly abridged with permission of author and publisher from *Canadian Public Administration*, Vol. 5, No. 1, March 1962, pp. 46-52. This paper was presented to the Thirteenth Annual Conference of the Institute of Public Administration of Canada, at Ste. Foy, Quebec, September 6-9, 1961.

1 B. Schwartz, *An Introduction to American Administrative Law*, Pitman, London, 1958, p. 180.
2 Canada, *Annual Report for the Fiscal Year 1959-1960*, The Canadian Pension Commission, p. 73.
3 Ontario, *Report of the Committee on the Organization of Government in Ontario*, 1959, pp. 51, 53, 55-56.
4 Great Britain, *Report*, 1st, 1959, Council on Tribunals, 1960, p. 4.

London, has pointed out that judicial attitudes to administrative tribunals have fluctuated widely. In early cases on judicial review, "the courts inclined to the view that in a conflict between the common law property rights of an individual and the statutory powers of a local authority to interfere with those rights, the benefit of any doubt in the statute was to be given to the individual — and that this was particularly so if the statute gave less than full compensation to the individual."[5] Thus, a classic example of a court's substituting its views on policy for those of administrators was the 1925 decision, *Roberts* v. *Hopwood*.[6] There the House of Lords struck down a borough council's minimum wage resolution even though the legislation had given the council authority to pay such wages as the council might wish. The council would be acting illegally, Lord Atkinson said, if they "allowed themselves to be guided . . . by some eccentric principles of socialist philanthropy, or by a feminist ambition to secure the equality of the sexes in the matter of wages . . ."

The 1939-45 War produced a marked change in this attitude. The courts seemed reluctant to curb any administrative action.[7] Possibly, since the end of the War, there has been a reaction. Certainly, recent speeches by some members of the bar have rallied the legal profession against the administrators. Speaking to the Commonwealth and Empire Law Conference in Ottawa in September, 1960, Donald McInnes of Halifax, President of the Canadian Bar Association, urged lawyers to preserve the rights of individuals "from the hand of ruthless and untrained administrative bodies." At the same conference, Robert F. Reid, a Toronto lawyer who has taught administrative law at the Osgoode Hall Law School, complained of "the absence of any effective control over the tribunals."[8]

How then can one distinguish the proper spheres of the administrator and the judge? Or to be more exact, is there an adequate test for the scope of judicial review?

Probably the test most frequently used by the courts in deciding whether to review is a distinction between "administrative," "ministerial" or "legislative" actions of a board on one hand, and "judicial" functions of a board on the other. Much of the emphasis upon the "judicial" nature of the tribunal has resulted from an opinion of Lord Justice Atkin (as he then was) in *Rex* v. *Electricity Commissioners*:

> Whenever any body of persons having legal authority to determine questions affecting the rights of subjects, *and having the duty to act judicially*, act in excess of their legal authority, they are subject to the controlling jurisdiction . . .[9]

---

[5] J. A. G. Griffith, "Judicial Attitudes to Administrative Powers", British Journal of Administrative Law, 41, 1954.

[6] [1925] A.C. 578.

[7] Griffith refers to *Liversidge* v. *Anderson*, [1942] A.C. 206.

[8] R. F. Reid, "Administrative Tribunals and their Function as a Legal System", *Proceedings*, Commonwealth and Empire Law Conference, Ottawa, September 1960.

[9] [1924] K.B. 171 at 205. My italics.

Another landmark in the history of this conceptual approach was the Report of the Committee on Ministers' Powers, which attempted to classify decisions by administrators as judicial, quasi-judicial, or administrative.[10] Court decisions discussing whether a particular tribunal is "judicial" or must act "judicially" are legion.[11]

Yet this conceptual alchemy has failed. In 1948, reviewing twenty-five years of Canadian administrative law, Dean (then Professor) F. R. Scott wrote:

> It must be remembered that the "act" of an agency exercising delegated powers may fall into one of a number of categories. It may be "legis-lative," "executive," "administrative," "judicial," "quasi-judicial," "minis-terial" — these are the terms most frequently used. In these concepts lies the heart of administrative law as presently practised. Which acts belong to which categories? What is the essence of each? It cannot yet be said that we have achieved much clarification of this problem.

More than twenty years and some dozens of cases and learned articles later, the Committee on the Organization of Government in Ontario recalled Dean Scott's words and commented:

> Nor have the members of this committee "achieved much clarification" of the problem and for this reason alone the answer to the question of which appeal provisions are appropriate to which acts is also obscure.[12]

A number of reasons for the failure can easily be found. The answers to at least three distinct questions are said to depend on whether an act is judicial or administrative. Is the conduct of the administrator to be required to conform to certain standards, generally known as the "rules of natural justice"? Are certain types of procedural remedy — certiorari, prohibition, mandamus — the proper methods for review of the action? Are the administrator's acts to be accorded certain privileges — for example, freedom from legal proceedings for defamation? The meaning of the term "judicial" will vary depending on the question being asked. It need not follow that because an administrator's functions are the kind where he should hold his hearings in public (i.e., that he should act "judicially"), that his acts should be reviewed by certiorari (i.e., that his acts are akin to "judicial" proceedings) or that he should be protected from legal actions if he makes libelous statements during his proceedings (i.e., that he should have "judicial" immunities). Nevertheless, the decision by a court that an

---

10 Great Britain, *Report*, Committee on Ministers' Powers, pp. 73-75, 81-82, 114.

11 See, for example, the following: *Local Government Board* v. *Arlidge*, [1915] A.C. 120 (esp. per Lord Haldane); *Franklin* v. *Minister of Town and Country Planning*, [1948] A.C. 87; *Nakkuda Ali* v. *M. F. de S. Jayaratne*, [1951] A.C. 66; *Re Ashby*, [1934] O.R. 421, [1934] 3 D.L.R. 565; *Re Brown and Brock*, [1945] O.R. 554; *Re Ontario Labour Relations Board*, [1952] 2 D.L.R. 302.

12 *Op. cit.*, p. 14.

administrative action is "judicial" for one purpose is often used in testing whether other administrative actions are "judicial" for other purposes.[13]

A major cause of vagueness in the use of the term "judicial" has been the lack of a convenient procedure for judicial review, and the continued use of the antiquated forms of certiorari, prohibition and the like. Historically, the prerogative writs of certiorari and prohibition were issued to control the action of inferior courts. Then, by analogy, the use of these remedies was extended to other bodies. This extension by analogy continued until the writs came to be applied to bodies plainly administrative, but called "judicial." Occasionally, however, a court failed to recognize that powers really administrative had been called "judicial" for the purpose of using the writs. The court said: "Here is a case indisputably administrative and not at all like a court case," and refused to issue a writ.[14] Thus the meaning of the term "judicial" was gradually extended, but occasionally construed in a narrower sense.

In the United States, this source of confusion was avoided by the Supreme Court decision in *Degge* v. *Hitchcock*,[15] refusing to recognize the extension by analogy of the use of certiorari. Certiorari, the case held, lay only against courts in the "strict sense of the word" and could not be used to review decisions of administrative agencies. In place of the prerogative writs, American administrative law developed the remedies of injunctions and declaratory judgments.[16]

To a limited extent, British and Canadian law has simplified the use of certiorari and the other prerogative remedies; following the recommendations of the Committee on Minister's Powers, prerogative writs were replaced by orders. Although the procedure for seeking such orders is relatively simple, the legal requirements for the orders are uncertain. The law concerning certiorari is still unduly complex. And the vagueness in the use of the term "judicial" still continues.

If, then, the use of the "judicial" — "administrative" distinction has proved unsatisfactory in providing a test for the scope of judicial review, what other test is there?

A frequently suggested test is that the courts should confine their review to questions of jurisdiction and questions of law. Since the question of an administrator's jurisdiction is itself a problem of interpretation of law, this suggestion would confine the courts to a review of legal questions — as to which the courts are presumed to be competent. This, basically, is the recommendation of the Franks Committee Report:

---

13 See J. Finkelman, "Separation of Powers: A Study in Administrative Law", U.T.L.J., 313, 1936 at pp. 321-322.

14 An example of such a case is *Nakkuda Ali* v. *M. F. de Jayaratne* [1951] A.C. 66, as Mr. H. W. R. Wade has shown in his article, "The Twilight of National Justice", L.Q.R. 67, 1951, p. 103.

15 229 U.S. 162, 1913.

16 Schwartz, *op. cit.*, pp. 177-178.

> . . . we have concluded that in general the appropriate appeal structure
> is a general appeal from a tribunal of first instance to an appellate
> tribunal, followed by an appeal to the courts on point of law.[17]

The Committee pointed out that the characteristics of tribunals which often give them advantages over the courts are "cheapness, accessibility, freedom from technicality, expedition and expert knowledge of their particular subject."[18] This last characteristic — the expertise of the tribunal — is the major reason for restricting judicial review to questions of law. To allow an appeal from an administrative tribunal to the courts on questions of fact "would constitute an appeal from a body expert in the particular subject to a relatively inexpert body."[19]

But is this distinction between law and facts a valid test for limiting the scope of judicial review? First, it seems to be based upon the questionable notion that the special competence of the courts lies in law-finding rather than fact-finding. But as Judge Jerome Frank has pointed out, the work of the courts in determining facts is far more significant than their work in finding the law. Secondly, the test makes the equally questionable assumption that the expertise of the administrator lies in his fact-finding skill rather than in his knowledge of the relevant law. Yet, if the reason for excluding judicial review of the fact-finding process is to be the expert knowledge of the administrative tribunal, then the same reasoning applies with even greater force to the law-finding process. The law which governs the actions of administrators is often not only complex and highly technical, but also not readily ascertainable by a person not an expert. The regulations and previous rulings on such a matter as tariffs or unemployment insurance coverage are not only beyond the ordinary judge's comprehension — the judge does not know or have access to the source books and references. There is no law library in Canada at present which has an adequate collection of administrative regulations and decisions. Thus, it is very doubtful whether the judges of the Exchequer Court, when they consider appeals from the Tariff Board — appeals limited to questions of law — have a knowledge of or ability to discover tariff law equal to the knowledge and resources of members of the Tariff Board.

Moreover, drawing the distinction between matters of law and matters of fact is extremely difficult. Thus, in interpreting the scope of the remedy of certiorari, the courts have found themselves gradually extending the meaning of "questions of law." Originally, certiorari was issued by the courts to curb acts of inferior tribunals beyond their jurisdiction. Then, in the case of *Rex* v. *Northumberland Compensation Appeal Tribunal*,[20] the English Court of Appeal held that a court can grant an administrative decision not only in cases where the tribunal has exceeded its jurisdiction,

---

17 Great Britain, *Report*, Committee on Administrative Tribunals and Enquiries, 1957 Cmd. 218, p. 29. The Committee also recommended retaining the prerogative orders.
18 *Ibid.*, p. 9.
19 *Ibid.*, p. 25.
20 [1952] K.B. 338.

but also where there are errors of law which appear on the face of the record.[21] By a further extension it is possible to hold that a finding not based on evidence is contrary to law. As Lord du Parq has said, "To come to a conclusion which there is no evidence to support is to make an error in law."[22] Authorities differ as to whether insufficient evidence can amount to an error in law, but it is still clear that the boundary between matters of fact and law has been blurred.

Clearly, however, the decision whether judicial review is to be restricted to some form of interpreting law and excluded from a review of administrative fact-finding should depend on the purpose of judicial review. For not only is judicial review calculated to prevent excesses of jurisdiction and illegal administrative action, but also judicial review — indeed, any system of review — encourages consistency of administrative decision and makes the tribunal of first instance take greater care. Again, appeals serve to satisfy the public that the administrative process is fair.[23]

Surely the crux of the matter is that some system of appeal is desirable, and that review by the judiciary is most acceptable to the public. If the courts are not to provide review, then who is? For some boards review by ministers or by the cabinet can be provided either directly (as in the case of the Board of Transport Commissioners[24]) or indirectly, by requiring ministerial or cabinet confirmation of a board recommendation, (as with the Board of Broadcast Governors[25] or the National Energy Board[26]). But this form of review can deal only with broad policies. And it raises very difficult problems concerning the degree of independence which should be given to the administrative tribunals. Broadly, the Franks Committee has recommended a greater degree of independence for British tribunals. The Committee specifically recommended against appeals to ministers.[27]

---

21 The *Northumberland Compensation Appeal Tribunal Case* has been followed in Canada in *Re Labour Relations Board (Nova Scotia)* [1952] 3 D.L.R. 42, affirmed by the Supreme Court of Canada sub nom, *Smith and Rhuland* v. *The Queen* [1953] 2 S.C.R. 95, [1953] 3 D.L.R. 690. This technique of holding that a manifest error in law amounts to a declining of jurisdiction has been of great importance in avoiding privative clauses. By extension, a board which violates a rule of natural justice can be held to be acting outside its jurisdiction and outside the protection of the privative clause. See the *Globe and Mail* case, *Toronto Newspaper Guild* v. *Globe Printing Company* [1953] 2 S.C.R. 18.

22 *Bean* v. *Doncaster Amalgamated Collieries Ltd.*, [1944] 2 All E.R. 279 at 283. See also Schwartz, *op. cit.*, p. 186.

23 Great Britain, Committee on Administrative Tribunals and Enquiries, *op. cit.*, p. 25. See also, J. A. G. Griffith, "Tribunals and Inquiries", Mod. L.R. 22, 1959, 125 at 140.

24 Railway Act, R.S.C. 1952, c. 234, s. 53(1).

25 Broadcasting Act 1958 Canada, c. 22, s. 12.

26 National Energy Board Act 1959 Canada, c. 46, s. 81 and National Energy Board Part VI Regulations, Regulation 8.

27 *Report*, Committee on Administrative Tribunals and Enquiries, *op. cit.*, p. 25. For the view that the desire to increase the independence of the tribunals was the main feature of the Committee's Report see Griffith, "Tribunals and Inquiries", *op. cit.*, *passim*.

In Canada, no analysis has been made of the degree of independence presently possessed by the tribunals, much less of the degree of independence which is desirable.[28]

44   The Ombudsman in Canada*

Donald C. Rowat
Henry F. Llambias

Canada shares the general characteristics of the parliamentary system that exists in the Commonwealth countries. Among its main features are: a union of executive and legislative powers in a politically dominant Cabinet, a single-member, single-vote electoral system that often throws up a huge parliamentary majority which gives obedient support to that Cabinet, a tradition of secrecy that permeates the whole administrative structure, and severely limited opportunities for the appeal or judicial review of administrative decisions. All of these lend support to the proposition that the citizens and Parliament need the help of an Ombudsman in any attempt to get at the facts regarding a complaint of maladministration or arbitrary administrative action.

In fact, there are good grounds for believing that the need for the Ombudsman institution in Canada is more pressing than in many other Commonwealth countries. As in the United Kingdom, the liberties of the subject are not entrenched in a written constitution. But Canada has fewer administrative tribunals, where decisions can be made in a judicial manner, and no Council on Administrative Tribunals. Also, she has inadequate legislative prescription of administrative procedure; many regulatory boards and commissions with power to decide cases but no provision for appeal to the courts; antiquated laws on Crown privilege, expropriation and liability; weak arrangements for free legal aid to needy citizens; and no formal procedures in either Parliament or the provincial legislatures for settling the grievances of individuals. In addition to all this, the federal division of powers means that the provisions protecting the citizens' rights against administrative action are worse in some provinces

---

[28] Justice Minister Davey Fulton, Attorney General R. W. Bonner of British Columbia, Premier Louis J. Robichaud of New Brunswick and Douglas Fisher, CCF Member of Parliament for Port Arthur, are reported to have agreed that governments should have the final say over decisions of the boards because the governments ultimately would be responsible to the people. *Montreal Gazette*, August 31, 1961.

* Reprinted with permission of authors and publisher from D. C. Rowat (ed.), *The Ombudsman*, University of Toronto Press, Toronto, 1965.

than in others, and that the administration of justice varies because it is divided between the federal government, which appoints and pays the judges, and the provinces, which appoint all magistrates and control the organization and civil procedure of provincial and lower courts.

Throughout the Commonwealth countries there seems to be a general attitude of complacency about the protection of the citizens' rights, perhaps engendered by the strength of the tradition of the 'rule of law'. People do not realize that due to the modern growth of administrative powers the meaning of this tradition has lost much of its content. In Canada, one of the most frequently voiced objections to the Ombudsman proposal is that it is not needed: citizens' rights seem to be adequately protected already, and one doesn't 'hear about' very many cases of persons who have been dealt with unfairly by the administration. The objectors do not appreciate that, since administrative action is secret, the great majority of such cases do not come to light. Only some of the most serious ones are revealed and, since they concern isolated individuals, often they are not widely publicized by the press and are soon forgotten by the public.

To meet this objection, the authors of this essay have made it their business to collect cases of maladministration, arbitrariness and outright injustice which have been publicly reported within the past few years and which were not adequately handled by existing machinery. These reveal a bewildering variety of examples of bureaucratic bungling at all three levels of government — federal, provincial and local; they range from simple (but none the less serious) cases of red tape such as failure to answer an inquiry or make a decision, to heart-rending stories of sane persons incarcerated for years in the cockroach-ridden mental wing of Montreal's Bordeaux jail.[1] We have collected about 60 such cases, most of which have occurred in the past three years. In all of them an Ombudsman could have improved the situation for the complainant, usually by finding out the true facts at a much earlier date, by obtaining either redress or a change in the decision, and by doing so with far less injurious publicity. In several, he would no doubt have secured administrative and perhaps even legislative reforms.

These cases, however, are ones that, by good fortune or the strenuous efforts of the complainant, happen to have been revealed. There are countless others that are never brought to light and in which the aggrieved persons may suffer years of heart-breaking frustration. This was demonstrated by the numerous letters that Professor Rowat received from aggrieved citizens when he wrote a magazine article and spoke on radio and television about the Ombudsman idea. Their cases are of much the same type that the Ombudsmen receive and investigate. (Aggrieved citizens in Britain similarly sent cases to Ombudsman Hurwitz in Denmark after he returned home from speaking about his office on television in Britain.)

---

[1] Henry F. Llambias, "Wanted — An Ombudsman", *Edge*, No. 2, Spring 1964, pp. 81-91; D. C. Rowat, "We Need a New Defense Against So-Called Justice", *MacLean's*, Vol. 74, January 7, 1961, pp. 10, 82-83.

Another indication of the volume of unsatisfied complainants is the number of cases handled by a voluntary organization called Underdog, recently organized in Toronto to help mistreated persons. In Underdog's first eighteen months of operation there were 173 cases involving government officials. Of these, 69 had to do with the federal government, 84 were provincial and 20 were municipal.[2]

On the basis of the Scandinavian experience, one can estimate that the total case-load for Ombudsmen at all levels of government in Canada might be about 7,000 per year, with perhaps 3,000 at the federal level alone. Even using the low Danish figure of about 10 per cent that require some kind of corrective action, this would mean that the number of cases of uncompensated administrative injustice in Canada must be at least 700 per year. However, these figures may be far too low because of the earlier-mentioned inadequacy of Canada's protections against arbitrary administration. Also, the federal division of the country into two levels of government causes administrative conflict and delay, and creates confusion for the citizens, who are likely to complain to the wrong level of government at first, thus increasing the total case load at both levels. Another significant difference from the Scandinavian countries is Canada's higher level of post-war immigration and the accompanying administrative problems of eligibility for admission and citizenship.

While opponents may admit that most of an Ombudsman's cases could not be handled by the courts in Canada, they frequently object that with the single-member district it is the job of the member of Parliament to handle such cases for his district. In effect, they say, Canada already has 265 Ombudsmen at the federal level of government, to say nothing of those at the lower levels. To investigate this argument — to find out how many and what kinds of complaints MPs receive, how they handle them and whether they think an Ombudsman would help — Mr. Llambias sent a questionnaire to all members of the House of Commons in the spring of 1964, and received 80 replies. Nine of these were refusals of information, of which two were from Ministers who declined to express any opinion for fear that this might be interpreted as Government policy. Although the remainder is probably a biased sample, in the sense that only the most interested and sympathetic MPs replied, it does reveal some interesting facts.

The MPs were asked to estimate 'how many complaints about some aspect of governmental administration in relation to individuals' they received per month from constituents, and there was a surprising scatter in the replies. Thirty-six MPs estimated they had fewer than 10 complaints per month while twelve said they received more than 30, and two indicated that they were burdened with as many as 65. The difference in the number of complaints seems to depend mainly on the rural or urban character of the constituencies and their total populations, which at present vary tremendously. The average number of complaints received by the forty-

2 Robert McKeown, "Why Canada Needs an Ombudsman", *Weekend Magazine*, January 11, 1964, p. 24.

four MPs who replied to this question was about 15. Extending this average to all MPs would mean that in total they received an estimated 4,000 per month, or nearly 50,000 per year. Even if we assume that it was mainly the overburdened MPs that replied, and that an average for all MPs would be closer to 10 per month, this would still mean a total of 32,000 complaints per year. The replies indicated that a surprising number of complaints concern provincial or local government and even non-governmental bodies. Only about 70 per cent relate to federal departments or agencies, so that complaints of the latter type may total about 22,000 per year.

To a question on whether the complaints concern the personality of officials, the manner of proceeding or the substance of the action taken, there was considerable variation in the replies. However, most of the MPs thought that about 10 per cent concern personalities, 35 per cent the manner of proceeding, and that a majority are directed to the substance of the action. It is likely that many of the latter deal with the reasonableness of a decision or the effect of a law or policy. These matters an Ombudsman would not ordinarily investigate. MPs would continue to handle such cases, as well as requests for help and information and demands for change in the laws or regulations.

When the MPs were asked to identify the areas of governmental activity into which complaints mainly fell, they named 41 different areas, departments and agencies. However, there was a heavy concentration on certain areas. Decisions regarding pensions seemed to cause the most trouble, appearing in 20 questionnaires. The next most common areas of complaint were citizenship and immigration, income tax, health and welfare, unemployment insurance, and veterans' affairs.

Questions were also asked on the efficacy of the existing procedure for handling complaints. It is interesting that there was considerable disagreement about whether being on the Government or Opposition side of the House made a difference to the success of a complaint, although a majority of the MPs felt that it made no difference. Perhaps the reason for this disagreement, as one stated, is that being on either the Government or Opposition side has advantages and disadvantages. While access to information is easier for Government MPs, they are reluctant to ask the Minister a question in the House for fear of embarrassing the Government. As one MP wrote, 'No questions to the Minister, as I am on the Government side!' An Opposition MP, on the other hand, is free to publicize a case and to press an attack on the floor of the House.

A crucial question was: 'Do you ever handle complaints which are settled in a manner unsatisfactory to you and/or the complainant?' To this the great majority (55 out of 63) answered yes, and many said that half or more of their complaints were settled unsatisfactorily. Various reasons were given for the shortcomings of the existing system. One stated bluntly, 'Insufficient time and secretarial assistance to deal with each complaint'. Another felt that the basic inadequacy of the system was the 'weakness of individual MPs who are unwilling to intercede on behalf of constituents'. A third believed that not all MPs had the 'experience or training to deal with some of the issues which arise', while two MPs pointed out that in most cases they could only obtain information at second-hand from the Minister or civil servant, since they lacked access to the files.

The MPs were then requested to describe one or more typical cases, or cases in which they felt that the Minister's explanation and/or the department's action was unsatisfactory. Although many MPs felt that they could not take the time to do this, the others went to the trouble of presenting a great variety of interesting and sometimes shocking cases. While space does not permit an analysis of these cases here, it is clear that many of them would fall within the competence of an Ombudsman.[3]

To the final question, whether they thought that a Parliamentary Complaints Commissioner (Ombudsman) would be of help, 53 MPs answered yes, 13 said no, and 2 were doubtful. Of this sample of 68, then, the proportion in favour of the Ombudsman exceeded three to one.

Because of the large number of unsatisfied grievances against administrative action in Canada, and the inability of members of Parliament to deal with them adequately as revealed by the questionnaire, interest in the Ombudsman proposal has been rising — especially since New Zealand's adoption of the scheme in 1962. As early as December of that year, Arthur Smith, a member of the majority Conservative party, presented to the House of Commons a private member's Bill for a Parliamentary Commissioner. As often happens with such Bills, it was not debated or voted on. Much the same Bill was introduced again in 1963, this time by R. N. Thompson, leader of the Social Credit Party, but its second reading was disallowed by the Speaker because a private member's Bill may not propose the expenditure of public funds. He introduced it again as Bill C-7 in February 1964, with provision for the Commissioner to be financed by private benefactions — a change obviously designed to circumvent the Speaker's previous ruling. This time it was successfully debated.[4] By then a royal commission had reported favourably on the idea[5] and a Liberal Government was in power. Being more sympathetic to the proposal, the new Government agreed to refer the Bill to a standing committee, which will probably support it in principle.

Bill C-7 is based on the New Zealand Act of 1962, but is a much simplified and condensed version. Only some of its main features are mentioned here. As in the New Zealand Act, the Parliamentary Commissioner's grounds for criticizing an administrative action are to be very broad. For example, he may make recommendations where he adjudges that an authority or officer is administering a law 'unreasonably, wrongly . . . or by using

---

3 Mr. Llambias has analyzed and outlined some of these cases in his MA thesis, "The Need for an Ombudsman System in Canada", Carleton University, Ottawa, 1964.

4 *Debates*, Commons, March 17, 1964, pp. 1,167-1,173.

5 The Royal Commission on Government Organization, *Report*, Vol. 5, Queen's Printer, Ottawa, 1963, pp. 94-95.

a discretionary power for an improper purpose, or on irrelevant grounds.'
The scope of his jurisdiction is to be even broader than that in New
Zealand. The judiciary and the Governor General acting on the advice
of the whole Cabinet are exempt from his purview, as in New Zealand,
but any other 'power or authority or officer', apparently including individual Ministers, can be investigated and criticized if need be. The authors
of the Bill were obviously unimpressed by the fears expressed in Britain
that an Ombudsman might interfere with ministerial responsibility, for
they included neither the proposal of the 'Justice' report that a Minister
should have power to stop an investigation or refuse to release departmental minutes, nor even the stipulation in New Zealand's Act that, where
an investigation relates to a recommendation made to a Minister, the
Commissioner must consult the Minister at his request. Unlike the provisions in New Zealand, his powers of inquiry, rather than being spelled
out in great detail, are simply said to be those of a commissioner under
the Inquiries Act, and his investigations are not required to be private;
no fee is required to make a complaint, no limits are placed on his power
to investigate the armed services, and his scope is not limited to only
those departments and agencies named in a schedule.

It is important to recall, however, that the jurisdiction of an Ombudsman created under federal law in Canada could not extend to the provinces
or municipalities. For this purpose each province would need to provide
its own Ombudsman. Realizing this, a number of provincial bar associations and legislative representatives have become interested in the idea,
and several provincial Governments are considering it. In the early spring
of 1964, for example, the Governments of Saskatchewan, Nova Scotia and
New Brunswick announced that the idea would be investigated. And in
May the Government of Ontario appointed a royal commission on human
rights and civil liberties. This inquiry arose out of a controversy stirred
up by that Government's ill-fated police bill, which would have given
the Ontario Police Commission power to question any suspect in secret
and to hold him in custody indefinitely if he refused to answer questions.
One of the royal commission's objectives is to explore the office of
Ombudsman.

Indeed, it is very likely that an Ombudsman will be established in one
of the provinces of Canada before it is adopted at the federal level. But
this is perhaps as it should be. One of the great advantages of a federal
system is that an experiment with a new idea or constitutional form can
be tried on a small scale in one of the states or provinces first. If it is
successful there, it will then spread to the others and can safely be adopted
by the central government.

The needs at the provincial level, however, are different, and therefore
the provincial and federal offices should not be mere carbon copies of one
another. Because the provincial governments are smaller, an Ombudsman
would get to know the senior officials personally so that he would be less
likely to criticize them. The Cabinet's control over the administration is

more direct, party patronage exerts a greater influence, and provincial Governments frequently have very large majorities in the legislatures for long periods of time. For these reasons, stronger provisions will be needed to ensure the Ombudsman's independence from the executive. Moreover, while there may be grounds for exempting the higher courts from an Ombudsman's supervision, the situation regarding the lower courts, which the provinces control completely, is different. The Chief Justice of the Supreme Court has some disciplinary control over the judges of the higher courts but any disciplining of magistrates must be initiated by a provincial Government. Because of the tradition that the executive should not interfere with judicial independence, provincial Governments rarely undertake to do this. Yet magistrates are often inadequately trained and inexperienced, and, because of the large volume of cases they must consider, frequently make decisions involving civil liberties that are too hasty, or delay making decisions so long that the delay amounts to a denial of justice. Theoretically, the appeal system should take care of such faults, but it is in the lower courts that the real 'underdog' most frequently appears — with no education, no money, no counsel, and no thought of appeal. The case for including the lower courts in a provincial Ombudsman scheme is therefore strong.

Another difference between the federal and provincial governments is that the latter control the local governments. Hence a provincial Ombudsman would need to have jurisdiction over decisions made by municipal officials. Indeed, it may be that the largest city corporations, such as Montreal, Toronto, and Vancouver, should each have an Ombudsman of its own, such as has already been proposed for Philadelphia.[6] On the other hand, the federal government controls the armed services. There is plenty of evidence that cases arise within them which need the aid of an Ombudsman. But perhaps the nature of military organization and the laws governing service personnel are sufficiently different to justify a separate office for military cases, as in Sweden, Norway and Western Germany. Although in most provinces a single Ombudsman may be adequate to handle the volume of work, one wonders whether this would be true at the federal level. The countries in which the Ombudsman system now exists all have small populations, and it may be that Bill C-7 copied New Zealand's scheme too directly in this respect. A plural Ombudsman, in the form of a Complaints Commission, would probably meet the need more adequately in larger countries like Canada.[7] Sweden, the biggest of the Scandinavian countries, is itself seriously considering this idea, now that the work of the Ombudsman and his Deputy is growing so rapidly.

Whatever adjustments may be required to make the institution coincide more neatly with conditions at the federal and provincial levels, there is

---

[6] See H. J. Abraham's essay.
[7] For further comments on the adjustments needed to fit Canadian conditions, see D. C. Rowat, "An Ombudsman Scheme for Canada", *Canadian Journal of Economics and Political Science*, Vol. 28, No. 4, November 1962, pp. 554-556.

no doubt of the need in Canada for an institution like the Ombudsman. Yet it is important to realize that such an institution cannot cure all administrative ills. It will work successfully only in a country, province or state that is already reasonably well administered. Where an administration is riddled with political patronage or corruption, the problem is too big for an Ombudsman, and a reform of the whole system is required. Even where this is not the case, the need for additional protections against arbitrary administrative action is now so great in most Commonwealth countries that other reforms will be needed if the institution is not to become overloaded. Canada, like other Commonwealth countries, is now living on its past reputation for 'the rule of law'. We are like the dog in the anonymous rhyme:

> There was a dachshund, one so long
> He hadn't any notion
> How long it took to notify
> His tail of his emotion;
> And so it was that, though his eyes
> Were filled with tears and sadness,
> His little tail went wagging on
> Because of previous gladness.

Faced with our failure to solve the problem of protecting the rights of the citizen in the modern administrative state, and with the progress made in solving this problem by other democratic countries, our eyes are 'filled with tears of sadness'. But our tails go wagging smugly on, because of previous gladness.

45   The Public Official—Parliament, The Public and the Press*

S. H. S. Hughes

There is a salutary tradition of long standing in Parliament that civil servants are not to be called to account individually and by name for the actions which they perform under the authority of a minister of the Crown, and only that minister (and perhaps his colleagues) can be assailed when things go wrong, or legitimately acclaimed when things go right. There was a time when public officials were not afforded this

* Reprinted with permission of author and publisher from *Canadian Public Administration*, Vol. 3, No. 4, December 1960, pp. 289-298.

protection; a time, needless to say, when ministers of the Crown were not yet responsible to Parliament, and in those far off days it was the custom, when either House felt that its prerogatives had been usurped or infringed, to call the offending functionary before its bar so that he might explain, apologize, and be admonished upon his knees. Many a modern antiquarian must have sighed over the passing of this golden age. It is hardly necessary to say that were this practice still followed, no minister could be impartially advised or efficiently served. None the less, this protection of the civil servant from specific and personal attack in Parliament is not always to his advantage. The very facelessness and namelessness of the men and women who conduct the day-to-day business of government have engendered the fear that legislative bodies are losing their grip upon administration, and that ministers no longer control the actions of their permanent advisers, but are themselves controlled by the views and the behaviour of the departmental officials for whom they are responsible. This fear, like all fears, is of course partly the product of illusion. But it would be dangerously complacent to assume that by merely guaranteeing the independence of the civil service we have reached the promised land. If we as a people become convinced that the real power in the State resides in the permanent officials, and that electoral changes have no real meaning in terms of policy and administration, then a deadly blow has been dealt to our parliamentary institutions and we are on the brink of that disillusionment and cynicism which has assailed so many famous democratic states before the final fragmentation of their political beliefs has plunged them into totalitarianism. I say, therefore, with diffidence but with conviction, that it should be the abiding concern of civil servants to communicate with Parliament as fully and frankly as it is in their power to do within the compass of their authority, so that members of all parties may discharge their duties to the people whom they represent with the aid of the most complete information and the most disinterested advice required in any given situation.

I do not want to be understood as suggesting that the general rule of conduct of civil servants in these matters does not comply with the highest counsels of perfection. I think that most members of Parliament would agree that they are well served in these matters, but that they are sometimes baffled by an atmosphere of reticence which is likely to pervade government departments when called upon to answer enquiries. I shall have more to say on this subject when I come to refer to tendencies and trends which seem to be characteristic of the present-day relationship between the public and its employees. For the present it is sufficient to say that of all the means of communication with the public, Parliament — because of its great constitutional authority, its ability to require the production of papers and to have these and ministerial explanations submitted to the test of debate — is far the most reliable. The reporting of parliamentary proceedings has, none the less, had a strange history. In that period of our common British constitutional history before the principle of ministerial responsibility was established, no reporting was allowed, for the well-known reason that the House of Commons, at least, feared any form of royal surveillance which might result in reprisals taken against its members by the Sovereign and his servants. Later on, and particularly during the nineteenth century, the reporting of parliamentary debates became not only a matter of official approval but of the widest popular acceptance. Thereafter I think we can discern a tendency for the press to give increasingly less prominence to proceedings in Parliament and to adopt a less objective attitude towards parliamentary reporting. For example, a member of the House of Commons may ask a question which raises a matter of public importance. The question is often in a form which suggests that he is just as anxious to impart information as to receive it. It may be of a provocative nature, and if it is it is assured of receiving prominence in the press. But what happens to the answer? This may take some time for a minister to furnish, because enquiries must be made of his civil service advisers, who in their turn must secure all the relevant information. When the answer is at length given in the House, it may well receive so little prominence in the press that the purpose of giving it, which is really to inform the public through Parliament, is almost entirely defeated. Of course the parliamentary representatives of the press will have done their best. It is not for them to say where and how their material will be published, and newspaper editors will say that it is their business, in order to serve the material interests of their publishers and their advertisers, to supply the public with news that is fresh, stimulating and even alarming. I do not quarrel with this explanation, but I merely say that it appears to the public employee that the press is nowadays more interested in rumour than in fact, and that the public, if it gets any at all of parliamentary proceedings, has an impression of charge and countercharge, and eventually of concealment.

It should not be assumed that members of the public services of Canada and its provinces tend, as a result, to undervalue the importance of the legislative bodies that represent the public which they serve. On the contrary, by the very nature of their duties, they are more appreciative of the representative function than most. But I do not think they are to be blamed if they have increasing recourse to direct communication with the public through all the media which are available, when the constitutional channels cease to be effective. We may expect an increasing reliance upon experts in the field of public relations, not only to deal directly with the press but to conduct costly and continuous advertising campaigns to attract public attention to departmental problems. This will result in the taxpayer having to pay to have his own elbow jogged, and I think it is fair to assume that the more often the jogging takes place the less sensitive his elbow becomes. We must not ignore the possibility that by the operation of some law of diminishing returns this type of communication will cease eventually to have any effect at all. However attractive speculation on this subject may be, I wish to consider with you for a moment the much more important problems involved in the day-to-day communication of public servants with men and women who come directly into contact with them, either personally or by correspondence.

We are all familiar with the paradox of public administration that being right 99 per cent of the time is no guarantee of success or even of safety. It is the hundredth or thousandth administrative process which, coming apart at the seams after a record of unbroken ease and tranquillity, threatens to condemn the whole system. In the field of communication about which we are speaking, there is nothing that succeeds like failure. Any casual acquaintance, so it seems, can wittily epitomize the civil service by giving you an example so exceptional in its circumstances and outlandish in its results that it is typical of nothing, but all the reasonable argument in the world will not serve to shake his conviction of its characteristic verisimilitude. This strange inversion of the law of averages is naturally encouraged by the press, which cannot be expected to resist news of the "man bites dog" variety. It is not surprising, therefore, that public officials become wary of giving anyone any more information than is absolutely necessary, and often much less than is desirable.

Here I think, in the public interest, certain simple rules can be laid down governing the direct relationships of civil servants with members of the public. First of all, a civil servant should be accessible, and wherever possible he should be at once available and not given to making members of the public wait simply to illustrate his intense preoccupation with other and more important matters. This rule can be applied to communication by letter by the simple expedient of ensuring that all letters from members of the public are at least acknowledged promptly, even if they cannot be answered immediately. We are all familiar with the delays that seem to overtake a great deal of official correspondence. A letter is received asking for information which the recipient does not have or cannot by himself supply. It is minuted from this person to that, and the assembling of information and the preparation of draft letters for signature by higher authority often takes a considerable time. When I was engaged in the practice of law I was irritated by the long silences which were apt to follow enquiries by letter from government departments, and was always agreeably surprised when my enquiries were promptly acknowledged, even though the information requested was not then forthcoming. I am still surprised, after experience of public administration in two jurisdictions, at the extent to which this simple and inexpensive form of courtesy is sometimes neglected. It is unnecessary to say that courteous and prompt replies go very far to creating a satisfied correspondent, even though the issue of his problem is not favourable to him. There is no doubt that the public service is improving in this respect, but I think it is still far from perfect.

In the second place, it is seldom possible to give too much information, provided that it is lawful to give it. This principle applies to internal communications within the service as well as contacts between the service and the public outside. The tendency to avoid candour, or to give too little information, is one of the most generally prevalent among public employees. I have heard various explanations of the reason for this lack of candour, and they all seem to stem from the apparent need for caution which an official feels must be observed in committing himself or his department in written dealings with the public or with other departments. This caution seems to reflect firstly the fear of being held responsible by superiors and secondly that of being held responsible by the law. It lies at the root of much that is unattractive and unglamorous about the public service and which gets departments of government described as inert and unenterprising. It is a great tribute to the resourcefulness of the legal profession that a letter from one of its members threatening to involve a government department or any of its members in legal proceedings frequently produces a gratifying state of perturbation, however empty the threat may be. I have had lawyers write to me and talk menacingly about Mandamus and Certiorari who clearly have about as much knowledge of the prerogative writs as I have about the theory of relativity. It is wise to remember that lawyers who have a case seldom tell you in advance where the lightning is going to strike. And since it is the law of libel which people seem to be afraid of when called upon to give information about the actions of individuals, it is also well to remember that telling the truth without malice is a good working rule of defence against the sometimes formidable weapons which that law makes available. When I was chairman of an administrative tribunal in Ontario which my colleagues and I had the great good fortune of establishing from the ground up, we were able to adopt as a principle, and implement in practice, the idea that all our files should be available to public scrutiny, and we even provided accommodation for the convenience of any member of the public who wanted to examine them. Needless to say, this attitude disarmed a great deal of curiosity and we were seldom troubled with many requests. Of course there will always be confidential papers which it will be constitutionally proper to make inaccessible, but as a rule of conduct as much information as can be given lawfully should be volunteered without hesitation, not only to establish good faith but also as a test of its accuracy and to separate rumour from fact. In personnel work particularly, it is easy to damage a man's character firstly by failing to test the accuracy of information which is apparently unfavourable to it and secondly by failing to divulge it and to allow the person affected to meet it with explanations. The inclination to conclude that it is better not to take a chance, and quietly close the file, is sometimes irresistible, but it is also an effective way of creating injustice.

The third rule of conduct which I would like to propound is that of consistency. I noticed recently in a magazine produced by a well-known manufacturer of business machines, among a number of other aphorisms, the following attributed to the latter-day American sage William Allen White, "Consistency", quoth he, "is a paste jewel which only cheap men cherish." The lot of the aphorist is a hard one, because so much sense has to be sacrificed to form, and wit and wisdom do not always go hand in hand. Making all the usual allowances for misquotation and removal from context, it would be difficult to find a more perverse observation, particularly when applied to the subject of administration. Consistency is as important in administration as it is in law, and a subject is as concerned with knowing how his rights will be interpreted as with what his rights are. Yet consistency has its drawbacks, as anybody who has the experience of being told "I cannot do this for you because if I did I would have to do it for everybody else" can testify. To each member of the public, his own problem is paramount, and it is of little comfort to him to be told that the requirements of consistency, in this respect, are all that stand between him and the beneficence of a warm-hearted civil servant who would otherwise be glad to help him. And yet here I think the public must be told emphatically that without consistency in administration there can be no real justice. A capricious, changing, unpredictable policy can only be a reflection of the minds of men who make it. It is only necessary to consider a situation where consistency is not observed, and which results in different treatment being given in individual cases where the facts and the law are the same, to realize that a position typified by the observation "I will do it for you but not for him" is indefensible. I labour this point because the cautious approach to so many questions which the need for consistency imposes upon members of the public service in all jurisdictions is one of the principal reproaches levelled at them by press and public alike.

Are there any special considerations applicable to communication with the public through the Press? I think it should be borne in mind that most of the trouble in this area — and for the civil servant it is frequently troublesome indeed — arises from the fact that the public official and the journalist often fail to speak the same language or think along the same lines. The official lives in a world where precision of thought and speech is valued for its own sake, and like the lawyer has developed conventions of expression which have significance primarily for his colleagues. The journalist is generally in a hurry and has been compelled, by the nature of his craft, to speak and write colloquially. He naturally distrusts the carefully-worded departmental press release and tries to instill some life into it with what he calls "background material," generally acquired directly from the official concerned with the business in question. The result of these communications, if not always a complete distortion of the facts, is often a perfunctory and incomplete reference to that to which the official has devoted considerable time and energy and thoroughly understands himself. The fact that he has taken the understanding of the journalist too much for granted and has perhaps failed to explain himself fully and exactly does not immediately occur to him, and he indignantly claims that he has been misquoted, when at the worst he may only have been misunderstood. But it is certain that he will protect himself in the future by saying less, or perhaps nothing at all.

The result of this type of contretemps is that many government agencies will only communicate with the press through clearly defined channels, which the press will not always accept as either fully informed or completely candid. Another barrier is accordingly erected between the public and the Public Service — a barrier which mutual distrust will keep firmly in place. If public officials had some experience of journalism, and journalists of the Public Service, it is probable that the former would be more forthcoming and lucid and the latter more judicious in the provision and use of information respectively. There is, however, no easy solution of this problem, and I will have to be content with two observations. In the first place, the provision of information to the press in as full and complete a form as possible by officials should be encouraged by their superiors, even though it be occasionally misused or neglected, provided always that timely precautions are taken against indiscretions injurious to the State. Secondly, journalists, by curbing the tendency to be prescient in speculation at the expense of the facts as they have found them to be, may well confer even greater benefits upon the public than they now do.

If we can therefore summarize the foregoing rules for communication with the public by the slogan, "Courtesy, candour and consistency," there remain to be discerned, wherever possible, the trends in present day relationships between the public service and its employers.

No one will seriously contend that the influence of political patronage in the recruitment and selection of public employees is not on the decline. Even in those jurisdictions where there are no statutory safeguards against its operation, there is a general inclination to avoid it and at the very least to pay lip-service to the principle of appointment and promotion by merit. The reasons for this are not far to seek. A system of competitive selection administered by an independent government agency is surer to win public acceptance than one which depends upon the mere reward of political services and support, and the type of political support which is only given in the expectation of such reward is seldom of decisive influence in the determination of electoral contests. Over and above these considerations are those of the efficiency and quality of the Public Service, which no representative government can afford to neglect.

But as the independence and security of the service becomes more strongly rooted in the traditions of impartiality and loyalty to the State, free from partisan bias, they are apparently threatened by a new set of suspicions. The facelessness and namelessness to which I have referred appear to be more alarming as the complexity of administration increases. Lobbyists and pressure groups, to use terms which have acquired meaning on both sides of the Atlantic Ocean, are not as well recognized in the framework of our public life as in the United States, but the techniques which they employ have acquired a respectable seniority in Canada. It is inevitable that the public official, protected by constitutional safeguards and required to give impartial advice to his political head, should acquire serpentine characteristics in the eyes of advocates of special interests. My own experience in the regulatory field persuades me that the business community occasionally resents that type of regulation which it understands to be restrictive of free enterprise, and is inclined to regard those who are charged with the responsibility of designing and enforcing it with feelings akin to those felt by Sinbad for the Old Man of the Sea. It is hard indeed to dispel the feeling that the public service is indoctrinated with economic and social beliefs not necessarily acceptable to the nation as a whole.

Nothing, in fact, is so provoking to press and public alike as the silence which is imposed by custom upon the operations of public officials, but the measure of public acceptance of the course of conduct of which that silence is eloquent is illustrated by the general condemnation of the public servant who speaks out for himself on a question of policy for which he is not responsible to a legislative body. We are fortunate indeed in the moderation and sense of responsibility displayed by the press of Canada in dealing with this type of provocation. One has only to look at sections of the British and American press to see how the independence of the Public Service can be threatened by irresponsible agitation. We do not suffer here from the daily and envenomed use of the term "bureaucrat," and the compulsive malevolence of widely syndicated commentators earning reputations for fearlessness by abusing the "civil service mentality." Since we are still citizens of a comparatively small country, it is well-recognized that the civil servant is like any other next-door neighbour who pays taxes to various public authorities, and pays them be it said without recourse to those provisions of the law which lighten the load upon the shoulders of those of his brethren engaged in mercantile pursuits. It would be idle to pretend, however, that the practice of abusing the public service on general principles cannot be matched with sincerity in this country. Assuming, for the purposes of argument, that it does not deserve abuse, there is always that significant element in any group of human beings who cannot accept the proposition that they are the authors of their own misfortunes. We are all familiar with this phenomenon, and it is especially noticeable in the field of personnel administration. It is apt to be aggravated proportionately when those who are expected to realize that they are, in fact, the authors of their own misfortunes become convinced that they are not in reality the masters of their own destinies.

It would seem to be an arguable proposition that hostility towards an individual is easier and more natural to develop than hostility towards a class. The characteristics of an individual are easy to observe, and the consequence of injustice to one not as calamitous as injustice to many. But the lessons of history tell us that hostility towards a class, like the Spartan helots or the Roman publicans or the Russian kulaks, is equally easy to develop, if not easier, because of a human tendency towards broad

*

generalization and the ease with which private virtues can be offset by submersion in a group or a common environment.

If we assume that the regulation of private activities by the State is increasing, and I submit that we are not justified in assuming the contrary, the tendency to attribute responsibility for its disagreeable aspects to those who administer and enforce regulation will increase correspondingly or perhaps disproportionately, depending upon the steps that are taken to excite public indignation. In a federal state like ours, with strongly established institutions of local government, the process may well be retarded, but the possibility of its development in advance cannot be ignored by anyone interested in public administration. We are accustomed to being told in this country that we are over-governed, that the increase in the numbers of public employees threatens our liberties and our finances, and that the size and number of government agencies must be reduced. We are well aware that many, if not all, of the same voices are raised in protest if any of the establishments complained about, or the services provided, are actually reduced or curtailed. Government agencies are on all sides urged to do more, but to do it with less. It is easy to speak with feeling on this subject from the point of view of the Civil Service Commission of Canada, which has to satisfy the appetites of government departments in its recruiting function and so often to thwart them in that of organization and classification. In the course of a close, not to say rigorous scrutiny of the Commission's operations early in 1959, the House of Commons Committee on Estimates recommended that the Commission embark on a course of action entirely commendable and salutary, which would, at a conservative estimate, have required the doubling of our personnel selection staff. Weighing the advantages of the recommendation against the propriety of a control agency indulging in such spectacular expansion, we had regretfully to decline, or at least postpone, contemplation of the course proposed. If we were wrong in this conclusion, we only succeeded in preventing or retarding a desirable development for the sake of an economy which may, in any event, be nullified by the external pressures of our national expansion.

Speaking generally, I foresee, as a concomitant of this expansion which is with us and around us at the present moment, a great increase in the duties and responsibilities of governments at all levels, accelerated perhaps by the inevitable tendency of our people to thrust more burdens upon them. I take my stand as firmly as anyone else on the side of free enterprise and the preservation of private rights, being always aware that never in our history have we been able to countenance enterprise in a state of perfect freedom or the ascendency of private rights over the eminent domain of public need. We live and move in a maze of contrivances, which could not by themselves and one by one survive the test of logic, at once as tenuous as the 49th parallel and as massive as the British North America Act. It follows, therefore, that there is no return for us to first principles of political theory, and that failing some inundation which will erase us as a nation from the page of history, we must follow the current of our national life down ever-widening but predetermined channels.

If such an increase in governmental responsibility and activity is inevitable, then I foresee a corresponding increase in the numbers and influence of the administrators and their executants who form the Public Service. There will be plateaux, as the doctors say, stages of temporary respite from this inexorable advance, and it will, I hope, be possible to preserve a just proportion between the enlargement of administrative function and the needs of a growing community. In consequence, there will be a very real danger that the tendencies which now seem to divide the public from its servants will become more marked and excite more feeling. I hope that the public and its great mentor, the press, will not take too lopsided a view of this process. There will always be safeguards against a "population explosion" among public employees. Legislative bodies and the executives which are responsible to them will no doubt continue to be concerned with the over-riding necessity of good husbandry in the raising and expending of public funds. Control agencies will continue to harry the empire builders. Enlightened statesmanship and a vigilant bench and bar will labour to preserve our characteristic and historic concern with the sanctity of private rights. In short, all the resources of democracy as we know it will be deployed against the advance of bureaucracy in the most invidious sense of that hard-worked word. We can only hope that the best traditions of public service will not be compromised in the struggle, and that a fully and fairly informed public will steadily survey the scene.

46   The Political Rights and Activities of Canadian Public Servants

W. D. K. Kernaghan

Until the 1960's, the approach of the Canadian federal and provincial governments to the extension of political rights to public servants was much less progressive than that of many other industrialized, democratic states. Despite the loosening of restraints on the political activity of Canadian federal employees in recent years, the conclusion of a comparative study conducted by a United States Government commission in 1967 was that

> Canadian restrictions of the political activities of civil servants have been stricter than those found in other British Commonwealth nations of

comparable development, such as Australia and New Zealand, and are presently far stricter than the regulations in Great Britain itself.[1]

Canadian literature on this important and controversial topic is virtually non-existent. This brief paper will introduce the subject through an inquiry into the theoretical debate on the granting of political rights to government personnel; a comparative analysis of the legal regulations in certain foreign states and Canadian provinces; and an examination of the evolution of political rights at the federal level of government in Canada.

In its application to the public service, the term *political rights* generally encompasses the rights to vote, to campaign in support of a candidate, to attend political meetings, to stand as a candidate in federal or provincial elections, to hold local office and to appeal against dismissal arising from real or alleged political activity. In addition, the citizen's crucial right to freedom of expression on political matters touches on the propriety of a public servant's action in criticizing government policy in the press or from the platform and in disclosing official information without authorization.

The dilemma posed by the question of political rights for government personnel is the need to reconcile the necessity for the political neutrality and administrative impartiality of public servants with the demand for equal rights for all citizens in a democratic state. The traditional arguments promoting the extension or limitation of the political rights of government employees are offered on behalf of the general citizenry, the political heads of executive departments, political parties and the public servants themselves.

Opponents to broadening the range of political rights contend, first of all, that overt political partisanship among government employees undermines public confidence in the impartial conduct of the nation's business. Moreover, they contend that the unabated expansion of the bureaucracy's influence in the policy-making process requires a public service free of political bias. Governments can discharge their responsibilities effectively and efficiently only if the bureaucracy is divorced from partisan affiliation since the political executive, who relies on administrative subordinates for counsel and policy implementation, must be assured of their integrity and loyalty. It may be argued further that government employees should not publicly criticize government policy, whether this criticism is based on knowledge available to the general public or on information available to public servants by virtue of their official position. Certainly, in the interests of state security, governments must impose heavy penalties on public servants who make unauthorized use of official documents. Another common argument for the restriction of political rights is that in accepting the advantages of security and generous fringe benefits accompanying government employment, public servants can realistically be expected to relinquish

---

[1] United States, *Report of the Commission on the Political Activity of Public Personnel*, United States Government Printing Office, Washington, D.C., 1968, Vol. 2, p. 162.

certain political rights enjoyed by other citizens. Finally, public servants must be protected against financial exploitation or coercion by a superior with party affiliations who can affect his subordinates' prospects for promotion.

On the other hand, advocates of the emancipation of public servants from political restraints are motivated in large part by the political sterilization of an increasing percentage of the population as the number of public servants continues to expand.[2] In a democratic society, the isolation of such a substantial proportion of the population from political activity must be offset by substantive and demonstrable benefits to the public interest. An especially powerful argument for the removal of political restrictions is that the public services contain a concentration of the best educated and best informed persons in the country. As a consequence of excessive limitations on the political rights of public personnel, the nation may be deprived not only of an articulate and knowledgeable expression of views on public issues but also of talented persons reluctant to accept employment which restricts their political activities. In addition, political parties may be obliged to exclude from active party membership and possible candidature persons whose intimate acquaintance with governmental problems is invaluable to the formulation of party policy.

The solution to this conflict between administrative nonpartisanship and the enjoyment of political rights is not a simple weighing of these opposing theoretical considerations or the application of one or the other set of arguments to particular countries. In practice, it is common for governments to evolve a position of compromise between the unworkable extremes of unrestrained political activity and absolute political sterilization. The measure of political activity accorded government employees in democratic societies may be depicted along a continuum between these two extreme poles.

On this continuum, the status of public servants in the United States approaches the extremity of complete exclusion from political activity. The *Hatch Act* of 1939 and its amendment in 1940[3] severely restrict the political activities of more than 4.5 million public servants at the federal, state and local levels of government.[4] The provisions of this federal statute apply to employees of state and local governments working on programs financed wholly or in part by federal loans or grants.

The narrow range of permissible political activities under the Act includes the right to vote; the right to express views "on all political

---

2 The number of public servants at all levels of Canadian government today amounts to 17.2 per cent or about one-sixth of the total labour force. See my article "Public Administration in Canada Today" in this book, p. 52.

3 53 United States, *Statutes*, 1147 (1939) and 54 United States, *Statutes*, 767, (1940).

4 *Report of the Commission on the Political Activity of Public Personnel, op. cit.*, Vol. 1, p. 11.

subjects and candidates"[5]; membership in political party clubs and attendance at political rallies and conventions; voluntary contributions to political parties and organizations; wearing political badges and displaying political stickers and signs on a car or at a home; participation in local non-partisan elections; and full political activity on matters "relating to constitutional amendments, referendums, approval of municipal ordinances, and others of a similar character".

A wider range of prohibited activities includes standing as a candidate for federal, state or local office; organizing or holding office in a political club; serving as a speaker, delegate or alternate to a party convention; campaigning actively for a political party or candidate through public speeches, the distribution of literature, the circulation of nominating petitions or participation in parades; engaging in official or partisan activity at the polls on election day or transporting voters to the polls; and soliciting political contributions. The penalty imposed for violation of these prohibitions is removal from office or suspension without pay for a minimum period of 30 days.

The Commission on the Political Activity of Public Personnel, appointed jointly by the President and both Houses of Congress in 1966, presented a three-volume report recommending the removal of many of the existing barriers to political activity.[6] The implementation of these recommendations would help to eliminate numerous abuses of the *Hatch Act* which have arisen partly from uncertainty among public servants as to the permissible and proscribed activities under the Act. One of the central proposals of the Commission was that "the law regulating political activity of government personnel should specify in readily understandable terms those political activities which are prohibited, and specifically permit all others."[7]

The British Government's attitude on the issue of political activity for public servants brings their position closer to the pole of unrestrained political activity. Yet this general statement must be severely qualified since a substantial number of British civil servants are barred from all but the most limited political activity. Following an evolution over 80 years in the direction of extending the scope of political activity, a reconciliation of views contained in the Masterman Committee Report[8] with the counterproposals of the staff side of a Whitley Council Committee led to the

---

[5] The United States Civil Service Commission has explained that this right "is subject to the prohibition that employees may not take any active part in political management or in political campaigns". *Political Activity of Federal Officers and Employees*, United States Civil Service Commission, Washington, D.C., May 1966, pamphlet 20, p. 12.

[6] See especially Vol. 1, *Findings and Recommendations*.

[7] *Ibid.*, p. 4.

[8] Great Britain, *Report of the Committee on the Political Activities of Civil Servants*, His Majesty's Stationery Office, London, 1949, Cmd. 7718, June 1949.

adoption in 1953 of a differentiated system of political rights for civil servants.[9]

The entire body of British civil servants was divided into three major categories labelled *politically free, intermediate* and *politically restricted* depending on their influence on policy making and their occupational relationships with the public. The politically free category comprises all employees working in the industrial civil service and those in the non-industrial civil service falling within the manipulative grades of the post office and the minor grades of messengers and cleaners. These civil servants are free to participate fully in national and local political activities although they must submit their resignations before nomination day if they stand for election. Moreover, they may be subsequently reinstated to the civil service on the fulfilment of certain conditions. The intermediate category embraces those civil servants performing clerical and typing responsibilities. These employees may take part in all political activities except candidacy for Parliament. Their political activities are subject, however, to the granting of departmental permission "according to the degree and nature of the conduct with the public involved"[10] and to the acceptance of a code of discretion. The politically restricted category includes all other civil servants, that is, those falling within the executive, the professional, the scientific and technical, and the administrative grades. Members of this restricted category will normally be permitted to take part in local political activities which are not associated with national political organizations. The political activities of this group are subject both to the acceptance of a code of discretion and the obligation to inform the department of election to a local government office.

The location of Canada's federal public servants on the continuum of political activity lies between the positions of the United States and Great Britain. Only during this decade has Canada taken the progressive measures necessary to achieve this status.

For 40 years following Confederation, the Canadian federal government was plagued by a heritage of patronage from the pre-Confederation era of colonial rule. The practices of appointment for party service, the use of government employees to promote partisan objectives, the holding of office at pleasure and rotation in office brought the government to the verge of the United States *spoils system*. Little advance toward the elimination of the evils of patronage was made before the *Civil Service Amendment Act* of 1908[11] which applied the merit principle to the inside service (civil servants in Ottawa) and imposed the penalty of dismissal for political activity. Patronage in the outside service continued apace, however, and the device of making temporary appointments on political grounds to the

9 Great Britain, *The Political Activities of Civil Servants*, Her Majesty's Stationery Office, London, 1953, Cmd. 8783, March 1953. See also Great Britain, (Treasury) *Establishment Circular* 26/53, August 14, 1953.

10 *Establishment Circular* 26/53, sec. 37(b).

11 Canada, *Statutes*, 7-8 Edw. VII, c. 15.

inside service almost destroyed the merit system during the following decade.

Then, in 1918, a new *Civil Service Act*[12] extended the merit system. Provision was made for admission by competitive examination to both the inside and outside services. The prohibition against political activity was reinforced by vesting exclusive power of appointment and promotion in the Civil Service Commission rather than in the politicians. Section 55 of the Act, which stood unaltered for 43 years, stated that

1. No deputy head, officer, clerk or employee in the Civil Service shall be debarred from voting at any Dominion or provincial election if, under the laws governing the said election, he has the right to vote; but no such deputy head, officer, clerk or employee shall engage in partisan work in connection with any such election, or contribute, receive or in any way deal with any money for any party funds.

2. Any person violating any of the provisions of this section shall be dismissed from the Civil Service.

Although the enforcement of the Act diminished substantially the magnitude of partisan political activity among government employees, Dawson wrote as late as 1936 that "political patronage is still the great enemy of civil service efficiency in Canada".[13]

Nevertheless, the effect of patronage on appointments to positions falling under the authority of the Civil Service Commission gradually dwindled to the point where by 1960, Hughes, then chairman of the Commission, could write that

. . . no one will seriously contend that the influence of political patronage in the recruitment and selection of public employees is not on the decline. Even in those jurisdictions where there are no statutory safeguards against its operation, there is a general inclination to avoid it and at the very least to pay lip-service to the principle of appointment and promotion by merit.[14]

In making reference to "those jurisdictions where there are no statutory safeguards", Hughes was alluding to the large numbers of public servants working in government positions and agencies which had over the years been exempted from the application of the inflexible and overcentralized controls of the *Civil Service Act*. Indeed, in 1960, only 131,953 persons out of a total civilian public service of 344,362 (less than 40 per cent) were subject to the provisions of the Act, including the restrictions on political activity.[15] Although the acceptance of the merit principle by exempt groups

---

12 Canada, *Statutes*, 8-9 Geo. V, c. 12.

13 R. M. Dawson, "The Canadian Civil Service", *Canadian Journal of Economics and Political Science*, Vol. 2, August 1936, p. 291.

14 S. H. S. Hughes, "The Public Official — Parliament, the Public and the Press", *Canadian Public Administration*, Vol. 3, No. 4, December 1960, p. 295.

15 Canada, Civil Service Commission. *Annual Report 1960*, Queen's Printer, Ottawa, 1961, Appendix B, *Composition of the Public Service as of September 30, 1960*, p. 34.

varies from agency to agency, political appointments and activities have been more common outside the confines of the *Civil Service Act*.

Also in 1960, the federal government, by Order-in-Council, conceded a public servant the legal right to participate in political movements and elections at the local level of government "if he has been granted leave without pay to do so or if his Deputy Minister finds that holding such office will not prevent the civil servant from properly discharging his duties. . . ."[16] A federal public servant may in addition receive leave without pay if he wins election to a full-time municipal office.[17]

The Province of Saskatchewan long preceded the federal government in removing certain deterrents to the political activity of public employees. As early as 1947, the Saskatchewan government bestowed on its employees generous political privileges. *The Public Service Act*[18] provides that no public servant may engage in political activity during working hours; use his authority to coerce any other employee into political participation or to make financial contributions to any political party; or indulge in political activities which might "impair his usefulness in the position in which he is employed". Aside from these minor restraints, the province's public servants are free to take part in political activity outside their regular working hours. Furthermore, a government employee who wishes to stand for public office may have 30 days leave of absence without pay before election day.

The 1958 *Report of the Civil Service Commission on Personnel Administration in the Public Service*[19] (the Heeney *Report*) proposed few modifications in federal legislation affecting political activity. The *Report* included proposals that public servants be permitted to act as poll officials under specified conditions and that a commission of inquiry be established to consider alleged instances of political partisanship. The revision of the *Civil Service Act*[20] in 1961 retained the longstanding prohibition against partisan work but incorporated the recommendation of the Heeney *Report* that an alleged violation of political activity be the subject of an inquiry. In all provinces except Saskatchewan, Ontario and Quebec, legal regulations or established practices affecting political activity are today identical or very similar to the federal procedure as it existed under this 1961 Act. The federal government was upstaged by the 1962 amendments to Ontario's *Public Service Act*[21] which liberalized previous regulations in the realm of political activity for a large proportion of the province's employees. Any public servant, other than deputy ministers and certain designated senior officials, may be a candidate or actively support another candidate

---

16 Canada, Memorandum, *Public Office — Municipal or Civic*, P.C. 1960 — 1121, August 12, 1960.
17 Canada, *Civil Service Regulations*, c. 71. *The Canada Gazette*, Vol. 96, No. 7, Ottawa, April 11, 1962, p. 396.
18 Saskatchewan, *Revised Statutes*, 1965, c. 52.
19 Queen's Printer, Ottawa, December 1958, pp. 93-94.
20 Canada, *Statutes*, c. 57.
21 *Statutes*, 1962-1963, c. 121.

for election to municipal office providing that such activity does not adversely affect the employee's performance on the job; does not harm the interests of the Crown; and is not affiliated with a provincial or federal political party. The employee shall, however, be granted a leave of absence without pay to stand for provincial or federal election or to campaign openly and to solicit funds in support of a provincial or federal party. An Ontario public servant who resigns on winning election may be reinstated if he ceases to be a political representative within five years and applies for reappointment within the subsequent three months.

According to the terms of the Quebec *Civil Service Act*,[22] a provincial civil servant may participate in federal or provincial political activities only on resignation from the civil service. If defeated in an electoral contest, the civil servant is entitled to reappointment to the service.

On the basis of the recommendations of a joint committee of the House of Commons and the Senate on employer-employee relations in the federal public service,[23] significant alterations in federal legislation regulating political activities were incorporated in the *Public Service Employment Act*.[24] Public servants are now permitted to attend political meetings and to contribute money to a candidate's campaign or to party coffers. The Public Service Commission has authority to approve requests for leave of absence without pay to enable any employee to seek nomination and election to federal, provincial or municipal office. These requests may be denied if the employee's usefulness would be impaired by such activity. Furthermore, in the event of election to office, the employee automatically vacates his position.

The very general language of the statute and the inadequacy of its coverage provides little specific direction to federal employees and leaves much discretion as to acceptable and forbidden political activities to the Public Service Commission. For example, the Act makes no reference to membership in political parties. In practice, however, federal employees may hold "inactive membership" in a political party, that is, they may be seen at party gatherings and rallies but may not be heard.

None of the Canadian legislation on political activity discussed to this point has treated the critical and delicate issue of the right of public servants to freedom of expression on political matters. The traditional, but informal, practice has been that government employees should maintain "a certain reserve" in their discussion of public questions. In 1965, a federal government actuary was dismissed for his public denunciations of the *Canada Pension Plan* which at the time was being debated in the House of Commons. The Appeal Board upheld the dismissal primarily on the grounds that the employee had special responsibilities "as a member of the civil service to uphold the constitutional laws and traditions and

---

22 Quebec, *Statutes*, 1965, c. 14.
23 Queen's Printer, Ottawa, 1966-1967.
24 Canada, *Statutes*, 1966-67, c. 71.

as an employee to refrain from conducting himself in a manner that would destroy his harmonious relationship with his employer". In addition, the Board noted that the employee's conduct in making "the representatives of the press and the public . . . witnesses to the unedifying spectacle of a senior civil servant attacking government policy . . . tended to make the discharge of the government's functions more difficult".[25]

The unauthorized disclosure of information by public servants is ordinarily regulated by the initial oath or affirmation of office and secrecy.[26] Severe penalties may be imposed under the *Official Secrets Act*[27] on government employees who make unauthorized use of official information, particularly the communication of a "code word, pass word, sketch, plan, model, article, note, document or information" to agents of a foreign power.

Comparative analysis indicates that the gradual extension of political rights to certain groups of government employees is not likely to injure the public interest through the reintroduction of appointment and promotion on partisan grounds. Canadian federal and provincial governments may benefit not only from granting a broader range of political rights but from a more explicit legislative statement of permissible and prohibited political activities. Canadian governments may also evaluate the procedure of differentiating among public servants for purposes of political activity based on the British or the Ontario model.

The federal government and certain provincial governments have moved a long way in the direction of an appropriate balance between the political neutrality and the individual rights of government employees. Yet, in a comparative context, not only with Great Britain but with several developed countries in Western Europe and Asia, Canadian laws and practices appear unduly restrictive. The accumulation of much more empirical data on the extent of political activity at all levels of Canadian government is essential, however, before further legislative modifications are made.

---

25 "Appeal of Mr. John W. Kroeker, Actuary 6 (Senior Actuary) against decision of Superintendent of Insurance to recommend dismissal under Section 60 of the Civil Service Act", INS-A-20, April 9, 1965, pp. 22-23.

26 The federal wording is as follows: "I, (A.B.) solemnly and sincerely swear (or affirm) that I will faithfully and honestly fulfil the duties that devolve upon me by reason of my employment in the Public Service and that I will not, without due authority in that behalf, disclose or make known any matter that comes to my knowledge by reason of such employment. (In the case where an oath is taken add, 'So help me God'.)" Schedule C of the *Public Service Employment Act*.

27 Canada, *Revised Statutes*, 1952, c. 198.

47　The Problem of Administrative Secrecy*

Donald C. Rowat

The growth of governmental secrecy as a result of the Cold War constitutes a serious threat to the effective working of modern democracies. This
was well illustrated by Herblock's famous cartoon in the United States
during the post-war era of McCarthyism and hysteria. John P. Citizen was
sitting before a stage, but all he could see in front of him was a closed
curtain with the official words stamped on it in huge letters: "SECRET,
CLASSIFIED, SHH!". At the side of the stage was the master of ceremonies, Mr. Government Secrecy, who was saying, "It's a great performance
going on, folks — take my word for it!".

The magnitude of the post-war secrecy problem for democracies was
revealed by the famous U-2 incident of 1960. During his election campaign, President Eisenhower had said, "We must take the people into our
confidence and thereby restore their confidence in government. We will
keep the people informed because an informed people is the keystone in
the arch of free government". Yet for two days after Krushchev accused
the Americans of air reconnaissance over Russia, Eisenhower felt that in
the interests of national security he had to lie to the American people and
to the world. And during the Cuban crisis of 1962, Arthur Sylvester, U.S.
Assistant Secretary of Defence, stated flatly that "the inherent right of the
Government to lie to save itself when faced with nuclear disaster is basic".

These examples are not meant to imply that the secrecy problem is
peculiarly American, or even mainly a result of the Cold War. In fact,
I believe the problem is more serious in other countries, including those
that have inherited the British parliamentary system, which has a strong
tradition of administrative secrecy. The United States has always had a
much more open system of administration than most other countries. For
this reason, the post-war pinch of military secrecy was felt much more
acutely by the public and the press in that country, and they were quick
to speak out against it. As a result of this outcry, many desirable changes
have come about there in recent years.

The principle followed almost everywhere else, however, is that all
administrative activities and documents shall be secret unless and until
the Government chooses to reveal them. The public has no right to know
the manner in which the Government is carrying out its trust. To the
average citizen, the civil service is anonymous, faceless and impervious.
He has no right of access to official information, even if he has a personal
interest in a case. He may get so little information about an administrative

* Reprinted with permission of author and publisher from *International Review of
Administrative Sciences*, Vol. 32, No. 2, 1966. A shortened and revised version of "How
Much Administrative Secrecy?", *Canadian Journal of Economics and Political Science*,
Vol. 31, November 1965, pp. 479-498.

decision against him that he has no way of knowing whether it was made by unfair procedures or for improper reasons. This situation is an irresistible temptation to arbitrary action by government officials.

In many countries various professional groups have been complaining about the adverse effects of administrative secrecy. But they usually point only to its effect in their own realm of activity without realizing that it is a more general and basic problem. One such group are the newspapermen and broadcasters. They complain that because of the anonymity of the administration, they must work in a crazy world of illicit purveyors of official information who, like gossipers, give them a story but insist either that they must not tell anybody, or that if they print it, they must not give its source. Newsmen also object to the many meetings of boards, commissions and local councils which are closed to the press and public. Scientists complain that the wall of military security prevents the free flow of information essential to scientific development. In the Commonwealth countries, lawyers complain about the tradition of Crown privilege: it is so extreme that the Government has a right to refuse administrative documents to a court even when they contain essential evidence.

In most countries historians and other scholars find that they have no right of access to public records. Often, no rules exist regarding the types or ages of documents which they may see, and the granting of access is entirely at the whim of the government department concerned. Most countries require their diplomatic documents to be locked away from public scrutiny for a ridiculously long period. Despite some recent loosening of the rules, France still requires forty-five years and Britain fifty. In deference to the British fifty-year rule, most other countries will not let their scholars study any diplomatic document involving Britain until after fifty years have passed. These rules are obviously unsuitable for a democratic age whose historians and social scientists are trying to help us to learn from our past mistakes. As a result, ways are found to evade the rules. Ministers make off with semi-public papers when they retire — some, like Winston Churchill, with the obvious intent of publishing. And favourites who can be trusted not to be too critical are invited to write official histories, or are given access to recent documents. This playing of favourites is in some ways worse than the strict rule that "everyone has lost and so no one shall have prizes", which is at least fair to all.

Indeed, there are so many indications of the undesirable effects of governmental secrecy that I believe the time has now come for questioning the whole principle. It has been inherited from an earlier system of absolute monarchy, and has been preserved by Governments and officials mainly for their own convenience.

The conflict between the tradition of secrecy and the needs of a modern democracy is shown by the simultaneous existence of the secrecy oath and publicity services. In many countries officials must swear an oath that they will not, without permission from the Government, disclose *anything* they

THE PROBLEM OF ADMINISTATIVE SECRECY   457

learn while at work.[1] At the same time, government departments maintain huge information services which pour a torrent of administrative publicity into the channels of communication. It is true that in a democracy there is a positive duty to bring administrative activities to the public knowledge. But the problem is that "hand-outs" have become a substitute for access. In Canada, for instance, the recent Royal Commission on Government Organization found that in 1962 the information services of the Armed Forces were manned by 190 officials, who spent hundreds of thousands of dollars painting the Armed Forces in a favourable light. In a single two-week period in 1961, they distributed 75 news stories and releases, over 1,300 radio, TV and film productions, and more than 2,500 photographic prints.[2] In most countries we are told only what the Government wants us to know and a "paper curtain" of secrecy is drawn across the rest. Even more disturbing, Governments sometimes control publicity in their own interest. Upon occasion they doctor and time news releases to favour the party in power and use promotion campaigns to cover mistakes.

We must face the fact that any large measure of governmental secrecy is incompatible with democracy. This is true for two reasons. First, it leads to distrust and fear on the part of the public. Yet the decisions at the very apex of our political systems are made secretly in cabinets and party caucuses. Hence, much of the political process is hidden from the people, and they can hardly be blamed if they imagine the worst. In Canada, for instance, where the contributions to political parties for election expenses are secret, recent scandals have led to the suspicion that the criminal underworld makes gifts to political parties. Second, the people cannot control their government without knowledge. Yet the means available to the opposition parties and the public generally to obtain information about administrative activities are usually woefully inadequate. Opposition members of Parliament sometimes have to dig vital information out of a reluctant Government. But often they don't know what to ask for because they don't know what is really going on behind the clouds surrounding Mount Olympus. Our systems of government seem to be based on the premise that we must trust the Government and hope for the best. This is entirely too paternalistic a concept for a democracy. Parliament and the public cannot hope to call the Government to account without an adequate knowledge of what is going on. Nor can they hope to contribute their talents to the process of framing new policy and legislation if that process is hidden from view.

---

[1] In Britain, the definition of "official" under the Official Secrets Acts is so broad that it includes ex-ministers, ex-soldiers and the employees of government contractors. The Acts have been used to prosecute, or threaten prosecution of, a disturbing array of unlikely persons, including ex-ministers in Parliament. See Clive Perry, "Legislatures and Secrecy", *Harvard Law Review*, Vol. 67, 1954, pp. 770-772.

[2] Canada, Royal Commission on Government Organization, *Report*, Vol. 3, Queen's Printer, Ottawa, 1962, p. 71.

Recent Improvement in the United States

The openness of American administration is in sharp contrast with the secrecy of many other countries. There has been a long and strong tradition of publicity in the United States. It has been quick to break with the secrecy of European diplomacy by publishing its documents at an early date even though they may contain information not yet made available by other powers. It is true that there has been a higher degree of secrecy in the United States since the war. But, as mentioned earlier, the Americans finally overcame the shock and fear of the Cold War which drove them to excessive secrecy. Newsmen and scholars gradually convinced the public in the face of solid evidence that security classifications and loyalty screenings had gone too far. They pointed out that those with a "security mentality" often were protecting obsolete technological information and at the same time interfering with the free flow of information essential to the development of science and military technology. Their obsession with secrecy was even preventing the necessary flow of information from one agency to another. Worse still, secrecy had provided an easy opportunity for agencies to hide mistakes. Americans also found that the difficulty with secrecy is that it has a disturbing way of feeding upon itself. One cause of this is that not only the originator of a classified document but all others using it must similarly be placed under wraps. Another cause is the over-classification of confidential documents. As many American writers have observed, there are serious penalties for an official who under-classifies a document but no one has ever been punished for over-classifying.

Although newspapers in the United States still complain about the "paper curtain" and especially "managed news", I believe it fair to say that the crisis of administrative secrecy has now passed in the United States. Many recent developments have been designed to contain the area of administrative secrecy and to balance its objectives against the larger objectives of national policy and the preservation of American democracy. The Americans are now far ahead of most other countries in their determination to solve the problem of administrative secrecy, and we have much to learn from them. Playing its traditional role as a check on the Executive, the American Congress deserves much of the credit for the new developments. Members of Congress became worried as early as 1955 that not enough information on matters of security and defence was being released to enable the public to discuss them intelligently and to influence government policies. A subcommittee of the House of Representatives began a systematic investigation and campaign designed to require government agencies to release information more freely and to make the American public aware of the problem. And a Senate subcommittee began hearings on remedial legislation. The Administration, too, particularly since Kennedy's regime, deserves some of the credit. But I think the most important factor has been a significant shift in public opinion regarding the evils of administrative secrecy.

One result, as is well known, has been more satisfactory screening procedures and a freer flow of scientific information. Important changes have also taken place regarding declassification and access to public documents. In 1953 an Executive Order reduced the number of agencies entitled to classify information and abolished the "restricted" classification. More important, a system was instituted in 1961 whereby classified documents are placed in one of four declassification groups. This means that the great bulk of classified documents now falls into a group which steps them down automatically every three years until the lowest of the secrecy classifications is reached. Thus any material in this group will be fully declassified at the end of twelve years.[3] The Commission on Government Security, which reported in 1957, even recommended the abolition of the "confidential" classification, as being a device for over-classification which retards scientific and technological progress.[4]

Access to other public documents has always been much freer in the United States than in most other countries. Since the war, the maximum period observed for most documents has been twenty years.[5] In 1961, however, President Kennedy stated in a famous letter to his secretaries that "any official should have a clear and precise case involving the national interest before seeking to withhold from publication documents or papers fifteen or more years old".[6] This letter has had a tremendous influence upon the accessibility of documents within the various departments and agencies. While some of them claim they do not have the facilities and staff to put the rule into full effect, they now regard this as their objective.

Perhaps even more significant has been the Senate's drive to amend Section 3 of the Administrative Procedure Act of 1946. This section purported — perhaps even was intended — to ensure full publication of rules and orders and to provide free access to most public documents. But the statement of exceptions was so broad that it has swallowed the rule. The Senate had been considering bills to amend this section since 1957. Finally, in 1964, it passed an amendment designed to emphasize the principle of full disclosure, to limit the exceptions, and to provide a court procedure whereby citizens and the press could obtain information wrongfully withheld. Although this amendment was not approved by the House of Representatives, it is before the Senate again this year and will very likely pass.

---

[3] The second group steps down from one degree of secrecy to another only every twelve years; the third group are extremely sensitive documents, to be downgraded on an individual basis; and the fourth group contains information over which the United States has no jurisdiction. A House subcommittee estimated that the new system could save $1 million a year. See U.S. Congress, House, *Fourteenth Report by the Committee on Government Operations*, Washington, D.C., 1963, Ch. V.

[4] U.S. Commission on Government Security, *Report*, Washington, D.C., 1957, section on document classification.

[5] See H. G. Nicholas, "Public Records: The Historian, the National Interest and Official Policy", and C. P. Stacey, "Some Pros and Cons of the Access Problem", *International Journal*, Vol. 20, 1964-65, pp. 34-44, at 43, and pp. 45-53.

[6] Quoted in Stacey, *ibid.*, p. 52.

Meanwhile, the House is considering a very similar bill to amend further the so-called "housekeeping statute", which gives the departments power over the custody of records.

There has also been a successful campaign to have the state legislatures enact similar legislation, as well as "open-meeting" laws. These laws grant the press and the public a legal right to attend meetings of state, county, and local government bodies. Thirty-seven states now have record-access laws providing for varying degrees of public access. Ten years ago only one open-meeting law existed in its present form. Twenty-nine states now have such a law. This is in sharp contrast with the situation at the provincial and municipal levels in Canada. After a detailed study of the new open-meeting legislation in the United States, the *Harvard Law Review* concluded that it "has neither revolutionized the conduct of state and local government nor brought it grinding to a halt . . . the presence of an audience has not in most cases restrained officials from giving full expression to their views, the problems concededly created by an irresponsible press have not been intensified . . . and the fear that officials would waste their time making speeches has proved largely unfounded".[7]

Despite all this recent activity in the United States designed to preserve and extend the traditional openness of American government, there has been very little discussion of similar problems in other countries. Few people elsewhere seem interested in whether documents are over-classified or when they will be declassified. Perhaps the reason is that it makes little difference; they will not be made available to the public anyway.

The Swedish Principle of Public Access

Let us now take a look at a country which has operated for many years under the reverse principle: Sweden. Since the principle of secrecy has been imbibed with our mother's milk, so to speak, we find it hard to believe that a country can get along without it. Swedish Professor Nils Herlitz has said that when he speaks in other countries about the Swedish principle of public access to documents, he is often amused by the reaction of his audience. While each listener "shows the courtesy not to make any observation, it is obvious that he ponders a question: Is this man unable to express himself intelligibly in my language, so that I have misunderstood him? Or is he mad?".[8] Professor Herlitz is certainly not mad, and it is

---

7 "The Press Fights for the 'Right to Know'" *Harvard Law Review*, Vol. 75, 1962, p. 1,219. The figures for the state laws are from "Comparative Digest of Access (Open Meetings, Records) Laws", No. 7, Freedom of Information Center, University of Missouri, Columbia, Missouri, March 1965, p. 1.

8 Nils Herlitz, "Publicity of Official Documents in Sweden", *Public Law*, Spring 1958, pp. 50-69, at p. 50. So far as I am aware, this is the only full-length article in English on the Swedish principle of open access. Hence I have had to rely on it almost exclusively. Professor Herlitz has confirmed to me that he knows of no other, although he has of course mentioned the principle in his other writings in English. I have been able to give only some highlights here; the whole article deserves to be read much more widely. He points out that Finland has a similar principle, though not as part of the Constitution.

indeed true that for almost two hundred years the Swedish Constitution has provided for open access to official documents and full information to any citizen about administrative activities.

This provision is so unusual, perhaps unique in the world, that one immediately thinks of the many circumstances under which secrecy is desirable. How can such a provision work successfully in practice? Are there not serious limitations upon its application? The answer is that of course there are limitations, and these are provided for in the Constitution itself. But the important point is that the *principle* has been reversed: whereas in most countries all documents are secret unless a specific authority is given for their release, in Sweden they are all public unless legal provision has been made for them to be withheld. The actual wording in the Constitution is as follows:

> To further the free interchange of opinion and general enlightenment, every Swedish citizen shall have free access to official documents. . . . This right shall be subject only to such restrictions as are required out of consideration for the security of the realm and its relations with foreign powers, or in connection with official activities for inspection, control or other supervision, or for the prevention and prosecution of crime, or to protect the legitimate economic interests of the State, communities and individuals, or out of consideration for the maintenance of privacy, security of the person, decency and morality.[9]

It will be noted that all of the general circumstances traditionally used as arguments against free access to administrative information are covered by this list of exceptions. It should also be noted that in general the right of free access is to prevail, and that this right shall be subject *only* to the exceptions listed. The Constitution goes on to say that the specific cases in which official documents are to be kept secret shall be "closely defined" in a special statute. As one might expect in a modern welfare state, this law, called the Secrecy Act, spells out an impressive list of matters that must be kept secret. But, as Professor Herlitz points out, "the detailed catalogue of the Secrecy Act has also a considerable effect *e contrario*. Since we have modern legislation providing for secrecy when it is necessary . . . it follows that where publicity is required, it must be properly and conscientiously adhered to. And publicity has nowadays a very strong support in public opinion, as a keystone of our constitutional system. It is a considerable and effective force felt in every section of social life".[10]

A full appreciation of the impact of the principle of open access can be gained only by giving some examples of the extensiveness of its operation. It applies, for example, to public documents kept by all sorts of administrative agencies, from government departments to police officers, administrative tribunals, and local governments. Even Parliament is under the rule; for instance, a citizen can demand to see the minutes of its com-

---

9 *Ibid.*, p. 51.
10 *Ibid.*, p. 53.

mittees. Moreover, anybody is entitled to ask for documents; he does not have to show that he has a legal interest in seeing them nor is he obliged to say for what purpose he wants them. To make sure that agencies do not purposely delay in answering a request, the Constitution provides that a requested document shall be "made available immediately or as soon as possible", and the courts in their judgments have taken this rule seriously.

The definition of "public document" includes not only those prepared but also those received by a public authority. And their availability to the newspapers has been organized as a routine service:

> Every day, in the great offices in Stockholm, for instance, documents which have been received will be brought to a room where representatives of the newspapers are welcomed to see them. A representative of the leading news bureau will never fail to appear, and through him a flood of news will go to the newspapers and to the general public.
>
> The purpose is this. Just as publicity in the courts all over the world makes it possible for everybody to know how justice is administered, the publicity of documents has the same effect in so far as documents reflect the activity of the authorities; the publicity shall provide [as the Constitution says] "general enlightenment."[11]

The principle of publicity is so firmly embedded in Swedish tradition that the Secrecy Act, government regulations, the courts, and the Ombudsmen for civil and military affairs, all place great weight on the need for free public access to administrative information. For instance, in the Secrecy Act itself and in government regulations the secrecy of documents is valid for only a specified period of time, and the restrictions are not valid for documents preserved in the courts. The Secrecy Act, far from stating that all documents of the Foreign Office and the armed services are to be kept secret, carefully enumerates those which may be kept secret temporarily. And in many cases the Ombudsman for military affairs has insisted upon publicity for information unjustifiably withheld by the military establishment. It is also noteworthy that most of the regulations for secrecy do not refer to documents containing administrative decisions. Here the rights of persons having an interest in seeing the documents have been upheld by the courts in a great number of cases. The principle of easy access is also upheld in a positive way by regulations which require special arrangements in order to facilitate easy access to documents by the press, scholars, interested parties, and the public generally. Most agencies, for example, keep up-to-date diaries in which information about documents received is easily available.

Another important feature of the Swedish publicity system is that under the Freedom of the Press Act a reporter or editor cannot be compelled to disclose his source of information. In fact, he is legally *prohibited* from revealing an informant's name without the latter's consent. Instead, the editor takes direct and personal responsibility before the law for what he

---

11 *Ibid.*, pp. 54-55.

prints. The only significant exception to this protection of informants is when an official has disregarded a clear statutory duty to keep a matter secret. In view of the recent controversies over a disclosure in Britain and the United States, the Swedish experience is instructive; the principle of protecting news sources has been an important device for providing access to official information wrongfully withheld from the public.[12]

An important consequence of the stress upon the principle of administrative publicity is the impact upon the administration itself. Professor Herlitz describes this impact as follows:

> In every step an authority takes, it feels that it is under public control, under the imminent danger of having its steps discussed and criticized. The publicity is always in the minds of the officials and makes them anxious to act in such a way that they will not be exposed to criticism. This situation will, in a way, make them cautious, perhaps sometimes over-scrupulous. But on the other hand, they will feel a certain amount of confidence. They need not be exposed to vague suspicions, since there is always an opportunity to control their work. And, after all, the wind which sweeps from without over the work of the authorities is not always harsh and unfriendly. If publicity is a plague to authorities which are inclined to take wrong steps, it may also give considerable support to other authorities, provide them with good information and prevent their being deceived by false information and unfounded pretensions. In a word, publicity creates, when it is effective, quite a peculiar atmosphere of openness and confidence in which administration has to work.[13]

Regarding the significance of the publicity principle for the people in a democracy, Professor Herlitz concludes:

> Our judgment on public affairs is facilitated; the public debate is given a firmer basis, whether we judge what the authorities think, or what they have done, or what they should do. . . .
>
> It would be an understatement to say that in Sweden publicity is generally and highly estimated. It would be more exact to say that it is regarded as indispensable. Whilst, in the eyes of other nations, publicity may look impossible and incredible, most Swedes, including many high lawyers, regard access to official documents as something like a natural right and believe that it has a counterpart in all civilized countries.[14]

And Mr. Bexelius, the Swedish Ombudsman, has said, "I have always maintained that free access to official documents is of far more importance for the legal security of citizens than is the office of Ombudsman".[15]

---

12 See Hilding Eek, "Protection of News Sources by the Constitution", *Scandinavian Studies in Law*, Stockholm, 1961, pp. 11-25. This essay also contains some additional information on access to documents.

13 Herlitz, *op. cit.*, p. 56.

14 *Ibid.*, pp. 55, 58.

15 Letter to the author, January 3, 1966.

Application of the Swedish Principle Elsewhere

I believe that the Swedes are right. The principle of open access to administrative information is essential to the full development of democracy. In spite of the enhanced need for secrecy in certain areas resulting from the Cold War, the logic of democracy demands that the long-term trend be in the direction of the principle of publicity. This trend may be seen in the growth of vast public information services for modern democracies, in the relaxation of the fifty-year rule, and in the steady development of legislation in the United States towards the Swedish principle of open access. For when essential information is withheld from the public, there is a grave danger that the discussion of public policy will be shallow and that the people will be unable to control their government. My recommendation, then, is that other democracies should prepare to abandon the principle of secrecy.

The Swedish publicity principle, like the Ombudsman system, has had considerable influence upon the other Scandinavian countries. After becoming a republic in 1919, Finland adopted the principle, though not as part of the Constitution. In Denmark, a commission appointed by the Prime Minister reported on the question in 1963. Eleven of the twenty members recommended that parties to an administrative case should be given the right of access to the file of the case, while the remaining nine favoured a system of full publicity on the Swedish model. The Danish Parliament enacted the majority's recommendation in 1964. In Norway, the Commission on Administrative Procedure, which reported in 1958, favoured the publicity principle, and another commission is now considering the matter. It is likely to recommend the adoption of the principle of access at least to the extent now provided in Denmark.

In Canada, one of our members of Parliament has at last recognized the writing on the wall by introducing a private member's bill designed to establish the publicity principle.[16] Though the bill is only one page long, it contains the main elements of the Swedish scheme. The first section states that "every administrative or ministerial commission, power and authority shall make its records and information concerning its doings available to any person at his request in reasonable manner and time". The second section provides the basic exceptions by stating that this rule does not apply to records that affect national security, that are exempted by statute from disclosure, and that concern trade secrets, nor to cases where the right to personal privacy excludes the public interest. Section three contains the important principle that the courts should determine whether any particular record or information is to be made public. Some such bill, as well as legislation requiring open meetings of regulatory boards, municipal councils, and similar public bodies, should be passed by all democratic legislatures, or even made part of the Constitution as in Sweden.

---

16 Bill C-39; first reading, April 8, 1965.

It is recognized, of course, that the principle of publicity could have a profound and far-reaching effect upon the operation of the cabinet system of government, especially in the Commonwealth countries. One immediately thinks of a whole series of disturbing questions. What would happen to the cherished traditions of cabinet secrecy and civil service anonymity? Would not free access be embarrassing to civil servants, politicians, and governments? Would it not make the cabinet system unworkable? What would happen to cabinet responsibility? My own view is that the fears implicit in these questions are largely unfounded. As with so many proposals for social change, the consequences predicted, based on fear, are likely to be greatly exaggerated. Sweden, after all, does have a parliamentary system of government with the cabinet responsible to the legislature. The need for anonymous administration as a prerequisite to the successful working of the cabinet system is no doubt overstressed. Many senior officials and regulatory bodies have a great deal of power; their official views and activities deserve to be known. Under the publicity rule a Government would still be able to issue directives to its officials and to semi-independent agencies for which it is responsible. But it could not do so secretly, and it would more surely be called to account for its actions. As for the likelihood of revelations in government documents being embarrassing to senior officials or politicians, the answer is that he who accepts public responsibility can expect to be criticized; it is well recognized that public life has no room for personal sensitivity. Besides, as Professor Herlitz has pointed out, officials are likely to give more considered judgments if they know that the record will be open to public view.[17] The Swedish experience also shows that ways can always be found to deliberate and to circulate information confidentially when this is absolutely necessary.[18] Provision would no doubt be made for the cabinet itself to continue its secret sessions.

An important benefit of open access is the participation of the public in the formation of policy. The public have a chance to criticize and discuss proposals *before* decisions are made. One of the disabilities of the secrecy system is that a Government has no easy way of testing public reaction to a measure before it is presented in almost final form to Parliament. Hence, the Government must resort to special devices like royal commissions to stir up interest and form a public opinion on proposed measures. In Sweden and some other countries of Western Europe, draft bills are made public and widely discussed with all interested groups *before* being presented to the legislature.

There is no doubt that cabinet responsibility would work somewhat differently under the principle of publicity. But this may be all to the good: it may make the cabinet *more* responsible. Many people in Britain have argued that under modern conditions ministerial responsibility is

---

17 Herlitz, *op. cit.*, p. 56.
18 *Ibid.*, pp. 61-63.

pretty much of a myth. Professor Finer has made a count of instances in the past century where ministers have been forced to resign as a result of parliamentary disapproval. He managed to produce only a handful of cases, and most of these were of doubtful validity as illustrations of the punitive effect of the doctrine of ministerial responsibility.[19] Professor Robson has noted that "party discipline can be wielded in such a way as to enable the Government to get away with even the most obvious and fearful blunders".[20] Under a system of administrative publicity, on the other hand, the Government is constantly exposed to criticism and must move much more carefully. Since it receives advice and suggestions from a much wider public, it acts much more wisely. And ministers must act with forthright propriety or their sins will be quickly discovered. Under the secrecy system, the Government's monopoly of information means that Opposition MP's are unable to find the soft spots. Since knowledge is power, Governments hide reports prepared by senior officials or other experts, and reveal them only if it is to their advantage. With the publicity rule this is not possible. As Professor Herlitz points out: "Bringing bills before Parliament, the Government . . . will never neglect to give [in its own presentation] part of the reports which have been gathered, often very abundantly, from different authorities. And it is usual for their views to become good weapons in the hand of the Opposition. It is an old saying that the Opposition has its best arsenal in the records of the Government".[21]

There are good grounds for the belief that, in most systems of government, the executive is too dominant. Being in a position to accept or reject proposed reforms, Governments naturally tend to reject proposals that would limit their own powers. Geoffrey Marshall has wittily suggested that to meet such contingencies Governments possess an all-purpose speech, with blanks to be filled in as required. The key phrases in this speech are, "incompatible with ministerial responsibility" and "inappropriate to our constitutional arrangements". It contains references to the adequacy of existing procedures, the importance of avoiding confusion between the executive and legislative functions, and a number of other clichés.[22] One can therefore confidently predict variations on this speech to be used against the principle of open access. Indeed, the principle represents such a break with our traditional wisdom that it is likely to be adopted only after considerable soulsearching, the lapse of several years, and the rise of an overwhelming pressure of public opinion upon Governments.

---

[19] Discussed in W. A. Robson, *The Governors and the Governed*, Louisiana State University Press, Baton Rouge, 1964, pp. 29-30.

[20] *Ibid.*, p. 31.

[21] Herlitz, *op. cit.*, p. 56.

[22] Geoffrey Marshall, "Ministerial Responsibility", *Political Quarterly*, Vol. 34, July 1963, p. 265.

Index